The SAGE Dictionary
of Statistics & Methodology

Fifth Edition

SAGE was founded in 1965 by Sara Miller McCune to support the dissemination of usable knowledge by publishing innovative and high-quality research and teaching content. Today, we publish more than 850 journals, including those of more than 300 learned societies, more than 800 new books per year, and a growing range of library products including archives, data, case studies, reports, and video. SAGE remains majority-owned by our founder, and after Sara's lifetime will become owned by a charitable trust that secures our continued independence.

Los Angeles | London | New Delhi | Singapore | Washington DC

The SAGE Dictionary of Statistics & Methodology

A Nontechnical Guide for the Social Sciences

Fifth Edition

W. Paul Vogt
Illinois State University

R. Burke Johnson
University of South Alabama

Los Angeles | London | New Delhi
Singapore | Washington DC

Los Angeles | London | New Delhi
Singapore | Washington DC

FOR INFORMATION:

SAGE Publications, Inc.

2455 Teller Road

Thousand Oaks, California 91320

E-mail: order@sagepub.com

SAGE Publications Ltd.

1 Oliver's Yard

55 City Road

London EC1Y 1SP

United Kingdom

SAGE Publications India Pvt. Ltd.

B 1/I 1 Mohan Cooperative Industrial Area

Mathura Road, New Delhi 110 044

India

SAGE Publications Asia-Pacific Pte. Ltd.

3 Church Street

#10-04 Samsung Hub

Singapore 049483

Copyright © 2016 by SAGE Publications, Inc.

Printed in the United States of America

Library of Congress Cataloging-in-Publication Data

Vogt, W. Paul.

[Dictionary of statistics & methodology]

The Sage dictionary of statistics & methodology : a nontechnical guide for the social sciences / W. Paul Vogt, R. Burke Johnson. — Fifth edition.

pages cm
Earlier editions published as: Dictionary of statistics & methodology : a nontechnical guide for the social sciences.

Includes bibliographical references.

ISBN 978-1-4833-8176-3 (pbk.)

1. Social sciences—Statistical methods—Dictionaries.
2. Social sciences—Methodology—Dictionaries.
I. Johnson, R. Burke.
II. Title.

HA17.V64 2016
300.1'5195--dc23   2015023616

This book is printed on acid-free paper.

Acquisitions Editor: Helen Salmon

Editorial Assistant: Anna Villarruel

Production Editor: Kelly DeRosa

Copy Editor: Sarah Duffy

Typesetter: C&M Digitals (P) Ltd.

Proofreader: Alison Syring

Cover Designer: Janet Kiesel

Marketing Manager: Nicole Elliott

SUSTAINABLE FORESTRY INITIATIVE

Certified Chain of Custody
Promoting Sustainable Forestry
www.sfiprogram.org
SFI-01268

SFI label applies to text stock

15 16 17 18 19 10 9 8 7 6 5 4 3 2 1

Contents

List of Figures

List of Tables

Preface

Almost all research studies contain technical terms that students and researchers do not know and, even worse, that they cannot easily look up. What is needed to lower the jargon barrier between readers and research is a handy reference work in which students and researchers can find quick definitions of a wide variety of statistical and methodological terms. We have tried to satisfy that need in this dictionary.

As in previous editions, our goal is to provide readers of research reports with a practical and nontechnical reference work. We are steadfast in keeping our eyes on the target of providing a source of concise, nontechnical definitions that readers can use to aid in their understanding of research. We have already used the term *nontechnical* twice in this preface, and it features prominently in our subtitle. What do we mean by it? Three things: First, definitions are written in clear, ordinary English; second, words are not initially defined with formulas; third, when more specialized terms are used in a definition, they are explained there and/or cross-referenced.

We conceive the word *methodology* in the title as including concepts from the qualitative, quantitative, and mixed methods traditions in research. And we believe it is important to define broader philosophical and theoretical terms users are likely to encounter in their reading as well as more technical concepts. Of course, this dictionary is not unabridged and all-inclusive. Nor is it a specialized encyclopedia with comprehensive articles and extensive references. Finally, the dictionary is not a how-to guide. But it can help you read encyclopedias and how-to guides.

We define elementary concepts more fully than advanced concepts and highly specialized terms. We do that because it would be impossible, no matter how long the volume, to explain advanced topics in detail. Our definitions of advanced concepts tend to be short and use terms that are likely to be unfamiliar to readers with elementary knowledge of statistics and methodology. But, by following the paths suggested by the cross-references, readers should be able to "work backward" until they reach definitions they understand. Conversely, the cross-references also suggest ways readers can "work forward" from elementary terms to more specialized topics.

Cross-references are also helpful to readers for another reason. As with any other "language," methodological and statistical discourse contains many synonyms (and even some homonyms). This means that one technique can be referred to in more than one way, sometimes even by the same author. We have paid close attention to reducing that source of confusion by cross-referencing synonyms.

Audience

We hope this volume proves useful to many explorers in the social and behavioral sciences and related applied fields such as education, management, business, nursing, and social work.

Since the original edition of this dictionary was published in 1993, a few other dictionaries have appeared (see "Suggestions for Further Reading"). While each of these volumes has its strengths, the book you have in front of you is the most useful for its intended audience, that is, readers trying to inform themselves about research terms and concepts so they can be effective consumers and, potentially, producers of research. That audience is a broad group, ranging from professionals who want to improve their practice by keeping up with the research in their fields to students trying to decipher research reports for the first time. Likewise, students planning to conduct their own research who can use a little help with the methodological terms in the research literature will find this dictionary useful.

Features

Without making detailed comparisons with other dictionaries, we will briefly list this one's noteworthy features.

- *Nontechnical.* By being nontechnical, this work adheres to one of the most basic rules of good dictionary writing: A definition should *never* contain terms more obscure than the one being defined. For example, definition of words by algebraic formula (very common in other dictionaries) is helpful for mathematicians but is of limited use for less specialized readers.
- *Self-contained.* Each term used in the definitions is itself defined in the dictionary. When other technical terms are used in a definition, they are cross-referenced. Readers with a good grasp of ordinary English will rarely if ever come to a dead end because they have looked up a word only to see it defined by a word they do not know and that they can look up only by consulting another volume.

- *Descriptive, not prescriptive.* Terms are described as they are actually used rather than how they "should" be used. Setting standards for proper use is important, but a dictionary is more valuable to readers when it is informative rather than normative.
- *Comprehensive.* Our goal is for this book to include everything that readers are likely to need to understand a research report. We have tried to make the book comprehensive in several ways.
  - Methodology and design terms are defined as well as terms relating to statistical analysis and measurement.
  - Concepts from qualitative research methods are covered (although somewhat less extensively) in addition to terms from quantitative traditions in research.
  - Elementary terms and concepts are defined, often extensively, not merely more specialized and advanced terms.
  - Related terms from theory (e.g., *postmodernism, positivism, constructionism*) and philosophy (e.g., *empiricism, nominalism, realism*) are defined. The rationale for these inclusions is, as always, that readers are likely to encounter such terms when reading research reports.

Sources

Where do the definitions come from? There are two main sources. It is a long-standing practice of dictionary writers to comb the relevant literature for terms and their use. As Dr. Johnson said of his famous 18th-century dictionary, we decide what to include by the "perusal of our writers." We have been systematic in our efforts to review relevant literature in the social sciences and to be alert to the appearance of new methods, new terms, and newly popular terms. But this book is not an unabridged dictionary, in which *any* use would justify inclusion. Rather, we have had to exercise judgment and include only fairly widespread terms.

The perusal of the works of methodology writers helped us find new terms for new methods. Just as frequently, new labels for existing methods have come into use. It is remarkably common in quantitative research to find that there are several terms used to describe the same concept or technique. This proliferation of synonyms is perhaps even more widespread in the field of qualitative methods, which is going through a period of rapid growth that has not yet been codified.

A second source is queries and suggestions by readers. Communications from readers of earlier editions have led to including previously omitted terms and to revising others. We greatly appreciate this help from people we think of as volunteer coeditors and look forward to receiving e-mails with more suggestions for improvement. Please send suggestions either to Burke Johnson at bjohnson@southalabama.edu or to Paul Vogt at wpaulvogt@gmail.com.

What's New in the Fifth Edition?

As with each edition after the first, in this volume, new terms are defined, new synonyms are included, and both are illustrated with new graphics. In total, over 500 new terms, definitions, and graphics have been added in the fifth edition. These additions reflect changing conventions in usage in methodological and statistical language in the social sciences. While we have shortened some entries and deleted some obsolete ones, very few terms from the earlier editions have been removed. The importance of classic terms persists even as new techniques and new terms describing methods are invented. Old terms linger on; new terms are created much faster than old ones die out.

We have also updated and expanded the "Suggestions for Further Reading" and the section "Useful Websites on Statistics and Methodology."

Another change in this fifth edition is one of format. Unlike previous editions, this one is available electronically as well as in hard copy, which expands accessibility and ease of use for many readers.

Acknowledgments

SAGE and the authors would like to thank the following reviewers:

Jann W. MacInnes, University of Florida

Alejandra Dubois, University of Ottawa

Ann M. Mayo, University of San Diego

Anita G. Welch, North Dakota State University

Brittany Landrum, University of Dallas

Keith F. Donohue, North Dakota State University

Notes for Users

1. Alphabetizing

Entries are in alphabetical order, using the letter-by-letter (not word-by-word) method. This means that when looking up terms and expressions made up of more than one word, you should ignore the spaces and hyphens between words. For example, "*F*," "*F* Distribution," and "*F* Ratio" are separated by several pages, not grouped together as they would be using the word-by-word method. The only exception to the letter-by-letter rule is entries with a comma, such as "Association, Measure of."

2. Greek Letters

Greek letters are anglicized, spelled out, and alphabetized accordingly. Consult the table "The Greek Alphabet" on the inside front cover for equivalents. For example, to find α, you would look under "Alpha."

3. Numbers

In terms containing numbers, the numbers are spelled out and alphabetized accordingly. For example, to find "2×2 design," look under "Two-by-Two Design."

4. Symbols

For symbols, consult the table "Frequently Used Symbols" on the inside front cover, get the equivalent in words, and look up the words in the ordinary way. For example, to find | |, you would look in the table to learn that this symbol means "absolute value" and then consult that entry in the alphabetical listing.

5. Multiple Meanings

If a term has more than one meaning, definitions are separated by letters—(a), (b), and so on—with the more common definitions coming first.

6. Synonyms

If more than one word is used to express the same or similar idea—such as dependent, outcome, and criterion variable—we have defined fully what we believe to be the most common term and briefly defined and cross-referenced the others. But we have not tried to stipulate the "proper" labels for concepts that appear under more than one name. Nor have we specified the "correct" use of terms that are used in different ways. We have attempted to be inclusive and descriptive, not prescriptive. This results in a more comprehensive dictionary, one that increases access to works in the social and behavioral sciences.

7. Cross-References

When an entry contains other terms defined in this dictionary, they are indicated by an asterisk (*). When studying any language, learners may sometimes be frustrated because they have to look up words in the definition of the term they just looked up. By writing the definitions in ordinary English whenever possible, we have tried to keep this unavoidable annoyance to a minimum. But it is unavoidable, especially in a dictionary of technical terms. Thus, many of the definitions in this dictionary use other methodological or statistical terms in their definitions; these are marked with an asterisk and defined.

About the Authors

W. Paul Vogt is Emeritus Professor of Research Methods and Evaluation at Illinois State University, where he has won both teaching and research awards. He specializes in methodological choice and program evaluation and is particularly interested in ways to integrate multiple methods. His other books include *Tolerance & Education: Learning to Live With Diversity and Difference* (Sage, 1998); *Quantitative Research Methods for Professionals* (Allyn & Bacon, 2007); and *Education Programs for Improving Intergroup Relations* (coedited with Walter Stephan, Teachers College Press, 2004). He is also editor of four 4-volume sets in the series SAGE Benchmarks in Social Research Methods: *Selecting Research Methods* (2008), *Data Collection* (2010), *Quantitative Research Methods* (2011), and, with Burke Johnson, *Correlation and Regression Analysis* (2012). His most recent publications include the coauthored *When to Use What Research Design* (2012) and *Selecting the Right Analyses for Your Data: Quantitative, Qualitative, and Mixed Methods Approaches* (2014).

R. Burke Johnson is a professor in the Professional Studies Department at the University of South Alabama. His PhD is from the REMS (research, evaluation, measurement, and statistics) program in the College of Education at the University of Georgia. He also has graduate degrees in psychology, sociology, and public administration, which have provided him with a multidisciplinary perspective on research methodology. He was guest editor for a special issue of *Research in the Schools* focusing on mixed research and completed a similar guest editorship for the *American Behavioral Scientist*. He was an associate editor of the *Journal of Mixed Methods Research*. Burke is first author of *Educational Research: Quantitative, Qualitative, and Mixed Approaches* (Sage, 2014, 5th edition); second author of *Research Methods, Design, and Analysis* (Pearson, 2014, 12th edition); coeditor (with Sharlene Hesse-Biber) of *The Oxford Handbook of Multimethod and Mixed Methods Research Inquiry* (2015); coeditor (with Paul Vogt) of *Correlation and Regression Analysis* (2012); and associate editor of *The SAGE Glossary of the Social and Behavioral Sciences* (2009).

A-B-A-B Designs   Single case research designs that alternate *baseline measures of a *variable with measures of that variable before, during, and after a *treatment. Such designs are used in single-subject or single-group or single-case *experiments usually having one treatment and no *control group. The "A" stands for baseline, the "B" for treatment. A-B and A-B-A designs are shorter versions of the A-B-A-B design. A-B-A-B designs are often used when it would be unethical to withhold a treatment from a control group. See *interrupted time-series design. The A-B-A and A-B-A-B designs are appropriate when reversal (i.e., return to baseline) is expected following withdrawal of the treatment condition. When reversal is not expected, a *multiple-baseline design is preferred.

For example, in order to see whether a treatment had an effect, patients' symptoms might be measured daily for four weeks. During the first week, there would be no treatment (baseline, A). Then the treatment (B) would be given for a week. In the third week, the treatment could be withdrawn, and a second baseline (A) would be established. In the fourth week, the treatment would be given again. If the goal is to reduce the baseline response level, the "signature" of an effective treatment is (A) high, (B) low, (A) high, (B) low; conversely, when the goal is to increase the behavior, the desired signature is low, high, low, high.

A-B-A-C-A Design   A single-case research design that begins with no treatment baseline measurement (A), followed by treatment B (B), followed by no treatment baseline measurement (hopefully with a return to baseline on the dependent variable), followed by a different treatment (C), followed by no treatment baseline. This design tests the relative impact of two different treatments (B and C). Reversal is needed for this design to provide the desired signature result needed to attribute causation (as in the A-B-A-B designs).

Abduction   The *logic of discovery by which a researcher explores the data (e.g., interview transcripts, observations) and creates or generates an explanation of a "surprising fact," finding, or problem. After provisional hypotheses are generated, they are tested, interpreted, and refined until the "best explanation" of all the data is obtained. Also called "inference to best explanation." This type of logic can include elements of both deductive and inductive logic, often used interactively. Abduction is often associated with research using *grounded theory. See *context of discovery. Compare *deduction, *induction.

Ability Parameter   (symbolized by θ[theta]) In *item response theory, θ is a latent variable; specifically it is the underlying capability or ability of the examinees. See *item characteristic curve, *item response theory.

Abscissa   (a) The horizontal axis (or *x*-axis) on a graph. See Figure A.1 for illustration. (b) A particular point or value on that axis. See *Cartesian coordinates.

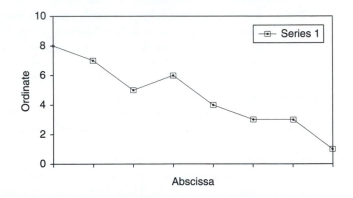

Figure A.1   Abscissa

Absolute Deviation   See *mean absolute deviation, *average deviation.

Absolute Frequency   The actual number of times a particular value occurs in a *distribution, as opposed to its *relative frequency or the *proportion of times it occurs.

Absolute Value (of a Number)   The value of a number regardless of its sign (positive or negative). Also called the "modulus."
   For example, the absolute value of +8 and −8 is the same, 8. Symbolized: |8|. (The absolute value is the positive value, since a number without a sign is positive.)

Absolute Zero Point   A value on a scale indicating that none of the variable being measured is present. See *ratio scale.

Abstraction A cognitive process in which common elements of diverse things are identified and pulled out of their context (abstracted) in order to study them. Doing this makes it possible to classify and analyze *data that could not otherwise be studied together. Abstraction increases a researcher's ability to generalize, but at the cost of some of the concrete details of each case.

For example, say you wanted to do a cross-national study of the relation of democracy to economic equality in modern nations. You might construct a "Democracy Index" (made up of measures of freedom of the press, open elections, independent judiciary, etc.) and an "Equality Index" (made up of measures of the distribution of income, wealth, employment opportunities, etc.). You would then collect the data, convert the values on each index to ranks, and compute the *correlation coefficient between the two rank-ordered indices. On the basis of this work you might determine that there is a general relationship between economic equality and democracy.

Only by using such abstractions as your Democracy and Equality Indexes can you work at a *level of generality high enough to make comparisons across nations. To the extent that you focused on the specific details of the local economic and political situations in each country, it would be more difficult to make a statement about the general relationship between democracy and equality.

Accelerated Longitudinal Design A combination of the methods (and their advantages and disadvantages) of *cross-sectional and *longitudinal studies in research on individuals over time. See *age effects, *stratified random sample, *cohort-sequential design. Also called *cohort-sequential design.

For example, say you want to study the effects of aging on some variable(s) over the 30 years from age 20 to age 50. Since you do not have 30 years to conduct your study, you cannot use a true longitudinal design and follow a group for 30 years (from age 20 to 50). You know that it is not justifiable simply to take a cross-sectional sample of subjects of different ages and assume that younger subjects will become like older subjects as they age. So you combine the two methods in an accelerated longitudinal design by taking samples of subjects aged 20, 25, 30, 35, 40, and 45 and following each group for five years.

Acceptance Error Another term for *beta error or *Type II error.

Acceptance Region The range of values of a test statistic that would lead to the "retention" or "acceptance" or a "failure to reject" the *null hypothesis. The opposite of the *regions of rejection.

Acceptance Sampling (a) In manufacturing, a process of sampling designed to accept or reject a group of products. (b) In *epidemiology, a method to identify subgroups, often defined by time in a population, followed by sampling from the subgroups.

For example (a), an inspector might examine 1% of items manufactured. On the basis of the number of defects in that sample, the inspector can infer what the rate will be in the entire production run (*population) and decide whether to accept or reject the entire run.

Accessible Population   The population of subjects from which you can draw a sample (and then ask to participate in your research study). Compare *target population.

Accidental Error   Error in measurement that cannot be predicted or controlled because the researcher is ignorant of its cause(s). Compare *bias, *random error.

Accidental Sample   A sample gathered haphazardly, for example, by interviewing the first 100 people you run into on the street who are willing to talk to you. An accidental sample is sometimes confused with, but is definitely not, a *random sample. The main disadvantage of an accidental sample is that the researcher has no way of knowing what the *population might be. See *convenience sample, *probability sample.

Accurate to *n* Decimal Places (or Digits)   A statement that indicates how *rounding is done.

For example, since $e = 2.71828 \ldots$, the approximation 2.7183 (with the 3 the result of rounding) is accurate to 5 decimal places or significant digits.

Acquiescent Response Style   The tendency of some research participants, quite apart from what they actually believe, to be agreeable and say yes to all statements in an interview or on a questionnaire. Also called "acquiescence bias." Compare *social desirability bias.

There is not much evidence that such yea-saying is very common. It is no more common, at any rate, than a nay-saying "quarrelsome response style." To guard against such biases, many question writers compose their *scales and *indexes so that persons have to answer questions in opposite ways to convey their beliefs—for example, asking for a yes or no response to both statements: "Abortion should be legal" and "Abortion should be illegal." This practice appears to reduce the acquiescent response style, but this benefit may come at the cost of reducing scale *reliability.

Action Research   A type of *applied research designed to find the most effective way to bring about a desired social change or solve a practical problem; it is usually conducted in collaboration with the subjects of the research. Compare *basic research, *evaluation research.

Active Consent   Type of *informed consent. It occurs when a person agrees to participate after being informed of the study's purpose, risks, potential benefits, procedures, alternative procedures, and limits of confidentiality. Compare *passive consent.

Active Control Equivalence Study An experimental research design including three groups, in which one group receives the treatment, a second group receives the "standard practice treatment," and a third group is an ordinary no treatment *control group. One goal of this design is to demonstrate that the new and active control treatments are equally effective. When the standard practice treatment is known to be effective, ethical issues can arise in the inclusion of a no treatment control group.

Active Control Trial A *clinical trial in which a *treatment is compared to another treatment rather than to a group receiving no treatment or a *placebo. See *active control equivalence study.

Active Variable An experimental or manipulated *independent variable, as opposed to one over which the researcher exerts no control. Compare *attribute variable, *background variable.

Actuarial Statistics Statistics used to calculate insurance rates and pensions (e.g., mortality rates, accident rates, life expectancy). They are used to estimate *risk.

Actuary A statistician specializing in *probability theory, particularly as it relates to calculating risks for insurance companies. Actuaries estimate the likely dividends companies will have to pay and therefore how high the premiums will have to be in order for them to make a profit. Actuaries were probably the earliest professional statisticians.

AD *Average deviation. See *mean absolute deviation (MAD).

Adaptation Period The period in an experiment or study when participants become accustomed to the setting and materials, such as instruments and equipment used in the research. The goal is to reduce effects of novelty to the situation and materials before beginning the experiment to determine cause and effect.

Adaptive Cluster Sampling Type of sampling sometimes used when cases are believed to be distributed into multiple clusters (e.g., geographic, spatial, temporal, low probability behaviors). Sampling is adaptively increased, such that when a cluster is likely found additional units are selected in that area before moving on in the search for additional clusters or "neighborhoods." Unbiased estimators are available with this sampling method. Adaptive cluster sampling is used in fields such as epidemiology, geology, and ecology.

Adaptive Sampling Any multistage sampling approach in which information is used from a prior stage to locate useful units in the following stage (e.g., *adaptive cluster sampling, *snowball sampling, *network sampling). The units to include in the study are not fixed in advance, but are accrued over stages.

Adaptive Testing   A computer-based testing procedure whereby subsequent items presented to test takers are selected based on their prior answers. The approach is used to obtain an estimate of ability/aptitude more quickly than through the use of full and parallel forms for every test taker. The method is used in standardized tests such as the GRE, LSAT, MCAT, and MAT.

Added Variable Plot   A graphic technique used to decide whether an additional *predictor (*independent) variable needs to be added to a *regression equation.

Addition Rule for Probability   States that, for mutually exclusive events, the probability of one event occurring or the other event occurring is equal to the sum of their probabilities. For example, in a deck of cards, the probability of a spade or a heart is the probability of a spade (13/52 = 1/4) plus the probability of a heart (13/52 = 1/4) = 1/4 + 1/4 = 2/4 = 1/2 = .5. Symbolized as $P(A \cup B)$, called probability of A union B, or probability of A or B. You can extend this logic to any number of events desired. If events are not mutually exclusive, then use the *general rule of addition; this adds to the above procedure subtracting the probability of the joint occurrence of A and B; this general formula is symbolized as $P(A \cup B) = P(A) + P(B) - P(A \cap B)$. See *mutually exclusive, *probability. Compare *multiplication rule for probability, *conditional probability.

Additive   Said of a relation or a *model in which the effects of the *independent variables on a *dependent variable can simply be added together to find their total effect. Contrast *interaction effect.

Additive Model   In social and behavioral statistics this term is used to refer to a statistical model that includes only main effects. The model assumes that each *independent variable (IV) operates constantly across the other IVs (has no *interaction effects) and that each quantitative IV is linearly related to the *dependent variable (DV; is a linear relationship). It's called an additive model because the effects of each independent variable are added in the linear combination, producing the predicted value of the DV. Compare *nonadditive mode, *multiplicative model.

Additivity Test   It is used to see if an *interaction effect needs to be added to a model with main effects only (i.e., *additive). It answers the question "Is the interaction statistically significant?" If the interaction effect is statistically significant, then a model with main effects plus interactions is appropriate and the interaction effects must be interpreted.

Adequate Sample   A random sample that is of sufficient size to be representative and provide enough statistical power for significance tests, including any subgroup analyses. We often say "the larger the sample, the better" and this is true with regard to reducing the *standard error, providing precise *confidence intervals, and maximizing *statistical power. However, cost also is an issue in sampling theory, and at some point increasing sample size brings diminishing or little or no return on investment. Therefore, one should select a sample that is "large enough" for the purposes at hand rather than as big as you can possibly make it.

Ad Hoc   Literally, Latin for "for this." Said of an explanation or a solution improvised for a specific purpose. Compare *planned comparisons.

Ad Infinitum   Latin for "to infinity" or continuing without end. Compare *limit.

Adjusted Goodness of Fit Index (AGFI)   A statistic sometimes used in *structural equation modeling to indicate model fit. It adjusts the *goodness of fit index (GFI) for the number of degrees of freedom relative to the number of parameters; that is, it rewards parsimonious models. Close model fit is indicated by GFI greater than or equal to .90. Because AGFI is heavily influenced by the sample size (bigger sample produces larger values), this index is not currently recommended for use by itself.

Adjusted Mean   In *general linear models (e.g., *ANOVA, *regression), the estimated parameters take into account or control for the other variables in the equation. When using one of these models (e.g., *ANCOVA), a predicted mean on the dependent variable (DV) for the levels of a categorical variable will be slightly different from the actual mean on the DV. This is because of statistical adjustment; adjustment only occurs, however, if the independent or predictor variables are correlated (i.e., when some *multicollinearity is present).

Adjusted R^2   An *R^2 (R-squared) adjusted to give a truer (population) estimate of the amount of variance in a *dependent variable that is accounted for by the *independent variables in a multiple *regression analysis. The adjusted estimate is always smaller; it is made by taking into account the number of independent variables and the sample size. Compare *coefficient of determination, *omega squared.

Adjusting for Baseline   Any technique in longitudinal studies that takes the starting point into account when reporting on the end point. For example, in studies of academic achievement, students' test scores at the end of the year might be compared to their scores at the beginning of the year in order to measure improvement. This can be done by using *difference scores or by *controlling for the earlier scores. See *value-added models.

Adjustment   Statistically removing the effects of a variable in which the researcher is not interested in order to focus better on variables that are of interest. Various statistical techniques can be used to make this adjustment. For example, a researcher who wanted to study the effects of ethnicity on income would probably want to adjust for other variables that could account for any association, such as education level. See *control for, *crosstabs, *regression analysis.

A

Admissible Hypothesis   A hypothesis that is open to consideration because it is not mathematically or logically self-contradictory or otherwise impossible.

Adoption Study   A type of research design used in developmental psychology to study the relative influence of genes/biology and environmental factors in human development (e.g., personality, intelligence). The design typically compares the relation of child characteristics to both biological and adoptive parents.

Affirming the Consequent   A *deductively invalid argument that takes the following form: If p then q; q; therefore p. This logic formed the basis of the *positivists' verificationism. It also was standard practice in most behavioral and social sciences. (If theory X is true, the hypothesized outcome will occur; the hypothesized outcome did occur; therefore theory X is true.) The philosopher of science Karl Popper provided a different and deductively valid approach called *falsificationism (showing what theories are not true), but his approach also had difficulties. Popper allowed only deductive or negative claims; he *rejected the use of induction,* but to show what theories are well supported over time requires *induction. Current practice in behavioral and social science uses a hybrid of verification (now called "confirmation") and falsification. Compare *falsificationism. *See modus tollens.

Age Cohort   A group of study participants, used in a *longitudinal study, of the same age (e.g., 6 years old) or age bracket (6–10 years old). See *cohort.

Age Effects   Outcomes attributable to subjects' ages or aging (becoming older), such as changes in cognitive processing with age. Compare *maturation effects.
   Age effects are often difficult to disentangle from other effects. For example, part of the difference between the social values of adults in their 70s and adults in their 20s is likely due to their ages (i.e., due to their becoming older). However, it is difficult to distinguish this age effect from *period effects (the 1960s was a very different historical period from today) and *cohort effects (the 1960s "baby boomer" generation is different from the generation Y "eco boomers" because of their different experiences).

Age Equivalent Score   A test score that reports the average chronological age at which the measured performance occurs. For example, if a child's performance indicates an age equivalent score of 8, that means the child's score is similar to that of average 8-year-olds.

AGFI   *Adjusted goodness of fit index.

Agglomerative Clustering   A type of *hierarchical clustering in which each case begins as its own cluster, and then, working in a bottom-up way, it is merged with similar "clusters"; the process continues until an optimal number of clusters is obtained. See *cluster analysis. Compare *divisive clustering.

Aggregate   A group of persons, or other *units of analysis, that have certain traits or characteristics in common without necessarily having any direct social connection with one another, such as the population of a city. Also called *aggregation. Compare *holism, *disaggregate.

For example, "all female physicians" is an aggregate; so is "all European cities with populations over 20,000." Gross national income is an aggregation of data about individual incomes.

Aggregate Data   Information about *aggregates or groups such as ethnic groups, social classes, or nations. Sometimes contrasted with *micro-data. See *level of analysis.

Aggregation   (a) A summary statistic based on data about individual cases or units, such as the mean score on a test calculated from individuals' test scores. (b) Data produced at a group level because they are not available at the individual level. See *ecological fallacy.

Aggregation Problem   The difficulty of predicting macro-level behavior from micro-level data. The term is used mainly by economists, but the problem pervades the social sciences. See *ecological fallacy, *level of analysis, *abstraction.

Agreement, Coefficient of   See *coefficient of agreement.

Agreement, Measure of   Any of several statistics used to summarize the degree of agreement between the rankings or classifications made by two or more observers. Examples include *Cohen's kappa and *Kendall's coefficient of concordance.

Ahistorical   Said of an interpretation, theory, or point of view that ignores the influence of the past on the present, that assumes the past is no different than the present, or that ignores time as a variable.

AI   *Artificial Intelligence.

AIC   *Akaike Information Criterion.

Akaike Information Criterion (AIC)   A *goodness-of-fit measure used to select among statistical models. It adjusts for the number of parameters; the greater the number, the bigger the adjustment or "penalty." The better the fit, the lower the value of the AIC. Compare *adjusted R^2 and *Bayesian information criterion.

Aleatory   Determined or characterized by chance, luck, randomness, or uncertainty. Sometimes, particularly in previous centuries, used in *probability theory; for example, "aleatory variable" means *random variable. More recently used in *qualitative research to mean uncaused or random.

Algorithm   (a) A set of clearly defined rules for solving a problem in a limited number of steps. In an ideal algorithm, if the rules are followed, the solution will require no judgment because it will automatically be correct. (b) Elements of or routines in a *computer program. Different statistical packages may use different algorithms for solving the same problem. (c) A formula. (d) Used broadly in methodological writing to mean any step-by-step procedure to solve a problem. Named after the 9th-century Arab mathematician and inventor of algebra Al-Khwarizmi, whose name in Latin was Algorithmi.

Alienation, Coefficient of   *Coefficient of alienation.

Allocation Bias   Misleading results arising from not validly allocating subjects to treatment and *control groups. See *randomized control trial.

Allocation Ratio   The ratio of the number of participants across the groups in an experiment. For example, if the experiment has two groups and has 15 participants per group, then the allocation ratio is 15:15. The number of participants across the two groups might also be proportional, as in 15:30; groups also can simply be unequal (neither equal nor proportional). When the allocation ratio is equal or proportional, the two *independent variables will be uncorrelated (i.e., no *multicollinearity will be present). This is a desirable feature because it simplifies the estimation of the unique effect of each independent variable and *variable ordering.

Allocation Rule   In *discriminant analysis, an algorithm for placing observations into categories.

All Subsets Regression   (also called **All Possible Subsets Multiple Regression/Correlation**) A method for selecting the predictor or *independent variables to include in a regression model. A computer program compares all possible combinations of predictor variables to determine which set of them performs best according to criteria determined by the researcher (e.g., largest R^2). Compare *stepwise regression.

Alpha (A, α)   (a) Usually called *Cronbach's alpha to distinguish it from the alpha in *alpha level. It is a measure of internal consistency or *reliability of the items in an *index. Cronbach's alpha ranges from 0 to 1.0 and indicates how much the items in an index are intercorrelated and thus presumed to measure the same construct. (b) Symbol for the *intercept in a *regression equation. (c) Symbol for an *odds ratio. (d) Symbol for "is proportional to."

Alpha Error   An error made by rejecting a true *null hypothesis (such as claiming that a relationship exists when it does not). Also called *Type I error, *false positive. See *beta error, *hypothesis testing.

Alpha Level   (a) The chance a researcher is willing to take of committing an *alpha error or *Type I error, that is, of rejecting a *null hypothesis that is true.

(b) If the null hypothesis is true, the alpha level is the probability that a Type I error (wrongly rejecting the null hypothesis) will be committed.

The smaller the alpha level, the smaller the *p value must be in order to reject the *null hypothesis. Thus, an alpha level of .01 is a more difficult criterion to satisfy than a level of .05. Also called *level of (statistical) significance. See *p value, *probability value, *probability level, *sampling error.

Alphanumeric Variable   A variable that can be expressed as a letter, number, or other symbol—or some combination of letters, numbers, and symbols.

Alternate Forms   Two or more versions of the same standardized test that measure the same construct and are identical in every way (e.g., equal difficulty and other psychometric properties) except that different items are used. Also called *equivalent forms or parallel forms.

Alternate-Forms Reliability   The consistency of test takers' scores on alternative/equivalent forms of the same test measuring the same thing. Those scoring high/low on one form should tend to be the same people scoring high/low on the other form. Also called *equivalent forms reliability. See *test-retest reliability.

Alternative Hypothesis   In *hypothesis testing (or *significance testing), any hypothesis that does not conform to the one being tested; it is the logical opposite of the *null hypothesis. If significance testing leads to the rejection of the null hypothesis, the researcher *tentatively* accepts the alternative hypothesis. Symbolized: H_1 or H_a.

For example, researchers conducting a study of the relation between teenage drug use and teenage suicide would probably use the null hypothesis of no relationship: "There is no difference between the suicide rates of teenagers who use drugs and those who do not." The null hypothesis says there is no difference in the suicide rates of the populations of drug users and non–drug users. The alternative hypotheses would be: "There is a difference in the suicide rates of the populations of drug users and non–drug users." It is the null hypothesis that is directly tested in hypothesis testing; therefore, if the sample data led to the rejection of the null hypothesis (that there was no statistically significant difference), the researcher would tentatively accept the alternative hypothesis.

Alternative Methodologies   A catchall term referring to any *nonexperimental and/or nonquantitative research. See *qualitative research.

Ambiguous Temporal Precedence   Situation in which a correlation is present between variables A and B, but it is not clear which is the cause and which is the effect.

AMELIA   A software program for imputing missing values. It is available at no cost as part of the *R statistics package. That plus its comparative ease of use has made it increasingly popular in recent years. It is based on *bootstrap methods. Named after a famous missing datum, Amelia Earhart, the celebrated pilot who disappeared in 1937. Compare *multiple imputation.

AMOS   Analysis of Moment Structures. A *statistical package used especially for *structural equation models.

Anachronism   An error made by affirming something that is chronologically impossible, such as by attributing *cause to something that followed the effect. Compare *ahistorical.

   For example, to claim that Keynes's writings influenced Adam Smith's theories would be an anachronistic mistake; it is impossible because Smith died long before Keynes wrote anything.

Analog   (Also spelled "analogue") Said of data or computers that use a system of representation that is physically analogous to the thing being represented. Compare *digital.

   For example, a thermometer can use height of a column of mercury to indicate heat; the higher the column, the higher the temperature. Or analog watches use the physical movement of hour and minute hands to represent the passing of time; the more the hands have moved, the more time has passed.

Analysis   (a) The separation of a whole into its parts so as to study them. (b) The study of the elements of a whole and their relationships. (c) Loosely, but perhaps most commonly, any rigorous study of anything. (d) In the context of *design and *measurement, the term is used broadly to mean statistical techniques. Compare *synthesis.

Analysis of Covariance (ANCOVA)   (a) An extension of *ANOVA that provides a way of statistically *controlling the effects of variables one does not want to examine in a study. These *extraneous variables are called *covariates, or control variables. ANCOVA allows you to remove covariates from the list of possible explanations of variance in the *dependent variable. ANCOVA does this by using statistical techniques (such as *regression) to *partial out the effects of covariates rather than by using direct experimental methods to control extraneous variables. ANCOVA is also conducted to provide an increase in the *power of the test (compared to an ANOVA) of the categorical independent variable. (b) More generally, ANCOVA is the special case of the *general linear model in which one has a single quantitative (*continuous) dependent variable and a mixture of categorical and quantitative independent variables.

   ANCOVA is used in experimental research studies when researchers want to remove the effects of some *antecedent variable. For example, pretest scores are used as covariates in pretest-posttest experimental designs. ANCOVA is also used in *nonexperimental research, such as surveys of nonrandom samples, or in *quasi-experiments when subjects cannot be assigned randomly to *control and *experimental groups. Although fairly widespread, the use of ANCOVA for *nonexperimental research is controversial.

All ANCOVA analyses can be handled with *multiple regression analysis using *dummy coding for the nominal variables; with the advent of powerful computers, this is a more efficient approach. Because of this, the traditional approach to ANCOVA is used less frequently than in the past.

Analysis of Covariance Structures   An alternate term for *structural equation modeling (SEM).

Analysis of Deviance Table   A table listing the key results of a *logistic regression (i.e., model, deviance, df, χ^2, G^2). The results show whether there is a change in deviance across models compared. Roughly analogous to an *analysis of variance *summary table.

Analysis of Unweighted Means   In the *analysis of variance and *analysis of covariance, these are what is obtained when the user selects *Type I sum of squares. This process allows the first categorical variable to account for variance in the dependent variable (DV) without controlling for the other independent variable (IV; which may be categorical or quantitative); then the effect of the second IV is added to the model, and the amount of variance in the DV it accounts for is tested. This approach gives unfair advantage to the initial IV and is not recommended. Instead, generally speaking, one should use an analysis of weighted means. Compare *Type III sum of squares.

Analysis of Variance (ANOVA)   (a) A test of the *statistical significance of the differences among the *mean scores of two or more groups on one or more *variables or *factors. It is an extension of the *t test, which can handle only two groups at a time, to a larger number of groups. More specifically, it is used for assessing the statistical significance of the relationship between *categorical *independent variables and a *continuous *dependent variable. The procedure in ANOVA involves computing a ratio (*F ratio) of the *variance between the groups (*explained variance) to the variance within the groups (*error variance). See *one-way ANOVA, *two-way ANOVA. (b) ANOVA is the special case of the *general linear model in which one has a single quantitative (*continuous) dependent variable and one or more categorical independent variables. ANOVA is equivalent to *multiple regression with *dummy coded *independent variables and a continuous dependent variable (e.g., it provides the same model R^2 and p value).

For example, a professor tried different teaching methods. He randomly assigned members of his class of 30 students to three groups of 10 students each. All three groups were given the same required readings, but class time was spent differently in each. Group 1 ("Discuss") spent class time in directed discussions of the assigned readings. Group 2 ("No Class") was excused from any obligation to attend classes for the first half of the semester, but they were given additional text materials they could use to help them understand the assigned readings. Group 3 ("Lecture") was taught by traditional lecture methods. The students' scores on the midterm examination are listed in Table A.1.

A

Students in the three groups obviously got different average scores. The professor wanted to know whether the differences were statistically significant, that is, whether they were bigger than would be likely due to chance alone. To find out, he entered the information from Table A.1 into his computer program and conducted an ANOVA. As Table A.2 shows, the results were statistically significant (at the $p < .001$ level); the teaching methods probably made a difference. Compare *factorial experiment, *two-way ANOVA.

A key limitation of ANOVA is that it indicates only whether a statistically significant difference exists among the group means, but it does not specify *which* differences are statistically significant. For that, researchers must turn to methods of *multiple comparisons. Also, most experts today recommend that one include an *effect size indicator to help interpret and communicate information about the size or magnitude of relationship.

How to Read an ANOVA Summary Table. "Source" means source of the variance. "Between groups" is explained variance, that is, explained by the

Table A.1   Analysis of Variance: Students' Midterm Scores, by Method of Instruction

	Group 1 Discuss	Group 2 No Class	Group 3 Lecture
	94	78	87
	92	76	85
	91	72	84
	89	71	84
	88	68	81
	88	68	80
	86	67	80
	86	66	79
	83	64	72
	83	60	68
Totals	880	690	800
Means	88	69	80

Table A.2   ANOVA Summary Table: Three Teaching Methods

Source	SS	df	MS	F
Between Groups	1820	2	910.00	35.10*
Within Groups	700	27	25.93	
Total	2520	29		

*$p < .001$.

treatments the different groups received. "Within groups" is unexplained or error variance, since differences among individuals within a group cannot be explained by differences in the treatments the groups received. "SS" is *sum of squares (total of squared *deviation scores). *Degrees of freedom are abbreviated as "*df.*" "MS" stands for mean squares, which are calculated by dividing the SS by the *df.* "*F*" is the *F* ratio of the MS between to the MS within, which is statistically significant at the .001 level ($p < .001$). (Note that it is common for such tables to be cut from research reports to save space.)

Analysis of Weighted Means   In the analysis of variance and analysis of covariance, this is what is obtained when the user selects *Type III sum of squares. This process tests the amount of variance uniquely explained or added to the model. The same process is used for all independent variables. It is the recommended approach, rather than the analysis of unweighted means. See *Type III sum of squares.

Analytic Approach   An analytical approach that studies a phenomenon by breaking the whole down into its component parts. For example, Isaac Newton showed that white light can be separated into multiple colored light streams, as seen in a rainbow. Compare *synthetic approach, *reductionism.

Analytic Induction   An approach in *qualitative research that develops theory by examining a small number of cases. Theory then leads to formulation of a hypothesis, which is tested through the study of more cases. This usually leads to refinement or reformulation of the hypothesis, which is then tested with further cases until the researcher judges that the inquiry can be concluded. Compare *negative case analysis.

Analytics   Most generally, a new term for quantitative *analysis or statistics; it is most often used in the context of *big data generated by or available on the Web. Since the last edition of this dictionary, universities have created numerous departments or programs of analytics—or reorganized and renamed existing departments and programs. Predictive analytics refers to quantitative *forecasting often using *ARIMA models.

Anchor   The words applied to points on a *rating scale. Sometimes only the end points are anchored (e.g., *low, high*), sometimes the middle point also is anchored (e.g., *medium, neutral*), and sometimes all points on a rating scale are anchored as in the following 5-point rating scale: 1 = *strongly disagree*, 2 = *disagree*, 3 = *neutral*, 4 = *agree*, 5 = *strongly agree*.

Anchor Test   Used to establish alternate forms reliability. For example, when just two alternate forms are of interest, one group of participants receives the first alternate form, a second group receives the second alternate form, and the anchor test items are provided to all participants. In the anchor test, the scores of groups one and two are compared to their scores on the common test items. The goal is to obtain alternate sets of items (alternate forms) that are equivalent and provide the same test scores. Compare *item response theory.

ANCOVA   *Analysis of covariance.

Anecdotal Evidence   Evidence, often in story form, derived from casual, unsystematic, and/or uncontrolled observation. Usually used to dismiss someone's evidence, as in "*mere* anecdotal evidence." Compare *case study methods, *narrative analysis.

Angoff Procedure   Using a panel of subject matter experts to judge the difficulty of items on a test and to produce cut scores for levels on it (e.g., proficient, at risk). There are several versions and considerable debate among measurement specialists about the merits of each. Compare *item response theory.

Animal Rights   The belief that animals have rights similar to humans and these rights should be protected in research. Animal rights include, for example, treatment with respect and freedom from pain and abuse by humans.

Anonymity   The assurance that individual participants in research cannot be identified. The strictest kind of anonymity means that the identities of participants are concealed even from researchers, as is possible when respondents return their completed questionnaires by mail with no identifying information. Many kinds of research, such as face-to-face interviews, make strict anonymity impossible. Then *confidentiality* of information about individual participants, including their identities, becomes the standard. While anonymity means that the researcher does not know subjects' identities, confidentiality means that the researcher knows but promises not to tell. See *research ethics, *institutional review board.

ANOVA   *Analysis of variance.

ANOVA Summary Table   A table showing the key results of an *analysis of variance test, including the source of the effect, sum of squares, degrees of freedom, mean square, F statistic, and p value. An example is shown in this dictionary at the entry *analysis of variance.

Ansari-Bradley Test   A two-sample nonparametric statistical test of the equality of variance or dispersion or spread of the data. The null hypothesis is that the amount of dispersion is equal in the two populations. It is recommended over an F test when the populations are not normally distributed.

Anscombe Residual   A type of residual or unexplained variance or error used in *generalized linear models. It is the transformation of the dependent variable that is the closest to normality, and it is then standardized to have a variance of 1 and a mean of 0, for ease of interpretation.

A

Antecedent   (a) A condition that precedes another and is thought to influence or to cause it. (b) The first term in a ratio. For example, in the ratio 14:1, 14 is the antecedent; 1 is the *consequent.

Antecedent Variable   A variable that comes earlier in an explanation or in a chain of causal links—as in a *path analysis. Sometimes used to refer to *background variable.

For example, if the dependent variable were occupation at age 50 and education level were the *predictor or independent variable, place of birth would be a variable antecedent to education.

Antedependence   With longitudinal or time-series or event history data, observations on a variable are said to be "antedependent" when later observations are independent of (not correlated with) preceding observations. Compare *autocorrelation.

Anthropometry   Research that involves measurements of the human body.

Anthropomorphism   Attribution of humanlike characteristics to nonhuman entities, as in "The research study collected survey data from the participants." The statement could avoid anthropomorphism by saying, "The researcher collected survey data from the participants."

Antilog   See *logarithm.

Antimode   The least common score or value in a distribution. Compare *mode.

Antinaturalism   The belief that using methods developed in the natural sciences is inappropriate in the study of human thought and action. Contrast *positivism.

A-optimal/A-efficient design   Type of *optimal design that focuses on obtaining the combination of independent variables that minimizes the average variance of the model parameter estimates of the dependent variable. See *efficiency, definition (b).

Apache Hadoop   Open-source *software used to store and analyze large *data sets. See *hadoop.

A Posteriori   Literally, Latin for "from what comes after"; said of conclusions reached by reasoning from observed facts (after observation) or of research that proceeds in an *inductive way. Loosely, *empirical. Compare *a priori, *post hoc comparisons.

A Posteriori Comparison   A comparison that a researcher decides to make after the data have been collected and studied. This is usually done because the results have suggested a new way to approach the data. See *post hoc comparison, *multiple comparisons. Compare *a priori comparison.

Apparatus   Physical equipment sometimes required to *operationalize independent or dependent variables, typically in experimental research.

A

Applications Software Computer programs designed for specific purposes (applications) such as word processing, accounting, or doing statistical analysis.

Applied Research (also called **Applied Science**) Research undertaken with the intention of applying the results to some specific problem, such as studying the effects of different methods of law enforcement on crime rates. One of the biggest differences between applied and *basic research is that in applied work, the research questions are more often determined not by researchers but by policymakers or others who want help. Virtually any *research design can be, and has been, used to conduct applied research. Types of applied research include *evaluation research and *action research.

Applied Statistics (a) Often used to refer to statistical analysis in the social and behavioral sciences. (b) A branch of mathematical statistics focused more on real-world problems than on pure mathematical problems, but it is still highly mathematical.

Apprehensive-Subject Role Behavior by research participants attempting to please the researcher but simultaneously becoming anxious about being evaluated. See *demand characteristics, *social desirability bias.

Approximation Error Another term for *rounding error.

A Priori Literally, Latin for "from what comes before." (a) Said of conclusions reached on the basis of reasoning from self-evident propositions—without or before examining empirical facts—or of research that proceeds in a mathematical or *deductive way. Loosely, theoretical. Compare *a posteriori. (b) Said of conclusions that can be known without experience, as in the solution to a mathematical equation or problem ($2 + 2 = ?$). (c) Used to describe preexisting (prior) conditions among groups of subjects, especially potential *confounding variables.

The expression is sometimes used to describe a conclusion for which someone believes there is no empirical evidence, as in "One conclusion is as likely to be true as the other, a priori, which is why we need to gather more data to resolve the question."

A Priori Comparison A comparison that a researcher decides to make before (prior to) performing the experiment or gathering the data. Designs incorporating a priori comparisons are usually considered stronger than those that use *a posteriori comparisons. See *planned comparison, *multiple comparisons, *Bonferroni test statistic.

A Priori Power See *prospective power.

A Priori Probability Another term for *theoretical probability. Contrast *prior probability.

Aptitude-Treatment Interaction A *trait-treatment interaction research design in which the researcher checks to see if the effect of a treatment varies according to a trait variable, where the measured trait is an aptitude such as verbal ability or manual dexterity. Aptitude-treatment interaction was the original term; *attribute-treatment and *trait-treatment were more general versions developed later. See *interaction effect.

Archival Data   (a) Data that were originally used for a research study, stored, and later used in additional research studies. Traditionally most archived data were quantitative, such as the large collection of the Interuniversity Consortium for Political and Social Research (ICPSR). Increasingly, qualitative data also are being archived and reused. (b) Any data used by a researcher that was not originally generated or collected by a researcher, such as data from government reports, newspaper archives, or Internet sources.

Archival Research   The study of existing records (archives). Often associated with historical research because, by definition, existing records will contain information about the past.

Archive   (often used in the plural) (a) A place where public records or other kinds of information are stored. (b) The information thus stored.

   *Database archives (such as the *Public Use Microdata Samples and the *General Social Survey) are increasingly important in social and behavioral research. Both quantitative and qualitative data can be archived, and both types of archive have a very long history.

Arc-Sine Transformation   A statistical transformation used to increase the homogeneity of variance of samples, that is, to make sample variances more similar across comparison groups. This transformation is done because equality of variances is a fundamental *assumption of several important statistical tests, such as *ANOVA. The transformation is used to change data made up of frequencies or proportions so that they can be more accurately analyzed with ANOVA or regression.

Area Sample   A kind of *cluster sample in which the clusters are selected on the basis of geographic units. Area samples use maps or GPS coordinates rather than lists to define the *sampling frames from which the sample is then drawn.

   For example, say you want to survey residents of California about their *attitudes concerning property taxes. You do not have a list of all California residents from which to draw a sample. You could divide the state into "areas" (such as *census tracts or voting districts) and take a *random sample of those areas. Then, within each of these selected areas, you could survey all (or a sample) of the residents on their attitudes.

Area Under the Curve (AUC)   (a) Inferential statistics that rely on probability distributions. For example, a *p value is the area under the curve at or beyond the calculated value of a test statistic. All possible events must occur under the curve; therefore, the area under the curve is 1.0 (or 100% if one wants to think in percentages). Areas under the curve can be calculated using integral *calculus, but in basic statistics we can find the desired areas in tables in the back of statistic books for common probability distributions such as t, F, χ^2, and z. (b) The area under a *receiver operator curve (ROC) is used for plotting results on a binary test, such as true positive versus *false positive rates, for example, having a disease and not having it.

A model that predicts a condition perfectly would be scored 1.0; one that predicts no better than chance is scored 0.5. The results are often depicted graphically, which may aid in interpreting data.

ARIMA Auto-regressive integrated moving average. A complex set of statistical techniques for *time-series analysis that combines *autoregressive analysis procedures with those of *moving averages. By using ARIMA models, the researcher is able to construct *trend lines that take into account both the *systematic error (autocorrelation) and the unsystematic or *random error (or *noise).

Well-known examples of findings based on this sort of work are the *seasonally adjusted figures for unemployment or consumer spending.

Arithmetic Mean See *mean.

Arithmetic Sequence A series of numbers that changes by a constant amount. Here is an example in which the difference is 6: 5, 11, 17, 23.

AR Model Abbreviation for autoregressive model. See *autoregressive.

Array (a) An ordered display of a set of observations, measurements, or statistics—such as a *frequency distribution. For example, the observed grade point averages 3.2, 2.2, 3.1, 3.6, 2.8 in *ascending order give the array {2.2, 2.8, 3.1, 3.2, 3.6}. (b) An arrangement of numbers in a *matrix. See *correlation matrix.

Arrow's Impossibility Theorem A logical demonstration by the economist Kenneth Arrow that when there are three or more alternatives, there is no way of deciding by voting how to consistently combine the distinct preferences of individuals in such a way that each of their preferences will be maximized. It short, it is impossible for society to make up its mind democratically about what it wants. The theorem is generally accepted as true and important in economics, social theory, political science, and *decision theory.

Artifact An artificial result. (a) A mistaken or *biased result produced by the measuring instrument rather than the phenomenon being studied. (b) Something the researcher created by the way he or she gathered or analyzed the *data, not a condition present in the *subjects. Examples include *halo effect, *Hawthorne effect, *John Henry Effect, *regression artifact, and *demand characteristics. See *self-fulfilling prophecy.

Artificial Intelligence A branch of computer science that studies ways of getting computers to simulate human thought, including such abilities as reasoning and learning from experience.

Ascending Order   Said of data arranged so that each item in a series is higher than (ascends) the previous items. Arranging data in that way can be an important step toward constructing a *frequency distribution or calculating a *rank correlation. Compare *descending order.

Ascertainment Bias   A term popular in medical research referring to sampling in a way that produces a sample that is not representative of the population. If a sample is the product of ascertainment bias, some groups are excluded from the sample, and, therefore, the sample is not a *representative sample.

ASCII   (rhymes with "passkey") American Standard Code for Information Interchange. This computer character set is used as a sort of Esperanto for *software. It enables a user of one software *program to translate what he or she has written into a language that can be understood by another software program. ASCII is widely used to transfer statistical data files from one computer or program to another.

Assessment   Sometimes used as a synonym of evaluation, but many authors make a distinction. Assessment refers to collecting data to measure performance; it is diagnostic and is the act of attaching a score to what one wants to measure. Assessment provides the input data required to make evaluative judgments. Assessment can be ongoing and is often formative (i.e., for purpose of improvement). Contrast *evaluation.

Assessment Research   Often a synonym for *evaluation research. When a distinction is drawn between the two, assessment frequently refers to measuring individual outcomes, while evaluation refers to studying the effects of programs. The two are routinely linked, because a common way to evaluate a program is to assess its effects on the individuals who participated in it. Compare *evaluation research.

Association, Measure of   Any *statistic that shows (in a single number) the degree of relationship between two or more *variables. Two broad types are those based on *proportional reduction of error in prediction, such as *lambda, and those based on departure from *statistical independence, such as *phi.

   Other examples of measures of association include *Pearson's correlation coefficient, *gamma, and *Cramer's *V*. Note that there can be considerable controversy about which measures of association are best to use for various purposes and kinds of data.

Association Models   In the analysis of *categorical data, models that analyze the observed frequencies in cross-classified tables so as to measure the strength of association between two or more ordered categorical variables. Compare *loglinear models, of which association models are a subcategory.

Association, Statistical   (a) A relationship between two or more *variables that can be described statistically. (b) Any of several statistical techniques (such as *correlations and *regression analysis) that can be used to describe the degree to which differences in one variable are accompanied by (associated with) corresponding differences in another variable. Such associations do not prove the presence of a causal relation, but they sometimes suggest that one may be present.

Association, Test of   Another term for *test statistic when applied to a *measure* of association, which indicates the size of the relation between two variables. Like any test statistic, a test of association tests for *statistical significance. A test of association estimates how likely (or unlikely) an empirical (i.e., observed/measured) association is under the assumption that the *null hypothesis is true.

Assumption   (a) A statement that is presumed to be true, often only temporarily or for a specific purpose, such as building a *theory. Compare *axiom, *hypothesis. (b) The conditions under which statistical techniques yield valid results.

For example, (a) researchers might make the assumption that there is no difference in the innate verbal ability of men and women so that they could use differences in grades in college-level literature courses to test a theory that college professors discriminate on the basis of sex.

For example, (b) most statistical techniques, such as *regression analysis and *ANOVA, require that certain assumptions be made about the data. Tests of *statistical significance for these procedures (regression and ANOVA) assume random samples or *random assignment to control and experimental groups, *homoscedasticity, and *normality. Serious violations of statistical assumptions can make the results misleading or meaningless.

Assumption of Equal Variances   Synonym for homogeneity of variances. See *homogeneity of variances, *Hartley's test, *Cochran's C test, *Levene's test, and *Brown Forsyth test. If violated, see *Tamhane's T2 and *Games-Howell post hoc tests. For multivariate version, see *homogeneity of variance-covariance matrices.

Assumption of Homogeneity of Slopes   See *homogeneity of slopes.

Assumption of Homogeneity of Variance-Covariance Matrices   See *homogeneity of variance-covariance matrices.

Assumption of Independence   See *independence of observations, *i.i.d.

Assumption of Normality   See *normality.

Assumption of Sphericity   See *sphericity.

Asymmetrical Distribution   A *skewed distribution.

Asymmetrical Test   Another term for *one-sided test of significance.

Asymmetric Measure   A measure of *association that has a different value depending on which *variable is treated as *dependent and which as *independent. Compare *symmetric measure.

*Lambda and *Somers's *d* are examples of asymmetric measures of association. A *regression coefficient is an asymmetric measure; a *correlation coefficient is symmetric.

Asymmetry The state of a *distribution that is *skewed or unbalanced.

Asymptote (a) A theoretical limit that a curve approaches but never reaches. (b) Any theoretical outer limit; see *limit. (c) A leveling off of performance quality or efficiency; see *learning curve.

Asymptotic Said of a curve that gets ever closer to a line but never touches it. For example, the *tails of a *normal curve are asymptotic to the *x*-axis.

Atomistic Fallacy An inferential error made about groups because it is based only on data about individuals. See *fallacy of composition, *ecological fallacy.

Attenuation A reduction in a measure of *association caused by measurement errors. Compare *artifact. Since no measurement is without error, attenuation is all but universal.

For example, in a study of consumer confidence and spending, neither measure will be perfect, which means that a correlation between confidence and spending will be too low (attenuated).

Attenuation, Correction for An adjustment made to *correlation coefficients to estimate more accurately what they would have been had error-free measurements been available. The greater the *reliability of the measures, the smaller the attenuation; the lower the reliability, the greater the attenuation and the correction.

Attitude A positive or negative evaluation of and disposition toward persons, groups, policies, or other objects of attention. Attitudes are inferred based on cognitive, affective, and behavioral categories. Attitudes are learned and relatively persistent. See *trait, *Bogardus Social Distance Scale.

Attitude Scale A series of questions designed to measure the strength of attitudes and beliefs. A common format for such measures is a *Likert scale. Compare *Guttman scale, *index.

Attribute (a) A *qualitative variable or trait, often used in contrast with a *quantitative variable or trait. This is the same basic distinction as that between *categorical (attribute) and *continuous (quantitative) variables. Compare *attribute variable. (b) In *conditional probability, the "given" or condition.

For example, (a) a person's physical sex is an attribute (or qualitative, categorical variable), while the number of square feet in his or her living room is a quantitative, continuous variable. Occupation is a variable; carpenter, teacher, and butcher are attributes or constants.

For example, (b) for the problem "What is the probability that a college sophomore will graduate, given that she is on the dean's list?" being on the dean's list is the attribute.

A

Attribute-Treatment Interaction (ATI)   Another term for *trait-treatment interaction and *aptitude-treatment interaction. The purpose of studying an ATI is to learn whether the effect of an attribute on a *dependent variable is the same or different for control and treatment groups. See *interaction effect.

Attribute Variable   A variable that is a characteristic or trait of a participant, which, therefore, researchers cannot manipulate but can only measure.

For example, in a study of the effects of age and vitamins on health, researchers could vary (manipulate) the amount and kind of vitamins participants received. However, they could not manipulate the participants' ages; they could only measure their ages.

Attrition   Losing subjects over the course of the research project. Also called "mortality." Attrition is a common problem in *longitudinal studies and may be a source of *external validity *bias if the subjects who are lost make the *sample less *representative of the *population. Attrition may be a source of *internal validity bias when comparison groups (e.g., experimental and control groups) become different because of differential loss of participants. Statistical methods for detecting attrition are uncontroversial but are probably used too infrequently. Statistical corrections for attrition bias are less clearly valuable.

Attrition is a frequent issue in *field experiments and *panel studies in which the same subjects are studied at two or more times. Attrition may occur, for instance, when subjects move and cannot be located. If many subjects are lost, and if they are in some way unusual in comparison to the remaining subjects, this makes it hard to draw valid conclusions about what happened to the group over time.

AUC   See *area under the curve.

Audit   Inspection of an organization's or an individual's records. The term was originally used to describe reviewing financial records, but it is increasingly used in social and behavioral research, especially in qualitative research, to mean examining the extent to which the methods of a study are sound and its findings confirmable. Audits can be external (done by an outside expert) or internal as a self-check on efficiency and effectiveness.

Audit Trail   A systematic set of records that allows someone conducting an *audit to reconstruct what was done, such as keeping track of changes made in a data file. The term is mainly used to describe documentation that allows financial transactions to be traced, but it is also used to describe researchers' records, especially in qualitative research. Sometimes called "paper trail." Compare *protocol.

Authenticity Criteria   Standards appropriate for judging the quality of research. Used especially in the context of *qualitative, *constructivist, and *postmodernist research.

Autochthonous Variability   Change that comes from influences within a causal system as opposed to from outside it. Compare *endogenous and *exogenous variables.

Autocorrelation   Correlation between members in a series of observations, such as weekly oil prices. Autocorrelation is present when later items in a *time series are correlated with earlier items. For example, the oil price for a particular week is usually more similar to that of the previous week than to the price several weeks prior to the measurement. More technically, autocorrelation occurs when *residual *error terms from observations of the same variable at different times are correlated. Such correlations or nonindependence can raise several kinds of interpretive problems. The problem with using autocorrelated data in a *regression analysis is that it violates the assumption of *independence of observations. Independence of observations is usually produced by random selection or random assignment, but this is not possible with a time-series variable. In regression analysis, autocorrelation can be reduced by using *generalized rather than *ordinary least squares to compute the *regression equation. Also called "serial correlation." See *multicollinearity, *ARIMA.

Autocorrelation Coefficient   The *Pearson correlation between a time-series variable (e.g., annual GDP) and a lagged (by one or more time points) version of itself (annual GDP lagged by one year). It shows the extent to which the time-series variable, lagged one or more periods, is correlated with itself. See *lagged dependent variable.

Autoregressive   Said of a series of observations in which the value of each depends (at least in part) on the value of one or more of the immediately preceding observations. Called autoregressive because one explains later observations by earlier ones; that is, one *regresses later values on earlier values. See *autocorrelation, *Markov chain, *time series.

Auxiliary Assumptions   Background assumptions that must be made when conducting any test of a theory or hypothesis. See *Duhem-Quine thesis.

Available Case Analysis   In missing data analysis, another term for *pairwise deletion.

Average   See *mean.

Average Deviation (AD)   (also called **Average Absolute Deviation**) A measure of the *variation in a group of scores. It is calculated by taking the *mean or average of the *absolute values of the *deviation scores (that is, the differences between the scores and their mean). The larger the average deviation, the greater the *spread of scores in a group of scores. An AD can also be, and often is, calculated on the basis of deviations from the *median. The AD is less commonly used as a measure of variation than are the *standard deviation and the *variance. Also called "mean deviation" and, most accurately, *mean absolute deviation.

A

Axial Coding   In *grounded theory and related forms of analysis, axial coding is used to organize data and data categories into a model or theory. By comparison, in *open coding, the data are organized into initial categories.

Axiom   A maxim or statement that is considered so accurate or self-evident that it is widely accepted as a foundation on which arguments can be built or a truth from which other truths can be deduced. Compare *assumption, *postulate.

   In contrast to mathematics, there are few genuine axioms in the social and behavioral sciences. Two statements that might qualify as axioms (at least for some researchers) are (1) "Out-group hostility breeds in-group solidarity" and (2) "People seek to maximize pleasure and minimize pain."

Axis   A vertical or a horizontal line used to construct a *graph. See *abscissa (*x*-axis), *ordinate (*y*-axis), *Cartesian coordinates.

b Symbol for an unstandardized *regression coefficient, usually a lowercase, italicized *b*.

Background Variables Aspects of subjects' or *participants' "backgrounds" that might influence other variables but will not be influenced by them. Background variables are usually demographic characteristics—such as age, sex, ethnicity, and parents' income—that the researcher cannot manipulate. Also called "subject," "organismic," "classification," and "individual-difference" variables. While there can be subtle differences among these usages, the basic idea is the same: Background variables can be causes, but they are not *independent variables, in some strict senses of that term, because they cannot be manipulated by a researcher. However, researchers can and frequently do *control for background variables. Compare *antecedent variable.

For example, your sex and your age (background variables) might influence your income (think of age and sex discrimination), but a change in your income certainly would not change either your sex or your age.

Backward Elimination A computer procedure for *regression analysis that is used to identify the set of *independent variables that are good (statistically significant) predictors of the *dependent variable and produce the best *fitting equation or model. Also called "stepdown selection." Compare *forward selection, *stepwise regression.

The routine is to begin the analysis with all the variables in the equation and remove (eliminate) them one at a time according to whether they meet specific criteria (levels of significance of their *F ratios). The variable with the smallest *partial correlation is examined first. If it does not meet the criterion, it is eliminated. Then the variable with the second smallest partial is examined, and so on until no more variables are eliminated.

Bagplot A bivariate version of a univariate *boxplot (*box and whisker plot). It attempts to summarize the bivariate data and the relationship between the variables. The "bag" part of the graph surrounds one half of observations. An example is shown in Figure B.1, where the two variables are GPA and starting salary.

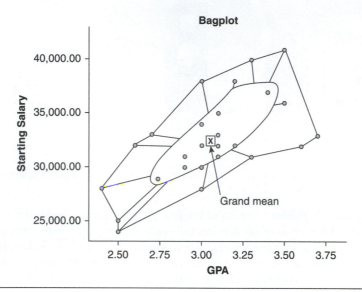

Figure B.1   Bagplot

Balanced Design   A *randomized-blocks design in which every *treatment appears in each block the same number of times. The same number of observations is made for each experimental condition. An *ANOVA is balanced when the number of subjects in each group is equal.

Balanced Scale   A *rating scale that has a negative and positive side of equal size, as in (1) strongly disagree, (2) disagree, (3) neutral, (4) agree, (5) strongly agree. Compare to *unbalanced scale.

Bar Chart   Another term for a *bar graph. Also called "bar diagram."

Bar Graph   A way of depicting *frequency distributions for *categorical (*nominal) variables, such as religious affiliation, ethnic group, or state of residence.
   The example in Figure B.2 on page 29 presents the Republican Party affiliation of a sample of survey respondents categorized by religious affiliation. About 31% of Protestants surveyed reported affiliation with the Republicans, roughly 17% of Catholics did, and so on. Note that the bars do not touch in a bar graph, as they do in a *histogram.

Bartlett-Box Test   One of several tests for *equality of variances of populations. *Cochran's C test, *Levene's test, and *Brown Forsythe test are also are used for this purpose. Also called "Bartlett-Box F test."

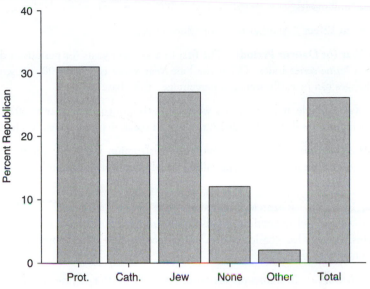

Figure B.2   Bar Graph

Bartlett's Test   (a) Commonly used in *factor analysis to test the *null hypothesis that all the correlations in the matrix to be factor analyzed are zero. If they are not significantly different from zero, a factor analysis is inappropriate. See *KMO test. (b) A test for equality of population variances in an *analysis of variance. It tests the null hypothesis that the population variances (i.e., the group variances) are all equal. One hopes to not-reject this null hypothesis.

Bartlett Test of Sphericity   Used in principle components analysis/factor analysis to test the null hypothesis that the correlation matrix of the variables is an *identity matrix (i.e., each variable is perfectly correlated with itself and the variables are uncorrelated with each other). One wants to reject this null; otherwise conduct of a factor analysis is inappropriate.

Baseline   (a) One or a series of measurements of the rate or level of some *variable in its naturally occurring state before an experimental *treatment is applied or before some measure of the effect of a new variable is taken. Compare *pretest. (b) In a single-subject design, measurement of the target behavior of the participant prior to presentation of the treatment condition and after the treatment is removed. See *A-B-A-B design. (c) The horizontal or *x-axis, also called the *abscissa.

For example, (a) if a political party wished to test the effects on party finances of a new advertising campaign, it could get baseline data by measuring the rate of contributions a week before the campaign started (the baseline) and compare that with the rate of contributions for the week after the campaign began.

Baseline Model   (in confirmatory factor analysis and structural equation modeling). See *null model.

Basement Effect   Another term for *floor effect.

Base Year (or Date or Period)   The first in a series of years (or periods or dates) in a *time-series index. Often the base year value is set at 100; subsequent changes can be easily seen as a percentage of the base year.

For example, if a price index were set at 100 for the base year of 2010, and the index moved to 140 by 2017, this would mean that prices went up by 40%.

BASIC   Beginner's All-Purpose Symbolic Instruction Code. A *programming language, intended for nonspecialists, widely used for writing microcomputer programs.

Basic Research   Research undertaken with the primary goal of advancing knowledge and theoretical understanding rather than solving practical problems. Also called "basic science." Often contrasted with *applied research. Sometimes called *pure research.

Bathtub Curve   In studies of *life expectancy, the death rate often looks roughly like a cross section of a bathtub. The death rate starts fairly high, declines rapidly until about age 5, then levels off for some decades before starting to climb rapidly again around age 50. See *life table.

Battery of Tests   A group or series of tests, usually psychological tests.

Bayesian   See *Bayesian statistical inference.

Bayes's Theorem   A method for evaluating the *conditional probability of an *event, particularly an unknown prior event, given that a known subsequent event has occurred. Bayes's theorem allows researchers to revise estimates of the probability of events using new evidence to do so. See *Bayesian statistical inference.

Bayesian Analysis   Data analysis in *Bayesian statistical inference.

Bayesian Decision Theory   A method of decision making and, by extension, of estimating probabilities that is based at least partly on expert opinion, called *subjective probability.

Bayesian Information Criterion (BIC)   Like the chief alternative, the *AIC, the BIC is a statistic used to select preferred statistical models from a set of models. It is a measure of goodness-of-fit that adjusts ("penalizes") for model complexity. A model with a smaller BIC statistic is generally superior to one with a larger BIC.

Bayesian Linear Models   A term sometimes used to describe *hierarchical linear models.

Bayesians   Researchers and statisticians who advocate the use of *Bayesian statistical inference.

Bayesian Statistical Inference   Methods based on a subjectivist rather than a frequentist understanding of probability. *Subjectivist* in this context means that a researcher begins with a personal assessment of uncertainty called a *prior probability. This is often based on evidence, but it is subjective in that it may vary among researchers. The prior probability is often described as the opinion of a rational individual given the evidence or as the decision of a rational person expressed as a probability distribution.

Bayesian methods *formally* combine the prior probability with data obtained from research—often called the "likelihood"—to reach a revised assessment of uncertainty called the *posterior probability. The posterior probability replaces the traditional *p* value. Because Bayesian methods are not tied to the assumptions of classical theory, they can be applied to problems with nonrandom samples and to samples too small for classical inference.

Prior probabilities are the key to Bayesian statistics. They are often based on previous research; if so, the method is referred to as "empirical Bayes," which bases the prior probability as much as possible on data. Both Bayesian approaches, standard and empirical, provide the researcher with formal ways of incorporating prior judgment or information into the process of making statistical inferences. This leads to more precise inferences and estimates, such as narrower confidence intervals (called "credible intervals" by Bayesians). Because it is rare, except in highly exploratory studies, for researchers not to have prior information with which to narrow the possibilities, the Bayesian advantage of being able to incorporate this knowledge into calculations can be considerable.

The Bayesian approach can be quite natural. For example, if the average life expectancy for men in a society is 80 years and you meet someone who is 82, you don't expect him to die 2 years ago. Rather, you take the prior information into account when you estimate his life expectancy. See *life table.

Although Bayes's theorem dates from the 1760s, it was not often used as a foundation for statistics until the 20th century. Bayesian methods became more common by the 1990s, particularly as specialized computer software became available for handling some of the intricate problems of their application to multivariate research. Bayesian methods have evolved into an approach to the whole of statistics and are no longer confined, as they tended to be before the 1990s, to alternative ways of computing confidence intervals.

The spread of Bayesian methods has been slow because they are more mathematically intricate than frequentist approaches. While it is easier to put Bayesian inferential conclusions into ordinary language, arriving at those conclusions is usually mathematically more challenging. Even though software is now freely available and many problems of applying Bayesian methods have been solved through the application of *MCMC methods of simulation, doing Bayesian analysis is still no simple matter for a researcher not well versed in mathematical statistics.

Before-After Design   Any research design in which the subjects are given a *pretest and a *posttest and an intervention between the pretest and posttest. See *one-group pretest-posttest design, *A-B-A-B designs, *repeated-measures designs.

Behavioral Checklist   A data collection instrument listing behaviors (broadly viewed) to be observed. If the behavior is present during the time, setting, and context, the observer places a checkmark beside the behavior.

Behavior Coding   Methods assessing the quality of *surveys by observing and coding the behaviors of interviewers and *respondents, such as whether the interviewer reads the question accurately and whether the respondent asks for clarification or refuses to answer.

Behavioral Diary   A data collection approach conducted by the research participant in his or her own places and life to examine and record the behavior of interest. Sometimes qualitative data are included about the participant's thoughts about the meaning of his or her behaviors, actions, responses, thoughts, and so on.

Behavioral Observation   A data collection approach conducted by the researcher to determine if certain behaviors (broadly defined) occur with research participants. The researcher often uses a *behavioral checklist to record observations for later analysis.

Behavioral Science   Study of the actions (behaviors) of human beings and other animals. Psychology is the primary discipline historically referring to itself as a behavioral science, probably due to the dominance of *behaviorism until the late 1970s, when cognitive psychology, neuropsychology, and other nonbehavioral subdisciplines gained increasing stature. Behavioral science tends to put more emphasis on individual behavior and traits, while the *social sciences focus more on institutions and culture. Examples of social sciences include sociology, cultural anthropology, economics, and political science.

Behaviorism   (a) A theoretical position in psychology and related disciplines contending that the only scientific subject matter is behavior—not beliefs, attitudes, desires, or other mental states. It is most commonly associated with the work of John B. Watson in the early 20th century and B. F. Skinner later. (b) Advocacy of research based on empirical, external observation of behaviors.

Behavior Sampling   See *event sampling.

Behrens-Fisher Test   An extension of the *t test of the *statistical significance of the difference between two means; it relaxes the requirement of equal population *variances. It is somewhat controversial and not widely used.

Bell-Shaped Curve   A symmetrical curve, usually plotting a continuous *frequency distribution such as a *normal distribution, which looks like a cross section of a bell. See *normal distribution for an illustration. The *student's *t* distribution is also bell shaped, although it is not often referred to as such.

Benchmark   Used to mean (a) highest standard or target, (b) a *baseline measure, or (c) a more reliable measure. Benchmarks are established through benchmarking processes that are aimed at determining what has been achieved by competitors or similar organizations focused on an issue or process or problem.

Beneficence   The principle of beneficence states that social and behavioral research should always have as its largest goal that it ultimately benefits others (not the researcher) and society.

Bernoulli Distribution   A type of *binomial distribution.

Bernoulli Hypothesis   The hypothesis that a person's decision about whether or not to take a risk is based not just on the probability of success but also on the value attached to the thing being risked (usually called *utility).

For example, if a person were considering investing $10,000, her decision would be based on the probability of losing the money and of making a profit. But it would also likely be based on how valuable or important the money was to her. If the $10,000 was her life's savings and all that kept her from starvation, her willingness to take a small risk (even with a strong probability of a large return on the investment) might not be very great.

Bernoulli Process   Two classes of events and their associated probabilities. See *Bernoulli trial.

Bernoulli's Theorem   In a *probability experiment, the larger the number of trials, the closer the *empirical probability will come to the *theoretical probability.

For example, the more flips of a fair coin, the closer the actual percentage of heads will be to the theoretical probability of 50%.

Bernoulli Trial   In *probability theory, a trial or experiment with two possible outcomes, such as heads/tails, win/lose, 7/not 7, death/survival. One of the two is usually called "success," and its probability is termed "p." The other is called "failure," and its probability is labeled "q." Since $p + q = 1.00$; $1 - p = q$; $1 - q = p$. Named after the Swiss mathematician Jacques Bernoulli (1654–1705).

Best Estimator   Any method of estimating a *population *parameter using specific optimizing techniques for calculations on the sample, such as the *least squares criterion or *maximum likelihood estimation methods. See *best linear unbiased estimator.

Best Fit   See *goodness-of-fit.

Best Linear Unbiased Estimator (BLUE)   The *regression coefficient estimator computed using the *least squares criterion when none of the *assumptions are violated. A BLUE will have a smaller variance than any other estimator of the *population parameter.

Best Practices   (a) In social and behavioral research, refers to approaches to solving problems individuals and groups face using the approach that works best according to empirical research. (b) In business, best practices are derived from *benchmarking activities analyzing different practices, including measurement, production, data analysis, and operational efficiency.

Beta (B, β)   Greek letter used to symbolize several statistical concepts, including (a) probability of a *Type II error, (b) standardized *regression coefficients, (c) *population parameters of unstandardized regression coefficients, and (d) the amount of a *latent trait, such as ability, in a *Rasch model.

Beta Coefficient   (a) A *regression coefficient for a *sample expressed in *standard deviation units (i.e., *z scores). Specifically, the beta coefficient indicates the standard deviation change in a *dependent variable associated with one standard deviation increase in the *independent variable—when *controlling for the effects of other independent variables. Also called *standardized regression coefficient and *beta weight. (b) A statistic summarizing the movement in the price of a particular stock compared to that of the stock market as a whole. The bigger the beta coefficient, the greater the volatility of the stock.

Note: A *regression coefficient expressed in nonstandardized units is usually symbolized by *b*. Usage is confusing because beta is also used to symbolize the population parameter of *b*.

Beta Error   An error made by accepting or retaining a false *null hypothesis—more precisely, by failing to reject the null hypothesis when it is false. This might involve, for example, claiming that a relationship does not exist between two variables when it in fact does. Also called a *Type II error and a *false negative. Compare *alpha error. See *hypothesis testing.

Beta Level   The probability of making a *beta error, that is, failing to reject a false *null hypothesis. Compare *alpha level.

Beta Weights   Another term for *standardized regression coefficients or *beta coefficients. Beta weights enable researchers to compare the size of the influence of *independent variables measured using different *metrics or scales of measurement. Also called "regression weights."

For example, imagine a *regression analysis studying the influence of age and income on attitudes. Subjects could be adults ranging in age from 18 to 80. Their annual incomes might vary from $4,000 for a high school senior working after school to $300,000 for a tax lawyer. By reporting years and dollars as *standard scores, rather than in the original metric, beta weights allow the researcher to make easier comparisons of the relative influence of age and income on attitudes.

Between-Group Differences   Usually contrasted with differences *within* the groups being studied in an *analysis of variance (ANOVA). Between-group differences are what the researcher is interested in; they are considered large only if they are large in comparison to *within-group differences. Also called "interclass variance."

For example, the results of an experiment are reported in Table B.1. The between-group difference (between the means of the groups) appears significant since it seems quite a lot larger than the differences among subjects within each group. Using ANOVA or a *t* test to test for statistical significance indicates that the means in Table B.1 are significantly different ($p < .001$).

Table B.1   Scores Illustrating Between-Group Differences

	Control Group	Experimental Group
	72	91
	71	89
	68	88
	67	86
	66	85
	64	83
Total	408	522
Mean	68	87

Between-Groups Design   Synonym of *between-subjects design.

Between-Groups Variance   In *ANOVA, the variation that is due to differences in the group means. The larger this variation, the greater the effect. It is obtained by dividing the between-group *sum of squares by the between-group *degrees of freedom. If you view the *F ratio as a signal-to-noise ratio, then the between-group variance is your estimate of the "signal." Compare *within-group difference or variance.

Between-Subjects Design (or ANOVA)   A research procedure that compares different participants in different groups. It is a design with a *between-subjects independent variable. Each score for the different levels of the *independent variable in the study comes from a different subject. Usually contrasted to a *within-subjects design, which compares the same subjects at different times or under different *treatments.

Between-Subjects Variable (or Factor)   An *independent variable or *factor for which each subject is measured at only one *level or under one *condition. See *within-subjects variable, *repeated-measures designs, *nested design.

Between Sum of Squares   A measure of *between-group differences. Symbolized: $SS_{between}$. It is calculated by squaring and summing *deviation scores. It is used in comparison to *within-group differences in an *analysis of variance. More specifically, the between and within sums of squares are first divided by their respective *degrees of freedom, which turns them into *mean squares (which are variances); the ratio of these two mean squares produces the F ratio. See *mean squares, *F ratio.

Bias   (a) Anything that produces *systematic* error in a research finding; causes of bias can range from poor data collection to flawed measurements to inappropriate statistical analysis. While the distortions due to systematic error continue to grow in the long run, *random* errors tend to balance out in the long run. See *biased estimator. (b) The effects of any factor that the researcher did not expect to influence the *dependent variable.

For example, suppose you wanted to survey the opinions of New York City residents (the population). If you stood on a busy street corner at noon and asked the first 200 people who walked by to respond to your survey, your results would almost surely be biased. Perhaps your corner is at an intersection where out-of-town conventioneers usually stay, or where only very poor people are found, or where men seldom pass by at that hour. You would be very lucky (and you would never really know) if some such factor were not at work to bias your results by making your 200 respondents unrepresentative of the general population of the city.

Biased Estimator   When the *expected value of a *sample statistic tends to over- or underestimate a *population parameter, it is called a biased estimator.

For example, the *standard deviation (SD) of a sample is a biased estimator; it underestimates the population standard deviation. To correct for that bias, when computing the SD, the *sum of squares is divided by $n - 1$, rather than n. This correction is not necessary when computing the SD of a population; it is needed only when using a sample statistic to estimate a population parameter.

Biased Sample   A sample selected by a nonrandom process. Compare *probability sample.

Bibliographic Impact Factor (BIF)   Also called impact factor. A measure of the influence of a research journal measured as the average frequency that its articles are cited by other research journals. Similar calculations are made for individual articles. Originally important in the natural sciences, the use of the BIF has spread to the social and behavioral sciences.

BIC   *Bayesian information criterion.

Bifactor Model   In *factor analysis, the assumption that the *variance can be analyzed into a general factor and some *mutually exclusive subfactors.

Big Data   Some data collection processes collect data on thousands or even millions of cases, producing very large data sets that require analysis techniques such as data mining, content analysis, and exploratory methods looking for patterns in the data. These large data, and their analysis, sets are popularly labeled "big data." Some examples are Facebook, Twitter, and Google+, which provide data independently generated by individuals rather than researchers. The data are analyzed by marketers and others for purposes such as individual-level targeted advertising. Cameras located on streets and continuously operating also provide big data. *Machine learning is also often associated with big data because it uses brute force computer searching and correlating algorithms to find seemingly meaningful patterns in the data.

Bimodal Distribution   A distribution having two *modes or peaks. Strictly speaking, for a distribution to be called bimodal, the peaks should be the same height. However, it is quite common to call any two-humped distribution bimodal, even when the high points are not exactly equal.

In Figure B.3, the number of students getting various scores on a 12-item test is plotted on the graph: 19 students got 4 correct, and another 19 got 8 right.

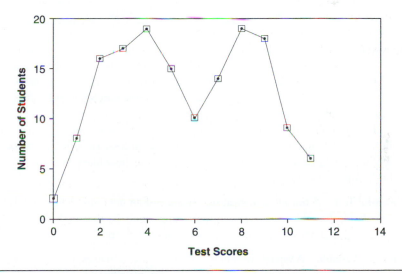

Figure B.3   Bimodal Distribution

Binary   (a) An adjective describing a number system or coding system that uses only two digits, generally 0 and 1. (b) A binary variable is one that can have only two possible values, such as sex (male or female); these are usually coded 0 and 1.

Binomial Distribution   A *probability distribution for a *dichotomous or two-
value *variable (*binomial* means "two names"), such as success/failure, profit/
loss, or in/out. Also called *Bernoulli distribution.

For example, suppose you take an ordinary deck of playing cards, shuffle it,
draw a card, note what you draw, replace the card, and repeat the process five
times. Say you record only one of two events: getting a club or not (clubs/not
clubs). The probability distribution is given in Table B.2. Reading it, you can
see that the probability of getting clubs on all five draws is very small (.0010).
The probability of getting exactly one club is .3955. To calculate the probability of getting two or more clubs, add together the probabilities of getting
exactly 2, 3, 4, and 5 = .3672.

Table B.2   Binomial Distribution: Probability Distribution for Drawing Clubs

Number of Clubs	Probability
0	.2373
1	.3955
2	.2637
3	.0879
4	.0146
5	.0010

Binomial Probability   (a) A kind of probability calculation used when there are
only two possible outcomes (*binomial* means "two names") for each of a series
of trials, such as heads/tails, win/lose, true/false. (b) The chances associated
with a series of trials when there are only two possible outcomes. See *binomial
distribution.

For example, suppose you are taking a true/false test tomorrow. There will
be a total of 25 questions. To pass you need to get at least 18 correct. You could
use binomial probability calculations to figure out how likely you are to pass
by *random guessing alone.

Binomial Test   A test of *statistical significance of an outcome that proceeds by
calculating how likely (*p value) a particular result is, that is, how much it
differs from chance as described by the *binomial distribution.

Binomial Variable   A variable with only two values or two "names" (a *dichotomous
variable), such as strong/weak, left/right, rich/poor, male/female.

Biometrika   Pioneering British statistics journal founded in 1901 by Karl Pearson
(of the Pearson correlation) in which many of the statistical techniques most
widely used today were first described. Many statistical tables (e.g., F, t, and chi-
square distributions) reprinted in the back of textbooks were originally put
together by the editors of this journal.

Biostatistics   Branch of statistics applied to biological research, especially in medicine and *epidemiology.

Biplot   A graphic technique for depicting both the values of variables and the differences among individuals.

Bipolar Factor   In *factor analysis, a factor that has both positive and negative *factor loadings. Such factors can be difficult to interpret.

Bipolar Scale   A scale in which the opposite ends represent contrasting concepts or antonyms, such as lazy and industrious. A *semantic differential scale is bipolar. Compare *unipolar scale.

Biquartimin   A method of (*oblique) rotation of the *axes in a *factor analysis.

Birth-Cohort Study   A birth cohort is a group of people born during a single year (e.g., 1983) or born during an interval of years (1981–1985). A birth-cohort study is a longitudinal study following a birth cohort across time. It is a type of *panel study. See *cohort. For example, the so-called millennials are the cohort of people born from 1980 through 1995.

Biserial Correlation   A *correlation coefficient computed between a *dichotomous and a *continuous variable. The dichotomous variable should be an interval-level variable that has been *collapsed to only two levels (such as high and low). The biserial correlation provides an estimate of what the correlation would have been if the collapsed dichotomous variable had been left as a continuous variable. The estimate is usually high. Abbreviated r_{bis}. Compare *tetrachoric correlation, *point-biserial correlation.

Biserial *r*   See *biserial correlation.

Bit   A binary digit (1 or 0). It is the smallest unit of information recognized by a computer. Several bits (usually 8) are combined to make a *byte.

Bivalence   See *principle of bivalence.

Bivariate Pertaining to two *variables only.

Bivariate Analysis   Analysis with just two variables, such as *Pearson correlation, *simple regression, *one-way ANOVA, *Cramer's *V.* Compare *univariate analysis, *simple multivariate, *full multivariate.

Bivariate Association   A relation (*covariation or *correlation) between two variables only. Among the many measures of bivariate association are *eta, *gamma, *lambda, *Pearson's *r,* *Kendall's tau, and *Spearman's rho.

Bivariate Correlation   Alternative name for *simple correlation.

Bivariate Distribution   The joint distribution of two variables. In a bivariate distribution, each member of a particular sample or population has a score on two variables—say, height (X) and weight (Y). This makes for three distributions: the distribution of height, the distribution of weight, and the distribution of the *covariance of height and weight, which is the bivariate distribution.

When a bivariate distribution is discussed, the *bivariate normal distribution* is what is usually meant, although several other meanings are possible. In a bivariate normal distribution, X is distributed normally, and so is Y. Also, and this is the nub of the matter, for any given value of X, the conditional values for Y are normally distributed. Likewise, for any given value of Y, the conditional values for X are normally distributed.

In most correlation research, a bivariate normal distribution is assumed. This assumption allows inferences about correlations to be extended to inferences about the *independence or the *dependence of the two variables. See *probability distribution, *normal distribution.

Bivariate Normality   The two-variable case of *multivariate normality. Most everyone is familiar with the *normal distribution for a single variable. It has the familiar bell-shaped distribution (but it is not the only bell-shaped distribution). The bivariate normal distribution is normal when viewed from the axis of either variable (i.e., for every point on the other axis). It is important because it is a test assumption in correlational analysis.

An example of bivariate normality is shown in the three-dimensional graph in Figure B.4; X and Y are the variables, and the height is the density of points on those two variables. If you were to slice this bivariate normal distribution into a cross section from the top down at any point on either the *x*- or *y*-axis, you would see a normal distribution. The distributions would be the widest at the center point of X or Y and would get narrower as you moved away from the center. The presence of a correlation between the two variables will make the distribution even more distinctive.

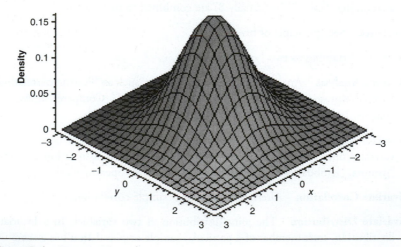

Figure B.4   Bivariate Normality

Bivariate Regression Coefficient   The regression coefficient obtained in *simple regression showing the relation between two variables only. The coefficient indicates the degree of relationship between two variables by estimating the change in the *dependent (*outcome) variable associated with a one-unit change in the *independent (*predictor) variable. Can also be viewed as the slope on a straight line (the change in Y divided by the change in X). The coefficient could estimate, for example, how much weight varies on average given a one-inch or one-centimeter increase in height. A *standardized regression coefficient in *simple regression is a *Pearson's r. See *simple regression, *regression equation. Compare *multiple regression analysis.

Biweight Mean   A measure of *central tendency designed to correct for extreme values by letting the researcher treat *outliers differently (that is, give them less weight) than other values. See *trimmed mean.

Black Box   Any mechanism whose internal workings are hidden. Said of input-output *research designs in which what happens in between is impossible to study or is ignored. Sometimes contrasted with a *clear box.

For example, studies of the effects of education on students often treat schooling as a black box. Students' characteristics upon entering and upon leaving are compared, but without directly considering which parts of the school experience might have produced any changes or how they could have done so.

Blank Experiment   An experimental *control produced by introducing an irrelevant treatment from time to time to keep subjects from becoming automatic in their responses.

Blinded Analysis   Diagnosis or analysis made from test or experimental data without direct contact with or knowledge of the subjects or when the person doing the analysis does not know which *treatment, if any, the various subjects received. The goal of such "blinding" is to eliminate bias. When those administering the treatment *and* those receiving it *and* those analyzing the results do not know who received the treatment, an alternative treatment, or a *placebo, then the procedure is called "triple blinded." Triple blinded is the ideal but is rarely achieved in practice. See and compare *single blind, *double blind, *triple blind. Sometimes called "masked" rather than blinded.

Blinding   See *blinded analysis.

Blind Review   In academia, professors submit manuscripts to be reviewed for potential publication in journals. When the reviewers do not know who wrote the manuscript, blind review is present. Blind review is standard operating practice for good journals. It is also widely used in reviewing grant proposals.

Block   (a) In *experimental design, a group of similar subjects receiving treatments. Blocking in experiments is equivalent to *stratifying on a categorical variable in surveys; it can help reduce variability due to extraneous causes. See *randomized-blocks design. (b) In *path or regression analysis, a group of variables (e.g., *background variables) that can be put in a causal order even while the individual variables in the block cannot be so ordered. See *recursive model.

Block Design   An experimental design in which subjects are grouped into homogeneous groups or categories that are called "blocks." In a randomized block design, participants in each block are then randomly assigned to the treatment conditions. In a post hoc block design, the blocking variable is determined during data analysis rather than during the study design. The goal of categorizing subjects into blocks is to reduce error variance, *control for the *blocking factor in the statistical analysis, and increase statistical power. See *matched pairs design and, for an example, *randomized-blocks design.

Blocking   The process of dividing participants into similar groups or locating participants that are similar on a variable and including the *blocking factor (a categorical *independent variable) in the *block design.

Blocking Factor   A categorical or ordinal independent variable with homogeneous cases within each level of the blocking factor, for example, a demographic or attribute variable. Blocking factors should be strongly related to the *dependent variable. Caution: If using blocking for precision or control and the control variable of interest is quantitative, do not categorize it, but leave it in its natural quantitative units and treat it as a *covariate.

Block Randomization   Process of constructing "arbitrary" subsets of a certain size and randomly assigning participants in each block to the experimental conditions to ensure a *balanced design, that is, a design with an equal number of participants in each treatment condition. For example, one might divide participants into blocks of 10, and randomly assign 5 participants to the control condition and 5 to the experimental condition, resulting in an equal number of participants in each treatment condition; this process is done for each of the blocks.

Block Sampling   (a) A sampling design in which respondents are grouped into representative categories or "blocks," which are then sampled. (b) Another term for *area sampling. Compare *cluster sampling, *stratified sampling.

BLS   Bureau of Labor Statistics.

BLUE   *Best Linear Unbiased Estimator. The linear estimator that is unbiased and has the smallest variance of all linear unbiased estimators.

An example is a *regression line or *regression coefficient computed using the *least squares criterion when none of the *assumptions are violated. Estimates so made will be more accurate, on average, than estimates using other criteria. Another example is use of the sample mean to estimate the population mean.

BMI   *Body mass index.

Body Mass Index   An individual's weight (in kilos) divided by the square of his or her height (in meters). Sometimes called the Quetelet index after its 19th-century inventor.

Bogardus Social Distance Scale   An attitude scale for measuring how closely people would be willing to associate with members of social and ethnic groups other than their own. Respondents are asked whether they would be willing, for example, to live in the same town as, in the same neighborhood as, invite home for dinner, and have a relative marry a member of the social group in question. Named after its creator, Emory S. Bogardus.

Boilerplate   Chunks of text (or other data) that are used repeatedly, word for word, in different documents. The term comes originally from old newspaper printing technology.

Bonferroni Technique (or Test or Inequality; also Bonferroni Adjustment Technique)   One of several methods for testing the *statistical significance of *multiple comparisons (such as a series of *t tests of the means of three or more groups). It involves adjusting the significance level needed to reject the *null hypothesis by dividing the *alpha level you want to use by the number of comparisons you are making. Using the Bonferroni technique helps the researcher avoid the increased risk of *Type I error that comes with multiple comparisons. Also called "Dunn's multiple comparison test." See *omnibus test. For a more liberal variation of the conservative Bonferroni technique, see *Holm's procedure, *Hochberg test.

For example, if a researcher wanted to use an alpha level of .05 and planned to make 6 comparisons, the new alpha level would be $.05 \div 6 = .008$.

A researcher using the so-called pseudo-Bonferroni technique uses a more rigorous alpha level but does so without actually calculating the precise level. This more casual practice is quite common. Researchers will often say something like "Because we made six comparisons, we used a more demanding significance level (.01 rather than .05)." Using the true Bonferroni technique, the researchers would have to conclude that their .01 level was not quite demanding enough.

Boolean Algebra   A form of algebra that deals with logical relations rather than numbers, or a form of symbolic logic similar to algebra. Some common Boolean operators are AND, OR, and NOT. Boolean algebra is important in computer design, set theory, *probability theory, and *qualitative comparative analysis (QCA). Named after the English mathematician George Boole (1815–1864).

Boot (or Boot Up)   To start a computer; to get it ready to work by loading the *operating system into its memory. Derived from the term *bootstrap*, as in "pull yourself up by your own bootstraps," meaning to get yourself going.

Bootstrap Methods   Procedures that provide alternative ways to estimate the variance and *standard error of a parameter by repeated *resampling from a sample. Bootstrapping is a *nonparametric approach to *statistical inference that can be applied to any data because it requires no assumptions about *underlying population distributions. See *jackknife method.

The phrase "pull yourself up by your own bootstraps," which tells you to rely on your own resources, is apt for these methods. The researcher's own resources are the sample. Rather than make assumptions about *underlying population distributions to estimate the standard error, one estimates on the basis of repeated random samples (with replacement) from one's sample. Taking 1,000 or more such samples is common. This resampling provides an estimate of what we *would have* gotten had we sampled repeatedly from the *population*. Since resampling from the population is almost never done, bootstrapping is a more empirical technique.

Borrow Strength   Tukey's term for a not "pure" but practical method for improving one's understanding of a phenomenon for which inadequate data are available. One borrows strength by using data from parallel but distinct phenomena for which data are more numerous. For example, if you wanted to know about the relation between two variables in a particular city, but the data on those variables were inadequate for that city, you could use data from similar cities as evidence. This would be to "borrow strength" from the rich data to use in circumstances where the data were less adequate.

Bounded Rationality   Decision-making model emphasizing limits (bounds) to the rational abilities of decision makers, whether managers, customers, or researchers. Bounds are produced by lack of complete information, insufficient decision time, limited information processing capability, emotions, and so forth. These limits make optimal decisions rare in principle as well as in practice. A common decision-making strategy used under conditions of bounded rationality is *satisficing*, or selecting and being satisfied with a "good enough" option or solution.

Bounds   Short for "confidence bounds," another term for *confidence limits.

Box-and-Whisker Diagram   A type of graph in which boxes and lines show a *distribution's shape, *central tendency, and *variability. The "boxplot," as it is often called, gives an informative picture of the values of a single variable and is helpful for indicating whether a distribution is *skewed and has *outliers. See *exploratory data analysis.

In Figure B.5 on page 45, two box-and-whisker diagrams are used for comparing two distributions. The grades of two groups of students on the same 60-item test are diagrammed. Here is some of the information necessary to interpret the diagrams. (Terms and symbols vary, but the following conventions are fairly common and illustrate the main concepts.)

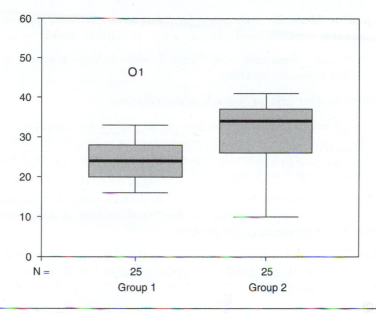

Figure B.5   Box-and-Whisker Diagrams

1. The upper and lower boundaries of each box (called *hinges) are drawn at the 75th and 25th *percentiles; this means that the box represents the *interquartile range (IQR), that is, the middle 50% of the values in the distribution.

2. The heavy line in the box (sometimes marked with an asterisk) shows the distribution's median.

3. The "whiskers" are the lines extending from the boxes. They reach to the largest and smallest scores that are less than 1 IQR from the ends of the boxes.

4. Any points beyond the high and low points of the whiskers are *outliers (if they are less than 1.5 IQRs from the end of the box) and are marked with an "O." If they are more than 1.5 IQRs from the end, they are extreme outliers and are indicated by an "E."

5. Comparing the two boxplots, we can see that the variability in Group 2 is greater than that of Group 1. Group 1's median score is lower than Group 2's. This is true despite the fact that the highest single score was earned by a student in Group 1 (the outlier, O1) and even though the lowest scores were earned by students in Group 2 (as is shown by its whisker).

Box-Cox Transformation   A family of data transformations for achieving linearity and *normality. Similar to *Box-Tidwell transformation, except that that transformation operates on the dependent rather than the independent variable.

Box-Jenkins Methods   Techniques for *time-series problems, particularly *forecasting economic trends; they are a type of *ARIMA model.

Box-Pierce test   A test used to determine if *autocorrelation is present in the errors of a time-series variable.

Boxplot   Another term for *box-and-whisker diagram.

Box-Score Method   An elementary first step in synthesizing research in *meta-analysis, named after its similarity to scorekeeping in baseball. Basically, one simply tallies the various research reports and whether each supports or fails to support the hypothesis being studied.

Box-Tidwell Transformation   Used to linearize the relationship of the dependent variable to the independent variables. See *transformations of data. Compare *Box-Cox transformation.

Box's Test   A test for *equality of variances in different populations. Also known as Box's M test. Used especially in MANOVA applications. See *homogeneity of variance-covariance.

Bracketing   (a) Another term for *collapsing data. (b) Providing upper and lower limits for a quantity. (c) In *qualitative research (especially in *phenomenology), considering an experience purely and apart from its prior associations and context.

Brainstorming   A method of problem solving that involves getting together a group of 5 to 10 persons to consider a problem. The participants are to suggest whatever ideas pop into their heads, no matter how weird, in the hope that a creative solution will be found. Compare *focus groups.

Brown-Forsythe Test   It is used to test the assumption of homogeneity of variances. The null hypothesis is that the population group variances are equal. Similar to *Levene's test except that the Brown-Forsythe uses the median in its formula and the Levene's uses the mean.

Bubble Plot   A type of *scatter plot used to depict three variables. Two of the three are shown in the usual way, as the intersection of the values of cases. The third is shown by the size of bubbles indicating the *data points.

Figure B.6 on page 47 shows an example in which the variables are the ages and incomes of respondents in different cities. The intersections of age and income locate the data points, and the cities' populations are indicated by the size of the data points or bubbles.

Buffer   (a) Unscored test items included to reduce interaction between other items. Compare *blank experiment. (b) In brains and computers, a place for (or a process of) storing information briefly until one has time to deal with it.

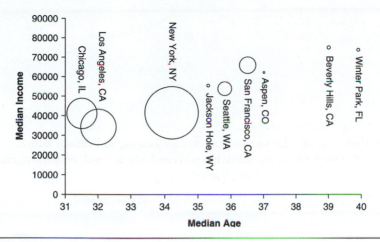

Figure B.6 Bubble Plot

Bump Hunting Looking at *spikes and *modes in frequency distributions that might indicate that some of the subjects are from different populations.

Byte A unit of information used by digital computers, usually equal to 8 *bits. For example, in *ASCII, the uppercase letter *B* is symbolized by the byte 01000010; *C* is 01000011.

C (a) A *programming language developed at Bell Laboratories. Because of its efficiency and because Bell Labs was barred from copyrighting the program, it is very widely used, especially by professional programmers. C⁺⁺ and C# are advanced versions. Compare *BASIC. (b) Symbol for *Pearson's contingency coefficient. (c) As a *superscript, symbol for *complement of; for example, $P(B^c)$ means the probability of the complement of B.

CAD   Computer-assisted design.

CAL   Computer-assisted learning.

Calculus   A branch of mathematics that analyzes rates of change, motion, minimization/maximization problems, and areas under curves and slopes of curves, including density curves (such as the *normal distribution, *t distribution, and *F distribution). The popular *least squares criterion, which estimates the best-fitting *regression line along with the *y-intercept and *regression coefficients, is based on differential calculus (it's a minimization problem), and the areas under the probability density curves in the back of your statistics book are based on integral calculus.

Callback   A return to *respondents in *survey research who were unavailable when the investigator first tried to contact them. Repeated callbacks can improve the *response rate and reduce *nonresponse bias.

Campbell Collaboration   An association of researchers working to establish an *archive of *meta-analyses of research in the social and behavioral sciences. See *Cochrane Collaboration.

Cancer Cluster   A set of cases in a geographic area over a specific period of time that has a greater than average occurrence of cancer. The cause could be "only chance" or it could be some other "real" factor that can be identified (e.g., environmental contaminants, a "sick building") causing the group to get cancer.

The idea can be used beyond cancer to refer to statistical clusters that might or might not be due to chance. See *Texas Sharpshooter fallacy.

Canon   (a) Accepted rule or standard. Compare *algorithm. (b) An authoritative list of books. In research *design and statistics, most lists of canonical works would probably include volumes by Ronald Fisher and Donald Campbell.

Canonical Analyses   Any of several methods for studying relations among sets of related variables, including *multiple regression analysis, *discriminant analysis, *MANOVA, and *canonical correlation analysis.

Canonical Correlation Analysis   A *full multivariate general linear model or form of *regression analysis for use with two or more independent variables and two or more dependent variables. The independent and dependent variables are each grouped into *linear composites or sets of variables; then correlations between those composites are calculated. Like other correlation coefficients, canonical coefficients range from -1.0 to $+1.0$. This coefficient is symbolized R_c. Today, canonical correlations are increasingly superseded by *structural equation models (SEM). Compare *factor analysis, *principal components analysis, and *MANOVA.

For example, suppose researchers were interested in the relationship of students' health to their school achievement. They might want to use several measures of health (e.g., number of absences due to illness, nutritional information, body weight, dental records, school nurse's evaluation) and several measures of achievement (e.g., grades, scores on a reading test, scores on a mathematics test, teacher evaluations). The relation of the two clusters of measures could be studied with canonical correlations.

Canonical Variate   What a set of variables is called in *canonical correlation analysis. Compare *factor.

Cap   In *set theory, the symbol ∩, meaning "and." It is used to indicate the *intersection of two sets. Compare *cup.

CAPI   Computer-assisted personal interviewing.

Capital   Productive wealth; resources one can use to generate income or additional resources. Compare *cultural, *human, and *social capital.

Examples of economic capital include the balance in an interest-bearing savings account or tools one could use to make products to sell. By contrast, human capital refers to individuals' knowledge or skills; social capital means resources arising from social interaction; cultural capital refers to benefits arising from social standing.

Capture-Recapture Sampling   A method of studying samples drawn from populations for which no *sampling frame exists. Originally developed in wildlife biology for the study of animal populations, variations have been developed for human populations, where it is more accurately called "contact-recontact" sampling. The best-developed related method for human populations is *respondent-driven sampling, which is an elaboration of *snowball sampling.

For example, researchers wanting to learn about the population of fish in a lake would catch a sample, mark it, and release it. Subsequent samples would note how many fish and of what types had been previously captured. With this information, it would be possible to estimate the size and composition of the lake's fish.

CAQDAS   Computer-assisted qualitative data analysis software. Software packages for assisting researchers in the *coding and sorting of qualitative data. Such software is used most often with text, such as interview transcripts. As with software for quantitative data analysis, the efficiency of qualitative software makes analyses that were once overwhelmingly time-consuming comparatively easy. It helps researchers analyzing large amounts of text to be more systematic and less impressionistic. Of course, no software, whether for qualitative or quantitative data, replaces intelligence and judgment in the interpretation of its output.

Carryover Effects   Lingering effects of an earlier experimental treatment that combine with the effects of a later treatment in a way that makes it difficult to assess the unique effects of the later treatment. Carryover effects are often a problem in *within-subjects designs. The technique of *counterbalancing controls for carryover effects, but it does not control for *differential carryover effects. See *practice effects, *A-B-A-B designs.

CARS   Computer-assisted reference service. Located at major research libraries in the United States, CARS enables users to search for bibliographic citations by topic in a large *database.

CART   Classification and regression tree. See *classification tree.

Cartesian Coordinates   The numbers associated with points on a graph. The graphs one typically sees in the social and behavioral sciences display only the upper right-hand corner of the Cartesian chart (the positive numbers only). Named after the French mathematician René Descartes (1596–1650).

In the example shown in Figure C.1 on page 52, four coordinates are plotted. Reading clockwise from the upper right, they are (1) $x = 5$, $y = 4$; (2) $x = 3$, $y = -5$; (3) $x = -4$, $y = -4$; (4) $x = -5$, $y = 4$.

To place a new number one starts at the "origin," which is the zero intersection of the x- and y-axes. For example, to place $x = 2$, $y = 4$, one would move to the right of the origin (horizontally) 2 spaces and move up 4 spaces (vertically).

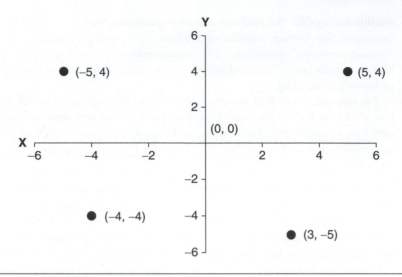

Figure C.1   Cartesian Coordinates

Cartesian Product   All the possible pairs of elements from two *sets.

   For example, if the two sets were two dice, the Cartesian product would be the 36 possible combinations of those two sets (dice): 1 + 1, 1 + 2, 1 + 3, and so on. See *underlying distribution.

Case   A *subject, whether an individual person or not, from which *data are gathered. A case is the smallest unit from which the researcher collects data. It is represented by a row (or *record) in a statistical program. The *sample size of a study equals its number of cases. Compare *unit of analysis.

Case-Cohort Design   A research design in which a random sample is drawn from a *cohort; the sample is used as a *comparison group for all the cases that occur in the cohort. Compare *resampling.

Case-Control Study   A method of studying an outcome by sampling cases with and without that outcome and studying their backgrounds. For example, in a study of lung cancer, the cases are individuals who have the disease. The controls are people who are similar in as many respects as possible, but who do not have the disease. The backgrounds of those with and without the disease are compared to understand the origins of the disease. A case-control study is sometimes called a *retrospective study, but the method can be used prospectively. Developed in *epidemiology, the method has many potential applications in the social sciences. Compare *matched case-control study.

Case-Oriented Research   Studies in which the focus is on in-depth investigation of one or a few cases rather than on the variables in many cases. See *case study methods; compare *variable-oriented research.

C

Case-Referent Study   Another term for *case-control study.

Case Study Methods   Gathering and analyzing data about one or a small number of examples as a way of studying a group, place, issue, or other phenomenon. When the goal is to generalize beyond the case, this is done on the assumption that the example (the case) is in some way typical of a broader or more general phenomenon. The case may be an individual, a city, an event, a society, or any other possible object of analysis. A wide variety of methods can be used to study the cases. An advantage of the case study method is that it allows more intensive analyses of specific empirical details. A disadvantage is that a limited number of cases makes it harder to use results to generalize to other cases. See *abstraction, *comparative method, *generalizability, *qualitative comparative analysis.

For example, a political scientist wishing to study why some candidates for public office are successful and others are not might study a particular election campaign in great depth in the hope of finding some general lessons about the electoral process.

Casewise Deletion   See *listwise deletion.

Catastrophe Theory   A theory of how living systems grow and differentiate. Long periods of slow change are punctuated by dramatic (catastrophic) change. Originally developed in biology in the 1970s by René Thom, it has been applied to sociological, linguistic, and economic change as well.

Categorical Data Analysis   Any of several methods used when the variables, especially the *dependent variables, to be analyzed are categorical rather than continuous (measured on an *interval or *ratio scale). These include the *chi-square test, *log-linear analyses, *logistic regression, and *probit regression.

Categorical Variable   A variable that distinguishes among subjects by sorting them into a limited number of categories, indicating type or kind, as religion can be categorized: Buddhist, Christian, Jewish, Muslim, Other, None. Breaking a continuous variable, such as age, to make it categorical is a common practice, but since this involves discarding information, it is usually not a good idea. The categories of a categorical variable should be exhaustive (cover all cases) and mutually exclusive (no case can fit into more than one category). Also called "discrete" or "nominal" variable. Compare *attribute, *continuous variable, *nominal scale.

Catell's Scree Test   A graphic way to decide on the number of important factors in a *factor analysis. See *scree plot for an illustration.

CATI   Computer-assisted telephone interviewing.

Causal Analysis   Statistical analysis of data collected for testing a *causal system or model. See *path analysis, *structural equation modeling.

Causal Conclusion   A conclusion drawn from a study designed in such a way that it is legitimate to infer *cause. Many people who use the term "causal conclusion" believe that an experiment, in which subjects are *randomly assigned to *control and *experimental groups, is the *only* *design from which researchers can properly infer cause. Other researchers, such as those who conduct *path analyses on nonexperimental data, do not agree with that restriction. Compare *correlational research design, *natural experiment, *ecological fallacy.

Causal Description   Causal description (or **descriptive causation**) is obtained when evidence (e.g., based on an experiment) shows that some program or complex treatment produces an outcome. See *black box.

The founder of the concept of *internal validity pointed out that experiments are the best way to show *descriptive causation or "local *molar causation." Internal validity has traditionally focused on local molar causation, that is, on demonstrating whether an experimental treatment condition, in its entirety (i.e., taken as a whole package with multiple contents), produced a particular outcome with a particular group of people. Contrasted with *explanatory causation. Causal generalizing requires *external validity.

Causal Diagram   A graphic representation of *cause and *effect relationships among *variables. Arrows indicate the direction of causal influence. The variables are called "nodes" and the arrows "edges." A causal diagram with no feedback loops is called "acyclic." Also called a *causal model. See *model and, for an example, *path diagram.

Causal Explanation   Focused on opening up the *black box, showing the processes by which something causes something else. Usually involves producing a causal model showing causal process via *intervening or *mediating variables and then testing that model with empirical data. Explanatory causation can also include determining variables that moderate a causal relationship. See *moderating effect.

Causal Heterogeneity   The existence of different causal patterns leading to the same effect or outcome. The opposite of *causal homogeneity.

Causal Homogeneity   The existence of only one path from a predictor or explanatory variable to an effect or outcome. This is usually a working *assumption in studies of causation. While causal heterogeneity can be demonstrated empirically, causal homogeneity is more often assumed.

Causal Hypothesis   A *hypothesis stating that changes in one variable (the *independent variable) produce changes in another variable (the *dependent or outcome variable).

Causal Inference   The process of drawing conclusions about cause-and-effect relationships. These inferences can be *inductive, *deductive, or some combination

of the two. Note that while *statistical inference is often used in causal inference, the two are not synonymous. The so-called fundamental problem of
causal inference arises because empirically based causal inference is ultimately
*counterfactual. For example, in an *experiment, the effect of a treatment
cannot be measured by *simultaneously* giving and not giving the treatment to
the *same* subjects. Therefore, in an experiment, a control group is used to
obtain an estimate of what would have happened (counterfactually) to the
experimental group *if it had not received the treatment*. Making strong causal
inferences or claiming the presence of causal laws is further complicated by
the lack of complete *determinism in the world and by the "problem of
induction," frequently discussed by philosophers of science, which states that
the future might not resemble the past. In sum, the making of causal inference is an important human and scientific activity, but it is not one that can
be conducted with certainty.

Causal Model   (a) A synonym for *causal diagram or *path diagram. The causal
model in explanatory research is not always depicted in a diagram by researchers, so you will often have to construct the depiction yourself. To do this, try
to answer the following question: What causal model is implied or implicit in
this explanatory research? (b) The deterministic part (i.e., *not* the error component) of an equation (e.g., a single *GLM) or set of equations (as in the
equations defining a *structural equation model) that mathematically define
the particular *causal system.

Causal System   A set of theoretical constructs and their causal interrelation-
ships. See *causal model, *nomological network.

Causal Variable   See *cause, *independent variable.

Cause   An event, such as a change in one variable, that produces another event,
such as a change in a second variable. See *necessary condition, *sufficient
condition.
    Before reading further, be forewarned. There is no concept in this diction-
ary more troublesome than "cause." Highly respected researchers disagree
about what constitutes a cause, whether we should even use the term, and
especially how restrictive a set of conditions must be met before it is legitimate
to talk of cause. Many social scientists, and even some philosophers, would
agree with the following. Others, naturally, would not.
    To attribute cause, for X to cause Y, three conditions are necessary (but not
sufficient): (1) X must precede Y; (2) X and Y must covary; (3) no rival explanations account for the covariance of X and Y. Statistical data can never *prove*
causation, but analysis of them can suggest, more or less strongly, that a causal
relation is present.
    Causal relations can be simple or multiple and *deterministic or *probabi-
listic. In simple causation, whenever the first event (the cause) happens, the

second (the effect) always does too. Multiple causation and *probabilistic causation are much more common in the social and behavioral sciences. Multiple causes may be such that any one of several causes can produce the same effect. For example, monetary inflation may be caused by rising wages, rising prices, declining productivity, or some combination of the three. Multiple causes may also be such that no one of them will necessarily produce the effect, but several of them in combination make it more likely. For example, prejudiced attitudes may be produced by repressive child rearing, general ignorance, low self-esteem, and/or lack of contact with people different from oneself.

Compare *descriptive causation, *explanatory causation, *nomological causation, *idiographic causation.

Ceiling Effect   A term used to describe what happens when many *subjects in a study have scores on a *variable that are at or near the possible upper limit ("ceiling"). The ceiling effect makes analysis difficult because it reduces the amount of variation in a variable. Compare *floor effect.

For example, suppose a group of statistics professors want to see whether a new method of teaching increases knowledge of elementary statistics. They give students in their classes a test, try the new method, and then give the students another version of the same test to see whether their scores went up. If one of the professors had students who knew a lot of statistics already and scored at or near 100% on the first test, she could not tell whether the new method was effective in her class. The scores of her students were so high (at the ceiling), they could hardly go up, even if the students learned a great deal using the new method.

Cell   (a) The space formed by the intersection of a row and a column in a statistical table. (b) Combination of levels of two or more independent variables. (c) Any single group in an *analysis of variance design.

For example, in Table C.1, each of the numbers (except for the 100s) is in one of the table's cells. The percentage of Seniors who plan to Seek Work is in one cell, as is the percentage of Juniors who Don't Know, of Sophomores who plan to go on to Grad School, and so on.

Table C.1   Cell: Students' Plans Upon Graduation, by Class

	Freshmen	*Sophomores*	*Juniors*	*Seniors*
Seek Work	73	58	57	58
Graduate School	5	11	18	30
Don't Know	22	31	25	12
Total	100	100	100	100

Note: Numbers listed are column percentages. These numbers are rates and are to be compared across each row to determine if a relationship between plans and class is present.

Cell Frequency   The number of cases that occur in a single cell of a *contingency table. For an example of cell frequencies, see *cell.

Cell Mean   The mathematical average value on the dependent variable for a treatment combination. For example, assume that you have two independent variables in a *factorial experiment design—specifically treatment condition (treatment vs. no treatment control) and gender (male vs. female). Assume the dependent variable is posttest score on a performance text. Since each independent variable has two levels, there are four groups or treatment combinations (male-treatment, male-control, female-treatment, female-control), and each of these groups has a cell mean (M_{M-T}, M_{M-C}, M_{F-T}, M_{F-C}).

Cell Percent   In a *contingency table, types of cell percents include total cell percent, column percent, and row percent. Cell percent is the number of cases in the cell divided by the total number of cases. Interpreting cell percents can be misleading when using one variable to predict values in the other variable in a contingency table; column or row percents are preferred because they provide *conditional probabilities or rates to be compared. For an example of cell percent, see Table C.10 with *contingency table. Also, see *row percent, *column percent.

Censored Data   Data that are incomplete in some way, as when certain values, usually extreme values, are unknown or ignored. Sometimes used as a synonym for truncation; when a distinction is made, censored usually refers to *measurements* that are incomplete, while truncation refers to incomplete *samples*. See *trimmed mean, *truncated distribution. Censored *subjects* occur because of *attrition, as when the effect of an intervention is unknown because the subject dropped out before it could be measured. In regression models data are *censored* if we observe all of the observations in the sample but the information on dependent variable is limited for some of the observations. We have complete information on all of the independent variables, but some of the information on the dependent variables is missing. A fixed value is assigned to the dependent variable when its value is missing.

Imagine, for example, a study conducted in 2020 of the college graduation rate of individuals entering college in 1995. Some people entering college in 1995 might not have completed college by 2020, but they could easily do so later on, after the end of the study. The data in this study would be censored; that is, the number of people from the 1995 *cohort who got their degrees after 2020 would be unknown. Specifically, it would be "right censored"; that is, the individuals did not graduate until *after* the observation period. In "left-censored" data, the outcome of interest occurs *before* the observation period. One method to handle censored data is the *Cox proportional hazard model.

Censored Regression Model   See *tobit analysis.

Census   (a) A complete count of an entire *population. (b) Collection of data from all members of a population—in contrast to a survey of a *sample (subset) of the population.

Census Tract   (also called **Census Block**) A small area of a city or other densely populated region in the United States formed to make gathering census data easier. Currently there are about eight million census blocks. Census tracts usually contain between 3,000 and 8,000 people (mean, 4,000). They are defined with the advice of local committees so as to approximate neighborhoods.

Centering   Transforming data by setting the mean of a series of scores to zero. One uses the *deviation scores rather than the raw scores of the variable. When the scores on the *independent variable are centered, the *intercept is the mean. Centered scores are widely used in *multilevel model data analysis. See *centroid.

Centile   Abbreviation of *percentile.

Central Limit Theorem   A statistical proposition to the effect that the larger a sample size, the more closely the *sampling distribution of a sum or a mean will approach a *normal distribution. This is true even if the population from which the sample is drawn is not normally distributed. A sample size of 30 or more will usually result in a sampling distribution for the mean that is very close to a normal distribution.

   The central limit theorem explains why *sampling error is smaller with a large sample than with a small sample and why we can use the *normal distribution to study a wide variety of statistical problems.

Central Tendency, Measure of   Any of several statistical summaries that, in a single number, represent the typical or average number in a group of numbers. Examples include the *mean, *mode, and *median. Compare *dispersion, *variability.

   A batting average is a well-known measure of central tendency in the United States. A grade point average might be a more important example for many college students.

Central Tendency (of a Distribution)   A point in a distribution of scores that corresponds to a typical, representative, or middle score in that distribution—such as the *mode, *mean, and *median.

Centroid   The concept of a *mean applied to multivariate data. (a) In regression analysis, the point that represents the mean on all variables. When all the independent variables have been centered (see *centering), the mean of each equals zero and the mean of all variables where they each equal zero is the centroid. (b) A *weighted average or *linear combination of the observed *dependent variables in a *MANOVA; it is a mean of the *vector of scores for all subjects. (c) In *factor analysis, the "centroid method" is a way to extract factors. (d) In a *discriminant analysis, the centroid is the mean *discriminant function score for each group.

CERES Plot   A graphic means of judging whether the *independent (*explanatory, *predictor) variables in a *regression analysis have a linear relation to the *dependent (*outcome, *response) variable. CERES stands for "combining conditional expectations and residuals."

Ceteris Paribus   Latin phrase meaning "other things being equal;" also often used to mean "if other things remain constant or unchanged." The phrase is generally used to qualify a conclusion, as in "This is true, *ceteris paribus,*" meaning this is true if other things are/remain equal/unchanged/constant.

    Many aspects of *research design (such as *random assignment to *experimental groups or statistically *controlling for a variable) can be seen as attempts to approach the goal of *ceteris paribus*. Assuming *ceteris paribus* is a kind of counterfactual reasoning important in causal analysis.

CF   *Cumulative frequency.

CFA   *Confirmatory factor analysis.

CFI   See *comparative fit index.

Chain   A series of values in which a value at one point depends in some way on the previous values in the series.

Chain Path Model   Said of measurements of a variable taken from the same sample at three or more different times when the cause of the value of the measurement for each time is the immediately previous measurement. Also called *Markov chain.

    For example, say we took measurements of some variable at four times, T1 → T2 → T3 → T4. Using a chain path model, we would assume the cause of the value at time 4 (T4) is T3, but T2 and T1 have no direct effect. Similarly, the cause of T3 is T2, but T1, while causing T2, has no direct effect on T3.

Chance Error   Another term for *random error. Compare *noise.

Chance Variable   Another term for *random variable and *stochastic variable; also called *variate.

Chance Variation   Another term for *random variation.

Change in R^2   The amount of variance in the dependent variable attributed to the addition of one or more variables in a general linear model. The difference between the full model with all the variables and the reduced model with the smaller set is the change in R^2.

Change Score   A score obtained by subtracting a *pretest score from a *posttest score. A more common approach, and one that can reduce measurement error, is to treat the posttest score as a *dependent variable in a *regression analysis and the pretest score as *one* of the *predictor variables. Also called *difference score and "gain score."

Changing-Criterion Design   A single-case experimental research design in which a research participant's behavior is gradually altered by changing the requirement for success during successive treatment periods. Because the research participant desires success, he or she alters his or her target behavior to be in line with the changing requirement. See Figure C.2.

Phase A	Phase B	Phase C	Phase D
Baseline	Treatment and initial criterion	Treatment and new (incremented) criterion (compared to Phase B criterion)	Treatment and new (incremented) criterion (compared to Phase C criterion)

Figure C.2   Changing-Criterion Design

Source: Johnson, Burke. *Educational Research: Quantitative, Qualitative, and Mixed Approaches.* Thousand Oaks, CA: Sage, 2013.

Chaos Theory   An umbrella term for several methods of analyzing extremely complex systems, especially systems with many dynamic variables resulting in *nonlinear effects. An example is the weather, which is difficult to predict accurately. Small changes in assumptions or small differences in initial conditions can lead to very different predictions of weather more than a few days into the future. The term "chaos" should not be taken to mean that the system involves random elements. According to the mathematics, the system is fully deterministic, but the seemingly chaotic or random behavior arises from the nonlinear equations governing the behavior of the system; cause-and-effect relations exist, but they are difficult or impossible to discover and model with conventional *linear and static equations. The complexity of systems in behavioral and social science suggests that chaos theory holds promise for analyzing them. See *fractal, *complexity theory, and *dynamicism.

Characteristic Root (or Value or Number)   Other terms for *eigenvalue.

Chebyshev's Theorem   Alternate spelling of *Tchebechev's theorem. There are others (e.g., Chebycheff, Tchebycheff).

Chi-Square Distribution   A family of theoretical *probability distributions, defined in part by their different *degrees of freedom (df); that is, they differ by the number of cases. The *mean of the curve is its df, and the *standard deviation is the *square root of $2 \times df$. Several statistical tests are based on this distribution, including the *chi-square test.

Chi-Square Index for SEM Used in *structural equation modeling to determine if the implied covariances are not very different from the true covariances as a measure of model fit. One does not want to reject the null hypothesis; that is, one wants the p value to be greater than .05. The null hypothesis states that population covariance matrix implied by the model is equal to the population covariance matrix.

Chi-Square Test A *test statistic for categorical data. As a test statistic, it is used as a test of *independence, but it is also used as a *goodness-of-fit test. The chi-square test statistic can be converted into one of several measures of association, including the *phi coefficient, the *contingency coefficient, and *Cramer's *V.*

The chi-square test is known by many names: Pearson chi-square, χ^2, chi^2, and χ^2.

The use of the chi-square test of independence, illustrated in the following example, occurs when a researcher wants to see if there are statistically significant differences between the observed (or actual) frequencies and the expected (or hypothesized, given the *null hypothesis) frequencies of variables presented in a *cross-tabulation or *contingency table. The larger the difference between the observed and expected frequencies, the larger the chi-square statistic. The larger the chi-square statistic, the less likely the observed difference is due just to chance, and the more statistically significant the finding is.

For example, say that a researcher gives a pass/fail test to a sample of 100 subjects, 42 men and 58 women; 61 subjects pass, and 39 fail. If the researcher were interested in whether there are differences in test performance by gender, she could use the chi-square test to test the *null hypothesis of no statistically significant performance differences between the sexes. To do so, she might arrange the information about her subjects in Tables C.2, C.3, and C.4, all on page 62. Table C.2 gives the total (or *marginal) frequencies for the two variables. Table C.3 shows what the (approximate) frequencies of passes and fails on the two tests *would have been* if the null hypothesis were true, that is, what you would expect if there were no differences on the exam between men and women. Table C.4 shows the actual or observed number of men and women who passed or failed the exam. Comparing Table C.3 and Table C.4, it is clear that the actual and expected frequencies are not identical. For example, 26 men were expected to pass, but only 19 did; 23 women were expected to fail, but only 16 did, and so on. But are these differences statistically significant; that is, are they unlikely to have occurred by chance? Conducting the chi-square test can tell you. The answer (calculations not shown) is that the null hypothesis of no difference between men and women should be rejected. The differences are greater than what would be expected by chance alone; they are statistically significant at the .01 level. See *chi-square test for independence.

Chi-Square Test for Independence Statistical test used with a *contingency table to determine whether two categorical variables are related (e.g., can one predict values of one variable given knowledge of the other variable?). The null hypothesis is that the two variables are not related (i.e., independent). See *chi-square test. Contrast with *goodness-of-fit test, for which chi-square also can be used.

Table C.2   Chi-Square Test (Marginal Frequencies)

	Pass	Fail	Totals
Men			42
Women			58
Totals	61	39	100

Table C.3   Chi-Square Test (Expected Frequencies)

	Pass	Fail	Totals
Men	26	16	42
Women	35	23	58
Totals	61	39	100

Table C.4   Chi-Square Test (Observed Frequencies)

	Pass	Fail	Totals
Men	19	23	42
Women	42	16	58
Totals	61	39	100

Chow Test   A *test statistic used to determine whether *regression equations differ significantly; also used to ascertain whether regression coefficients change over time (e.g., period 1 versus period 2). It is based on the *F test.

CI   *Confidence interval.

Circular Reasoning   A logical fallacy in which the so-called proven conclusion is contained in or assumed by one or more of the premises. It's called "circular reasoning" because, basically, one claim depends on a second, which in turn depends on the first. Also called "begging the question." Compare *tautology.

For example, "Unemployed people are lazy. How do we know this? Because they are unemployed, which proves they're lazy; if they weren't lazy, they'd have jobs."

Class Boundary   See *class limits.

Class Frequency   The number of observations of a particular *variable that fall in a given *class interval.

C

For example, if researchers were studying income distribution in a particular city and 2,149 individuals earned between $30,000 and $39,999, the class frequency for the class interval $30,000–39,999 would be 2,149.

Classical Statistical Inference   What most researchers mean by "statistical inference." Also called the "frequentist school" of statistics. Views probability as the long-run expected frequency of an event or process occurring (e.g., it would expect a coin to come up heads 50% of the time *in the long run*). Assumes that the true population parameter (e.g., the population mean) is fixed and it must be estimated using sample data. The word "classical" is often added to make a contrast with *Bayesian statistical inference.

Classical Test Theory   The original test and measurement theory used to assess the reliability and validity of psychological and educational tests. It assumes that an observed test score is equal to a true score component (the actual ability, trait, etc.) plus a measurement error component, and the error is assumed to be random across measurements. *Ontologically speaking, it assumes there is a single true score to be estimated and that we hope to estimate it better and better over time. Although it is considered outmoded today, it is still widely used for simpler problems in testing and measurement. For instance, many college instructors use it to interpret students' results on examinations. *Item response theory and *Rasch modeling are more modern and sophisticated alternatives.

Classification Tree   Method for predicting the category of an object from the values of its predictor variables. The outcomes are depicted, visually, in classification trees. Classification trees are often used in *data mining. Classification trees are used for categorical dependent variables; CARTs, or "classification and regression trees," are used for continuous dependent variables. See *decision tree and *tree diagram for examples.

Classification Variables   Another term for *background variables.

Classificatory Variable   A *categorical variable, that is, one that values a variable by classifying or categorizing—such as upper/middle/lower class or jumbo/large/medium/tiny shrimp. Compare *nominal and *discrete variables.

Class Interval   A convenient grouping of the data on a *continuous variable that makes the data easier to interpret; the interval between the boundaries (or limits) of a class, such as between 21 and 40 million in the following example. By turning continuous variables into *categorical variables, class intervals make it possible to do *frequency distributions and *cross-tabulations—at the cost, however, of discarding detailed information.

For example, Table C.5 on page 64 classifies 236 countries with indigenous inhabitants by population size. This makes it easier to see the big picture, easier than if we used a list of all the nations and their exact populations. On the other hand, a major disadvantage of using classes is that it obscures large differences,

Table C.5   Class Interval: Distribution of Nations by Population Size (2003)

Population (in millions)	Number of Countries
Less than 1	81
1–20	106
21–40	20
41–60	10
61–80	4
81–100	4
More than 100	11

such as the one between Mauritius with a population of about 1 million and Australia with over 19 million, both of which are grouped in the same category.

Class Limits   The upper and lower values of a *class interval. Also called "class boundaries."

Clear Box   The opposite of *black box. Producing a "clear box" enables you to understand how a program operates; it is the goal of theory-driven research and evaluation. Michael Scriven (a prominent figure in the field of program evaluation) coined the term, even though he is a critic of this approach to evaluation.

Clinical Significance   *Practical significance in a clinical setting. Usually contrasted with *statistical significance. See *effect size. A small effect may be statistically significant but too small to be clinically significant.

Clinical Trial   The term originated in medicine and refers to a *prospective *experimental study comparing the effect of a treatment by using a treatment group and control group composed of human beings. See *double-blind procedure, *randomized clinical trial, *randomized control trial, *nonrandomized clinical trial. Contrast with *retrospective, *case-control study.

Cliometrics   The application of statistical methods and economic theories to the study of history. Named after Clio, the muse of history. Compare *econometrics.

Closed-Question Format   Format used with closed-ended questions. In surveys, researchers most often offer subjects a limited number of predetermined responses to questions (closed format) rather than allow them to choose their own words for answering questions (*open-question format).

For example, "What sort of job is the president doing overall? (a) Excellent (b) Good (c) Fair (d) Poor (e) Don't know." Using the closed-question format means that a respondent who wants to say, "Very good for foreign policy, but not so hot on domestic issues," is forced to select among options (a)–(e).

Closed System   A theoretical system that does not admit evidence or arguments from different perspectives. In other terms, a causal system that allows no *exogenous causal variables.

Freudianism, Marxism, and *behaviorism have been accused of being closed systems. Indeed, most theoretical systems have been so accused—by opponents.

Cluster Analysis   Any of several procedures in *multivariate analysis designed to determine whether individuals, cases, or other units of analysis are similar enough to be grouped into clusters. The individuals within a cluster are similar on some variable(s), while the clusters are dissimilar from one another. Compare *MANOVA, *canonical correlation, *discriminant analysis, *individual centered analysis. See *hierarchical clustering.

Cluster Randomizing   Randomly assigning groups rather than individuals to a study's *control and *experimental groups. For example, one might assign classrooms rather than individual students to receive or not receive a treatment. Compare *cluster sampling, *group randomized trial.

Cluster Sampling   A method for drawing a *sample from a *population in two or more stages. It is typically used when researchers cannot get a complete list of the members of a population they wish to study but can get a complete list of groups or clusters in the population. It is also used when a *random sample would produce a list of subjects so widely scattered that surveying them would be prohibitively expensive. Generally, the researcher wishes to use clusters containing subjects as diverse as possible. By contrast, in *stratified sampling the goal is often to find strata containing subjects as similar to one another as possible.

The disadvantage of cluster sampling is that it is less efficient than directly sampling individual units; that is, *sampling error is increased. Each stage of the process also increases *sampling error. In *one-stage* cluster sampling, clusters are randomly selected from the set of all clusters, and all individual units in the selected clusters are included in the total sample; in *two-stage* cluster sampling, a second stage of sampling is added where individual units are randomly selected from each of the selected clusters. The margin of error is larger in cluster sampling than in simple or stratified random sampling, but since cluster sampling is usually much easier (cheaper), this error can be compensated for by increasing the sample size. If all clusters are of equal size, cluster sampling is an equal probability of selection method and therefore produces representative samples. If clusters are not of equal sizes, statistical adjustments must be made. See *central limit theorem.

For example, suppose you wanted to survey university students on social and political issues. There is rarely a complete list of all students in a country. But there are complete lists of all universities in a country. You could begin by getting such a list of universities (which are "clusters" of students). You could then select a *probability sample of, say, 50 universities. Once these clusters were identified, you could go to each school and get a list of its students; students to be surveyed would be selected (perhaps by simple *random sampling) from each of these lists. Note that this is an example of two-stage cluster sampling because sampling also was conducted within each cluster. If all of the students in the 50 randomly selected universities had been included in the final sample, one would have a one-stage cluster sample.

COBOL COmmon Business Oriented Language. A *programming language. Compare *BASIC, *C, *FORTRAN.

Cochrane Collaboration A group of medical researchers who conduct systematic reviews (*meta-analyses) of the research literature in medicine and make the reviews available to the public, other researchers, and medical practitioners. It is the model for a similar group in the social sciences, the *Campbell Collaboration.

Cochran's C Test One of several tests for *equality of variances. Another is *Levene's test.

Cochran's Q Test A variant of the *chi-square test used for samples that are not *independent, that is, for *within-subjects designs. It is an extension of *McNemar's chi-square test to research problems with three or more *correlated samples.

Code (a) Rules specifying how data are to be represented. See *codebook. (b) Rules for converting data from one form to another—usually from the form in which they were collected to a form that is easier to analyze. See *coding. (c) A *computer program, as in "She wrote the code for that operating system."

Codebook A list of *variables, their definitions, their type, definitions for each value of a categorical variable, and explanation of how they have been coded so that they can be read and manipulated by a computer. Also called a "coding frame." See *coding.

   For example, a typical entry in a codebook would be: Variable 1, Sex: 1 = female; 0 = male.

Coding (a) "Translating" data from one language or format into another—often to make it possible for a computer to operate on the data thus coded. (b) Reducing textual and visual data (e.g., many pages of text or videos of observations) to summary codes and categories to aid in analyzing and understanding the large amount of data. Some coding schemes (e.g., *a priori codes) are decided before data are collected, especially when the data are easily defined and measured. In *qualitative research (in contrast to quantitative research), coding is often done after the data are collected; the codes, called *inductive codes, are generated by the researcher during data analysis. In contrast to quantitative research, qualitative research coding focuses on categories rather than variables (see *variable analysis). A familiar example of inductive coding would be reading transcripts of interviews, line by line, and constructing codes as needed; during this analysis, the researcher continually devises and revises the coding system and produces a cumulative qualitative *codebook listing all of the codes and their labels and definitions. Computer software packages are often helpful with this kind of coding. See *qualitative data analysis software, *effects, *dummy, and *contrast coding. (c) Writing a set of instructions telling a computer how to handle data. See *programming.

For example, (a) if one of your variables were "race," you might code it as 1 for "black," 2 for "white," and 3 for "other." (b) In an interview transcript about an organization's work environment, the string of words "manager X treats me unfairly" might be coded as "management complaint," and "there are too many cliques here" might be coded as "cliques." (c) "Arrange data in ascending numerical order" could be coding that instructs a computer about how to handle a data file.

Coefficient (a) A number used as a measure of a property or characteristic. (b) In an equation, a number by which a variable is multiplied.

For example, (a) a coefficient showing inequality between incomes could be calculated by dividing the larger income into the smaller. Thus, if the average (mean) income of men working full-time were $25,000 per year, and that of women working full-time were $15,000, the coefficient of inequality between men and women would be 15,000/25,000 = .6. (b) In the equation $\hat{Y} = 10 + 3.2X$, 3.2 is a coefficient. See *regression coefficient.

Coefficient Alpha See *Cronbach's alpha.

Coefficient of Agreement (a) A measure of the relation of a single item on a *scale or an *index with the rest of a scale or index. See *Cronbach's alpha. (b) A measure of the similarity of one rating to another. See *interrater reliability.

Coefficient of Alienation (a) A measure of the lack of relationship between two *variables. It is sometimes symbolized k or k^2. Usage, and therefore the meaning, varies. When the coefficient of alienation is high, it is hard to make predictions about one variable by knowing the value of another. The stronger the correlation between two variables, the weaker the coefficient of alienation will be. (b) A measure of how poorly a *model fits actual data. The lower the coefficient, the better the fit.

The coefficient of alienation is equal to 1 minus the *coefficient of determination, that is, to $1 - r^2$ or $1 - R^2$. That means that the coefficient of alienation is the complement of the coefficient of determination (i.e., taken together, they add up to 1). See *coefficient of nondetermination.

Coefficient of Concentration Another term for *Gini coefficient.

C

Coefficient of Concordance   Another term for *Kendall's coefficient of concordance.

Coefficient of Determination   A statistic that indicates how much of the *variance in one variable is determined or explained by one or more other variables; more strictly, how much the variance in one is associated with variance in the others. With just two variables (e.g., one dependent and one independent), it is calculated by squaring the *correlation coefficient. With one dependent and two or more independent variables, it is calculated by squaring the *multiple correlation coefficient (which, after squaring, is sometimes called the "coefficient of *multiple* determination" rather than the simpler "coefficient of determination"). In *bivariate analyses it is abbreviated r^2, and in *multivariate analyses it is abbreviated R^2. Also called "index of determination." See *strength of association.

For example, one might find a statement like the following in a research report: "Education level attained explains 22% of the variance in adult occupational status ($r^2 = .22$)."

Coefficient of Equivalence   A measure of *reliability used for two or more forms or versions of a test to determine the extent to which they yield the same (or equivalent) results. It is a *correlation between the two forms and is a widely used gauge of the reliability of *standardized tests. See *reliability coefficient, *Cronbach's alpha.

Coefficient of Multiple Determination   Term sometimes used to refer to the *coefficient of determination in multiple regression (i.e., when there are two or more independent or predictor variables).

Coefficient of Nondetermination   That part of the *variance that cannot be explained or accounted for by the measured effects of the *independent variable(s). Symbolized: $1 - r^2$ or $1 - R^2$. Also called the *coefficient of alienation. See *error term. Compare *coefficient of determination.

Coefficient of Relative Variation (CRV)   A measure of *dispersion used to compare across samples with different *means and *units of measurement. It is computed by dividing the *standard deviation of a *distribution by its *mean. Compare *z score.

Coefficient of Stability   A measure of *reliability calculated by retesting the same subjects with the same test. Also called "test-retest reliability." It is often used when alternate forms of a test are not available. One problem with this *reliability coefficient is determining the appropriate length of time between the test and the retest. If it is too short, subjects may remember items; if it is too long, subjects may change in the interval. See *history effect. Compare *coefficient of equivalence.

Coefficient of Total Determination   In *regression analysis, the proportion of the total variance in the *dependent variable explained by the *independent variables. Symbolized R^2. Also called *coefficient of determination.

C

Coefficient of Variation   A measure used to compare the dispersion or variation in groups of scores. To obtain the coefficient of variation (CV), one divides the *distribution's *standard deviation by its *mean. The CV is appropriate only for scores measured on a ratio scale. Compare *Gini coefficient.

Cofactor   A variable that has a particular effect in combination with another variable.
> For example, some infectious diseases, such as hepatitis B, increase susceptibility to noninfectious diseases, such as liver cancer. Compare *interaction effect.

Cognitive Interviews   Interviews conducted by survey researchers in which respondents are asked about the mental processes they used when answering survey questions. The goal is to determine whether the respondent understood the survey questions to mean what the researcher intended them to mean. Sometimes called the "think-aloud technique." See *content validity.

Cognitive Science   The interdisciplinary study of cognition, that is, the processes of acquiring, creating, and disseminating knowledge. It comprises in varying proportions cognitive psychology, computer science (*information theory, artificial intelligence), philosophy (*epistemology), linguistics, and neuroscience.

Cohen's _d_   A standardized mean difference *effect size measure; it standardizes using standard deviation of the pooled scores of the control and experimental groups. See effect size, definition (b). Compare *Glass's Delta.

Cohen's Kappa   A measure of *interrater reliability for *categorical data. This percentage-of-agreement measure corrects for chance or random agreement. Kappa is 1.0 when agreement is perfect; it is 0.0 when agreement is no better than would be expected by chance. See *reliability coefficient.

Coherence   A measure of the strength of association of two *time series.

Coherency Principle   In *Bayesian analysis, the belief that *subjective probabilities, often described as betting odds, follow the usual laws of probability.

Cohort   A group of individuals having a statistical factor (usually age) in common.
> For example, all persons born in 1990 form a cohort.

Cohort Analysis   Studying the same *cohort over time. See *panel study, *time-series analysis.
> For example, individuals who graduated from high school in 2005 form a cohort whose subsequent educational experiences could be followed in a cohort analysis. For example, how many went on to college immediately? How many went on eventually? Of those who attended college, how many went to a 2-year college? How many to a 4-year college? How many graduated? And so on.

Cohort Effects   The effects of membership in a cohort, usually an age group. Also called "generation effects." Often contrasted with *period effects, which are the effects of living during an era regardless of individuals' ages.

C

For example, it is often claimed that being an adolescent in the 1950s affected people's attitudes quite differently than being an adolescent in the 1960s.

Cohort-Sequential Design   A combination of *cross-sectional and *longitudinal designs, usually to test for generation or *cohort effects and *age effects. Compare *accelerated longitudinal design.

For example, in Table C.6 the rows allow longitudinal comparisons, while the columns provide for cross-sectional analysis. The *cells contain the ages of the subjects.

Table C.6   Cohort-Sequential Design: Ages and Dates of Measurement of Subjects

	Year of Measurement				
Birth Year	*1985*	*1990*	*1995*	*2000*	*2005*
1980	5	10	15	20	25
1985		5	10	15	20
1990			5	10	15
1995				5	10
2000					5

Cohort Study   A study of the same group (cohort) over time, but not necessarily of the same individual members of that group. Contrast *panel study, in which the same individuals are studied at each stage.

For example, you might draw *probability samples from the cohort of 1994 (those born in that year) in the first three presidential election years in which they were eligible to vote: 2012, 2016, 2020. You would be unlikely to study the same individuals more than once.

COLA   Cost of living adjustment. An increase in wages or benefits, usually based on an index of consumer prices. See *Consumer Price Index.

Collapsing   Combining groups or categories of a variable in order to reduce their number. Also called "bracketing." See *class interval.

For example, suppose we surveyed 100 people about the number of movies they saw last year and got the following results. Table C.7 on page 71 uses five categories. Table C.8 on page 71 collapses the five categories into two.

Collider Variable   In a *causal diagram, a variable directly affected by two or more other variables, as in the following: $X \rightarrow C \leftarrow Y$. C is the collider. Term used by Judea Pearl in his distinctive graphing approach to causal analysis. Collider variables complicate causal analysis.

Collinear   Having a common line. See *multicollinearity.

Table C.7   Collapsing (Five Categories): Number of Movies Seen Last Year

0–5	22
6–10	18
11–15	12
16–20	28
20+	20

Table C.8   Collapsing (Two Categories): Number of Movies Seen Last Year

0–15	52
16+	48

Collinearity   The extent to which *independent (or *predictor) variables in a *regression analysis are correlated with one another. Collinearity causes problems in analysis because it makes it difficult to study the separate effects of independent variables. Synonym for the more traditional and more widely used term *multicollinearity. See *intercorrelation, *tolerance.

Column Marginals   See *marginal frequency distributions, *row marginals.

Column Percent   The number of cases in the cell (in a *contingency table) divided by the number of cases in the column; the percents in each column add to 100%. Column percents are *conditional probabilities or rates and should be compared across the columns in each row. Examples of column and row percents are shown in Table C.10 with the definition of *contingency table. Compare *cell percent, *row percent.

Combination   See *permutation.

Combinatorics   The study of the ways items in a *set can be arranged, selected, or combined. For example, if there were 5 candidates for 2 awards, such as first and second place, 10 distinct combinations of winners are possible.

Commonality Analysis   Methods of separating the effects of correlated *predictor variables in multiple *regression analysis and other multivariate techniques. The problem addressed by commonality analysis is estimating how much of the variance in the *outcome variable can be explained by each of the predictors, while controlling for the other predictors, and how much can be explained by all the predictors taken together. See $*R^2$.

Common Factor   A *factor that appears in two or more variables. A factor appearing in only one variable is called a "specific factor." See *factor analysis.

Common Factor Variance   The variance shared by two or more *factors. See *communality, *factor analysis.

Common Logarithm   A *logarithm using base 10.

Common Metric   A scale of measurement shared by more than one study or into which the results of several studies have been transformed. *Transformation to a common metric is usually accomplished using *standard scores; this is done in a *meta-analysis because it allows the results of different studies to be compared.

Common Variance   Variance shared by two or more variables. Two empirical indicators of the same factor (e.g., a dimension of mental ability) would be expected to have a good deal of common or overlapping variance and thus to correlate highly. See *reliability.

Communality   In factor analysis, the proportion of the total variance that is *common factor variance (that is, shared by two or more factors). It is calculated by summing the squared *factor loadings (see Table C.9) of a variable. Symbolized h^2.

Table C.9   Communality

	Factor 1		Factor 2
Loadings	.70		.10
Loadings squared	.49	+	$.01 = .50 = h^2$

Communication Theory   The study of the transfer of information. It tends to emphasize parallels between the ways humans and computers do this. Compare *information theory, *artificial intelligence, *cognitive science.

Comparative Case Study   Two or more cases are studied intensively and compared for similarities and differences to obtain a broader understanding of a phenomenon and to construct and test a theoretical explanation; especially popular in political science research. See *case study methods.

Comparative Fit Index (CFI)   A statistic used in *structural equation modeling to indicate model fit. It is an incremental fix index, measuring the increase in fit relative to a baseline model (usually an independence/null/not related model). Close model fit is indicated by CFI values greater than or equal to .95.

Comparative Method   The study of more than one event, group, or society to isolate factors or *variables that explain patterns. The term is most often used to describe *case study research with a small number of cases and cross-national research. However, almost all systematic research is comparative in the broad sense of the term. Experimental research, for example, involves comparing *control and *experimental groups. The term "comparative

C

Computational Formula   Statistical formula constructed for ease of hand computation instead of for understanding of a statistical concept. Most statistics books no longer include these formulas and instead include *definitional/conceptual formulas.

Computer-Intensive Methods   Statistical methods that rely heavily on computers. While they might be theoretically possible without using computers, these methods are practically impossible without assistance from machines. As computers increase in power, "intensive" methods take less time. See *computer simulation, *resampling methods.

Computer Program   A set of instructions written in a form a computer can read ("machine readable") that tell it how to perform specific tasks.

Computer Simulation   Using a computer to build a *model of what would happen in a real-world situation under certain conditions. Computer simulations are used in a wide variety of fields, from economic forecasting to demography. Compare *Monte Carlo methods.

Concentration, Coefficient of   See *Gini coefficient.

Concentration Ratio   Any of several measures of the extent to which economic activity in an industry is concentrated in a small number of firms. If the activity were monopolized by one firm, the ratio would be 1; if it were controlled equally by 100 firms, it would be .01. Compare *Gini coefficient.

Concept   An abstract idea expressed in language (or other symbol system). It often implies generalization from particulars—although Plato would not agree. Qualitative researchers tend to treat concepts as categories, and they are sometimes used as building blocks in *grounded theories. Quantitative researchers often transform concepts into *variables for empirical study and statistical analysis. Compare *construct, a term used more often in quantitative research to express the same idea (concept) as "concept."

   For example, if you saw an unusual breed of dog for the first time, you would probably still recognize it as a dog—even though you had never seen it before—because it would fit into your general concept or idea of what a dog is. Compare *schema.

Conceptual Formula   See *definitional formula.

Conceptualism   The middle or compromise position in the theory of universals. *Nominalism held that only particulars exist (e.g., particular chairs, triangles). *Realism held that universals exist independently of us. Falling in the middle, conceptualism is the position that universals exist in our minds and particulars exist in actual objects.

Conceptualization   Specifying what we mean by the *concepts we will use in a research project. In quantitative research, this is often a step on the way to *operational definitions.

Concomitant Variable   A variable a researcher wishes to *control for. Often an *attribute or a *trait of subjects. Also called *covariate.

Concomitant Variation   Said of two or more phenomena that vary together, or covary. See *correlation, *covariance, *cause, *Mill's methods for causation.

Concordance, Coefficient of   See *Kendall's coefficient of concordance.

Concurrent Validity   A way of determining the *validity of a measure by seeing how well it correlates with (agrees or "concurs" with) some other measure the researcher believes is valid.

   For example, if psychologists wanted to see whether a new IQ test were a valid measure of intelligence, they could correlate subjects' scores on the new test with their scores on an old IQ test that they thought was a good measure of intelligence. If the scores were highly correlated, this would be evidence of the validity of the new test—or, at least, that the two tests were measuring the same thing.

Condition   A *treatment or a *level of an *independent variable (or combination of more than one independent variable) in an *experiment.

   For example, a study comparing the effects of drugs A, B, and C has three conditions (Drug A, Drug B, Drug C). The independent variable (drug treatment) has three levels (A, B, and C).

Conditional Distribution   The distribution of the values of one variable at each of the values of another variable or variables. See *bivariate distribution.

   For example, the distribution of weight in a population is conditional upon the distribution of height (tall people tend to weigh more than short ones). If we compared the distribution of weights of people 5 feet tall with that of people 6 feet tall, we would be comparing two conditional distributions; specifically, we would be comparing weight conditional on height = 5 with weight conditional on height = 6. A *regression equation predicts the mean of the conditional distribution of the dependent variable for every value of the independent variable(s).

Conditional Effect   Another term for *interaction effect. It is used especially in *regression analysis to distinguish it from general effects; "interaction effect" is the more common term in the context of *ANOVA.

   For example, going to college improves earnings for all groups (general effect), but the improvement may be greater for some groups (conditional effect).

Conditional Event   In *probability theory, an event that can occur only in conjunction with another event. See *conditional probability. Contrast *independent event, *complement.

   For example, say you rolled a pair of dice one at a time. Getting a total of 9 (the conditional event) after the second roll is conditional upon the first die having come up 3 or higher.

Conditional Odds   *Odds that take into account other variables. Compare *conditional probability.

For example, the odds (unconditional) of graduating from high school in a particular state might be 80% to 20%, or 4 to 1. Taking into account the variable sex, the conditional odds for females might be 85% to 15%, or 5.67 to 1.

Conditional Probability   (a) The chance that an event will occur, given that some other event has already occurred. Symbolized: $p(B|A)$, which is read, "the probability of event B, given event A." (b) The chance that one condition exists given that another does. See *Bayesian statistical inference.

For example, (a) the probability of drawing an ace at random from a deck of 52 playing cards is 4 out of 52, or 1 out of 13. Say you drew a card, got an ace, and did not put it back in the deck. Call that draw event A. What is the conditional probability (given event A) of drawing another ace (event B)? Since you did not replace the first ace, the (conditional) probability of drawing a second ace is 3 out of 51 or 1 out of 17. Compare *gambler's fallacy.

An example of (b) might be the likelihood that a patient has HIV, given that his blood test is positive. See *sensitivity.

Conditioning Effect   Another term for *interaction effect.

Conditioning on (a Variable)   In the context of *causal analysis, to condition on means to control for. One can condition on variables by methods such as *matching, *stratifying, or *regression.

Confederate   Someone who pretends to be a subject in an *experiment, but who is actually helping the experimenter in some way.

Confidence Band   The region between the lower and upper *confidence limits.

Confidence Bounds   Another term for *confidence limits.

Confidence Coefficient   Another term for *confidence level. It is 1.0 minus the *alpha level. Thus an alpha level of .05 results in a confidence coefficient of .95.

Confidence Interval (CI)   A range of values of a sample *statistic that is likely (at a given level of probability, called a *confidence level) to capture a *population parameter. The interval that will include the population parameter a certain percentage (*confidence level) of the time in the long run (over repeated sampling). In other words, a range of values with a known probability of including or capturing the true population value. The wider the confidence interval, the higher the confidence level. If you want a more precise (i.e., narrower) confidence interval, you will have to use a lower level of confidence. See *confidence level for an example. The CI is an interval estimate; compare *point estimate.

It is common to say that one can be 95% confident that the confidence interval contains the true value. Although this is the usual way to report confidence intervals and limits, it is not technically correct (in *frequentist statistical

C

inference, which is typically used, but it is correct in *Bayesian statistical inference). Rather, it is correct to say: Were one to take an infinite number of samples of the same size, on average 95% of them would produce confidence intervals containing the true population value.

Confidence Level   A desired percentage of the scores (often 95% or 99%) that would fall within a certain range of *confidence limits. It is calculated by subtracting the alpha level from 1 and multiplying the result times 100 (e.g., 100 × (1 − .05) = 95%).

For example, say a poll predicted that if the election were held today, a candidate would win 60% of the vote. This prediction could be qualified by saying that the pollster was 95% certain (confidence *level*) that the prediction was accurate plus or minus 3% (confidence *interval* = 57% to 63%). *Ceteris paribus* (i.e., other things equal), the larger the sample, the narrower the confidence interval or margin of error.

Confidence Limits   The upper and lower values of a *confidence interval, that is, the values defining the range of a confidence interval. See *confidence level for an example.

Confidentiality   See *anonymity for explanation of anonymity and confidentiality.

Confirmation Bias   A tendency to search for information and interpret information in a way that supports our prior beliefs and hypotheses. Researchers must use strategies (such as *blinding, *reflexivity, and *negative case analysis) to help prevent this problem.

Confirmatory Data Analysis   The statistical testing of hypotheses and theories during data analysis for statistical significance. Contrast with *exploratory data analysis. See *confirmatory factor analysis.

Confirmatory Factor Analysis   *Factor analysis conducted to test hypotheses (or confirm theories) about the factors one expects to find. It is a type of or element of *structural equation modeling. Compare *exploratory factor analysis.

Confirmatory Research   Research focused on hypothesis and theory testing rather than on generating new hypotheses and theories. Confirmatory research takes more of a deductive or top-down approach to research, while, in contrast, exploratory research relies on an inductive or bottom-up approach. Contrast with *exploratory research.

Conflict Theory   A perspective on society and social relations contending that the main determinant of social phenomena is the tendency of individuals and groups to have opposing interests over which they come into conflict. Although traditionally focused on class and wealth inequality, today it targets many additional inequalities such as gender, race, ethnicity, sexual orientation, and other international and intranational differences that lead to differences in wealth and power or result in prejudice and discrimination. Among the many classical authors who could be called conflict theorists, Karl Marx and Max Weber are probably the best known. Compare *functionalism.

Confound (a) To study combined treatments in such a way that their separate effects cannot be determined. (b) A variable that obscures, or makes it impossible to interpret, the relations among other variables. See *confounded.

For example, to study the effects of fertilizer on your lawn growth when the fertilizer must be applied with water is to confound the effects of watering and of fertilizing. Water is the confound.

Confounded Said of two or more *variables whose separate effects cannot be isolated.

For example, if Professor X used Textbook A in her classes and Professor Y used Textbook B, and students in the two classes were given achievement tests to see how much they had learned, the *independent variables (the textbooks and the professors' teaching effectiveness) would be confounded. There would be no way to tell whether any observed differences in achievement (the *dependent variable) between the two classes were caused by either or both of the independent variables in this flawed study.

Confounding Variable A variable that obscures the effects of another. In a high-quality research study, the researcher does his or her best to identify and control for confounding variables. See *confound and *confounded for examples. Compare *suppressor variable.

Conjoint Analysis An approach to market research in which the market researcher has subjects rate their preferences for different prototypical versions of an entire product. The comparisons are made two at a time (called paired comparisons). The different versions of the product presented in each paired comparison have different combinations of attributes (e.g., a red auto with a manual transmission and a six-cylinder motor vs. a red auto with an automatic transmission and a four-cylinder motor). This approach of examining complete packages is considered more holistic than rating each attribute abstractly and separately (rate different colors, then rate different transmissions, then rate different engine types). A weakness is that this process is demanding and tedious for subjects when they are asked to compare many different pairs with only very slight differences. Also, the number of paired comparisons becomes very large as the number of attributes and levels of attributes increase. The data are usually gathered with survey research instruments (questionnaires). The results are used in designing and producing products that are considered likely to be purchased by consumers.

Consensual Validation The use of agreement (consensus) of two or more experts to determine whether a statement is true or valid.

Consent   Synonym for *informed consent.

Consequent   The second term in a ratio. In the ratio 3:2, 2 is the consequent. The first term (3) is the *antecedent.

Consequential Validity   Present when a researcher or test administrator understands the likely implications of using a particular test with an individual or group of people. Often the focus is on unintended negative consequences that could arise from using a test or measurement, such as an adverse effect on a particular social group. In this sense, the concept refers to *in*validity. More broadly, it is present to the degree that use of a test has maximal positive and minimal negative intended and unintended psychological and social consequences.

Conservative (Measure or Estimate)   Said of a statistic that tends to underestimate; that is, if it errs, it is more likely to do so by being overly cautious. See *post hoc test.

For example, *omega squared is a conservative measure of *strength of association, because it is more likely to underestimate than to overestimate that strength—especially in comparison with *eta squared, which can sometimes overestimate the strength of an association.

Consistent Estimator   A sample *statistic (estimator) that tends to get closer to the true population *parameter as the sample size increases. Also, as the sample size increases, a consistent estimator has a smaller variance. See *central limit theorem.

Constant   (a) A measure or value that is the same for all units of analysis. (b) A quantity that does not change value in a particular context. (c) In a *regression equation, the *intercept (also called *regression constant and *y*-intercept) is often referred to as "the constant"; the *beta coefficients are also constants, but are less often so called. Compare *variable, *universal constant.

For example, (a) in research that studied variables explaining unemployment among women only, sex would be a constant; all subjects (units of analysis) are female. An example of (b) would be the sex of the inmates in a federal prison for men, which does not vary over time. For definition (c), the value of *a* would be the constant in the regression equation $\hat{Y} = a + bX + e$.

Constant Comparison   A method of *qualitative data analysis particularly associated with *grounded theory. As data are being coded and analyzed, the researcher continually compares conclusions drawn from the earlier stages to data from the later stages. For example, initial review of some interview transcripts will suggest coding schemes and interpretations. With each additional transcript reviewed, these schemes and interpretations are compared and revised if needed.

Constrained Parameter   In *SEM, model parameters (e.g., path coefficients, error coefficients) can be fixed, constrained, or freely estimated. Constrained parameters are parameters the researcher sets to have the same value even though they still must be empirically estimated. This procedure is sometimes used in multi-group confirmatory factor analysis to determine if a model positing the same structure across groups has good fit. Compare *fixed parameter, *freely estimated parameter.

Construct   (a) Something that exists theoretically, but is not directly observable. (b) A *concept developed (constructed) for describing relations among phenomena or for other research purposes. (c) A theoretical (not *operational) definition in which concepts are defined by researchers in ways they believe are meaningful.

For example, intelligence cannot be directly observed or measured; it is a construct. Researchers infer the existence of intelligence from behavior and use *indexes (such as size of vocabulary or the ability to remember strings of numbers) to "construct" a measure of the construct, intelligence.

Constructionism   A research perspective that emphasizes that knowledge claims are constructed; specifically, they are constructed so as to satisfy the social needs and interests of the knowers, including researchers. Since different social groups will have different needs and interests, their definitions of knowledge will vary accordingly. Constructionism is thus socially *relativist, and its proponents reject most claims of *objectivity. Also called "social constructionism."

Constructivism   A theory of learning formally developed by Piaget. His research indicated that children learn by constructing their knowledge on the basis of their experiences. More subjective versions of constructivism have much in common with *constructionism, though the latter tends to stress social more than individual influences on what counts as knowledge. Constructivism is especially popular among *qualitative researchers.

Construct Validity   The extent to which *variables accurately measure the constructs of interest. In other words, how well are the variables *operationalized? Do the *operations really get at the things we are trying to measure? How well can we generalize from our operations to our construct? In practice, construct validity is used to describe a *scale, *index, or other measure of a variable that *correlates with measures of other variables in ways that are predicted by, or make sense according to, a theory of how the variables are related. See *concurrent, *content, *convergent, and *criterion-related validity. Absolute distinctions among these kinds of validity are difficult to make, in large part because procedures for assessing them tend to be similar, if not identical. *Convergent and *discriminant validity, for instance, are used as tests of construct validity.

For example, if you were studying racist attitudes, and you believed that racism (the construct) was more common among people with low self-esteem, you could put together some questions that you thought were a good *index

C

of racism. If subjects' scores on that index were strongly (*negatively) correlated with their scores on a measure of self-esteem, this would be evidence that
your index had construct validity. The index is more likely to be a good measure of racism if it correlates with something your theory says it should correlate with than if it does not. All this assumes, of course, that your theory is
right in the first place about the relation between self-esteem and racism *and*
that you have valid measures of racism and self-esteem.

Consumer Price Index   A measure of the average change over time of a fixed
group of goods and services. It is used to gauge inflation. In the United States,
data for this index are collected monthly or bimonthly from about 50,000
households by the Bureau of Labor Statistics. See *base year.

Consumption Function   The relation between consumption and other variables—such as income, wealth, and interest rates—expressed as a formula
(function). Generally, consumption is a function of (increases with, is caused
by) income. See *production function.

Contamination   Refers to research situations in which data or variables or levels
that should be kept separate come into contact. For example, the treatment
and control groups might interact or the *independent and *dependent variables measure the same or similar things. See *confounded.

   Dirty test tubes in the chemistry lab are the classic example. A more common example in the social and behavior sciences could occur when researchers
know subjects' scores on an *independent variable before they measure them
on the *dependent variable; that knowledge could influence (contaminate) the
second measurement. See *double-blind procedure.

Content Analysis   Any of several research techniques used to describe and systematically analyze the content of written, spoken, or pictorial communication—
such as books, newspapers, television programs, or interview transcripts.
The techniques are often, though not necessarily, quantitative in orientation
because enumeration or counting is often involved. Qualitative analyses of
content more often go by names such as *discourse analysis and *narrative
analysis.

   For example, in a series of interviews you could ask people open-ended
questions about different ethnic groups. Later the audiotapes of these interviews could be transcribed (perhaps entered into a computer program) so that
the number of positive and negative adjectives used by interviewees when
talking about various ethnic groups could be counted.

   A famous early use of content analysis dates from the 1960s. Statisticians
used word frequency analysis to identify previously unknown authors of some
of the *Federalist Papers.*

Content-Referenced Test   Another term for *criterion-referenced test.

C

Content Validity (or Content-Related Validity)   (a) A measure has content validity to the degree that its items accurately represent the thing (the "universe") being measured. Content validity is not a statistical property; it is a matter of expert judgment. Compare *construct, *concurrent, and *convergent validity. (b) In *factor analysis, the degree to which a group of measured variables estimates a *latent variable.

For (a), it is easier to give clear examples of *in*validity than of validity. For example, a test of American history that contained only questions about Civil War battles would not be content valid; its questions would not be representative of the entire subject.

Context of Discovery   The creative, psychological part of research in which the researcher comes up with, discovers, or generates a hypothesis, explanation, or theory. (Sometimes called the "logic of discovery.") See *abduction, *induction.

Context of Justification   The part of science in which the researcher empirically tests a hypothesis, explanation, or theory to determine whether it should be considered true and added to the stock of scientific knowledge. (Sometimes called the "logic of justification.") See *hypothesis testing.

Contextual Effects   The impact on individuals of operating in certain contexts (e.g., geographical, temporal, social). These effects are usually studied with *multilevel models or *hierarchical linear modeling. Compare *cohort effects, *conditional effects.

For example, attending a secondary school in which most of the other students plan to go to college (one context) might influence a student differently than attending a secondary school in which very few students planned to go to college (another context). Otherwise similar students, attending different types of secondary school, might have different propensities to attend college. If so, that would be an example of contextual effects.

Contextual Interaction   The interaction of an independent variable (e.g., treatment and control) with a contextual effect. Researchers are learning that context influences many statistical relationships, and therefore it is important to search for contextual interactions. Reality can be quite complex and contextual and situational. *Mixed methods research is quite useful for identifying contextual interactions.

Contingency   A relation between variables such that one determines or depends upon (is contingent upon) another. See *conditional probability.

Contingency Coefficient   Short for *Pearson's contingency coefficient, which is a measure of *association for *categorical variables, usually as displayed with a *contingency table. Compare *Cramer's *V,* a more versatile and accurate measure for categorical variables.

Contingency Effect   Another term for *conditional effect or *interaction effect.

C

Contingency Question   Type of question in a survey instrument that directs different types of respondents to different follow-up questions depending on their response. For example, "Are you currently pregnant?" should be preceded by a contingency question asking for the respondent's sex, and only females should be directed to the question about possible pregnancy. Contingency questions usually lead to skipping directions, a frequent source of respondent error: "If you answered yes to question 14, skip ahead to question 17." Also called a filter question.

Contingency Table   A table of frequencies classified according to two or more sets of values of *categorical variables. Also called a *cross-tabulation. It is called a contingency table because what you find in the rows (the usual place for the *dependent variable) is contingent upon what you find in the columns (the usual place for the *independent variable). Identification and interpretation of relationships between categorical variables via contingency tables is enhanced by including *column percents (the percentages in each column sum to 100%) and *row percents (the percentages in each row sum to 100%). To determine if there is a relationship between the two variables with column percents, one should compare across each row; with row percents, one should compare down each column. This procedure also produces the relevant *risk ratios. See *categorical data analysis, *cell percent, *column percent, *row percent.

For example, Table C.10 shows the results of a survey of 700 individuals concerning their religious affiliations and attitudes about legal abortion. Table C.11 on page 83 adds the gender of the respondents; it is an example of a multivariate (more than two variables) contingency table.

Table C.10   Contingency Table (Bivariate): Religious Affiliation and Attitude Toward Legal Abortion

Favor Legal Abortion	Religion			Total
	Catholic	Protestant	Other	
Yes	63	278	73	414
	9.00 (cell %)	39.70 (cell %)	10.43 (cell %)	
	15.22 (row %)	67.15 (row %)	17.63 (row %)	100 (row total)
	31.03 (column %)	70.20 (column %)	72.28 (column %)	
No	140	118	28	286
	20.00 (cell %)	16.86 (cell %)	4.00 (cell %)	
	48.95 (row %)	41.26 (row %)	9.79 (row %)	100 (row total)
	68.97 (column %)	29.80 (column %)	27.72 (column %)	
Total	203	396	101	700
	100 (column total)	100 (column total)	100 (column total)	100 (cell total)

Table C.11   Contingency Table (Multivariate) With Cell Frequencies: Attitude Toward Legal Abortion by Gender and Religious Affiliation

| | Gender | | | | | | | |
| | Women | | | | Men | | | |
Favor Legal Abortion	Catholic	Protestant	Other	**Total**	Catholic	Protestant	Other	**Total**
Yes	40	140	51	231	23	138	22	183
No	64	58	23	145	76	60	5	141
Total	104	198	74	376	99	198	27	324

Continuity Correction   See *Yates's correction (for continuity).

Continuous Variable   A variable that can be expressed by a large (often infinite) number of points or values. Loosely, a variable that can be measured on an *interval or a *ratio scale. Compare *categorical variable.

Deciding whether to treat data as continuous can have important consequences for choosing statistical techniques. Ordinal data are often treated as continuous when there are many ranks in the data, but as categorical when there are few. See *discrete variable for further discussion.

For example, height and grade point average (GPA) are continuous variables. Persons' heights could be 69.38 inches, 69.39 inches, and so on; GPAs could be 3.17, 3.18, and so on. In fact, since values always have to be rounded, theoretically continuous variables are measured as discrete variables. There is an infinite number of values between 69.38 and 69.39 inches, but the limits of our ability to measure or the limits of our interest in precision lead us to round off continuous values.

GPA is a good example of the difficulty of making these distinctions. It is routinely treated as a continuous variable, but it is constructed out of a rank order scale (A, B, C, etc.). Numbers are assigned to those ranks, and the numbers are then treated as though they were an interval scale.

Contour Plot   A two-dimensional representation of a three-dimensional surface. Contour plots are used on maps to indicate the variations in altitude in the area depicted. In social and behavioral research, they are used to show relations among variables, as in a *regression analysis.

Contrast Coding   A technique for coding *categorical variables to facilitate *planned comparisons between groups that are orthogonal. Unlike *dummy coding, which uses a series of 1s and 0s for a multiple-category variable, contrast coding might use −1, 0, and +1 or other codes as long as they sum to zero. Also called *orthogonal coding. Compare *effects coding. Table C.12 describes the uses of the three most common types of categorical variable coding. Note that all three approaches to coding can be used for planned comparisons. The disadvantage of using contrast coding for planned comparisons is that one might not be able to make all of the comparisons of theoretical interest in a set of orthogonal comparisons.

Table C.12   Contrast Coding: When to Use Different Forms of Coding for Categorical Variables

Type of Coding	When to Use
Contrast Coding	To construct planned comparisons between groups that are orthogonal
Dummy Coding	To compare each group's mean to the mean of the group getting all zeros
Effects Coding	To compare each group's mean to the overall mean

Control   (a) To eliminate the effects of *extraneous or *confounding variables. This can be done either by *random assignment in an *experiment or by statistical simulation in nonexperimental research. See *hold constant and *net effects. (b) Application of social science knowledge to produce desirable physical, social, and behavioral outcomes (e.g., *reduction* in illness, violence, and poverty; *increase* in learning, productivity, and job, life, and customer satisfaction).

Control Card   A series of instructions for a computer program telling it what operations to perform on a particular set of data. So called because these instructions (and the data) were at one time entered on computer punch cards. The cards have disappeared, but the term lingers.

Control for   Any one of several ways of statistically subtracting the effects of a variable (a *control variable) to see what a relationship would have been without it. See *hold constant.

    For example, to compare the average incomes of various ethnic groups, we might wish to control for education level. In that way we could measure the effects of ethnic group membership apart from differences in the educational levels among the groups. This would be important, for example, if we were showing how much of the difference in income persisted even when people from different groups had the same education level. See *analysis of covariance and, for an example, *crosstabs, Table C.16.

Control Group   In experimental research, a group that, for the sake of comparison, does not receive the *treatment the experimenter is interested in studying. In an *experiment, the control group is used to estimate the *counterfactual (i.e., what the experimental group would have been like if it had *not* received the treatment). Compare *experimental group (also called *treatment group).

For example, a psychologist studying the effects of television violence on attitudes about violence might give subjects a questionnaire (the *pretest) to measure their attitudes, randomly divide them into two groups, and show a video of a violent program to one half (the experimental group) and not show the video to the other half (the control group). The attitude questionnaire would then be administered again (the *posttest), and the researcher would compare the results of the experimental and control groups to see if the violent video caused a change in the experimental group's attitudes about violence.

Controlled Trial   A *clinical trial in which a new treatment is compared with another treatment (rather than no treatment), usually the standard treatment against which the new treatment is being compared.

Controlled Variable   A term occasionally used for an *independent variable, so called because independent variables are controlled by experimenters.

Control on   Another way of saying *control for.

Control Variable   An extraneous variable that you do not wish to examine in your study; hence you *control for it. Also called *covariate. This may be done by assignment to control and experimental groups or statistically by such methods as *partial correlation, *ANCOVA, or *regression analysis.

Convenience Sample   A sample of subjects selected for a study not because they are *representative but because it is convenient to use them or easy to obtain their consent to participate—as when college professors study their own students. Compare *accidental sample, *bias.

Oddly, using this term sometimes tends to legitimize bad practice. Researchers occasionally say, "A convenience sample was used to gather the data," as though this hard-to-justify method were a reasonable option among the many types of samples such as *random, *systematic, *stratified, and so on.

Convergent Validity   The overlap between different tests that presumably measure the same *construct. Present to the degree that scores on a measure of a construct are strongly correlated with an independent (different) measure of the same construct. See *concurrent validity, *construct validity, *discriminant validity.

Converging Evidence   Said of the results of multiple methods or multiple studies that lead to the same conclusion. Compare *meta-analysis, *triangulation.

Conversation Analysis   An area of research that draws from psychology and sociology to investigate the rituals, competencies, and layers of meaning employed by speakers in verbal interactions. Conversation analysis emphasizes naturally occurring conversations as opposed to verbal interactions in formal interviews.

Cook's Distance (*D*)   The standardized difference between two sets of fitted values; used to identify *influential observations. It measures change in the set of regression coefficients that would result if a particular case were removed. According to one popular rule of thumb, you should worry about the influence of a case when its *D* value is greater than 1. See *leverage, *outlier detection.

Coordinates   Numbers that can be used to plot points on a graph. See *Cartesian coordinates for an example.

Correction for Attenuation   Adjusting a *correlation to estimate what it would have been had the correlated variables been measured without error. See *attenuation.

Correct Model Specification   See *model specification.

Correlated Groups   See *correlated groups design.

Correlated Groups Design   A *research design in which some of the *variance in the *dependent variable is produced by a correlation between groups of subjects—or among sets of their scores. Compare *independent samples (or groups). Different tests of statistical significance are required when the groups are correlated rather than independent.

A common form of this research design is a before-and-after study. For example, fifth graders are given a vocabulary pretest. Then they receive an experimental vocabulary enrichment program. At the end of a semester, they are given the vocabulary test again (a posttest). The dependent variable is the scores on the posttest. A good part of the students' scores on the posttest could be explained by their pretest scores. For example, students with very large vocabularies before the study would still have large vocabularies after it was over. Thus, regardless of the treatment they receive, the scores of students on the pretest and posttest will almost certainly be somewhat correlated and probably highly correlated. The correlated-groups *t* test corrects for the fact that large mean differences are less likely when the groups are correlated.

Correlated-Groups *t* Test   Synonym for *paired samples *t* test.

Correlated Samples   Two or more samples in which members of the separate samples share a characteristic or relationship with one another—husband-and-wife pairs, for example. See *correlated groups design. A *t* test for correlated samples, not the test for *independent samples, should be used with such a design.

Correlated-Samples *t*   Synonym for *paired samples *t* test.

Correlation   The extent to which two or more things or variables are related ("co-related") to one another. This is usually expressed as a *correlation coefficient.

Students sometimes misinterpret a warning about correlations found in elementary textbooks—correlation does not equal causation. We have seen students take this warning so literally as to believe that two correlated variables cannot possibly be causally linked under any circumstances. Less erroneous, but even more widespread, is the mistaken view that a correlation between two variables provides no evidence whatsoever about cause. The evidence from correlations is often weak by experimental standards, but it is evidence, often important evidence, that it would be foolish to ignore. Disciplines as diverse as economics and epidemiology are heavily based on correlational evidence. Textbook warnings would be more accurate were they to read: Correlation does not *necessarily* indicate causation. Another way of putting this is to say that correlation is necessary but not sufficient for causation; if one wants to make a claim of causation between two variables, the variables *must* be related, but the researcher also needs to establish the time ordering of the variables and rule out any plausible rival explanations of the observed relationship. See *necessary condition.

Correlational Research Design   A design in which the variables are not manipulated. The researcher uses measures of *association to study their relations. Also called *nonexperimental research. The term is usually used in contrast with *experimental research.

Correlation Cluster   A group of variables that correlate with one another. Compare *factor analysis.

Correlation Coefficient   A number showing the degree to which two *variables are related. Correlation coefficients range from −1.0 to +1.0. If there is a perfect *negative correlation (−1.0) between A and B, then whenever A is high, B is low, and vice versa. If there is a perfect *positive correlation (+1.0) between A and B, then whenever one is high or low, so is the other. A correlation coefficient of 0 means that there is no relationship between the variables. (A zero correlation may also occur when two variables are related but their relationship is not *linear; see *eta.) See also *association, measure of, *correlation matrix, *regression analysis, *scatter plot.

There are numerous ways to compute correlation coefficients depending on the kinds of variables being studied. Among the most common are the *Pearson product-moment, *Spearman rho, and *Kendall tau. The term "correlation" is used by some to refer to any measure of association and by others to refer only to the association of variables measured at an *interval or *ratio level.

Graphically, a correlation is the degree to which two variables form a straight line when plotted on a *scatter diagram. The examples in Figure C.3

C

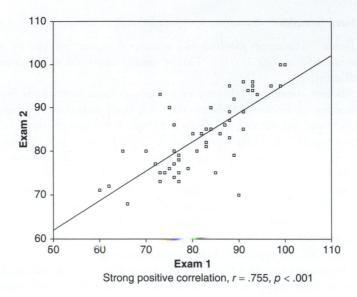

Strong positive correlation, *r* = .755, *p* < .001

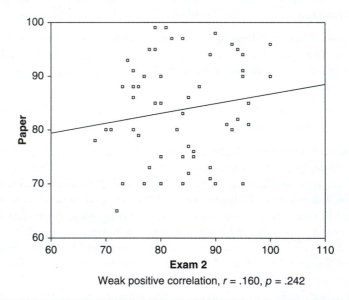

Weak positive correlation, *r* = .160, *p* = .242

Figure C.3   Correlation Coefficient

show a strong positive relation (.755) and a weak positive relation (.160). The line through the pattern of points in each scatter diagram is the *regression line, which is the straight line that comes closer on average to the points than any other possible line.

Correlation Matrix A table of *correlation coefficients that shows all pairs of correlations of a set of variables. Compare *covariance matrix.

In the following example, correlations between subjects' age, income, and scores on two attitude scales are shown. Note in Table C.13 the series of diagonal correlations of 1.00. These figures reflect the fact that a variable always correlates perfectly with itself. These correlations are often omitted, as they are in Table C.14, since they are self-evident. The upper-right (or lower-left) portion of the table is usually omitted as well, because it just repeats (as a sort of mirror image) what is printed in the lower left. In short, most correlation matrices are simplified to look like Table C.14, not Table C.13.

Table C.13 Correlation Matrix (Full; With Redundant Data)

	Age	*Income*	*Scale 1*	*Scale 2*
Age	.00	.49	.74	.68
Income	.49	.00	.33	.42
Scale 1	.74	.33	.00	.91
Scale 2	.68	.42	.91	.00

Table C.14 Correlation Matrix (Abbreviated; Without Redundant Data)

	Age	*Income*	*Scale 1*	*Scale 2*
Age				
Income	.49			
Scale 1	.74	.33		
Scale 2	.68	.42	.91	

Studying either table, you could conclude that the two scales were highly correlated (.91) with one another and that the scores on the scales were more strongly correlated with age (.74 and .68) than they were with income (.33 and .42).

Correlation Ratio A kind of correlation—symbolized by and commonly known as *eta squared—that can be used when the relation between two variables is not assumed to be *linear. It is a measure of *strength of association that is independent of the form of the relation—unlike Pearson's *r*, which shows only a linear relationship between variables.

Correlogram A graphic representation of *autocorrelation, that is, of a variable's correlation with itself over time. Correlation is plotted on the vertical (or *y*) axis, and time is indicated on the horizontal (or *x*) axis.

Correspondence Analysis Graphical methods of depicting the degree of association in *cross-tabulations.

Cost-Benefit Analysis (also Benefit-Cost Analysis) Economic approach to program evaluation. In cost-benefit analysis, costs and benefits are measured and converted into a common monetary unit (present-value dollars). The ratio of total present-value dollar benefits to total present-value dollar costs is calculated, yielding the *benefit-cost* (B-C) *ratio*. The breakeven point on the B-C ratio is 1. If the ratio is greater than 1, the benefits are greater than costs, and the program or object of evaluation should be adopted; if the ratio is less than 1, it should not be adopted. Because turning benefits into monetary units is difficult, economists often use *cost-effectiveness* analysis instead of cost-benefit analysis. In cost-effectiveness analysis, the benefits are left in their natural (nonmonetary) units. The ratio of a benefit to cost shows how much of that benefit one obtains per dollar spent—this is sometimes called the "bang for the buck." Comparatively, the program providing the biggest "bang for the buck" is preferred. Both cost-benefit and cost-effectiveness analysis are used to study program *efficiency, which is contrasted with program *effectiveness.

Count Data Statistical information obtained by counting the number of occurrences of categorical variables rather than by measuring variables on a numeric *scale.

Counterbalancing In a *within-subjects *factorial experiment, presenting *conditions (*treatments) in all possible orders to avoid *order effects. See *Latin square.

For example, an experimenter might wish to study the effects of three kinds of lighting (A, B, and C) on performance of a visual skill. Subjects could first be placed in Condition A and be given a test of the skill; then they could be put in Condition B and get a second test, and so on. By Condition C and the third test, subjects' scores might go up simply because they had the practice of the first two tests. Or their scores might go down because they became fatigued.

The effects of practice and fatigue could be counterbalanced by rotating the lighting conditions so that subjects would experience them in all possible orders. Since there are six possible orders (ABC, ACB, BAC, BCA, CAB, CBA), subjects could be divided into six groups, one for each possible order.

Counterbalancing controls for *carryover effects and *order effects, but it does not control for "nonlinear" or "interactive" effects such as *differential carryover effects.

Counterexample An example that conflicts with or disproves a general statement, as when the statement "All women hate to study statistics" is countered by the example of Mary, a woman who loves to study statistics.

Counterfactual (Conditional) A statement of what "would have" happened had something occurred that did not in fact occur.

For example, the statement "Had the New York stock market crash of 1929 not occurred, the worldwide depression of the 1930s would have been over by

1932" is a counterfactual conditional. Counterfactuals play an important role in theorizing about *cause. In an experiment including a treatment and control group, the no-treatment *control group performance is used as an estimate of what the treatment group would have been like if it had not received the treatment. In a one-group pretest-posttest design, the pretest is used as the estimate of the counterfactual condition.

Covariance   A measure of the joint (or co-) *variance of two or more variables. See *covariation, *analysis of covariance. A covariance is an unstandardized *correlation coefficient r. The covariance is very important in calculating many multivariate statistics. See *covariance matrix.

For example, suppose we want to see if there is a relation between knowledge of politics (variable X) and political tolerance (variable Y). Our tests of these two variables are each measured on a scale of 1–20. We give the two tests to a *sample of 10 people. The scores and the calculation of the covariance are shown in Table C.15. Column 1 assigns a number to each individual taking the two tests. Columns 2 and 4 are their results on Test X and Test Y. Columns 3 and 5 subtract the mean of each variable from each individual's score (to get the *deviation scores). Column 6 shows the *product of multiplying Column 3 times Column 5 (the *cross product). You total Column 6 and divide by the number of cases minus 1 ($10 - 1 = 9$) to get the covariance of X and Y (Cov_{XY}), which equals 11.4. The *correlation r is a standardized version of the covariance, which for these data equals .79.

Table C.15   Covariance (Example of How to Compute)

Column 1 Case	Column 2 X	Column 3 $X - \bar{X}$	Column 4 Y	Column 5 $Y - \bar{Y}$	Column 6 $(X - \bar{X})(Y - \bar{Y})$
01	18	5	16	4	20
02	9	−4	10	−2	8
03	12	−1	11	−1	1
04	17	4	14	2	8
05	13	0	13	1	0
06	8	−5	13	1	−5
07	17	4	16	4	16
08	14	1	11	−1	−1
09	16	3	13	0	0
10	6	−7	4	−8	56
Total	130	0	120	0	103
Mean	13		12		11.4
					(covariance)

C

Covariance Analysis   See *analysis of covariance.

Covariance Components Models   See *hierarchical linear models.

Covariance Matrix   A square matrix formed of the covariances of variables. This is directly comparable to the *correlation matrix, since correlations are standardized (expressed in *z scores) covariances. For both matrices, the numbers on the diagonal are variances. For correlations, the variance is always 1.0. Although the nonstandardized numbers, especially the variances, of the covariance matrix can be very large and hard to manipulate, the covariance matrix is more useful for many statistical applications, such as *structural equation modeling. Also called *variance-covariance matrix.

Covariance Structure Models   See *structural equation modeling, *analysis of covariance structures, *LISREL models, *confirmatory factor analysis.

Covariate   (a) Another term for a continuous *independent variable. (b) A variable other than the *independent (or *predictor) variable that correlates with the *dependent (or *outcome) variable. Typically, the researcher seeks to *control for (statistically subtract the effects of) the covariate (b) by using such techniques as *multiple regression analysis (MRA) or *analysis of covariance (ANCOVA). Also called "concomitant variable."

Covariation   A state that exists when two things—such as the price and the sales of a commodity—vary together. Measures of *association are designed to capture the degree of covariation. See *covariance, *correlation.

Cover Story   Untrue accounts of the purposes of research sometimes told to the subjects of the research. Such deception is sometimes considered necessary in psychological research if subjects' knowledge of the true purposes of the research might *confound the results. See *debriefing and *dehoaxing.

Cov_{XY}   *Covariance of X and Y.

Cox-Mantel Test   A *nonparametric test for comparing two survival curves. If the two curves vary randomly rather than systematically, then the test statistic, C, is normally distributed.

Cox Proportional Hazard Model   A type of Cox regression used in survival analysis to estimate the effect of fixed covariates on the hazard of an event. For example, the CPH model estimates the effect of a variable such as sex on the odds of death at a particular point of time during the period that subjects are observed. Because this model assumes the odds are proportional across all time periods, it cannot be used with time-varying covariates.

Cox Regression   A group of regression methods that are used to analyze *survival data that are *right censored. It can be used with both fixed and time-varying covariates. The most commonly used type of Cox regression is the *Cox Proportional Hazard Model.

Cox-Snell Residuals   Statistics used in a method of assessing the quality of a statistical model in a *survival analysis.

CPI   *Consumer Price Index.

CPS   *Current Population Survey.

Cramer's *V*   A measure of *association for *categorical variables based on the *chi-square statistic. It ranges from 0 to 1 and allows meaningful comparisons of chi-square values from tables with different sample sizes and different numbers of *cells. Compare *phi coefficient and *Pearson's contingency coefficient, which are also based on chi-square but are applicable to a more limited range of problems.

Criterion   (a) Short for *criterion variable, that is, the *outcome or *dependent variable. (b) In testing, the specific content or standard against which examinees' performances are compared.

Criterion Contamination   The part of a criterion or test that is not relevant to the theoretical construct of interest. This is due to the presence of some items that measure a different construct and were incorrectly included. The irrelevant items "contaminate" the test. See *criterion deficiency, *criterion relevance.

Criterion Deficiency   Characteristic of a test present when the test does not include items to measure certain parts of the theoretical construct. The test is "deficient." For content and construct validity, items need to be added. Compare *criterion contamination.

Criterion Group   A group used to validate a test because its characteristics are known. See *validity.

For example, if we wanted to validate a screening test for prospective locksmiths, we could give the test to master locksmiths to see if they performed well on it. If they did not perform well, the test probably would not be a valid measure of skills needed to be a good locksmith.

Criterion-Referenced Test   A test that examines a specific skill (the criterion) that students are expected to have learned or a level (the criterion) that students are expected to have attained. Unlike a *norm-referenced test, it measures absolute levels of achievement; students' scores are not dependent upon comparisons with the performance of other students. Also called a "content-referenced test."

Criterion-Related Validity   The ability of a test to make accurate predictions. The name comes from the fact that the test's validity is measured by how well it predicts an outside criterion. Also called "predictive validity." See also *concurrent validity, which is often held to be another aspect of criterion-related validity.

For example, the extent to which students' SAT scores predict their college grades is an indication of the SAT's criterion-related validity.

Criterion Relevance   The part of a criterion or test that is "relevant" to the theoretical construct of interest. This part of the test has construct validity, overlapping with the construct, in contrast to other items on the test marked by *criterion contamination (i.e., that do not measure the construct). When constructing a test, the goal is for all of the items to have criterion relevance (i.e., for the actual and theoretical criteria to be equivalent).

Criterion Scaling   A method of reducing the number of categories of *categorical and *ordinal variables in a *multiple regression analysis. The goal is to make the analysis more manageable by reducing the number of coded *vectors. The technique gets its name from the fact that it involves using the *mean of each group on the criterion (dependent) variable. It is often used in *repeated-measures designs.

Criterion Variable   Another term for *dependent or *outcome variable. The term is usually used for nonexperimental studies. In such usage, the *independent variable is called the *predictor or *explanatory variable.

Critical Ratio   The formula that gives the values that define the *critical region.

Critical Region   The area in a *sampling distribution representing values that are "critical" to a particular study (see Figure C.4). They are critical because when a *sample statistic falls in that region, the researcher can reject the *null hypothesis. (For this reason, the critical region is also called the "region of rejection.")

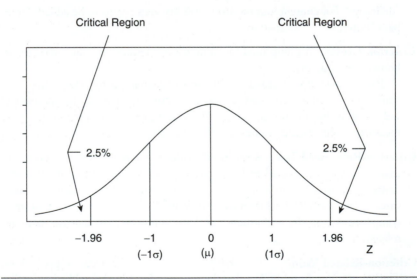

Figure C.4   Critical Region

Critical Theory   A term applied to several approaches to research and scholarship, most of which blend *relativism with left-wing political commitment. Often associated with the work of J. Habermas, critical theory stresses the distinction between the natural and the social sciences and thus rejects *positivism. Similar to *conflict theory in its distaste for societal inequalities (class, gender, ethnicity, etc.). Variants include critical ethnography, critical pragmatism, critical race theory, and so on. See *Geisteswissenschaften.

Critical Values   (a) The values that determine the *critical regions in a *sampling distribution. The critical values separate the obtained values that will and that will not result in rejecting the *null hypothesis. See Figure C.4 under *critical region.

(b) Tables of values for *test statistics that, when exceeded, enable the researcher to reject the null hypothesis. Such tables are used to interpret the results of *t tests, *chi-square statistics, or *F ratios. The values on such tables are in the *metric of these tests; they are not expressed in *raw data.

For example, when a normal distribution with an *alpha level of .05 is used as a test of significance, the critical value is plus or minus 1.96. If the *test statistic is greater than 1.96, then the null hypothesis is rejected.

Cronbach's Alpha   (called **coefficient alpha** by Cronbach) A measure of internal *reliability or consistency of the items in an *instrument, *index, or *scale. It is a widely used form of *Kuder-Richardson formula 20 (KR-20), but unlike KR-20, it can be used for test items that have more than two answers, such as *Likert scales. Cronbach's alpha is the measure of the *intercorrelation of the items and estimates the proportion of the variance in all the items that is accounted for by a common *factor. Like other *reliability coefficients, it ranges from 0 to 1. Scores toward the high end of that range (e.g., above .70) suggest that the items in an index are measuring the same thing. Also called "alpha coefficient" and "coefficient alpha."

Cronbach's alpha is replacing KR-20 because it is more versatile. An alpha on dichotomously scored items gives the same reliability score as KR-20. Despite its popularity, due in part to its ease of use, researchers, including Cronbach, have long stressed its limitations; the most commonly suggested alternatives are based on *generalizability theory.

Cross-Case Analysis   Another term for *comparative method.

Cross-Cultural Method   See *comparative method.

Crossed Factor Design   The usual way two or more factors are combined in a *factorial design. When every level of one factor appears within every level of the other factor(s), they are said to be (completely) crossed. The opposite of crossed is "nested." See *nested design for illustrations of the two designs.

Cross-Lagged Models   *Regression models for longitudinal or *panel data. The technique is designed to determine whether *independent variables at one session or *wave are related to or affect *dependent variables in the next wave of data gathering.

C

Cross-Lagged Panel Design   A nonexperimental longitudinal research design that is relatively strong for establishing cause and effect. Two variables are measured, one believed to be the *independent variable (IV) and the other believed to be the *dependent variable (DV), and these variables are measured at two times. This allows six correlations to be computed: IV and DV at time 1, IV and DV at time 2, IV at time 1 with IV at time 2, DV at time 1 with DV at time 2, and the "cross lagged correlations" of (a) IV at time 1 with DV at time 2 and (b) DV at time 1 with IV at time 2. If the correlation between the IV at time 1 and the DV at time 2 is significantly greater (i.e., a > b) than the correlation between the DV at time 1 and the IV at time 2, then it is concluded that it is likely that the IV is causing the DV rather than the other way around.

Cross-Level Inferences   Making inferences about one *level of analysis based on data about another, such as making inferences about individuals based on data about groups. See *ecological fallacy, *multilevel modeling.

Crossover Design   A type of *longitudinal or *within-subjects experimental study in which subjects receive different treatments at different times. Treatments are allocated randomly. The simplest version involves two groups of subjects and two treatments. Group 1 is given treatment A and then, after an interval, treatment B. Group 2 is given B, then A. Also called a *reversal design.

Crossover Interaction   Another term for *disordinal interaction.

Cross Partition   A combination of two or more *partitions.
   Say, for example, we were studying unemployment rates. We could look at them in general (for all people), or we could partition the data by group. We could examine unemployment among men and women (one partition) or among different ethnic groups (a second partition). Cross partitions would combine the first two partitions (gender by ethnicity) so that we could study groups such as white women, Hispanic men, and so on.

Cross Products   Short for cross-products deviation scores. A step in the calculations to determine the *covariance; the cross products are obtained by multiplying the *deviation scores of one variable times those of another. See Column 6 of Table C.15 under *covariance for an example.

Cross-Products Ratio   Another term for *odds ratio.

Cross-Sectional Data   Data gathered at one time. Compare *longitudinal data, *time-series data.

Cross-Sectional Study   A study conducted at a single point in time by, so to speak, taking a "slice" (a cross section) of a population at a particular time. Compare *panel study, *longitudinal study, *cohort-sequential design.
   Cross-sectional studies provide only indirect evidence about the effects of time and must be used with great caution when drawing conclusions about change. For example, if a cross-sectional survey shows that respondents aged 60–65 are

more likely to be racially prejudiced than respondents aged 20–25, this does not necessarily mean that as the younger group ages it will become more prejudiced—nor does it necessarily mean that the older group was once less prejudiced.

Cross-Sequential Design   See *cohort sequential design.

Crosstabs   Short for *cross-tabulations ("tabs") or *cross-partitions. A way of arranging data about categorical variables in a matrix (or *contingency table) so that relations can be more clearly seen. This is not to be confused with a *factorial table in which two or more variables are related to a third. While not all researchers make these distinctions in the terms, the concepts are quite distinct. Compare *contingency table. Also called "crossbreaks."

For example, Table C.16 is a crosstabs table. It shows the relation between race and graduation rates and sex and graduation rates. Table C.17, on the other hand, is a factorial table that shows the influence of two variables (sex and education level) on a third variable (average annual income).

Table C.16   Crosstabs Table Showing the Percentage of High School and College Graduates Among Persons Aged 25–29, by Race and Sex (2002)

	High School or More	Bachelor's Degree or Higher
Men	84.7	26.9
Women	88.1	31.8
Whites	85.9	29.7
Blacks	86.6	17.5

Table C.17   Factorial Table (Compared to Crosstabs Table) Showing Median Annual Income of Full-Time Workers 25+ Years Old, by Sex and Education Level (2000)

	High School	Bachelor's Degree or Higher
Men	$34,303	$61,868
Women	$24,970	$42,706

Cross-Tabulation   A way of presenting data about two variables in a table so that their relations are more obvious. Also called a *contingency table or a *crosstabs table (see Tables C.16 and C.17 under that entry for examples). A cross-tabulation can be used for *categorical variables only and shows the joint *frequency distributions of the two variables. Compare *factorial table.

Cross-Validated Multiple Correlation   A multiple correlation coefficient (symbolized: R) that has been examined on a *training sample and a test sample to increase confidence in its size and reliability. The average of the two

C

multiple correlations is the final multiple correlation to be used as the estimate of the population multiple correlation. See *cross-validation.

Cross-Validation   Using one *sample or one part of a sample (called the "training sample") to develop a theory and select appropriate statistics and then using another sample or part of a sample (called the "test sample") to validate the theory and the performance of the statistic. Cross-validation is important because using the same data to develop a theory and to test it is a form of circular reasoning or *tautology.

Crucial Experiment   An experiment or other study that decisively tests a theory or hypothesis. There is some controversy about whether any one experiment can be crucial in this sense, particularly in the social and behavioral sciences.

CRV   *Coefficient of relative variation.

Cultural Capital   Cultural resources (such as verbal fluency and educational credentials) that one can use to obtain income or other resources. Compare *capital, *social capital, *human capital.

Cultural Relativism   The belief that human thought and action can be judged only from the perspective of the culture out of which they have grown.

For example, a person who is generally opposed to male chauvinism, but who is also a cultural relativist, might conclude that one should not condemn male chauvinism if it could be seen as an integral part of the culture of a particular ethnic group. Of course, this relativistic judgment could itself be relative to another cultural group, middle-class Western intellectuals, perhaps.

Cumulative Frequency (and Cumulative Frequency Distribution)   For any value or *class interval in a *frequency distribution, the total up to and including that value or interval is its *cumulative frequency*. Cumulative frequency is often symbolized as *cf*. The set of cumulative frequencies shows the *cumulative frequency distribution*.

For example, the grades of 43 students on an examination are shown in Table C.18. The cumulative frequency for the class interval 70–79 is 13, which is the total up to and including that interval (4 + 9 = 13). The set of cumulative frequency values in the table (i.e., 4, 13, 31, 43) shows the cumulative frequency distribution.

Table C.18   Cumulative Frequency: Final Examination Grades of 43 Students

Interval	Frequency	Cumulative Frequency
A 90–99	12	43 (4 + 9 + 18 + 12)
B 80–89	18	31 (4 + 9 + 18)
C 70–79	9	13 (4 + 9)
D 60–69	4	4

Cumulative Frequency Polygon A graphic representation of a *cumulative frequency distribution. In Figure C.5, a more detailed version of the data from Table C.18 is graphed. Figure C.6 on page 102 under *cumulative standard normal distribution is another example.

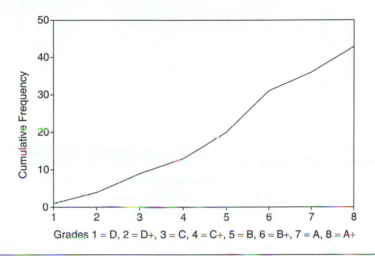

Figure C.5 Cumulative Frequency Polygon

Cumulative Scale A *scale, strictly speaking. See *summated scale, *Guttman scale, *index.

Cumulative Standard Normal Distribution (CSND) If you remember the normal distribution and the corresponding percentile scores, the concept of the CSND is easy to understand. A score that is 2 standard deviations below the mean ($z = -2.0$) would fall in the 2nd percentile and would have a cumulative frequency or probability of 2%. A score 2 standard deviations above the mean ($z = +2.0$) would be in the 98th percentile and have a cumulative probability of 98%, and so on. The left side of the CSND looks like any other standard normal distribution, but the curve reverses direction at the midpoint. The CSND is used in *probit regression. Figure C.6 shows an empirical distribution that closely approximates a CSND.

Cup In *set theory, the symbol ∪ meaning "or." It is used to indicate the *union of two sets. Compare *cap.

Current Population Survey (CPS) An annual survey conducted by the U.S. Census Bureau. About 60,000 households are sampled and studied, mainly about income and employment status.

Curvilinear Regression Another term for *polynomial regression. See *spline regression.

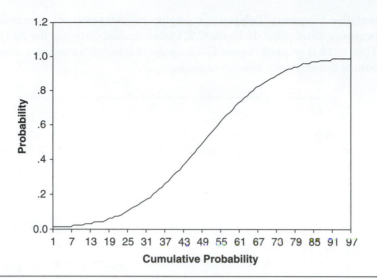

Figure C.6   Cumulative Standard Normal Distribution

Curvilinear Relation (or Correlation)   A relationship between two *variables that when plotted on a graph forms a curve rather than a straight line (a *linear relationship). See *eta, *polynomial regression analysis.

For example, the relation between physical strength and age is curvilinear. As children get older, they tend to get stronger, and this continues into adulthood; but as adults get older, they tend to get physically weaker. Figure C.7 graphs the relation between age and grip strength for a sample of males aged 5 to 70.

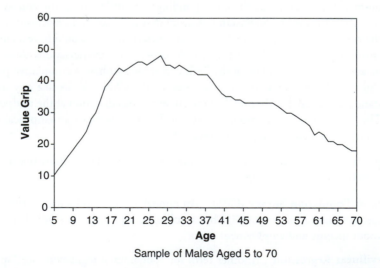

Figure C.7   Curvilinear Relation

Cut Point   A value in a series of values used to divide the series into parts. Cut points are often controversial and believed to be arbitrary. Controversy often surrounds points very near (just above or just below) the cut point. One familiar example is the passing score on an examination.

CV   (a) *Critical value. (b) *Coefficient of Variation.

Cybernetics   A discipline specializing in the study of communications systems, particularly as they relate to control mechanisms, as when computers run robotic assembly lines. Compare *artificial intelligence, *information theory.

Cycle   Any regular variation (down and back up or up and back down) in *time-series data, usually after *seasonal adjustments have been made.

Cyclical Data   *Time-series data arranged on a measurement scale in which the numbers or categories recur, as 12 o'clock is followed by 1 o'clock, December 31 by January 1, and so on. Special statistical techniques are required to describe and analyze most types of cyclic data. Compare *seasonal variation, *secular trend.

D (a) Used to symbolize a wide variety of *difference scores, such as the difference between ranks when computing *Spearman's rho. (b) Abbreviation for *deviance. (c) Short for *Cook's *D*. (d) Abbreviation for a standardized *effect size index, also called *Cohen's *d*. It reports the difference between the *means of two groups in terms of their common *standard deviation. When $d = 1.00$, for example, the mean of one group is one standard deviation above that of the other group. A lowercase *d* is used for the *parametric statistic; an uppercase *D* is used for the *nonparametric statistic. See *Somers' *d*, *Kim's *d*, *D* test.

D^2 Symbol for the *Mahalanobis distance statistic, which is a widely used test for multivariate *outliers.

Dandekar's Correction A method of adjusting the calculation of a *chi-square statistic for a *two-by-two table. Compare *Yates's correction.

Dashboard A summary page on a website displaying data and usually allowing the user to link to (or to "drill down" to) more detailed data; the term comes from the analogy to an instrument panel in an automobile.

Data Information collected by a researcher; any organized information. ("Data" is the plural term; the singular is "datum," but usage varies.) Data are often thought of as statistical or quantitative, but they may take many other forms as well, such as transcripts of interviews or videotapes of social interactions. Nonquantitative data such as transcripts or videotapes are often *coded or translated into numbers to make them easier to analyze. See *primary source, *secondary data. The term "data" is used in many ways. One distinction in U.S. copyright law is that data are facts and thus cannot be copyrighted; however, different compilations or presentations of data may be copyrighted. Whether "pure" data, apart from human manipulation, exist is a matter of some dispute among researchers.

D

Database   (a) A collection of data organized for rapid search and retrieval, usually by a computer; often a consolidation of many records previously stored separately. (b) Sometimes used loosely to mean *sample size.

Data Cleaning   The process of editing a *data set to prepare it for analysis. It involves correcting data (when possible), such as locating data entry mistakes (e.g., a 6 on a 5-point scale) or finding impossible responses (e.g., a male answering a *contingency question about pregnancy), checking questionable *outliers, and possibly using data *imputation for missing data. It sometimes involves deleting data, such as irrelevant variables or data in incomplete *cases or *records. See *raw data.

Data Curve   A line formed by connecting the *data points on a graph. For an example, see *frequency polygon.

Data Dictionary   See *codebook.

Data Dredging or Data Fishing   This occurs when a researcher hunts in a data set for any statistically significant relationship—one that has a sufficiently low *p* value. When the *alpha level is set at .05, five out of 100 tests will be statistically significant (on average) even when the null hypothesis is true. An example of data dredging would be running many statistical tests when one has no theory or hypothesis. Typically only a few of such tests will be statistically "significant." If one reports the "significant" relationships as if they had been hypothesis tests and fails to inform the reader, this is deceptive and unethical, because the processes of this data analysis have been concealed from the reader of the research. See *data mining, *p* hacking.

Data Entry   The process of preparing data for use by a computer or of putting data into a computer, usually by using a keyboard.

Data File   A collection of *data records organized for retrieval and analysis, usually stored in computer program format. For example, SPSS saves data in a .sav file. When opened, a data file often appears as a data matrix.

Data Filter   Criteria used to select data for inclusion in a data file that will be analyzed.
      For example, in a study of average incomes of full-time workers to be drawn from a large database, you might use the status "unemployed" or "age less than 16" as a filter to reduce the size of your data file. Unemployed people, by definition, or people under 16 years of age, by law, cannot be employed full time.

Data Matrix   A grid for storing and subsequently locating data, usually in a computer format.
      For example, suppose you surveyed five people and asked each of them four questions. The results of the survey could be put in the type of data

matrix shown in Table D.1. The rows (or *records) represent the persons interviewed (the *respondents, *cases) and the columns (or *variables) their answers to the questions. In Table D.1, the "a" shows the location (the *cell) where respondent 01's answer to question 1 (Q1) would be entered, "b" shows where respondent 02's answer to Q2 would be placed, and "c" shows where respondent 05's answer to Q4 would be placed.

Table D.1 Data Matrix for Four-Item Hypothetical Survey (Excluding Data Values)

		Question		
Respondent, Case, or Record	Q1	Q2	Q3	Q4
01	a*			
02		b*		
03				
04				
05				c*

*See definition of "Data Matrix" for explanation of these letters.

Data Mining "Digging" around in a large *database to discover relationships among variables or, sometimes, until you find a statistical association that "demonstrates" something you would like to demonstrate. With the increasing availability of huge databases and powerful computer programs, the importance of data mining has grown greatly. See *data dredging. Compare *analytics, *big data, *fishing expedition, p hacking. Contrast *hypothesis testing.

Data Point An individual piece of data, a datum. Often, the point at which two values intersect on a graph, as in the *line graph in Figure D.1 on page 108, where the data point for a person who is 66 inches tall and weighs 150 pounds is circled.

Data Reconstruction In *meta-analysis, any of various methods for using research findings to calculate data not reported. This is done so that the person doing a meta-analysis can compare or combine the results of different studies that do not report their results in the same way.

One common form of data reconstruction occurs when a study reports the total number of subjects and the percentage of them that fall into various categories (e.g., "Of the 1,500 people interviewed, 52% were females, 18.6% of whom had 4 or more years of college education"). A researcher could reconstruct the absolute numbers from these percentages: 780 females were interviewed; 145 of them had 4 or more years of college.

Data Record A grouping of data for one case. In a data file, there is one record for each *subject or *case in a study. A record is part of a *data file. The columns indicate the location of the data about each variable for each case, as in Table D.2,

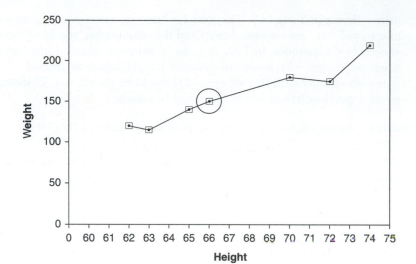

Figure D.1 Data Point

Table D.2 Data Matrix Showing Three Data Records

	Fields (With Numerical Data Included)		
	Variable 1 *(Age)*	*Variable 2* *(Height)*	*Variable 3* *(Weight)*
Case/Respondent/Record 1	27	72	173
Case/Respondent/Record 2	35	70	180
Case/Respondent/Record 3	25	63	125

which gives the age, height, and weight for three subjects. For example, the number 27 is the variable 1 value for case 1; it was written into the field for that variable; 72 and 173 were written into the other two fields for case 1.

Data Reduction Summarizing large amounts of data, usually by *descriptive statistics such as measures of *central tendency, but also by *factor analysis and *principal components analysis, as well as by graphical techniques.

Data Screening See *data cleaning.

Data Set A collection of related *data items, such as the answers given by respondents to all the questions on a survey instrument. Compare *data file, *data matrix, *database.

Datum Singular of *data. The value of a single *variable for a single *case. An individual number, symbol, or other item of information, such as $4.25, 72 inches, or 91%. See *cell, *data point.

D

Debriefing   Explaining the purposes of an experiment to subjects after their participation in it is over. This is required, legally as well as ethically, especially when the experiment has involved deceiving subjects or has in any way put them at risk of some harm. See *dehoaxing, *desensitizing.

Decidable   Said of problems that are solvable, particularly with an *effective procedure or an *algorithm.

Decile   One of the 9 points that divides a *frequency distribution into 10 equal parts. Of the cases, 10% fall below the first decile, 20% below the second, and so on.

For example, if there were 120 million wage earners in the United States, a researcher might divide them into ranked 10ths (or deciles) of 12 million each, the lowest-earning 10th, the second lowest-earning, and so on. This would facilitate comparisons, such as of the average earnings of people in different deciles.

Decile Range   The difference between the 9th and 1st decile; the middle 80% of a distribution. Compare *interquartile range.

Decision Error   A mistake made when deciding whether to reject the *null hypothesis. See *Type I error, *Type II error.

Decision Function   A rule of procedure that specifies whether sufficient data have been collected or whether further observations need to be made. See *decision rule. Compare *sequential sampling.

Decision Problem   (a) A problem requiring a yes or no answer. (b) The problem of figuring out whether a problem is *decidable.

Decision Rule   (a) A statement specifying when a statistic we are about to compute will lead us to reject or not reject the *null hypothesis. (b) Any procedure for making a decision. See *decision function.

An example of (a) would be a rule such as the following: If the *p value for the *test statistic for the observed difference between the diabetes mellitus rates for the samples of ethnic groups A and B is less than .05, we will reject the null hypothesis of "no difference between the two populations" from which the data were randomly selected. Examples of (b) include the criteria used to *operationalize a variable, such as "We will record only rates that increase or decrease, not those that remain stable" or "To be elected, a candidate need only obtain the most votes; a majority is not required."

Decision Table   A table depicting the alternatives to be considered in a given problem, along with the outcomes of each alternative and action(s) to be taken.

For example, suppose you went to a doctor who told you that you had a terrible degenerative disease. The *probability is very great (.90) that it will kill you within in a year. You can reduce your chances of death from the disease (but only somewhat, to .80) by a radical change of diet. There is an operation, but it is risky: 50% of those who have the operation are cured, but 50% die on the operating table. Table D.3 shows your options and the likely outcomes.

Without any other information, it looks as though your "best" choice might be to have the operation, but "best" in this case, as in so many others, must ultimately be based on your subjective values, not arithmetic.

Table D.3   Decision Table

Options	Outcomes, Probabilities of Survival
Do nothing	.10
Change diet	.20
Operation	.50

Decision Theory   An interdisciplinary area of research that focuses on how to select good ways of making decisions based on evidence. The basic method is to compare costs and benefits (often called *utilities) and study these along with the *probability of the various alternatives. Decision theory originated in problems of economic decision making, but it has become increasingly associated with statistics and hypothesis testing. See *game theory, *minimax strategy.

Decision Tree   A graphic representation of the alternatives in a decision-making problem.

For example, suppose you were considering buying some high-risk stock. The cost of the stock is $5,000. If the company in which you are investing is successful, your stock will be worth $40,000. If it fails, you will lose the $5,000. On the basis of past performance of such companies, you estimate that the probability of success for this one is .10, or 10%. The solution to the problem of whether to invest can be summarized in a decision tree like the one in Figure D.2.

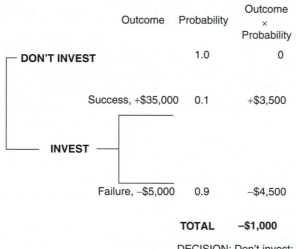

Figure D.2   Decision Tree

D

Decode To translate or determine the meaning of *data that have been *coded.

Decomposition (a) Splitting a *time series into its component parts: *trends, regular *fluctuations, and random fluctuations. (b) A similar division of a *correlation coefficient or a *regression coefficient into direct effects, indirect effects, and dependence on common causes. Compare *partitioning of variance. See *effects analysis.

Deconstructionism An approach ("method" would not be appropriate) to studying texts that rejects the assumption that texts have logical meanings and argues for "demystifying" texts instead of deciphering them. The focus is on breaking down, rather than building up. Meaning is found more in difference rather than in similarity or agreement. One strategy is to show that a particular word has no essential meaning, that it has multiple meanings, and that it fails in the particular context being critiqued. Interpretations of texts are little more than word games according to proponents of deconstructionism, such as Jacques Derrida.

Deduction (a) A conclusion that follows logically from known (or assumed) principles, that is, a conclusion arrived at using *deductive methods. (b) The process of reasoning that moves from general principles to conclusions about particular instances. See *deductive. Compare *induction, *abduction, *dialectic.

Deductive Said of conclusions derived by deductive reasoning rather than by data gathering, or research methods using such reasoning. A *hypothesis is often arrived at by deduction from a *theory or other assumed truth; the hypothesis can then be tested using *inductive (data-gathering) research methods. Here is an example:

1. Prejudice is the product of ignorance.

2. Education reduces ignorance.

3. Therefore, the prejudice level will go down as education level goes up.

The assumptions or theories are (1) and (2); (3) is the deduction. It can be turned into a research question or hypothesis. For instance, one could do survey research to see whether education levels and prejudice levels vary *inversely. Are people with low levels of education more likely to give prejudiced answers to survey questions, and vice versa?

Default (a) In computer jargon, said of a disk or a drive or a value. It is the one the computer *software assumes you mean when you do not tell it otherwise, that is, when you "default" on your obligation to specify what you mean. (b) In statistical packages, the default procedure is used unless the user specifies a different one to be employed. Default procedures are

D

often a reasonable place to start an analysis, but it is unwise to use them without investigating whether the default is most appropriate for your particular analysis problem. (c) The term is sometimes used more broadly, as in "The default *alpha level used in this research is .05." This means "Unless I say otherwise, it is .05."

Definitional Formula   Also called conceptual formula. Statistical formula provided in statistics books to explain a concept such as sum of squares or covariance. Contrasted with a *computational formula that is algebraically equivalent to the definitional formula, and is simpler for purposes of calculation, but is not as useful in defining and understanding the basic concept. See *computational formula.

Degrees of Freedom   Usually abbreviated "*df.*" The number of values "free to vary" when computing an inferential statistic. It's the number of pieces of information that can vary independently of one another or, alternatively stated, the number of unconstrained observations used in calculating an estimate. For example, when using the sample variance to estimate the population variance, you first have to calculate the sample mean, which puts a "constraint" on the data values. Specifically, if you have the value of the sample mean, then using basic algebra, you can determine the value of the last data point from the mean and the other $(n - 1)$ data points. Therefore, there are only $n - 1$ values that are "free to vary" (i.e., $df = n - 1$). In inferential statistics, estimators and test statistics (which follow a known probability distribution such as chi-square, t, or F) all require the use of a df value. In *z tests, degrees of freedom are not used, but you have to know the population variance (which you rarely do) to use this statistic. See *chi-square test, statistic, *F ratio, *t test.

Many people find the concept of df difficult, but the practical application is relatively easy; that is, statistics texts contain clear rules for how to calculate and use the df to interpret a statistic.

The degrees of freedom in a *cross-tabulation provide a clear example. The df are computed by multiplying the number of rows minus 1 times the number of columns minus 1: $df = (R - 1)(C - 1)$. Thus, the more categories the variables are broken into, the higher the degrees of freedom.

For example, suppose a professor with 130 students gave a test and tabulated the scores. Table D.4 on page 113 is a *two-by-two (2×2) table; it has two rows and two columns. Using the formula, $df = (R - 1)(C - 1) = (2 - 1)(2 - 1) = 1 \times 1 = 1$. Table D.4 has 1 df, which means, among other things, that if you know one of the *cell values and the totals (or *marginals), you can figure out the other three. For instance, if 40 men passed, it is easy to figure out how many men failed ($70 - 40 = 30$), how many women passed ($90 - 40 = 50$), and how many women failed ($40 - 30 = 10$).

Table D.4 Degrees of Freedom (2 × 2 Table): Sex by Test Grade

	Pass	Fail	**Total**
Men			70
Women			60
Total	90	40	130

Table D.5 Degrees of Freedom (2 × 5 Table): Sex by Test Grade

	A	B	C	D	F	**Total**
Men						70
Women						60
Total	20	50	20	30	10	130

Table D.5 is a 2 × 5 table. Using the formula $df = (R - 1)(C - 1) = (2 - 1)(5 - 1) = 1 \times 4 = 4$. This means that if you know four of the cell values and the marginals, you can compute the other six—because they are no longer free to vary once four are determined.

Dehoaxing   A form of *debriefing of subjects in an experiment after their participation is concluded. When the experimental design requires deceiving ("hoaxing") subjects about themselves, dehoaxing involves convincing them that they have been deceived. The idea is to eliminate any undesirable effects the deception might have had. Compare *desensitizing. Dehoaxing should also be considered after a *participant observation study in which the investigator has not revealed that she or he was doing research.

For example, if a learning experiment involved studying the effects of believing that one is not good at learning a particular subject, the researchers might give all participants an aptitude test. The *experimental group might be told that they did quite poorly and demonstrated low aptitude, regardless of how they actually performed. The *control group might not be informed one way or another about their scores. Then, both groups could be given the same kind of learning task to see whether the experimental group (those who had been falsely told they had low aptitude) performed any differently than the control group. It is generally considered the researcher's ethical responsibility in such circumstances to dehoax the participants, to convince them that they were deceived and that, in this example, they are not in fact low in aptitude. It may sometimes be difficult to convince participants; the researcher's credibility can be reduced by the fact that he or she has just admitted lying: "I was lying before, but now I'm going to tell you the truth."

Deliberate Sampling   Type of nonprobability sampling. Another term for *quota sampling. See *purposive sampling.

Delimiting Variables   Variables that specify the nature of a population or a sample. For example, a sample of female college students would have three delimitations: female, student, and college.

Delphi Technique   A method of survey research developed by the RAND Corporation requiring repeated surveying of the same respondents on the same issue or problem; after each round of surveying, the answers are shared so that the respondents can work toward an informed consensus. In business, sometimes called "jury of executive opinion."

   For example, managers in a large organization might be sent questionnaires asking them to rank a list of the organization's priorities and to explain their reasoning. Later surveys (usually a minimum of four rounds) provide each respondent with information about how the others have answered questions on the prior surveys.

Delta (Δ, δ)   A Greek letter most often used to symbolize one form or another of difference. Compare *D. For example, delta-L^2 is the difference between two L^2s. Delta-R^2 indicates the change in R^2 attributable to adding an *independent variable to a *regression equation.

Demand Characteristics   Any of the numerous potential cues available to participants in experimental research, regarding the nature and purpose of the study, that might influence the subjects' reaction to the experimental treatment.

   For example, an experimenter might, without realizing it, nod encouragingly when participants act in ways that seem to be supporting the research hypothesis; the experimenter seems to be "demanding" certain behavior from participants. One way to reduce this problem is to use *double-blind procedures.

Demography   The study of *variables characterizing human populations (e.g., births, deaths, health, fertility, migration) and the social and economic variables that cause them to change. Demographic variables are often used by researchers in other disciplines as *background variables.

Dendrogram   A kind of *tree diagram representing shared characteristics of cases; similar cases are categorized onto separate branches. It is used in *cluster analysis.

Denominator   Another term for the *divisor in division; the part of a fraction that is below the line.

Density Curve   A graphic representation of a distribution of scores or values that takes the form of a smooth curve. It indicates the proportion of scores in a distribution as the area under the curve. The total area is 1.0. If, for example, 30% of the scores in a distribution fell between 65 and 85, then those scores would be represented by 30% of the area under the curve. *Normal curves are the best-known examples, and like all density curves, they are idealized or theoretical rather than exact representations of actual distributions.

Density Function   The equation for a theoretical *probability distribution for a continuous *random variable; in statistics, it's a synonym for *probability density function, which, when plotted, forms a *density curve. See *probability distribution. Compare *probability density function, *probability mass function.

Deontology   Ethical theory emphasizing duty or moral obligation based on some universal code, such as the Golden Rule or Immanuel Kant's categorical imperative. Deontological ethics do not allow variation in practice; if killing is wrong, for example, then there are no exceptions (e.g., war, death penalty, late-term abortion). What is ethically wrong does not vary by context or consequences. Compare to *ethical skepticism, *utilitarianism.

Dependent Event   In *probability theory, said when the occurrence of one event changes the probability that a second will take place; the probability of the second event is then "dependent" upon the first. See *conditional probability. Compare *independent event.

Dependent Interviewing   In *panel studies, in which *respondents are reinterviewed, dependent interview questions are those based on answers to questions from an earlier session (*wave). For example, "Last year you said that when you finished college, you were planning to go to graduate school. What are your current plans?"

Dependent Samples   Another term for *correlated samples or groups. Said of research groups that are not drawn independently from a population. Dependent samples occur most commonly in before-and-after studies when two measures are taken on the same subjects. Dependent samples require different *test statistics than independent samples.

Dependent Samples *t* Test   Synonym for *paired samples *t* test.

Dependent Variable   (a) The presumed effect in a study, so called because it "depends" on another variable. (b) The variable whose values are predicted or explained by the *independent variable, whether or not caused by it. Also called *outcome, *criterion, and *response variable.

For example, in a study to see if there were a relationship between students' drinking of alcoholic beverages and their grade point averages, the drinking behavior would probably be the presumed cause (independent variable); the grade point average would be the effect (dependent variable). But it could be the other way around—if, for instance, one wanted to study whether students' grades drive them to drink.

D

Note: Some authors use the term "dependent variable" only for *experimental research; for *nonexperimental research they might use (or argue that others should use) *criterion variable or *outcome variable. Most commonly, however, dependent variable is used in both experimental and nonexperimental research.

Derivation Sample   A sample used to obtain an initial statistical model. Researchers do not want their statistical models to be dependent upon a particular sample because of sample biases and chance factors. Therefore, they sometimes start by using a derivation sample. Then they use the obtained model on a new sample to test the model. As an example, a researcher might conduct an *exploratory factor analysis on a derivation sample and then conduct a *confirmatory factor analysis on a validation sample. Compare *validation sample. See *training data (or sample), *cross-validation.

Derived Statistics   Statistics calculated on the basis of other (simple or primary) statistics. Compare *raw data.

For example, say you had *data describing the total number of murders last year in all U.S. cities and the total populations of those cities. You could use those primary statistics to compute the murder rates—statistics derived by dividing the number of murders in each city by its population. Other examples of derived statistics include *percentile ranks and *standard scores. Compare *data reconstruction.

Descending Order   An order than begins with the highest value and moves to the lowest. The opposite is *ascending order.

Descriptive Causation   See *causal description.

Descriptive Discriminant Analysis   The terms "descriptive discriminant analysis" and "predictive discriminant analysis" (DDA and PDA) distinguish two purposes and uses of *discriminant analysis. DDA is a follow-up procedure to *MANOVA to describe the effect of the grouping variable on the linear composites of the dependent variables identified by the MANOVA. Compare *predictive discriminant analysis.

Descriptive Research   Research that describes, usually in detail, phenomena as they exist. Descriptive research is usually contrasted with *experimental research, in which environments are controlled and *subjects are given different *treatments. It is also contrasted with research that comes to *causal conclusions or inferences. Note that *inferential (not only descriptive) statistics may be used in descriptive research, as may measures of association such as correlation and regression based on sample data.

Descriptive Statistics   Procedures for summarizing, organizing, graphing, and, in general, describing quantitative data. Often contrasted with *inferential statistics, which are used to make inferences about a *population based on the data in a *sample drawn from that population. Descriptive statistics are sometimes contrasted with analyses of causal relations. Compare *exploratory data analysis.

Descriptive Survey Research Sometimes survey research is said to be descriptive. That can be true, as in polls whose goal is to estimate specific population characteristics based on sample data. However, it is important to understand that survey research also can be used in predictive and explanatory research to make predictions and test hypotheses and theoretical models. In short, one can have descriptive, predictive, and explanatory survey research.

Deseasonalizing Statistically removing the seasonal variation component from *time-series data. Often reported as "seasonally adjusted," as in "The seasonally adjusted unemployment rate for July was at a 5-year low."

Desensitizing A form of *debriefing subjects after their participation in an experiment. The purpose of desensitizing is to enable subjects to cope with any negative information they may have acquired about themselves as a result of an experiment. Compare *dehoaxing, *Milgram experiments.

Design Short for *research design, that is, the plan a researcher will follow when conducting a study. Examples include survey, experimental, interview, observational, and archival designs. See *protocol.

Design Effect (or Factor) The influence of a sampling design, such as *cluster sampling or *stratified sampling, on a study's *standard error. Usually reported as a comparison to what the standard error would have been with *simple random sampling.

Determination, Coefficient of See *coefficient of determination.

Determinism The theory that all events and behaviors are determined or caused by prior events, conditions, and the operation of natural laws. Under the assumptions of strict determinism, there are no random events, and people do not have free will. "Soft" versions of determinism exist, which might be thought of as "influence-ism"; these are more common among social and behavioral scientists than the strict variety.

Deterministic Model A *causal model that contains no random or probabilistic elements; one in which all causes and values are known (or assumed) and all the *variance in the *dependent variable(s) can be explained. Quantitative deterministic models contain no *error term. Compare *stochastic model. In research on categorical events, a deterministic model is one employing necessary and/or sufficient causal conditions rather than probabilistic causation.

Detrended Normal Plot A scatter plot used to check visually the assumption that one's sample is drawn from a normally distributed population. If the sample is from a normal population, the points should form no pattern. Also called "detrended probability plot." Compare *normal probability plot, *Shapiro-Wilk test.

Detrending   To adjust or *control for trends in one's data caused by *variables in which one is not interested. Often used with time-series data.

   For example, in a study of the effects of education level on productivity level, you might find that the trend toward increasing education was associated with a trend toward increasing productivity. But productivity can also go up for reasons unrelated to education, such as increased capital investment. By controlling any trends toward increased capital investment, you could then focus better on the relation of education to productivity.

Deviance   A measure of the degree to which a *model explains the *variation in a set of data when using *maximum likelihood estimation. Compare *deviation score. It involves comparing the *saturated and *unsaturated models. Abbreviated *D*.

Deviant Case   In *case study methods, a term used to describe a case that differs dramatically from the set of cases under consideration. Compare *outlier.

Deviate   Another term for *deviation score.

Deviation Score   A statistic indicating how much the *mean score of a group of scores differs (deviates) from an individual score. It is obtained by subtracting the group mean from the individual score. Also known as an *error score. See *covariance for an example.

df   *Degrees of freedom.

DFBETA   Statistic used to detect an outlier or extreme case. It shows how much a regression coefficient (slope) changes when the case is removed. In simple regression, there is a DFBETA for each case; in multiple regression, there will be a DFBETA for each case for each of the coefficients. If the value is positive, then the original coefficient is larger when the case is included (the case "pulls up" the coefficient); if it's negative, then the original coefficient is smaller when you include the case. According to one rule of thumb, if the absolute value of a DFBETA for a case is greater than $2/\sqrt{n}$ (where n is the number of cases), then you might have an outlier. Compare *DFFITS.

DFFITS   Statistic used to detect an outlier or extreme case. It shows how much the case's own *predicted Y value changes when it is excluded. According to one rule of thumb, you have an outlier when the DFFITS value (ignoring the sign) is greater than $\sqrt{2(p \div n)}$ (where n is the number of cases and p is the number of predictor variables plus 1). Compare *DFBETA.

Diachronic   Said of research that studies events as they occur or change over time. Often contrasted with *synchronic. Compare *panel study, *event history analysis.

Diagnostic Test   A procedure in medicine, psychology, or education designed to determine whether a subject has a particular condition or the extent of that condition. Diagnostic *validity refers to the accuracy of the procedure at correctly categorizing and measuring cases. See *sensitivity, *specificity.

Diagnostic Test Study Medical study used to determine if a medical procedure is useful in assessing the probability of a particular patient condition.

Diagraph Short for *directed graph.

Dialectic A method of reasoning that proceeds by developing contradictions to propositions and then discovering ways to resolve those contradictions so as to discover new ideas and advance thought. Although employed by many philosophers since ancient Greece, the dialectic is perhaps best known as it was used by Karl Marx, who held that history progresses dialectically through the conflict of opposing classes.

Diary Method A method of data collection in which participants keep a journal or diary, and in it they record, during each day of the week, what the researchers ask them to record, such as their thoughts, behaviors, events, and so on. Diaries can vary from unstructured to highly structured, depending on the research study. Diaries have traditionally been paper-and-pencil methods, but recordings and Internet links are also increasingly used.

Dichotomized Variable A continuous variable that has been divided into two categories. For example, one might use income data to create two categories, poor and not poor. Compare *dichotomous variable, in which the two categories occur naturally; that is, they are not created by the researcher. The distinction between dichotom*ized* and dichotom*ous* variables is important when selecting appropriate measures of *association.

Dichotomous Variable A *categorical variable that can place subjects or cases into only two groups, such as male/female, alive/dead, or pass/fail. Compare *dichotomized variable.

DIF *Differential item functioning.

Difference-in-Differences Estimation A group of methods used in *natural experiments to assess the likely impact of a program, policy, intervention, or event. Trends in an outcome variable in units (cities, nations, etc.) that have been affected are compared to trends in those that have not been affected. The simplest model is two groups measured at two times (before and after). The difference in the before-after difference is the estimation of the effect. Pioneered in *econometrics, difference-in-differences estimation is widely used in policy research in other disciplines.

Difference of Proportions A method for comparing proportions for *dichotomous variables. One proportion is subtracted from the other. The result ranges from −1.0 to +1.0, with zero indicating that the two variables have identical conditional probabilities on a dependent variable.

For example, a study of a medical treatment that resulted in Cure or No Cure could use difference of proportions to describe results for men and women. If the proportion of women treated who were cured was .60 and the proportion of men was .45, then the difference of proportions would be .15.

Difference Scores Measurements obtained by subtracting pretest (before) from posttest (after) scores. Sometimes called "gain scores," even when the goal is to lower the score, for example, to reduce the time to complete a task or to lose weight. Also called "change scores."

Difference scores are often standardized by transforming pretest and post-test scores into *standard scores before subtracting. The size of the difference is often adjusted by *controlling for *nuisance variables.

Difference Sign Test A test of *time-series data to see if a *linear trend exists. It is calculated by counting the number of times the series increased—for example, the number of times the Dow Jones average went up over the past year. See *sign test.

Differential Carryover Effect A complex type of *carryover effect, such as when a particular treatment affects subjects' performance in a later condition in one way but in another way when the treatment is followed by a different condition. *Counterbalancing does not control for differential carryover effects.

Differential Item Functioning (DIF) In *item response theory (IRT), differential item functioning occurs when test items function differently for different groups with the same total test score, such as ethnic and *SES groups; that is, when different individuals or groups with the same test score or ability have different probabilities of giving correct responses to the different items. IRT can be used to find items for which such differences do not exist, which is a goal of good test construction.

Diffuse Comparisons Techniques used in *meta-analysis to compare the amount of heterogeneity in the analyzed studies' *significance levels and *effect sizes. The more heterogeneity or "diffuseness," the harder it is to integrate the studies. See *focused comparisons. Compare *divergent validity.

Diffusion of Treatments A threat to the *validity of a study occurring when subjects in one condition receive some of the treatment from a different treatment condition or arising from communication among the subjects, such as when the communication results in the experimental *treatment being spread ("diffused") among *control group subjects. Also called "diffusion effect." Contrast with *double-blind procedure.

For example, if a new technique were being tested in a chemistry laboratory to see if it led to quicker and more accurate analyses, it could be tried out by a sample of the lab workers. They would be the *experimental group. The rest of the workers would be the *control group. To measure the effectiveness of the new technique, the productivity and efficiency of the two groups of workers would be compared. But if the experimental group liked the new technique and told their friends in the control group about it, and they also started using it, the validity of any comparison between the two groups would be doubtful at best, because of the diffusion effect.

Digital Data   (a) Information represented by numbers (digits) such as time on a digital watch; often contrasted with *analog data such as time represented by movement of a watch's hands. (b) Loosely used to mean *binary, as in "digital computer," that is, a computer that uses information represented in the form of 1s and 0s. The 1s and 0s represent electronic computer switches that are "on" (1) or "off" (0).

Dimension   (a) A single variable or factor. For example, a unidimensional test measures a single variable or factor, and a *multidimensional test measures two or more variables or factors. (b) Clusters of related *indicators. For example, for the dimension public health, the indicators could be the infant mortality rate, average life expectancy, the rate of access to medical treatment by citizens, and so on.

Dimensionality   The number of aspects or "dimensions" a *construct has. Is "tolerance," for example, one attitude or a cluster of related attitudes? If it is one attitude, it is said to be a unidimensional construct; if more than one, it is a multidimensional construct.

D Index   See *D.

Direct Correlation   Another term for *positive correlation, that is, a correlation in which the values of the variables tend to move in the same direction. Compare *inverse correlation.

Directed Graph   A pictorial representation of a *dominance matrix used in *game theory and similar problems.

   The example in Figure D.3 on page 122 shows who won in a chess tournament among four players. An arrow indicates the winner. Anne, for example, won her match with Carl. See dominance matrix for a table showing the same data.

Direct Effect   The effect of one variable on another, without any intervening or mediating variables in the causal chain. Depicted as "A➔B," where changes in variable A are theorized to cause changes in variable B. Compare *indirect effect. See *path analysis, *structural equation modeling.

Directional Hypothesis (or Test)   An *alternative hypothesis that specifies the direction of difference between means (greater or smaller) or specifies the direction of relationship (positive or negative). Sometimes called a *one-tailed test. Directional tests have slightly greater *statistical power than nondirectional tests, but at the cost of having to ignore a large effect or relationship found in

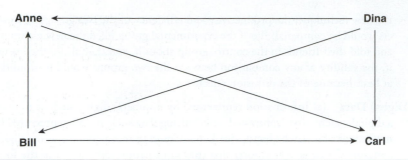

Figure D.3   Directed Graph

the opposite direction from the originally hypothesized direction (which impedes the discovery function of science). When in doubt about which to use, most research methodologists and many statisticians recommend using nondirectional tests (even when you have a directional *research hypothesis).

For example, say the null hypothesis in significance testing were that there is no difference in manual dexterity between Group A and Group B. An example of a directional alternative hypothesis would be that Group A's average dexterity quotient is greater than B's.

Directionality   A feature of research studies distinguishing whether they gather data from the past to draw conclusions now (*retrospective studies) or plan to gather data about events in the future to draw conclusions at a later time (*prospective studies).

Directionality Problem   Uncertainty about the direction of causal relations among variables, especially in *correlational research designs. (The difference between "directionality" and "direction"? Three syllables.)

For example, if aggressive people watch lots of violence on TV, that could be because TV causes them to be aggressive or because aggressive people choose to watch violent programs or both. Or neither, but that is a different issue. See *spurious correlation.

Directional Statistic   A statistic that varies depending on the direction of causation or, in other terms, which variable is independent and which dependent. *Regression is directional; *correlation is not. The regression coefficient for supply and demand differs depending on which is the predictor (independent) variable and which the outcome (dependent) variable. The correlation between supply and demand does not so vary; it is nondirectional.

Directly Proportional   Approximately speaking, two variables are directly proportional when they are *positively related (and inversely proportional when they are negatively related). More precisely, in mathematics, variables X and Y are directly proportional when Y is a constant multiple of X as in Y = CX, where C is the constant. For example, if C = 4 then the following X,Y pairs would result: (1,4) (when X is 1, Y = 4), (2,8) (when X is 2, Y = 8), (3,12), (4,16), and so forth. Note that in the example, the ratio of Y/X (the slope) is always equal to 4. In the example, as values on one variable increase, values on the other variable also increase; the values on the variables move in the same direction. Compare to *inversely proportional. Also compare *positive relation and *negative relation.

Direct Relationship (or Correlation)   A relation between two *variables such that when the value of one goes up or down, so does the other. Also called *positive relationship. Compare *inverse relationship.

For example, hours spent studying and grade on an examination might be directly related; that is, the more hours students study, the better they do, and the fewer, the worse.

Disaggregate   To separate, for purposes of analysis, the parts of an *aggregate statistic. Compare *decomposition.

For example, if we were interested in trends in average SAT scores over the past 20 years, we might want to disaggregate the data so that we could look at separate trends for males, females, blacks, whites, students in and not in college preparatory programs, and so on. Or we could disaggregate by studying different dimensions of the test.

Disattenuated Correlation and Regression Coefficients   According to classical measurement theory, obtained correlation and regression coefficients are viewed as being somewhat smaller than they should be because the calculated values are weakened by measurement unreliability. Disattentuated statistics correct for this unreliability. Simple formulas are used to adjust the coefficients slightly upward, making them larger. The adjusted coefficients indicate what the relationship would have been if perfect reliability were present in measuring variable X and variable Y. See *attenuation.

Discourse Analysis   Any of several methods for studying talk, conversation, and, more broadly, verbal communication. The general approach is to treat utterances not so much as stores of meaning to be deciphered but more as acts or performances to be interpreted.

Discrete Time Event History Analysis   A method for estimating the impact of time-varying covariates (independent variables that change over time such as "Are you employed?" or "Are you married?") on the hazard of an event using discrete measures of time (monthly, daily, yearly data). Contrasted with other survival methods that use continuous time measures such as *Cox regression. Note, non-time-varying independent variables would be variables like sex, race, and country of origin.

Discrete Variable   Also called "discrete random variable." Commonly, another term for *categorical (or *nominal) variable. Compare *continuous variable.

D

More formally, a discrete variable is one made up of distinct and separate units or categories. When a variable is discrete, only a finite number of values separate any two points. While all categorical variables are discrete, in some usages there might be dispute about whether to label particular variables discrete or continuous. This matters because it determines appropriate statistical techniques.

For example, the number of people in a family is clearly a discrete variable. So is the outcome of flips of a coin; if you flip a coin 10 times, you can't get 3.27 tails. But the distinction is not always so clear. Take personal income. It looks like a continuous variable, and it is usually treated as one in research. Millions of possible values stretch from zero to Bill Gates's income. More strictly, however, income is discrete. Income does not come in units smaller than one cent; there is only one value between $411.01 and $411.03 ($411.02). Thus, while income is measured on a *ratio scale, it is a discrete variable. By contrast, weight is a truly or a strictly continuous variable. No matter how close two individuals' weight, there is always an intermediate value, although an ordinary scale might not capture it. Because of limits in how accurately we can measure, all measurements are discrete in practice.

Discriminant Analysis (DA)   A form of *regression analysis designed for classification into predefined groups. It allows two or more *continuous *independent variables (or *predictor variables) to be used to place individuals or cases into the categories of a *categorical *dependent variable. DA also provides a means of calculating a weighted combination of all independent variables so as to be able to cut the dependent variable into discrete categories. Also called discriminant "function" analysis. Called "multiple" discriminant analysis when subjects are to be placed in more than two categories. Compare *logistic regression.

DA was originally used for classification work such as deciding whether a collection of thigh bones dug up by paleontologists belonged to early hominoids, chimps, or baboons. Continuous variables, such as the bones' length, weight, and circumference, were used to "discriminate" among them and place them in the right categories.

As a second example, illustrating another use of DA, suppose a researcher wanted to use data about previous secondary school students to figure out which current students were and were not likely to graduate. The categorical dependent variable would be graduation yes/no. The continuous predictor variables might be number of days absent, grade point average, score on a verbal ability test, and so on. A successful discriminant analysis would enable the researcher to predict, with some accuracy, who would be likely to graduate and who would not, as well as to compare the relative importance of each of the predictor variables.

Discriminant Function   A combination of the observed *independent variables in a *discriminant analysis that aids in distinguishing (discriminating among) categories of the *dependent variable. Like *factors in a factor analysis and *canonical variates, discriminant functions are ways of dealing with groups of related variables and relating them to other variables. See *structural equation modeling.

Discriminant Validity   A measure of the *validity of a *construct. It is high when the construct does not *correlate with other, theoretically distinct constructs. Discriminant validity is sometimes called "divergent validity" and is the mirror image of *convergent validity.

For example, suppose researchers are writing a questionnaire containing several questions designed to measure the construct "patriotism." They worry that respondents may just be giving the answers they think are "proper" or that they think the researchers want to hear (*social desirability bias). So the researchers include questions that measure the construct "socially desirable responding." If the two measures were not correlated, the measure of patriotism would have more discriminant validity; that is, it would be unrelated to a measure of something to which it should not be related if it were valid.

Disjoint Sets   In *set theory, sets with no common elements (i.e., sets that are "joined by" no common elements), such as the set of all males and the set of all females.

Disordinal Interaction   Said of an *interaction effect when the lines on a graph plotting the effect cross. When the lines do not cross, the interaction is called *ordinal. The graphs in Figures D.4 and D.5 on page 126 show a disordinal and an ordinal interaction, respectively. In neither case are the lines parallel. If they were parallel, there would be no interaction. In the ordinal interaction, the lines *would* cross if extended further. The fact that they are not extended to that point could mean that the researcher was not interested in those levels of the variables—in the example, no more than 10 treatments of fertilizer and, of course, by logical necessity, no fewer than 0 treatments.

Say a gardener had 9 rows of tomatoes with 9 plants in each row. She planted 3 different brands of tomato plant, A, B, and C, in 3 rows each. She gave each of the 9 "columns" of tomatoes a different number of doses of fertilizer and kept a record of the total weight of tomatoes produced by each brand of plant at each dose level, as shown in Table D.6 on page 126. Up to a certain point, fertilizer increases the tomato crop, but for different brands it does so at different rates, which means there is an interaction effect. The graph in Figure D.4 shows a disordinal interaction; the graph in Figure D.5 shows an ordinal interaction.

Dispersion, Measure of   A statistic showing the amount of *variation or spread in the scores for, or values of, a *variable. When the dispersion is large, the scores or values are widely scattered; when it is small, they are tightly clustered. Two commonly used measures of dispersion are the *variance and the *standard deviation. A measure of dispersion always implies the presence of a measure of *central tendency, such as a *mean. For example, the standard deviation measures deviation *from the mean.*

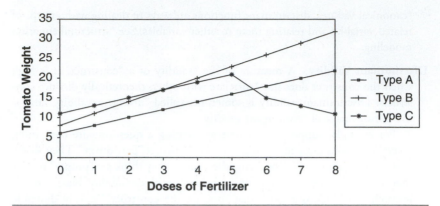

Figure D.4   Disordinal Interaction of Plant Type and Fertilizer Dose

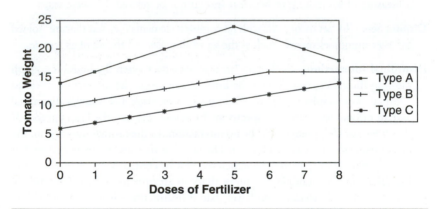

Figure D.5   Ordinal Interaction of Plant Type and Fertilizer Dose

Table D.6   Design Layout of Plant Type and Fertilizer Dose

Type	Rows ↓	Columns →	0	1	2	3	4	5	6	7	8
						Doses					
	1		A	A	A	A	A	A	A	A	A
A	2		A	A	A	A	A	A	A	A	A
	3		A	A	A	A	A	A	A	A	A
	4		B	B	B	B	B	B	B	B	B
B	5		B	B	B	B	B	B	B	B	B
	6		B	B	B	B	B	B	B	B	B
	7		C	C	C	C	C	C	C	C	C
C	8		C	C	C	C	C	C	C	C	C
	9		C	C	C	C	C	C	C	C	C

Dissimilarity Index   An alternative to the *Gini index often used as a measure of neighborhood segregation. The index indicates the percentage of a group that would have to move to achieve a proportional residential pattern in a geographic region.

Distance   Sometimes used in statistics to mean difference, as when the distance between two populations is the difference between their means. See *Mahalanobis distance.

Distractor   A multiple-choice question typically has four answers to choose from. One answer is the correct answer, and the others are said to be distractors. The goal of a distractor is to distract the uninformed test taker (who has not achieved the learning outcome) away from the correct answer. The distractor must be false in a good and fair multiple-choice question. Distractors also are used in research sometimes to keep participants from engaging in certain tasks (e.g., to prevent cognitive rehearsal).

Distribution   A ranking, from lowest to highest, of the values of a *variable and the resulting pattern of measures or scores, often as these are plotted on a graph. Usually either a *probability distribution or a *frequency distribution. See *array, *kurtosis, *normal curve, *sampling distribution, *skewed distribution.

For example, if researchers recorded the closing sale price of all stocks traded on the New York Stock Exchange on a given day and arranged the prices in *ascending order so that they could study patterns in the prices, they would have constructed a distribution.

Distribution-Free Statistics (or Tests)   Another term for *nonparametric statistical tests; so called because they do not require assumptions about the form of the distributions of the *populations from which *samples are drawn. Examples include the *chi-square and *Wilcoxon tests. See *bootstrap methods.

Disturbance   Another term for *noise in *information theory; broadly used to mean *random error.

Disturbance Term   See *error term.

Divergent Validity   Another term for *discriminant validity.

Diversity Index   A measure of the degree to which different categories in a *population occur with unequal frequencies. If there is only one category in the population, the value of the index is zero. Compare *Gini index.

Dividend   In division problems, the number that is divided by the *divisor or *denominator. The part of a fraction that is above the line. Also called the *numerator.

Divisive Clustering A type of *hierarchical clustering. In this type, all cases together begin as a single cluster; then, splits are made, recursively, until an optimal number of clusters is obtained. See *cluster analysis. Compare *agglomerative clustering.

Divisor A quantity used to divide another quantity (the *dividend). The part of a fraction that is below the line. Also called the *denominator.

DK Common abbreviation for "Don't Know" in survey research.

Domain (a) A subgroup of a *population that is of special interest to the researcher *sampling it. (b) The content area studied in a *domain-referenced test. (c) In set theory, a set of numbers that can serve as a replacement for a variable; also called "replacement set." See *function.

Domain-Referenced Test A type of achievement test that measures a person's absolute level of performance in a specific area or "domain," such as long division or 20th-century economic history. Domain-referenced tests usually measure content areas more specifically defined than other achievement tests. Compare *criterion-referenced test, *norm-referenced test.

Domain Sampling Sampling of items, such as questions for a questionnaire, in a particular subject area or *domain.

For example, a researcher might be interested in the domain of respondents' attitudes toward affirmative action. Rather than studying all possible questions that are pertinent, the researcher would take a representative sample of the questions in the domain (which, in this usage, is a *population of items).

Dominance Analysis A method of *variable ordering, that is, determining the relative importance of the independent variables in a set of independent variables. The technique specifically examines the change in R^2 as a result of adding an independent/predictor variable to all possible subset regression models and produces a general dominance weight to be compared with that produced for the other independent variables.

Dominance Matrix A table showing winners and losers (or analogous relations) in a *game theory or similar problem.

For example, Table D.7 on page 129 shows the winners and losers in a chess tournament (1 = yes/win, 0 = no/lose). Reading across the rows we can see, for instance, that Ann beat Carl, but lost to Bob and Dot. Or reading down a column, we can see that Dot lost none of her matches, while Carl lost all of his. See *directed graph for another way to show the same data.

D-Optimal/D-Efficient Design D-optimal approaches are probably the most commonly used *optimal design approaches, which aim to make research designs, especially experimental designs, most effective. The goal of a D-optimal research design is to retain a balance of the levels of the independent

Table D.7   Dominance Matrix of Chess Tournament Results

		Loser			
		Ann	Bob	Carl	Dot
Winner	Ann	-	0	1	0
	Bob	1	-	1	0
	Carl	0	0	-	0
	Dot	1	1	1	-

variables, that is, the regular appearance of all levels of each independent variable, and, simultaneously, to minimize the amount of correlation between the variables.

DOS   Disk Operating System. One of the earliest of the personal computer operating systems; computer software that coordinates *software's demands on *hardware. Like other operating systems, DOS makes a kind of "map" of the disks so as to manage, store, and keep track of files. Other operating systems include UNIX, OS, and Windows.

Dose-Escalation Study   See *dose-ranging trial.

Dose-Ranging Trial   (also called **Dose-Escalation Study**) Typically a *phase 1 randomized clinical trial used to compare the relative effectiveness and tolerance (without toxicity) of different doses of a drug or other experimental ingredient expected to produce changes in the dependent variable (e.g., effect of low dose, medium dose, and high dose on clinical depression or ADHD symptoms).

Dose-Response Relationship   The correlation between the amount, frequency, or duration of a treatment and the amount of observed outcome. Usually expected to be a *positive correlation (i.e., as dose increases, so does response). For example, the more sessions of a remedial reading program attended, the more improvement in reading one would expect to see. Often used in program evaluation and epidemiology.

Dot Plot   A graphic representation of the distribution of one variable only; this is distinct from the typical scatter plot, which shows the relation of two variables. Each value is represented by one dot, as shown in Figure D.6 on page 130. Compare *stem-and-leaf display, *bar graph.

Double-Barreled Question   A single question that asks about two or more objects. Here is an example that asks about two objects: "Are teachers' and politicians' salaries too low?"

Double-Blind Crossover Trial   A type of *repeated-measures design that also uses a double-blind procedure. All participants receive the active treatment

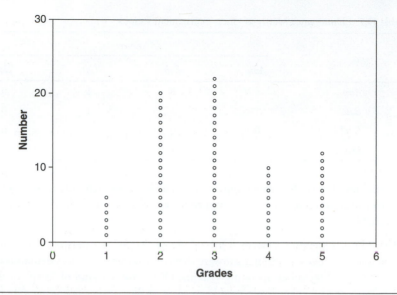

Figure D.6 Dot Plot

and control conditions at different times, in different orders, and neither the participant nor researcher can identify the condition in which a participant resides. See *crossover design, *double-blind procedure.

Double-Blind Procedure   A means of reducing *bias in an *experiment by ensuring that both those who administer a *treatment and those who receive it do not know (are "blind" to) which subjects are in the *experimental and *control groups, that is, who is and is not receiving the treatment.

For example, in a study of the effectiveness of various headache remedies, 80 headache sufferers could be *randomly assigned to four groups. Group A would receive aspirin, Group B ibuprofen, Group C acetaminophen, and Group D a *placebo. The pills might be color-coded, but otherwise look the same so that the experimenter handing them out would not know which subjects were getting which, and, of course, the subjects would not know. When subjects experienced pain, they would be given pills depending on their group and then asked about the relief they got from their pills. Their responses would be data used to evaluate the effectiveness of the various remedies. If the experiment used true double-blind procedures, the researchers analyzing the data would not know, until after they had reached their conclusions, which group received which remedy; they would only know, say, that on average the blue pills worked better than the red ones. See *triple-blind procedure.

Double Sampling   A procedure in which two samples are taken, the first to learn information to design the second. For example, in *stratified sampling, the first sample could be used to estimate the sizes of the strata to be used in the second sample.

Double-Tailed Test Another name for a *two-tailed test, that is, one for which the *region of rejection of the null hypothesis is made up of (usually equal) areas at both ends of the *sampling distribution. See illustration under *region of rejection. Compare *one-tailed test of significance.

Download To transfer data from a data storage device or computer to another computer.

Drill Down To move to increasingly specific submenus in a program (e.g., from Analysis to Compare Means to ANOVA to Repeated-Measures ANOVA). More generally, to concentrate on more specific categories or methods of analysis.

D Test Also called the "Kolmogorov-Smirnov D test." A test of the *statistical significance of the difference between two *frequency distributions. It is a *nonparametric statistical test.

Duhem-Quine Thesis (or Quine-Duhem Thesis) In philosophy of science, the idea that a single hypothesis can never be fully tested in isolation because many *auxiliary assumptions must be made and because any hypothesis is embedded in a holistic network or web of beliefs. This is one reason that alternative explanations will probably always exist and experts will keep arguing. The problem applies to both the *falsification and the verification or confirmation of hypotheses.

Dummy Coding A way of *coding *categorical variables such that membership in a category is indicated by a 1 and nonmembership by a 0. So called because the zero is silent ("dumb") about nonmembership. One advantage of dummy coding is that it allows researchers to use statistical techniques that assume *interval-level data on variables measured only at the *nominal or *ordinal levels. See *dummy variable. Compare *effects coding, *orthogonal coding, *contrast coding (and see that entry for a table on when to use different coding methods).

Dummy Table An empty or blank table (one that "says" nothing) constructed before data are collected and into which the data will be put once they are collected.

Dummy Variable A *dichotomous variable *dummy coded 1 to indicate the presence of an attribute and 0 to indicate its absence. Example: 1 = female; 0 = not female. This coding facilitates the use of *interval-level statistical techniques, which could be harder to interpret if the variable were coded otherwise, such as female = 2, male = 1. Also called "indicator variable." See *dummy coding, *multiple classification analysis.

When a variable has more than two categories, a series of dummy variables are used. For example, say we wanted to use *regression analysis to study the effects of three kinds of growing conditions (A, B, C) on weight (Y) of pump-kins. The coding would be condition A: 1 = yes; 0 = other than A; and B: 1 = yes; 0 = other than B. The results of weight (Y) by condition for 15 cases put in dummy variable form are shown in Table D.8. Upon examining the table, you might well ask: Whatever happened to C? C is not included because it is deduced from the coding of A and B. Indeed, it *must* not be included since the number of dummy variables must be 1 less than the number of categories in order to avoid perfect *multicollinearity. No need to worry, however, because the third category (C) appears in the y-intercept, and the regression equation produces the correct predicted values for A, B, and C.

Table D.8   Dummy Variable Coding

Case	A	B	Y
01	1	0	20
02	1	0	21
03	1	0	23
04	1	0	22
05	1	0	18
06	0	1	15
07	0	1	12
08	0	1	11
09	0	1	19
10	0	1	17
11	0	0	24
12	0	0	26
13	0	0	29
14	0	0	28
15	0	0	29

Duncan's Multiple-Range Test   A test used after conducting an *analysis of variance (ANOVA) to determine which sample means differ significantly from one another. See *multiple comparisons.

Dunnett's C and T3 Post Hoc Tests   Post hoc adjustments for comparison of pairs of means that do not assume *homogeneity of variances. There is not much difference between these two procedures. In the case of unequal vari-ances, these tests tend to be more liberal (i.e., more statistically powerful) than Tamhane's T2 but less statistically powerful than Games-Howell. Some claim

Games-Howell is too liberal. Compare to *Tamhane's T2 and *Games-Howell post hoc tests.

Dunnett's Test A method of controlling for *Type I errors when *multiple comparisons are made. It compares each of a number of *treatments with a *control. Like other such *post hoc methods (e.g., *Tukey's, *Duncan's, *Scheffé's), Dunnett's test adjusts the size of the *critical value used to determine whether an observed difference between two means is statistically significant. Compare *Bonferroni technique.

Dunn-Sidak Modification A revision of the *Bonferroni technique for multiple tests of significance.

Dunn's Multiple-Comparison Test Another term for the *Bonferroni test statistic; a method for multiple comparisons of *treatment effects in *regression analyses and *ANOVA designs. It adjusts (downward) the *alpha level depending on the number of comparisons. See *Bonferroni for an example.

Duration Analysis Another term for *survival analysis. See also *event history analysis.

Duration Recording Measuring the amount of time a particular behavior lasts, such as using a stopwatch to record how long research subjects spend talking to one another.

Durbin *h* Statistic A variation on the *Durbin-Watson statistic used to detect *autocorrelation in a *regression. Unlike the Durbin-Watson statistic, however, the Durbin *h* statistic is appropriate when one has a *lagged dependent variable.

Durbin-Watson Statistic A diagnostic test for *autocorrelation, or serial correlation, in a *time-series, *OLS *regression analysis. The larger the autocorrelation, the less reliable the results of the regression analysis. The range of the Durbin-Watson statistic is 0 to 4, and a value of 2 is expected when there is no (first-order) autocorrelation. According to one rule of thumb, values between 1.5 and 2.5 are usually acceptable.

DV Abbreviation for *dependent variable.

Dyad Two persons interacting; often thought of as the most elementary sociological unit.

Dynamicism A relatively new and popular approach to artificial intelligence and machine learning on which the system continually learns through its interaction with the environment. It is based on a "connectionist" model of information processing whereby ideas and memories are distributed throughout the brain or operating system, as opposed to being located in specific places (the modular approach).

D

Dynamic Model   In economics and related disciplines, a model in which at least one variable is measured over time; contrasted with "static model," which does not incorporate a time element.

Dysfunction   Any element of a system that hinders the overall operation of the system, as hostility between groups in a society might impede the functioning of the society. See *functionalism.

E (a) Usually lowercase *e*, the symbol for *error, or *error score (lowercase epsilon, ε, also is commonly used to signify error). See *residual. (b) Uppercase *E*, *expected value, as in $E(x) = .33$, which means the expected value (i.e., long-run average) of *x* is .33. (c) Lowercase *e*, the symbol for the "universal constant," or "Euler number" (2.7182818 . . .), which is an *irrational number that is the base of natural *logarithms that is used in many calculations, such as figuring compound interest. The formula for this *e* is $1 + 1/1! + 1/2! + 1/3! + 1/4! . . . .$ See *factorial; compare *pi. (Note that there is also a Euler constant, gamma.)

Ecological Correlation   A correlation between two variables based on grouped data such as averages for a geographical area or for social groups. One can commit an *ecological fallacy by using such correlations to draw conclusions about individuals.

For example, the correlation between the gross national income for various nations and average education level for those nations would be an ecological correlation. Such a correlation would not, however, be valid evidence for an individual to use in deciding whether she should continue an education in hopes of earning a higher income.

Ecological Fallacy   An error of reasoning committed by coming to erroneous conclusions about individuals based only on data about groups, especially groups based on geographical areas, such as residents of cities. Compare *Simpson's paradox, in which individual-level associations are changed by aggregation.

For example, if crime rates were higher in areas with a high concentration of elderly people, you would be committing an ecological fallacy if you concluded that elderly individuals are more likely to commit crimes.

Reasoning in the opposite direction, from data about a few individuals to generalizations about groups, is also a widespread form of fallacious thinking, sometimes called *fallacy of composition or the *atomistic fallacy.

Ecological Inference Problem   The difficulties in avoiding *ecological fallacies are sometimes referred to in this way, usually by those who do not think that reasoning from data about groups to conclusions about individuals is necessarily fallacious in all cases.

Ecological Validity   (a) A kind of *external validity referring to the generalizability of findings from one group or context or setting to another. Usually used when a study does not meet the criterion. Compare *population validity. (b) The extent to which a measurement taken in an experiment or on a survey reflects what subjects do in real life.

For an example of (a), studies of 19-year-old college students might not be generalizable to 19-year-olds who are not attending college. If a study made such generalizations from one group or context to the other, it could be lacking in ecological validity. An example of (b) would be having subjects rate each of the four candidates in the upcoming primary election on a scale of 0 to 10. Having them pick one candidate would be more ecologically valid for generalizing about the likely results of the election, because picking one candidate is what voters would have to do on Election Day.

Econometrics   (a) The application of statistical methods to economic data, usually to forecast economic trends and decide among policies. (b) The branch of economics applying statistical *models, often models based on multiple *regression, to economic problems.

EDA   *Exploratory data analysis.

Edge   In causal graphs, an arrow connecting two variables or events. A single-headed arrow is called a "directed edge."

EFA   *Exploratory factor analysis.

Effect   (a) Broadly, a phenomenon believed to have been caused, influenced, or determined by another phenomenon, as when inflation is held to be the effect of declining productivity. (b) In *analysis of variance (ANOVA), effect refers to differences among group *means, differences presumably caused by treatments received by the groups. *Main effects are differences among group means for levels of a *variable (*factor) apart from the effects of other variables. *Interaction effects occur when the effect for one factor (variable) differs depending on the levels of another factor. See the example at *disordinal interaction.

Effects are often discussed as *total* effects, often measured by *zero-order correlation. Total effects are composed of *direct* effects (i.e., those that are not mediated or that remain after the effects of *mediating variables have been removed) and *indirect* effects (i.e., effects mediated or transmitted by *intervening variables). Direct effects plus indirect effects add up to total effects.

E

Effect-Cause   The situation in which what is thought to be the *dependent variable causes changes in the *independent or predictor variable. This can be a serious problem in correlational research. See *ambiguous temporal precedence.

Effect Coding   See *effects coding.

Effect Coefficient   In *path analysis, the total effect (that is, direct plus indirect effects) of an *independent variable on the *dependent variable. Compare to *path coefficient.

Effectiveness   Ability to achieve goals well, or the degree to which intentions are achieved. For example, in biomedical research, effectiveness answers the question of whether a procedure, service, or intervention works when it is used broadly under "normal" field conditions (i.e., "Does the locally demonstrated causal effect generalize broadly?"). In *evaluation research, it refers to the causal impact of a particular program. See *impact assessment. Effectiveness is contrasted with *efficiency, which addresses the issue of amount of output relative to input. For example, efficiency is present when relatively small amounts of resources (money, time, effort) are required to produce a sizable outcome.

Effectiveness Research   (also called **Effectiveness Studies**) Effectiveness research is conducted to determine how well an intervention works in actual practice, in real-world conditions, where many variables are not held constant, where adherence to protocol is somewhat incomplete. It sometimes uses weaker designs than *RCTs. It is contrasted with *efficacy research. See *pragmatic trial research.

Effective Procedure   A series of steps that work in solving problems, an *algorithm.

Effect Modifier   A characteristic of research subjects that interacts with a *treatment; thus another term, and a clearer one, for *moderating variable. For example, if a treatment had stronger (or weaker) effects for younger than for older people, age would be an effect modifier. Note that a *confounding or *third variable also can be an effect modifier. The term is more often used in epidemiology than in the social sciences.

Effects Analysis   The effect of an independent variable on a dependent variable, controlling for other independent variables. Trying to determine what the relation between two variables would be with prior or *exogenous variables controlled. See *partial regression coefficient, *elaboration, and the final paragraph of *effect.

Effects Coding   (also called **Effect Coding**) A way of coding *categorical variables in a *regression analysis. It uses 1, 0, and −1, unlike *dummy coding, which uses only 1 and 0. Effects coding gets its name from the fact that when it is used with experimental research data, the *regression coefficients show the effects of the treatments. Compare *contrast coding, *orthogonal coding.

Effect Size (ES)   (a) Broadly, any of several measures of association or of the magnitude or strength of a relation, such as *Pearson's correlation coefficient squared (i.e., r^2) or *eta squared or *semipartial correlation squared. ES is often thought of as a measure of *practical significance, but it is better thought of as one important piece of information to use when making a judgment of practical significance. (b) A statistic, often abbreviated *d* or Cohen's *d*, indicating the standardized difference in outcome for the average subject who received a *treatment as compared to the average subject who did not (or who received a different level of the treatment). This statistic is often used in *meta-analysis. In psychological research, Cohen's *d* is sometimes referred to as *the* effect size statistic, but it is in reality one of many. *Glass's delta and *Hedges's *g* are alternatives. (c) In *statistical power analysis, ES is the degree to which the *null hypothesis is false (i.e., it refers to the status of the *populations* that you are studying). See *power of a test.

Efficacy Research   (also called **Efficacy Studies** or **Efficacy or Explanatory Trial**) It is contrasted with effectiveness research. Efficacy research uses *RCTs to determine how well a treatment intervention works under ideal conditions. It answers the question "Does the intervention work in an ideal setting, when fully and accurately implemented according to the intervention manual?" Compare *effectiveness research, *pragmatic trial research.

Efficiency   (a) In *research design, said of a procedure that uses fewer resources for the same results or that gets more results using the same resources. (b) In statistics, efficiency is a highly desirable property of an *estimator of a *population *parameter (e.g., the sample mean and the mode are competing estimators of the population mean). Efficiency is a property of the *variance of an estimator's *sampling distribution relative to that for a competing estimator (e.g., mean vs. mode). A particular estimator is an efficient, unbiased estimator if for any specific sample size the variance of the estimator is smaller than the variance for any other estimator—the sample mean meets this criterion; the mode does not. The smaller the variance, the better the estimator because it gives you more precise estimates. (You can reduce the variance of any estimator by simply increasing the sample size.) Compare *consistent estimator, *effectiveness. (c) In economics, a measure of cost per unit of output; the lower the cost per unit, the higher the efficiency. See *cost-benefit analysis. Compare *effectiveness.

Efficient Design   See *optimal design.

Efficient Estimator   See *efficiency (b), *estimator. Among *unbiased estimators, the one with the smallest *variance is called the "best" or "most efficient" estimator. See *BLUE.

Eigenvalue   A statistic used in *factor analysis to indicate how much of the variation in the original group of variables is accounted for by a particular factor.

E

It is the *variance of a matrix and the sum of the squared *factor loadings of a factor. Eigenvalues of less than 1.0 are usually not considered significant. Usually symbolized lambda (Λ). Also called "characteristic root" and "latent root."

Eigenvalues have similar uses in *canonical correlation analysis and *principal components analysis.

Elaboration   A process of studying *correlations or relationships between *variables by observing how they are affected when *controlling for the effects of other, *intervening variables. Elaboration is used to uncover *spurious correlations and identify intervening variables, moderating variables, and suppressor variables. Compare *effects analysis.

Elasticity   Percentage change in one *variable divided by percentage change in another variable. If you take the natural log of the *DV and *IVs in a regression, the regression coefficients are in elasticity units, showing the percentage change in the *dependent variable given a one percentage unit change in the *independent variable. Used most often in economics.

Element   (a) In *set theory, any one of a set's members. (b) In *matrix algebra, an individual value. See *vector.

Elementary Event   See *event, elementary.

Elementary Unit   Another term for *unit of analysis, the point at which one analyzes (breaks down) the subject matter no further. For example, in a study of cities or of families and their characteristics, cities and families would be the elementary units, not the individuals living in them.

Emic   *Culturally relative approaches to the study of anthropology that stress participants' understanding of their own culture. It's the "insider's viewpoint." Derived, by an indirect route, from the linguistics term phon*emic*. Usually contrasted with *etic, which refers to the "objective outsider's viewpoint." The emic-etic distinction was made by Kenneth Pike in the 1950s when he drew an analogy to the linguistics concepts of phon*emics* (study of meanings) and phon*etics* (study of sounds).

Empirical   Said of *data based on observation or experience and of findings that can be verified by observation or experience. Often contrasted with "theoretical." Compare *deductive, *objective.

Empirical Bayes Procedure   Estimation or prediction based on *Bayesian inference when the *prior probability is based on data rather than entirely on subjective judgment.

Empirical Generalization   A statement about observable regularities made without an attempt at explanation. Such factual statements can sometimes be useful, but without being explained by a *theory, they may add little to science. Compare *middle-range theory.

An example of an empirical generalization is "Men in their 20s have a high rate of killing themselves and others in automobile accidents." There are many possible explanations for this empirical generalization. Say we theorized that young men are socialized to a subculture that defines traditional manhood as reckless disregard for personal safety. If this theory is true, it could be used to explain other aspects of young men's behavior (such as smoking, drinking, participating in violent sports). Furthermore, with our theory about traditional male culture, we could make predictions about other groups. For example, as women become more integrated into male-dominated society, their auto death rate should go up (along with their drinking and smoking rates). Or we might predict that the auto death rate for men somewhat outside traditional male culture (such as homosexual men) would be lower.

Empirical Probability Probability values based on an empirical process or experiment. For example, if you tossed a fair coin 10 times, you would theoretically/mathematically expect that 5 of the tosses would be heads and 5 would be tails. However, it is an "empirical question" as to how many heads (and tails) will occur in any given set of 10 tosses. Empirical probability is based on what you observe; theoretical probability is based on what you would expect mathematically. Empirical probabilities often converge with *theoretical probabilities in the long run. Empirical probabilities (based on experiments and experiences), once determined, are often used in making judgments about the probability/likelihood of future events. Compare *theoretical probability.

Empirical Probability Distribution A distribution based on data you collect or based on a simulated data collection process that you carry out.

For example, when producing *frequency distributions, most statistical packages provide a column showing the percentages for the numbers (in addition to the frequencies). That column shows the "percentage distribution," which you can transform into an empirical "probability" distribution by dividing by 100 (remember, percentages vary from 0 to 100, but probabilities are proportions, that is, numbers that vary between 0 and 1).

Empirical Question A question, such as a typical research question, that requires data to be collected to determine the answer to the question. Researchers "let the data speak" to answer their questions, rather than confidently claiming we have the answer. The answers to most questions require empirical evidence. That's why in social science we often say that we "love our data" or we "let the data speak."

Empirical Test Collecting and analyzing data and examining the results to determine the answer to a question. This is what is done in *hypothesis testing (we state the hypothesis and then conduct an empirical test of the question).

Empiricism   (a) The prominent epistemology stating that all knowledge comes from experience. (b) Any approach to research relying heavily on observation, experience, and experiment. Historically, empiricism has been the primary epistemology of the social and behavioral sciences. In its strong form, empiricism includes the belief that empirical research is the only approach that yields true knowledge. Compare *rationalism, *positivism.

Empty Cells   A problem in research using *cross-tabulations that arises from having too many categories or too few subjects. Whenever a category has no subjects that fit into it, you have an empty cell. See *cell.

For example, suppose you survey a *sample of 100 people on their attitudes. You are interested not only in overall response of the sample but also in the attitudes of different groups of people. Among the groups you think are important are gender, age, race, education, and occupation. It is clear that with only 100 people answering your survey, you would not have many people in each category. Some will almost surely be empty (e.g., white, female, blue-collar workers over 60 with more than 12 years of education). Of course, you might have several people in that category, but if you do, you will be short of people in other categories.

Empty Set   A *set that contains no *elements. Also called "null set."

Encode   To put into a *code, as by assigning numbers to categories. Encoding always involves simplifying observations. See *coding.

Endogenous Variable   A *variable that is caused by other variables in a causal system. Generally contrasted with *exogenous variable. See *path diagram. In Figure E.1, Child's Aspirations, Child's Education, and Child's Income are endogenous. Parents' Education and Parents' Aspirations are *exogenous.

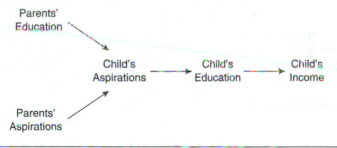

Figure E.1   Endogenous Variable

Entails   Said of a statement that must logically or inevitably or necessarily follow from another statement. "A entails B" means that if A is true, B must also be true. Such entailment is very rare in the social and behavioral sciences. Compare *necessary and *sufficient conditions.

Entry Criteria   See *inclusion criteria.

E

Epidemiology   The study of health problems in a population, especially infectious diseases. Many research issues in epidemiology are parallel to research issues in the social sciences, especially the study of problems that require using nonexperimental designs to make causal inferences.

Epistemology   Literally, "the study of knowledge." That branch of philosophy concerned with the nature and criteria or standards of knowledge. Methodological debates in the social and behavioral sciences are often the result of differences of opinion about epistemological issues and often raise epistemological questions. Methodology can be understood as applied epistemology—applied to researchers' problems. The two most influential epistemologies over the past 200 years or so are *empiricism and *rationalism. Compare *ontology.

EPSEM   *Equal probability of selection method.

Epsilon (E, ε)   Symbol for the *random error component in a *regression equation.

Epsilon Squared   Another term for *adjusted R^2.

EQS   A statistical program designed for *structural equation modeling. Compare *AMOS, *LISREL.

Equality of Variances   (also called **Homogeneity of Variance** and ***Homoscedasticity**) A basic assumption of several statistical tests (e.g., *t test, *ANOVA) that the variances in the populations sampled are substantially equal; when the assumption is violated, this may require either data *transformation or using a *nonparametric test. See *heteroscedasticity for a graphic illustration.

Equal Probability of Selection Method (EPSEM)   Any *sampling procedure in which all members of the *population have an equal probability of being included in the sample. Includes simple random sampling, proportional stratified random sampling, systematic sampling (when *periodicity is not present), and cluster sampling (if the clusters are of equal size or if the clusters are selected so that their probabilities of selection are proportional to their sizes). Compare *probability sample.

Equal Probability Sampling   Approach to sampling that uses an *equal probability of selection method (EPSEM).

Equation   A formal statement that two mathematical expressions, placed on either side of an equal sign (=), are equal, such as $12 \times 9 = 108$, or $\hat{Y} = bX + a$. Compare *model, *function.

Equifinality   Different starting points or causes or conditions can ultimately lead to the same end point or outcome. Equifinality indicates complexity in social/behavioral reality, such as that of individuals with different and complex life trajectories. Compare *multifinality.

Equipoise   Situation in which the researcher does not know which treatment condition will work better (e.g., a new treatment versus a control or traditional treatment). In this situation it is unambiguously ethical to conduct a *randomized clinical trial.

Equivalence, Coefficient of   See *coefficient of equivalence.

Equivalence Study   A research study designed to show that two or more treatment conditions have the same or similar outcomes. Typically one of the treatments is new and the other is known to be effective.

Equivalent Forms   Synonym for *alternate forms.

Equivalent-Forms Reliability   Synonym for *alternate forms reliability.

ERIC   Educational Resources Information Center. Managed by the Institute of Education Sciences, ERIC indexes and abstracts journal articles (in *Current Index to Journals in Education*, or CIJE) and other documents and research reports (in *Resources in Education*, or RIE).

Error   (a) The difference between a true value and an observation, measurement, or estimate of that value. (b) The difference between a predicted or estimated score and an observation; this is often called a *residual or *deviation score. Symbolized as e or E or epsilon (ε). Note that in statistics, "error" usually does not mean mistake; rather, it means something closer to imprecision or currently unexplained. But see *Type I error, which is a mistake.

Statistics originated in the study of error. The discipline was initially developed to handle errors in astronomical observations, which, like most of the social sciences, is an observational, not an experimental, science. Because error in measurement and coding are inevitable, dealing with error remains the foundation of statistical techniques.

Error Bars   Graphic representations of uncertainty in a measurement. They either depict the confidence limits around a measurement or 2 standard deviations on either side of it. An example showing 95% confidence intervals around the mean points is shown in Figure E.2 on page 144.

Error of the First Kind   Another term for *Type I error.

Error of the Second Kind   Another term for *Type II error.

Error Score   The difference between the actual value of a case on a variable and an estimated value such as a *mean. Also called *residual or *deviation score.

For example, say that the average (mean) verbal GRE score for students in your department was 560 and your score was 580. If the head of your department used the mean score to predict your score, the error score for you would be 20 (580 − 560 = 20).

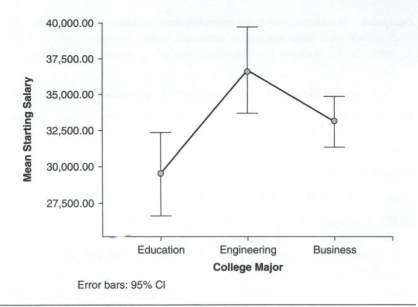

Figure E.2 Error Bars

Errors-in-Variables Problem The problem of measurement error in *independent/predictor variables in *linear regression. When present, this kind of measurement error will produce biased regression coefficients.

Error Sum of Squares In *analysis of variance, the *within-group sum of squares, that is, the part not explainable by the *treatment effects. Also called "residual sum of squares." See *error variance.

Error Term The part of an *equation indicating what is unexplained by the *independent variables. The error term specifies how big the *unexplained part is. Also called the *residual term since it is what is left over after one subtracts from the total *variance in the *dependent variable the part that is explained by the independent variables. When subjects in an experiment are randomly assigned, differences among them become part of the error term. Also called "disturbance term."

Error Variance Any uncontrolled or unexplained variability, such as *within-group difference in an *ANOVA. Also called *random error, "random variance," and *residual. The error variance is the variance of the *error term.

ES *Effect size.

Essentialism Used pejoratively to indicate an erroneous belief that one can accurately describe the essence of persons, concepts, or things. Sometimes used as a synonym for stereotyping found in racism or sexism. The term has its roots in older discussions (especially those of Plato and Aristotle) in *epistemology and especially *ontology concerning the nature of *concepts and their relationship to things. See *conceptualism.

Estimate   The value of an *estimator.

For example, we might use the *mean daily caloric intake of a *sample of adults to estimate the mean daily caloric intake of a *population of adults. The sample mean is our estimator; if we calculated it to be 2,570, then 2,570 would be the estimate given us by our estimator.

Estimation   Using a *sample *statistic to determine the probable value of a *population *parameter. See *inferential statistics. Estimation is used when the researcher is not testing a hypothesis. Obtaining a point or interval estimate of a population parameter, rather than its *statistical significance, is the goal in estimation. In other words, in estimation the researcher does not state a hypothesis about the population parameter, whereas in hypothesis testing the researcher does.

For example, let's say you wanted to know the average (*mean) verbal SAT score of students at your university. Rather than going through the files and getting the *data for several thousand undergraduates, you could take a *random sample of, say, 200 files. Suppose the mean verbal SAT score of those 200 students was 553. If you used that average score to estimate the score of the population of all students, this would be a *point estimation. If you said that the interval between 533 and 573 was 95% likely to capture the mean score of the population, this would be *interval estimation.

Estimator   (a) Any formula that can be used to make an *estimate. (b) A *sample statistic that is used to determine the probable value of a *population parameter, as one might use a known *mean value of a sample to estimate the value of the population mean. See *estimate, *estimation. Good estimators should be consistent, *unbiased, and *efficient.

Eta (H, η)   A *correlation coefficient that does not assume that the relation between two variables is *linear. Thus, it can be used to express a *curvilinear relationship. It can be used only with categorical independent variables and a continuous dependent variable (as in ANOVA). Eta is read in the same way as other correlation coefficients. Also called *correlation ratio. Compare *Pearson's r. See *polynomial regression analysis.

Eta Squared   A measure of how much of the *variance in a *dependent variable (measured at the *interval level) can be explained by a *categorical (nominal, discrete) *independent variable. Eta squared can be interpreted as a *PRE measure; that is, it tells us how much better we can guess the value of the dependent variable by knowing the independent variable. Overall Eta squared in *ANOVA is analogous to *R^2 in multiple regression; it is an estimate of the variance associated with all the independent variables taken together. Eta squared also can be computed for each independent variable, showing the amount of variance added by each separate variable.

E

Ethical Skepticism   Ethical theory denying the possibility of any concrete and inviolate moral code. Ethical judgments must be made individually, in particular situations, based on one's own value system. It supports the position of cultural relativism, that social values vary by culture and there is no universal set of "true" or correct values. Compare *deontology, *utilitarianism.

Ethics   Principles of good conduct, such as *deontology, *ethical skepticism, and *utilitarianism. In the context of research, ethics usually refers to the protection of research subjects from physical or mental harm. It also refers to researchers' honesty in reporting results. See *institutional review board.

Ethics Committee   See *institutional review board.

Ethnographic Research   A major method of *qualitative or *mixed methods research focusing on the description of the social or cultural life of particular groups of people based on direct, systematic observation, such as becoming a participant in the particular social system. Ethnographic research is most closely associated with anthropological research but is widely used in other fields as well. See *descriptive research, *participant observation.

Ethnography   Type of qualitative research focused on discovering and describing the culture of a group of people. Its roots are in anthropology.

Ethnology   The comparative study of cultural groups.

Ethnomethodology   A type of *ethnographic research in sociology founded by Harold Garfinkel. It focuses on the commonsense understanding of social life held by ordinary people (the "ethnos"), usually as discovered by *participant observation. Often the observer's own methods of making sense of the situation become the object of investigation.

Ethology   Research methods stressing observation and detailed descriptions of behavior in natural settings. The term originally referred to the study of animal behavior, but it has come to be used in research on human behavior when the methods are strongly observational and minimally interpretive. See *ethnographic research.

Etic   (a) Methods of study in anthropology stressing material, rather than cultural, explanations for social and cultural phenomena. (b) The viewpoint of the social scientist or "objective outsider," as in a researcher attempting to study and describe a cultural group. Compare *emic, with which etic is usually contrasted.

For example, an anthropologist using an etic approach might look for the origins of cannibalism in a need for protein; an emic-minded colleague might stress the reasons given by the members of a group practicing cannibalism in the attempt to explain what cannibalism means to them from their perspective. Perhaps a group had religious needs that cannibalistic rituals satisfied.

E

Etiology   The study of causes, usually but not exclusively causes of diseases.

Euler's Constant   An *irrational number, usually symbolized gamma (γ), with a value of 0.577216 . . . .

Evaluation   Sometimes used as a synonym for assessment, but many authors make a distinction. Evaluation uses assessment data to make value judgments and decisions about programs, processes, products, and performance. Evaluative judgments might include, for example, that a teacher or a program is not meeting the required standard or benchmark and should, therefore, be terminated. Contrast with *assessment. See *evaluation research.

Evaluation Research or **Evaluation**   Investigations, using any of several methods, designed to test the *effectiveness or impact of a social program or intervention. In addition to impact, evaluation research sometimes assesses program need, program theory, program implementation, and program efficiency. It is often conducted by interdisciplinary teams of researchers. Evaluation research is a type of *applied research. Also called "program evaluation." Compare *assessment research.

Evaluation research became important in the 1960s with the expansion of social welfare programs in that decade and has become a routine requirement of federal programs in the United States.

Examples of evaluation research include studies designed to tell whether a school desegregation plan improved intergroup harmony, whether new sentencing guidelines deterred crime, or whether driver education reduced fatal accidents.

Event   In *set theory, any single or group of *elementary events. A *subset. Also called "event class" or "compound event" to distinguish it from an elementary event.

For example, if the elementary event were the 7 of clubs in a deck of cards, an event would be the 7s, the clubs, or the black cards.

Event, Compound   An *event made up of two or more events. Either *union or *intersection of sets is a compound event.

For example, hiring an employee who is highly motivated *and* talented is a compound event.

Event, Elementary   In *set and *probability theory, a single *data point in or element or member of a *sample space; the outcome of a repeatable process (such as flipping a coin and recording the event). Also called "simple event."

For example, the 7 of clubs would be an elementary event in a deck of cards (the sample space). A particular college student would be an elementary event in the *population (or sample space) of all college students.

Event History Analysis   Methods for studying the movement over time of subjects through successive states or conditions by asking them to remember biographical data (an alternative approach uses *archives containing longitudinal data) about the occurrence, timing, and duration of events in their lives. The goal of the research is to study change from one state to the next and how long each of the states lasts. "Events" are changes from one categorical state to another. For example, one could use event history analysis to study marital status, with the states or conditions being unmarried, married, divorced, remarried, widowed. See *longitudinal study, *time-series data, *survival analysis.

By contrast, *panel studies, which also study subjects over time, use successive *waves of surveys or interviews. Since they do not usually investigate what happened between the waves, panel studies can be thought of as a series of cross sections of the same group. See *cross-sectional data.

Event Sampling   The recording of when a particular event occurs and conducting systematic observation during and directly after the specific event occurs (e.g., observing students when the teacher asks for questions or sends someone to the principal's office). Compare with *time-interval sampling.

Event Space   Another term for *sample space.

Evidence-Based Practice   Said of practice in medicine, and by extension in other fields such as education, that is based on the systematic review of the most current research in the field. Goal is to identify and implement practices and policies said to "work" according to the "best available evidence."

Exact Identification   Synonym for *just-identified.

Exact Test   See *Fisher's exact test.

Exclusion Criteria   A list of the characteristics that prevent research participants from eligibility to participate in a research study.

Exclusive   See *mutually exclusive, *exhaustive.

Exhaustive   Said of a group of conditions, events, or values of a variable that, when taken together, account for (or "exhaust") all possibilities.

For example, age categories 0–19, 20–39, and 40-plus are exhaustive; everybody fits into one of them. On the other hand, Christian, Hindu, Islamic, and Jewish is not an exhaustive list of religious affiliations. It could be made so, however, by adding Other and None to the list. Compare *mutually exclusive.

Existing Data   Data that can be used in research, such as *personal documents* (i.e., anything written, photographed, or recorded for private use), *official documents* (i.e., anything written, photographed, or recorded for official use), *physical data* (i.e., anything created or left by humans), and *archived data* (i.e., data originally used for research purposes and then stored). Compare *tests, *questionnaires, *interviews, *focus groups, *observation, *secondary data. See *research design.

Exogenous Variable   A variable entering from and determined from outside the system being studied. A causal system says nothing about its exogenous variables. Their values are given, not analyzed. Also called "prior variables." See *endogenous variable. In *path analysis, cause is illustrated by a unidirectional arrow →. If a variable does not have a unidirectional arrow pointing at it, it is exogenous. An exogenous variable is the first link in a causal chain; subsequent links are *endogenous. See Figure E.1.

For example, say we were studying the relation of hours spent practicing to score in an archery contest. Subjects' dexterity and strength might be related to their scores, but these would be exogenous variables for the purposes of the study.

Expected Frequency   In *contingency table problems, the frequency you would predict ("expect") if you knew only the *marginal totals and if you assumed the *independence of the variables. With the *chi-square test, the expected frequency is the predicted value when the *null hypothesis is true.

For example, suppose that in a *sample of 100 adults you had 60 women and 40 men, and 70 of the 100 adults had graduated from high school and 30 had not. You could put the results in a contingency table as in Table E.1.

Table E.1   Expected Frequency

	Men	Women	Total
Graduates	a	b	70
Nongraduates	c	d	30
Total	40	60	100

Given this information, you can compute the expected frequency for each of the cells, a, b, c, and d. To find the expected frequency for a cell, multiply its row marginal (total) by its column marginal (total) and divide the result by the total number of subjects. For example, the expected number of women high school graduates (cell b) would be $60 \times 70 = 4{,}200/100 = 42$. You would expect 42 of your sample to be female high school graduates. If your expected frequencies were significantly different from the actual, observed frequencies (you could determine this with a *chi-square test), you could conclude that there was probably some relationship between the variables such that one sex was more likely to have graduated from high school.

Expected Value   (a) The *mean value of a variable in repeated samplings or trials. (b) The mean of the *sampling distribution of a statistic. Usually symbolized E, as in $E(X)$, which means the "expected value of X."

The idea grew out of gamblers' calculations of how much they could expect to win (or lose) in a fair game, in the long run, with a bet of a certain size. Say you play roulette, making 1,000 bets of $1 on your favorite number.

Each time you win, you get $35; each time you lose, the croupier takes your dollar. Your odds of winning on most wheels are 37 to 1, which means that in the long run you will lose about $55 for every 1,000 bets. If you tried the experiment once, you might do considerably better or worse. But if you tried it many times, your average result for each 1,000 bets would be to lose about $55. The more times you made the 1,000 bets, the closer your average would get to the expected value of a $55 loss.

Note that the expected value is not necessarily the most common (modal) value. It can even be an impossible value. If, for example, a variable can have a value of either 1 or 2, the expected value is 1.5, a value that never occurs.

Experience Sampling Method   Any of several methods that require subjects to record what they are doing or thinking or how they are feeling at times specified by a researcher. Subjects might be asked to enter data into a log when beepers they are wearing sound.

Experiment   (a) In behavioral research, a study undertaken in which the researcher has control over some of the conditions in which the study takes place and control over (some aspects of) at least one *independent variable being studied. The independent variable is manipulated rather than only observed. *Random assignment of subjects to *control and *experimental groups is the most important characteristic of a very strong experiment (called *randomized experiment, or RCT). Compare *natural experiment, *quasi-experiment, *secondary analysis, *descriptive research.

(b) In probability theory, an experiment is an act or a process that leads to a single outcome (an elementary *event) when that outcome cannot be predicted with certainty, such as flipping a coin or asking potential customers whether they would consider buying a particular product.

For example, if you interviewed moviegoers as they exited a theater to see if what they saw influenced their attitudes, this would not be an experiment (a); that's because you had no control over who the subjects were or what film they watched or the conditions under which they watched it. On the other hand, if you chose a room and a film and randomly assigned subjects to control and experimental groups, showed a film expected to affect certain attitudes to the experimental group only, and interviewed all subjects afterward about the relevant attitudes, that approach would be much more experimental.

Experimental Design   The art of planning and executing an *experiment (a). The greatest strength of an experimental research design, due largely to *random assignment, is its *internal validity; one can be more certain than with any other design about attributing *cause to the *independent variables. The greatest weakness of experimental designs may be *external validity; it may be inappropriate to generalize results beyond the laboratory or other experimental context. See *research design.

Experimental Error   Differences in results among experiments repeated using identical procedures. When experiments are repeated, the results are rarely if ever exactly the same—even if the experiments are well designed and the experimenters make no mistakes. Compare *error term, *random variation.

Experimental Group   A group receiving some *treatment in an experiment. Data collected about subjects in the experimental group are compared with data about subjects in a *control group (who received no treatment) and/or another experimental group (who received a different treatment).

Experimental Realism   The extent to which engaging in an experimental intervention is engaging and realistic and meaningful to the research participants and elicits natural actions and responses. Compare *mundane realism.

Experimental Research   The type of research that includes a *manipulated independent variable. Compare *nonexperimental research.

Experimental Unit   The smallest independently treated unit of study. Compare *unit of analysis.

For example, if 90 subjects were randomly assigned to three *treatment groups, the study would have 3 experimental units, not 90.

Experimenter Bias   Problems caused in an experiment because of the researcher's expectations, hopes, preconceived beliefs. This can result in errors of observation and interpretation, and can affect attitudes and behavior of research participants.

Experimenter Drift   A slow and unconscious, but systematic, change in how a researcher conducts an experiment over time leading to bias in results. See *observer drift.

Experimenter Effect   (a) A type of *confounding effect that occurs when different experimenters working on the same experiment administer different *treatments or *conditions. (b) Any bias introduced by experimenters' expectations. Compare *Pygmalion effect.

For example, say Al, Betty, and Chuck were running an experiment on subjects' reaction time as influenced by three types of visual cues (A, B, C). If Al always administered cue A, Betty cue B, and Chuck cue C, it would be impossible to tell if differences in subjects' reaction times were due solely to differences in the cues or in part to the way the experimenters administered them. Al, Betty, and Chuck should rotate. Compare *counterbalancing.

Experimentwise Error Rate   (also called **Experimentwise Alpha**) The probability of committing a *Type I error (if the null hypothesis is true) in the full set of *multiple comparisons made in a single experiment. Holding this error rate at the traditional alpha level (e.g., .05) is a very conservative approach to significance testing (especially if one has many independent variables in the study. Therefore, it is often (but not always) recommended that the researcher focus on the familywise error rate rather than the experimentwise error rate. Compare *familywise error rate.

Expert System   A computer *program modeled on the experience of human experts in decision making and problem solving. An expert system is a form of *artificial intelligence and has been used in such diverse fields as medical diagnosis, *data mining, and investment banking.

Explained Variance   Variance in the *dependent variable that can be accounted for by (statistically associated with) variance in the *independent variable(s). The goal of research is to explain variance. In the words of Stanley Lieberson, "Happiness is variance explained." Contrast *error variance.

Explanatory Causation   See *causal explanation.

Explanatory Research   Research that seeks to understand variables by discovering and measuring causal relations among them. Sometimes used to describe *experimental versus *correlational, *exploratory, or *descriptive research designs. Often contrasted with *predictive research, especially in discussions of *regression analysis.

Explanatory Survey Research   See *descriptive survey research for a comparison of descriptive, predictive, and explanatory survey research.

Explanatory Trial   *Randomized clinical trial focused on determining how and why a drug produces an effect in an ideal setting. Similar to *efficacy research.

Explanatory Variable   An *independent variable, especially in *regression analysis. Term often used when a researcher is using regression for the purpose of explanation. See *predictor variable and *regressor.

Exploratory Data Analysis (EDA)   Any of several methods, pioneered by John Tukey, of discovering unanticipated patterns and relationships, often by presenting quantitative data visually. The *stem-and-leaf display and the *box-and-whisker diagram are well-known examples. Compare *hypothesis testing, *data mining, *elaboration.

Exploratory Factor Analysis   *Factor analysis conducted to discover what *latent variables (factors) are behind a set of variables or measures. Generally contrasted with *confirmatory factor analysis, which tests theories and hypotheses about the factors one expects to find.

Exploratory Research   Said of research that looks for patterns, ideas, or hypotheses rather than research that tries to test or confirm hypotheses. Contrast with *confirmatory research.

Exponent   A symbol written above and to the right of another symbol to indicate how many times it should be multiplied by itself. Example: 7^3 means $7 \times 7 \times 7 = 343$. See *power.

Exponential Growth   Loosely, very rapid growth; during an economic crisis, the rate of inflation might double every month from 2% to 4% to 8% to 16% to 32% to 64% from January to July; such an increase would be said to be exponential.

Exponential Smoothing   Statistical technique in *time-series analysis used to smooth out (reduce error variation) of a set of time-series data points and give more weight to more recent points on the time-series variable. Compare *moving averages.

Ex Post Facto Explanation (or Hypothesis)   An explanation about what the facts "will" look like that is offered after they have been collected. This is legitimate in *exploratory research. In other circumstances it can be a dubious practice. Compare *retrospective study.

Ex Post Facto Research Design   (a) Any investigation using existing data rather than new, original data gathered specifically for the study. This means that causes will be studied after (post) they have had their effect. (b) Any *nonexperimental research design that takes place after the conditions to be studied have occurred, such as research in which there is a *posttest but no *pretest. Researchers often try to compensate for the lack of a pretest or *baseline data by *matching subjects or otherwise *controlling for variables that might have influenced outcomes. See *case-control study.

Exposure   Term in medical research indicating that a research participant has a particular risk factor.

Externalities   Unintended, incidental, or external outcomes or effects (positive or negative)—usually economic effects. For example, one of the externalities of a honey farm is that the bees will pollinate neighboring plants. An externality of a new shopping mall in a town could be increased traffic congestion.

External Reliability   See *reliability.

External Validity   The extent to which the findings of a single research study apply beyond that study. It's another term for *generalizability.
   For example, some external validities include *population validity (generalizing from a sample to a population or generalizing across all subgroups within a single population), *ecological validity (generalizing across different settings), *temporal validity (generalizing across time), *treatment variation validity (generalizing across slight variations of the treatment), and outcome validity (generalizing across slightly different dependent variables).

Extraneous Variable   Any condition not part of a study (that is, one in which researchers have no interest) but that could have an effect on the study's *dependent variable. (Note that in this context, "extraneous" does not mean unimportant.) Researchers usually try to *control for extraneous variables by experimental isolation, by randomization, or by statistical techniques such as *analysis of covariance. Sometimes called "nuisance variable."

Extraneous Variance   Variance caused by an *extraneous variable.

Extrapolation   Inferring values by projecting *trends beyond known evidence, often by extending a *regression line. Compare *interpolation.

Suppose, for example, that you had some measures of the daily high temperatures for a week in June, as shown in Table E.2.

If you guessed that the temperature on Sunday would be 84, that would be an extrapolation. If you guessed that Wednesday's temperature was 76, this would be an *interpolation, which is generally a safer kind of inference.

Table E.2   Extrapolation of Temperature

Mon.	Tues.	Wed.	Thur.	Fri.	Sat.	Sun.
72	74		78	80	82	

Extrema   *Extreme values.

Extreme Outlier   See *outlier, *box-and-whisker diagram.

Extreme Values   The largest and smallest values in a distribution of values. See *range. Compare *outlier.

f   (a) Lowercase *f*, the usual symbol for *frequency in a table depicting a *frequency distribution. (b) The symbol for *function, as in $Y = f(X)$. (c) Symbol for *sampling fraction.

F   Uppercase *F*, the test statistic that is computed, for example, when conducting an *analysis of variance. See *F distribution, *F ratio.

FACAN   Sometimes used as an acronym for *fac*tor *an*alysis.

Face Validity   Logical or conceptual validity; so called because it is determined by whether, "on the face of it," a measure appears to make sense. In determining face validity, one often asks expert judges whether the measure seems to them to be valid. The term is also used to describe whether a test or survey seems reasonable to those being tested or surveyed; if not, they may be less motivated to complete it carefully. See *prima facie evidence.

Fact   A piece of information believed to be true or to describe something real. Facts are empirical and particular rather than abstract and general, and many stated facts can be checked; historical facts are often more difficult to check and validate. Compare *objective, *data.

Factor   (a) In *analysis of variance, an *independent variable. (b) In *factor analysis, a cluster of related variables that are a distinguishable component of a larger group of variables. See also *latent variable. (c) A number by which another number is multiplied, as in the statement "Real estate values increased by a factor of 3," meaning that they tripled. (d) In mathematics, a number that divides exactly into another number. For example, 1, 2, and 4 are factors of 8, since when you divide each of them into 8, the result (quotient) is a whole number. See *factoring.

Factor Analysis (FA)   Any of several methods of analysis that enable researchers to reduce a large number of *variables to a smaller number of variables, or *factors, or *latent variables. A factor is a set of variables, such as items on a survey, that can be conceptually and statistically related or grouped together. Factor analysis is done by finding patterns among the variations in the values of several variables; a cluster of highly intercorrelated variables results in a factor. *Exploratory factor analysis was the original type. *Confirmatory factor analysis developed later and is generally considered more theoretically advanced. *Principal components analysis (PCA) is sometimes regarded as a form of factor analysis, although the mathematical models on which it is based are different. While both FA and PCA have strong advocates, the two techniques tend to produce similar results, especially when the number of variables is large. See *variable-centered analysis.

For example, factor analysis is often used in survey research to see if a long series of questions can be grouped into shorter sets of questions, each of which describes an aspect or factor of the phenomenon being studied. See *index (c), *latent class analysis.

Factor Equations   In *factor analysis, equations analogous to *regression equations describing the regression of observed (*manifest) variables on unobserved (*latent) variables. Factor equations have no *intercept, or rather, the intercept is fixed at zero.

Factorial   Said of a whole number (positive integer) multiplied by each of the whole numbers smaller than itself. It is usually indicated by an exclamation point. Factorials are used extensively when calculating probabilities because they indicate the number of different ways individuals or other units of analysis can be ordered. See *permutation.

For example, 5 factorial, or 5!, means $5 \times 4 \times 3 \times 2 \times 1 = 120$. Therefore, 5 individuals can be ordered in 120 different ways.

Factorial Analysis of Covariance   Label or name for a *GLM with one quantitative *dependent variable, two or more *categorical independent variables, and one or more quantitative independent variables (called *covariates).

Factorial Analysis of Variance   An *analysis of variance (ANOVA) with two or more *factors or independent variables, allowing *interaction effects to be computed and studied. It is contrasted with a single factor or *one-way ANOVA.

Factorial Experiments or Designs   Research designs with two or more *categorical *independent variables (*factors), each studied at two or more *levels. Some definitions also require that participants be randomly assigned to the conditions forming at least one of the independent variables. The goal of factorial designs is to determine whether the factors combine to produce *interaction effects; if the treatments do not interact with one another, their combined effects can be obtained simply by studying them one at a time and adding the separate effects. See *analysis of variance, *main effect.

For example, a study of the effects of a drug administered at three doses or levels (factor 1) on male and female (factor 2) subjects' psychological states (dependent variable) would be a factorial design. There would be an interaction effect between the drug and gender if, say, at some level(s) the drug had a different effect on men's and women's psychological states.

Factorial Invariance   Pattern present in *factor analysis results when the *simple structure is relatively constant across different subpopulations and across new samples of data.

Factorial Plot   A graph of two or more *independent variables (factors) in which nonparallel lines for the levels of a factor indicate the presence of an *interaction effect. See *disordinal interaction and *interaction effect for examples.

Factorial Table   A table showing the influence of two or more *independent variables on a *dependent variable. See *summary table.

Factorial Validity   Factorial validity is present when the hypothesized factor structure is confirmed in an empirical test as in *confirmatory factor analysis. As another example, finding factorial invariance would suggest that a test has factorial validity.

Factoring   Breaking a number into its *factors, that is, breaking it into parts that, when multiplied together, equal the number.
  For example, 24 can be factored into 2×12, 3×8, and 4×6. Each of these numbers (2, 3, 4, 6, 8, 12) is a factor of 24.

Factor Loading Matrix   Contains the factor loadings when the rotation is *orthogonal and is usually used to interpret and name each factor. When the rotation is *oblique, the factor loading matrix is split into the two matrices: *factor pattern matrix and *factor structure matrix.

Factor Loadings   Loadings obtained in *factor analysis and used to interpret the *factors (b). They are analogous to *regression (*slope) coefficients (specifically, *partial regression coefficients) and indicate the unique contribution of each factor to the variance of an observed variable. The higher the loading, the closer the association of the item with the group of items that makes up the factor. When *orthogonal rotation is used, they are the simple *correlations between each observed *variable and each factor. Loadings greater than .3 or .4 are generally considered meaningful. See *factor equation, *structural coefficient.

Factor Pattern Matrix   In *factor analysis with *oblique rotation, a table showing the *loadings of each variable on each factor. It shows the unique relationship between each factor and the observed variables. The factor *pattern* matrix is usually used to interpret and name each factor. See *factor structure matrix. Compare *factor loading matrix.

F

Factor Rotation   Any of several methods in *factor analysis used to "rotate" or transform the initial factors to make them easier to interpret. The desired outcome of a factor analysis is to obtain a pattern of loadings that has a *simple structure. The *transformation procedure "rotates the factor axes" and increases the size of large factor loadings and decreases the size of small ones. *Oblique rotation produces factors that are allowed to correlate; *orthogonal rotation produces factors that are not allowed to correlate. "Orthogonal" in this context simply means uncorrelated. While each method has strong advocates, oblique and orthogonal rotation tend to produce similar results, especially when the number of variables is large.

Factor Score   The score of an individual on a factor after the factor has been identified by *factor analysis.

Factor Structure Matrix   In *factor analysis with *oblique rotation, a table showing the *loadings of each variable on each factor. See *factor pattern matrix. Compare *factor loading matrix.

Fail-safe *N*   Concept used in a *meta-analytic study that found a statistically significant relationship (i.e., it's relevant when the *effect* that has been averaged across the set of included studies is statistically significant). It is the number of no-relationship studies (i.e., null studies) that would have to be located and added to the already analyzed set of studies in order to change the currently statistically significant meta-analytic result into a non–statistically significant result. For example, in a meta-analysis that found a statistically significant effect, the fail-safe *N* might be 93, meaning that 93 additional no-relationship studies would have to be added to make the currently statistically significant finding become non–statistically significant. The larger the fail-safe *N*, the more confidence one can place in the original significance finding because it is unlikely (or it should be unlikely) that the researcher has failed to locate a very large number of null studies.

Failure   In *probability theory, one of the two ways a *Bernoulli trial can turn out. For example, in flipping a coin, tails might be called *success and heads failure. While the designations are mostly arbitrary, the term "failure" is reserved for occasions when the predicted event does not occur.

Faithful-Subject Role   Research participants' behavior that attempts to fully and honestly follow the researcher's directions and protocol, even if they can anticipate the researcher's hypotheses. Compare *apprehensive-subject role, *good-subject role, *negative-subject role.

Fallacy of Composition   An error of reasoning made by assuming that some trait or characteristic of an individual must also describe the individual's group. Also called "atomistic fallacy." Compare *ecological fallacy.

For example, if you knew one or several white males who were unsympathetic to affirmative action, it would be a fallacy of composition to assume that all white males were equally unsympathetic.

Fallibilism   The philosophical doctrine, developed by C. S. Peirce, to the effect that all knowledge claims, scientific or otherwise, are always fallible or open to question. See *falsificationism, *Heisenberg's uncertainty principle.

False Alarm   See *signal detection theory.

False Negative   Said of a test that wrongly indicates the absence of a condition—for example, the test shows that you don't have cancer when in fact you do. Originating in medical testing, the term has broader use today. Compare *false positive, *Type II error, *specificity.

False Positive   Said of a test that wrongly indicates the presence of a condition—for example, the test shows that you do have cancer when in fact you do not. Originating in medical testing, the term has broader use today. Compare *false negative, *Type I error, *sensitivity.

Falsifiability   Said of theories that can be subject to tests that could prove them to be false. Those who believe in *falsificationism contend that only falsifiable theories are truly scientific.

Falsificationism   The doctrine, originating with Karl Popper, that we can only refute ("falsify") theories; we can never confirm them. A good theory is one that we have tried—repeatedly, but unsuccessfully—to disprove or falsify. Compare *null hypothesis.

Familywise Error Rate   (also called **Familywise Alpha**) The probability of committing a *Type I error (if the null hypothesis is true) in a particular set of *multiple comparisons. "Family" in this context means group or set of "related" statistical tests.

For example, in a one-way *ANOVA the categorical variable might have three *levels (A, B, C), and if the overall significance test is statistically significant, the researcher might conduct three post hoc comparisons (AB, AC, BC) to see which of the groups were different—this set of post hoc comparisons would be a family. If you set your *alpha level at .05 and make these three comparisons, the probability of familywise error is roughly .15 (.05 + .05 + .05 = .15). It is recommended to hold the alpha error rate for this family at .05 (rather than using the "inflated alpha" rate of .15). Therefore, researchers must use one of the many techniques available for adjusting the familywise rate back down to .05, such as the *Bonferroni technique or the *Scheffé test. See *post hoc comparison.

Note that familywise error rate can be different from the *experimentwise error rate. For example, in a two-way ANOVA, you might have three families of comparisons, one for the multiple comparisons associated with each main effect and one for the *interaction effect. Some recommend that rather than focusing on families of comparisons, one should hold the alpha rate to .05 for the entire experiment rather than for each of the three families. See *experimentwise error rate.

Fan Spread   When the scores or values for two groups grow further apart with the passing of time; plotting this on a graph results in a figure resembling a fan and is called a "fan spread." See *interaction effect.

FASEM   Factor analytic structural equation modeling. See *structural equation modeling, *analysis of covariance structures, *LISREL. The proliferation of names for identical or highly similar techniques is due to the relative newness of the techniques and, perhaps, to the desire of *software companies to come up with distinctive brand names.

Fat-Tailed Distribution   A data distribution that departs from the *normal distribution by having more cases at the high and low ends of the range of values (i.e., in the tails of the distribution). Distributions of stock prices that fluctuate greatly have fat tails. By comparison with the normal distribution, the *t distribution is fat-tailed. Also called "heavy tailed."

F Distribution   A popular *theoretical probability distribution. More formally, it is the distribution of the *ratio of two independent (chi-square) variables, each of which has been divided by its *degrees of freedom. See *F ratio, *chi-square distribution. The distribution is perhaps most widely used in or closely associated with *analysis of variance, where it is used to assign *p values. Named after Sir R. A. Fisher.

Feasibility Study   A preliminary investigation to determine the possibility of successfully conducting a larger program, procedure, or study. Compare *pilot study. Sometimes called a "proof of concept study."

Fidelity   See *implementation fidelity.

Field   (a) A place for doing research that is not a laboratory or library but is a naturally occurring place, such as if one studies insect life in a meadow or a human interaction in a particular social organization. (b) In a computer program, a place for a specific piece of information in a *data record, usually marked by a column. *Variables are arranged vertically by column or field across all the cases; cases are arranged horizontally by row or record. See *data record for an example.

Field Experiment   An *experiment in a natural setting (the "field"), not in a laboratory. The researcher in a field experiment does not create the experimental situation, but he or she does manipulate it. School classrooms are a common location for field experiments. See *quasi-experiment, *natural experiment.

Field Notes   A record, usually written, of events observed by an *ethnographic researcher. The notes are taken as the study proceeds. Because field notes will later be used for analysis, they should be as close to comprehensive (perhaps even stenographic) as possible.

Field Research (or Study)   Research conducted in a real-life setting, not in a laboratory. The researcher neither creates nor manipulates the subject of study but rather observes it. See *field experiment, *participant observation, *ethnographic research.

File   Any *program or *data set in a computer's memory.

File Drawer Problem   In literature reviews and *meta-analyses, a problem of *validity that arises because study results that are not *statistically significant may often go unpublished; they might be put in researchers' file drawers and be unavailable for review and analysis. This would *bias any meta-analysis, which would tend to overestimate the proportion of research containing statistically significant findings. See *publication bias.

Filter   In the context of *time-series analysis, a procedure for converting one time series into another. The most widely known example is the *moving average.

Filter Question   See *contingency question.

First-Order Factor   Type of factor obtained in a standard *exploratory factor analysis. Contrasted with the factors obtained in a *second-order *factor analysis. Theoretically, third and even higher order factors are possible.

First-Order Interaction Effects   Said of the *interaction of two *independent variables. Second-order interaction effects take place among three independent variables. Higher orders are possible, perhaps even common, but are difficult to interpret. Also called a *two-way interaction or an A × B interaction. See *interaction.

First-Order Partial   Said of a *partial correlation or a *partial regression coefficient that *controls for the (*linear) effect of one *independent variable. A second-order partial controls for two, a third-order for three, and so on. A *zero-order correlation controls for no other variables.

Fishbone Diagram   A diagram that looks a little like a fishbone, or a fish spine, used to show causes (grouped into categories) of an event or problem (see Figure F.1 on page 162). The specific idea was created by Kaoru Ishikawa in the 1960s and used in quality management work.

Fisher's Exact Test   A *test statistic for measures of *association that relate two *nominal (usually *dichotomous) variables. It is used mainly in 2 × 2 frequency tables when the *expected frequency is too small to trust the use of the *chi-square test. The result is an exact p value, such as $p = .11$, not a range of

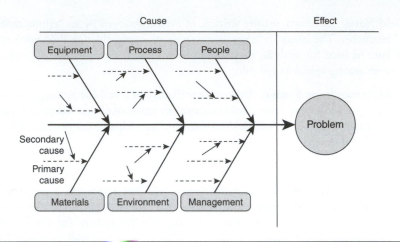

Figure F.1 Fishbone Diagram

Source: User: FabianLange/Wikimedia Commons/CC-BY-SA-3.0/GFDL.

values, such as $p < .05$, obtained from a distribution table in the back of a statistics book. The Fisher exact test is a *permutation test. See *bootstrapping, *phi coefficient, *Yates's correction.

Fisher's LSD Test   A test of statistical significance used in *post hoc or *multiple comparisons. LSD is short for "least significant difference." The two-step procedure is (1) to test the omnibus null hypothesis that a set of means are all equal and (2) if this null hypothesis is rejected, then conduct post hoc t tests on the different pairs of the means. It's a controversial test; one rule of thumb is to use the LSD test only when you have three groups *and* it is conducted following a statistically significant *omnibus test in *ANOVA. See *Scheffé test.

Fisher's Z   (a) A measure of *effect size often used in *meta-analysis. Symbolized: Z_{FISHER}. (b) A *logarithmic *transformation of *Pearson r correlation coefficients so that *confidence limits can be constructed for an observed correlation and for testing the difference between two observed correlation coefficients. It also can be used for *significance tests for the correlation coefficient, although the *t distribution is often used for testing the null hypothesis that the population correlation is zero. Also called *r-to-Z transformation. Sometimes abbreviated Fisher's Z_r. See *r-to-Z transformation for more information.

Fishing Expedition   Any random looking around in the data gathered in a study to see if you can find some significant relationship. This is generally considered bad practice, especially if one is reporting the results of *significance tests. See *post hoc comparisons. However, there are good ways to go "hunting" (vs. bad ways to "fish") for interesting relationships. See *exploratory data analysis, *data mining, *elaboration.

F

Fit   Refers to how closely observed *data match the relations specified in a hypothesized *model or how closely they correspond to an assumed distribution. See *goodness-of-fit.

Fit Index   See *goodness-of-fit.

Five-Number Summary   A way of describing a distribution of data associated with *exploratory data analysis. It is made up of the smallest value, the largest value, the median, the 25th percentile, and the 75th percentile. These are the values used to construct a *box-and-whisker diagram.

Fixed-Effects Model   The typical *ANOVA design in which the populations studied are (or are treated as) fixed categorical variables—users of Drug A, B, and C, for example. The *independent variables and their *levels are determined (fixed) by the researcher. Also called "Model I ANOVA." See *random effects model in which the researcher uses a random procedure to select the different levels of treatment.

   Fixed effects, such as male/female, do not vary within groups. Random effects, such as height and weight, do vary. *Mixed-effects models investigate both fixed and random effects in the same study. See *multilevel modeling.

Fixed Factor   Said of a variable in a *factorial *ANOVA design when the *levels of the variable are categorical or are categorized.

Fixed Parameter   In *SEM, model parameters (e.g., path coefficients, error coefficients) can be fixed, constrained, or freely estimated. Fixed parameters are those that the researcher sets to a specific value (e.g., 0 or 1) and are not estimated in the empirical analysis. For example, if one does not want to estimate a particular relationship, the parameter can be fixed at 0. Compare *constrained parameter, *freely estimated parameter.

Floor Effect   A term used to describe a situation in which many subjects in a study have scores at or near the possible lower limit (the "floor"). This makes analysis difficult since it reduces the amount of variation in the variable. Compare *ceiling effect.

   For example, a study of counseling strategies to reduce suicidal tendencies could be more difficult to conduct with subjects who were black women in their 30s since this group has a very low suicide rate, one that could be hard to reduce further. It might be easier to conduct the study with white men in their 60s since they have a higher suicide rate.

Flow Chart (or Diagram)   A graphic illustration of progression through a system or the steps of a procedure. Used extensively in such fields as manufacturing and computer processing. See *logic model.

   The simple example from psychology shown in Figure F.2 on page 164 briefly suggests the steps by which some environmental stimuli might be "processed" to go into long-term memory.

> Environmental stimuli → Initial perception → Short-term memory → Long-term memory

Figure F.2   Flow Chart

Flow Graph   Another term for *path diagram.

Fluctuations   In *time-series data, any short-term back-and-forth movements that are unrelated to long-term *trends. See *spike, *moving average.

Sometimes fluctuations are so frequent and large it makes trends difficult to see. Global warming is an example. Even if the planet is gradually getting warmer, it still gets very cold in the winter (regular fluctuation), and sometimes the temperature can be quite low for a few days in the summer (random, nonpredictable fluctuation).

Focused Comparisons   Techniques of *meta-analysis for comparing *significance levels and *effect sizes by measuring the extent to which the studies' results are explained by an *independent variable.

Focus Group   A qualitative research tool pioneered in the 1940s and 1950s by Robert K. Merton, who called it the "focused group interview." The basic technique involves having about a dozen persons engage in an intensive discussion focused on a particular topic. It has been used extensively in market research among potential customers ("What would you think of a product like this?") and in planning political campaigns ("What do you see as this candidate's main weakness?"). It is increasingly used by survey researchers to help them design questionnaires. Members of focus groups tend to be similar to one another, sharing a trait of interest to the researchers, such as potential customers for a product or likely voters for a candidate.

Follow-up Tests   Another term for *post hoc comparisons.

Forecasting   Predicting future events or quantities, such as the inflation rate next year, on the basis of information about past events or quantities. Forecasting is often contrasted with *estimation, by which one tries to determine the size of some existing quantity. Compare *prediction. See *ARIMA, *indicators.

Researchers forecast *events* (Will an election take place?) or *event timing* (When will the election occur?) or *outcomes* (Who will win the election?) or a *quantity* (What percentage of the electorate will vote for the Social Democrats?).

Forest Plot   A graphic used in *meta-analysis to show an effect size for a research relationship across multiple published research studies. It displays the *confidence interval bars (see *error bars) from the studies in the meta-analysis as well as an overall confidence interval.

Formal Theory   Theory that uses symbols (logical or algebraic) rather than a natural language (like English or French) to state its propositions. Formal theorists manipulate formulas, not words. Their goal is to use symbols that will work in any context, to use forms that are not dependent on content, and to produce logically consistent systems.

Formative Evaluation   *Evaluation research undertaken to find ways to improve, redesign, or fine-tune a program in its early stages. The focus is on the program's processes more than its outcomes, and the techniques are often *qualitative. Compare *summative evaluation.

Form Invariance   Outcome obtained in *confirmatory factor analysis when the hypothesized model fits across two or more groups. It is a desirable *psychometric characteristic of a test/assessment instrument, and it must be determined empirically.

Formula   A general *rule, principle, or statement of a relationship, usually expressed in mathematical or logical symbols. See *function.

FORTRAN   Short for FORmula TRANslator. One of the earliest *programming languages used for writing computer programs. Using commands such as "DO," "GO TO," and "READ," it "translates" English into a language a computer can use.

Forward Selection   A computer method or algorithm for *variable selection in *regression analysis. The goal of variable selection is to obtain a subset of variables that accounts for a large amount of variance. This procedure might be used when a researcher has a very large number of variables and desires to find a smaller set for the purpose of prediction. This method should not be used in explanatory research. Compare *backward elimination and *stepwise regression. Also called "step-up selection." Statisticians seldom recommend using such computer routines, especially forward selection by itself.

For example, if you had 20 potential independent variables, the computer program would estimate 20 *simple regressions (one for each independent variable) and choose the "best" one, that is, the one that has the highest R^2 (explains the largest percentage of the variance in the dependent variable). Then this variable would be tried in combination with the remaining 19 to find a second that (in a *multiple regression equation) produces the "best" pair (the pair with the largest R^2). Then the computer would use those two and search for a third, and so on until adding more variables no longer leads to a statistically significant increase in the R^2.

Fractal   A geometric structure such as a curve or surface that possesses a fractional dimensionality. Rather than being one-dimensional such as a line or two-dimensional such as a plane, a fractal can have a dimensionality between one and two. Such structures possess properties of self-similarity in which each part of the structure is a miniature version of the whole. Examples of such self-similarity are branches of a tree, which resemble the whole tree, and the pattern of vortices in turbulent water, which resembles the pattern of the vortices in the rushing river. Such structures often occur as a result of the recursive application of a process. An example of such a process is "Take a line segment, divide it into thirds, and throw away the middle third." Repeated application of this process to each segment produced by the previous one produces the Cantor set, whose dimensionality is log(2)/log(3). Fractals have application to image compression, fluid dynamics, and *chaos theory.

Fractile   Any division of a *distribution into equal units or fractions, such as fifths (*quintiles), tenths (*deciles), or hundredths (*percentiles). See *quantile.

Fractional Factorial Design   An experimental design that is not fully crossed; that is, some of the possible treatment combinations (cells) are omitted. An example is a *nested design configuration. Compare *crossed factor designs, *fully-crossed factor design.

Frame   See *sampling frame.

F Ratio (or Value or Statistic)   The ratio of explained to unexplained variance in an *analysis of variance, that is, the ratio of the *between-group variance to the *within-group variance. Sometimes viewed as a signal-to-noise ratio. To interpret the F ratio, you need to consult a table of F values for a particular level of *statistical significance at the number of *degrees of freedom in your study. Or if you use a statistical package, the software will provide you with a p value based on the F distribution to use in determining statistical significance. Named after Fisher, the inventor of analysis of variance. See *F test.

Freedom From Harm   An ethical principle in social research, stating that participation in the research study will not physically or mentally harm the research participant. See *ethics.

Freedom to Withdraw   An ethical principle in social research, stating that the research participant has the right and is completely free to exit the study at any time without negative judgment or repercussion. See *ethics.

Free Listing   An interview technique in which respondents are asked to list as many examples or characteristics of a phenomenon as they can think of in a limited time (e.g., 10 minutes). They might be asked to name all the types of bad behavior in children they can think of or all the traits of a good candidate for public office and so on. Differences among respondents of different ages, genders, social classes, ethnicities, and so on can often be quite revealing.

Freely Estimated Parameter   In *SEM, model parameters (e.g., path coefficients, error coefficients) can be fixed, constrained, or freely estimated. Freely estimated parameters are those whose values are unconstrained and empirically determined, rather than set by the researcher. Examples are correlations, error variances, structural coefficients, factor variances, and factor loadings to be empirically estimated. Compare *fixed parameter, *constrained parameter.

Frequency   The number of times a particular type of event occurs (such as the number of days it rained last year) or the number of individuals in a given category (such as the number of males under 21 years old who got speeding tickets this month).

Frequency Curve   (a) A smooth curve or *line graph depicting the data in a *frequency polygon. (b) The curve representing a *probability density function.

Frequency Distribution   A tally of the number of times each score occurs in a group of scores. More formally, a way of presenting *data that shows the number of cases having each of the *attributes of a particular *variable.

For example, the frequency distribution of final exam grades in a class of 50 students might be: 8 As, 20 Bs, 19 Cs, 1 D, and 2 Fs. In this example, the variable is final grade; the attributes are A, B, C, D, and F; and the frequencies are 8, 20, 19, 1, and 2. Compare *stem-and-leaf display.

Table F.1 presents a more elaborate frequency distribution of the data for these final exam scores. See the definitions of the various column heads (*class interval, *relative frequency, and so on) for more detail.

Table F.1   Frequency Distribution: Final Examination Grades in a Class of 50 Students

Final Grade	Class Interval	Frequency (f)	Relative Frequency	Cumulative Frequency	Cumulative Relative Frequency
A	90–99	8	.16	50	1.00
B	80–89	20	.40	42	.84
C	70–79	19	.38	22	.44
D	60–69	1	.02	3	.06
F	50–59	2	.04	2	.04

Frequency Function   See *probability density function.

Frequency Polygon   A *line graph connecting the midpoints of the bars of a *histogram.

The frequency polygon in Figure F.3 on page 168 depicts the same data as in Figure H.2 (on page 189) under *histogram.

Frequentism   (a) An approach to studying probability that views probability as the frequency with which events occur in the long run. The approach relies on mathematical and empirical models of how estimators operate over "many"

F

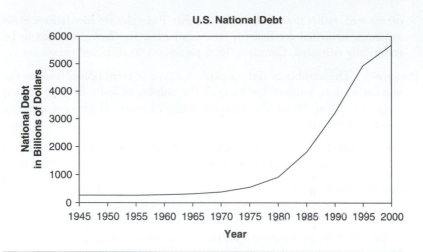

Figure F.3   Frequency Polygon

trials or "all possible trials" or an infinite number of trials (depending on the application). (b) A person who advocates the approach in (a). Frequentist methods are usually contrasted with *Bayesian methods. The primary statistical packages used in much behavioral and social science (e.g., SPSS, SAS, R) rely on *frequentist inference methods, although Bayesian methods are increasingly included in the standard packages.

Frequentist Inference (or Probability)   The most often used approach to statistics in behavioral and social science for conducting *significance tests, *hypothesis tests, and *confidence intervals. The frequentist approach is based on the assumption that a statistic has been calculated an infinite number of times; see the discussion at *sampling distribution. The main alternatives are *Bayesian inference and *resampling methods, such as *bootstrapping.

Friedman Test   A *nonparametric test of *statistical significance for use with *ordinal data from *correlated groups. It is similar to the *Wilcoxon test, but it can be used with more than two groups. It is an extension of the *sign test and is a nonparametric version of a *one-way, *repeated-measures ANOVA.

Friedman Two-Way Analysis of Variance   A *nonparametric alternative to the standard (i.e., parametric) *two-way analysis of variance. The analysis is conducted on ranks rather than on fully quantitative data. The null hypothesis is that the population medians across the groups are equal. The alternative hypothesis is that the population medians are not all equal. The test does not make the assumption of *normality.

F Scale   A measure of the authoritarian personality (F for fascism) created in the aftermath of World War II by T. Adorno and colleagues. Not to be confused with the *F* ratio or *F* test.

F Statistic   See **F* ratio, **F* test.

F Test   A test of the results of a statistical analysis, perhaps most closely associated with, but by no means limited to, *analysis of variance (ANOVA). The *F* test yields an **F* ratio or *F* statistic. This is a ratio of the *between-groups variance (or *explained variance) to the *within-groups variance (or *unexplained variance). To tell whether a particular *F* ratio is statistically significant, one can consult an **F* distribution table. The table approach is less and less frequently used, because computer programs routinely calculate the *F* ratio and report its *observed level of significance (i.e., **p* value). See *analysis of variance for an illustration. When the *F* test is applied to a regression equation, the *null hypothesis is that all the regression coefficients are zero or that *$R^2 = 0$.

Full Multivariate   (form of the *general linear model) The generic name for any general linear model that has two or more continuous dependent variables. A few examples are *canonical correlation, *multivariate analysis of variance, *multivariate analysis of covariance, and *factor analysis. If dependent variables are not continuous, see *generalized linear model.

Fully Crossed Factor Design   See *crossed factor design.

Fully Recursive Model   Said of a *recursive *path analysis model when all the variables are connected by arrows, that is, when they are causally linked. Also called "just-identified model." (See Figure F.4.)

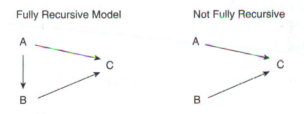

Figure F.4   Fully Recursive Model

Function   (a) A *variable that can be expressed in terms of another variable; also, a variable that varies with another variable. The term is often used loosely, if not very correctly, to mean a *cause. For example, "Learning is a function of time spent studying" means that spending time studying causes learning. The functional relationship can be expressed in an equation: $L = f(T)$, where L stands for learning and T for time spent studying and f means "is a function of."

(b) A mathematical expression of a relation between *independent variables and a *dependent variable; a formula or *equation such as a *regression equation.

(c) A *rule for turning each member of one *set into a member of another set. For example, $y = f(x) = 4x + 2$ says that to convert a number from set X into a number in set Y, you multiply the number (x) times 4 and add 2 to it. Thus, the number 1 in set X would be 6 in set Y, 2 would be 10, 3 would be 14, and so on.

(d) In *set theory, a functional relation exists when each *element, x, in one set, X, is paired with an element y in set Y; this is written $y = f(x)$, meaning "y is a function of x." The set X is called the "domain," and the set Y is called the "range." A function can be plotted on a graph if for every value of x there is exactly one value of y. In the equation $y = f(x)$, Y is the *dependent variable and is plotted on the *y-axis, and X is the *independent variable plotted on the *x-axis.

Functionalism   Short for "structural-functionalism." A perspective on research in sociology and anthropology based on the assumption that social phenomena that are widespread and long-lasting probably fulfill a social function. Hence, to explain a social form (structure), a functionalist will look for its usefulness for maintaining the society. Functionalism is an idea borrowed from anatomy, where the same assumption is made: Anatomical structures are said to exist for a functional reason; the reason that, say, the kidney has the shape (structure) it does is that it could not function (well) otherwise.

For example, a functionalist might study income inequality (the structure) in a society by looking for the ways it was functional for the society as a whole. Perhaps inequality increases motivation and thus stimulates the overall productivity and economic well-being of the society. Compare *conflict theory.

Functional Relationship   A relation that can be expressed in an *equation. Can be *linear or *curvilinear. See *function.

Funnel Plot   In *meta-analysis, a graphic method of detecting *publication bias. The *sample sizes are plotted against the *effect sizes of the studies. If publication bias is absent, the resulting graphic should be close to symmetrical and shaped roughly like a funnel or pyramid. See *file drawer problem.

Fuzzy Set   Said of *sets, or groups of variables, in which the extent of membership in the set is not precise. Since a set is a clearly defined group, a fuzzy set is a group the definition of which is allowed to vary or that can be hard to *operationalize. In "fuzzy logic," truth is viewed as a matter of degree rather than always requiring a binary (true or false) conclusion; this rejects necessary application of the *principle of bivalence. Based on complicated mathematics, fuzzy sets are sometimes used by analogy in the social sciences to discuss variables that are difficult to quantify, such as the degree of democracy in comparative studies of nations' political systems. See *complexity theory.

G   Sometimes short for *gamma.

G^2 Symbol for the *likelihood ratio test of *goodness-of-fit. The larger the sample, the more G^2 tends to approximate the *chi-square distribution. The lower the G^2 for a particular independent variable, the more it contributes to the explanation of the dependent variable.

Gabriel's STP   One of several ways to adjust *significance levels in *multiple or *post hoc comparisons to reduce the chance of *Type I error. STP stands for "simultaneous test procedure." See *Tukey's HSD test.

Gain Scores   See *difference scores.

Gambler's Fallacy   The mistake of treating *independent events as though they were *dependent.

The familiar example has to do with tossing a fair coin by a fair person. If after five consecutive heads you conclude that a sixth toss is more likely to come up tails, you are committing the gambler's fallacy. You are assuming that the sixth toss is dependent on the previous five, when, in fact, each toss is independent of the others.

Or suppose you shuffle an ordinary deck of cards and draw a card from it at random. The card is red (a heart or a diamond). You replace the card, reshuffle the deck, and draw a second card; this too is a red card. You repeat the process and draw a third red card. You commit the gambler's fallacy if you believe that because you drew three red cards in a row, your fourth draw is more likely to be a black card. Because you replaced the card and reshuffled each time, each draw was an independent event; that is, it had no influence on subsequent events (and was not influenced by prior events). On the other hand, had you not replaced the red card each time, that would have made drawing a black card more likely. See *sampling with replacement.

The confusion arises in part from the fact that the best estimate, made before you begin, of your *probability of drawing four red cards in a row is

G

quite low: .0625. But your best estimate of drawing four red cards in a row, given that you have already drawn three and replaced them, is .50. See *geometric distribution.

Games-Howell Post Hoc Test Post hoc adjustment for comparison of pairs of means that adjusts for violations to the assumption of *homogeneity of variances or equal variances. This is a popular test when variances are unequal and group sizes are unequal. This test operates by incorporating group variances and sample sizes into its formulation. Compare *Tamhane's T2, *Dunnett's T3, Dunnett's C adjustments.

Game Theory A branch of mathematics that studies competitive games in which each player wants to figure out the best way to play games given a specified set of rules. The games in question have to be strategic games, that is, not games of pure chance but games based on knowledge, including knowledge of what the other players are likely to know. Game theory has been widely applied as a model of human decision making and action in such fields as economics and military strategy. See *maximin strategy, *minimax strategy, *zero-sum game.

Gamma (Γ, γ) (a) Sometimes called "Goodman and Kruskal's gamma." A *measure of association for *ordinal variables. It is a *symmetric *PRE statistic. Gammas range from −1.0 to +1.0. When calculating gamma, the ranks of the ordered categories are not treated as interval scales. Compare *Spearman's rho. (b) *Euler's constant; it is the basis of the gamma distribution, which can be used to model highly *skewed data.

For example (a), if knowing how a sample of citizens ranked on one variable, such as opinion about gun control (strongly opposed, opposed, in favor, strongly in favor), always enabled you to predict how they would rank on attitude toward the death penalty (strongly opposed, opposed, and so on), the gamma indicating the association between those two variables would be −1.0. But since there are probably people who oppose both gun control and the death penalty, the gamma might be something more like −.80.

Gantt Chart A type of bar chart used to plan projects, especially to schedule tasks and keep track of whether they are being completed on time.

Gap Statistic A statistic for estimating the number of clusters in a *cluster analysis.

Garbage In, Garbage Out See *GIGO.

GARCH Generalized autoregressive conditional heteroscedasticity. GARCH models are used to describe and predict the volatility of financial *time-series data. See *ARIMA.

Gaussian Distribution Another term for *normal distribution.

Gauss-Markov Theorem   A theorem stating that if the *error terms in a *regression analysis are uncorrelated and have equal variances, then the *regression coefficients and *Y-intercept (as determined using the *least squares criterion) are better (i.e., more *efficient) than any other unbiased estimators. In other words, the theorem provides some justification for using the regression coefficients and intercepts that are commonly used in behavioral and social research.

Geisser-Greenhouse (or Greenhouse-Geisser) *F* Test   An *F test that adjusts the critical value upward in a *repeated-measures ANOVA to correct for violations of the *sphericity assumption. (a) One version of this test is the lower-bound adjustment, which produces a larger critical-F value and is relatively conservative. (b) Another version of the test, which is more popular today and is computed by statistical packages such as SAS and SPSS, is the epsilon hat (ε̂) adjustment. It also produces a larger critical-F but not as large as the one produced by the lower-bound adjustment. To the computer user, the result is an adjusted p value (i.e., it will be a little larger to the degree that sphericity is violated, making it a little more difficult to reject the null hypothesis). Another adjustment procedure designed to improve on the epsilon hat adjustment is the *Huynh-Feldt correction.

Geisteswissenschaften   German for "human sciences" (literally, "spiritual" or "mental" sciences), including the social and behavioral sciences as well as the humanities. The term has mostly been used in contrast to the natural sciences (*Naturwissenschaften*). Classic debates about research methods in Germany in the 19th and 20th centuries centered around the question of whether these two broad categories of science can or should use the same or different methods. Advocates of the distinctiveness of the human sciences were among the most important early critics of *positivism. See *Verstehen.

Gender   (a) As a variable, gender can be a synonym for "sex," one that some researchers consider more polite or correct. (b) Gender can also refer to the socially constructed (as opposed to biologically given) roles, attitudes, beliefs, and behaviors that society expects of women and men.

General Effect   The impact of a *variable on another that does not take into account differences among groups. See *effect. Compare *conditional effect, *interaction effect.

For example, graduating from college improves average earnings for all (general effects), but it does so more for some groups (conditional effects).

Generalizability   The extent to which you can come to conclusions about one thing (often, a *population) based on information about another (often, a *sample). Compare *external validity, *inferential statistics.

For example, when a national burger restaurant wants to see whether a new sandwich will sell, it promotes the sandwich in a few communities that are

G

assumed to be representative of the nation. If that assumption is correct, the company can accurately generalize from the sales figures in the handful of communities to how the new product will sell in the rest of the country.

Generalizability Coefficient   An index of reliability used in *generalizability theory, ranging from 0 to 1, indicating how reliably a score would occur in randomly selected settings and situations with different people in the universe of generalization. It's an *intraclass coefficient and index of score variance in the universe of scores relative to *error variance.

Generalizability Theory   An alternate way to estimate *reliability suggested by Cronbach; it identifies the different sources of *error in a measure rather than simply estimating the total error. The procedures for doing this are complicated, which might be why most researchers continue to estimate reliability using simpler statistics, such as *Cronbach's (same statistician) alpha.

Generalization   (a) A statement covering all the members of some group or class. (b) The process of coming to such a conclusion by *inference; the inference is usually *inductive. See *external validity.

   Few issues are as central or as controversial in the social and behavioral sciences as the characteristics of (true or probable) generalizations and the best methods of arriving at them. See *theory.

Generalized Least Squares (GLS)   An alternative estimation procedure (e.g., to the use of *ordinary least squares) in *regression analysis; it is used when there is a nonrandom pattern to the *error terms, specifically, *heteroscedasticity and *autocorrelation. When these problems are present, GLS is more *efficient (b) than *OLS.

Generalized Linear Models   Statistical techniques used when certain assumptions of the *general linear model are not met, as when the dependent variable is not continuous and not distributed normally. These nongeneral features of the dependent variable are general*ized,* often by logistic *transformations. In this context, transformations of the dependent variable are called *link functions; they specify how the dependent variable is to be modeled. *Logistic regression and *log-linear models are examples; so are *probit models.

Generalized Maximum Likelihood Ratio Test   A statistic formed by comparing the *maximum likelihood of drawing a particular *sample if a particular hypothesis were true to the maximum likelihood of drawing that sample if that hypothesis were not true.

General Linear Model (GLM)   A statistical model (most easily shown with matrix algebra) with a set of statistical *assumptions that includes many special cases such as *regression, *correlation, *analysis of variance, and *analysis of covariance. In the *simple multivariate form, the full range of methods used to study the *linear relations between one continuous dependent variable and one or more independent variables, whether continuous or categorical. It also can model curved relationships between Y and X variables by including transformed variables. The model is "general" in that the kind of independent variable is not specified. Once the independent variable(s) is specified, the particular special case will be known; for example, having two categorical independent variables is the special case commonly known as *two-way ANOVA. A convenient way to classify general linear models is into three forms: (1) the bivariate form, which has a single continuous dependent variable and a single independent variable requiring a single vector (i.e., a continuous independent variable or a dichotomous independent variable); (2) the *simple multivariate form; and (3) the *full multivariate form.

The basic idea is that the relation between a dependent variable and the independent variables can be expressed as a linear equation containing a *term for the weighted sum of the values of the independent variables—plus a term for everything that we do not know about, which is called an *error term. The method used to decide how much weight to give to the independent variable(s) is the *least squares criterion. Despite its name, *polynomial regression analysis is a special case of the GLM. That's because the word "linear" in general linear model technically means *inherently linear,* and many nonlinear (e.g., *curvilinear regression) and multiplicative relations (*interaction effects) are easily transformed into an inherently linear model.

You can get a good practical feel for the general linear model by spending a few hours calculating by hand standard deviations, Pearson correlations, regression equations, t tests, and F tests. You will quickly discover that many of the steps in these calculations are generally the same.

General Rule of Addition in Probability   See *addition rule.

General Social Survey (GSS)   An annual or biannual survey of a representative sample of (about 1,500) American adults conducted by the National Opinion Research Center. Respondents are asked numerous questions about their backgrounds and their opinions about many social and political issues. The results of these surveys are available to, and are widely used by, other researchers for *secondary analyses.

General Systems Theory   See *systems theory.

Generation Effects   The effects on individuals of growing up in or being members of the same generation or age group. See *cohort effects.

GenStat   Short for GENeral STATistics, a statistical package used especially by researchers working with biological and environmental statistics.

Geographic Information System (GIS)   A computer system (hardware and software) for collecting, storing, and analyzing spatially organized data, such

G

as populations in geographic areas. It has been used to classify areas by, and to identify concentrations of, most social characteristics.

Geometric Distribution   A *probability distribution of the number of *failures before the first *success in a series of trials, each with only two possible outcomes (*Bernoulli trials). See *Pascal distribution.

For example, Table G.1 gives the probability of getting tails on the first, second, and additional flips of a coin and of getting a heart on the first, second, and additional draws (with *replacement) from an ordinary deck of cards. Consulting the table, you can conclude, for instance, that only about 3% of the time would you need five flips of a coin to get a tail. Only about 8% of the time would you need to draw five cards before getting a heart. In these two examples, as with all geometric distributions, the most probable number of trials (before obtaining the first success) is always 1.

Table G.1   Geometric Distribution: Probability of Getting the First Success on Each Trial

Trial	Tails	Heart
1	.50	.25
2	.25	.1875
3	.125	.1406
4	.0625	.1055
5	.03125	.0791

Geometric Mean   See *mean.

Geostatistics   Branch of statistics in geology, earth science, geography, epidemiology, and other interdisciplinary areas interested in the interconnection of time, space, place, natural/physical reality, and other environmental variables for understanding and making sense of our complex and dynamic world.

GFI   See *goodness-of-fit index.

Giga   A prefix indicating a multiple of 10,000,000,000; thus, a gigabyte is 10,000,000,000 bytes.

GIGO   Short for "garbage in, garbage out." A brutal way of putting an undeniable principle: No matter how good your computer and your statistical analysis package, if you put poor *data (data that are neither *reliable nor *valid) into your computer, it will give you poor results.

Gini Index (or Coefficient)   A measure of inequality or dispersion in a group of values, such as income inequality in a population. It ranges from 0 to 1, with larger coefficients indicating greater dispersion or inequality. It is calculated by taking the mean difference between all pairs of values and dividing the result by 2 times the population mean. The Gini statistic is derived from the *Lorenz curve. Sometimes called the "coefficient of concentration" or "Gini ratio."

Glass's Delta A standardized measure of *effect size used in research and *meta-analysis; it is a mean-difference measure that standardizes using the standard deviation of the control group. Compare *Cohen's *d*, *Hedges's *g*.

Glejser Test A test statistic used to detect *heteroscedasticity in the *residuals of a *regression equation. See *Goldfeld-Quandt test.

GLIM Generalized Linear Interactive Modeling, a *statistical package.

GLM Abbreviation for the *general linear model *and* for *generalized linear models.

Global Sometimes used to mean general or pertaining to all variables; not necessarily having anything to do with a sphere or a worldwide phenomenon.

GLS *Generalized least squares estimation.

GNI *Gross national income.

GNP *Gross national product.

Gödel's Proof (or Goedel's Incompleteness Theorem) A theorem published by Kurt Gödel in 1931 proving that for logical systems (systems based on axioms, theorems, and rules of inference) satisfying certain broad criteria, it is impossible to establish their completeness and consistency. There are two versions of the theorem. The first says that within a system there will be true theorems that cannot be proven. The second says that if a system has a theorem stating that the system is consistent, then it is not consistent. Philosophically, the incompleteness theorem negatively impacted the efforts of logicians such as Bertrand Russell to establish arithmetic as a form of logic. Gödel showed that there were statements, in particular "This statement cannot be proven," that, if true, could not be proven or, if false, could be proven but were not true. In either case, the logical system in which the statement was made was incomplete or inconsistent. Practically speaking, Gödel's proof is sometimes taken to suggest that we can never have certainty in our knowledge because axioms have to be assumed and even logical systems lead to contradictions. Compare *Heisenberg's uncertainty principle.

Going Native In anthropological or *qualitative research, especially *participant observation, said of investigators who lose their *objectivity and essentially become members of the culture they are studying. Participant observation requires that researchers become members of the groups they are studying—at least to *some* extent. Controversy and difficult judgments occur when trying to specify to *what* extent.

Goldfeld-Quandt Test One of several statistical tests to detect *heteroscedasticity in the *residuals of a *regression equation.

Gold Standard   Used loosely to mean the best, state-of-the-art methods for research problems. Perhaps most often used to refer to *randomized clinical trials as the gold standard for showing cause and effect. Ironically, in monetary policy, where the term originated, the gold standard is recognized as ineffective and has long been abandoned by all major nations.

Gompertz Curves   Growth curves that are shaped like an elongated letter *S*, moving left to right on a graph. The curve describes a growth rate that is initially small, increases for a time, and then levels off. Compare *J curve.

Goodman and Kruskal's Gamma   See *gamma.

Goodman and Kruskal's Lambda   See *lambda (b).

Goodman and Kruskal's Tau   A measure of association for categorical variables. It is a *PRE measure.

Goodness-of-Fit   How well a *model, a theoretical distribution, or an *equation matches actual *data. See *goodness-of-fit test.

   For example, in *regression analysis, the question is: How closely does the *regression line (formed of the *predicted Y values) come to summarizing the observed scores? The *coefficient of determination, or R^2, is a measure of the goodness-of-fit for a regression line. In the graph in Figure G.1, line A fits the data better (is "gooder") than line B.

Goodness-of-Fit Index (GFI)   A statistic used in *structural equation modeling to indicate model fit. It is an absolute-fit index, ranging from 0 to 1, indicating the proportion of covariances in the sample data matrix that are explained by

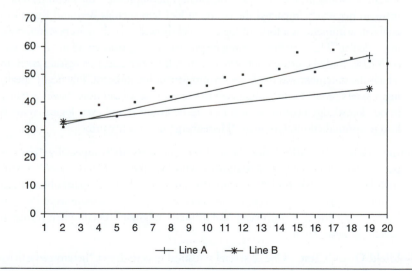

Figure G.1   Goodness-of-Fit

G

the model. Close model fit is indicated by GFI greater than or equal to .90. Because GFI is heavily influence by the sample size, this index is not currently recommended for use by itself.

Goodness-of-Fit Test A statistical test to see whether a model fits a set of data or whether the observed data match a theoretical expectation. The most commonly used test is the *chi-square test: The bigger the chi-square statistic, the poorer the fit; the smaller the better. That is because a small chi-square statistic indicates a small difference between the model and the data. The *likelihood ratio test is also used as a measure of goodness-of-fit. See also *Kolmogorov-Smirnov test.

For example, say a researcher wants to know if bankruptcies are randomly distributed throughout the year. The theoretical distribution in this case would be equal probability; the *expected frequency would be that 1/12 of the bankruptcies occur in each month (with slight adjustments for the longer and shorter months).

Good-Subject Role Research participants' behavior attempting to support the researcher's hypotheses and other *demand characteristics. Compare *apprehensive-subject role, *faithful-subject role, *negative-subject role.

Google Scholar An online reference tool for finding sources by author and/or topic. Unlike similar reference tools it is available for free to anyone with an Internet connection and is used increasingly by many researchers, including by scholars of scholarship. Some controversy exists as to whether its quality is as high as more established and specialized citation indices.

Graeco-Latin Square An extension of the *Latin square method of allocating *treatments in a *within-subjects *factorial experiment. The extension is done by adding a different Greek letter to the Latin letter in each cell. As with the Latin square method, the goal is to *counterbalance *order effects.

Grand Mean The mean of the means (or simply the mean of all of the data) on the *dependent variable. In *analysis of variance, the *between-group variance indicates variation of group means relative to the grand mean.

Granger Causality Techniques in *regression analysis of *time-series data in economics to investigate whether variables that are statistically associated are causally related. The method involves taking into account the fact that causes do not operate instantaneously; they take time, and these time lags are incorporated into the model. See *cause, *confounded, *lurking variable.

Graph A diagram showing the values of a *variable or showing a relationship between variables. For examples, see *bar graph, *curvilinear relation, *histogram, *frequency polygon, and *correlation coefficient.

Graphic Rating Scale A *rating scale that includes visual/graphical information such as a numbered line (e.g., 1 to 5; 0 to 10) with endpoints labeled and sometimes additional points labeled or "anchored." A graphic rating scale can be used with a single item, or multiple dimensions to be rated can be included as rows under the graphic rating scale. An example is shown in Figure G.2.

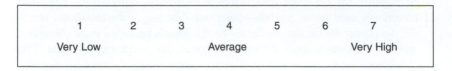

| 1 | 2 | 3 | 4 | 5 | 6 | 7 |
| Very Low | | | Average | | | Very High |

Figure G.2   Graphic Rating Scale

Grid Sampling   A form of *cluster sampling in which the clusters are the areas marked off by a grid, such as map coordinates. It is increasingly common to use GPS (global positioning system) technology to identify the areas.

Gross   The amount before any deductions. For example, gross income is income before deducting expenses. Compare *net.

Gross National Income (GNI)   The total of a nation's earnings from all sources in a year. It is a common method of calculating the same information as the *gross national product. By definition, GNI and GNP are identical.

Gross National Product (GNP)   The total value of a nation's output of goods and services in a year. It is a frequent *indicator of a nation's economic health. See *gross national income.

Grounded Theory   A method for inductively generating and constructing an explanatory theory based on data (usually qualitative data). The theory usually grows out of extensive interviewing and direct observation in a *natural or *nonexperimental setting. The term is used loosely to mean any theory based on (grounded in) data. Although the idea of inductively generating explanations goes back to at least Aristotle's time, grounded theory as a formal research method is usually viewed as starting with the sociologists Barney Glaser and Anselm Strauss and their 1967 book *The Discovery of Grounded Theory: Strategies for Qualitative Research.* Both the method and the conclusions reached by using it are labeled "grounded theory," as in "Grounded theory was used to produce this grounded theory." See *a posteriori, *inductive.

Grouped Data   Data recorded as number of cases in each *class interval. Compare *raw data, *aggregate

Group Effect   The influence on individuals of being members of one group rather than another, such as the effect on one's earnings of being female. See *contextual effects, *t test, *analysis of variance.

Grouping   Another term for *collapsing.

Group Matching   Used to equate comparison groups so that they have a similar frequency and the same mean on one or more *extraneous variables. In contrast, *individual matching identifies similar individual pairs to be assigned to each group. Compare *individual matching.

Group Randomized Trial   A method in which groups, not individuals, are assigned randomly to experimental or control conditions. All individuals in each group receive the same condition. For example, if 40 university classes were the sample in which a new teaching technology were to be tested, and the researchers randomly selected 20 of these classrooms to use the new technology and the other 20 continued to use standard methods, this would be a case of a group randomized trial. Note that statistical adjustments are necessary when using this common method of randomizing rather than individual randomization. Compare *quasi-experiment, *cluster randomizing data.

Growth Curve Analysis   (also called **Growth Curve Modeling**) Statistical methods for studying development over time, originally for uncovering trajectories in the biological development of individuals. Also called "latent curve models" and "latent trajectory models." The models are developed using either *multilevel modeling or *structural equation modeling. See *time series, *longitudinal studies.

GSS   *General Social Survey.

Guttman Scaling   A method of scale construction created by Louis Guttman. Although he originally designed it to be used after the data were collected to see if the items in an *index could be arranged as a *scale, that is, in the order of the strength of the items, he also used it for scale construction. For example, national surveys often ask questions about abortion roughly as follows:

Do you favor a woman's right to have an abortion if

1. having the baby would threaten her life?

2. the fetus is deformed?

3. she is too poor to care for the child properly?

4. she does not want any more children?

If these items form a Guttman scale, the vast majority of people who answer the questions will do so in a scalar pattern: People who say yes to question number 4 will also say yes to questions 3, 2, and 1; those who say yes to number 3 will also say yes to 2 and 1, but not necessarily to 4, and so on. If these items do not form a scale, there will be no pattern to the answers: People who say yes to number 4 will be as likely as not to say no to numbers 3, 2, and 1. See *Bogardus social distance scale.

H   The usual symbol for the statistic computed for the *Kruskal-Wallis test of statistical significance.

H_0 Symbol for the *null hypothesis.

H_1 A symbol for the *alternative hypothesis.

h^2 Symbol for the *communality of an item (or indicator or variable) in a *factor analysis.

H_a A symbol for the *alternative hypothesis. See *research hypothesis.

Hadoop   An open source software for storing, sharing, and processing *big data with multiple users.

Halo Bias (or Effect)   A tendency of judges to overrate a performance because the subject did well in an earlier rating or when rated in a different area. Also used to mean the tendency to make more favorable judgments about physically attractive people, an effect that has been studied in areas such as job performance ratings and sentencing of convicted criminals.

For example, say a student has taken two courses from a professor and has done exceptionally well in each. In a third course, she writes an ordinary paper. This paper might receive a higher grade than it deserves because the student's earlier good work creates a halo effect.

Hanning   A technique for *smoothing data in a *trend line. You can smooth time-series data using the Hanning function. Compare *running medians, *moving average.

Haphazard Sampling   A nonsystematic, nonrandom sampling method based on ease and convenience of selection. It produces *biased samples, rather than *representative samples. See *convenience sampling.

Hard Sciences   Natural sciences, especially physics and chemistry. Often contrasted with soft sciences such as psychology, sociology, political science, and

H

economics. Some scholars think this distinction indicates a real difference; others dismiss it as mere "physics envy." If one views "hardness" as using quantitative research methods, then economics and psychology are harder sciences because they have used these methods longer than the sciences such as sociology, anthropology, and political science. Another view of "hardness" is the degree to which a discipline reduces its explanations to the kind found in the hard sciences; for example, neuropsychology and biological psychology would be relatively hard in this sense. Many researchers studying qualitative data have no desire to be hard scientists and prefer to be practitioners of the human sciences. Compare *verstehen, *geisteswissenschaften.

Hardware   In computer jargon, the physical components of a computer; the machine without any operating instructions or *software.

Harmonic Mean   A *measure of central tendency used mainly in comparing average rates. See *mean for details.

Hartley F$_{max}$ Test   Synonym for *Hartley's test.

Hartley's Test   A measure of the *equality of variances of several populations. The *null hypothesis is that the samples come from populations with equal variances. When using this test to check for the *assumption of equality of variances in an *analysis of variance, the assumption is satisfied when the null is not rejected (i.e., is retained). See *Box's test.

Hartley Test for Homogeneity of Variance   Synonym for *Hartley's test.

Hash   Short fluctuations in *time-series data.

Hawthorne Effect (or Reactivity)   A tendency for subjects of research to change their behavior simply because they are being studied. So called because the classic study in which this behavior was discovered was in the Hawthorne plant in Illinois. In this study, workers improved their output regardless of changes in their working conditions. Compare *John Henry effect. See *artifact.

Hazard   (a) Sometimes used to mean chance or *probability. (b) A cause of possible loss. The word comes from Arabic for a dice game. Compare *survival analysis.

Hazard Function   A measure of how likely an individual is to experience an event (death, illness, etc.) given the age of the individual and given that the individual has not yet experienced the event. Originally developed in medical research, this measure of *risk is used more broadly now. Compare *survival function.

Hazard Plot   Plot where the horizontal axis is time and the vertical axis is rate or cumulative hazard or probability. The plotted function shows the hazard rates (e.g., deaths) across time. For example, in *survival analysis one might create a functional plot with mortality rate on the Y axis and age on the X axis to show changes over age.

Hazard Rate   An estimate of the probability of failure of a system or of a component over time. Also called "hazard ratio." See *hazard function.

Hedges's _g_   A standardized measure of *effect size used in research and *meta-analysis; it is a mean-difference measure that standardizes using the pooled standard deviation of the control and experimental groups. Compare *Cohen's _d,_ *Glass's delta.

Heisenberg Uncertainty Principle   We cannot simultaneously measure the position and momentum of a particle (e.g., an electron) at any single point in time. Because we cannot measure properties of a particle without affecting it, we cannot know (we must be uncertain about) what it might be like without our interference, when we are not studying it. The idea is that as we increase our precision of measurement of one property in a pair (such as position and momentum), our precision of measurement of the other property decreases. This is a principle of quantum reality, but it has been extended by some writers to very different areas and methods of research, such as *participant observation.

Helmert Contrast   A comparison technique in *analysis of variance in which the mean of each level of a *factor (*categorical variable) is tested against the mean of the remaining levels.

Helsinki Declaration   Ethical principles for research, especially research involving human subjects. An extension of principles first importantly codified in the *Nuremberg code.

Herfindahl Index   A measure of concentration or control or dominance, usually of firms in a sector of the economy. A low value indicates that there are many firms in relation to the industry (industry is not very concentrated), and a high value indicates high concentration or dominance or control by one (monopoly) or a few (oligopoly) firms in the industry or economic sector. Often used as a measure of competition (or lack thereof). Compare *Gini index.

Hermeneutics   A philosophical theory of interpretation, originally of written texts and especially of biblical passages, but now used more broadly. Most significantly developed and used in Germany. Compare *_Verstehen_.

Heterogeneous   Generally, mixed or diverse. Used to describe *samples and *populations with high *variability. See *variance, *standard deviation.

Heteroscedasticity   Heteroscedasticity is present when the variance of the dependent variable, _Y,_ is not constant at the different levels of the independent variable; alternatively stated, it is present when the error variance is not constant at the different levels of the independent variable. Comes from _hetero-,_ meaning other or different, and _scedasticity,_ meaning tendency to scatter. Heteroscedasticity violates the *assumption of *homoscedasticity or *equality of variances. This violation, if serious enough, compels the use of *nonparametric statistics

H

or use of data *transformations or more advanced estimation procedures (e.g., *generalized least squares, *weighted least squares).

Although there are statistical tests to detect heteroscedasticity, it is common to check for it using scatter diagrams, such as Figure H.1. The pattern of points shows that the variances (departures from the line) for the dependent variable are very similar (*homo-*) at the low levels of the independent variable (years of experience), but the distances from the line are quite different (*hetero-*) at its upper levels. Another popular graph used to look for heteroscedasticity is one with *standardized residuals as the vertical (Y) variable and *predicted Y as the horizontal (X) variable—you look to see if the width changes for different values of predicted Y.

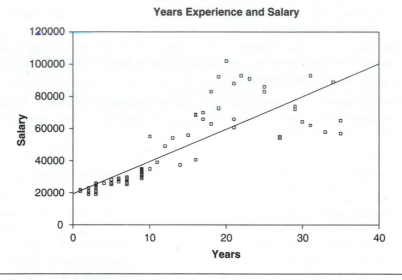

Figure H.1   Heteroscedasticity

Heterotrait-Heteromethod Coefficient   In a *multitrait-multimethod matrix, this coefficient indicates the strength of correlation between two tests that are different on both traits and methods of measurement. For example, it might be the correlation between self-esteem measured with a 10-item *summated scale with self-efficacy measured with an observational rating scale.

Heterotrait-Monomethod Coefficient   In a *multitrait-multimethod matrix, this coefficient indicates the strength of correlation between two tests that are different on traits but not methods of measurement. For example, it might be the correlation between self-esteem measured with a *summated scale with self-efficacy also measured with a summated scale.

Heuristic   (a) Generally, instructive or pedagogical. (b) Having to do with methods that aid learning by exploratory or trial-and-error methods; said of a *computer program that can learn from its mistakes (by eliminating trials that do not work) and/or that can teach people how to use the program by learning from their mistakes. (c) A rule of thumb; a procedure for making decisions. Compare *algorithm.

Heuristic Assumption   An *assumption made more because it is useful for teaching or research purposes than because it is believed to be true.

Heywood Case   Situation in *SEM or *factor analysis where a standardized loading (*path coefficient), a correlation, or a commonality is greater than one or the error variance is negative. Often caused by incorrect model *specification, multicollinearity, extraction of too many factors, and/or an insufficient sample size.

Hexadecimal Notation   A number system that uses the ten digits 0–9 and the six letters A–F. It is useful in computer programming.

Hierarchical Clustering   Methods for generating clusters (i.e., groups of similar cases on designated variables) in *cluster analysis. Hierarchical clustering includes both the "bottom-up" approach known as *agglomerative clustering and the "top-down" approach known as *divisive clustering.

Hierarchical Linear Models (HLM)   Statistical models; alternatives to single-equation *OLS regression models. The key idea is that in contrast to traditional regression models, which analyze data at one level of analysis, HLM models allow for the variance in the dependent variable to be analyzed and partitioned at more than one level. They are often used when data are found in *nested variables.

For example, in many education studies, students are nested within classrooms, and the classrooms are nested within schools. Part of the variability in performance on an educational intervention might be due to the intervention or control condition being implemented by different teachers/classrooms and by different schools/cultures. Variability in performance created by such nesting can be analyzed using HLM. Some variables can show different impacts depending on how they are analyzed. Typically, HLM models have either two or three levels of nesting. So, for example, we might look at schools within districts and districts within states.

Also called *multilevel modeling (MLM), "covariance components models," "Bayesian linear models," and, mostly by economists, "random coefficients models." HLM is widely incorporated into software used for these analytic techniques, and as is frequently the case, the techniques are commonly referred to by the brand name of the software. "Multilevel modeling" is probably the most generic term. Other software packages—such as SAS, SPSS, and R—also are used for HLM analysis.

Hierarchical Models   Two or more models arranged so that each higher model contains all the components of the next lower model plus at least one additional component. See *multilevel models.

Hierarchical Regression Analysis   (a) A method of regression analysis in which *independent variables or *blocks of independent variables are entered into the regression equation in a sequence specified by the researcher in advance.

The hierarchy (order of the variables) is determined by the researcher's theoretical understanding of the relations among the variables (e.g., perhaps the variables are meaningfully divided into a block of background variables and a block of cognitive-processing variables). Hierarchical techniques are contrasted with *simultaneous regression (where all the independent variables are entered at the same time as one *block or set). Hierarchical analysis is also contrasted with *stepwise regression, in which the order of entry of the independent variables is determined by a computer program according to a criterion (for example, the *semipartial correlation of each independent variable with the dependent variable). Hierarchical and simultaneous regression are used in explanatory and predictive research, but stepwise is used only for predictive research and, in particular, for the purpose of *variable selection. None of these techniques should be confused with *hierarchical linear models, which deal with nested variables.

(b) A type of *regression model that assumes that when a higher order *interaction term is included, all the lower order terms (*main effects) are also included.

Higher Order ANOVA   An ANOVA with three or more *independent variables.

Higher Order Factor   A general factor or dimension that is said to incorporate or explain lower order factors. For example, general intelligence is believed to incorporate multiple subtypes (lower level) of intelligence.

Higher Order Interaction Effects   Interaction effects between more than two *independent variables. See *first-order interaction effect.

Whenever a *factorial experiment has more than two *factors or independent variables, higher order interactions are possible, and the number of possible interactions increases rapidly as the number of factors increases.

Higher Order Partials (or Correlations)   Fully, "higher order partial correlations." Correlations that *control for more than one *variable in a complex, *multivariate relationship. A *zero-order correlation controls for no other variables; a *first-order partial controls for one, a second-order correlation for two, and so on. All beyond the first order are higher order. Compare *partial relation.

For example, when computing a correlation between persons' education levels and their incomes, a researcher might wish to control for other variables that could influence the relationship between education and income. If three variables were controlled (e.g., age, sex, and ethnicity), the correlation would be a higher order (third-order) partial correlation.

High-Level Language   *Software for programming computers. The programmer writes programs in the high-level language, which then "translates" the program into language that the machine (*hardware) can understand. For example BASIC, C, COBOL, and FORTRAN are relatively high-level languages, and an assembler is a lower "machine" language that communicates in zeros and ones. High-level languages are easier to work with. One can view programs such as

Windows, Word, SPSS, and SAS as being very high-level languages in which the user has to do very little to get the computer to do a lot of processing.

Highspread   The range of values between the *median and the highest value in a *distribution. Compare *lowspread.

Hill's Criteria for Causality   A set of criteria elaborated by the epidemiologist Austin Bradford Hill sometimes applied in the social sciences, particularly when social scientists are studying health-related issues. When the criteria (Hill called them "considerations") are met, one can have greater confidence that a causal inference is true. See *cause.

The criteria, briefly, are these: The cause always precedes the effect; a consistent relation exists between the presumed cause and effect; a strong statistical association exists between the two; the presumed causal relation is very specific; the relation is plausible and coherent in light of current knowledge of the variables and theories of their functioning; and the causal relation can be reproduced in laboratory experiments.

Hinge   The point in a *distribution that divides the scores at the 1/4–3/4 mark. The lower hinge is the score at the 25th *percentile, that is, the point in a distribution above which 3/4 of the scores are located. The upper hinge (at the 75th percentile) is the point with 1/4 of the scores above it and 3/4 below it. See *exploratory data analysis, *box-and-whisker diagram, *five-number summary.

Histogram   A graph with frequency shown by the height of contiguous bars, used for *variables measured at the *interval and *ratio levels (see Figure H.2). Because the data in a histogram are interval or ratio, the bars should touch; in a *bar graph for *nominal or *ordinal data, the bars do not touch.

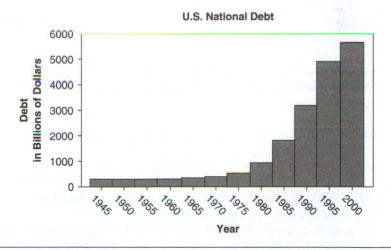

Figure H.2   Histogram

Historical Prospective Study   Somewhat of an oxymoron ("historical prospective"), but the label is used to refer to a longitudinal design in which some or all of the data are from the past. It is a *longitudinal study in form, but data already collected from the past are located and used in constructing the study.

Historical Sciences   Disciplines in which *cause and *effect are separated by relatively long periods—including, but not limited to, topics taught in traditional history courses.

   For example, geology is a historical science; the formation of continents takes millions of years. On the other hand, while chemical reactions occur over time, the amounts of time are usually very small by human standards, so chemistry is not considered a historical science. In psychology, personality development, which takes years, could be thought of as a historical science; perception, which takes milliseconds, would not be. Compare *longitudinal study.

Historicism   (a) The original form of *cultural relativism stressing that different eras can be understood *only* in their own terms. Like the strong form of *relativism, it can lead its adherents to doubt all claims to knowledge. Compare *anachronism. (b) Search for historical laws to use in predicting the future. (c) Historical reductionism, that is, the belief that the explanation of every event boils down to the impact of its historical development; descriptive accounts of history provide a sufficient explanation of all events (sociological, economic, psychological phenomena are determined by history).

Historigram   A line-graph used with time-series data. The horizontal or X axis is time, and the vertical or Y axis is the dependent or outcome variable of interest. For example, the X axis might be years 1950 to 2015 and the Y axis might be GNP. This is the standard plot used to show the pattern of data over time.

History Effect   An event that intervenes in the course of one's research and makes it difficult, if not impossible, to interpret the relations among *independent and *dependent variables. Usually listed among *threats to validity, especially *internal validity. See *extraneous variable, *confounding variable.

   Suppose a city government begins an experiment with sensitivity training (*independent variable) to improve intergroup relations (*dependent variable) among its employees. Using a *one-group pretest-posttest design, attitudes are measured before the training begins and are to be measured again after 10 weeks. In the 9th week, a dramatic event occurs that could influence subjects' attitudes (such as a race riot or a controversial affirmative action ruling). Any pre-to-post differences in attitudes measured after the 10th week of training could be due to the training, or the training effects might have been affected by the event (the history); there is no way to tell.

   History effects are not necessarily dramatic. In fact, they are perhaps more of a problem when they are less striking and can more easily go unnoticed.

History effects are a potential threat to validity for any nonlaboratory study that lasts more than a few hours.

HLM   *Hierarchical linear modeling or models.

Hochberg Test   A modification of the Bonferroni adjustment technique for multiple statistical tests (e.g., *multiple comparisons). It involves ordering the null hypotheses for the various comparisons according to their *p values. You check the largest p value and compare it with alpha. If it is statistically significant then the remaining p values are significant. If it is not statistically significant, then check the hypothesis with the second highest p value and compare it with a critical value of alpha divided by the number of tests minus 1. If this is statistically significant, then the remaining hypotheses are significant. If it is not statistically significant, then move to the next hypothesis with the next largest p value and compare it to a critical value of alpha divided by the number of tests minus 2. Continue this process (increasing the subtraction by an increment of one each time) until determining which null hypotheses can be rejected or not. Compare *Bonferroni technique, *Holm's procedure.

Hold Constant   (a) To "subtract" the effects of a *variable from a complex relationship so as to study what that relationship would be if the variable were in fact a *constant. Holding a variable constant essentially means assigning it an average value. See *control for and *partial out, which are equivalent expressions for the same mathematical operations. (b) Another way to hold a potentially confounding variable constant is to conduct the research with participants of only one type on the potentially confounding variable; one could, for example, conduct the research only with females (or only with males) if gender is a potentially confounding variable. The problem with this strategy, however, is that it decreases *external validity.

For example (a), in a study of managerial behaviors and their effects on workers' productivity, a researcher might want to hold the education of the managers constant. This would especially be the case if she had reason to believe that different kinds or amounts of education might lead managers to behave differently. The dependent variable in this example would be worker productivity, type of managerial behavior would be the categorical variable of interest, and education level of manager would be the independent variable controlled for. An *analysis of covariance or *regression would be used for this statistical analysis.

Holism   An *assumption that groups, collectivities, or wholes can be more than, or different from, the sum of their individual parts. This leads to an approach to research that stresses studying wholes or complete systems, rather than analyzing individual parts. Compare *reductionism, *methodological individualism.

For example, a holist might say that an organization, such as General Motors, exists independently of the individuals who work for or own it. After all of the individuals who today own or work for General Motors quit, retire, die, or sell their stock, the corporation could still exist—as long as those people were replaced by others. Since General Motors is not just the sum of its parts, it makes sense, holists would say, to talk of GM "wanting," "planning," "deciding," and so on. Such desires, plans, and decisions are not reducible merely to those of individuals.

Holm's Procedure   A modification of the *Bonferroni adjustment technique for multiple statistical tests (e.g., *multiple comparisons). It involves ordering the null hypotheses for the various comparisons according to their *p values. You check the smallest p value first and see if it is less than alpha divided by the number of comparisons (α/n). (If you use an alpha of .05 and want to conduct up to 5 tests, then the critical point is $.05/5 = .01$.) If it is not, then testing stops; but if it is, then the first null hypothesis is rejected, and the researcher moves to the next smallest p value and its null hypothesis. In this second stage, however, one uses $\alpha/(n-1)$ as the rejection point. (This time the critical point would be $.05/(5-1) = .05/4 = .0125$.) If the second p value is not less than $\alpha/(n-1)$, then testing stops; but if it is, then the second null hypothesis is rejected, and one proceeds to the third smallest p value and uses $\alpha/(n-2)$ as the cutoff point. (This time, the rejection point will be $.05/3 = .017$.) This process continues until either a nonsignificant finding is reached or the last null hypothesis has been rejected. This procedure is less conservative than the traditional Bonferroni adjustment technique. Also called the "Bonferroni-Holm procedure." Compare *Hochberg Test.

Homogeneity of Regression   Synonym for *homogeneity of slopes.

Homogeneity of Slopes Assumption   In a traditional *analysis of covariance, the researcher desires to interpret the main effect for the categorical independent variable. When this is the case, the categorical variable should not interact with the covariate because interpretation would be difficult if not impossible. To test the assumption, simply make sure the interaction effect is not statistically significant.

Homogeneity of Variance-Covariance Matrices Assumption   An assumption required when conducting *multivariate analysis of variance. In *MANOVA there is a grouping *independent variable and multiple quantitative *dependent variables. In MANOVA, the homogeneity of variance-covariance assumption states that the different groups constituting the independent variable have equivalent *variance-covariance matrices. This means the *covariances among the same dependent variables are equal for the different groups, and the variances for the same dependent variables are equal for the different groups. It's the multivariate analog of *homogeneity of variances or *homoscedasticity. The assumption is tested using *Box's test.

H

Homogeneity of Variances   An assumption that populations from which samples have been drawn have equal variances. If this assumption is not true, *test statistics cannot be trusted. If violated, one can use adjustment tests such as *Tamhane's T2, *Dunnett's T3, *Games-Howell, and *Dunnett's C. Also called the *equality of variance assumption and homoscedasticity assumption. See *homoscedasticity and, for an illustration, *heteroscedasticity.

Homogeneous   Generally, the same or similar. Used to refer to *populations and *samples that have low *variability. Compare *heterogeneous.

Homoscedasticity   Assumption that the error term has a constant variance across each of the levels of the independent variable or predicted y. It is one of the key *GLM assumptions and applies to techniques such as *regression analysis, *ANOVA, and *ANCOVA. It is also called *equality of variances assumption. The word comes from *homo-*, meaning the same or equal, and *scedasticity*, meaning tendency to scatter (skedaddle?). *Parametric statistical tests usually assume *homoscedasticity. If that assumption is violated, results of those tests will be of doubtful validity. See *heteroscedasticity for a graphic representation. *Homogeneity of variances is the term used when the dependent variable is continuous and the independent variable(s) is categorical or grouped; homoscedasticity is the term used when the dependent variable is continuous and the independent variable(s) is/are continuous.

Honestly Significant Difference (HSD) Test   See *Tukey's honestly significant difference test.

Hot Deck   A method of *imputation for *missing values. Missing values are imputed (i.e., replaced) based on the data of similar cases that have values for the variable question. See *AMELIA.

Hotelling's t^2 Test   An extension of the *t test to *multivariate research problems. It is used when you have one dichotomous independent variable and two or more continuous dependent variables. Also called Hotelling's T^2 (uppercase T) test.

Household Sample Survey   A survey of the individuals living in households. The *unit of analysis may be households or individuals; in the latter case, the method is a form of *cluster sampling. Household surveys are widely used in developing countries, which are less likely to have census data on individuals usable for creating a *sampling frame.

HRAF   *Human relations area file.

HSD Test   See *Tukey's honestly significant difference test.

Human Capital   A kind of *capital (resources that can produce income) that exists within persons rather than external to them. Knowledge, skill, and strength are examples of human capital. Economists often think of education as an investment in human capital. Compare *cultural capital.

Humanistic   A stance taken by *qualitative researchers that empirical research and writing should focus on humans as individuals, acting freely (and often passionately), rather than as just natural scientific or physical objects.

Human Relations Area File (HRAF)   A collection of anthropological information about hundreds of human cultures throughout the world divided into several hundred categories of information. The HRAF is widely used by researchers doing *secondary analyses of data on cross-cultural topics.

Hume's Law   Position of David Hume that it is impossible to derive an "ought" from an "is"; that is, facts cannot imply values. It is the strong version of the separation of facts and values. How would you answer this question: If facts are true or false, then what are values? Hume's law provides an epistemologically skeptical answer. Also called the "is-ought problem." Compare *thick concepts.

Huynh-Feldt Correction   The assumption of *sphericity is made for some significance tests (e.g., *repeated-measures ANOVA). When this assumption is violated, the obtained critical value and its associated p value cannot be trusted. The Huynh-Feldt procedure is a relatively powerful procedure for correcting the critical-F value and p value. The p value will be a little larger depending on the degree of violation of sphericity. For small sample sizes, however, the Huynh-Feldt correction can be a little liberal with regard to Type I error, and in this case, the *Geisser-Greenhouse epsilon hat adjustment is recommended.

Hypergeometric Distribution   A *probability distribution used for studying *sampling without replacement, that is, when each selection (or trial) changes the probability of the outcome of the next. Each member of the population can be categorized into one of two classes, such as success/failure or yes/no.

Hyperplane   A plane of three or more dimensions. While hard to picture, hyperplanes are a widely used concept in *multiple regression. See *regression plane for an illustration.

Hypothesis   A tentative answer to a research question; a statement of (or conjecture about) the relationships among the *variables that a researcher intends to study. Hypotheses should be testable statements of relations. In such cases, they are usually thought of as predictions that, if confirmed, will support a *theory. See *alternative hypothesis, *null hypothesis, *research question.

For example, suppose a social psychologist theorized that racial prejudice is due to ignorance. Hypotheses for testing the theory might be as follows:

If (1) education reduces ignorance, then (2) the more highly educated people are, the less likely they are to be prejudiced. If an attitude survey showed that there was indeed an *inverse relation between education and prejudice levels, this would support or confirm the theory that prejudice is a *function of ignorance.

Hypothesis Testing   The classical approach to assessing the *statistical significance of findings. Basically, it involves comparing empirically observed *sample findings with the theoretically expected finding that would occur if the *null hypothesis were true. To make this comparison, the researcher computes the *probability of the observed outcome if the observed outcome were only due to chance or *random error. Also called *null hypothesis significance testing (NHST). See *alpha error, *beta error.

For example, suppose you wanted to study the effects on performance of working in groups as compared to working alone. You get 80 students to volunteer for your study. You assign them randomly to two categories: those who work in teams of 4 students and those who work individually. You provide subjects with a large number of math problems to solve and record the number of answers they get right in 20 minutes. Your *alternative or *research hypothesis might be that people who work in teams are more efficient than those who work individually. You indirectly test your research hypothesis by determining whether the empirical evidence suggests that you should reject your null hypothesis—your null hypothesis would be something like "There is no difference between the average score of students who work individually and those who work in teams." If you rejected your null hypothesis, you would conclude that the alternative hypothesis is probably true.

The outcomes of a decision in hypothesis testing are often depicted in a matrix like the one in Table H.1. (Compare the similar matrix illustrating *signal detection theory.)

Table H.1   Possible Outcomes of a Hypothesis Test

		Your Decision	
		Retain the Null*	Reject the Null
Reality	Null Hypothesis Is True	Correct retention	Type I (alpha) error, wrong rejection
	Alternative Hypothesis Is True	Type II (beta) error, wrong retention	Correct rejection

*Note: Although hypothesis testing uses the language of "retain null" versus "reject null" in its decision logic, it is usually recommended to interpret the "retain null" decision as a "fail to reject null" decision.

H

Hypothetico-Deductive Method   A name philosophers of science sometimes use to describe the general logic of research that uses *hypothesis testing to draw its conclusions. The basic steps are these: Use *theory to infer or deduce a testable hypothesis; deduce the observable outcomes that must occur if the hypothesis is true; gather data and use statistical inference to test the statistical significance of the hypothesis. The result will support or not support the theory, depending on the outcome of the hypothesis testing.

ICC   *Intraclass correlation.

Ideal Index   An index computed by taking the *geometric mean of two indexes. The goal is to have the *biases in the two indexes offset one another. Sometimes called "Fisher's ideal index."

Idealism   The *ontological position that mind (ideas), not matter, is most fundamentally real. An idealist would argue that all knowledge necessarily comes from the mind. Its conceptual opposite is *materialism or *physicalism.

Ideal Type   A term introduced by Max Weber to refer to a pure conceptual type or *model. "Ideal" does not refer to the best or most desirable; rather, it means "pertaining to an idea." In modern English usage, "conceptual type" would capture Weber's meaning. See *concept, *construct, *thought experiment.

   For example, one could describe an ideal-typical bureaucracy; this would be as conceptually pure a bureaucracy as one could imagine, that is, an organization that worked only according to bureaucratic principles. An ideal type is used as a category or a concept to guide research. Thus, if you defined how a pure (ideal type) bureaucracy would work, you could use this as a standard for comparison to actual organizations to see how bureaucratic they were. Without such a standard, it would be difficult to say whether an organization had many or most of the characteristics of a bureaucracy or whether one organization was more bureaucratic than another.

Identification Problem   An analytic difficulty that arises in *regression analysis and *structural equation modeling when one has an *underidentified model. It occurs when one has more unknowns than can be independently estimated from the available data. This problem most frequently occurs with causal *models and *factor analysis. See *just-identified model.

Identity Matrix   A matrix in which all the elements on the diagonal are 1 and all the other elements are 0. See *matrix algebra.

Ideology   A system of beliefs held by a group that tends to serve the interests of that group. In research reports, one generally reserves the term "ideology" for positions one really does not like at all.

Idiographic   Used to describe research that deals with the individual, singular, unique, or concrete. Idiographic is often contrasted with *nomothetic. Compare *generalizability.

Idiographic Causation   Causation viewed locally or historically, as of causes of specific events and actions; includes unique and intentional causes, such as an act of an individual agent to produce a specific outcome. Idiographic causation is of most interest to practitioners and qualitative researchers because it is what occurs in particular local contexts and it is what, one hopes, an individual agent can directly affect; it is contrasted with *nomothetic causation.

i.i.d.   Abbreviation for "independent and identically distributed." Mostly used in mathematical statistics to refer to random variables that are independent of one another and are produced by the same theoretical probability distribution. It also occurs in random sampling, when each selection (case 1, 2, etc.) is viewed as a random variable (as a random and independent event, with each having the same theoretical probability distribution). This is important because it is what happens in random sampling, and the process produces independence of observations, which is one of the key assumptions used in inferential statistics. This sort of i.i.d. is not present in time series or *correlated groups designs because more than one observation is made on the same case.

Illusory Correlation   See *spurious correlation. Also called "nonsense correlation."

Impact Assessment   A variety of evaluation research that focuses on the short- and long-term effects (planned and unplanned) of a program, intervention, or other action. Originally used to refer to assessing the environmental impact of proposed activities, such as erecting new buildings in a wilderness area, and subsequently to the social impact of new programs. "Impact assessment" is now used generally to refer to the broader consequences of a planned action.

Impact factor   See *bibliographic impact factor.

Implementation Fidelity Assessment   Determination of the degree to which an intervention was conducted exactly as specified and is consistent with procedures in the program manual, including its goals and structures. When new social/educational/medical programs are demonstrated to work via empirical research, they are taken to new sites for use. At least in the beginning, the program needs to be replicated or implemented exactly as designed to give it a good chance of success. Having said that, sometimes small context-driven modifications are needed to make a program work locally.

Implicit Measures   Indirect measures of psychological states, traits, and conditions. They are used as indicators of variables that might not be accurately measured more directly. The kind of physiological measures used by lie detectors are one example. Another category clocks the amount of time it takes subjects to answer questions about different topics; response time is taken as an implicit measure of attitudes about those topics. See *proxy variable.

Imputation   Methods of replacing missing values in a data set. The simplest is *mean substitution, in which the missing value for a case is replaced with the mean score of the other cases. For example, if teachers' income were a variable in your study and you were missing the incomes for a few teachers, you could use the mean for the other teachers as an estimate of the missing values. Methods of imputation are controversial; some researchers recommend deleting cases with missing values and argue against any imputation, but this can result in dramatic loss of data and *statistical power. See *listwise deletion, *missing values procedures, *multiple imputation, *extrapolation, *interpolation, *AMELIA.

Incidence Rate   Incidence is the rate at which new cases of something (crime, marriage, disease, etc.) occur during a particular time period. The incidence rate is often used in epidemiology. One way to calculate this rate is as follows:

$$\frac{\text{Number of new cases or events in the particular time period}}{\text{Size of the population at the beginning of the time period}}$$

Compare *prevalence.

Inclusion Criteria   A list of the characteristics that research participants must have in order to be eligible to participate in the study.

Incomplete Block Design   An experimental design in which all treatment conditions do not occur in all levels of the *blocking variable. Some treatment-blocking combinations are excluded. This strategy might be used when there is a very large number of treatment combinations. See *fractional factorial design. Compare *complete block design.

Incomplete Counterbalancing   Approach to *counterbalancing using fewer than all possible sequences; it requires different groups of participants to take the different sequences. Compare *complete counterbalancing. For example, if there are three treatment conditions, complete counterbalancing would require ABC, ACB, BCA, BAC, CAB, CBA, but incomplete counterbalancing might use only ABC, BCA, and CAB. (For the interested reader, a formula for determining the ordering of treatments in incomplete counterbalancing is 1, 2, n, 3, $(n-1)$, 4, $(n-2)$, 5, and so forth.)

Increment   A small change in the value of a variable—often a positive change. A negative change is sometimes called a decrement.

Independence   (a) In *probability theory, a state in which the occurrence of one event does not change the probability of another event, that is, when one event does not depend on another. The numbers in a table of random numbers are independent. (b) A key assumption of many statistical tests is that the *residuals or *errors are independent; this condition can usually be produced by random sampling or random assignment. (c) In statistics and research design, two variables are independent when the value of one has no effect on the value of the other. (d) More generally and loosely, two variables are said to be independent when measures of association between them are small and not *significant. However, statistically associated variables may also be independent, such as your age and the price of cheese over the past 20 years. Compare *gambler's fallacy, *sampling with replacement, *orthogonal.

Independence of Observations   A key assumption in many statistical tests in inferential statistics. It is present when the selection of one observation is unrelated to the selection of another observation, as in random sampling or random assignment. Independence of observation is *not* present when the cases on a variable are correlated in some way, such as when *autocorrelation is present. See *i.i.d.

Independent Event   In probability theory, said of an occurrence that is not *conditional upon or conditioned by another. See *independence, *dependent event.

Independent Samples (or Groups)   Groups or samples that are unrelated to one another, that is, when the measurements of subjects in one group have nothing to do with the measurements of subjects in the other group. Independent samples and observations are an assumption of many statistical tests; if they are not independent, different procedures should be used. See *paired samples *t* test.

   For example, individuals put into different treatment groups by *random assignment would be independent. By contrast, subjects assigned to treatment groups according to the time of day they arrived at a clinic would not be independent. Early risers might have traits in common, as might people who arrived in the evening (they might work during the day). Also, students sampled from the same school would not be independent samples of all students because students in the same school would be likely to have some things in common. Compare *between-subjects variable, *correlated groups design.

Independent Samples *t* Test   A *t* test for comparing the means of two *independent samples. Compare *paired samples *t* test.

Independent Variable   The presumed *cause in a study. Also, a variable that can be used to predict or explain the values of another variable. A variable manipulated by an experimenter who predicts that the manipulation will have an effect on another variable (the *dependent variable).

   Some authors use the term "independent variable" for experimental research only. For these authors, the key criterion is whether the researcher can manipulate the variable; for nonexperimental research, these authors use the term *predictor variable or *explanatory variable. However, most writers say "independent variable" when they mean any causal variable, whether in experimental or nonexperimental research. Some even use it in pure *forecasting, in which no causal connection is implied, as when variations in the starting date of the migrating season are used to predict the severity of winter temperatures.

Index (a) A number, often a *ratio, meant to express simply a relationship between two variables or between two measures of the same variable. (b) A composite measure (a group of individual measures) that, when combined, is meant to indicate some more general characteristic. This type of index is similar to certain types of *scales, and the terms are sometimes used interchangeably.

For example (a), indexes measuring access to medical school for various groups could be calculated by dividing a group's percentage of students in medical school by its share of the population of medical school age. If, say, women made up 50% of the 21- to 25-year-olds and were 40% of the medical students, their access index would be 0.8 (40/50 = 0.8). Or if white males were 40% of the 21- to 25-year-old population and were 56% of the medical students, their index would be 1.4 (56/40 = 1.4).

For example (b), in survey research, political tolerance might be measured by an index composed of six questions about whether the respondent favored such things as free speech for religious outsiders, the right to demonstrate for political radicals, and so on. Scores on the index could range from 0 (for those answering none of the questions in the tolerant way) to 6 (for those answering all of the questions in the tolerant way). This kind of index is used to measure an *ordinal variable.

Indexization Adjusting wages, taxes, Social Security benefits, and so on to an *index number, such as the *Consumer Price Index.

Index Number A measure of change for comparison to a particular *base year or date in a *time series. The base year is often set at 100. Used most often with economic variables. See *Consumer Price Index, *Laspeyres index.

Indicator (a) A specification of how we will recognize or measure a *concept, as an IQ test could be taken as an indicator of the concept of intelligence. (b) A variable that can be used to study another variable because it affects or is correlated with it, as absenteeism could be an indicator of employee (dis)satisfaction. Clusters of related indicators are *dimensions. See *indicator variable, *social indicators.

Indicator Variable (a) Another term for *manifest variable, that is, an observable variable one uses to study a *latent (unobservable) variable. (b) Another term for *dummy variable.

Indices   An alternative way of pluralizing *index, more traditional than "indexes."

Indirect Effect   The effect of one variable at the starting end of a causal chain on a later variable in a causal chain by way of one or more *intervening or mediating variables occurring between the first and last variables. Mediating variables in indirect effects are sometimes said to "explain" the relationship between the initial and the later variables. For a depiction of an indirect effect, see *mediating variable.

Indirect Proof   Demonstrating the truth of a conclusion by showing that its logical opposite is self-contradictory or contradicts known truths. The idea might be expressed this way: It has to be true, because anything else is logically absurd.

Individual Differences   Differences that vary across two or more individuals, such as traits, aptitudes, personality, behaviors, performance, and other characteristics. For example, self-esteem varies across people. Compare *intraindividual differences.

Individual-Difference Variables   Psychological traits and states on which individuals differ, such as intelligence, self-esteem, parenting style, and personality type. These kinds of variables are extensively studied in psychology and related fields.

Individual Matching   See *matched pairs. Compare *group matching.

Induction   The logical process of moving from particular information to general conclusions. This would include using statistical methods to form generalizations by finding similarities among a large number of cases. The generalizations derived in this way are probabilistic. For example, if 90% of the members of the U.S. Congress were lawyers, the chances of any individual member of Congress being a lawyer would be 9 out of 10. Compare *abduction, *deduction.

Inductive   Said of research procedures and methods of reasoning that begin with (or put most emphasis on) observation and then move from observation of particulars to the development of general theory or *hypotheses. Often used to describe *grounded theory. Compare *empirical, *deductive.

Inductive Generalization   A general claim made on the basis of particular cases; concluding that a pattern exists in a population based on sample data. Sampling theory rests on the ideas that, first, inductive generalizations are important and, second, some sampling methods are better than others for producing trustworthy inductive generalizations. Inductive generalizations are part and parcel of inferential statistics. Also called "statistical generalizations."

Inductive Statistics   Another term for *inferential statistics.

Inference   The act of combining information (logical propositions, empirical facts, empirical generalizations) with careful thought and reasoning (inductive, deductive, abductive) to produce a new idea, generalization, or claim.

For example, statistical inferences are based on empirical data that have been analyzed using the appropriate techniques (sometimes multiple techniques enabling one to view the data in different ways). More generally, inferences made by behavioral and social scientists are statements based on the preponderance of the best evidence we have available.

Inferential Statistics   Statistics that allow one to draw conclusions or inferences from data. This means coming to conclusions (e.g., estimates, generalizations, decisions, predictions) about a *population on the basis of data describing a *sample. See *statistical inference.

Inflated Alpha   An alpha error rate greater than alpha (e.g., greater than .05) because of the conduct of *multiple *t* tests. See *multiple comparisons. Compare *familywise and *experimentwise error rates.

Influence Statistics   In *regression analysis, statistics designed to assess the effect (influence) of particular observations on the *regression coefficients. See *regression diagnostics.

Influential Observation (or Case)   A piece of data or a case that would, if removed from the other data, greatly change conclusions drawn from the data, especially in *regression analysis. Often an *outlier.

Informant   A term mostly used in qualitative research to refer to a person who provides the researcher, often an anthropologist doing *field research, with useful information about the inside goings-on of a group of which the informant is a member. The term is not considered pejorative in this context. Informants are distinguished from *subjects and *respondents by their greater degree of personal interaction with the researcher.

Information Theory   A statistical and mathematical theory of communication dealing with the nature, effectiveness, and accuracy of transmitting information between humans, between machines, and between humans and machines.

Informed Consent   Principles for protecting human research subjects based on the Nuremberg Code of the 1940s and the Helsinki Declaration of the 1990s. In brief, before agreeing to participate in research, and before giving researchers permission to proceed, potential subjects must be informed, prior to any treatment, of the possible risks of participation and that they may withdraw at any time. The process of informing potential subjects and their consent must be documented. Most controversies over informed consent revolve around whether truly informed consent is possible. Can potential participants in the research fully understand the procedures and risks? Compare *active consent, *passive consent.

Instantiate   To provide an instance of. A synonym for "actualize" or "bring into empirical being." For example, an instantiation of "a car" is your automobile, and an instantiation of "a triangle" is one that you draw on a piece of paper.

Institute for Social Research (ISR)   Founded by Rensis Likert and located at the University of Michigan, the ISR is perhaps best known as the parent organization of the Survey Research Center (SRC).

Institutional Research   What researchers in higher education often call *evaluation research, especially research on their own institutions. The research is usually designed to help administrators of a higher education institution plan and make decisions.

Institutional Review Board (IRB)   A screening panel for research projects that must by law be in place at any U.S. institution receiving federal funding. Its focus is protecting human subjects from potential harm caused by research. Research conducted by faculty must have IRB approval before being conducted. See *research ethics.

Instrument   Any means used to measure or otherwise study subjects. In the language of social and behavioral research, an instrument can call to mind a mechanical device (as it does in ordinary language—a dentist's drill, a saxophone), but it is used more broadly to include written instruments, such as attitude *scales or *interview schedules. In survey research, the *survey instrument* is usually a *questionnaire, an *interview schedule, or an *interview protocol.

Instrumentalism   The philosophical belief that *theories are not direct statements of truth about the real world, but rather are tools or instruments to help scientists explain phenomena, make predictions, and produce changes in the world. Instrumentalism was held by both *positivists and pragmatists. Instrumentalism is sharply criticized by *realists, who view theories as true or false.

Instrumental Variable   A variable used to replace an independent variable in a *regression equation when the independent variable is highly correlated with the *error term. A good instrumental variable will be highly correlated with the independent variable that it is replacing but will not be correlated with the error term. Instrumental variable estimation is an important way of compensating for the lack of random assignment to control and experimental groups in *quasi-experiments and *natural experiments. Compare *propensity score matching.

Instrumentation   A section in a research report or journal article where the researcher discusses the data collection instruments used, including their currently known *psychometric properties and reasoning, e.g., reliability, validity, factor structure, performance with different groups of participants, and reasons why the instruments are believed to operate appropriately with current participants.

Instrumentation Effect   Threat to *internal validity in single group designs (e.g., pretest-posttest design), whereby changes in the *dependent variable occur from pretest to posttest because of changes in the measurement instrument. An example would be *instrument drift; another example would be a researcher/observer becoming tired over time (*observer drift).

Instrument Drift   Label applied to physical or mechanical measurement instruments that change performance over time. Instruments need to be checked for this problem to make sure they perform to required standards, and recalibrated as needed. Compare *observer drift.

Intact Group   An existing group of research participants that cannot be readily separated in a research study (e.g., a classroom of students, people living in a specific dormitory). These kinds of groups are problematic because participants cannot be randomly assigned to them; they exist as wholes. If a treatment is given to one intact group and not the other, the difference on the dependent variable might be due to existing differences between the intact groups rather than to the treatment condition. See *selection bias, *selection threat, *group randomization trial.

Integer   A whole number, whether negative or positive: 1, 2, 4, and 5 are integers; 1.2 and 4/5 are not.

Intention-to-Treat Analysis (ITA)   In an ITA, data are analyzed according to the treatment conditions to which they were initially randomly assigned, rather than based on the treatment conditions they are believed to have actually received. For example, if some participants in the treatment group don't follow protocol or don't comply in some way, their data are still used (if available) during analysis. This approach fully respects the assignment process but ignores additional useful information such as knowing whether protocol was appropriately followed or knowledge of the actual type or amount of treatment received.

Interaction Effect   The combined effect of two or more *independent variables on a *dependent variable that is not accounted for by the simple sum of their separate effects. In other terms, interaction effects occur when the relation between two variables differs depending on the value of another variable. An interaction is present between two independent variables when the relationship between one independent variable and the dependent variable changes at the different levels of the other independent variable—the relationship, in a sense, "depends on" the level of the second independent variable. The presence of a statistically significant interaction effect makes it difficult to interpret main effects. Also called "conditioning effect," "contingency effect," "joint effect," and "moderating effect." Compare *main effect, *additive relation, *moderator variable.

When two independent variables interact, this is called a *first-order inter-action or a *two-way interaction; when three independent variables interact, it is a second-order interaction or a *three-way interaction; and so on. Interaction effects can be *ordinal or *disordinal; see the entries under those terms for more details.

For example, suppose a cholesterol reduction clinic had two diets and one exercise plan. The first independent variable, type of diet, is dichotomous (Diet A and Diet B); the second independent variable, amount of exercise, is continuous (varying from 0 to 25). Exercise alone was effective, and dieting alone was effective. As can be seen in Figure I.1, for patients who did not exercise, the two diets worked about equally well. Those who went on Diet A and exercised got the benefits of both; however, those who combined exercise with Diet B got a bonus, an interaction effect. All patients could benefit by dieting and exercising, but those who followed Diet B and exercised benefited more.

One also sees an interaction effect when the treatments interact with *attributes of the people being studied, such as their age, sex, or personality type; these interactions are often referred to as *moderating effects. The diet and exercise example illustrates the interaction of two kinds of treatments (diet and exercise).

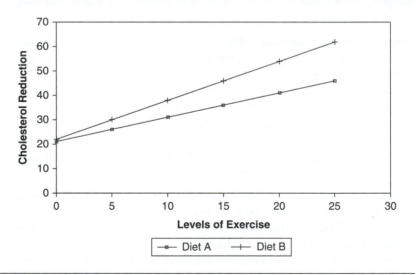

Figure I.1 Interaction Effect

Intercept   The point at which a *regression line crosses (or "intercepts") the vertical (y) axis, that is, when the value on the horizontal (x) axis is zero. Put another way, the intercept is the expected value of the *dependent variable when the value of the *independent variable is zero. Also called "y-intercept." See *regression constant and *constant (c). When there are multiple independent variables, "constant" is a more accurate term.

Regression lines can also cross the *x*-axis, producing an *x*-intercept, but this is rarely discussed. In *multiple regression, the *y*-intercept is the mean value of the *dependent variable for a case with a value of zero on all the *independent variables.

If we had 100 students' scores on an exam and asked them how many hours they spent studying for the exam, we could make a scatter plot of the data and draw the regression line as in Figure I.2. The point at which the line crosses the vertical axis is the intercept. It is around 70. The regression coefficient or *slope is 0.8, which means that, on average, for every hour a student studied, his or her estimated score went up a little less than a point. Note that no student actually claimed not to have studied at all. We might estimate that a student who had not studied at all would score 70 on the exam, but that would be an *extrapolation from the data, not a real value in the data set.

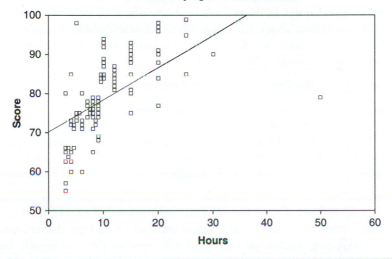

Figure I.2   Intercept

Interclass Correlation   An ordinary *correlation. The term *inter*class is used to distinguish it from an *intra*class correlation (ICC).

Interclass Variance   Another term for *between-groups differences in *ANOVA. By extension, *intra*class variance refers to within-groups differences.

Intercoder Reliability   Synonym for *interrater reliability.

Intercorrelation   A correlation between variables; sometimes restricted to correlation between *independent variables, as contrasted with a correlation between an independent variable and a dependent variable. See *multicollinearity.

Interim Analysis Term used in *qualitative and *mixed methods research to refer to the cyclical process of collecting data, analyzing the data, collecting more data, and so forth in a single research study. This contrasts with the more traditional procedure of conducting an analysis once, at the end of the study.

Intermediary Variable Another term for *mediating variable or *intervening variable.

Internal Consistency The extent to which items in a *scale are *correlated with one another and, by extension, the extent to which they measure the same thing. See *Cronbach's alpha.

Internal Reliability The extent to which items in an *index or *scale (such as questions on a test of a particular *domain of knowledge) give similar results. See *Cronbach's alpha, *reliability coefficient.

Internal Validity The extent to which the results of a study (often an *experiment) can be attributed to the *treatments rather than to flaws in the research design. In other words, internal validity is the degree to which one can draw valid conclusions about the *causal* effects of one variable on another. It depends on the extent to which *extraneous variables have been controlled by the researcher. Compare *external validity.

Interobserver Reliability Synonym for *interrater reliability.

Interpolation The act of estimating an unknown value by using its position among a series of known values. Compare *extrapolation.

For example, if the average weight of 5-year-olds in a sample were 50 pounds, and the average weight of 7-year-olds were 70 pounds, we might interpolate that 60 pounds would be the average weight of 6-year-olds in the sample.

Interpretation/Interpretive Methods Understanding evidence or giving it meaning through a process of analysis and reasoning. In social research, it usually refers to accounts of human thought and action from the standpoint of those being studied—as contrasted with viewing them exclusively from the standpoint of the researcher. See *in vivo coding, *emic, *etic, *thick description, *Verstehen.

Interpretive Phenomenological Analysis (IPA) A new type of phenomenology that is more attuned to situated, interpreted, group-based, and particularistic lived experiences rather than on transcendental experiences desired by traditional phenomenology (i.e., experiences that everyone has in common). Compare *phenomenology.

Interquartile Range (IQR) The middle half of a distribution. A measure of *dispersion calculated by taking the difference between the first and third *quartiles (that is, the 25th and 75th percentiles). Also called "midspread." See *box plot, *hinge. Compare *standard deviation. Also called the "middle 50."

Interrater Reliability   Agreement or consistency among raters; the extent to which raters judge phenomena in the same way. Ratings often involve assigning numbers to qualitative assessments. Olympic judges provide a familiar example. Although all the judges of an Olympic performance rarely award it exactly the same score, a very high level of agreement (interrater reliability) is common. Interrater reliabilities are usually measured by *correlation coefficients. See *Cohen's kappa.

Interrupted Time-Series Design   An approach that requires researchers to examine trends in the *dependent variable before, during, and after an intervention or *treatment to identify a change in the dependent variable after onset of the treatment (the "interruption"). The purpose is to avoid such *threats to validity as *maturation effects and *pretest sensitizing. The *history-effect threat to validity is not eliminated, however. The method is often used in clinical settings to study a single subject. See *difference-in-differences estimation.

Suppose, for example, that the management of a company thinks that productivity will go up if employees attend a special training seminar (the *treatment). To see whether the seminar is effective, the design shown in Table I.1 is used. Repeated pretesting (weeks 1–3) establishes a *baseline and helps reduce *Hawthorne effect bias. Repeated posttesting helps establish whether any improvements in productivity occur and last beyond the first posttest week (week 5).

Table I.1   Interrupted Time-Series Design

Week 1	Week 2	Week 3	Week 4	Week 5	Week 6	Week 7
Pretest	Pretest	Pretest	Treatment	Posttest	Posttest	Posttest

Interscorer Reliability   Synonym for *interrater reliability.

Intersection   In *set theory, the overlapping of two or more sets; said of the elements in the set of intersection. If set A includes all college professors and set B includes all married people, then the intersection will include all college professors who are married. Symbolized *cap, as in $A \cap B$. Pronounced "A intersection B" or "A and B." See *Venn diagram.

Intersubjective Agreement   A state that exists when a group of people (subjects) agree or have something in common (e.g., language, norms). It is a main criterion of *objectivity in science. Refers to the social part of human reality (e.g., language, institutions, culture).

Interval Estimate   An estimate that includes a range of scores. Compare *point estimate. See *confidence interval.

For example, the following statement contains an interval estimate: "If the election were held today, we estimate that Candidate A would get between 51%

and 57% of the vote." By contrast, a point estimate would read, "If the election were held today, we estimate that Candidate A would get 54% of the vote."

Interval Scale (or Level of Measurement)   A scale or measurement that describes variables in such a way that the distance between any two adjacent units of measurement (or "intervals") is the same, but in which there is no absolute or true zero point. Strictly speaking, scores on an interval scale can meaningfully be added and subtracted, but not multiplied and divided. Compare *ratio scale.

For example, the Fahrenheit temperature scale is an interval scale because the difference, or interval, between, say, 72 and 73 degrees is the same as that between 20 below and 21 below. Since there is no true zero point (zero is just a line on the thermometer), it is an interval, not a ratio scale. There is a zero, of course, but it is not a true zero; when it's zero degrees outside, there is still some warmth, more than when it's 20 below.

To take another example, if on a 20-item vocabulary test Mr. A got 12 right and Mr. B got 6 right, it would be correct to say that A answered twice as many correctly, but it would not be correct to say that A's vocabulary was twice as large as B's—unless the test measured all vocabulary knowledge and getting a zero on it meant that a person had no vocabulary at all (in that case, the test would be an example of a ratio scale).

Intervening Variable   A variable that explains a relation, or provides a causal link, between other variables. Also called "mediating variable," "intermediary variable," and "causal mechanism." Compare *moderating variable, *effect modifier, *suppressor variable.

For example, the statistical association between income and longevity needs to be explained, since having money by itself does not make one live longer. Other variables intervene between money and long life. For instance, people with high incomes tend to have better medical care than those with low incomes. Medical care is an intervening variable; it mediates the relation between income and longevity. Figure I.3 shows this graphically.

Income $\rightarrow$ Medical Care $\rightarrow$ Longevity

Figure I.3   Intervening Variable

Intervention   The experimental condition, *manipulated by the researcher, that is theorized to impact the *dependent or outcome variable. The intervention is tested in intervention research, typically by comparison with a control group.

Interviewer Effects   Influences on the responses of persons being interviewed that stem from the characteristics of interviewers. Respondents may answer questions differently depending on the accent, age, gender, and so on of the person asking the questions. Few systematic studies of such effects have been conducted; most of these have found the effects to be quite modest but stronger in face-to-face interviews than in telephone interviews.

Interview Protocol   A list of questions and instructions for how to ask the questions. It is used as a guide when interviewing respondents.

Interviews   Data collection method in which an interviewer asks an interviewee questions. It is one of the major methods for collecting empirical data. Compare *tests, *questionnaires, *focus groups, *observation, *secondary or existing data.

Interview Schedule   A list of questions and spaces to write down the answers. It is used by interviewers to record respondents' answers. Compare *questionnaire.

Intraclass Correlation (ICC)   A measure of homogeneity among the members of a group, class, or cluster. It is often used as a measure of *interrater reliability. Several different procedures for calculating ICCs exist; they are used for measuring reliability in different circumstances, such as different numbers of raters. The ICC is used in *multilevel models to indicate the proportion of the total variance attributable to variables at different levels. Also called "intracluster correlation."

Intraclass Variance   Another term for *within-group differences in *analysis of variance. See *interclass variance.

Intraindividual Differences   Differences within single individuals (rather than across different individuals) on more than one trait, aptitude, behavior, performance or other characteristic, or on one of these characteristics across time. For example, a person might have high social intelligence but moderate mathematical intelligence, or a person's social anxiety might change over time. Compare *individual differences.

Invariance   (a) The condition of being unchanged by specific mathematical *transformations, as an invariant *factor. For example, if you double the values of two variables, the *correlation between them does not change; it is invariant. (b) In *structural equation modeling, invariance is the process of determining whether the coefficients (e.g., factor loadings, regression coefficients, variances, means, intercepts) are statistically similar across multiple groups.

Inversely Proportional   Two variables are inversely proportional when they are *negatively related (and two variables are *directly proportional when they are *positively related). In mathematics, variables X and Y are inversely proportional when $Y = C/X$, where C is a constant. For example, if $C = 40$, the following X,Y pairs result (1, 40), (2, 20), (3, 13.33), (4, 10). As you can see, as X becomes larger, Y becomes smaller; the variables move in opposite directions as in a *negative relationship.

Inverse Relation (or Correlation)   A relation between two variables such that when one goes up, the other goes down, and vice versa. Also called *negative relation. Compare *direct relationship, *positive relation.

For example, the relation between the female employment and fertility rates tends to be inverse (or negative): The higher the female employment rate, the lower the fertility rate. See *linear relation for another example.

Inverse Sine Transformation   Synonym for *arc sine transformation.

Inverse Transformation   Synonym for *reciprocal transformation.

In Vivo Coding   In verbal data, coding that uses the participants' own words, rather than the researchers' terms and concepts.

IPA   *Interpretive phenomenological analysis.

Ipsative Measure (or Scale)   A *rank order scale in which a particular rank can be used only once. The opposite is usually called a "normative" scale.

For example, if you gave raters the following instructions, the results would be an ipsative scale: "Here are 11 movies. Rank them from best to worst, giving the best a 10, the next best a 9, the next an 8, and so on down to the worst, which gets a 0." By contrast, if you said, "Here are 11 movies. Rate them on a scale of 0 to 10," you would be asking for a normative scale. One rater could think the movies were all excellent and give them all 10s and 9s; another might believe they were all terrible and give them all 1s and 2s.

When several raters use an ipsative scale, the means, medians, and standard deviations of their rankings are always the same. But when several raters use a normative scale, this is not necessarily (and rarely is) the case.

IQR   *Interquartile range.

IRB   *Institutional review board.

Irrational Number   A number with infinite, nonrepeating decimals, such as pi or the square root of 2 (1.414213562 . . .). It is said to be irrational not because it is wacky, but because it cannot be exactly expressed as a *ratio of whole numbers. For example, 22/7 comes close to, but does not exactly equal, pi (3.14159265 . . .). Compare *rational number.

Irregular fluctuations   One of the four components of *time-series data. It is the random or unpredictable part of the time series. In time-series analysis, the data are analyzed until this is the only remaining component. It is the "noise" that remains unexplained in the data. Compare *secular trend, *seasonal variation, * cyclical.

IRT   *Item response theory.

Isomorphic   Having a form or structure similar to something else. Said of a *theory that can be deduced from another theory because the two are logically equivalent. Said of measurements when big units of measurement are used to measure big things and small units are used to measure small things.

For example, we don't measure the distance from Los Angeles to San Francisco in inches or centimeters; we could, but we don't, because the measurement scale and the thing measured would not be isomorphic.

Is-Ought Problem   See *Hume's law.

Item Analysis   In testing research, the study of questions (test items) based on individuals' responses to the questions. See *item response theory, *Rasch modeling.

Item Characteristic Curve (ICC)   Used in *item response theory. For each item on a test there is an item characteristic curve that plots the probability of providing a correct response to the item for each ability level on the measured trait.

Item Difficulty   To make a judgment of item difficulty, one first calculates the following ratio for each item: number of test takers who answered the item correctly divided by the total number of test takers who provided an answer. This index shows the proportion of test takers who answer the item *correctly*; therefore, higher scores indicate easier items, and lower scores indicate harder items (it's an inverse measure of difficulty). If the rate for one item was .8 and for another term was .1, then the second item was more difficult because only 10% got it right; in contrast, fully 80% got the first item correct. The optimal item difficulty depends on the purpose of the test and whether it is *criterion-referenced or *norm-referenced.

Item Discrimination   Tests and research instruments are designed to discriminate among subjects on the qualities being measured. Therefore, psychometricians and researchers often calculate an index of item discrimination. There are many indexes of item discrimination available. One popular index (called D) compares the strongest group with the weakest group (determined by the researcher) on each item; the preferred items are those showing a large difference. Another index is the item-to-total correlation, whereby, for each item, the researcher correlates individuals' item scores with their total test scores. A *biserial or *point biserial correlation coefficient is used. Strong positive correlations are desirable, although values of .10 to .50 are often considered acceptable.

Item Distractor   See *distractor.

Item Parceling   A process used in *SEM to create multiple indicators for a unidimensional construct. It is used with survey instruments that have multiple items measuring the same construct. The researcher assigns items to specific "parcels" or clusters based on theory or statistical procedures. For example, if a measure of attachment contains nine items, in order to create a latent variable of attachment the researcher creates three parcels of three items each, which will serve as indicators for the latent attachment variable.

Item Response Theory (IRT)   A group of methods designed to assess the *reliability, *validity, and difficulty of items on tests. The assumption is that each of the items is measuring some aspect of the same underlying (*latent) ability, trait, or attitude. IRT is important for determining equivalency of tests (such as two versions of the same proficiency exam) as well as for determining individuals' scores. IRT uses a version of *logistic regression as its basic tool, with the dependent variable being the log of the odds of answering questions correctly. It is often contrasted with the older, and simpler, *classical test theory. See *differential item functioning and *Rasch modeling.

Item-Total Correlation   Relation between scores on a single item on a test and the total test score. These correlations should be high if the test is reliable and measures a single construct, and if the item has discrimination power. Items with relatively high values (e.g., greater than .4) discriminate well. Items with negative or low item-total correlations indicate problematic items.

Iteration   Generally, a repetition. (a) Any procedure in computation in which a set of operations is repeated, such as each time an *estimate is obtained in a series of estimates. (b) A method of successive approximation in which each step is based on the results of the preceding steps.

IV   Abbreviation for *independent variable.

Jackknife Method A way to estimate *standard errors and *confidence intervals. The basic approach is to take repeated random subsamples, without replacement, of one's original sample, eliminating one or more data observations each time. The main advantage of the method is that it requires no assumptions about *underlying distributions; it is thus a *nonparametric or *distribution-free method. See *bootstrap methods, which are an extension of the jackknife, and *resampling.

J Curve (or J-Shaped Distribution) (a) A curve describing a *frequency distribution that looks roughly like an uppercase letter *J*, that is, with minimum frequency at low levels of the *x*-axis and rapidly increasing frequencies at higher levels. Examples of such curves are often found illustrating the frequency of adherence to a norm or compliance with a standard of behavior. (Depending on how a relationship is graphed, the *J* may be in its normal upright position or, as is often the case, lying on its side.) (b) A curve describing the relation between a nation's balance of payments (imports relative to exports) and the value of its currency; as the value of the currency goes down, the balance of payments goes down for a while but then goes up, slowly at first, then rapidly, which results in the J shape.

Jittering A method of making *scatter plots easier to interpret when many data points are identical. It involves adding a tiny amount of random variation to the points so that they are not on top of one another and can be seen.

John Henry Effect A threat to research validity occurring when persons in a *control group (those who are not receiving an experimental *treatment) take the experimental situation as a challenge and exert more effort than they otherwise would; they try to beat those in the *experimental group. This, of course, negates the purpose of having a control group.

For example, in order to see if a new power tool were worth the investment, a supervisor in a construction firm might provide some workers (the experimental group) with the new power tool; the rest of the workers (control group) continue using the old tool. The workers using the old tool might work much harder to show that they were just as good and should get the new tool too. They might actually produce more, even though under ordinary conditions (not influenced by the John Henry effect), workers using the new tool would be more productive.

Joint Contingency Table   A table illustrating how two or more *independent variables jointly affect a *dependent variable.

For example, Table J.1 gives the unemployment rates (dependent variable) by year for different age and race groups (independent variables). Unemployment is jointly affected by age, race, and year. The table shows that African Americans and young persons were more likely to be unemployed and that rates for all groups went down in the 1990s and back up after 2000.

Table J.1   Joint Contingency Table: Unemployment Rates (1994–2004)

	Whites		*Blacks*	
Year	*All*	*Aged 16–19*	*All*	*Aged 16–19*
1994	5.7	16.0	13.1	32.7
1996	4.9	15.4	10.6	33.5
1998	4.0	11.8	9.4	29.7
2000	3.4	11.1	8.0	23.1
2002	5.1	14.5	10.0	31.3
2004	4.9	14.1	10.5	32.9

Note: Figures are for January of each year.

Jointly Independent   Two variables (X and Y) are said to be jointly independent of a third variable (Z) if their *joint probability distribution is uninfluenced by the value of Z.

Joint Probability   The probability of the *intersection of two or more events; it's the probability that the events occur together.

For example, the probability of drawing (from a normal deck) a card that is a club is 1 out of 4 (or .25), and the probability of drawing a 7 is 1 out of 13 (or .0769). The *joint* probability of drawing a card that is both a club and a 7 is 1 out of 52 ($1/4 \times 1/13 = 1/52$) or .01923 ($.25 \times .0769$).

Judgment Sampling   A procedure in which a researcher makes a judgment that a *convenience sample (e.g., volunteers) might be similar enough to a *random sample that it could make sense to use statistical procedures designed for use on random samples. Selecting a sample according to the researcher's judgment of its representativeness is recommended only when a *probability sample is impossible or highly impractical, as it often is. Judgment sampling is very common when selecting interviewees or sites for observational research. See *purposive sample.

Just-Identified Model Another term for a *fully recursive model (i.e., one that is neither *underidentified nor *overidentified). In *SEM, a model in which the number of variables and the number of parameters to be estimated are equal. Unique parameter estimates are available in this type of model. Also called a *saturated model and an "exactly identified model." See *recursive model. Compare *overidentified model, *underidentified model.

k (a) Lowercase *k*: common symbol for the number of groups or *samples in a study. (b) Common symbol for the number of independent variables in a regression model.

K (a) Uppercase *K*: the usual symbol for a *coefficient of alienation. (b) Symbol for *kernel.

Kaplan-Meier Analysis A method of *survival analysis. A ratio is calculated of the surviving subjects (or those without an event) to the total number of subjects at risk for the event. Each time a subject has an event, the ratio is recalculated. It is common to graph change in the ratio over time in a Kaplan-Meier curve. Comparing curves for treatment and control groups is an effective way to depict the effects of a treatment. Like other forms of survival analysis, Kaplan-Meier analysis originated in medical studies but has since been widely applied in social and behavioral research. The 1958 article in which Kaplan and Meier first described their method is by some counts the most highly cited work in the field of statistics—cited over 44,000 times according to *Google Scholar.

Kappa (K, κ) See *Cohen's kappa.

Kappa Coefficient See *Cohen's kappa, which is a measure of *interrater reliability.

Kendall's Coefficient of Concordance A *nonparametric statistical test of the agreement among sets of rankings; symbolized: *W*. *W* can range from 0 (no agreement) to 1 (complete agreement). See *interrater reliability.

For example, if we wanted to see how much seven wine tasters agreed (were in "concord") about their rankings of a dozen different wines, we could use Kendall's coefficient.

Kendall's (Tau) Correlations One of three measures of *association (tau a, tau b, tau c) between two *ordinal variables. This type of *correlation between ordinal variables is used when the ranks of the ordered categories are not

K

treated as interval scales. It is generally considered better than *Spearman's rho because of the way it deals with tied ranks. Compare *Somers's *d*.

Kernel Methods   Methods for estimating *probability density functions. The kernel occurs in the integral equations of calculus.

Kilobyte   A measure of computer memory. Literally "1,000 *bytes" but actually 1,024 bytes.

Kim's *d*   A measure of *association between two *ordinal variables used when the ranks of the ordered categories are not treated as *interval scales. Contrast *Spearman's rho.

K-Means Clustering   Method of determining a single level of mutually exclusive clusters in cluster analysis. It assigns sets of cases to clusters that are near the cluster *centroid (mean on the clustering variables). The user can specify the number of k clusters to be examined, although some solutions will work better than others. Compare *hierarchical clustering.

KMO Test   Kaiser-Myer-Olkin test. An indicator of the strength of relationships among variables in a correlation matrix. It is arrived at by calculating the correlations between each pair of variables after *controlling for the effects of all other variables. Compare *Bartlett's test. The KMO statistic can range from 0 to 1; .70 is often considered a minimum for conducting a *factor analysis.

Known Group Validity   Evidence for validity obtained by checking to see if groups that are theoretically known (or presumed) to differ on a construct actually differ on the measurement instrument in the hypothesized direction. For example, one could obtain validity evidence of a problem-solving instrument by determining that it correctly classifies test takers into the known expert problem solvers versus weak problem solvers.

Kolmogorov-Smirnov Tests   *Nonparametric tests (for *ordinal data) of whether two distributions differ and whether two samples may reasonably be assumed to come from the same population; they are *goodness-of-fit tests. A one-sample version tests the hypothesis that the sample came from a population with a specific distribution, usually the *normal distribution.

KR-20 and KR-21   Abbreviations for *Kuder-Richardson formulas 20 and 21.

Kruskal-Wallis Test   A *nonparametric test of *statistical significance used when testing more than two independent samples; symbolized: *H*. It is an extension of the *Mann-Whitney *U* test, and of the *Wilcoxon test, to three or more independent samples. It is particularly useful for samples of differing sizes. It is a nonparametric *one-way ANOVA for rank order data and is based on *medians rather than *means.

Kuder-Richardson Formulas (20 and 21)   Measures of the internal consistency or *reliability of tests in which items have only two possible answers, such as agree/disagree or yes/no. Formula 21 is a simplified and easily computable version of formula 20. Both give conservative (low) estimates of a test's reliability. KR-20 estimates the outcome of taking all possible orders (*permutations) of questions on a test, computing a *split-half reliability coefficient for each of these orders, and finally taking the means of those coefficients. Compare *Spearman-Brown formula and *Cronbach's alpha.

Kurtosis An indication of the extent to which a distribution departs from the bell-shaped or *normal curve by being either pointier (leptokurtosis) or flatter (platykurtosis), as shown in Figure K.1. Platykurtic distributions are sometimes referred to as "fat tailed."

Kurtosis can be expressed numerically as well as graphically. Computer programs often provide such numbers. The basic rule for interpreting them is that negative numbers mean flatter than normal and positive numbers mean more peaked than normal. The kurtosis number for a normal distribution is 0. According to one rule of thumb, a distribution is approximately symmetric when kurtosis is ± ½, and it's highly skewed when kurtosis is ± 1.

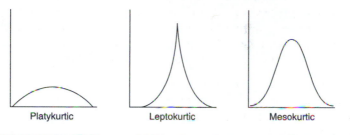

Platykurtic   Leptokurtic   Mesokurtic

Figure K.1   Kurtosis

L Symbol for *logit.

***L*²** Symbol for the *maximum likelihood ratio chi-square statistic.

Laboratory Research Any of several methods of isolating subjects so as to *control *extraneous variables. Often considered to be synonymous with *experimental research, which includes manipulation of the independent variable. The advantage of the laboratory method in the social and behavioral sciences is also its disadvantage. Subjects can be isolated from contexts that might influence their behavior; hence, the researcher can focus on those *independent variables of interest. However, it may be difficult to generalize results to situations outside of the laboratory, since people seldom act in isolation from context. In other words, using laboratory research sometimes means trading a gain in *internal validity for a loss in *external validity. See *randomized clinical trial.

Laddering An approach to in-depth interviewing whereby the interviewer continually probes and asks follow-up questions, moving "up the ladder," to understand an attitude, value, behavior, or belief in all of its complexity, understanding the way the participant thinks and experiences it. In one version, an initial question is asked and then follow-up questions focus on attributes of the attitudinal "object," its consequences, and values surrounding the object. Sometimes ladder-like graphs or maps are produced to depict the results.

Lagged Dependent Variable A variable constructed from a time-series dependent variable, where the values on the new (lagged) variable are the values on the original variable held back by one or more time points. Assume that the values on the dependent variable (for times 1 through 5) are 50, 55, 57, 63, and 67; the values on the dependent variable lagged by one time point are 50, 55, 57, and 63. The lagged variable is subsequently used to help predict the dependent variable; that is, the lagged version of the dependent variable (y_{t-1})

L

is used to predict the nonlagged version (y_t) of the same dependent variable. This is a useful prediction strategy because the past usually is a good predictor of the present. Last year's dependent variable becomes one of this year's independent variables.

Lagged Independent Variable   An independent variable is lagged by one or more time points, and the new lagged independent variable is used to help predict the values on the dependent variable. For example, the dependent variable, y, might be the number of new housing starts, and the independent variable, x, might be the prime interest rate. If it is believed that the interest rate at the previous period is a good predictor of the number of housing starts in the current period, then x_{t-1} rather than x_t would be used as the predictor variable.

Lagging Indicator   An indicator in which general trends show up only after a time, lagging behind other indicators. Contrast *leading indicators.

For example, one common lagging indicator is average length of time individuals are unemployed. It goes down as the economy gets stronger, but usually not right away.

Lagrange Multiplier Test   (also called **Score Test**) Used in econometrics and regression, a test for dealing with model specification problems. As an example, the null hypothesis is that the hypothesized or preferred model is adequate and the alternative hypothesis is that an alternative model identified in the data has better fit (e.g., a model with additional variables in it fits better, a model with autocorrelation allowed fits better). Often multiple alternative models are specified and tested with this test. See *omitted variables bias.

Lambda (Λ, λ)   (a) Common symbol for *eigenvalue. (b) Goodman and Kruskal's lambda, which is a *measure of association appropriate to use when the *variables being described are *categorical (*nominal or *discrete). Lambdas range from 0, when knowing one variable tells you nothing about another, to 1.0, when knowing one always enables you to predict the other. Lambda is a *Proportional Reduction of Error measure.

For an example of (b), say that a statistics professor had 40 students in a class, 20 women and 20 men. The professor gave a pass/fail test; 22 students passed and 18 failed. Of the 22 students who passed, if 11 were men and 11 were women, there would be no association between the two variables; knowing the sex of students wouldn't help predict whether or not they passed. The lambda would be 0. But suppose that 20 of the 22 who passed were female and 2 were male (and therefore that all 18 who failed were male). Then there would be a strong association between sex and success on the test. Knowing students' sex would most often enable us to tell whether they passed or failed. The lambda in this example is .89. This means that our prediction is 89% better when we know the students' sex.

Laspeyres Index   One of the earliest methods of calculating *index numbers and *base years for *time-series indexes, particularly for tracking prices and measuring inflation. The formula is still used today to compute the *Consumer Price Index (CPI) in the United States. A standard "basket" of goods is purchased; its cost is compared with the cost of the same basket at a baseline date. The index is a *weighted average, with the prices of some goods in the base period more heavily determining the index number.

LASSO   Least absolute shrinkage and selection operator. A criterion used in *ridge regression.

Last Observation Carried Forward (LOCF)   A method for imputing missing values by replacing the missing data with the most recently available data. Often used in *longitudinal studies when subjects drop out. Like *listwise deletion and *mean substitution, it is widely used but not to be recommended if more advanced methods, such as *multiple imputation, are possible for the data set. Compare *nearest neighbor imputation. See *AMELIA.

Latent Class Analysis (LCA)   A method similar to *factor analysis but used with *categorical variables. It is based on the assumption that categorical *latent variables (groupings) may underlie discrete observations. While factor analysis is used to discover continuous *latent variables, LCA is used to find discrete categories or "classes" of latent variables, based on manifest questionnaire items that have categorical, not continuous, answers. Like factor analysis, LCA may be exploratory or confirmatory.

Latent Class Models   Models designed to discover whether complex relations between observed categorical variables can be explained by relationships between unobserved or *latent variables. For example, unlike traditional regression models, latent class regression models contain one or more independent variables that are categorical *latent* (i.e., unobserved variables). Other types include latent class cluster models and latent class factor models.

Latent Class Regression (also **called Regression Mixture Modeling**)   A combination of *latent class analysis and *regression that classifies a sample into an optimal number of classes (sort of like cluster analysis) and estimates the regression model within each of the classes. It is used when heterogeneity is expected in the data, that is, when it is expected that subpopulations exist in the population. It can be used when variables are nominal and mixed (nominal and quantitative). It identifies regression models that work for different segments or subpopulations.

Latent Curve Models   See *growth curve analysis.

Latent Factor   See *latent variable.

Latent Function   In *functionalism, a purpose or use of a social phenomenon that is not obvious (it is hidden or "latent") to social actors. Researchers hypothesize its existence to explain otherwise mysterious phenomena. Researchers looking for latent functions are looking for *latent variables.

Men's neckties might be a good example. At one time they were presumably scarves meant to keep one warm. But today they are worn indoors in well-heated buildings and even on very hot days when it is uncomfortable to do so. Keeping warm cannot be the function they fill; it cannot explain their widespread use. Nor can neckties be wholly explained by their decorative function since there are many ways men could decorate themselves (such as wearing a brooch pinned to the collar). But all except neckties are considered socially inappropriate—for men, but not women, at least in some circumstances. So what is the latent function of necktie wearing? Latent functions are always speculative since, like all latent variables, they are hard to study and measure directly. But one might hypothesize that by wearing a necktie, a man makes the following kind of statement: "I am a serious person. I recognize that this is an important social context (work, a formal social event), and by dressing appropriately, I show you that I am the kind of person who can be trusted to do the right thing. Were I not wearing a tie, you might imagine that I am frivolous or rebellious."

Latent Growth Curve Analysis   A structural equation modeling technique in *growth curve analysis. Requires longitudinal data with at least four time points. It allows one to look at changes in means and intercepts for latent variables over time.

Latent Mixture Modeling   See *latent class regression.

Latent Profile Analysis   Methods used to discover discrete latent categories using continuous observed variables. See *latent class analysis.

Latent Structure   A pattern of relations among variables that is not directly observable but is hypothesized to exist so as to explain variables that are observable. See *latent variable, *factor analysis, *structural equation models.

Latent Trait Analysis   Methods for discovering continuous latent variables using categorical observed variables. See *latent class analysis.

Latent Variable   An underlying characteristic that cannot be observed or measured directly; it is hypothesized to exist so as to explain variables, such as behavior, that can be observed (*manifest variables). Latent variables are also often called *factors, especially in the context of *factor analysis. Compare *latent function, *latent class analysis, *structural equation models.

For example, if we observed the votes of members of a legislature on spending bills for the military, medical care, nutrition programs, education, law enforcement, and promoting business investment, we might find underlying patterns that could be explained by postulating latent variables (factors) such as conservatism and liberalism.

Latin Square   A method of allocating subjects, in a *within-subjects design, to *treatment group orders. So called because the treatments are symbolized by

Latin (not Greek) letters. The main goal of using Latin squares is to avoid *order effects by rotating the order of treatments. A criterion for constructing a Latin square is that each treatment must appear exactly once in each possible sequential order. See *counterbalancing, *Graeco-Latin square.

In the example shown in Table L.1, A, B, C, and D are treatments. There are 4 subjects and 4 orders of treatment. Subject 1 would receive the treatments ABCD in that order, the order for subject 2 would be BDAC, and so on. Note that a Latin square must be square (i.e., the number of rows and columns must be equal). The number of subjects must equal or be a multiple of the number of treatments—in this example, 4, 8, 12, 16, and so on. Notice that the criterion listed above is met because each treatment appears exactly once in each sequential order; for example, treatment A appears first for subject 1, second for subject 3, third for subject 2, and fourth for subject 4. When there are 4 treatments, as in our example, there are 576 possible Latin squares. See *randomized-blocks design, of which the Latin square is an extension.

Table L.1 Latin Square

	Order			
	1st	*2nd*	*3rd*	*4th*
Subject 1	A	B	C	D
Subject 2	B	D	A	C
Subject 3	C	A	D	B
Subject 4	D	C	B	A

Law (a) A statement about the relations among *variables that has been frequently confirmed and that seems to hold under all circumstances. While a law is generally thought to be more certain than a theory, the difference between law and theory is sometimes little more than a matter of accidents of usage (e.g., the *law* of supply and demand, but the *theory* of evolution). Usage varies considerably. (b) Sometimes law is used to mean universal theoretical or *empirical generalization; in that usage, a law would describe but not explain the regularity; a theory would explain it.

Modern social and behavioral scientists rarely refer to their generalizations as laws; they use "theory" almost to the exclusion of "law" to refer to statements about regular relations among variables.

Law of Averages The principle that *random errors in measurement will tend to balance one another out (for an *unbiased estimator); that is, they will as often be above as below the true values. Also, as *sample size increases, the sample *statistic becomes a better estimate of the population *parameter. Compare *law of large numbers, *central limit theorem.

L

Law of Large Numbers   Description of how larger *samples are better (more representative) of the *populations from which they were drawn—specifically, the more cases you select, the more likely it is that your sample *mean will equal the population mean. This law holds only if one uses a method of sampling that is not *biased. Any *equal probability of selection method will suffice, but *simple random sampling is usually assumed; increasing the size of biased samples leads to little or no improvement. Compare *central limit theorem.

Law of Parsimony   See *Ockham's razor, *parsimony.

Leading Indicators   Events likely to precede other events that researchers want to *forecast. Usually used in the phrase "leading *economic* indicators," but the concept is also useful in other fields that use *time-series data. Contrast *lagging indicator.

Learning Curve   The tendency to learn how to do something more efficiently the more often you do it. That is, the rate of learning produces a curve over time. When graphed, the learning curve may be steep or not steep for tasks that are and are not likely to be learned quickly with repetition. The concept is widely used in manufacturing, where the focus is on the unit cost of production, but it can be applied to other sorts of learning as well.

Least Significant Difference (LSD)   A post hoc comparison test used in *analysis of variance and *analysis of covariance when comparisons are made among three groups. If there are more than three groups, a different *alpha adjustment procedure should be used because LSD will be too liberal (i.e., p values will be too small and sufficient adjustment will not occur). The LSD test is like conducting unadjusted t tests on the data; the adjustment comes into play by requiring that the *omnibus test be statistically significant before using the LSD p values. See *post hoc comparison. (Also the type of "adjustment" preferred and used in experimentation by the late Harvard psychologist Timothy Leary during the psychedelic 1960s.)

Least Squares Criterion (or Principle)   This is used in calculating the values of many estimators. The criterion says to use the sample data to produce the values that minimize the sum of the squared errors (i.e., provide estimates with the "smallest error").

For example, if you have data on only one continuous variable, then using the sample mean will provide the smallest variance (e.g., compared to the mode and median). In *regression analysis, the procedure is called *ordinary least squares (OLS), and it produces the "best-fitting" straight regression line and the best estimates of the population Y-intercept and regression coefficients. Although OLS is the most frequently used estimation procedure, there are many others such as *maximum likelihood estimation, *generalized least squares, *weighted least squares, and method of moments. See *general linear model.

Least Squares Regression   Another name for *regression analysis. This name emphasizes that a standard *regression analysis is based on the *least squares criterion (i.e., the estimated coefficients are those that minimize the sum of squared error in the data and produce the *line of best fit).

Left Censoring   This occurs in *event history analysis (also known as *survival analysis and failure time analysis) when the time at which the subject entered the risk set for experiencing the event is unknown. In studies of recidivism, the data are left censored if the time of release from prison is unknown. These cases are problematic because it is not possible to compute how long the subject was at risk for experiencing an event. Note that data can be right censored or left censored or both, but left censoring is a more difficult problem to resolve. Compare *right censoring.

Lemma   A *theorem that has been proven and then used to prove another theorem.

Leptokurtic   More peaked than a *normal curve. See *kurtosis for an illustration.

Level   A *treatment or a *condition of an *independent variable (IV) in an experiment. A particular value of an IV in a study. "Level" implies amount or magnitude in ordinary language, and it is used that way in experiments too. If subjects were given 10 cc, 15 cc, or 20 cc of a medication, those would be the three levels. But "level" is also used for *categorical variables, such as medications A, B, and C, where the three are different in kind, not different in amount of the same thing.

Level of Analysis (or Aggregation)   If we were to study the United States, we could look at individuals, neighborhoods, counties, states, or regions. Individuals would be the lowest level of analysis or aggregation; regions would be the highest. The lower the level of analysis, the higher the level of specificity tends to be, and vice versa. See *level of generality.

Level of Generality   The breadth of statements or generalizations.

Take, for example, statements that apply to deviance, crime, and theft. Theft, a specific type of crime, is at the lowest level. Crime is a more general category than theft, but it is less broad than deviance, which includes crimes but can also be taken to mean any departure from ordinary behavior (see Table L.2).

Table L.2   Level of Generality

Level	Example
Low	Theft
Middle	Crime
High	Deviance

Level of Measurement   A term used to describe measurement scales in terms of how much information they convey about the differences among values—the higher the level, the more information.

According to the popular measurement typology developed by S. S. Stevens, there are four levels of measurement. Arranged in order of mathematical strength, from the highest to the lowest, they are *ratio, *interval, *ordinal, and *nominal. It is possible to describe data gathered at a higher level with a lower level of measurement, but the reverse is not true. For example, one can express income in dollars and cents (ratio level) or with ordinal descriptions like high, medium, and low income.

It is important to be aware of the level of measurement you are using because statistical techniques appropriate at one level might produce ridiculous results at another. For example, in a study of religious affiliation, you might number your variables as follows: 1 = Catholic, 2 = Jewish, 3 = Protestant, 4 = Other, 5 = None. The religion variable is measured at the nominal level. The numbers are just convenient labels or names; one cannot treat them as if they mean something at the interval level; one should not add together a Jewish person (2) and a Protestant person (3) to get an atheist (5).

Considerable controversy exists concerning which statistics can validly be used to analyze variables measured at different levels of measurement. The debates usually revolve around questions of how serious a distortion occurs when one violates particular *assumptions presumed by certain statistical techniques. As in constitutional law, so too in statistics there are strict and loose constructionists in the interpretation of adherence to assumptions.

Level of Significance   Synonym of *alpha level. Compare *observed level of significance, *p value, *statistical significance.

Level of Specificity   See *level of analysis, *level of generality.

Levene's Test   A test for *homogeneity (equality) of variances in distributions. Often used prior to conducting an *ANOVA and in interpreting the results of a *t test. The importance of Levene's test lies in the fact that ANOVA and the t test (among other statistical techniques) assume equality of variances. An ANOVA or a t test is not valid if the assumption is not met. If sample size is large, Levene's test can be very sensitive; it also is sensitive to violations of normality. Therefore, the following descriptive rule of thumb is sometimes recommended: Homogeneity is *not* seriously violated if the ratio of the largest within-group variance to the smallest within-group variance is less than 4 or 5.

Leverage   A measure of the influence of a case or observation on the regression model. A large leverage indicates the presence of an *influential observation, specifically indicating that the particular observation or case has a large impact on one or more of the regression coefficients. According to one rule of thumb, you should worry about and carefully examine cases with a leverage value greater than $2k/n$ (where k is the number of independent variables plus 1 and *n* is the number of subjects). *Mahalanobis distance is leverage multiplied by ($k - 1$), where k equals the number of cases. See *Cook's distance.

Leverage Point (or Case)   In *regression diagnostics, an *outlier among the *independent (*predictor) variables that is large enough to importantly affect the interpretation of the regression equation.

Liar's Paradox   A paradox that arises from someone making a statement such as "I am lying" or "This statement is false." If the statement is true, then it is false; and if it is false, then it is true.

Lie Scale   A set of items in an instrument designed to determine if the respondent has been untruthful. For example, to detect lying, the same item with slightly different wording might be used or something bogus might be provided to see the type of response given by the participant. In psychology, a historically well-known lie scale is the L scale in the MMPI (Minnesota Multiphasic Personality Inventory).

Life Course   A term to describe the regular periods in a typical life span, such as infancy, adolescence, adulthood, middle age, and old age. In medical and psychological research, it has long been recognized that certain conditions are influenced by one's stage in the life course.

Life Expectancy   The predicted number of years yet to be lived by persons of a particular age. The older the person, the shorter the life expectancy. This is calculated by taking the average number of years lived by persons in a particular birth *cohort at a given time or time interval. Life expectancies are based on *cross-sectional data, which means that using them to make predictions about future life expectancies is based on the assumption that future rates will be affected by the same variables as those at work at the time the cross section was taken. See *life table.

Life Table   A table showing *life expectancy at various dates and for different groups, usually birth *cohorts.

For example, Table L.3 on page 232 is a simplified life table that shows the life, death, and expectancies per 100,000 for a hypothetical (but not unrealistic) population. In row 1 we start with 100,000 persons, aged zero to 1 year, of whom 650 die by the end of the period. The survivors are expected to live another 79 years. Then 100,000 minus 650 leaves 99,350 survivors in row 2, of whom 150 die. Those who make it to the end of the period are expected to live 78 more years. Many things can be seen in this table. For example, infancy (years 00 to 01) is much more hazardous than early childhood (ages 01 to 05). If children make it through their first year, they are quite unlikely to die until adulthood. It is not until people are much older (in their 40s) that the death rate again approaches that of infancy. Looking at a later point in the age spectrum, in row 16, we see that people who survive into their 70s can expect to live another 15 years on average.

Table L.3 Life Table

	A. Number of Years*	B. Number Living	C. Number Dying	D. Expected Years to Live
1	00–01	100,000	650	79
2	01–05	99,350	150	78
3	05–10	99,200	80	75
4	10–15	99,120	90	70
5	15–20	99,030	220	65
6	20–25	98,810	240	60
7	25–30	98,570	300	55
8	30–35	98,270	430	50
9	35–40	97,840	600	46
10	40–45	97,240	840	41
11	45–50	96,400	1,200	36
12	50–55	95,200	2,000	32
13	55–60	93,200	3,000	27
14	60–65	90,200	5,000	23
15	65–70	85,200	7,000	19
16	70–75	78,200	9,600	15

*00–01 years means date of birth to day before first birthday; 01–05 means first birthday to day before 5th birthday; and so on.

Likelihood (*L*)   The *probability of observed results (in a *sample) given the estimates of the *population parameters. In other words, the *conditional probability of observed frequencies or values given expected frequencies or values. It is perhaps most widely used as a way to determine the *goodness-of-fit of a *logistic regression model. See *likelihood ratio, *maximum likelihood estimation.

Likelihood Ratio (LR)   (a) As the name implies, the LR is a *ratio of two *likelihoods, specifically the ratio of two likelihoods given two different hypotheses about the data. It is the ratio of the outcome if the *alternative hypothesis is true to the outcome if the *null hypothesis is true. It is often used as a *test statistic for comparing models, specifically two nested models. The smaller the LR, the stronger the relationship.

   (b) In medical research and practice, the LR is used to describe the accuracy of medical tests. It is a measure of the relation of the *sensitivity and the *specificity of a medical test. There is both a negative and a positive version, for negative and positive test results. A negative LR, especially if it is 0.1 or less, is considered good evidence to rule out a diagnosis. A positive LR, especially if it is 10.0 or higher, is considered good evidence to rule in a diagnostic result.

Likelihood Ratio Chi-Square   Short for *maximum likelihood ratio chi-square.

Likert Scale   A widely used scaling method developed by Rensis Likert (pronounced LICK-ert). (a) In its larger sense, it refers to a *summated scaling technique pioneered by Likert in the late 1920s. Respondents are given a series of statements and asked to respond to each by saying whether they 1 *strongly disagree*, 2 *disagree*, 3 *agree*, or 4 *strongly agree*. Each person's responses for the set of items are summed, providing a single scale score representing their value on the construct. (b) In its smaller sense, a Likert scale refers to the use of an *ordinal (some would say *interval) 4- or 5-point rating scale with each point anchored or labeled. This usage probably arose because in addition to pioneering the use of the summated scaling procedure, Likert used a 5-point approval rating scale. His original approval scale looked like this (although we start with the negative on the left side and move to the positive on the right side today):

Strongly Approve	Approve	Undecided	Disapprove	Strongly Disapprove
1	2	3	4	5

Today the term "Likert scale" has become somewhat confused because it might refer to either (a) or (b), and the reader is sometimes left wondering. Wording on rating scales today varies considerably. The width of rating scales tends to vary from 4 to 11 points. By constructing the appropriate *anchors, rating scales can be used to address many kinds of attitudinal variation, such as intensity about agreement, amount, effectiveness, importance, satisfaction, and so forth.

Summated scales and rating scales are the most widely used attitude scale types in the social sciences. Summated scales are comparatively easy to construct and tend to have high reliabilities.

Lilliefors Test   A *test statistic for the hypothesis that a sample has been drawn from a population that is normally distributed. It is a modification of the *Kolmogorov-Smirnov test.

Limit   (a) In mathematics, a theoretical end point that can be ever more closely approached, but never quite reached. For example, if we added the fractions $1/2 + 1/4 + 1/8 + 1/16 + 1/32$ and so on, each time adding half of the previous fraction to the string, then the more we added, the closer we would get to the limit of 1.0—but we would never reach it. Compare *asymptote.

(b) In *probability theory, the larger the number of trials, the closer the *empirical probability gets to the limit or the *theoretical probability. The more times we flipped a fair coin, the closer the proportion of heads would get to the limit of .5, or the closer the ratio of heads to tails would get to 1:1.

Lindquist Type I ANOVA   A *two-way, *mixed-design ANOVA, that is, an *ANOVA with one within-subjects variable and one between-subjects variable. E. F. Lindquist discussed seven mixed ANOVA design types in his 1953 book *Design and Analysis of Experiments in Psychology and Education*. Reference to "Lindquist-type designs" was popular in older behavioral science literature but is not used much anymore.

Linear   Of, relating to, or resembling a straight line.

Linear Algebra   A broad category of algebra including *matrix algebra.

Linear Combination   If when two variables are graphed they form a straight line, they are called a "linear combination." A *dependent variable (y) is a linear combination of two or more independent variables when a *linear equation can be used to describe the relation between the dependent variable and the independent variables. In a *GLM, *predicted-y or y-hat ($\hat{y}$) is a linear combination of the independent variables. The correlation between observed y (which is the dependent variable) and predicted y (which are the values predicted by the equation for each subject) is the multiple correlation coefficient.

Linear Dependence   Said of a variable that depends on another in the sense that it can be derived from the other using a *linear equation. When *independent variables have a great deal of linear dependency, this raises the problem of *collinearity. See *function. A desirable condition in a regression or *GLM occurs when the dependent variable is strongly linearly dependent on the independent variables but, at the same time, the independent variables are not linearly dependent on each other.

Linear Equation   An equation that can be plotted on a graph as a straight line. Such an equation contains no *powers higher than 1, and the variables (a and b in the following example) are combined by addition or subtraction, not by multiplication or division.

For example, $y = a + 2b$ is linear, but $y = a + b^2$ is not.

Linear Function   A *linear relation expressed as a *linear equation, that is, one that does not contain terms with powers.

Linear Model   (a) A model assuming linear relationships between quantitative independent variables and a quantitative dependent variable. (b) An assumption of regression that the coefficients are inherently linear. See *linear regression analysis.

Linear Regression Analysis   (a) A method of describing the relationship between one continuous dependent variable and one or more independent variables, usually using *OLS estimation. With just one independent variable, a "best-fitting" line is often graphed, or with two independent variables, a plane is sometimes depicted in a graph. The line or plane averages or summarizes the relationship. Frequently, the result is expressed in a *regression equation. (b) Sometimes the term "linear regression" is used to refer to cases in which the relationship between the dependent and independent variables is required to be linear. (c) More generally, as in the term *general linear model, the word "linear" refers to a requirement for *inherently linear* models, that is, models in which the relationships are either linear *or* can be expressed in a linear form by transforming and/or adding "variables" to the model.

*Curvilinear regression and *polynomial regression are terms used to contrast with (b). Because of the slightly different meanings of the word "linear," linear regression analysis is more often referred to as *regression analysis.

Linear Relation (or Correlation or Association)   A relationship that, when plotted on a graph, forms a straight line. It forms a straight line because the direction and the rate of change in one variable are constant with respect to changes in the other. Compare *curvilinear relation, *monotonic relation.

For example, if a baker notices that whenever he raises the price of a loaf of bread by 5 cents, sales drop by 10 loaves, and every time he lowers the price by 5 cents, sales go up 10 loaves, the relationship between price and sales (graphed in Figure L.1) is linear. This is also an example of an *inverse (or negative) relation, since when one variable goes up, the other goes down. Such relations are seldom perfectly linear as in this example. The *linear equations used to describe real-world relations are approximations. (Note that the baker makes a bigger profit selling 130 loaves for $1.00 than 250 loaves at 40 cents each.)

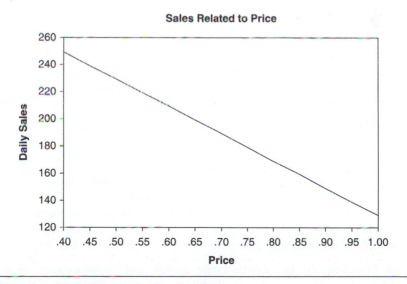

Figure L.1   Linear Relation (or Correlation)

Linear Transformation   Changing a number, a group of numbers, or an equation by adding, subtracting, multiplying, or dividing by a constant. The best-known example is probably multiplying *proportions by 100 (the constant) in order to change ("transform") them into percentages. Called "linear" because when you plot the old values against the new on a graph, the result is a straight line. Compare *nonlinear transformation, and see that entry for an illustration.

Linear Trend   Sometimes used to mean *correlation, often in medical research, as in "The linear trend ($r = .47$) has a p value of .023."

Line Graph   A graphic depiction of data relying on one or more lines. The lines can be *linear or *curvilinear. For example, grade point averages might be plotted on a line graph, as in Figure L.2.

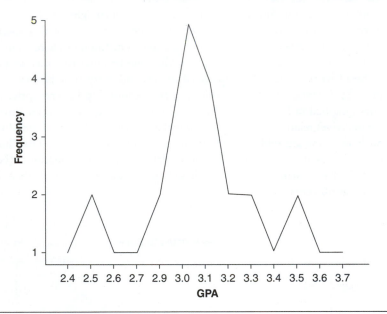

Figure L.2   Line Graph of Grade Point Average

Source: Johnson, Burke. *Educational Research: Quantitative, Qualitative, and Mixed Approaches.* Thousand Oaks, CA: Sage, 2013.

Line of Best Fit   The regression function or line that fulfills the *least squares criterion. Geometrically, there is only a line in a bivariate regression (i.e., a regression with one dependent variable and one independent or predictor variable). When there is more than one independent or predictor variable, it is helpful to think of the best-fitting function because the geometry becomes complex and increasingly difficult to depict as the number of variables goes up.

Link Function   In *generalized linear models, the *transformation of the *dependent variable. It connects (links) the nonlinear *outcome variable with the *linear combination of the *predictor variables. For example, in the *OLS formula $Y = a + bX_1 + bX_2$, the Y term is transformed. The kind of transformation (*logit, *probit, etc.) is called the "link function."

LISREL   Linear Structural Relations. A *computer program used for analyzing *structural equation models (SEM). The software brand name has become so well known that it is sometimes used for the methods of analysis as well as for the technology for executing them. Compare *EQS, *AMOS.

LISREL can be used to analyze causal models with multiple indicators of *latent variables and structural relations among latent variables. This analysis (SEM) is more powerful than simple *path analysis, because bias due to random measurement error in the multiple indicators of the latent variables is corrected. It goes beyond the more typical *exploratory factor analysis and allows the researcher to conduct *confirmatory factor analyses. See *canonical correlation analysis.

List Sample   Another term for *systematic sample.

Listwise Deletion   Completely removing a case from the calculation of *coefficients when that case has any datum missing. Only cases with values for all variables are used. This is the default in many statistical packages. It is in some ways a radical procedure, because it can decimate a sample. Also called "casewise deletion." Compare *pairwise deletion, *mean substitution, *multiple imputation.

For example, consider the *data matrix in Table L.4 with 4 cases and 3 variables in which there is no datum for Case 1 on Variable 1. Computer programs using listwise deletion will not use Case 1 at all, whereas those using pairwise deletion will use it to compute a correlation between Variable 2 and Variable 3. Pairwise deletion is often preferred because it retains more data for use in calculations. A third option is *mean substitution. In this example, the mean score of the other cases on Variable 1 (11.67) would be used as an estimate of the missing number. No one of these procedures is very satisfactory, although there is some dispute about which is worst. See *multiple imputation, *AMELIA.

Table L.4   Listwise Deletion

	Variable 1	Variable 2	Variable 3
Case 1	–	15	40
Case 2	10	16	42
Case 3	12	17	48
Case 4	13	20	47

Literature Review   A survey and interpretation of theoretical books/articles and empirical research findings (the "literature") on a particular topic, usually to prepare for undertaking further research on the subject. The literature review is often done a second time to help one interpret unexpected results. A *meta-analysis is a literature review in which the completeness of the survey is stressed and statistical techniques are used to summarize the quantitative findings. Meta-analyses are sometimes called "systematic" reviews, which are often contrasted with "traditional" or "narrative" reviews. Also called "research review."

LLR   *Log-likelihood ratio.

LN   Abbreviation for natural (not base 10) *logarithm, usually lowercase, *ln*.

Loading   A statistic that shows relation between observed variables and factors. There are a variety of types of loadings. See *factor loadings, *factor pattern matrix, *factor structure matrix, *communality.

Local Independence   In research on *latent variables, such as *factor analysis and *latent class analysis, local independence is the mathematical assumption that the latent variables account fully for the associations between the observed items. For example, in factor analysis, all of the variance in the items is explained by the factor including the items.

Local Regression   Method for fitting a regression line or curve that makes no assumption about the shape of the line or curve. Rather, it follows the pattern of the data points, including any small (local) bends in and clusters of data points. One method for local regression is the *loess method.

Lods   Short for *log odds ratio. Logarithm of an *odds ratio, usually the ratio of the odds of observed to expected values. Compare *logit, which is the log of the odds, rather than of the odds ratio.

Loess   Short for *lo*cally weighted regression. Method for fitting smooth curves to a set of data. It uses *weighted least squares, which reduce the influence of extreme outliers. Also spelled "lowess" with the *w* standing for "weighted."

Log   See *logarithm.

Log$_e$ Symbol for natural *logarithm, **ln*.

Logarithm   An *exponent of a number indicating the *power to which that number must be raised to produce another number.

For example, the log of 100 is 2, because 10^2 (10×10) equals 100; the log of 1,000 is 3, because 10^3 ($10 \times 10 \times 10$) equals 1,000. The log of 47 is 1.6721 because $47 = 10^{1.6721}$. The "anti-log" (or inverse log) turns the relation around; for example, antilog 2 = 100; antilog 3 = 1,000; antilog 1.6721 = 47. Logarithms were invented in the 17th century to ease the burden of calculations. Rather than multiply and divide large numbers, researchers could add and subtract their logs.

When "log" or "logarithm" is used without qualification, it sometimes means "common logarithm," that is, logarithm using base 10, as in the examples above.

Statisticians more frequently use the "natural" (or "Napierian") logarithm (abbreviated *ln*), where the base is the *universal constant *e* (2.71828). The *ln* is widely used in *transformations to make data more closely resemble the *assumptions of statistical techniques, especially in *logistic regression. See *logit, *log-linear analysis.

Logarithmic Transformation   The logarithm of the dependent variable and/or independent variable. The most popular logarithmic transformation is the natural log, although log base 10 also is used. This type of transformation is especially popular in *econometrics. The transformation is helpful for skewed, nonnormal, and slightly nonlinear data. Note: This transformation can be used only with nonnegative values. See *logarithm.

Logical Positivism   The variety of *positivism most closely associated with the Vienna Circle of philosophers in the 1920s and 1930s and their followers. To the extent that "positivism" has any meaning beyond a vague and usually pejorative label used by qualitative researchers to describe narrowness and rigidity in scientific assumptions, it means the theories of philosophers such as Rudolph Carnap and A. J. Ayer. The logical positivists have always provoked considerable indignation, in part because of their propensity to say that most of what others wrote was technically "nonsense" or by definition "meaningless."

Logic Model   In *evaluation research, a graphic representation of the program elements (inputs) and their relationships that indicates how they will function to produce program proximal (short-term) and distal (long-term) outcomes. Logic models serve as frameworks for evaluation researchers as well as plans for program managers. Also known as *program theory; see that entry for further discussion.

Logic of Discovery   Commonly used synonym for *context of discovery. Refers to the creative activities and thinking that occur when one attempts to generate or discover new knowledge.

Logic of Justification   Commonly used synonym for *context of justification. Refers to theory or hypothesis *testing* in order to provide justification of knowledge claims and allow one to take on the claim of knowledge in a relatively strong sense (as in knowledge that has been tested and shown to be true via research).

Logistic Model   See *logit analysis/models.

Logistic Regression Analysis   Also known as "logit regression" and even sometimes "logistical regression." A kind of regression analysis often used when the *dependent variable is *dichotomous and scored 0, 1. (It can also be used when the dependent variable has more than two categories, in which case it is called "multinomial.") It is usually used for predicting whether something will happen or not, such as graduation, business failure, heart attack—anything that can be expressed as event/nonevent. Independent variables can be categorical or continuous in logistic regression analysis. *Ordinary least squares regression can be used when the *independent variables are dichotomous, but this is not good practice when the dependent variable is dichotomous. Rather than using *OLS methods, logistic regression estimates parameters using *maximum likelihood estimation.

A logistic regression coefficient represents the effect of a one-unit change in an *independent variable on a dependent variable—specifically, on the natural log of the odds of the dependent variable being in category 1 when the dependent variable is *dummy coded (1, 0). For example, heart attack might be coded 1 and no heart attack coded 0. You can use this logistic regression coefficient much as you use a *partial regression coefficient using OLS. Specifically, you would check to see if (1) it is a statistically significant predictor of the dependent variable and (2) the coefficient shows you the relationship between the independent variable and the dependent variable after controlling for the other independent variables in the equation. (The difference is in the type of units in which the relationship is expressed; in logistic regression, the units express probability or likelihood.) A positive logistic regression coefficient indicates that as values on the independent variable *increase* (controlling for the other independent variables), the probability of the category coded 1 on the dependent variable increases. A negative coefficient says that as values on the independent variable *decrease* (controlling for the other independent variables), the probability of the category coded 1 on the dependent variable increases. In short, if the dependent variable is heart attack (0 = no heart attack, 1 = has heart attack), then you would want to decrease your values on independent variables with positive coefficients (e.g., smoking, eating fatty foods) and increase your values on independent variables with negative coefficients (e.g., exercising, moderate red wine consumption). Conversely, if you are in school and the dependent variable is graduation (0 = not graduate, 1 = graduate), you would want to increase your values on variables with positive coefficients and decrease your values on variables with negative coefficients because you want to increase your likelihood of graduating.

Logistic regression is an increasingly popular alternative to *discriminant analysis because it requires fewer statistical assumptions. See *logit analysis/models.

Logit   Short for "logistic probability unit" or the natural "*log of the *odds." A *logistic regression analysis yields a probability of an event; that probability is transformed into an odds; the natural log of that odds is taken to get the logit. See *logit analysis/models. Compare *probit regression analysis.

Logit Analysis/Models   A type of *log-linear analysis similar to multiple *regression analysis. It is used when both the independent variables and the dependent variable are *dummy (*dichotomous) variables. It is used for predicting a categorical dependent variable on the basis of two or more categorical independent variables. If one or more of the independent variables are continuous, then *logistic regression analysis is used. Compare *probit regression analysis.

The terms "logit model" and "log-linear model" are sometimes used interchangeably, but it is more precise to say that the logit model is a particular type (probably the most commonly used type) of the log-linear model.

Log-Likelihood   The *logarithm of the *likelihood, which is more often used than the simple likelihood when conducting a *maximum likelihood estimation.

Log-Likelihood Ratio (LLR)   A common *test statistic used for *logistic regression and *probit regression. The LLR is multiplied by −2. The test statistic is often written −2LLR or −2 LOG LR.

Log-Linear Analysis/Models   Methods for studying relations among *categorical (*nominal) variables in contingency tables. So called because they use equations that are transformed, by taking their natural logs, to make them linear. Log-linear techniques make it possible to conduct multivariate analyses of categorical data. Log-linear analysis uses *odds rather than *proportions, as is done in the more familiar *chi-square tests. Log-linear models are capable of handling several nominal variables and their relations in a way that approximates *analysis of covariance structures. The results of a log-linear analysis can be analyzed either by the usual chi-square *goodness-of-fit test or by the *likelihood ratio test.

Log-linear models are an advance over the older *chi-square test of independence, because unlike the chi-square test, log-linear analysis can handle complex patterns of *interaction among the variables. The distinction between dependent and independent variables does not apply in log-linear analysis. Some texts say that none of the variables is a dependent variable; others say that all of them are. In sum, the researcher attempts to explain the cell counts in each cell by examining the interactions of the variables in the remaining cells.

Log Odds   Another term for *logit, that is, the natural log of the odds. Note that *independence when using a log odds is 0, unlike for an *odds and in a *logistic regression analysis, where independence, or no effect, is 1.

Log-Rank Test   A statistical test for comparing sets of data in a *survival analysis. The technique involves comparing the ages of those who have survived to those who have not to see whether a *treatment has increased survival time.

Longitudinal Data   Data from multiple points across time. Compare *cross-sectional data.

Longitudinal Study (or Design)   A study over time of a variable or a group of subjects. See *panel study, *event history analysis, *prospective study, *microgenetic design. Contrast *cross-sectional study.

The National Educational Longitudinal Study of eighth graders started in 1988 (NELS88) is a well-known example. Investigators began with a national cohort of 25,000 eighth-grade students from 1,000 schools whom they surveyed extensively. Every few years, the same students were contacted again to learn what they studied in high school and whether they graduated, whether and where they went to college, whether they graduated, what employment they found, how much money they were making, and so on.

Lord's Paradox   A type of *Simpson's paradox that can occur when *change scores among preexisting groups are studied.

Lorenz Curve   A graphic representation of inequality or dispersion in a *frequency distribution. The cumulative percentages of a *population (such as income earners) is plotted against the cumulative percentage of another variable (such as percent of income earned). The more the curve departs from a straight line at a 45-degree angle, the greater the inequality. See *Gini coefficient, which is 2 times the distance between the curve and the diagonal line.

The graph in Figure L.3 uses a Lorenz curve to plot the degree of inequality in Society A and Society B. Income inequality is greater in B than in A.

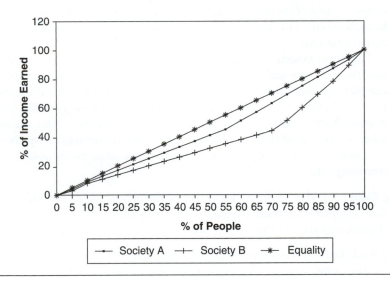

Figure L.3   Lorenz Curve

Loss to Follow-Up   In clinical trials research, "loss to follow-up" occurs when the participant drops out of the study and is not available during a follow-up to the study. Also called *attrition.

Lowess   See *loess.

Lowspread   The range of values in a *distribution between the *median and the lowest value. Compare *highspread, *boxplot.

LR   *Likelihood ratio.

LSD Post Hoc Test   In statistics and methodology, this does *not* refer to lysergic acid diethylamide! Please see *Fisher's LSD test.

Lumpers Versus Splitters   An informal term for important opposed tendencies of some researchers to group related phenomena and others to emphasize differences in categories of phenomena. For example, lumpers tend to be optimistic about the appropriateness of international comparisons; splitters think that such comparisons inevitably ignore too many important differences.

Lurking Variable   A third variable that causes a *correlation between two others—sometimes, like the troll under the bridge, an unpleasant surprise when discovered. A lurking variable can be a source of a *spurious correlation. See also *confound. Compare *covariate, *latent, *mediating, and *moderator variables.

For example, if researchers found a correlation between individuals' college grades and their income later in life, they might wonder whether doing well in school increased income. It might, but good grades and high income could both be caused by a third (lurking or hidden) variable such as tendency to work hard.

L

M   Symbol sometimes used for the *mean (of a *sample). For example, publications using the *Publication Manual of the American Psychological Association* may use *M* rather than $\bar{X}$.

Machine Learning   The ability of a computer program to improve its functioning on the basis of newly acquired or generated data—in brief, to learn from experience.

Macro   Prefix meaning "big." Used in economics and sociology to mean broad social, institutional, or system-level analyses or variables, such as the behavior of the economy as a whole. Usually contrasted with *micro, which refers to small-group or individual phenomena, such as individuals' job skills. Sometimes "meso" or "meso-level" is added between macro and micro, referring to intermediate or middle level. Compare *molar.

MAD   *Mean absolute deviation.

Magnitude of Effect   See *effect size.

Mahalanobis Distance   Abbreviated D^2. The difference (or "distance") between populations. It is the most common test for the presence of multivariate *outliers. It can be seen as a multivariate version of the standardized mean difference *effect size measure *d*, though it was developed long before *d*. See *leverage. It is the distance between each case and the *centroid, which is the group multivariate mean. Cases that are significantly different at the $p < .001$ level are considered multivariate outliers. See *multivariate outlier.

Main Diagonal   The diagonal in a matrix moving from the top left to the bottom right. An example is seen in the table given with the *correlation matrix entry. In a correlation matrix, the main diagonal includes all 1s because it shows the correlations of the variables with themselves.

Main Effect   The effect of an *independent variable on a *dependent variable; the effect of an independent variable uninfluenced by (without controlling for the effects of) other variables. Used in contrast with the *interaction effect of two or more independent variables on a dependent variable. It is difficult to interpret main effects in the presence of interaction effects. See *simple effect.

Main Effects Only Model   A statistical model (e.g., in ANOVA or regression) in which terms are included only for main effects. Interaction effects are excluded, as are any curvilinear effects. A main effects model is a simple model, but it might overlook important interaction effects. Therefore, the *additive test should usually be conducted to make sure a *nonaddative model is not more appropriate for one's data. Compare *main effects plus interaction model.

Main Effects Plus Interaction Model   This starts with a *main effects model and adds terms for *interaction effects. For example, in a two-way ANOVA a main effects only model would statistically test for the main effects of the two independent variables. However, a main effects plus interaction model would also include a significance test for the two-way interaction term. Interestingly in ANOVA, interaction terms are typically included as standard operating procedure, but in regression the interaction terms are often omitted even though they are easily included. It is recommended here that the reader always consider the possibility of interaction effects in regression as well as in ANOVA, as well as in other statistical models. See *nonadditive model, *interaction effect. Compare *main effects only model, *additive model.

MANCOVA   *Multivariate analysis of covariance; an extension of *ANCOVA to problems with multiple *dependent variables.

Manifest Function   The obvious, ostensible, or purported use or purpose of a social phenomenon—usually contrasted with its *latent function. See *functionalism.

For example, the manifest function of the death penalty might be deterrence. If you asked its supporters, this might be the reason (manifest function) they would offer for favoring it. But if there is little convincing evidence that the death penalty deters crime, a functionalist might look for latent (hidden) functions to explain the widespread support for capital punishment. Satisfying an urge for revenge might be the latent function.

Manifest Variable   A variable that can be directly observed. Often assumed to indicate the presence of a *latent variable. Also called an "indicator variable." See *factor analysis, *structural equation modeling.

For example, we cannot observe intelligence directly; it is a latent variable. But we can look at indicators such as size of vocabulary, success in one's occupation, IQ test score, ability to play complicated games such as chess or bridge well, and so on.

Manipulated Variable   Another term for *independent variable in experimental research. Also called "treatment variable." Compare *predictor variable. In *experimental research, you manipulate the independent variable(s); in *observational research, you do not.

M

Manipulation   Administration of an active substance or treatment to research participants. The outcome for the group experiencing the intervention is usually compared with a control group that does not receive the active substance or new treatment. An active "manipulation" is part of every experimental research study and helps in determining cause and effect. In contrast, in nonexperimental research the researcher measures/observes naturally occurring phenomena/variables without actively manipulating them. See *experimental research. Compare *nonexperimental research.

Manipulation Check   Part of a pilot study to make sure an intervention or treatment is strong enough or has the intended effect. For example, if an experiment in social psychology were designed to measure the effects of subjects' anger on their perceptions, a manipulation check would ascertain whether in the pilot study the treatment succeeded in making subjects angry.

Mann-Whitney *U* Test   A test of the *statistical significance of differences between two groups. It is used when the *data for two *samples are measured on an *ordinal scale. It is a *nonparametric statistics equivalent of the *t test. Although ordinal measures are used with the Mann-Whitney test, an underlying continuous distribution is assumed. This test is also used instead of the t test with interval-level data when researchers do not assume that the populations are normal. It is similar to the *Wilcoxon test, which is a different test but yields the same p value.

MANOVA   *Multivariate analysis of variance; an extension of *ANOVA to research problems with multiple dependent variables. Compare *MANCOVA.

Marginal Distribution   See *marginal frequency distribution.

Marginal Effect   In *regression analysis, a marginal effect is the expected change in a *dependent variable given an infinitely small change in a continuous *independent variable.

Marginal Frequencies   See *marginal frequency distributions.

Marginal Frequency Distributions   Frequency distributions of grouped data in *cross-tabulations or *contingency tables. So called because they are found in the "margins" of the table. Often called "marginals" for short.

   For example, researchers polled a sample of city residents about whether they favored busing to achieve school desegregation. They *cross-tabulated the answers by the race of the *respondents; the results are shown in Table M.1 on page 248. The totals are the marginal frequency distributions. The "row marginals" are 155 and 293; the "column marginals" are 187 and 261. These marginals could be used to calculate the *expected frequencies to use in a *chi-square test of the *statistical significance of the findings. Doing so yields a chi-square statistic of about 51, which at 1 *degree of freedom is statistically significant ($p < .001$).

Table M.1   Marginal Frequency Distributions

		Black	White	*Total*
Favor Busing	*Yes*	103	52	155
	No	84	209	293
	Total	187	261	448

Marginally Significant   Just barely or almost significant. Sometimes used to describe research results that fail to exceed the *critical value needed to be *statistically significant but that come close enough that the researcher wants to talk about them anyway.

Marginal Means   Weighted means of the cells across either the rows or columns. For example, in a 2 × 2 ANOVA there are four cell means, two column marginal means (the mean of the observations in each column), and two row marginal means (the means of each row).

Marginal Probability   The sum of the cell (i.e., joint) probabilities for a particular row or column in a *contingency table. Marginal probabilities are often shown in the margins of a table such as Table M.2 on page 249. A margin probability calculation depends only on the frequencies in the margins of a table. See *expected frequency, *marginal frequency distributions.

For example, suppose you randomly sampled 1,000 adults in a large city and obtained from each of them their sex and weight. Your sample included 600 men and 400 women; therefore, the marginal probabilities for sex would be .60 and .40. Your sample also was divided into 300 members who were overweight and 700 who were not; therefore, the marginal probabilities for weight are .30 and .70. The bold numbers in Table M.2 highlight the four marginal probabilities. One use of the marginal probabilities is to determine the expected frequency of the cells under the assumption that the row and column variables are independent (i.e., assuming that weight and sex in our table are not associated). You can get the expected cell frequency by multiplying the relevant row and column marginal probability values and multiplying that by the total sample size. The expected frequency for overweight males is found by multiplying its row marginal (.3) by its column marginal (.6), which is .18, and multiplying this by the sample size (1,000)—the expected frequency (if weight and sex are not related) is 180 people. The other expected frequencies are shown in the table. Here is the key point: The *expected frequency for each of the cells, if sex had no relation to being overweight, would be 180, 120, 420, and 280. If the actual, *observed frequencies departed significantly from these expected frequencies, you would conclude that sex and being overweight are related in the population sampled.

Table M.2 Marginal Probability: Overweight by Sex, Expected Frequencies in Cells

	Men	*Women*	**Total**	
Overweight	180	120	300	**.30**
Not Overweight	420	280	700	**.70**
Total	600	400	1,000	
	.60	**.40**		

Marginals (a) Totals of rows or columns in a *contingency table or *cross-tabulation. See *marginal frequency distributions. (b) Having to do with a small change or difference, often a change of one unit. See *marginal utility.

Marginal Totals See *marginal frequency distributions.

Marginal Utility The additional benefit that comes from obtaining a small (marginal) or one-unit increase in some good, given the amount that you already have.

   For example, the benefit or utility of a glass of cold water on a hot summer day might be very great. The value to you of a second glass of water would probably be less great. After you drank the third or fourth glass of water, the marginal utility of one more would probably decline to almost nothing.

Margin of Error A range of likely or allowable values. Although the term is widely used to report the results of survey research, in statistics the margin of error is usually expressed as a *confidence interval. Confidence intervals are usually determined by adding and subtracting the margin of error to the estimated value (to find the upper and lower limits, or width of the confidence interval). Sometimes, the full width of the confidence is called the margin of error. In both cases, it refers to the error placed around the predicted value to help users of statistics make more intelligent statements about statistical estimates obtained from samples.

Markov Chain *Time-series model in which an event's *probability is dependent only on the immediately preceding event in the series and this dependence is the same at all stages. The general idea is that the state of a system in the future will be unaffected by its past, except its immediate past. Also called "Markov process," "Markovian principle," and *chain path model.

   For example, if every year in a particular state, 5% of city dwellers moved to the suburbs and 2% from the suburbs moved to the city, eventually the proportions would stabilize (with the same number moving each way) at around 29% city and 71% suburbs, no matter what the original proportions.

Markov Chain Monte Carlo (MCMC) Methods Computer-intensive methods used for simulating large arrays of correlated observations. MCMC is a group of popular techniques for fitting complex models. Originally developed in physics, the techniques are now widely used in the social and behavioral sciences. The computer simulations are used to find probability distributions and are especially important in *Bayesian statistical inference.

Masking   See *blinding.

Matched Case-Control Study   A *case-control study that includes some form of matching to equate the groups, such as *individual matching, *group matching, or *propensity score matching.

Matched Pairs Design   A *research design in which subjects are matched on characteristics that might affect their reaction to a *treatment. After similar pairs of individuals are determined, one member of each pair is assigned at random to the group receiving treatment (*experimental group); the other group (*control group) does not receive treatment. Without random assignment, matching is considered a much weaker research practice because the groups are matched or equated on only a single variable. Also called *individual matching or "subject matching." Matching is a special case of blocking; see *block.

   For example, if professors wanted to test the effectiveness of two different textbooks for an undergraduate statistics course, they might match the students on quantitative aptitude scores before assigning them to classes using one or another of the texts. An alternative, if the professors had no control over class assignment, would be to treat the quantitative aptitude scores as a *covariate and control for it using an *ANCOVA design.

Matched Pairs *t* Test   Synonym for *dependent samples *t* test and *correlated samples *t* test.

Matching   See *matched pairs.

Materialism   The *ontological position that matter is the only reality and that other sorts of phenomena, such as ideas and social values, are reducible to or are merely expressions of material reality. Today, materialism is sometimes called *physicalism* in order to incorporate nonmaterial entities such as gravity, light (photons), and structural relationships. Compare *idealism.

Matrix   Any rectangular array of data into rows and columns. See *correlation matrix, *matrix algebra, *vector.

Matrix Algebra   Rules for adding, subtracting, multiplying, and dividing matrices. Its advantage is that it allows one to treat matrices as single objects. It is widely used in *regression analysis and other multivariate methods, because it greatly simplifies the calculations needed when there are more than two independent variables. See *vector.

   Table M.3 on page 251 shows a very simple matrix operation, how to add two matrices, $A + B$, to get a third, C. Many students find it interesting when they first learn that some of the rules of arithmetic do not hold in matrix algebra; for example, in algebra A times B is equal to B times A (i.e., $AB = BA$), but in matrix algebra this commutative law for multiplication does not apply!

Table M.3   Matrix Algebra: Adding Two Matrices

	A		+		B		=		C	
	4	8		4	3			8	11	
	9	6	+	2	4	=	11	10	
	1	2		8	6			9	8	

Maturation Effect   A *threat to *internal validity that occurs because of change in subjects over time. See *extraneous variable. Compare *history effect.

For example, to study the effects of a college education on social and political attitudes, we might ask entering students to complete an attitude survey. Three-and-one-half years later, we could ask the same students (now seniors) to answer the same survey questions. Any changes might be due to the effects of college, but they also might be due to the fact that the students have gotten older (matured) since we first surveyed them.

Mauchley's Test for Sphericity   Some statistical tests require the *assumption of *sphericity. For example, sphericity is required if *repeated-measures ANOVA F tests are to be valid. Mauchley's test is used to determine if the assumption of sphericity has been violated—the null hypothesis for Mauchley's test is that the assumption is met. Therefore, one hopes that Mauchley's test is not statistically significant. If it is statistically significant, there are, fortunately, several strategies available to correct for the violation. See *sphericity, *Geisser-Greenhouse, *Huynh-Feldt.

Maverick   An *outlier so extreme that it is doubtful that it could belong to the *population being studied.

Maximin Strategy   In *game theory, a strategy in which players try to maximize their minimum winnings or returns. Compare *minimax strategy.

An example might be concentrating one's investments in low-yield, but very safe, government bonds.

Maximum Likelihood Estimation (MLE)   Statistical estimation procedure (an alternative to *OLS) for estimating the *population parameters most likely to have given rise to the observed *sample data. In many cases OLS and MLE will produce the same values of the coefficients. MLE is an integral part of *SEM and *generalized linear models. It is also often used in *log-linear models to estimate *expected frequencies in *contingency tables.

M

Unlike OLS, which minimizes a criterion, MLE maximizes a criterion. Specifically, OLS methods work by minimizing the sum of squared differences between observed and predicted scores. MLE chooses as the estimates of the parameters the values for which the probability of the observed scores is the highest. See *likelihood. The basic procedure in MLE is as follows: For each possible value a parameter might have, compute the probability that the particular sample statistic (observed values) would have occurred if it were the true value of the parameter. Then, for the estimate, pick the parameter for which the probability of the actual observation is greatest.

Maximum Likelihood Ratio Chi-Square (MLRCS)   A test of the *statistical significance of *confirmatory factor analyses, *SEM models, and other statistical results that can be expressed as *likelihoods. Abbreviated L^2. The larger the value of this statistic, the poorer the fit of the model to the observed data. Unlike the ordinary (Pearson) chi-square, the MLRCS can be *partitioned.

Maxplane   A method of *oblique rotation of the axes in *factor analysis.

MCA   *Multiple classification analysis or *multiple correspondence analysis.

MCAR   Missing completely at random. See *missing at random.

MCMC Methods   *Markov Chain Monte Carlo methods.

McNemar's Chi-Square Test   A variation on the chi-square test used for samples that are not *independent but are related in some way, as in before-and-after studies, and when the outcome variable is *dichotomous. See *correlated groups design, *Cochran's Q test.

MD   Abbreviation for *median, and, less commonly, for *mean absolute deviation.

Mean   (a) Average; most widely used measure of location or central tendency; it has the desirable mathematical property of minimizing the *variance. To get the mean, you add up the values for each case and divide that sum by the total number of cases (e.g., the average of 1, 2, and 3 is $(1 + 2 + 3)/3 = 2$). For sample data, often symbolized as M or as $\bar{X}$ ("X-bar"). When used without specification, "mean" refers to the *arithmetic* mean. For another example of how to calculate an arithmetic mean, see *mode. Much less commonly used are the *geometric* mean and the *harmonic* mean.

(b) The *geometric mean* is computed by taking the nth root of the product of n scores (e.g., the square root of 2 scores, the cube root of 3). For example, to get the geometric mean of 5, 7, and 9, you multiply $5 \times 7 \times 9 = 315$ and take the cube root to get 6.8, which is somewhat smaller than the arithmetic mean (7.0) for the same scores. The geometric mean is useful for such tasks as averaging *skewed data and *indexes.

(c) The *harmonic mean* of a series of numbers is calculated by dividing n by the sum of the *reciprocals of the numbers. For example, to get the harmonic mean of 40 and 60, you add 1/40 plus 1/60 and divide the result into 2, for a

M

harmonic mean of 48. Like the geometric mean, the harmonic is always smaller than the arithmetic; also, the harmonic is always less than the geometric. For instance, the harmonic mean of 5, 7, and 9 is 6.6.

Mean Absolute Deviation (MAD)   A measure of *dispersion. It is calculated using the *absolute values of the *deviation scores—not the squares of the deviation scores as is done when computing the *variance and *standard deviation. Also called *average deviation and "mean deviation."

Mean Square Error   Another term for *mean square residual.

Mean Square Residual (MSR)   The *sum of squared errors divided by its degrees of freedom (to convert the sum of squares into a variance). MSR is the average of the residuals (i.e., errors) in squared units. Taking the square root of MSR produces the standard deviation of the errors (called the *standard error of estimate), which indicates how big the errors tend to be in regular (i.e., nonsquared) units; for example, if this standard error is 2.1, then the observed values tend to be about 2.1 points different from the value predicted by the model. Another term for *variance of estimate.

Mean Squares (MS)   Short for the mean of the squared *deviation scores, that is, the *variance. The *variance is most often referred to as the MS in an *ANOVA. In ANOVA, the *F test is based on the ratio of the MS explained (i.e., between-groups MS) to the MS error. In ANOVA, the *sum of squares (SS) is converted to mean squares by dividing the SS by its *degrees of freedom.

Mean Substitution   A procedure used when some values for *cases are missing. It involves replacing missing values with the mean of the values from the other cases. See *listwise deletion for an example.

Measurement   (a) Assigning numbers or symbols to things, usually to characteristics of *variables. (b) The subdiscipline concerned with how to assign numbers or symbols to variables. Compare *coding.

People often think of measurement and statistics as being the same thing, but there is a distinction: Measurement is how we get the numbers on which we then perform statistical operations. If we do not have good measurement, the statistical result is *GIGO. See *level of measurement.

Measurement Class   Another term for *class interval.

Measurement Error   Inaccuracy due to flaws in a measuring instrument, due to mistakes of those using it, or simply due to random or chance factors. Measurement error is inevitable since perfect precision is impossible. If measurement errors are *random, they will cancel one another out in the long run; however, if they are *systematic,* they will result in bias or invalidity rather than just reduced reliability. See *random error, *sampling error. Compare *bias.

For example, if a research team were studying the effects of stress on blood pressure, and the pressure gauge were not *perfectly* accurate (it never is), this would lead to measurement error.

Measurement Invariance   This occurs when scores on the construct or latent variable have the same meaning across two or more groups. This must be established before making comparisons and assuming common meaning. There is the potential for a lot of research in this area in the future. One example is *factorial invariance.

Measurement Model   In *structural equation modeling, latent variables are specified using two models: the measurement model and the structural (or causal) model. The *measurement model* shows the relationships between the *latent variables and their observed indicators. The *structural model* shows the relationships among the latent variables and is the substantive theory to be tested. Measurement and structural models are shown in Figure M.1.

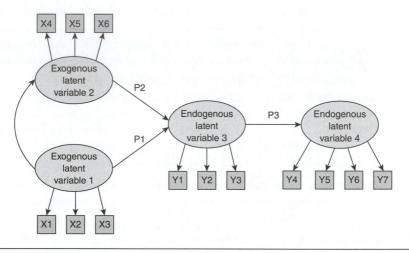

Figure M.1   Example of SEM of Measurement and Structural Models

Measurement Scale   An ordered reference standard used to quantify constructs or attributes, such as a 5-point scale or a 0-to-10 scale. See *scale, *scale development.

Measurement Theory   A branch of applied mathematics focused on how to assess and measure constructs, and determining their psychometric properties and how they operate in theory, research, and practice. Currently the two most common measurement theories are *classical test theory and *item response theory.

Measure of Association   See *association, measure of.

Measure of Central Tendency   Numerical value considered typical of the values of a quantitative variable, indicated by indices such as the *mean, *median, and *mode.

Measure of Variability   Numerical value that provides information about how much variation is present or how spread out the data values are, indicated by indices such as the *range, *standard deviation, and *variance.

Mechanism   The process or steps that lead to an event or outcome. Often the underlying determinants (i.e., *intervening or *mediating variables) that "explain" a *statistical association, as in a causal mechanism. Compare *descriptive causation, *explanatory causation.

Median   The middle score or measurement in a set of ranked scores or measurements; the point that divides a distribution into two equal halves; the 50th percentile. When the number of scores is even, there is no single middle score; in that case the median is found by taking the mean of the two middle scores. See the example at *mode.

Median Absolute Deviation   An estimate of variability spread of scores in a distribution. It is computed by subtracting the median of a distribution from each of the absolute values of the scores in a distribution and then taking the median of the resulting scores. Compare *mean absolute deviation, which like the median absolute deviation is also abbreviated as MAD.

Median Test   A *nonparametric test of significance to determine whether two *samples, measured on an *ordinal scale, come from populations having different medians. The null hypothesis is that the samples come from populations with the same median. The *chi-square test is applied to the proportions of the samples above or below the median. See *Mann-Whitney U test.

Mediating Variable   Another term for *intervening variable, that is, a variable that "transmits" the effects of another variable. Compare *interaction effect, *moderator variable.

   For example, parents transmit their social status to their children directly. But they also do so indirectly, through education, as in Figure M.2, where child's education is the mediating variable. See *path diagram.

Parents' Status → Child's Education → Child's Status

Figure M.2   Mediating Variable

Mediational Process   Process seen in the operation of one or more *intervening variables occurring between the initial *independent variable and the final *dependent variable at the end of a causal chain. The mediational process helps "explain" the relationship between the independent and dependent variables.

Mediator   Synonym for *intervening variable.

M

MEDLINE   Abbreviation for Medical Literature Analysis and Retrieval System Online, a bibliographic database that is widely used for identifying published medical research and obtaining data for *meta-analysis of health-related topics.

Megabyte   One thousand *kilobytes, or 1,024,000 *bytes.

Member Check (or Validation)   The practice of researchers submitting their data or findings to their *informants (members) in order to make sure they have correctly represented what their informants told them. This is perhaps most often done with data such as interview summaries; it is less often done with interpretations built on those data. This procedure is most widespread in *qualitative research.

Memos   (a) Term used by some researchers to describe what is more tradition-ally called *field notes. (b) In *grounded theory, memo writing is more often thought of as a step between field notes and drafting the research report. In this context, the memos are sometimes called "theoretical memos"; in these memos the researcher writes down thoughts and insights about the developing theory during conduct of the study and analysis of the data.

Meso   Latin for "middle," "intermediate," or "in between." For example, "Meso-america" falls in between and connects North and South America. Used in social science theory to refer to a middle level of theoretical analysis falling between *micro and *macro levels or theories. Sometimes refers to attempts to interrelate the micro and the macro. For example, social psychology can be helpful in connecting psychology and sociology.

Mesokurtic   See *kurtosis for definitions and comparison of leptokurtic, platykurtic, and mesokurtic.

Meta-analysis   Quantitative procedures for summarizing or integrating the find-ings obtained from a *literature review on a topic. Meta-analysis is, strictly speaking, more a kind of *synthesis than analysis, and it is also called "research synthesis." The meta-analyst uses the results of individual research projects on the same topic (perhaps studies testing the same *hypothesis) as *data for a sta-tistical study of the topic. The main controversies about meta-analysis have to do with identifying studies that are appropriate to synthesize, that is, with specifying which studies are truly studying the same hypotheses, treatments, and populations as well as using the same methods of investigation, such as *RCTs.

Meta-analytic Path Analysis   This is a three-step process. First, a meta-analysis is conducted to produce a meta-analytic correlation matrix of all of the vari-ables of interest. Second, a path analysis theoretical/structural model is speci-fied based on understanding of other models in the literature. Third, the model is tested using the correlations.

Metadata   Data that provide information about an information resource, includ-ing where and how it is stored as well as the design and sampling methods used to collect it. For example, a web developer might provide metadata about the website content (keywords, questions, topics). Metadata about a website or source also is sometimes included in search results, providing information to help users know whether the website will be of interest. As another example, the information in the front of a book (copyright, ISBN, publisher) is metadata. Last, the National Security Agency's definition of metadata concerning the phone calls it has monitored includes the following: the phone number, as well as the location, time, and duration of the call—but not the call itself. The data are the content of the call; the location, time, duration, and other elements are the metadata.

Metamodel   A model of models. For example, the second author of this book (Johnson) examined multiple implicit and explicit models of evaluation utilization, and from these he constructed a new metamodel based on all of the models.

Metaphysical Explanation   An explanation not subject to physical (or observational or behavioral) tests. The term is most often used loosely by social and behavioral scientists to mean "unscientific," "hard to understand," and/or "highly unlikely."

Metaregression Analysis   Technique used in meta-analysis to determine what factors moderate or interact with the observed *effect sizes. It helps answer this question: "Why does the effect size vary across studies?" The dependent variable is effect size and the predictor variables are characteristics of the research studies (e.g., individual differences variables, environmental or contextual variables, type of research method used in the study). It can also be used to investigate subgroup effects.

Metatheory   Theory about theory. Used for comparing and evaluating theories, or for just thinking about theories.

For example, a theoretical account of the *epistemological presuppositions of *logical positivism and *constructionism would be a metatheoretical work.

Methodological Individualism   The *assumption that all generalizations about groups can be explained by (or reduced to) facts about individuals. Sometimes also called—more often by its opponents than its friends—*reductionism. Methodological individualism is often contrasted with *holism.

For example, take the statement "Teachers' middle-class values often make them unable to respond to the needs of lower-class children." Methodological individualists would say that this statement makes no sense apart from the values of individual teachers and the needs of individual students; "middle-class" and "lower-class" are merely convenient generalizations that, when valid, summarize what we know about individuals.

Methodological Pluralism   The argument that the use of multiple methodologies (including quantitative and qualitative) to understand a phenomenon is good practice and provides greater understanding. It warns against the use of monomethods or monomethodologies because of their relative limitations. It is very similar to *multimethod research and *mixed methods research.

Methodology   (a) The study of research methods, from general problems bordering on history and *epistemology to specific comparisons of the details of various techniques. See *research design. (b) Sometimes a verbose way of saying "method," as in "This article employs an interesting methodology." In that case, the difference between "method" and "methodology" is three syllables.

Method Variance   The effects (*bias) that different methods of measurement have on data collection—for example, written surveys versus face-to-face interviews. One argument for *multimethod and *mixed methods research is that by using more than one method, the biases of individual methods are likely to cancel one another out.

Metric   Any standard or scale of measurement: inches, seconds, minutes, dollars, test scores, kilograms, and so on. The term is often used in a statement such as "Results are reported in the original metric," meaning that they have not been *transformed or *standardized.

Metric Variable   A variable that can be measured on an *interval or *ratio scale.

Micro   Prefix meaning "small." See *macro, *meso.

Microdata   Data about variables within a behavioral unit, such as an individual or a corporation. Microdata are often contrasted with *aggregate data, which are about groups of behavioral units such as individuals grouped by race, sex, or class or corporations grouped by economic sector.

Microgenetic Design   A type of *longitudinal design used in development science. Compared to traditional longitudinal designs, microgenetic designs use shorter periods (e.g., months, weeks, or days rather than multiple years between measurements). The goal is to observe changes in participants rather than just document the results of changes. The researcher hopes to determine exactly *how* changes take place. Observations should be made repeatedly before, during, and after the specific times of rapid developmental change. During times of expected transition, long and intensive observations are made. The scheduling of observation and measurement will depend on the kinds of developmental changes one wants to study; some changes occur over long periods, while some occur over shorter periods. Uses both quantitative and qualitative research methods.

Middle-Range Theory   Robert K. Merton's term for theory describing relations at modest levels of *abstraction, or middling *levels of generality—somewhere between an *empirical generalization and a *metatheory. Middle-range theories are, as Goldilocks put it, "just right," not too atheoretical like empirical generalizations, but not too hard to test like metatheories.

M

Midmean   The mean of the *midspread, that is, the mean of the middle half of the values in a distribution.

Midrange   The mean of the largest and smallest values in a sample.

Midspread   Another term for *interquartile range, that is, scores that range from the 25th through the 75th percentiles.

Milgram Experiments   A series of studies of individuals' willingness to "just follow orders," even when doing so appeared to require hurting other people. These studies of obedience to authority were controversial both because of their shocking findings about how many people would be willing to obey evil orders and because the methods used may have put the subjects of the studies at risk of psychological harm. The experiments are often cited as an example of violating *research ethics. See *debriefing.

Mill's Joint Method of Agreement and Difference   The combined use of the method of agreement and the method of difference in an attempt to locate a factor or event that is both necessary and sufficient. The method of agreement is used to show a necessary condition (i.e., a factor that must be present for the outcome to occur); everything else is not necessary for the outcome. The method of difference is used to show a sufficient condition (i.e., a factor that will produce the outcome); everything else is not sufficient for outcome. Mill argued that the combined logic would indicate a factor that is both necessary and sufficient for producing the outcome of interest. See *cause.

Mill's Method of Agreement   If everyone in a set of heterogeneous cases has the outcome of interest (e.g., a particular disease), then the cause is the one factor (other than the disease) that they have in common.

Mill's Method of Concomitant Variation   If the outcome of interest varies along with variations in a factor, then that factor might be the cause. See *concomitant variation.

Mill's Method of Difference   If two groups (e.g., a treatment and a control group) are the same on all characteristics except one, then that one factor or variable is the cause of the difference between the groups on the outcome that one group has but the other group does not. This logic is used in experimental research.

Mill's Method of Residues   If one knows that part of a phenomenon is due to a specific causal factor, then one can infer that the rest of the phenomenon is due to other causal factors. This is one interpretation of *unexplained variance in science.

Mill's Methods (of Causation)   J. S. Mill (1806–1873) discussed five methods for reasoning about causation. They are the method of agreement, the method of concomitant variation, the method of difference, the method of residues, and the joint method of agreement and difference.

M

Minimax Strategy   In *game theory, a strategy whereby players try to minimize their maximum losses. Compare *maximin strategy.

An example of how this strategy could be applicable is designing power plants to avoid nuclear accidents. It might be wise to reduce the odds of melt-down (maximum loss) to the lowest possible level, even if that must come at the cost of raising the odds of occasionally spewing small amounts of radioactive particles into the air.

MINITAB   A *software package for statistical analysis often used for teaching statistics. Compare *SPSS and *SAS.

Missing at Random   When *missing data occur in ways that do not *bias samples, they are said to be missing at random. If the missing data have no systematic pattern (are randomly distributed), they cause only small problems for the researcher. In practice, it is frequently difficult to know whether missing data are missing at random. Distinctions are often made between data missing *completely* at random (called MCAR), missing *partly* at random (called, confusingly, missing at random, or MAR) in ways that can be handled with *missing values procedures (called MAR), and biased data in which the values are missing *not* at random and cannot be imputed (called MNAR).

Missing Data   Information not available for a subject (or case) about whom other information is available—as when a *respondent fails to answer one of the questions in a survey. For an example, see *listwise deletion. Missing data is a problem in virtually all research projects and is usually a more serious challenge to the accuracy of estimates and conclusions than most researchers realize. See *multiple imputation for a description of procedures for correcting for missing data. See also *AMELIA.

Missing Values Procedures   Statistical methods for dealing with *missing data. See *listwise deletion, *pairwise deletion, *mean substitution, and *multiple imputation.

Misspecification (or Model Misspecification)   An error in model building (e.g., *SEM) and statistical analysis (e.g., *regression analysis) made by constructing a *model that excludes a *variable that ought to have been included—or includes one that ought to have been excluded. In regression analysis, the former is called the *omitted variable* problem and is very serious because it leads to *biased estimates. Good theory or an understanding of all the relevant variables is required for "proper model specification." Compare *identification problem. Sometimes also called, respectively, LOVE for "left out variable error" and RAVE for "redundant added variable error." Again, of the two, LOVE is the bigger error because it is harder to detect and correct.

Mixed ANOVA   This form of ANOVA combines (mixes) at least one *between-subjects variable and at least one *within-subjects variable. In other words, subjects are measured only one time on some variables (e.g., gender) but more than once on others (e.g., scores before and after an experimental intervention). Also called "split-plot" ANOVA. Sometimes called *mixed design or "mixed model ANOVA." See *repeated-measures ANOVA, *mixed designs (b).

Mixed Designs   (a) *Factorial designs in which the number of *levels of the factors is not the same for all factors. (b) Synonym for *mixed ANOVA. (c) Factorial *multiple regression analyses based on at least one *between-subjects variable and at least one *within-subjects variable. It combines *repeated measures (for the within-subjects variables) and one-time measures (for the between-subjects variables). (d) ANOVA with a mixture of *fixed and *random effects independent variables (also called *mixed model ANOVA).

Mixed-Effects Model   An ANOVA or *regression design combining a *random-effects model for some variables and a *fixed-effects model for other variables. Also called "Model III ANOVA." See *multilevel modeling.

Mixed Factorial Study or Experiment   Research in which the number of *levels of the *factors (or *independent variables) differs from one factor to another.

Mixed Methods Research (or Mixed Research)   Inquiry that combines or mixes *quantitative and *qualitative research approaches, logics, philosophies, or methods. Mixed methods research is often considered important for avoiding *method variance. (a) In its "weak form," mixed methods research involves the use of both quantitative and qualitative methods in a single study (e.g., you might conduct an experiment with objective measures *and* then conduct phenomenological interviews after the experiment). (b) In its "strong form," mixed methods research refers to the combining or mixing of quantitative and qualitative *epistemologies, *ontologies, or *paradigms; this "philosophical mixing" is sometimes considered more difficult than the mixing of methods because, for example, it is difficult for a single researcher to shift his or her "worldview." See *triangulation, *multimethod research, *paradigm.

Mixed-Model Analysis of Variance   (also called **Mixed Effects ANOVA**) (a) An ANOVA with at least one *fixed effects *factor and one *random effects factor. (b) Sometimes used to refer to a *mixed ANOVA.

Mixed Sampling   The use of a combination of (i.e., two or more) sampling methods to obtain the sample to be used in a research study. For example, one might first take a random sample of clusters and then use systematic sampling to select the elements within each cluster. Sampling experts often get creative in finding the *multistage sampling design that works best for their purposes.

Mixture Modeling   Modeling the existence, characteristics, relationships, and effects of a "mixture" of subgroups within a population. It includes *latent class analysis and *latent profile analysis.

M

MLE   *Maximum likelihood estimate or estimation.

MLM   *Multilevel models or modeling.

MNAR   Missing not at random. See *missing at random.

Mobility Table   A table showing persons' social or occupational status at two different times. Most commonly, individuals are cross-classified according to a parent's occupation (origin) and their own first occupation (destination).

   Suppose we sampled 2,000 of the adult men in a large city and asked them two questions: When you were growing up and going to high school, what was your father's occupation? What was your first full-time job? If we assigned levels to the occupations and entered the results in a mobility table, it might look something like Table M.4. The bold numbers on the diagonal are non-mobile sons, that is, sons who have the same rank as their fathers. Cells to the lower left of the diagonal show the numbers of upwardly mobile sons, while those to the upper right of the diagonal show the downwardly mobile.

Table M.4   Mobility Table: Father's Job by Son's First Job

		Son's First Job					
		Upper	Upper Middle	Middle	Lower Middle	Lower	**Total**
Father's Job	Upper	**75**	120	45	60	3	303
	Upper middle	50	**80**	55	65	5	255
	Middle	65	80	**90**	170	10	415
	Lower middle	90	70	90	**300**	45	595
	Lower	30	20	25	167	**190**	422
	Total	310	370	305	762	253	2,000

Mode   The most common (most frequent) score in a set of scores. See *bimodal distribution.

   For example, if students' scores on a midterm were distributed as in Table M.5 on page 263, the mode would be 90, the *median 81, and the *mean 74. Be sure to avoid the mistake of confusing the modal category with the number of individuals in the category, the "modal frequency." The mode is the score or the category, in this case, 90; it is not the number of students earning that score, in this case, 3.

Model   (a) A representation or description of something (a phenomenon or set of relationships) that aids in understanding or studying it. (b) In statistics, a model typically refers to an equation, a set of equations, or a causal model shown pictorially (e.g., *path diagram). (c) A set of statistical or relational assumptions constructed and varied to study empirically what occurs

Table M.5 Students' Midterm Scores: Mean, Median, and Mode

Student 1	94
Student 2	90
Student 3	90 } ←the most common score (mode)
Student 4	90
Student 5	81 ←the middle score (median)
Student 6	70
Student 7	65
Student 8	56
Student 9	30
Total	666 666 divided by 9 = 74 (mean)

for each combination of assumptions, as a computer simulation might model economic developments or as role-playing might model social interaction. Compare *ideal type, *paradigm, *theory.

Usually the purpose of constructing a model is to test it. For an example of a graphic causal model, see *path diagram. Perhaps the most common form of model is an *equation, which is a model that states a theory in formal, symbolic language, as in a *regression equation.

Model I ANOVA   See *fixed-effects model.

Model II ANOVA   See *random-effects model.

Model III ANOVA   See *mixed-effects model.

Model Building   Selecting the variables (*independent, *predictor, *mediating, *moderating, *dependent, *endogenous, and and/or *exogenous variables) to be used in a statistical model. The model can be built a priori (i.e., before analysis of data) based on prior literature and understanding, the model can be built in an exploratory way where the "best" model is fitted to the sample data, or the model building process can use both a priori and exploratory procedures. Two major kinds of models built are *predictive models and *explanatory models. In model building, typically, several models will be compared.

Model Fit Assessment   (a) In statistical analysis we specify models (e.g., path models, *t* test, ANOVA, ANCOVA, regression models) to be tested for their fit to observed empirical data. Model fit assessment is the determination of this fit according to one or multiple criteria such as amount of *variance explained, minimal *mean square residual error, *goodness-of-fit, *effect size, and consistency with known theory. (b) In *structural equation modeling, model fit is determined using multiple indices, including *chi-square (fit is indicated when the null is retained), *comparative fit index, *goodness-of-fit

M

index, *Tucker-Lewis index, *root mean square error of approximation, and *weighted root mean square residual.

Modeling   A term sometimes used to describe building a statistical *model.

Modeling Effect   A term used in experimental research where participants attempt to give the responses they believe the experimenter would give to stimuli.

Modeling Strategies in SEM   One approach to *structural equation modeling is the *one-step* approach: specify the measurement and structural models and test the combined models and quit. There are additional approaches identified in the literature: (a) *two step* (specify and test the measurement model and then test the structural model); (b) *four step* (start with an exploratory factor analysis, follow with confirmatory factor analysis, test the structural equation model, modify the structural equation model, and retest); and (c) *jigsaw piecewise* approach, where one goes back and forth, fitting the pieces of the model individually and then together as a whole until the process produces a desired theoretical model that also fits the data.

Model Misspecification   When the researcher identifies and tests the wrong statistical model, it is called model *mis*specification—this would be a model specification error. Compare *misspecification, *model specification.

Model Specification   This is perhaps the most important rule in statistical analysis; it says that the researcher stated/specified/tested the correct statistical model, that is, the model that has the correct variables in it and the correct statistical test for those variables was used in the analysis. This leads to something of a "catch 22," since learning what the correct variables in fact are is one of the purposes of building and testing a model.

Moderated Mediation   *Moderation occurs when a relationship between two variables (X and Y) varies across the levels of a moderator variable, and *mediation occurs when a *mediator variable occurs between two other variables in a causal chain. Moderated mediation occurs when a pattern of mediation occurs, but either the X to mediator relationship or the mediator to Y relationship is moderated by a moderator variable, as in the following two graphs:

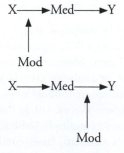

Moderated Multiple Regression   A *multiple regression with two or more *independent or *predictor variables that also includes one or more *interaction effect terms. For example, with two independent variables, a *two-way interaction can be included; with three independent variables, three two-way and one *three-way interaction terms can be included. Interaction terms can be included in any *GLM (e.g., regression, ANCOVA, ANOVA).

Moderating Effect   Another term for *interaction effect. Also called "conditioning effect" and "contingency effect." Typically, the term "moderating effect" is used when the treatments or independent variables interact with *attributes of the people being studied, such as their age or sex. When two treatments or independent variables have a joint effect, this is more often called an "interaction effect," not a moderating effect. See *effect modifier.

Moderating Variable   See *moderator variable.

Moderator (Variable)   A variable that influences ("moderates") the relation between two other variables and thus produces a *moderating effect or an *interaction effect. Compare *mediating variable.

For example, perhaps the relationship between college GPA and starting salary upon graduation is moderated by job interview skills, as shown in Figure M.3.

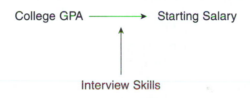

Figure M.3   Moderator (Variable)

Modification Index (MI)   In *structural equation modeling (and many other statistical procedures) the software provides suggestions for obtaining a better-fitting model using "modification indices." The index typically indicates the extent to which the model would be improved by deleting or adding a parameter. One should be careful, however, in modifying models based on these suggestions because it capitalizes on chance and sample-specific idiosyncrasies and can give the appearance of a good-fitting model that will not replicate on a new, independent sample.

Modular Arithmetic   A system of arithmetic for integers (whole numbers) in which the numbers repeat when reaching a particular value called the *modulus. A familiar example is the 12-hour clock; 10 o'clock plus 10 hours is not 20 o'clock; it is 8 o'clock because one starts counting again at the modulus (12); modular arithmetic is very important in cryptography and Internet security.

Modulus (a) Another term for *absolute value. (b) The factor by which a *logarithm of a number in one base is multiplied to obtain the logarithm of the number in another base. (c) A number in *modular arithmetic.

Modus Ponens A valid deductive argument or rule of inference in the form: If A exists, then so does B; A exists; therefore, B exists also (i.e., if p then q; p; therefore q). From the Latin meaning "method of affirming."

Modus Tollens A valid deductive argument or rule of inference in the form: If A exists, then so does B; B doesn't; therefore neither does A (i.e., if p then q; not q; therefore not p). From the Latin meaning "method of denying." Popper's *falsificationism is based on modus tollens: If theory T is true, then outcome Y will occur; outcome Y did not occur; therefore theory T is false. Popper's falsificationism can also be used with a universal law (e.g., all copper wire conducts electricity; the copper wire sample just tested did not conduct electricity; therefore, the law (about copper wire) is false. See *indirect proof.

Molar Loosely, "big." Said of research concerned with whole systems (an entire program) or categories of subjects (large units of analysis), rather than the characteristics of the individuals making up the categories or systems. Usually contrasted with *molecular. See *macro.

Molecular Loosely, "little." Having to do with parts rather than wholes, with simple rather than complex systems, with small rather than large units of analysis. Compare *molar. Molar and molecular are used more often in psychology than in sociology or economics. In the latter two disciplines, a similar concept is captured by the *macro-*micro distinction.

Moment The mean of the *deviation scores for a *variable raised to a particular power. The *sum of squares is the most familiar example; its mean gives the *variance. Moments can be used for computing measures that describe a distribution; the first moment is used to calculate the *mean, the second the *variance, the third *skewness, and the fourth the *kurtosis of a distribution.

Monotonic Relation Said of a relation between two variables in which an increase in one always ("monotonously") produces an increase (or decrease) in another. A monotonic relation is often, but not necessarily, a *linear relation; it might involve a curved line in which larger increases are interrupted by periods of smaller increases. Both positive and negative relations will be monotonic as long as the sign of the slope remains either positive or negative; that is, a straight or curved line will be monotonic as long as there is no reversal of direction. Compare *curvilinear relation, *nonmonotonic linear relation.

Figure M.4 on page 267 shows examples of monotonic and nonmonotonic relationships.

Monte Carlo Methods Any generating of *random values (most often with a computer) in order to study statistical *models. Monte Carlo methods involve producing several sets of artificial data and using these to study the properties

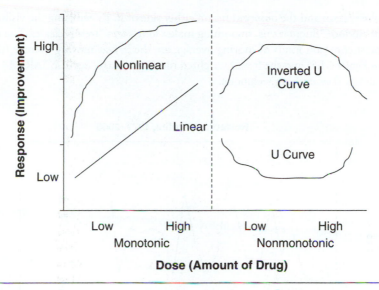

Figure M.4   Monotonic and Nonmonotonic Dose-Response Relationships

of *estimators. Many Monte Carlo methods involve *resampling or repeated simulations. See *random variable. Compare *jackknife, *bootstrapping. *Markov Chain Monte Carlo methods are an extension.

For example, statisticians who develop a new theory want to test it on data. They could collect real data, but it is much more cost-efficient, initially at least, to test the theory on sets of data (often hundreds of sets of data) generated by a Monte Carlo computer program.

Morbidity Rate   "Morbidity" means illness or disease. The morbidity rate is (a) the frequency with which a disease occurs in a population in a given year (often reported as per 1,000 or per 100,000 people) or (b) another name for *incidence rate of a disease, which is slightly different from (a). It does not refer to *prevalence rate or *mortality rate.

Mortality Effect   Another term for *attrition, or losing subjects in the course of a study, as in an experiment when some subjects withdraw. If those who opt out are different from those who stay (and there is no way to know for certain), this will compromise the *validity of the study.

Mortality Rate   The number of deaths occurring in a period of time (usually 1 year) as a *proportion of the number of persons in the *population.

Mortality Table   Another term for *life table.

Moving Average   In *time-series analysis, a method of *smoothing the line representing the data. Individual observations are replaced by a *mean of each observation and the observations on either side of it. By reducing the visibility of random *fluctuations, smoothing makes long-term *trends clearer. The two most common kinds of moving average are the 3-year moving average (used in Figure M.5) and the 5-year weighted moving average. See also *ARIMA, an advanced smoothing technique.

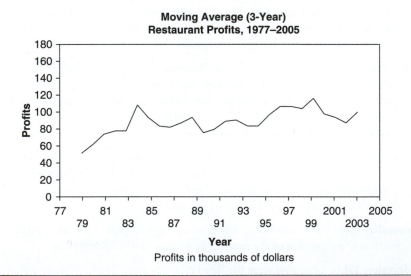

Figure M.5   Moving Average

M

MRA   *Multiple regression analysis.

MS   *Mean squares.

MSA   Short for SMSA, that is, *standard metropolitan statistical area.

MSR   Mean square residual. See *variance of estimate.

MTMM   Short for multitrait-multimethod models. See *multitrait-multimethod matrix.

Mu (M, μ)   Lowercase mu is used to symbolize a *sample *mean, and uppercase mu is used to symbolize a *population mean.

Multicollinearity   In *multiple regression analysis, multicollinearity exists when two or more *independent variables are highly *correlated; this makes it difficult, if not impossible, to determine their separate effects on the *dependent variable. The *tolerance and the *VIF are two methods of detecting multicollinearity. Also called *collinearity. See *intercorrelation, *tolerance.

Multidimensionality   Having more than one aspect or dimension. Said of complex (i.e., multidimensional) constructs. Often used to describe attitudes.
  For example, say a survey asked respondents for their overall attitude toward a presidential candidate. Any answers they give would likely mask the fact that their overall assessment was a composite of many dimensions (e.g., attitudes about the candidate's positions on foreign policy, welfare, and so on, as well as attitudes about his or her personal integrity, leadership qualities, and the like). In one sense, it is unrealistic to treat a complicated cluster of attitudes, some of which might be positive and others negative, as though it had only one dimension. In another sense, however, we often have to treat an "attitude object" on the basis of an overall attitude. In the case of a presidential candidate, this is especially clear. One must ultimately vote for or against—or not vote. The same kind of problem—a multidimensional issue requiring a monodimensional decision—can apply to many choices, such as whether to return to school or to accept a job offer.

Multidimensional Scaling (MDS)   A method of using space on a graph to indicate statistical similarity and difference. Pairs of variables with the highest correlations are plotted closest together; those with the lowest correlations are furthest apart. MDS involves treating social or psychological distance as physical distance, using graphical distance to draw a map of how individuals' attitudes or characteristics cluster.

Multifinality   The same starting point or cause or initial conditions can lead to different end points or outcomes. It shows complexity in social/behavioral reality, such as that of individuals with their different and complex life trajectories. Compare *equifinality.

M

Multigroup Confirmatory Factor Analysis   Analysis used to check for measurement or *factorial invariance across groups or subpopulations.

Multigroup Structural Equation Modeling   Analysis used to determine if a *structural equation model is *invariant or consistent across groups or subpopulations.

Multilevel Model (MLM)   A model that includes a hierarchy of *nested effects so as to disentangle the influences of different levels. The goal of an MLM is to explain a *dependent variable at one level with predictor variables at more than one level. For example, a multilevel study of the effects of schooling on academic achievement could study the effects on student learning (Level 1) of a particular classroom (Level 2), which is located in a given school (Level 3), which is influenced by the policies of the district (Level 4) in which the school is located. Models with more than three levels are possible but rare. MLMs can also be used to study repeated observations of individuals over time, in which case the observations (Level 1) are nested within the individuals (Level 2). MLMs are often considered more realistic because they explicitly incorporate social context into explanations of outcomes. MLMs are also called "mixed models" or *mixed-effects models (not to be confused with *mixed methods research), because they always include both fixed and random effects. MLMs are also called *hierarchical linear models (HLMs) after a popular software for conducting multilevel modeling.

Multimethod-Multitrait Models   A version of *confirmatory factor analysis in which each factor (trait) is measured in several ways (methods) in order to reduce the distortion that any single measure always contains. Compare *mixed methods research, *triangulation. See *multitrait-multimethod matrix.

Multimethod Research   (a) Research that combines two or more methods of *design, *measurement, or *analysis and usually hopes for a convergence of evidence, enabling a single strongly supported conclusion. The logic is that using more than one method is important for enabling the researcher to reduce biases likely to be associated with a single method. See *method variance, *triangulation, *convergent validity. (b) Sometimes used as a synonym for *mixed methods research (or mixed methodology or mixed research). The key difference is that mixed methods research focuses on mixing quantitative and qualitative approaches (philosophies, data, methods, etc.) but multimethod research does not emphasize the quantitative versus qualitative distinction. For example, the use of multiple quantitative approaches (such as surveys and experiments) or multiple qualitative approaches (such as interviews and participant observation) would be multimethod but not mixed methods research.

Multinomial Distribution   A *probability distribution used to calculate the probabilities of distributions of discrete events that have more than two outcomes.

Suppose, for example, that at a certain college 40% of the students were freshmen, 30% sophomores, 20% juniors, and 10% seniors. Say we drew a random sample of 10 students (with replacement) and got 2 freshmen, 3 sophomores, 5 juniors, and 0 seniors. The multinomial distribution could give us the probability of getting exactly that *sample distribution. That probability, by the way, is .0035.

Multinomial Logistic Regression   (also called **Multinomial Logit**) Type of logistic regression analysis used when the dependent variable is nominal with three or more levels. The independent variables can be categorical or quantitative. It is a generalization of *logistic regression with a dichotomous dependent variable. Multinomial logistic regression essentially compares multiple groups through a series of binary logistic regressions.

Multi-operationalize   To *operationalize a *construct in more than one way, that is, to measure a construct in more than one way.

For example, academic success of college students (the construct) could be measured by (operationalized as) grade point average, graduation, and/or rank in graduating class.

Multiple-Baseline Design   Design frequently used when an *A-B-A-B design is inappropriate because of the problem of non-reversal. That is, the multiple-baseline design can be used when behavior does not undergo reversal following withdrawal of the treatment condition. Reversal is needed in an A-B-A-B design to get the high-low-high-low (or low-high-low-high) pattern of response that is the distinctive signature of an effective treatment. In a multiple-baseline design, one would use an A-B (baseline followed by treatment) design for three subjects (or so) and stagger the onset of the treatment across the subjects.

You would conduct baseline measurement of behavior on all three subjects, then start the treatment for just the first subject while continuing to measure the behavior of the other two subjects. The behavior for this first subject should show a distinctive change (e.g., increase or decrease depending on the purpose of the treatment). Then, after a period of time, while the first subject continues to receive the treatment, the treatment is started for the second subject, but not the third. At this point, the behavior of the second subject should show a distinctive change (just as first subject's did earlier). Finally, after a period of time, the treatment is started for the third subject, at which time this subject's behavior should show the same distinctive change.

In this design, the behavior does not need to revert; the distinctive causal signature is shown by the behavior changing across the subjects exactly when the treatment is started at the different times. See Figure M.6 on page 272.

Multiple Classification Analysis (MCA)   A technique used when the *independent (or *predictor) variables are "classificatory" (i.e., *nominal, *categorical, or *discrete) and the *dependent variable is measured on an *interval or *ratio scale. MCA results in *coefficients (etas and betas) that are *weighted according to the number of cases in each category of the independent

		Phase 1	Phase 2	Phase 3	Phase 4	Phase 5
	A	Baseline	Treatment	Treatment	Treatment	Treatment
Different people, different	B	Baseline	Baseline	Treatment	Treatment	Treatment
behaviors, or different settings	C	Baseline	Baseline	Baseline	Treatment	Treatment
	D	Baseline	Baseline	Baseline	Baseline	Treatment

Figure M.6   Multiple Baseline Design

Source: Johnson, Burke. *Educational Research: Quantitative, Qualitative, and Mixed Approaches.* Thousand Oaks, CA: Sage, 2013.

variables. MCA is an alternative to using *dummy variables with regression analysis; it is often used to handle ANOVA designs in which there are an unequal number of cases in the cells.

Multiple Classification ANOVA   Term for ANOVA designs using two or more *independent variables or *factors. Also called *factorial ANOVA. Contrast *one-way ANOVA.

Whatever the label, such designs allow the researcher to test for *interaction effects among the independent variables.

Multiple Cohort Study   A *cohort study that includes two or more cohorts for the purpose of cross-cohort outcome comparisons.

Multiple Comparisons   Several comparisons made from one set of data; most often discussed in regard to *ANOVA, in which they are frequently called *post hoc comparisons. After obtaining a significant F statistic in an ANOVA, which tells the researcher that at least two means among treatment groups are significantly different, multiple comparisons involve looking among the possible comparisons between means, trying to learn *which* differences are statistically significant. Several techniques exist for conducting such multiple comparisons while limiting the problem of inflated *Type I error. See and compare, for example, *Tukey's HSD test, *Scheffé test, *Bonferroni adjustment technique.

Multiple Correlation   The correlation between the dependent variable and one independent variable (in *simple regression) or a linear combination of independent variables (in *multiple regression). The object is to measure the combined influence of two or more independent variables on a dependent variable. R is the symbol for a multiple correlation coefficient. Because R is a correlation coefficient, it can be squared to determine the variance explained. Therefore, R^2 gives the proportion of the variance in the dependent variable that is explained by the action of all of the independent variables taken together. R^2 is known as the *coefficient of determination. The multiple R in a regression is the Pearson r of the *predicted scores (predicted using all the independent variables) with the actual scores. Obviously, the closer the predicted scores to the actual scores, the larger the multiple R.

For example, researchers could use multiple correlations to measure the combined effects of age, ethnicity, and years of education on individuals' incomes.

Multiple Correspondence Analysis (MCA)   An extension of *principal components analysis for use when the variables are categorical rather than continuous.

Multiple Discriminant Analysis   See *discriminant analysis.

Multiple Imputation (MI)   *Missing value techniques that involve imputing each missing value several times. This leads to several sets of "complete" data. MI techniques are far superior to older and simpler methods such as *listwise deletion or *mean substitution. Briefly, MI uses computer randomization techniques to impute several data sets, usually 5 to 10. Each data set is analyzed, and parameter estimates are computed. Then the multiple estimates (such as *regression coefficients and their associated *standard errors) are combined by taking their means to make the final estimates of the population parameters. *AMELIA, which uses bootstrapping methods to compute the imputations, is the easiest to use of the multiple imputation packages at the time of this writing (but computer software evolves rapidly).

*Maximum likelihood (ML) techniques available in popular *SEM software packages, such as AMOS and LISREL, can also be used to impute missing values. ML techniques provide another modern and advanced method for imputing missing data. However, MI may often be preferable. It handles small sample sizes and large numbers of variables better than ML, requires fewer distributional assumptions, and has fewer problems than ML with larger proportions of missing data. But both MI and ML are far superior to most of the older, simpler methods.

Multiple R   See *multiple correlation.

Multiple Regression   See *multiple regression analysis, *multiple regression equation.

Multiple Regression Analysis (MRA)   Any of several related statistical methods for evaluating the effects of more than one *independent (or *predictor) variable on a *dependent (or *outcome) variable. Since MRA can handle all ANOVA problems (but the reverse is not true), some researchers prefer to use MRA exclusively. See *regression analysis. MRA answers two main questions: (1) What is the effect (as measured by a regression coefficient) on a dependent variable (DV) of a one-unit change in an independent variable (IV), while controlling for the effects of all the other IVs? (2) What is the total effect (as measured by the R^2) on the DV of all the IVs taken together?

Multiple Regression Equation   An equation that uses more than one *predictor variable (or *independent variable) to explain or predict a single *criterion variable (or *dependent variable). The *coefficient for any particular predictor variable is an estimate of the effect of that variable while *holding constant the effects of the other predictor variables.

The generic multiple regression equation looks like this:

$$Y = \beta_0 + \beta_1 X_1 + \beta_2 X_2 + \ldots + \beta_k X_k + \varepsilon \text{ or, alternatively,}$$
$$\hat{Y} = \beta_0 + \beta_1 X_1 + \beta_2 X_2 + \ldots + \beta_k X_k$$

where,

Y is the dependent variable;

β_0 is the Y-intercept (this is sometimes symbolized with α);

β_1 through β_k are the regression coefficients for the k independent variables;

X_1 through X_k are the k independent variables;

ε is the random error term; and

$\hat{Y}$ is the *predicted value of Y.

The *sample* multiple regression equation is based on sample data, and it is used to estimate the *population* regression equation. Roman letters are often used for the former and Greek letters for the latter, as in the following:

$$Y = a + b_1 X_1 + b_2 X_2 + \ldots + b_k X_k + e \text{ or, alternatively,}$$
$$\hat{Y} = a + b_1 X_1 + b_2 X_2 + \ldots + b_k X_k$$
$$Y = \beta_0 + \beta_1 X_1 + \beta_2 X_2 + \ldots + \beta_k X_k + \varepsilon \text{ or, alternatively,}$$
$$\hat{Y} = \beta_0 + \beta_1 X_1 + \beta_2 X_2 + \ldots + \beta_k X_k$$

Sometimes lowercase x and y are used in the *sample* multiple regression equation rather than uppercase X and Y.)

When you run a regression program, the computer takes the observed data on the dependent Y variable and the independent X variables and, using *OLS estimation, it produces *estimates* of the parameters in the population regression equation (β_0 through β_k).

Multiple Time-Series Design   A *time series or *interrupted time-series design that has more than one group. For example, the following is a single or basic interrupted time-series design:

$$O_1 \quad O_2 \quad O_3 \quad O_4 \quad O_5 \quad X \quad O_6 \quad O_7 \quad O_8 \quad O_9 \quad O_{10}$$

but the next is a multiple time-series design:

$$O_1 \quad O_2 \quad O_3 \quad O_4 \quad O_5 \quad X_{\text{Treatment}} \quad O_6 \quad O_7 \quad O_8 \quad O_9 \quad O_{10}$$
$$O_1 \quad O_2 \quad O_3 \quad O_4 \quad O_5 \quad X_{\text{Control}} \quad O_6 \quad O_7 \quad O_8 \quad O_9 \quad O_{10}$$

In contrast to the basic interrupted time-series design, for which the *history effect is a threat to *internal validity, the multiple time-series design controls for the history effect,

Multiple Treatment Interference   (a) Threat to *external validity. When multiple treatments are administered to participants in a *repeated measures design, the results can be generalized only to participants that have received the same treatments in the same order (this is a threat to *external validity). The problem of order can be eliminated by using *counterbalancing. (b) Note that receiving multiple treatments also can be a threat to *internal validity if data are collected at only two points and different/multiple treatments occur in between the two points. In this case the different treatment effects cannot be disentangled, and either one must consider the effect of the treatments in combination, as a "package," or separate studies must be conducted for each treatment.

Multiple t Tests   When there are three or more means or groups to be compared, multiple t tests are required. The use of multiple t tests leads to an inflated *alpha. One simple way to deal with this problem is to use the *Bonferroni technique (e.g., if you have 3 groups [and need to conduct three pairwise t tests] then use an adjusted alpha level of $.05/3 = .0167$ for each t test).

Multiplication Rule for Probability   This rule states that the probability of the intersection (or joint occurrence) of two events is equal to the product of their separate probabilities. For example, in a deck of cards, the probability of a spade and a king is the probability of a spade ($13/52 = .25$) times the probability of a king ($4/52 = .76923$) $= 13/52 * 4/52 = 52/2704 = .019$. Symbolized: $P(A \cap B)$, called probability of A intersection B or probability of A and B. You can extend this logic to any number of events desired. Compare *addition rule for probability, *conditional probability.

Multiplicative Model   A model (e.g., a *GLM) including separate terms for two or more *independent or *predictor variables that also includes terms for *interaction effects or *multiplicative relations. See *non-additive model. Contrasted *additive model.

Multiplicative Relations   A term for *interaction effects, curvilinear effects, and other more complicated functional relations that can be modeled via a *general linear model. The term is most often used when the research is *nonexperimental. So called because to analyze the effects of the variables, some of the variables must be multiplied by each other (e.g., $X_1 X_2$) or by themselves (e.g., $X_1 X_1$). In the experimental research literature, multiplicative is often contrasted with an *additive model that does not include an interaction effect.

Multiplier Effect   The tendency for an increase in investment or spending to have an effect that grows (multiplies) beyond the original amount spent or invested. The "multiplier" is a number expressing the extent of the multiplier effect. The term is used mainly in economics, but the concept of this kind of feedback effect has applications in other fields.

Multisite Study   A research study conducted at multiple locations for purposes of replication, check for generalizability of findings, and check for the need of contextual adjustments to the intervention due to complex *contextual interactions and *contextual effects.

Multistage Sampling   Any sampling design that occurs in two or more successive steps or stages. The term is often used when *cluster sampling or *area sampling is involved in one or more of the stages. In practice, the basic sampling methods (*stratified, *cluster, *simple random, *systematic) are often combined to form more complex but more useful sampling designs. A key goal is for the multistage approach to be an *equal probability of selection method so that all individuals in the population have an equal probability of selection. Each stage in multistage sampling includes a *sampling error component.

For example, suppose we wanted a sample of third-grade students in U.S. schools. We might do something like the following. First, stage one, we would take a (perhaps *stratified) sample from the roughly 15,000 school districts in the United States. Then, stage two, we could sample elementary schools within the districts chosen in the first stage. Then, stage three, we could sample third-grade classes within the schools. Finally, stage four, students within the sampled classes would be sampled. This would be a four-stage cluster sample.

Multistrategy Research   Another term for *mixed methods research, specifically combining quantitative and qualitative methods.

Multitrait-Multimethod Matrix   A *correlation matrix used to examine the *convergent and *discriminant validity of a *construct. The matrix contains correlations among two or more constructs (traits) measured in two or more ways (methods). See *heterotrait-heteromethod coefficient, *heterotrait-monomethod coefficient.

Multivariate   Pertaining to three or more variables. In nearly all cases the prefix "multi-" and the word "multiple" can be used interchangeably.

Multivariate Adjustment   A synonym for *statistical control.

Multivariate Analysis (Methods)   Any of several methods for examining multiple (three or more) *variables at the same time—usually two or more *independent variables and one *dependent variable. Usage varies. (a) One stricter and more traditional usage reserved the term for *designs with two or more dependent variables. In this usage, analyses with multiple independent but single dependent variables would be called multi*variable,* not multi*variate.* (b) More commonly, multivariate analysis applies to designs with more than one independent variable or more than one dependent variable or both. Case

M

(a) is sometimes referred to as the *full multivariate form of the general linear model, and case (b) is referred to as the *simple multivariate form of the general linear model.

Whichever usage you prefer, multivariate analyses allow researchers to examine the relation between two variables while simultaneously *controlling for other variables. Examples include *path analysis, *factor analysis, *principal components analysis, *multiple regression analysis, *MANOVA, *MANCOVA, *structural equation modeling, *canonical correlations, and *discriminant analysis.

Multivariate Analysis of Covariance (MANCOVA) An extension of *ANCOVA to research problems with multiple *dependent variables. See *MANOVA.

Multivariate Analysis of Variance (MANOVA) The extension of *ANOVA techniques to studies with multiple *dependent variables. MANOVA allows the simultaneous study of two or more related *dependent variables while taking into account the correlations among them. If the dependent variables are not related, there is no point in doing a MANOVA; rather, separate ANOVAs for each (unrelated) dependent variable would be appropriate.

For example, to study the effects of exercise on at-rest heart rate, you could use ANOVA to test the (null) hypothesis that there is no difference in average heart rate of three groups: women who never exercise, who exercise sometimes, and who exercise frequently. MANOVA makes it possible to add related dependent variables to the design, such as mean blood pressure and respiratory rates of the three groups.

Multivariate Normality Said of the values of two or more variables when each variable in a multivariate analysis *and* all linear combinations of those variables are distributed normally. See *bivariate normality to view a three-dimensional graph of the bivariate case of multivariate normality. Multivariate normality is an *assumption of many multivariate analyses, but one that can be difficult to test. When data are not normal or multivariate normal, the researcher should consider *transforming the data to be analyzed or using *nonparametric techniques, such as *bootstrapping.

Multivariate Outlier An *outlier in multidimensional space because of the inclusion of multiple variables. A popular measure for identifying multivariate outliers is the *Mahalanobis D^2 measure. As a rule of thumb, D^2/df values greater than 3 in small samples and 4 in large samples may be designated as possible outliers. Individual variable scores that are not outliers constitute part of multivariate outliers; for example, if we measured the ages, weights, and heights of members of a population, an age of 4 years, a weight of 200 pounds, and a height of 72 inches would all be reasonable individual measures, but an individual with such scores on the variables would be a multivariate outlier; a 200-pound, 72-inch 4-year-old would be a very unusual individual. As with

M

univariate outliers, such scores can sometimes be data entry errors; perhaps the individual listed as 4 years old was in fact 40 or 44.

Multivariate Research   Research that is based on multiple (more than two) variables can be called multivariate research. Contrasted with *bivariate research. In the *general linear model, a model with a single dependent variable and two or more independent variables (or a categorical independent variable with three or more levels) is called the "simple multivariate form of the GLM" and a model with two or more dependent or criterion variables is called the "full multivariate form of the GLM."

Multivariate Statistics   The set of statistical techniques that allow for the analysis of three or more variables. See *multivariate research. Contrasted with *bivariate analysis/statistics that focuses on analysis of only two variables at a time. A few examples of multivariate statistics are *multiple regression, *factor analysis, *multivariate analysis of variance, *discriminant analysis, *multidimensional scaling, and *cluster analysis.

Mundane Realism   The extent to which an experimental intervention is similar to real life outside of the laboratory. An important generalizability question for experiments is: Does the intervention resemble a real-life situation? Mundane realism is useful for *external validity. Compare *experimental realism.

Mutually Exclusive   Said of two events, conditions, or variables when both cannot occur at once.

For example, subjects in a study cannot be both female and male, nor can they be both Protestant and Catholic, for those are mutually exclusive categories. However, they could be both female and Protestant because those are not mutually exclusive groups. Researchers using categorical variables should be certain that their categories are mutually exclusive—and *exhaustive.

n   Number. Usage varies; among the most common meanings of the lowercase *n* are (a) number in a sample, as opposed to in a population, and (b) number of cases in a subgroup.

For example, consider the following from a research report: "We interviewed a random sample of college graduates ($N = 520$) to get their opinions on several issues; males were 45% ($n = 234$) of the sample." This means that a total of 520 graduates were interviewed; 234 of them were in the male subgroup.

N   Number. Usage varies; among the most common meanings of the uppercase *N* are (a) number of subjects or cases in a particular study, (b) number of individuals in a population, and (c) number of variables in a study.

N!   *N* *factorial. For example, 5! (5 factorial) means $5 \times 4 \times 3 \times 2 \times 1 = 120$.

NA   Abbreviation for "not applicable" or "no answer."

Napierian Log   Another term for "natural log." See *logarithm, *LN.

Narrative Analysis   Any of several approaches, mostly qualitative, to studying textual materials structured as a story, that is, an account of events held together by a common theme, usually including the passage of time. What was new about narrative analysis when it became important in the 1980s and 1990s was less its methods and more its subject matter. Narrative analysis made individuals' "stories" an important object of research.

Natural Experiment   A study of a situation happening naturally, that is, without the researcher's manipulation, that approximates an experiment; variables occur naturally in such a way that they have some of the characteristics of *manipulation of the independent variable or, in some cases, *control and *experimental groups. The opposite of a natural experiment would be an "artificial experiment." Although this term is rarely used, it does capture the essence of the laboratory: an environment artificially purified of variables in which the researcher is not interested. Compare *natural setting, *observational research, *correlational research, *quasi-experiment.

For example, a solar eclipse provides astronomers with opportunities to observe the sun that they cannot provide for themselves by experimental manipulation. Or a comparison was once made between the number of dental cavities in a city with naturally occurring fluoridated water and a similar city without fluoridation. Or comparisons between children's vocabulary growth during the school year versus during the summer months allow researchers to separate the effects of schooling from those of the children's home lives. Perhaps the original natural experiment was conducted by John Snow in the 1850s when he used the method to discover the cause of cholera.

Naturalism   The epistemological belief that the social and human sciences should conduct their research with the same aims and methods as scientists who study other natural, but nonhuman, phenomena. This approach also claims that philosophical quagmires (e.g., Are unobservable entities real?) should be decided based on experience and "scientific reasoning" rather than on philosophical logic. Also called "scientific naturalism" and "scientific realism." See *hard sciences, *positivism, *realism. Compare *naturalistic inquiry, *naturalistic observation.

Naturalistic Inquiry   The epistemological belief, commonly held in *qualitative research, that individual and social life should be studied in natural settings, as it occurs in real life, and not in a laboratory or where people are interacting with a researcher.

Naturalistic Observation (or Research)   Observation or research done in a *natural setting (in the *field) without any control or manipulation of the setting by the observer. The goal is to study people in their settings as they occur naturally, when they are not being studied.

Natural Logarithm   See *logarithm.

Natural Setting   A research environment that would have existed had researchers never studied it. Used also to refer to behaviors and events that occur in those settings. See *natural experiment.

Among examples of social phenomena that seem to demand study by social scientists but that are not easy to put in a laboratory or otherwise manipulate are elections, unemployment, monetary inflation, riots, wars, poverty, kinship structures, marriage practices, and so on. These generally have to be studied in their natural settings, using observational rather than experimental techniques, or not studied at all.

Natural Units of Measurement   Units of measurement or scales that have not been *transformed or *standardized. For example, saying that 1 year of experience leads on average to $600 of income expresses the relation in natural units of measurement. By contrast, saying that a 1 *standard deviation increase in experience leads on average to 0.23 standard deviation increase in income does not describe the relation in the units that people "naturally" use when discussing these variables. See *original metric.

Nay-Saying   The type of *response set that says no or responds negatively to a series of questions regardless of the question content. The results cannot be used because the items or questions might not have been considered individually or sufficiently; a *lie scale can help verify the problem.

N-by-M Design   Said of a *factorial research design in which each of the factors has more than two *levels. N and M stand for the number of levels of each factor, for example, a 2 × 3 design. By convention (from matrix algebra), the rows are often listed first, followed by the columns, as in r × c (rows by columns). A factorial layout with two rows and three columns would be a 2 × 3 design.

NCE   Abbreviation for *normal curve equivalent.

N-Choose-K   Short for the number of *samples of a particular size (K) that can be chosen from a given number (N) or *population of items. The terminology is often used in the explanation of *sampling distributions.

Nearest Neighbor Imputation   A method of *missing data imputation used when location is an important variable. It is widely used in survey research. The datum (or data) comes from the "donor" respondent that is closest according to some measure of distance. See *multiple imputation.

Necessary Condition   In causal analysis, a *variable or event that must (necessarily) be present for another variable or event to occur. Also called "necessary cause." See *cause.

A necessary condition may or may not be *sufficient to produce an effect. For example, for it to snow, it is necessary that the air temperature be 32°F or colder, but that is not sufficient; cold air is only one of the necessary conditions.

Negative Binomial Distribution   In *probability theory, the *distribution of the number of *failures prior to the first *success (or other specific number of successes) in a sequence of *Bernoulli trials. Compare *Pascal distribution.

Negative Case Analysis   A procedure used in *qualitative and mixed research for revising a *grounded theory, or conclusions, or hypotheses. One might begin with a hypothesis (about, say, the causes of urban riots) and systematically study many examples looking for disconfirming instances. As these are found, one revises the hypothesis or developing theory in light of the negative evidence, resumes the search, and continues until no further disconfirming cases are found. Compare *indirect proof.

Negative Number   A number that is less than zero; it is indicated by a minus sign in front of it; for example, –8 is minus or negative 8, as in 8 degrees below zero.

Negative Relation (or Correlation)   A relation between two *variables such that whenever one increases, the other decreases, and vice versa; also called *inverse relation.

Note that there is nothing "bad" or unfavorable about a negative relation; it is negative only in the sense that it is expressed by a negative number. For example, increasing the number of police patrols in an area might reduce its crime rate. Compare *positive or direct relationship.

Negative Results   Said of a study that does not produce *statistically significant findings. This usage can be misleading, particularly when the lack of statistical significance can (when replicated multiple times) be a substantively ("positively") important discovery.

For example, a study that found no significant difference between groups that were believed to be different on some variable could make a positive contribution to our understanding of those groups. See *publication bias.

Negative-Subject Role   Research participants' behavior attempting to disconfirm the researcher's hypotheses by behaving in the opposite way. Compare *apprehensive-subject role, *faithful-subject role, *good-subject role.

Nested Case-Control Study   Design, where cases with the characteristic of interest (e.g., a disease) is present in a *cohort (e.g., people born during the years 1970–1974) are identified, and then, for each of these cases, matched controls are identified and selected that do not currently have the characteristic of interest (e.g., disease). See *case-control study.

Nested Design   (a) Said of a *factorial design in which *levels of one factor appear within only a single level of another factor. The opposite of such "nested factors" are "crossed factors" (see *crossed design). (b) A synonym for *hierarchical models.

In the examples (a) shown in Tables N.1 and N.2 on page 283, the speed of solving problems (*dependent variable) is studied as it is influenced by two factors: levels of difficulty (A) and types of reward (B). In both the crossed and the nested designs, there are three levels of difficulty. In the crossed design, there are two types of reward; in the nested, there are six. In the nested design, levels of reward B1 and B2 appear only in (are nested in) level A1. In the crossed design, on the other hand, B1 and B2 appear at all three levels of A, but B3 through B6 do not appear at all.

Nested Variables   Said of variables located inside other variables—such as neighborhoods nested in cities, cities nested in states. See *nested designs, *multilevel models, *hierarchical linear models.

Table N.1 Nested Design

Difficulty	A1		A2		A3	
Reward	B1	B2	B3	B4	B5	B6

Table N.2 Crossed Design

Difficulty	A1		A2		A3	
Reward	B1	B2	B1	B2	B1	B2

Net   Remaining after deductions. Net income, for example, is income after expenses have been deducted. Compare *gross.

Net of   After having *controlled for the effect(s) of some variable(s). Also called "net relationship."

For example, phrasing such as the following often occurs in research reports: "The influence of education level on political attitudes, net of the effects of age and region of residence. . . ." This means: The influence of education on attitudes, having subtracted (*controlled for) any effects of respondents' age and where they live.

Network Analysis   Techniques for studying persons interacting in groups. Developed originally by anthropologists, this has become more widespread in political science, psychology, and sociology. The people interacting are studied in terms of the direction, frequency, duration, content, and so on of the interactions. The groups of interactors are studied in terms of their size, density, and so on. Also called social network analysis. Sometimes called, especially in older works, *sociometry. See *directed graph.

Network Sampling   Another term for *snowball sampling.

Neural Net or Network   Statistical and computer techniques used to try to replicate, and thus understand, the processes by which the brain learns.

Newman-Keuls Test (or Procedure)   A test for statistical significance used with multiple *post hoc comparisons. See *omnibus test, *Duncan's multiple range test, *Tukey's HSD.

Neyman-Pearson Theory   The general theory of *hypothesis testing, so named after its most important originators (Jerzy Neyman and Egon Pearson). They built on Fisher's pioneering work on "significance testing" and provided a null versus alternative "hypothesis testing" decision logic (with its Type I and Type II errors occurring when the wrong decision is made). They argued there are two states of the world (the null is true or false) and two actions can be made (reject the null or fail to reject the null). Before testing the null hypothesis, one

N

must set the *Type I error rate (.05 is a popular *alpha rate in social and behavioral science) *and* one should attempt to set the Type II error rate (*beta level) by selecting the appropriate sample size (.20 is a generally accepted rate, although it often is not achieved in practice). According to Neyman and Pearson, one should select the unbiased statistic that minimizes the beta level at a given alpha level (selected by the researcher). Despite their concern about statistical power, it would take the work of Jacob Cohen and others, several decades later, to raise social and behavioral researchers' consciousness about Type II errors and power. See *hypothesis testing, *Type I error, *Type II error, *power of a test.

Noise   In *information theory, any random disturbances to communication. The term originated from the analogy with static interfering with a radio transmission. This popular term is used broadly to refer to any *random error, such as *fluctuations around a *trend line in a *time series.

Nominal   (a) In name only; for example, a researcher who talked of "a merely nominal distinction" would be referring to a difference in labels or names that concealed an underlying similarity. (b) The lowest *level of measurement in S. S. Stevens's classification of nominal, ordinal, interval, and ratio scales of measurement.

Nominalism   A philosophical doctrine to the effect that abstract *concepts (e.g., justice, virtue, nothingness) are simply convenient labels or names. They do not refer to real entities. Only particulars (e.g., a just person), not universals (e.g., a Platonic "form"), ultimately exist; names are merely human creations. Compare *conceptualism, *realism, *methodological individualism, *holism.

Nominal Scale (or Level of Measurement)   A scale of measurement in which numbers stand for names but have no order or value. See *categorical variable.

For example, coding female = 1 and male = 2 would be a nominal scale; females do not come first, two females do not add up to a male, and so on. The numbers are merely labels.

Nominal Variable   Another term for a *categorical (or a discrete or a qualitative) variable. An example is religious affiliation: Buddhist, Christian, Jewish, Muslim, Other, None. See *nominal scale.

Nomographic   See *nomothetic.

Nomological Net   When a *concept or *construct is defined in terms of other concepts or constructs, those other concepts or constructs are its nomological net; they allow one to name it.

Nomological Network   A *causal system or its depiction. The root *nomo* is from the Greek, meaning "lawful"; hence, the term refers to a lawful network.

Nomothetic   Sometimes called "nomographic." Said of research that attempts to establish general, universal, abstract principles or *laws. Also used to describe relations among variables as well as the research that tries to discover them. Nomothetic is often contrasted with *idiographic. Compare *etic, *emic.

Nomothetic Causation   The traditional scientific view of causation whereby variables are said to be causally related. Scientific laws are sometimes viewed causally. Nomothetic causation is interested in abstract relationships, or what is sometimes called the "view from nowhere." Particular empirical data are studied to, over time, develop a better understanding of nomothetic causation. The idea is similar to what one might call "scientific explanation," in that events occur because of the operation of general or natural laws. Nomothetic causation (also called "nomological causation") is contrasted with *idiographic causation.

Nonadditive   Said of a relation such that its total effect cannot be obtained by adding up its separate effects. An example is a *multiplicative relation (which is usually treated as a synonym for nonadditive). See *additive, *interaction effect.

For example, when there is an *interaction effect among the *independent variables in a study, the relation among those variables and with the *dependent variable is nonadditive.

Nonadditive Model   Refers to statistical models that include not only main effects but also interaction effects. In a nonadditive model, the separate effects of the independent variables thus don't add up to the predicted value (they are nonadditive); interaction terms must be included to account for the interaction effect. A model that includes main effects and interactions is also called a "main effects plus interaction model." See *multiplicative model. Compare *additive model.

Nondetermination, Coefficient of   See *coefficient of nondetermination.

Nondirectional Hypothesis   An *alternative hypothesis that does not state a direction of relationship. It might, for example, state that two group means are not equal, or three group means are not all equal, or there is a non-zero correlation. Compare *directional hypothesis.

For example, suppose that in an experiment on speed of vocabulary learning, the *null hypothesis is that there is no difference between males and females. A *directional* alternative hypothesis would be that one or the other sex learns faster. A *nondirectional* test would determine whether there was a statistically significant difference between the males and females studied, but it would not specify in advance what that difference was hypothesized to be.

Nonequivalent Comparison-Group Design   A popular *quasi-experimental research design. It includes a treatment group and a dissimilar (nonequivalent) untreated comparison group, both of which are administered a pretest and a posttest measure of the dependent variable (see Figure N.1 on page 286).

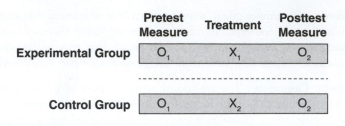

Figure N.1 Nonequivalent Comparison Group Design

Source: Johnson, Burke. *Educational Research: Quantitative, Qualitative, and Mixed Approaches.* Thousand Oaks, CA: Sage, 2013.

Nonexperimental Design A research design in which the researcher observes or measures subjects without altering or controlling their situation. In experimental research, the investigator controls the *independent variables and assigns subjects to treatments, but this cannot be done in nonexperimental research. Also known as *correlational research, *observational research, and "noninteractive research." Compare *experiment, *descriptive research, *natural experiment, *quasi-experiment.

Nonexperimental Research A type of quantitative research that often attempts to provide evidence of cause and effect but is weaker than *experimental research for that purpose. The approach is called *non*experimental because it lacks the defining characteristic of experimental research, which is the use of a *manipulated independent variable.

Non-inferiority Trial A *clinical trial conducted for the purpose of showing that the efficacy a new treatment (with some new advantages, such as easier to use, safer, cheaper) is no worse than the standard treatment protocol.

Nonlinear Equation (Model) An equation that cannot be plotted on a graph as a straight line. Such an equation contains *powers higher than 1 and/or interaction effects; that is, the variables are combined by multiplication.

For example, $y = a + 2x$ is linear, but $y = a + x^2$ is not linear (x^2 expresses a quadratic relation).

Nonlinearity In *chaos theory and *catastrophe theory, nonlinearity refers to events that are not proportional to their causes, particularly when small causes lead to big events.

Nonlinear Regression A regression problem in which the *parameters are not linear, which prevents the use of the *least squares criterion. The word "nonlinear" here refers to an *inherently nonlinear* model (i.e., it cannot be transformed into an inherently linear model). Many nonlinear relations can be transformed into an *inherently linear* regression model and used in regression analysis. This occurs when the nonlinearity occurs in the *variables rather than in the *parameters. Common transformations of variables that can produce inherently linear models are squaring and cubing variables (for quadratic and cubic relationships in *polynomial regression), multiplying variables (for interaction effects), and taking reciprocals and logs of variables to straighten out certain functional forms. See *spline regression.

Nonlinear Relationship   A relationship between two variables that, when plotted on a graph, does not form a straight line. See *curvilinear relationship.

Nonlinear Transformation   A *transformation of data such that when the original and the transformed data are plotted against one another on a graph, this does not result in a straight line. See *linear transformation.

The most common nonlinear transformations are done with logs, roots, and powers. These transformations change the relative distances between the data points in the original data.

The graph in Figure N.2 on page 288 shows a series of scores (1, 2, 3, 4, etc.) that have been transformed in two ways. When they are doubled (2, 4, 6, 8, etc.) and plotted against the originals, this results in a straight line. When the original scores are squared (1, 4, 9, 16, etc.) and the results of that transformation are plotted against the original scores, this results in the curved line shown in the upper graph. A different curve occurs when using one of the most common transformations in statistics, the natural log of the scores; this transformation is depicted in the lower graph.

Nonmaleficence   Ethical principle stating that research should do no harm to its research participants and others.

Nonmonotonic Relation   A relation that changes direction. An example is a parabola (e.g., a half circle facing up or a half circle facing down). In a parabola, the *slope* will shift from positive to zero to negative all on the same curve. A graph showing contrasting monotonic and nonmonotonic relationships is provided with *monotonic relation.

Nonorthogonal Designs   *Factorial designs are said to be nonorthogonal when the *cells, or *treatment groups, have unequal or nonproportional numbers; in other words, designs with unequal or nonproportional cell frequencies. When this is the case, the *independent variables will be correlated (i.e., non-orthogonal). Also called "unbalanced" designs. Compare *orthogonal.

Nonparametric   See *nonparametric statistics.

Nonparametric Regression   A flexible set of methods of regression analysis in which the form of the function expressing the dependence of the response variable on the predictors isn't specified in advance of fitting a regression model to the data. This approach is not *nonparametric in the traditional sense of the word (i.e., requiring fewer distributional assumptions). In nonparametric regression, "nonparametric" has a completely different meaning—it refers to estimating a regression function (typically the mean function) directly rather than estimating the parameters of a pre-specified equation, known up to a few parameters.

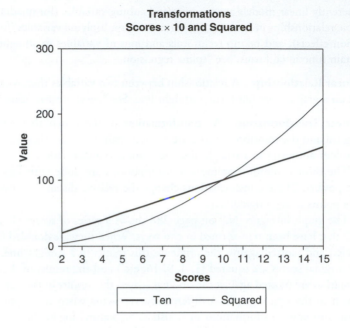

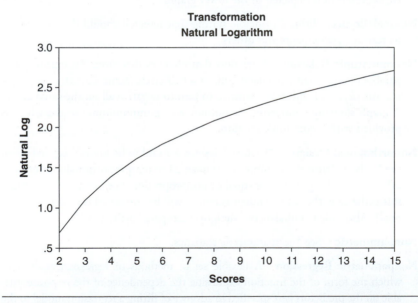

Figure N.2 Nonlinear Transformation

Nonparametric Statistics (a) Traditionally, true nonparametric statistics referred to procedures in which one was not interested in population parameters. (b) More generally, this term refers to statistical techniques designed to be used when the *data being analyzed depart from the distributions that can be analyzed with *parametric statistics. In practice, this most often means data measured on a *nominal or an *ordinal scale. Although nonparametric statistics require *fewer* assumptions than parametric statistics, they are not assumption-free. For example, independence of observations or random selection is assumed in many nonparametric statistics. Nonparametric tests generally have less *power than parametric tests. The *chi-square test is a well-known example. See *log-linear analysis, *logistic regression. Also called *distribution-free statistics.

Nonprobability Sample   A residual category or label for everything that is not a *probability or random sample. The one thing all types of nonprobability samples have in common is that it is not possible to estimate *sampling error when using them. Though often computed, tests of statistical significance are nonsense with nonprobability samples. Many things can be learned from research using nonprobability samples, but statistical significance is not one of them. See *convenience sampling, *judgment sampling.

Nonrandomized Clinical Trial   A *clinical trial in which participants are not randomly assigned to intervention and control groups (e.g., the participants themselves or the researcher might decide which groups participants will be in). See *clinical trial, *phase I, *phase II. This design is much weaker for establishing cause and effect than a *randomized clinical trial (RCT) design.

Nonrandomized Design   Any *experiment in which random assignment to groups is not present. For example, see *case-control design, *nonequivalent comparison-group design, *time-series design. Compare *randomized experiment, *RCT.

Nonreactive Measure   Synonym for *unobtrusive methods. It is a label for measurement whereby the participant cannot engage in any sort of *reactivity because he or she is unaware that data are being collected that will ever be used in research (e.g., public records, content analysis, erosion measures, accretion measures, existing statistics). From the standpoint of researchers, "nonreactive" means that they do not interact with research subjects.

Nonrecursive Model   A causal model that postulates that a variable can, at different times, be both a cause and an effect; that is, there is a reciprocal relationship between two or more variables. See *simultaneous equations, *recursive model.

For example, if you believed that education increases knowledge and that knowledge increases individuals' tendency to seek more education, you would be postulating a nonrecursive causal model.

Nonresponse Bias   The kind of bias that occurs when some subjects choose not to respond to particular questions and when the nonresponders are different in some way (they are a non-*random group) from those who do respond. See *missing values procedures.

N

For example, in a survey about taboo sexual practices, those who do not answer may be different from those who do; their missing information will bias the results.

Nonsense Correlation   A statistical association between variables that has no basis in reality, such as the correlation between the speed of data processing and the price of sunglasses over the past 20 years, which is a strong *inverse correlation. See *spurious relation.

Non Sequitur   Latin for "it does not follow." An argument in which the conclusion does not follow from the premises.

NORC   National Opinion Research Center. Located at the University of Chicago, the organization is best known for conducting the *General Social Survey.

Norm   A standard of performance. In social life, an expected standard of behavior. In *standardized testing, the norm is determined by recording the scores of a large group, such as a sample of elementary school students. When subsequent students take the test, the norms (or standards) for them will be those of the larger reference group (that is, the group on which the test was "standardized"). Thus, for example, the expected *mean for subsequent students taking the test is the mean achieved by the original large sample of elementary students.

Normal Curve   See *normal distribution.

Normal Curve Equivalent (NCE)   A *standardized scale of scores developed by the U.S. Department of Education. Test takers scoring at the *mean get an NCE of 50, persons scoring in the 1st *percentile get a score of 1, those in the 99th percentile a score of 99. The *standard deviation for the NCE is 21.06. Compare *z score.

Normal Distribution   A theoretical continuous probability distribution in which the horizontal axis represents all possible values of a variable and the vertical axis represents the probability of those values occurring. The scores on the variable (often expressed as *z scores) are clustered around the *mean in a symmetrical, unimodal pattern known as the bell-shaped curve or normal curve (see Figure N.3 on page 291). In particular, if a distribution is normally distributed, then 68.26% of the cases (or area under the curve) will fall within 1 standard deviation, 95.44 will fall within 2 standard deviations, and 99.74 will fall within 3 standard deviations. This idea is summarized as the "68-95-99.7 percent rule." In a normal distribution, the mean, *median, and *mode are all the same number. There are many different normal distributions, one for every possible combination of mean and *standard deviation. Also sometimes called the "Gaussian distribution."

Since the *sampling distribution of many statistics tends to be a normal distribution, the normal distribution is widely used in *statistical inference. For small samples, the *student's t distribution (which is also "bell shaped" but not "normal") is preferable. See *region of rejection.

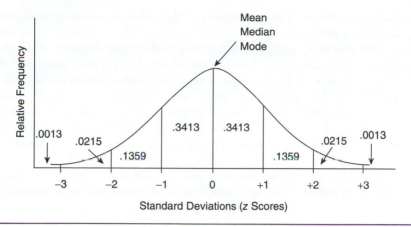

Figure N.3   Normal Distribution

Normality   A statistical assumption that values are normally distributed; it is important in many statistical tests. For example, in general linear models, the residuals (errors) are assumed to be normally distributed. Alternatively stated, the dependent variable values are assumed to be normally distributed at each level of the independent variable.

Normalization   (a) *Transforming the values of variables so that they approximate a normal distribution. This is done mostly so that statistical tests that *assume normally distributed variables can be used. (b) In matrix algebra, normalizing is a type of vector transformation.

Normalization of Scores   Converting original scores into scores on a standard scale. Often this is done by using the *percentiles of the scores and, assuming a *normal distribution, expressing these as deviations from the mean of a normal distribution. Thus the 50th percentile of the original scores would be treated as being at the mean, the 98th percentile would be treated as being at 2 *standard deviations above the mean, and so on.

Normalized Standard Scores   The *standard scores of a distribution that have been *transformed so that they approximate a *normal distribution.

Normal Probability Plot   Graphic method, using *scatter plots, to examine the assumption that your data come from a *normal distribution. The plot shows the relation of an empirical distribution's scores to the expected scores if the data were normally distributed. The scores are put in rank order and form the X-axis. The Y-axis is the proportion of scores less than or equal to each score. If your sample is drawn from a normally distributed population, the points in the plot will approximate a straight line. Plots can be drawn by hand using normal probability paper, but it is much more common to use

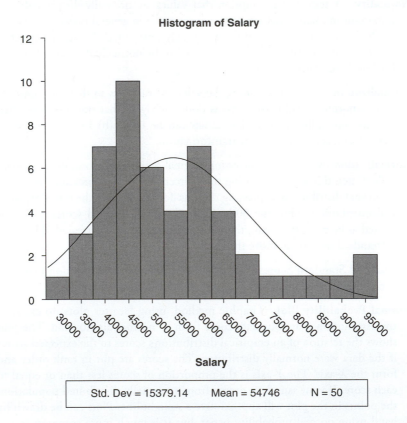

statistical software. The main types are *detrended normal plot, *P-P plot, and *Q-Q plot.

The plots in Figure N.4 on pages 292-294 all examine the same data on the salaries of 50 individuals. First the salaries are depicted in a *histogram. A *normal curve with the distribution's mean and standard deviation is superimposed on the histogram; this provides one way to judge the normality of the distribution. Next come two pairs of graphics: a P-P plot and its accompanying detrended plot, and a Q-Q plot and the detrended plot derived from it. On the one hand, the multitude of graphic and statistical tests for normality (see *kurtosis, *symmetry) is an indication of how important the assumption of normality is for many statistical procedures. On the other hand, many parametric statistical tests (e.g., ANOVA) are said to be "relatively" *robust to minor or even moderate violation of normality. Furthermore, because of the *central limit theorem, some statistics (e.g., means, difference between means, regression coefficients) tend to be normally distributed even when they come from nonnormal populations, given a reasonably large sample size.

Histogram of Salary

Std. Dev = 15379.14   Mean = 54746   N = 50

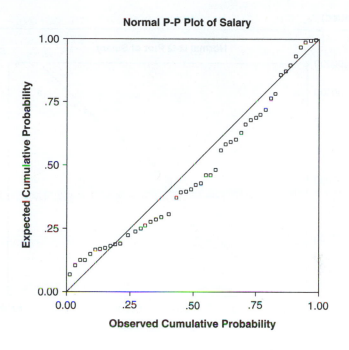

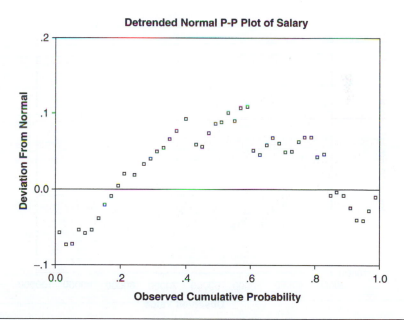

(Continued)

(Continued)

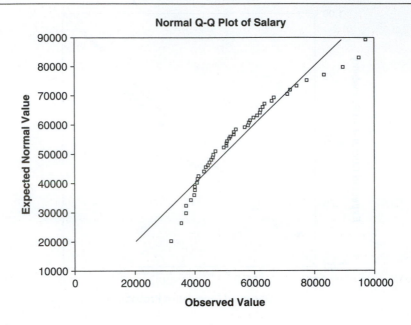

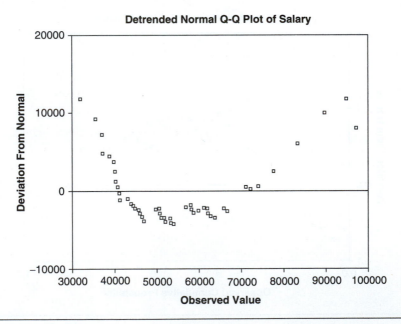

Figure N.4   Normal Probability Plots (P-P and Q-Q)

N

Normative   Pertaining to norms or standards. This term is often used to refer to *prescribing* norms, standards, or values—as opposed to describing them.

Normative-Empirical Research   Research undertaken with the goal of learning how to improve what is being studied (e.g., increase in job satisfaction, reduction in inequality, reduction in mental illness). Compare *action research, *formative evaluation.

Normative Scale   Generally any evaluative scale. Often used in contrast with *ipsative scale.

Norming Group   The specific group for which a researcher or test publisher provides evidence for test *validity and *reliability.

Norm-Referenced Test   A test in which the scores are calculated on the basis of how subjects did in comparison to (relative to) others taking the test (others' scores provide the norm or standard). The alternative is some absolute standard or criterion. Compare *criterion-referenced test, *norm.

NS   Not significant (not statistically significant, that is).
For example, the finding "$F = 2.38$, ns," means that the F ratio for that particular result was not large enough to reach *statistical significance.

Nu (N, v)   A lowercase nu (v) is often used to symbolize *degrees of freedom. v_1 stands for the degrees of freedom in the numerator when computing an *F statistic; v_2 stands for the denominator.

NUD*IST   Non-numerical Unstructured Data Indexing, Searching, and Theorizing. An older and once popular software for qualitative data coding and analysis. Its new version is called *NVivo.

Nuisance Variable   Another term for *extraneous variable. Compare *covariate, *lurking variable.

Null Finding   In *null hypothesis significance testing (also called *hypothesis testing), the null finding occurs when the researcher fails to reject the *null hypothesis. This is also called the "null result." It is a non–statistically significant result, that is, any difference between means or in an observed relationship is probably just due to chance factors rather than due to a real phenomenon (unless a *Type II error was made).

Null Hypothesis (H_0)   The hypothesis that is directly tested in hypothesis or significance testing. A hypothesis that a researcher hopes to reject ("nullify"), thereby substantiating its opposite. Often the hypothesis that two or more variables are not related or that two or more *parameters (e.g., means for two different groups) are not the same. The "null" does not necessarily refer to zero or no difference (although it usually does); rather, it refers to the hypothesis to be nullified or rejected. In accumulating evidence that the null hypothesis is false, the researcher

N

indirectly demonstrates that the variables are related or that the statistics are different. The null hypothesis is the core idea in *hypothesis testing. Compare *research hypothesis, *directional hypothesis, *falsificationism, *indirect proof.

The null hypothesis is something like the presumption of innocence in a trial; to find someone guilty, the jury has to reject the presumption of innocence. To continue with the analogy, they have to reject it beyond a reasonable doubt. The "reasonable doubt" in hypothesis testing is the *alpha level.

Null Hypothesis Significance Testing (NHST)   The longer name for *significance testing or *hypothesis testing. This name is sometimes used to remind the user that it is the *null hypothesis that is directly tested, not the *alternative hypothesis. The researcher rejects the null hypothesis when the *p value is less than the *alpha level, that is, when $p < \alpha$. For example, if the alpha level were set at .05 (meaning the researcher is willing to make a Type I error at most 5% of the time), then one would reject the null if the p value were less than .05; directly following this rejection, the researcher would tentatively conclude that the alternative hypothesis is true. Note: Some researchers and statisticians use the rejection rule $p \leq \alpha$, which can sometimes impact the statistical decision (e.g., if p is equal to .05 within rounding, then the null is rejected). One rule used in conjunction with the $p \leq \alpha$ criterion is that the p value must round to a number smaller than .051 (e.g., .0504 would be statistically significant according to this position; .0505 would not).

Null Model   In *CFA and *SEM, one has a strong (i.e., good-fitting) model when the empirically observed covariances/correlations are not very different from the covariance/correlation matrix implied/produced by the theoretical model. Therefore, one wants there not to be a statistically significant difference between these two sets of covariances or correlations. A chi-square test is used for this, and the "null model" or "baseline model" is that the two sets of covariances/correlations are equal. We do not want to reject this null hypothesis, but unfortunately this test is sensitive to sample size and even small differences can lead to statistically significant differences.

Null Set   In *set theory, an *empty set.

Numerator   In a fraction, the number above the line; the number into which the *denominator is divided.

Numerical Variable   Another term for *quantitative variable or *continuous variable.

Nuremberg Code   Standards for carrying out research on human subjects; written after the trials of Nazi war criminals following the Second World War revealed inhumane practices in medical experiments. See *institutional review board, *research ethics.

NVivo   A popular software program for qualitative data coding and analysis. Because it is the updated version of the program called NUD*IST, the NV in NVivo is sometimes taken to mean "new version." See *qualitative data analysis software.

Objective   Said of a type of research or a finding that resembles an object in that it exists independently of the beliefs and desires of researchers or subjects. "Objective" is often used to refer to matters of empirical fact rather than opinion. For example, people might disagree about whether a judge's ruling was fair, but they would be more likely to agree about the "objective fact" that she ruled against the plaintiff.

There should in principle be a high level of agreement about objective phenomena. But such consensus is fairly rare in social research, largely because people often disagree over whether a particular sort of research or phenomenon is "really" objective. In practice, objectivity usually boils down to the level of consensus (i.e., intersubjective agreement). If nearly everyone agrees that something is an objective fact, it becomes more or less true by intersubjective definition. On the other hand, if there is much disagreement, it is hard to maintain that something is objectively true. This has led some writers to cease using the word "objectivity" in social affairs and to replace it with *intersubjective agreement. Compare *subjective, *subjective methods, *subjective phenomenon.

Objectivism   The belief that objective science is possible and desirable. The term is usually used by people who think objective science is *not* possible; it is sometimes used as a straw person construction to knock down and, using a binary logic, to claim that everything is therefore subjective (a position that sounds much like philosophical *idealism).

Objectivity   (a) Those who think objectivity is possible often describe it as an approach that emphasizes fairness, accuracy, and lack of bias. (b) Those who think objectivity as defined in (a) is not possible often say that claims of objectivity are an attempt to disguise the self-interested conclusions of the powerful and privileged. See *relativism.

Oblique   Not at right angles; at an angle greater or less than 90 degrees. Used in *factor analysis and other research designs to refer to variables that are *correlated or not *independent of one another. In such cases in factor analyses, one uses oblique *factor rotation to allow the discovery of correlated factors. Compare *orthogonal.

Oblique Factor   A factor that is correlated with one or more other factors in a *factor analysis.

Oblique Factor Rotation   In *factor analysis the initial factor solution is "rotated" to obtain a clearer solution or *simple structure. In oblique rotation the factors are allowed to correlate. Compare *orthogonal rotation. See *oblique factor.

Observable Variable   A variable the values of which can be directly observed; contrast with a *latent variable, the values of which have to be inferred. For example, height is directly observable (although always with *measurement error), but wisdom must be inferred from indirect evidence. See *structural equation modeling.

Observation   The method of data collection in which the researcher watches or observes subjects and records what he or she sees in field notes. Compare *questionnaires, *interviews, *focus groups, *observation, *secondary or *existing data, *tests.

Observational Research   Any of several research designs in which the investigators observe subjects but do not interact with them as they would have to, for example, in interviews. Compare, however, *participant observation.

Usage varies. Some call almost any *nonexperimental research observational; others reserve the term for investigators who observe in a *natural setting, do not identify themselves as researchers, and do not participate in what they are observing. On the other hand, virtually all research is observational in one way or another; experimenters observe subjects as much as *participant observers do.

Observation Coding System   The use of a structured, a priori set of codes, labels, or categories to mark specific events, behaviors, phenomena, and other occurrences that may or may not occur during the observation period. Definitions and strategies for use are provided for each code. The researcher therefore knows what to focus on during the observation and enters the field with a set of codes.

Observed Frequencies   When conducting a *chi-square test, the term is used to describe the actual data in the *cross-tabulation. Observed frequencies are compared with the *expected frequencies, that is, the frequencies you would expect if the *independent variable had no effect. Differences between the observed and expected frequencies suggest a relation between the *variables being studied. See *marginal probability.

0

Observed Level of Significance   Synonym for *p value. The p value is empirically obtained in statistical testing. Could also be called "empirical significance." The observed level of significance (i.e., the p value) is compared to the *alpha level when making the determination of whether a finding is statistically significant. The observed level of statistical significance says nothing about a finding's *substantive or *practical significance; there are no statistical tests for substantive or practical significance!

Observer Bias   Inaccuracy that sometimes occurs when observers know the goals of the research or the hypotheses being tested and that knowledge influences their observations. Compare *blind analysis, *experimenter effect.

Observer Drift   The tendency, especially in lengthy research studies, for observers to become inconsistent in the criteria they use to make and record their observations. This causes a decline in the *reliability and possibly *validity (if it occurs in a systematic direction) of the data they collect.

Ockham's Razor   A philosophical doctrine to the effect that theories and explanations should be as streamlined as possible. All other things equal, the simplest theory (for example, the explanation with the fewest predictors) is the best. Named after William of Ockham (1285–1349). The principle is more often called *parsimony today.

OCLC   Online Computer Library Center. A national bibliographic center in the United States for library materials containing, among other things, information about which libraries own which books. A kind of computerized national "card catalog."

Odd-Even Reliability   Similar to *split-half reliability except the test is divided into halves using the odd-even rule (i.e., odd items form one half and even items the other half) for determining *internal consistency reliability. The scores from the two halves are correlated and adjusted using the *Spearman-Brown formula to obtain the odd-even reliability coefficient.

Odds   The *ratio of *success to *failure in *probability calculations.

For example, the odds of drawing, at random, a heart (success) from an ordinary deck of cards are 13 to 39, or 1 *to* 3, usually written 1:3. By contrast, the *probability (likelihood of success) of drawing a heart is .25, or 1 *out of* 4.

Odds Ratio (OR)   A *ratio of one *odds to another. The odds ratio is a *measure of association, but unlike other measures of association, 1.0 means that there is no relationship between the variables. The size of any relationship is measured by the difference (in either direction) from 1.0. An odds ratio less than 1.0 indicates an *inverse or negative relation; an odds ratio greater than 1.0 indicates a *direct or positive relation. Also called "cross-products ratio" after a method of computing this statistic. See *logistic regression. See *risk ratio for an example comparing the odds ratio and the risk ratio.

0

An *adjusted* odds ratio is an OR computed after having controlled for the effects of other predictor variables. An unadjusted OR would be a *bivariate OR.

Official Statistics   National census or survey data of the population collected by government agencies. Most nations assemble these data and make them available in statistical abstracts or other publications.

Ogive   A graph of a *cumulative frequency distribution, so called because it resembles an architectural arch of the same name. Also called *sigmoid or S-shaped distribution.

OLS   *Ordinary least squares.

OLS Regression   The most common type of regression analysis; it uses the *least squares criterion for producing the parameter estimates. When not otherwise specified, "regression" usually means OLS regression.

Omega Squared (Ω^2, ω^2)   A measure of effect or proportion of *variability in the *dependent variable that is accounted for by variability in the *independent variable. Omega squared ranges from 0 to 1. When it is 0, knowing X (the *independent variable) tells us nothing at all about Y (the *dependent variable). When it is 1, knowing X lets us predict Y exactly. The omega squared for a particular set of data will yield an estimate smaller than either *eta squared or *R^2. Omega squared is an adjusted eta squared. Compare *adjusted R^2.

Omitted Variable Bias   Mistakes made by leaving important causal variables out of an explanation. In nonexperimental research, this is a serious violation and produces *biased estimators. It is less of a problem in experimental research if the study is properly controlled (i.e., if random assignment is used); this is because in a randomized experiment, the researcher can set up a relatively closed situation in which only one or a few variables are manipulated and all others are held constant. See *specification error, *misspecification. Sometimes called LOVE for "left out variable error."

Omnibus Test   An overall test to determine whether there are any *statistically significant differences among three or more *treatment groups—such as the *F ratio used to test the results of an *analysis of variance when there are more than two groups. Omnibus tests are general; since they average all pairs of comparisons, they cannot specify what kinds of differences exist among which groups. Because of this feature, additional testing is usually needed following an omnibus test. In a *one-way ANOVA, there is one omnibus test. In a *two-way ANOVA, three omnibus tests are initially tested (factor 1, factor 2, and interaction). See *planned comparisons, *post hoc comparisons.

One-Factor ANOVA   Another term for *one-way ANOVA.

One-Group Pretest-Posttest Design   Relatively weak experimental research design in which a treatment condition is administered to a single group of subjects between a pretest and a posttest of the dependent variable. It's a specific type of *before-and-after design. Compare *A-B-A-B designs, *interrupted time-series design, *repeated-measures designs.

Pretest	Treatment	Posttest
O_1	X	O_2

Figure O.1   One-Group Pretest-Posttest Design

One-Parameter IRT model   Another term for a Rasch model. See *Rasch modeling, *item response theory. Compare *two-parameter IRT model, *three-parameter IRT model.

One-Sample t Test   Statistical significance test using the t probability distribution whereby the observed mean is compared to a hypothesized population value. For example, one might compare the GRE average for a particular university to the national average to determine if it is significantly different.

One-Sample z Test   Statistical significance test using the z probability distribution whereby the observed mean is compared to a hypothesized population value. The one-sample z test can be used instead of the *one-sample t test if the population variance is known and/or the sample size is large.

One-Sided Test   Another term for *one-tailed test, or one in which the *alternative hypothesis is *directional.

One-Tailed p Value   The p value for a *one-sided test. This p value is obtained by dividing the regular p value by 2. For a right-tailed test, it is the probability that the computed value of the test statistic (e.g., t, z, chi-square) would be equal to or greater than its observed value in the predicted direction, under the assumption that the null hypothesis is true. Compare *two-tailed p value.

One-Tailed Test of Significance   A *significance test in which the chances of making a *Type I (or alpha) error are located entirely in one tail of the *probability distribution. Also called "one-sided test." Some distributions, notably the F distribution, allow for only one-tailed tests. Compare *two-tailed test.

One-Way ANOVA   *Analysis of variance with only one *independent variable (IV) or *factor. Also called "single-classification" and "one-factor" ANOVA. Compare *factorial designs. Two-way ANOVA has two IVs; three-way, three IVs; and so on. A common confusion is between the number of variables and the number of categories of the variables. A one-way ANOVA examines only one independent variable, but that variable can have several categories. For example, comparing mean differences on a religiosity scale of six groups

0

(Buddhists, Christians, Jews, Muslims, None, and Others) would be a one-way ANOVA, not a six-way ANOVA.

One-Way Design   See *single factor design.

Ontology   (a) The philosophical study of the nature and characteristics of reality, or what exists. (b) A particular theory about the nature of reality; *idealism, *materialism, and *realism are ontological theories. Methodological disputes are often based in ontological disagreements. W. V. O. Quine argued that scientists must make an "ontological commitment" to the reality of the things they study; they must be committed to the variables and their particular values if they are to be committed to their theories. Two of the most influential ontological positions are *materialism and *idealism. Compare *epistemology.

Open Coding   See *axial coding, *grounded theory.

Open-Ended Interview   An interview in which the interviewee is asked *open-ended questions (i.e., questions answered in the participant's own words that go beyond simple "yes" or "no" answers). The interview can be *unstructured, *semistructured, or *structured.

Open-Ended Question   See *open-question format.

Open-Question Format   A survey or interview format that allows respondents to answer questions as they choose. The questions are open-ended. Unlike a *closed-question format, it does not provide a limited set of predefined answers.

Operating System   In computers, the *program that controls the other programs and coordinates their interactions with one another and with *data files. Examples include DOS, OS, Windows, and Linux.

Operational Definition (or Operationalization)   (a) A description of the way researchers observe, measure, and code a *variable; so called because it specifies the actions (operations) that will be taken to measure the variable. Operational definitions are not necessarily quantitative, although they are often thought of that way. For example, an interviewer might identify interviewees on a scale from very reluctant to eager to participate and answer questions; operationalizing the scale would involve specifying the criteria the researcher used to categorize interviewees thusly. (b) The criteria used to identify a variable or condition. According to the prominent 20th-century research methodologist Donald Campbell, the term "operationalization" is preferred. Campbell disagreed that empirical operations literally define variables. Practically speaking, "operationalization" and "operational definition" are viewed as synonyms.

Operationalizations are important for communication among researchers. They make *intersubjective agreement (or objectivity) possible because research studies can be clearly communicated, comprehended, and replicated; operationalizations are always imperfect, usually by being artificial or too narrow. See *operations, *operationalize, *construct.

For example, the operationalization of an overweight person in a research study might be one whose *body mass index (BMI) is over 25. However, some highly muscled individuals have BMIs over 25 and would not fit this operationalization of overweight, suggesting that a better operationalization would be needed in a study that included highly muscled individuals.

Operationalization   See *operational definition.

Operationalize   To constitute a *variable in such a way that it does a good job of measuring, identifying (or "operating on"), or representing a theoretical construct of interest. When you operationalize a variable, you answer the questions: How will I know it when I see it? How will I record or measure it?

For example, in a study of the academic achievement of poor schoolchildren, "poor" could be operationalized as eligibility for a subsidized lunch program and "achievement" as a score on a particular standardized test. Like all operationalizations, these are imperfect definitions.

Operational Research   Another term for *operations research.

Operations   *Variables *instantiated in such a way that they can be defined, manipulated, and measured and, at the same time, adequately represent the constructs of interest. Such operations are ways to study more general *constructs or *theories. Also called *operational definition or "operationalizations."

For example, one of the ways the general construct of "job satisfaction" could be studied would be to use the absenteeism rate as a *proxy measure or operation of satisfaction (lower absenteeism rates would indicate higher satisfaction). See *construct, *operational definition, *operationalize.

Operations Research (OR)   A general approach to the scientific study of the activities (operations) of complex systems such as large corporations. Quantitative criteria are often used, and techniques are usually drawn from several disciplines, to make decisions about ways to increase the efficiency of the system as a whole. See *decision tree, *evaluation research.

Opinionnaire   A type of *questionnaire including multiple statements on which participants state their opinions (e.g., 5-point agreement scale, sometimes a simple yes/no) about aspects of a topic or opinion "object." Popular in political and public opinion research.

Opportunity Cost   What one has to give up or postpone in order to do something else. Informally speaking, it means "trade-off."

For example, deciding to use all your spare time to practice the piano means that you will not have any left to practice the violin. Or pursuing an advanced university degree might involve giving up an opportunity to take a good job.

Opportunity Sampling   Synonym for *convenience sampling, but a synonym that can suggest something beyond the mere convenience of the researcher, as when a researcher attends a group's national convention to obtain a sample of members of the group (e.g., social workers, statisticians, police officers, urologists).

Optimal Design   Experimental researchers use optimal designs when it is not fea-
sible (whether due to safety, cost, or complexity of design) to test all conditions
in a *fully crossed factor design. The goal is to select the best combination of
variables, or levels of variables, that meets the needs of the researcher and minimizes some statistical criterion (e.g., the maximum variance of the predicted
value). The term *efficient design* is alternately used to account for the difficulty of
identifying the single optimal design. Types include *A-optimal and *D-optimal.

OR   (a) *Odds ratio or (b) *operations research.

Oral History   Historical evidence and research based on memories of witnesses
to events as these are reported in interviews, rather than memoirs or other
written records.

Order   The number of variables controlled or held constant in studies of the relations between two variables. For example, a zero-order correlation is a correlation
between two variables without introducing any controls. A first-order correlation
controls for one variable, a second-order correlation for two, and so on.

Order Effects   (a) In experiments where subjects receive more than one *treatment (a *within-subjects design), the influence of the order in which they
receive those treatments (e.g., the effect of receiving a treatment first, second,
etc.). Order effects may *confound (make it difficult to distinguish) the treatment effects. To avoid this problem, experimenters often use *counterbalancing; see that entry for an example. (b) In survey research, when *respondents
are asked more than one question about the same topic, the order in which the
questions are asked can influence the answers. One example in which researchers experimented with question order involved asking U.S. respondents, during the Cold War, whether Russian newspaper reporters should be able to
travel freely in the United States in order to gather information. Most respondents said no—unless they had first been asked whether U.S. reporters should
be able to travel freely in Russia to gather information.

Order of Magnitude   The size of something expressed as a multiple of a number, usually in powers of 10.

Order (of a Matrix)   The number of rows and columns in a matrix; also called
its "dimensions."

Ordinal   Refers to ranking or ordering. *See ordinal scale.

Ordinal Interaction   Said of an *interaction effect that, when plotted on a
graph, produces lines that do not intersect. Since the lines of any interaction
effect are not parallel, those of an ordinal interaction *would* intersect if they
were extended far enough, perhaps beyond the range of values of interest to
the researcher. See *interaction effect and *disordinal interaction for a fuller
definition and illustrations.

Ordinal Scale (or Level of Measurement)   A way of measuring that ranks subjects (puts them in an order) on some variable. The differences between the

ranks need not be equal (as they are in an *interval scale). Team standings or categories on an attitude scale (highly concerned, very concerned, concerned, etc.) are examples.

A question that sometimes arises in statistical analyses is whether ordinal variables ought to be considered *continuous. A rule of thumb is if there are many ranks, it is permissible to treat the variable as continuous, but such rules of thumb leave much room for disagreement.

Ordinal Variable   A variable that is measured using an *ordinal scale, such as shirt sizes: small, medium, large, and extra large. See *Kendall's tau, *Spearman's rho.

Ordinary Least Squares (OLS)   A statistical estimation method of determining a *regression equation, that is, an equation that best represents the relationship between the dependent variable and the independent *variables. See *least squares criterion. Compare *generalized least squares, *maximum likelihood estimation.

Ordinate   The vertical axis (or *y-axis) on a graph. Compare *abscissa (the horizontal axis) and see that entry for an illustration.

Organismic Variables   Variables indicating a physiological or psychological process occurring in subjects; sometimes refers to *background variables.

Original Metric   Said of data that have not been transformed from the units of measurement used to gather them. See *natural units of measurement.

Original Research Report   A publication or other document based on primary data gathered by the researchers who wrote the report, not a publication based on somebody's else's research. See *secondary source.

Orthogonal   (a) Intersecting or lying at right angles. (b) Used broadly to mean *independent or uncorrelated. Uncorrelated *variables are said to be orthogonal since, when plotted on a graph, they form right angles to one of the *axes (if there is no variance in one of the variables). More specifically, "at right angles" means "not correlated" because the cosine of the angle made by two lines is the *Pearson correlation, and the cosine of a 90-degree angle is zero. (c) Research designs are called orthogonal if there is an equal or proportional number of subjects in each group.

Orthogonal Coding   A method of coding in ANOVAs and *regression analyses. It is used to make *planned comparisons and test *hypotheses about the effects of *treatments on group *means. When one conducts a set of orthogonal comparisons/contrasts, each comparison is orthogonal or uncorrelated with the other comparisons, thus resulting in zero multicollinearity, which is a desirable property from a statistical point of view. Unfortunately, one might not be able to make all of the theoretically desired planned comparisons in a set of orthogonal comparisons. Also called *contrast coding. See that definition to compare orthogonal coding to *effect and *dummy coding.

Orthogonal Contrast   See *orthogonal coding.

Orthogonal Rotation   In *factor analysis, said of a *factor rotation when the axes are kept at right angles or uncorrelated; that is, when the factors are rotated to help clarify/simplify the *factor structure of the set of items, the resulting factors will not be correlated. Compare *oblique.

Outcome Variable   Another term for *dependent variable, used mainly in non-experimental research to refer to the presumed effect. Often used to describe the dependent variable when evaluating the effects of a treatment or an intervention. Also called *criterion variable and *response variable.

Outlier   A subject or other unit of analysis that has an extreme value on a *variable or a combination of variables or has a large *residual value. Outliers are important because they can distort the interpretation of *data or make misleading a statistic that summarizes values (such as a *mean). Outliers may also indicate that a sampling error has occurred by including a case from a population different than the *target population. See *skewed distribution, *trimmed mean, *Mahalanobis distance, *multivariate outlier. See *box-and-whisker diagram for a graphic illustration.

For example, you might want to get the average (mean) income of households in your neighborhood so that you could argue that yours was not a rich neighborhood and it should not be subject to a tax hike. Your results might be something like those in Table O.1. The outlier is Household 9. It raises the mean to $86,000, even though most households in the neighborhood do not earn even half that amount. To make your best case, you could either recompute the mean excluding Household 9 (which would give you a figure of $36,250) or use the *median income ($38,000). Since the median is more *resistant to the effects of outliers, it is more accurate than the mean as a measure of *central tendency for your neighborhood.

Table O.1   Outlier: Household Income in Our Neighborhood

Household 1	$22,000	
Household 2	$27,500	
Household 3	$28,000	
Household 4	$35,000	
Household 5	$38,000	←——Median
Household 6	$40,000	
Household 7	$49,000	
Household 8	$50,500	
Household 9	$484,000	←——Outlier
Total	$774,000	774,000/9 = $86,000 (mean)

Outlier Detection   Many procedures are used for identifying outliers or *influential cases. Of the many available, here are *a few:*

Univariate outliers (*frequency distribution, *box-and-whisker plot; compare case with median)

Bivariate outliers (*scatter plots, *standardized residual, *DFBETA, *studentized deleted residual)

Multivariate outliers (*Cook's distance, *leverage, Mahalanobis D^2, and many plotting techniques such as plotting the standardized residuals by predicted Y)

Outlying Case   Another term for *outlier.

Overall Regression Equation   A *regression equation in which terms for *interaction effects are included, that is, in which *product variables are calculated and product terms included. Also called the "main effects plus interaction model."

Overfitting (a Model)   Building a *model with too many predictor variables given the number of cases or the number of outcome variables to be studied. The problem arises when a statistical model is overly complex or has too many *degrees of freedom given the amount of data available.

Overidentified Model   Present in *SEM, when the number of variables is greater than the number of parameters to be estimated. This difference in the number of parameters is the degrees of freedom. *Overidentification is a good situation* because it allows theoretical models to be tested and compared and allows fit indices to be computed for the models.

Overmatching   Refers to problems that can occur in *matching when too many or the wrong matching variables are used (e.g., variables not related to the dependent variable), resulting in a loss of *efficiency.

Overparameterized Model   A model with more *parameters to be estimated than observations with which to make the estimations. Comparisons among U.S. states have a maximum *N of 50, but there are many more than 50 variables about states that one might wish to estimate. Compare *overfitting.

Oversampling   A technique in *stratified sampling in which the researcher purposively selects a disproportionately large number of subjects from a particular group (stratum). Most often researchers oversample in a stratum that would yield too few subjects if a simple *random sample were used. *Weighting is often used to adjust for oversampling so that the full sample will still be representative of the population.

For example, if one were to conduct a survey to compare the attitudes of male and female nurses, simple random sampling might select too few males for analysis.

P (uppercase and lowercase *P*, usage varies considerably) (a) Symbol for sample proportion, that is, the frequency of a particular event divided by the size of the sample. For example, if the sample were 20 coin flips, 9 of which came up heads, the sample proportion for heads would be .45 (9 heads/20 flips); $P = .45$.

(b) In path analysis, the symbol for a path, usually written with subscripts indicating the particular path and the direction of causal influence. For example, p_{32} means the direct effect of variable 2 on variable 3.

(c) *Probability value, or *p value. Often the exact p value is reported in empirical reports, although some journals prefer to rely on a traditional expression such as $p < .05$. For example, using the traditional notation, $p = .04$ is reported as $p < .05$. The p value is a very important concept in statistics. Technically speaking, a p value is the probability of the observed value of the test statistic (or a more extreme value) *if the null hypothesis were true*. Researchers reject the null hypothesis (the "chance variation" hypothesis) when the p value is very small (traditionally .05 or smaller, which is the *alpha level or *significance level). In other words, when the p value is "small," the researcher believes that the result was not due merely to chance. For example, $p = .001$ means that the observed statistic would occur, in the long run, only once every thousand times.

ρ Lower case Greek letter *Rho.

Page's *L* Test A test of the statistical significance of the effects of ordered categorical independent variables, such as the effects of high, medium, and low levels of a treatment on an outcome measure.

Paired Comparison Method See *paired comparison scaling.

Paired Comparison Scaling Data collection technique in which subjects are presented with two objects at a time and asked to select one object in the pair according to a criterion such as preference, most appealing, or congruence with one's beliefs (e.g., Coke or Pepsi?). Used in some scales (e.g., the Narcissistic Personality Inventory) and in data collection for *conjoint analysis.

Paired Samples   A method of assigning subjects in an experiment that puts subjects into groups of two based on some characteristic relevant to the study. Frequently used in epidemiological research (e.g., *case-control studies). When possible, one member of each pair should be assigned at random to the *experimental group and the other to the *control group. See *matched pairs.

Paired Samples *t* Test   A *t* test used to compare samples that are *correlated, such as scores of the same subjects on a *pretest and a *posttest. The opposite is an *independent samples *t* test. Also called a "correlated groups *t* test," "matched-pairs *t* test," or "dependent *t* test." This test is not related to the paired samples method of assigning subjects.

For example, a program designed to raise achievement scores is implemented. After the conclusion of the program, to see whether the means of the pretest and posttest scores were significantly different, the *t* test for pairs should be used.

Pairwise   Two at a time, as when the *means of groups are compared in pairs, two at a time.

Pairwise Comparison   Comparing two (but not more than two) individual or group scores. Compare *omnibus test.

Pairwise Deletion   Removing a case from the calculation of a *correlation coefficient (or other statistic) when it has missing values for one of the *variables. The pairwise procedure does not reject the case altogether but only sets it aside for the pair of variables for which information is missing. Also known as "available case analysis." Compare *multiple imputation for better procedures and *listwise deletion (another inefficient and biased but widely used method), and see the latter entry for an example.

Panel Data   Data from the same group of people collected at multiple points in time moving forward. See *panel study.

Panel Study   A *longitudinal study of the same group (or "panel") of subjects. Compare *cohort analysis, *cross-sectional study. A panel study surveys the same individuals at different times, whereas a cohort study usually uses independent samples from the same group/cohort at different times. Because of this difference, a panel study is sometimes thought of as a true longitudinal study, a cohort study is an approximation.

Paper-and-Pencil Test   A test or questionnaire that is a paper copy and is completed by the respondents. This is becoming somewhat less common now that the Internet is being used more and more frequently to collect survey data.

Paradigm   A group or discipline's general orientation, worldview, or way of seeing its subject matter. This meaning, today the most common in the social and behavioral sciences, was introduced by Thomas Kuhn. Originally, "paradigm" referred to an example in grammar showing a pattern in a conjugation or declension (e.g., ring, rang, rung; sing, sang, sung; bring, brang, brung [woops!]). Compare *schema, *model.

Physics around the time of Einstein is said to have undergone a "paradigm shift"—from one understanding of the discipline and the world it studied to a radically different one. Fields such as psychology, political science, and sociology are sometimes referred to as "multiparadigm" disciplines, since there are several competing ways of understanding those disciplines and their problems.

Paradox of Inquiry A puzzle in research that can arise when one wants to study an unknown subject. In the *Meno,* Socrates is asked (roughly): How can we seek something if we don't know it, and if we already know it, why would we seek it?

This paradox has important parallels to analytical problems in the social and behavioral sciences, most clearly to *specification error in *regression and *path analysis. If you do not have the "right" model, you cannot measure the effects of variables, but there is no way to know if you have the right model apart from the measured effects of variables.

Parallel Analysis (a) In mixed methods research, the analysis of the qualitative and quantitative data separately. Integration comes during interpretation of results. (b) A procedure used in *factor analysis for determining the number of factors to use. A set of random data with the same number of variables is produced and *eigenvalues are determined. The number of factors to be retained should be the number of eigenvalues that is greater than the number obtained with the random data. In factor analysis, parallel analysis is used in combination with the more popular *scree plot approach.

Parallel Distributed Processing Information processing involving a large number of units working simultaneously. Refers to both how the brain is thought to work and how some computer networks do.

Parallel Forms Synonym for *alternate forms or *equivalent forms.

Parameter Most broadly, a parameter is either (a) a limit or boundary or (b) a characteristic or an element. The word has many general and technical uses.

In statistics, a common use of "parameter" is for a characteristic of a *population, or of a distribution of scores, described by a *statistic such as a *mean or a *standard deviation. For example, the mean (average) score on the midterm exam in Psychology 201 is a parameter. It describes the population composed of all those who took the exam. Population parameters are usually symbolized by Greek letters such as σ (lowercase sigma), not Roman letters such as *s*, which are used for sample statistics.

In computers, the most common use of "parameter" is as an instruction limiting or specifying what you want the computer to do. For example, if you typed the following into your computer: "delete files 4, 7, & 9," "delete" would be the command, and "files 4, 7, & 9" would be the parameters.

P

In mathematics, "parameter" means an unknown that may vary. In the equation $Y = bX + e$, b and e are parameters.

Parameter Estimation   Inferring a *population characteristic (parameter) from information about a *sample. Stated differently, researchers generalize from sample statistics (e.g., sample mean, sample correlation) to population parameters (e.g., population mean, population correlation). They are usually interested in populations, but they study samples out of necessity and practicality. In the social and behavioral sciences, *OLS is, perhaps, the most popular method of parameter estimation used in *inferential statistics; others, which are popular in more specialized domains, are *MLE, *GLS, and *WLS.

Parametric   See *parametric statistics.

Parametric Statistics   Statistical techniques designed for use when *data have certain characteristics—usually when they approximate a *normal distribution and are measurable with *interval or *ratio scales. Also, statistics used to test hypotheses about *population parameters. Compare *nonparametric statistics or *distribution-free statistics.

Parsimony   Generally, frugality or thriftiness. Used in methodological writing to mean a principle for choosing among explanations, theories, models, or equations: The simpler the better; less is more. Of course, applying this standard makes most sense when the explanations one is choosing among are about equally good except for their degree of simplicity. See *Ockham's razor.

For example, the smaller the number of predictor variables used to predict an outcome variable, the more economical or parsimonious the prediction equation.

Part Correlation   Another term for *semipartial correlation. One variable (A) is correlated with another variable (B), and a control variable (C) is partialed out from variable (A) but not from variable (B). Alternatively stated, it is the Pearson correlation between an "unresidualized" variable B (i.e., C is *not* partialed out of it) and a "residualized" variable A (i.e., C *is* partialed out of it). Not to be confused with *partial correlation (which is where variable C is partialed out of *both* A and B).

Partial Correlation   Called "partial" for short. A correlation between two *variables after the researcher statistically subtracts or removes (*controls for, *holds constant, or "partials out") the linear effect of one or more other variables. The opposite of a partial relation is not a "whole" relation but rather a simple relation, that is, one uncomplicated by considering other variables. See *covariate, *control variable, *part correlation, *semipartial correlation.

Sometimes symbolized as pr; in another notational system, the distinction is indicated by r with subscripts. For example, $r_{12.3}$ means the correlation between variables 1 and 2 when variable 3 is controlled; $r_{13.2}$ means the correlation between 1 and 3 when 2 is controlled. Another way to put it: $r_{12.3} = .27$ means the correlation between variables 1 and 2 would have been .27 had all the subjects been alike with respect to variable 3.

Partial Eta Squared   An effect size indicator that examines the impact of a treatment independent of other effects in the model. It is common in some statistical analysis programs (such as SPSS), which is likely the reason for its popularity. Actually, partial eta squared is not as intuitive as *eta squared and *omega squared (which are estimates of the percentage of total variation associated with each variable or effect). Technically, partial eta squared is the effect sum of squares (e.g., main effect, interaction effect) divided by the sum of squares for the effect plus the error sum of squares. For better (more interpretable) percentage of variation effect size indicators, see *eta squared and *omega squared. For a good standardized mean difference effect size indicator, see *Cohen's *d*.

Partial Least Squares (PLS) Path Modeling   PLS is most easily understood in contrast to standard *SEM. In standard SEM, the process minimizes the difference between the observed and reproduced covariance matrices, but in PLS the procedure maximizes the explained variance in the dependent or endogenous variables. Practically speaking, *SEM is preferred when one has an a priori theory and wants to test the theory, and PLS is used for empirical theory development and prediction. PLS makes fewer assumptions, not assuming that data are normally distributed. PLS can be used with a smaller number of participants, fewer indicator variables, and ordinal data. As with all *exploratory techniques, the standard warning applies: The procedure may capitalize on chance factors and characteristics unique to the specific sample data. Currently, SEM is more popular than PLS.

Partial Least Squares Regression   A merging of the techniques of multiple regression with those of *principal components analysis that is especially useful when researchers want to predict dependent variables from a very large number of independent variables.

Partialling   See *partial out.

Partial Out   To *control for or *hold constant. In a *simple multivariate *GLM or *multiple regression, the coefficient for one independent variable reflects the relationship between that *independent variable and the *dependent variable "controlling for" or "partialling out" the effects of all other independent variables that are included in the equation. In partial correlation analysis, partialling refers to controlling for or partialling out an extraneous variable from the either the independent and the dependent variables (in partial correlation) or from the independent variable only (in semipartial correlation). See *partial correlation, *partial relations, *semipartial correlation.

P

Partial Regression Coefficient   A *regression coefficient in a *multiple regression equation. So called because each regression coefficient in a multiple regression equation shows the relationship between the particular independent variable and the dependent variable controlling for all other independent variables in the equation. An observed partial regression coefficient estimates the population regression coefficient. The value of each partial regression coefficient shows the average change in the dependent variable associated with a one-unit change in the independent variable—when "partialling out" (*controlling for) the effects of the other independent variables. Also known as the (partial) regression weight and the (partial) slope coefficient.

Partial Relations   Called "partials" for short. (a) Relations among variables discovered by dividing a sample into "parts" or subsets to test for (or *control for) the effects of additional variables. (b) More generally, relations between two variables with one or more other variables controlled, whether or not they are controlled by the partial table technique.

For example, say we did a survey and found that young adults (aged 20–39) were less likely to be racially prejudiced than older adults (aged 40–59). We thought the differences might be due not only to age but also to the fact that older adults tended to be less educated than younger adults. We could see if that were true by "partialling"; that is, we could divide the total sample into a more educated group (13+ years of schooling) and a less educated group (12 or fewer). We could then recompute the level of prejudice and the effects of age in each of the two parts of the sample. By comparing the *partial tables produced in this way, we could get a better understanding of the partial relationships between education and prejudice, between age and prejudice, and between education and age.

Partials   Short for *partial relations and *partial correlations.

Partial Table   A subtable of *cross-tabulations for two *variables formed on the basis of the outcomes on a third (*control) variable. See *partial relations.

For example, if we computed a cross-tabulation table for coffee drinking and heart disease, we might want to *control for sex by constructing separate sub- or partial tables for men and women.

Participant   A synonym, and newer term, for a research *subject or *respondent. Compare *informant.

Participant Observation   A kind of investigation in which a researcher participates as a member of the group studied. Sometimes the researcher informs the group that she or he is an observer as well as a participant, and sometimes the researcher pretends to be an ordinary member. Ethical dilemmas most often arise in the latter case, that is, when researching "undercover." See *ethnographic research.

Participants' Rights (also called subjects' rights)   Rights that are protected by researchers and *institutional review boards. Some examples of participants' rights are informed consent, freedom from risk and harm, freedom to withdraw from the study, freedom from coercion, minimal deception, understanding of potential costs and benefits, right to privacy of identity (confidentiality or anonymity), qualified researchers and staff, respect for the dignity of the participants, and knowledge of who can be contacted for concerns.

Participatory Evaluation   Approaches to program *evaluation research that include program staff and clients in the process of evaluation, often as part of a *formative evaluation. The conceptual opposite of participatory evaluation would be an external audit for purposes of *summative evaluation.

Participatory Research   (a) Research in which organization members or staff (and sometimes even research subjects) work with the researcher in making decisions and conducting the research. Popular in evaluation, *qualitative research, *action research (called "participatory action research"), and other areas. (b) Another term for *participant observation, more associated with sociology than with anthropology.

Partition   (a) Two or more subdivisions or categories of a *factor. For example, if class is the factor, upper, middle, and lower could be partitions. (b) In *set theory, to divide a *universal set into subsets that do not intersect and that exhaust all the elements in the universal set. (c) In *analysis of variance, to break the total *variance of observations into parts for purposes of *analysis. The variance is partitioned into an explained part, which is due to *regression or to differences between groups, and an unexplained part (called *error or *residual variance), which comes from differences among subjects within groups. (d) In *multiple regression, to divide the explained variance (R^2) into parts accounted for by different independent variables or groups of independent variables.

PASCAL   A programming language. Like BASIC, C, COBOL, FORTRAN, and others, it is used to write computer programs.

Pascal Distribution   A *probability distribution used to calculate the number of *trials necessary to get a particular number of *successes. Also called *negative binomial distribution. Compare *binomial distribution, *geometric distribution.

For example, we would use a Pascal distribution if we were interested in the number of flips of a fair coin (trials) it would take to get a total of 10 heads. The probability of getting 10 heads in just 10 or 11 flips would be very small; so would the probability of needing 40 or more flips to get 10 heads.

Passive Consent   Type of *informed consent. It's an indirect form of consent sometimes used with children. Consent is provided by the parent's or guardian's *not* returning the form. The consent form says to return it only if the child is not to participate and that consent is otherwise granted. Compare *active consent.

P

Passive Deception   The process of not telling participants every detail of the study, especially the hypotheses and details that might affect their expectations and performance on dependent variables. Although lack of deception is a goal, some deception is often needed for research purposes and allowed by *IRBs.

Path Analysis   A kind of *multivariate analysis in which causal relations among several *variables are represented by graphs (*path diagrams) showing the "paths" along which causal influences travel. The hypothesized causal relationships are stipulated by the researcher and then tested for adequacy. The computer is used to calculate *path coefficients, which provide estimates of the strength of the relationships in the researcher's hypothesized causal system or "theoretical model." In path analysis, researchers use data to examine the accuracy of causal models. A big advantage of path analysis is that the researcher can calculate direct and indirect effects of independent variables.

Path analysis is an early form of *structural equation modeling. A path analysis includes a *structural model but not a *measurement model; relationships among observed indicators, rather than *latent variables, are tested in path analysis. See *measurement model for definitions of measurement and structural models.

Path Coefficient   A numerical index of the strength and direction of the relations between pairs of *variables in a *path analysis, with any other variables having direct paths into the same dependent or endogenous variable held constant. Each path coefficient indicates the *direct relationship* between the originating variable and the variable that receives the arrow. For example, in the model A→B→C, there would be a path coefficient on the arrow connecting A to B (indicating the direct relationship between A and B), and there would be a path coefficient on the arrow connecting B to C (indicating the direct relationship between B and C). In this model, A has no *direct* effect on C, but it does have an *indirect* effect on C through the mediating variable B. Path coefficients are *standardized regression coefficients (*beta weights); that is, they are regression coefficients expressed as *z scores. If unstandardized path coefficients are included, they are usually called *path regression coefficients. See *path diagram.

Path Dependence   Said of an event or process at one time that has been strongly constrained by prior events or that greatly limits the possibilities of subsequent events. Finding path dependence is a key element of causal analysis in some types of case study methods.

Path Diagram   A graphic representation of a hypothesized causal model. Also called "flow graph" and "theoretical model."

For example, the path diagram in Figure P.1 on page 317 shows the effects of educational and other *background variables on children's occupational achievement.

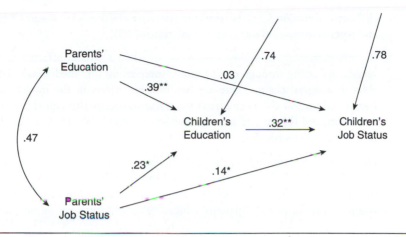

Figure P.1   Path Diagram

How to Read a Path Diagram

1. Examine the variables in the model. Parents' education and parents' job status are *exogenous variables (because they are not caused by any variables in the model), and children's education and children's job status are *endogenous variables because they are affected by one or more variables within the model. (The curved, two-headed line indicates that while there is a correlation between parents' job status and education [.47], no causal assumptions are made about these exogenous variables.)

2. Identify *direct effects*. Each *path coefficient shows the direct effect. There are five direct effects in our model. Parents' education directly affects children's education and children's job status. Parents' job status also directly affects children's education and children's job status. Also, children's education directly affects children's job status.

3. Determine the magnitude and direction of the direct effects. The numbers on the lines (i.e., *path coefficients) are *beta weights. Therefore, they are expressed in standard deviation units. For example, the .32 on the line between children's education and job status means that every 1.0 standard deviation increase in children's education level leads to a .32 standard deviation increase in child's job status controlling for the direct effects of parents' education and parents' job status (since these variables also have arrows going directly to children's job status). Here is a ranking of the direct effects from strongest to weakest: parents' education on children's education (.39), children's education on children's job status (.32), parents' job status on

children's education (.23), parents' job status on children's job status (.14), and parents' education on children's job status (.03).

4. Identify *indirect effects*. Indirect effects occur when a variable affects a later variable by acting through one or more *intervening (or *mediating) variables in a causal chain. There are two indirect effects in the model: (a) Parents' education affects children's job status indirectly through children's education, and (b) parents' job status affects children's job status indirectly through children's education.

5. Determine the magnitude of the indirect effects. This can be computed by multiplying the path coefficients involved in the indirect effect. For example, to get the indirect effect of parents' education on children's job status, you multiply the effect of parents' education on children's education (.39) by the effect of children's education on children's job status (.32). This gives you an indirect effect of .12 (.39 × .32 = .1248).

6. Determine which paths are statistically significant. The asterisks (*, **) indicate the *statistical significance of the path coefficients. For example, .23* means that the coefficient is significant at the .05 level, whereas .39** is significant at the .01 level. To determine whether an indirect effect is statistically significant, use the *Sobel test (or use a computer package such as *AMOS, *EQS, or *LISREL). Note that researchers sometimes will eliminate any nonsignificant paths and then re-estimate the model (see *theory trimming).

7. Determine the amount of variance in each endogenous variable explained by the direct effects on it. One way to do this is to locate the number on each *residual path that enters the model from outside the system (often abbreviated *e* or *u*); actually, these are used to determine the amount of the endogenous variable's variance that is *not* explained. For example, to find the percentage of variance in children's job status that is not explained by the direct effects, you need to square its residual path coefficient: .78 × .78 = .608; this means 60.8% of the variance in children's job status is unexplained. If you prefer to think in terms of what *is* explained, just subtract 60.8% from 100% and note that 39.2% of the variance in children's job status is explained. For the other endogenous variable in our model (children's education), 54.76% of its variance is unexplained (and 45.24% *is* explained) by the direct effects on it.

8. Most important of all, determine what the model means theoretically and practically speaking. Our model shows a sociological reality (that children's education is significantly influenced by their parents and that children's education affects their eventual job status). Practically speaking, we would want to follow this model up with new research to determine what additional factors can be identified to help increase children's educational attainment (because it is practically impossible to affect the parents' education and job status).

P

Path Regression Coefficient   Term for an unstandardized regression coefficient in a *path analysis. Compare *path coefficient.

Pattern Recognition   Methods of classification that allow researchers to discover patterns among the values of variables, most importantly *cluster analysis and *discriminant analysis.

Pattern Variable   A *nominal or *categorical variable whose categories are made of combinations ("patterns") of other nominal variables. Pattern variables are often used to study *interaction effects. See *contingency table.

   For example, if we know the employment status (employed/unemployed) and the sex (male/female) of a group of subjects, we could construct a pattern variable with four levels: employed women; unemployed women; employed men; unemployed men.

PC   Percent correct. Not to be confused with politically correct (or private corporation or prince consort).

PCA   *Principle components analysis.

PDI   *Percentage difference index.

PDF   (a) *Probability density function. (b) Portable document format, usually lowercase pdf. The files are created with Adobe software. They are easily sent over the Internet, downloaded, and printed, but they cannot be modified with the free version of the software.

Peacock Effect   The tendency of males in a study, such as a social psychology experiment or a focus group, to show off for the females.

Pearson's Chi-Square Statistic   What is usually meant when "chi-square" is used without qualification. See *chi-square test. Compare *likelihood ratio chi-square. Also called, chi-square*d*, since the statistic is squared before interpreting.

Pearson's Contingency Coefficient   A measure of association that can be used when both the *dependent and *independent variables are *categorical. Symbolized: *C.* It is based on the *chi-square statistic and was originally an extension of the *phi coefficient to tables with more than four *cells. See *Cramer's *V.*

Pearson's Correlation Coefficient   More fully, it is called the "Pearson product-moment correlation coefficient." More briefly, Pearson *r.* Even more briefly, *r.*

   A statistic, usually symbolized as *r,* showing the degree of *linear relationship between two *variables that have been measured on *interval or *ratio scales, such as the relationship between height in inches and weight in pounds. It is called "product-moment" because it is calculated by multiplying the *z scores of two variables by one another to get their "product" and then calculating the average (mean value), which is called a "moment," of these products. Note: The Pearson *r* is rarely computed this way; the preceding is known as the "definitional," not the "computational," formula. See *correlation coefficient.

P

Pearson's correlation is so frequently used that it is often assumed that the word "correlation" by itself refers to it; other kinds of correlation, such as *Kendall's and *Spearman's, have to be specified by name.

Correlation and regression are often discussed together. This is because correlation is a special case of regression. Pearson's *r* is a *standardized regression coefficient (or *beta) between two variables. The essential link between the two is most easily discussed by referring to a scatter diagram that includes a regression line. The regression line is the (straight) line that comes closest to the points on the diagram. One can view the correlation as the degree to which the points come close to the line, because the stronger the correlation, the more tightly the points will be around the line; if the correlation were perfect (−1.0 or +1.0), all points would be on the line. A little more technically, the correlation would be the slope of the regression line *if the variables were standardized* (i.e., converted into *z* scores); this "standardized line" would pass through the point of origin (point 0,0) on the graph.

In Figure P.2, showing the association of education levels and birthrates in 100 countries, the points are clearly arranged in a linear pattern. Since the line and the pattern of points run from the upper left to the lower right, the correlation is negative, as is the regression coefficient. The correlation coefficient is −.84. This is also the *standardized* regression coefficient. The *unstandardized* regression coefficient is −3.7, which means that, on average, for every 1-year increase in mean years of education in a country, the birthrate goes down by 3.7 per 1,000. See *intercept for another example.

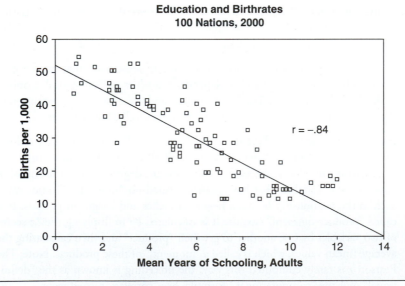

Figure P.2   Pearson's Correlation Coefficient

Pearson's *r*   See *Pearson's correlation coefficient.

Peer Review   Examination and evaluation of a researcher's submitted grant, manuscript for publication, or protocol to be used in a study by the "peers" of the researcher (i.e., by similar-level people working in the same field).

Percent   Per hundred; one part in one hundred; one part of a whole that has been divided into one hundred parts. If you multiply a *proportion times 100, you get a percentage.

Percentage Change   Number frequently reported in survey research. It is calculated by taking the difference between the first and second values, dividing this difference by the first or base value, and multiplying the result by 100. For example, if the average weight for a group of subjects was 274 upon entering a 1-year weight-loss program (pretest value) and 221 at the end of the program (posttest value), the *percentage change* would be $[(274 - 221)/274] \times 100 = -0.1934 \times 100 = -19.34$, or a reduction of a little more than 19%. Compare *percentage difference index.

Percentage Difference Index (PDI; or Percentage-Point Difference)   An index calculated by subtracting one percentage from another. For example, if 30% of the voters in your town wanted to replace the property tax with a sales tax and 70% were opposed, the PDI would be $30 - 70 = -40$.

Percentage Frequency Distribution   A *frequency distribution converted to percentages, showing the percentage (not the number) of cases having each of the *attributes of a particular *variable. See *relative frequency distribution.
   For example, say that in Economics 101, 22 of the students got As, 36 Bs, 29 Cs, 11 Ds, and 2 Fs. The variable is grade; the attributes are A, B, C, D, and F; and the percentage frequency distribution is 22%, 36%, 29%, 11%, and 2%.

Percentage Point Difference   See *percentage difference index.

Percentaging Rule   This rule says that in cross-tabulations, percentages should be calculated within the categories of the *independent (not the *dependent) variable. In a contingency table with just two variables, it says the following:

- If the percentages are calculated down the columns (i.e., if each column adds to 100%), then make comparisons across the rows.
- If the percentages are calculated across the rows (i.e., if each row adds to 100%), then make comparisons down the columns.

These rules produce *risk ratios and help to determine if the variables are related. A *chi-square test will tell the reader if an apparent relationship is statistically significant.

Percentile   (a) In a set of ordered scores, a set of divisions that produces exactly 100 equal parts. (b) A point along a continuum of scores that divides the scores into two groups, below and above the point. For example, the 60th percentile is the point below which 60% of the scores fall. See *quartile, *quantile.

Percentile Rank   A measure of relative standing in a group; it indicates rank by telling what percentage of those being measured fell below that particular score.

For example, if you scored at the 74th percentile on some part of the Graduate Record Examination (GRE), this means that your score cuts off the bottom 74% of the distribution; your score exceeded that of 74% of the others who took the test (or, sometimes, 74% of those on whom the test was *standardized).

Period Effects   Influences on people of a particular historical era or time (period). Compare *age effects, *cohort effects.

For example, living in a period in which the presidency was held by political conservatives for two decades may have influenced Americans' attitudes toward their government.

Periodicity   (a) Said of something that recurs regularly, that is, that has periods. (b) A problem that can occur in *systematic sampling when the *sampling frame is organized into ordered subsets (with the same number of people in each subset) and the length of the subsets coincides with k (the sampling interval).

For example, a high school principal might ask each teacher to provide a list of students in each class ranked by grades. The principal might then attach these lists and form one long sampling frame. If the classes were the same size (say, 25 students) and if (say) every 25th student were selected, the final sample might include only students with high grades (or only students with low grades). The moral of this example is to not attach multiple ordered lists when constructing a sampling frame.

Permutation   (a) An ordered sequence of *elements from a *set. (b) The process of changing the order of an ordered set of objects.

A permutation is often contrasted with a *combination*. AB and BA are two different permutations of A and B, but they are the same combination. The mixed doubles team of Jane and Dick is the same team (combination) as Dick and Jane. But if Jane is first in a contest and Dick is second, that is a different result (permutation) than if Dick is first and Jane is second. Note that for any set of two or more objects, the number of permutations is greater than the number of combinations, because many permutations are just reorderings of a single combination.

Permutation Tests   A category of *distribution-free tests of statistical significance. They use techniques similar to the *bootstrap, but rearrange ("permute") the sample rather than sample with replacement. Permutation tests are also known as "exact tests" because they are used to calculate an exact *p value directly—as distinct from using test statistics, such as a t test, that yield values that are interpreted to obtain a p value.

For example, in an experiment one could compute the means for the control and experimental groups. That is the original data. Then one would look at *every* possible permutation (or a very large sample of, say, 1,000) of the ways the assignment to control and experimental groups could have been made. For each of these permutations, the means would be recalculated. Comparing the 1,000 recalculated means to the original means yields an outcome that is the exact probability of getting the original mean. If 14% of the mean differences between the experimental and control group permutation samples differ by as much as or more than the difference between the original control and experimental groups, then the *p* value = .14.

Permutation tests are particularly handy for small samples. Although invented by Fisher in the early 20th century, they became practical for large data sets only with the advent of high-speed computers. Permutation tests have the same appeal as bootstrap methods—they are based on empirical sampling distributions rather than on theoretical assumptions about sampling distributions.

Per-Protocol Analysis   Analysis of clinical data only from the participants that followed the protocol as directed (i.e., those that adhered to the treatment plan exactly as required) and exclusion of other participants.

Personal Probability   Also called *subjective probability; a person's judgment or degree of belief that something will occur. This is contrasted with the method of estimating probability that is built on the empirical frequency of the event in the past. See *Bayesian statistics.

Person-Centered Analysis   Data analysis focused on relationships among natural groups of individuals (rather than variables), such as *cluster analysis, *latent class analysis, *latent growth curve analysis, *latent class regression, *latent profile analysis, *latent class regression, and *mixture modeling. The person-centered approach is designed to look at configurations of variables as they act together in the whole person, allowing the study of complexity as it exists in the world. Contrasted with *variable-centered analysis.

Person-Time   Total time devoted summed over persons. For example, if 3 researchers each devote 20 hours to a project, the project takes 60 hours of person-time. Similar calculations are made for the persons who are subjects of the research.

PERT   Program evaluation and review technique. A method for planning a complex activity sometimes used to plan research projects. Originally used by the U.S. Navy to produce the Polaris missile. A PERT document lists the specific tasks to be accomplished, the resources needed to accomplish them, the costs of those resources, and the start and end times for each of the tasks. Sometimes called the "critical path method."

***p* Hacking**   When the **p* value for one's hypothesis is greater than the *significance level, one fails to reject the *null hypothesis. *p* hacking occurs when a researcher attempts to find a way to get around this result. This might be done by changing the alpha level post hoc, using a different method of post hoc alpha adjustment, deleting outliers, using a different approach to missing values (e.g., trying different approaches to data imputation), changing parameters in a structural equation model based on fit indices, and so on. This is dishonest and unethical if any such steps are concealed from the reader of the research.

Phase I Study   Initial small-scale, exploratory clinical research designed to determine safety, appropriate dose, and side effects of new drugs or devices.

Phase II Study   Clinical research (comparative observational and small trials) designed to determine the efficacy of a range of doses of a new drug or device on specific illnesses and side effects, and whether research needs to advance to later phases. Compare *efficacy research, *effectiveness research.

Phase III Study   Large-scale clinical trial designed to determine the efficacy and effectiveness (often compared to standard treatments) of a new drug or device as well as to determine safety, side effects, and common treatment variations. Compare *efficacy research, *effectiveness research.

Phase IV Study   Clinical research done after a drug or device has been approved. It is designed to gather information on long-term use and long-term effects, and effectiveness among different populations.

Phenomenology   A philosophical doctrine established by E. Husserl in the early 20th century that has had considerable influence in the social sciences, particularly sociology. Husserl stressed the rigorously descriptive, but introspective, study of how people perceive and understand the world. Today, phenomenology is one of the major methods of qualitative research. It focuses on documenting how subjects experience a particular phenomenon (e.g., the death of a loved one, being a gifted child, any other "experience" that might be described from the subject's inner perspective). Phenomenology currently has a large international following. *Ethnomethodology is one descendent of phenomenology. See *IPA.

Phi (Φ, φ)   See *phi coefficient.

Phi Co   Short for *phi coefficient.

Phi Coefficient   A type of *correlation or measure of *association between two *variables used when both are *categorical and one or both are *dichotomous. Phi is a *symmetric measure. It is based on the *chi-square statistic (specifically, to get phi, you divide chi-square by the sample size and take the square root of the result). Compare *Cramer's V, which is a better measure when tables have more than four *cells. See also *Pearson's contingency coefficient.

For example, to compute the correlation between sex (male/female) and employment status (employed/unemployed), you could use a phi coefficient. You couldn't use it for age and income, because neither of these is dichotomous or categorical.

Physicalism   The newer name for philosophical *materialism. It says that the world is most essentially composed of matter and other physical reality (e.g., structure, relationships, nonmaterial particles such as photons). Physicalism is a popular type of ontological reductionism in the *hard sciences, reducing reality to physics (chemistry also is reduced to physics). Neuropsychology is more satisfied with the doctrine of physicalism than, perhaps, sociology and anthropology. Its ontological opposite is *idealism.

Pi (Π, π)   (a) A Greek letter used to symbolize a mathematical constant used in important statistics formulas, such as the formula for the normal curve. It is the ratio of the circumference of a circle divided by its diameter, approximately 3.14. (b) Pi is also used to symbolize a *proportion in a *population; the sample proportion is symbolized: *P*.

Piecewise Regression   A regression model or line that includes separate parts, allowing different forms of relationship between the independent and dependent variable in different places of the line. For example, part of the relationship might have a steep slope, part a flatter slope, and part a curve. When a relationship varies like this, the relationship needs to be analyzed in parts with more than one slope. An example is shown in Figure P.3. See *loess.

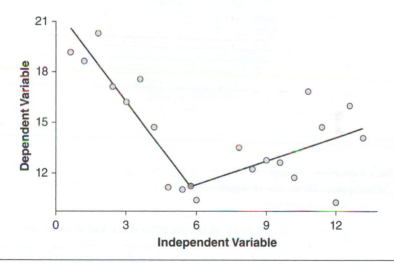

Figure P.3   Piecewise Regression

Pie Chart   A circle with areas ("slices") marked to represent the proportion of total units in each category.

The two pie charts in Figure P.4 on page 326 show each continent's percentage of the world's total land area and population.

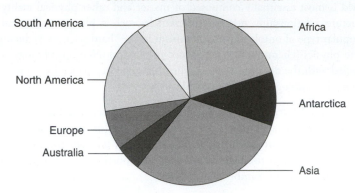

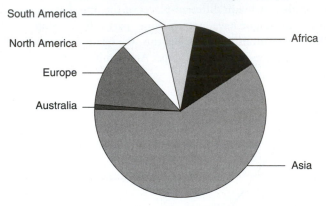

Figure P.4   Pie Chart

Pillai's Criterion   A *test statistic that is very *robust and not highly linked to *assumptions about the *normality of the *distribution of the data. Used in several *multivariate tests.

Pilot   A preliminary test or study to try out procedures and discover problems before the main study begins. This enables researchers to make important corrections and adjustments. It is a research project's "dress rehearsal."

In a pilot, the entire study with all its instruments and procedures is conducted in miniature (e.g., on a small sample). By contrast, a *pretest (b) is used to assess some part of an instrument or procedure.

Placebo (also called Placebo Control)   In experimental research, a *treatment given to a *control group that is meant to have no effect; it is used in comparison to the treatment that is being tested. See *double-blind procedure.

For example, in an experiment on the benefits of a drug, the control group might be given a sugar pill (the placebo) that resembles the drug being tested, while the experimental group would be given the drug.

Placebo Effect   Improvement in the condition of sick persons that cannot be attributed to the physiological effect of the treatment that was used but is due, rather, to their (mistaken) belief that they received an effective treatment (e.g., the medicine rather than the sugar pill). Compare *Hawthorne effect.

Placebo Group   The group in an *RCT that received the nonactive or inert substance called the placebo (e.g., a sugar pill). This group is compared to the group getting the active ingredient to see if the intervention produces change in the outcome variable. The placebo group provides an estimate of the *counterfactual or what one would expect if the active pill were *not* taken. See *causal inference.

Plagiarism   Scientific misconduct whereby a researcher uses the ideas, words, or results of someone else without proper attribution; it is a form of theft.

Planned Comparisons   Comparisons between the *means of categories of one or more *independent variable in *regression analysis or *analysis of variance. So called because they are specified at the outset of the research, before the *data are gathered. Used in theory/hypothesis-driven research. Also called "a priori comparisons." They do not require *omnibus testing; rather, one goes to directly testing each planned comparison. Planned comparisons might be simple *pairwise comparisons or more *complex comparisons. Compare *omnibus test, *post hoc comparisons, *multiple comparisons.

The advantage of planned comparisons is that the researcher can move directly to comparisons of interest without first doing an *omnibus test. Such comparisons involve less risk of *Type I error than do post hoc comparisons. Unplanned comparisons are often suggested by the data generated in the research. See *factor analysis.

Platykurtic   Flatter than a *normal curve. See *kurtosis for an illustration.

Pluralism   The belief that research methods often seen as incompatible aren't necessarily so. Quantitative versus qualitative and explanation versus understanding are typical of the dichotomies pluralists reject or think are overemphasized.

Point Biserial Correlation   A type of correlation to measure the *association between two *variables, one of which is *dichotomous and the other *continuous. Compare *biserial correlation, *widespread biserial correlation.

Point Cloud   A *scatter diagram on which three variables are plotted. The goal is to depict a three-dimensional relationship. See *regression plane.

Point Estimate   An estimate made by computing a *statistic that describes a *sample; this is then used to estimate a *population *parameter. The term "estimate," used without specification, almost always means point estimate. Compare *interval estimate, *confidence interval.

For example, you could survey a sample of students in your department to get their opinion about the statistics requirement. Say that on a scale of 0 to 10, the sample of students gave the statistics requirement a *mean rating of 4.0. You could then conclude that 4.0 would be the best estimate of the mean score of the population; that is, it is your best (point) estimate of what the mean score would have been had all the students been polled. An interval estimate might be that the value for the population is probably between 2.0 and 6.0.

Poisson Distribution   A *probability distribution that can be used for a statistical test when the number (N) of cases is very large and the probability (p) is very small.

For example, suppose the murder rate in U.S. cities is .0001, or 100 murders per 1 million residents. Say that Our Town, a city of 500,000 people, had 80 murders last year. A simple calculation shows that Our Town's rate is higher than the typical rate (80/500,000 = .00016, or 160 murders per million). But a more interesting question perhaps is whether 80 murders is higher than what could be expected by chance if ours is a typical town. We could use the Poisson distribution formula to find out. If Our Town is typical, then a total of 80 murders in a year has a probability of about .24. We might conclude that 30 murders more than the average rate could be expected by chance and that there was nothing atypical about Our Town. However, if the number of murders had been 120 instead of 80, we would probably come to a different conclusion, since the probability of 120 murders in a typical city of 500,000 would only be .04.

Poisson Process   A mathematical description of *random events that pertains when events occur randomly in such a way that for each small interval of time, one event or zero events, but not two events, can occur.

Poisson Regression   Type of regression analysis used when the dependent variable is an event count variable (rather than a continuous variable), often of a rare event (e.g., deaths from cancer in a cohort over a specific period of time). As many independent variables or predictors as needed can be used. The output is similar to *logistic regression. A Poisson regression model is sometimes called a *log-linear model, most often when it is used to analyze *contingency tables.

Policy Analysis (Research)   The study of social, political, economic, educational, and other policies. The goal is to discover alternative policies for resolving a public problem. Policy analysts are often closely allied with *evaluation researchers. Compare *applied and *basic research.

Table P.1 on page 329 shows one way to divide up the non–basic research domain.

Table P.1   Policy Analysis/Research Compared to Other Types

Type of Research	Typical Question Asked
Policy	What should we do?
Applied	How should we do it?
Evaluation	How well did we do it?

Polychoric Correlation   Measure of association between two *ordinal level (ordered category) variables. The variables are assumed to be quantitative, but measured as observed ordinal variables. The range is −1 to +1, just as in a regular *Pearson correlation coefficient.

Polychotomous categorical variable   A *nominal or categorical variable that has three or more categories.

Polygon   From the Greek for "many sided." A line graph drawn by connecting the midpoints of the bars of a *histogram. Also known as a *frequency polygon; see that entry for an illustration.

Polynomial Equation   An equation in which one or more of the variables is raised to a *power greater than 1. See *linear equation, *polynomial regression analysis.

For example, the regression equation $Y = a + bX + bX^2 + bX^3$ is a polynomial because X is raised to the second and third powers. The highest power of a term gives the equation its "degree" or "order." The example equation is thus a third-order (or third-degree) polynomial equation.

Polynomial Regression Analysis   *Curvilinear regression analysis, that is, regression analysis for relations that are or are suspected to be nonlinear. So called because the regression equation is constructed to fit an observed curvilinear (nonlinear) relation. A *polynomial equation is used, but the nonlinearity is in the variables, not the parameters (i.e., it is still an *inherently* linear model). For example, to fit a regression model to a set of data with one curve in it, you would use the following regression equation: $\hat{y} = b_0 + b_1 x + b_2 x^2$, where x is the single independent variable. If the data had two turns in the curve, this equation would be used: $\hat{y} = b_0 + b_1 x + b_2 x^2 + b_3 x^3$. The more turns in the regression line, the higher the power of the terms in the equation must be for the variable. Compare *spline regression. Table P.2 on page 330 summarizes some of the terminology used with polynomial regression.

Polytomous Variable   A *categorical variable with more than two categories, literally with "many divisions," as in marital status: single, married, divorced, widowed. Also spelled "polychotomous."

Pooled Cross-Sectional Analysis   A type of analysis conducted by combining ("pooling") two or more *cross-sectional studies. This pooling is most often

Table P.2 *Polynomial Regression*

Turns of Regression Line	*Order or Degree*	*Number of Terms*	*Type of Analysis*
0	First	1	Linear
1	Second	2	Quadratic
2	Third	3	Cubic
3	Fourth	4	Quartic
4	Fifth	5	Quintic

done for one of two reasons: (1) to increase overall sample size beyond what is available in a single cross-sectional sample or (2) to study the effects of the passage of time by comparing samples drawn in different years.

Pooled Variance   Combining multiple variances into one estimate. *Weighting might or might not be used in constructing a pooled estimate. When weighting is used, the separate variances are weighted by their respective degrees of freedom (sample sizes minus 1), giving more weight to variances from larger groups. When group sizes are the same, there is no difference in a weighted and unweighted variance.

Population   A group of persons (or institutions, events, or other subjects of study) that one wants to describe or about which one wants to generalize. In order to generalize about a population, one often studies a *sample that is meant to be *representative of the population. Also called *target population and a *universe.

Population Distribution   The data distribution for all of the cases in a population. Contrasted with *sample distribution, *sampling distribution.

Population Parameter   A statistical characteristic of a population, such as a population *mean or a population *correlation. Population parameters are usually symbolized by Greek letters; the Roman (English) alphabet is often used for *sample statistics. Consistency is not perfect, however, as Greek letters are sometimes used for both statistics and parameters.

Population Pyramid   A graphic means of describing the sex and age distribution of a population. Like a *box-and-whisker diagram, it is particularly useful for comparing different distributions. The examples in Figure P.5 on page 331 compare two countries with quite different age distributions. In Mexico, the modal age group is 0–4. In the United States, it is 35–39.

Population Standard Deviation   A measure of how much the values of a population's variable tend to deviate from the mean. The square root of the *population variance.

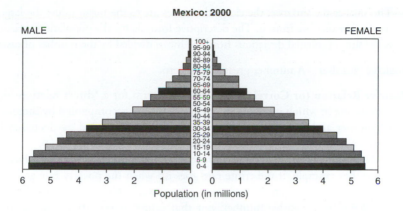

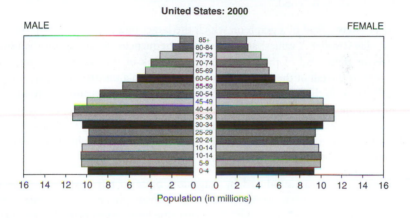

Figure P.5   Population Pyramid

Population Validity   A type of *external validity or *representativeness, focusing on whether one can make valid statements about the target population based on the sample data; population *in*validity describes research in which criteria for population validity are not met. Statistically speaking, the use of random sampling techniques (*EPSEM) is important for population validity. Compare *ecological validity.

For example, studies in which the samples are composed solely of college sophomores might not be validly generalizable to the population of all adults, or even young adults.

Population Variance   The variance in a population that is either (a) estimated from a sample variance or (b) calculated directly from population data (if available). It describes the average spread or variability in a population's scores in squared units.

P

The smaller the variance, the closer the scores are to the mean value; the larger, the further they are from it. The descriptive formula for the population variance is the sum of squared deviations from the mean divided by the number of cases.

Positive Number   A number greater than zero.

Positive Relation (or Correlation)   Another term for a *direct relationship, that is, one in which increases in one *variable are accompanied by increases in another and decreases in one variable are accompanied by decreases in another. Compare *inverse relationship, *negative relation.

Note that "positive" in this context does not mean beneficial or advantageous. For example, if the crime rate goes up when the poverty rate goes up, the correlation between the two rates is "positive," which means only that the correlation is a positive number, not that crime or poverty or the relation between them is "good."

Positive Skew   Said of a graph on which the larger frequencies bulge up on the left side (smaller X values) and the smaller frequencies are found on the positive (or right) end of the *x-axis. You can think of the "skew" as being the direction the tail of the distribution is pulled. With a positive skew, the bump or bulge is on the left but the tail is "pulled to the right" because of a few large or extreme values (*outliers) on the x-axis variable. For example, the distribution of scores on a difficult test would have a positive skew, while the scores on an easy test would be negatively skewed. Also called "right skew." For an illustration, see *skewed distribution.

Positivism   A term introduced by Auguste Comte to refer to the *empirical study of phenomena, especially social or human phenomena. Comte contrasted the "positive knowledge" (i.e., scientific knowledge) gained in this way with the less scientific knowledge obtained earlier in history by *metaphysical explanations and religion. See *scientism.

The term has had several meanings since it was introduced by Comte in the early 19th century and repopularized by the Vienna Circle of philosophers in the 1930s (see *logical positivism), and it has always been the object of debate. Loosely speaking, positivism includes a belief, held by some people, that one can study scientifically and/or with quantitative data things that other people believe cannot or should not be studied in this way, such as religion, emotions, ideas, art, and morality. More strictly speaking, positivism holds that facts and values are fully separate and that the only things we can *know* are those that can be observed. See *Hume's law.

Positivism is used by some *qualitative and *humanistic researchers to label *quantitative researchers, who are seen as not just believing in the usefulness of science but believing in *scientism, which is the position that *only* science can produce useful, interesting, or valid knowledge about humans and society. Today, few researchers consider themselves to be positivists because of its negative connotation. The more accurate term today is *postpositivism, which refers to a more sophisticated and reasonable version of positivism.

Posterior Probability In *Bayesian inference, an investigator's opinion, expressed as a probability, after research has been done and data gathered assessing the investigator's *prior probability opinions. It is the probability of a hypothesis given the evidence, or $P(H|E)$, read "probability of H given E"—this is the probability many people want from traditional hypothesis testing. However, traditional hypothesis testing, and in particular the p value, provides the probability of the evidence (e.g., an observed value of a statistic) given the assumption that the null hypothesis is true, or $P(E|H)$, read "probability of the evidence given the null hypothesis." See *null hypothesis. Compare *probability value.

Post Hoc Comparison A test of the *statistical significance of differences between group *means calculated after ("post") having done an *analysis of variance (ANOVA) or a *regression analysis that shows an overall difference. See *multiple comparisons, *omnibus test, *fishing expedition. Also called "post hoc test," "a posteriori comparison," and "follow-up test or comparison." Compare *a priori comparison, *planned comparison.

The *F ratio of the ANOVA tells you that some sort of statistically significant differences exist somewhere among the groups being studied. Subsequent—post hoc—analyses are meant to specify what kind and where. Since these comparisons are not part of the original study design (otherwise they would be *planned comparisons), some researchers consider them of doubtful validity. Such comparisons are easiest to justify for *exploratory research; they should not be used to test *hypotheses.

Post hoc comparison is a generic term for several kinds of analyses. *Least significant difference (LSD), *Tukey's HSD, *Bonferroni technique, and *Scheffé test are well known. Others include the *Newman-Keuls test, *Sidak technique, and *Duncan's multiple-range test. The LSD test is the least *conservative (but can only be used when there are three groups), followed by Duncan's; Scheffé's is the most conservative and is rarely used today because of its lack of statistical power. When there are many groups, the following are recommended: *Holm's procedure and *Hochberg test. In any case, the general procedure is the same: After you get a significant overall or omnibus test result, you look for differences among groups to explain it. Because the comparisons are multiple and carry with them increased risk of *Type I error, the *critical value of the test statistic is raised to compensate and thus to reduce that risk.

Post Hoc Hypothesis See *post hoc theorizing.

Post Hoc Power   See *retrospective power.

Post Hoc Test   Synonym for *post hoc comparison.

Post Hoc Theorizing   "After this" theorizing; that is, existing data are used to "test" theories that were originally constructed to describe that very same data. While this would be bad practice in experimental research, more latitude may be justifiable in nonexperimental work, especially exploratory studies. But in all cases, good practice is to test a theory with a new set of data, not the data used to develop the theory.

Postmodernism   A broad term covering a multitude of loosely related beliefs that have in common a distrust of "modern science" and, more broadly, "modern" ways of thinking that stress "rationality." Its adherents tend to be especially critical of any sort of *positivism. Perhaps the most common traits of postmodernists are a celebration of *relativism and a focus on *difference* rather than on similarity and patterned behavior. Using a statistics analogy, postmodernists are not interested in the mean; instead, they are interested in the variance and outliers (i.e., in documenting and discussing and promoting differences among people, ideas, theories, ideologies, and interests).

Postpositivism (or Neopositivism)   An updated and improved version of classical and logical *positivism. For example, postpositivism recognizes that research is not fully value-free. Objectivity is viewed as an ideal. Postpositivists today also tend to take more of a *realist stance about theoretical concepts and about entities that are useful but cannot be directly observed, such as subatomic particles.

Posttest   A test given or measurement taken after an experimental *treatment. Compare *pretest, with which the results of a posttest are usually compared.

Postulate   A conjecture or other statement considered to be an essential starting point in a chain of logical reasoning. While there can be subtle distinctions, it is generally accurate to say that *assumption, *axiom, and postulate refer to the same basic concept.

Power   The number of times a number is multiplied times itself, usually written as an *exponent. See *polynomial equation.
     For example, 8^2 is 8 to the second power and means $8 \times 8 = 64$; 8^3 is 8 to the third power and means $8 \times 8 \times 8 = 512$.

Power of a Test   Broadly, the ability of a technique, such as a statistical test, to detect relationships. Specifically, the probability of rejecting a *null hypothesis when it is false—and therefore should be rejected. The power of a test is calculated by subtracting the probability of a *Type II error from 1.0. The maximum total power a test can have is 1.0; the minimum is zero; .8 is often considered an acceptable level for a particular test in a particular study. Also called *statistical power. See *prospective power, *retrospective power.

Power Transformation   *Transformation of a variable by taking a power of its values, as by squaring or cubing it. See *polynomial regression for examples.

P-P Plot   Probability-probability plot. A graphic method of comparing two *probability distributions by plotting one against the other, often for comparing a normal distribution with sample data to determine whether the sample data are normally distributed. Compare *Q-Q plot. See *normal probability plot, *probability paper, *probability plots.

PR   An abbreviation for *probability.

Practical Significance   Said of a research finding that one can put to use, that can change practice. Usually contrasted with (mere) *statistical significance, which means that the null hypothesis (usually of no effect) was rejected; closely related to *substantive significance. "Clinical significance" refers to practical significance in a clinical setting, for example, an effect that is large enough to be a reasonable treatment option. There are no statistical tests for practical significance, although they usually take into account *effect size or size of *dose-response relationship, *efficiency, and contextual considerations of applying a finding. Ultimately, whether something is practically significant is a matter of judgment.

Often researchers talk of a low level of practical significance to describe a finding that is too large to be likely due to chance alone (i.e., one that is statistically significant), but not large enough to be of use. Sometimes, however, the practical significance of a finding can be great even when it is not large. For example, the statistical *association between amount of exercise and longevity is quite modest. But it is practically significant for two reasons: (1) Longevity is important (literally a matter of life or death), and (2) unlike many other variables that affect longevity, we have considerable control over the amount we exercise.

Practice Effects   Influences on the outcomes of a study that occur when subjects are tested more than once. Subjects may get adept at the task as a result of such practice—or bored with it and consequently less proficient.

Practice Trial   Early stage of a *clinical trial when participants become familiar with the setting and procedures before engaging in the full study. Any data collected during a practice trial are not included in the final data set.

Pragmatic Trial Research   *Effectiveness research using a *randomized controlled trial design. Sometimes called a "practical trial" because it attempts to determine effectiveness in actual clinical practice (where there is some natural variation in protocol use) rather than under strictly standardized conditions. The focus is on what will work in practice. See *effectiveness research. Compare *efficacy research,

Pragmatism   A philosophical movement that grew up in the United States in the late 19th century that had a good deal of influence on how social scientists viewed their work. Skeptical of broad truths (see *fallibilism), pragmatists held that knowledge is defined by usefulness; the ultimate test of a proposition is whether it "works," particularly in helping individuals solve practical problems.

PRE   Abbreviation for *proportional reduction of error.

Precision   In epidemiology, the degree to which measurements are not subject to *random error. Compare *reliability. See *specificity, *sensitivity. Contrast *validity, which means accuracy.

Preclinical Trial   A research study before clinical trials with humans, such as research with other animals, tissues, and cells.

Predetermined Variable   A variable in a *path analysis whose cause or causes are not specified. Such variables may be connected to other predetermined variables with curved, two-headed path lines. Also called *exogenous variables. See *path diagram for an illustration.

Predicted Value   See *predicted Y (or $\hat{Y}$).

Predicted Y (or $\hat{Y}$)   The value of the *dependent variable (Y) as predicted by a *regression or *GLM equation. It is based on the linear combination of the *intercept and the *independent variables for each case.

   For example, if the regression equation were $y = 1 + .45x_1 + .82x_2 + e$, then the predicted Y equation is $\hat{y} = 1 + .45x_1 + .82x_2$ (that is, the same numbers minus the e or error estimate). If the observed values for one person were 1 on x_1 and 2 on x_2, then the person's predicted y would be $\hat{y} = 1 + .45(1) + .82(2)$ or 3.09. The predicted Y value is determined this way for each person or case in the data set. Notice that the actual Y value minus the predicted Y value is called the *residual (it's the error).

Prediction   The term "prediction" has two common meanings in research: (a) using data to make a statement about the future, as in *forecasting, and (b) the more common meaning, and the one that sometimes confuses novice researchers, which refers to using data to "predict" outcomes that have already occurred, as in some *regression analyses. For example, one might use data about members of the entering class of 2012 to "predict" their likelihood of graduation in 2016. Obviously in such cases one is studying statistical associations among variables in the past, not "predicting" in the ordinary sense of the term. One could, however, use the equation developed by studying past data about the class of 2012 to predict graduation rates of future classes.

Prediction Equation   Another term for a *regression equation, that is, an equation that predicts the value of one variable on the basis of knowing the value of one or more other variables. A prediction equation is a regression equation that does not include an *error term. See * proportional reduction of error.

Predictive Analytics   Attempting to predict the future from the past to guide policy and business decisions. In business, a major goal is to predict consumer behavior. These predictions are often based on the *data mining of *big data.

Predictive Criterion-Related Validity   Evidence of validity based on the relationship between scores on the focal test collected at one time and later scores on a criterion of interest. For example, the GRE (test) is used to predict student performance in graduate school (criterion). To the degree that the GRE makes accurate predictions, it is said to have predictive criterion-related validity.

Predictive Discriminant Analysis (PDA)   In PDA a set of variables is used to predict membership into a categorical variable; the goal is to have a good "hit rate," classifying cases into their correct categories. This task also can be accomplished using *logistic regression, and some prefer logistic regression because it makes slightly fewer population assumptions. Compare *descriptive discriminant analysis.

Predictive Research   Said of an investigation whose goal is to forecast (predict, but not explain) the values of one variable by using the values of one or more other variables. Usually contrasted with *explanatory research, in which the goal is to understand the *causes behind relations, to test theory-based hypotheses to develop a theory, or sometimes to compare the effectiveness of two theories to explain variance in a dependent variable. In other terms, the goal in predictive research is to estimate a future value of a dependent variable; in explanatory research, it is to estimate the *partial regression coefficients that are interpreted as showing the degree of effect or causal relation for each variable, controlling for the other variables. For some authors writing about research methods, the distinction between explanatory and predictive research amounts to a dichotomy between *experimental research (which can be explanatory) and other kinds, especially *correlational research (which cannot). The debate over whether only experimentalists can make valid causal generalizations, and thus do explanatory research, is sometimes quite heated and more than a little self-interested.

Predictive Survey Research   See *descriptive survey research for comparison of descriptive, predictive, and explanatory survey research.

Predictive Validity   The extent to which a test, scale, or other measurement predicts subsequent performance or behavior. Also called *criterion-related validity.

Predictor Variable   Loosely, another name for *independent variable or *cause. The term is often used when discussing *nonexperimental research designs such as *correlational studies. See *explanatory variable. Compare *criterion variable.

P

PRESS Statistic   Predicted residual sum of squares. A technique used to estimate how widely a *multiple regression model can be generalized and to compare models. Values range from zero to 1.0, with those closer to 1.0 indicating a higher level of *generalizability.

Pretest   (a) A test given or measurement taken before an experimental *treatment begins; more generally, a "before" measure in a before-and-after study. By contrasting the results of the pretest with those of the *posttest, researchers gain evidence about the effects of the treatment. (b) A trial run used to assess some part of an *instrument or procedure. Compare *pilot.

Pretest-Posttest Design   A one-group design that includes pretest measurement of the dependent variable, the administration of an intervention, followed by posttest measurement of the dependent variable. The researcher determines if change occurred from pretest to posttest. This one-group design has multiple *threats to *internal validity, including *history, *maturation, *testing, *instrumentation, and *regression artifacts.

Pretest Sensitizing   Unintentionally influencing the results of the *posttest by giving a pretest. Compare *practice effects, *order effects.
        For example, the pretest could influence the posttest results if subjects have been alerted to what the researcher is interested in or if they learn skills on the pretest that they can later use on the posttest.

Prevalence   A measure of occurrence of a disease or other phenomenon. It is the total number of people or cases with the particular condition in a specific area or place at a specific point in time. Compare *incidence rate.

Prevention Research   Research focused on identifying effective interventions or ways to prevent future pathologies such as high blood pressure and mental illness. Focus often is given to identifying high-risk individuals, including markers of risk. Both *risk and protective factors are determined for future intervention with individuals considered at risk. *Best practices based on empirical evidence are used for interventions.

Prevention Trial   Medical research studies used to determine how to prevent future pathologies with high-risk participants.

Prima Facie   Latin for "at first sight" or "true on first view"; true unless demonstrated otherwise by subsequent evidence.

Primary Analysis   Original analysis of the data in a research study. Compare *secondary analysis (re-analysis of data gathered by others) and *meta-analysis (analysis of analyses).

Primary Data   New data collected by the researcher in a research study. Contrasted with *secondary data, which are already collected data that might be reused in a research study.

Primary Prevention Research   Research focusing on the prevention of problems/ disorders before they occur. Compare *secondary prevention research, *tertiary prevention research.

Primary Source   An original source of *data; one that puts as few intermediaries as possible between the production and the study of data. Compare *secondary source.

For example, the primary sources for the study of the use of metaphor in Shakespeare would be works written by Shakespeare; secondary sources would be books about Shakespeare. "Primary" is often a matter of degree than kind; for instance, Shakespeare's original manuscripts would be more primary than a 20th-century edition of his works.

Principal Components Analysis (PCA)   Methods for undertaking a *linear transformation of a large set of observed correlated variables into a smaller set of uncorrelated *latent variables. This makes analysis easier by grouping data into more manageable units and eliminating problems of *multicollinearity. Principal components analysis is similar in aim to *factor analysis (FA), but it is an independent technique; advocates of the two methods stress the differences rather than the similarities, and debates between them are often highly contentious. However, the outcomes produced by the two methods are usually quite similar, especially when the number of observed variables is large. A key difference between the two is that in PCA, the observed variables are elements (components) of the latent variable, as lung capacity and blood pressure are components of the latent variable health. In FA, by contrast, the latent variable *causes* the observed variables, as a personality trait might cause responses to a psychological test. See *discriminant analysis, *canonical correlations, *cluster analysis.

Principle of Beneficence   See *beneficence.

Principle of Bivalence   States that every statement or proposition is either true or false and there are no other alternatives.

Principle of Indifference   If you want to state how probable something is, some knowledge of *prior probability is needed. If you don't have any useful information about probability before making your guess, the principle of indifference says to assume that all outcomes are equally likely (called the "uniform distribution").

For example, if two outcomes are possible, then you would consider the probability of each to be .5 (or 50% likely). The principle is used in *Bayesian statistical inference.

Principle Investigator   The lead researcher for a project; he or she has ultimate responsibility for proposal, design, conduct of the study, analysis and dissemination of the results, and dealing with any issues that arise surrounding the study.

Principle of Nonmaleficence   States that research should do no harm to its research participants and others.

Principle of Parsimony   States that researchers should follow *Ockham's razor and strive for *parsimony.

Prior Distribution   The *prior probability distribution showing one's believed probability before new data are collected and incorporated into a revised *posterior probability distribution. See *Bayesian statistical inference.

Prior Probability   In *Bayesian inference, the opinion of an investigator who states an opinion as a probability before (prior to) a research study. On the basis of the study, the researcher revises the opinion in light of the data collected in order to arrive at a new *posterior probability. Also called "priors." This prior probability can be based on extensive evidence, but it is "subjective" in the sense that it can vary from one researcher to the next.

Priors   (a) *Prior probabilities or prior distributions in *Bayesian inference. (b) *Prior variables in a causal model.

Prior Variable   Another term for *exogenous variable.

Prisoners' Dilemma   In *game theory, a classic illustration of competition when information is imperfect. The situation involves two prisoners accused of committing a crime together. They are questioned separately. If both refuse to confess, they will do better than if both confess. If one confesses and the other does not, the one who confesses goes free while his or her partner goes to jail. A remarkable number of findings have been built on the mathematical and logical analyses of this and similar simulations of competition.

Probabilistic   (a) Said of research that focuses on *probabilities rather than, for example, universal *laws or truths. Contrasted with *deterministic. (b) Said of a causal relationship in which change in one *variable increases the *probability of change in another variable but does not invariably produce the change. Compare *necessary condition, *sufficient condition.

For example, age at marriage and divorce are negatively correlated, but that does not mean that all people getting married at younger ages end up divorcing, and it does not mean that no individuals getting married at older ages will end up divorcing. It is an *empirical generalization, not a mathematical law.

Probability   Like "cause," probability is a controversial concept; different, and opposed, camps of statisticians study probability, most importantly the *frequentists and the *Bayesians. The definitions that follow generally cover both. (a) The likelihood that a particular event or relationship will occur; the *proportion of tries that are *successes. More formally, out of all possible outcomes, the proportionate expectation of a given outcome. Values for statistical probability range from 0 (never) to 1.0 (always). Probability statistics cannot be negative numbers because something cannot be less than totally unlikely. See *p* value, *likelihood ratio, *Bayesian inference. (b) The field of mathematics devoted to the study of probability as defined in (a).

For example, the probability that a person drawing a card at random from a deck of 52 playing cards will select a red card is 26/52, or .5. The probability of drawing a heart is 13/52, or .25; for an ace, it is 4/52, or .077.

Probability, Conditional   Said of situations in which the probability of one event (A) depends on (is conditioned by) another event (B). Symbolized: *p*(A|B), which is read as "the probability of A given B." Contrast *independence. See *p* value.

For example, the probability of contracting the AIDS virus is conditional upon contact with an infected person: *p*(AIDS|CONTACT). The greater the number of such contacts, the greater the probability of getting the disease.

Probability Density Function (PDF)   Depicted in a distribution showing the magnitudes of probability for a *continuous *random variable (i.e., a variable that can take on an infinite number of values in any given range). These magnitudes are called "densities," and the "function" is a formula for drawing a *histogram or *line graph depicting the densities. Alternatively stated, a PDF is a mathematical equation that defines the line graph showing the distribution of a continuous variable. The height at each point is its "density" or, roughly speaking, its relative frequency (the higher, the more probable). Technically speaking, probability is not calculated for a point on a continuous distribution; determining probability in this case requires integration (via *calculus) to determine the area around a point, between two points, or beyond a point— this is how the "distribution tables" you see in the back of statistics books are produced. See *probability distribution (b), *frequency curve. Compare *probability mass function.

Probability Distribution   (a) All of the outcomes in a distribution of research results and each of their probabilities (*empirical probability distribution). (b) The number of times we would expect to get a particular number of *successes in a large number of trials (theoretical probability distribution). The most important of the theoretical probability distributions are the *binomial, *normal, *Student's *t*, *chi-square, and *F* distributions. These distributions also can be shown empirically. Theoretical distributions are compared with observed, empirical distributions to judge the probability that the latter could have occurred by chance alone. For a *continuous variable, an empirical probability distribution is based on intervals. For example, a probability distribution for income could be the percentage of households whose incomes fell in each of the following intervals: less than $25,000 per year, $25,001 to $30,000, $30,001 to $35,000, and so on. For *discrete variables, the probabilities are *relative frequencies. See *binomial distribution for an example. Compare *probability density function, *probability mass function.

P

Probability, Empirical   An actual count of the number of events of a particular type divided by the total number of possible events. Usually contrasted with *theoretical probability.

For example, if we had a perfectly balanced coin, the theoretical probability of tossing the coin and getting tails is .50, that is, 1 out of 2 (1/2). But if we actually flipped the coin, say, 200 times, we might get 96 tails and 104 heads. The empirical probability—describing what actually happened—would be .48 for tails, that is, 96 out of 200 (96/200 = .48). As we increase the number of trials (coin flips), the empirical probability tends to get closer to the theoretical probability.

Probability, Joint   The probability of two or more events occurring together.

For example, the probability of drawing a spade from an ordinary deck of 52 playing cards is 13 out of 52, or .25. The probability of drawing a jack is 4 out of 52, or .0769. The joint probability of drawing a card that is both a jack and a spade is calculated by multiplying the probability of a spade (.25) times the probability of a jack (.0769). The product, .25 × .0769 = .01923, is the joint probability of drawing the jack of spades.

Probability Level   The *alpha level below which the *null hypothesis is rejected; this value or level is the chance of making a *Type I (or *alpha) error when the null hypothesis is true.

Probability Mass Function (PMF)   In contrast to *probability density functions, which define continuous *random variables, probability mass functions define *discrete random variables* (i.e., random variables that take on a countable number of values). A PMF provides the exact probability that the random variable (e.g., X) will take on a particular value.

For example, in a single toss of a die, the probability of a 5 is 1/6 or .167. Two required properties of all PMFs are (a) the probability of any single value of the random variable is between 0 and 1 and (b) the sum of the probabilities of all the values of the discrete random variable must equal 1. Our single toss of the die meets these two properties: (a) .167 falls between 0 and 1, and (b) the probability of each of the six possible values (1, 2, 3, 4, 5, 6) sum to 1 (.167 + .167 + .167 + .167 + .167 + .167 = 1). The height of a PMF for a particular value of X is its probability or "mass."

Probability Paper   Graph paper calibrated so that the values of a *cumulative frequency distribution fall on a straight line if the data being graphed are normally distributed. Less used today than computerized graphics equivalents. See *normal probability plot, *P-P plot.

Probability Plots   Graphic techniques for comparing probability distributions, usually to determine whether a data set is normally distributed. See *normal probability plot, *probability paper, *P-P plot, *Q-Q plot.

Probability Sample   A *sample in which each case that could be chosen has a known probability of being included in the sample. Often a *simple random sample, which is an equal probability sample (see *EPSEM). At some point, *random selection is part of the process of every probability sample.

Probability Sampling   Synonym for *random sampling.

Probability Statistics   Techniques for calculating the likelihood (*probability, usually expressed as a *p* value) that particular events will occur.

   Probability statistics are the bridge from *descriptive statistics about *samples to *inferential statistics about *populations. After calculating a descriptive statistic for a sample, one then calculates the probability that this statistic would have occurred by chance alone. If that probability is low, then one can reasonably infer that what is true of the sample is probably true of the population as well. See *sampling distribution, *statistical inference.

Probability, Subjective   A guess or feeling about some probability that is not based on any precise computation. However, it may be a reasonable, if not computational, assessment by a knowledgeable person. See *Bayesian inference.

   For example, an experienced member of a parole board might say, "I really believe that, on the basis of his attitude, and his record in the work release program, this prisoner is a good risk; we should give him a chance." Or the loan committee at a bank might conclude, "Given that several competing businesses are nearby and that previous establishments at this location have gone out of business, we feel that the probability of failure is high and, therefore, we recommend against the loan."

Probability, Theoretical   The expected or predicted likelihood that a particular event will occur. See *probability, empirical.

Probability Theory   A branch of mathematics dealing with how to estimate the chances that events will occur. Compare *decision theory, *risk.

   In a way, probability theory, especially the *frequentist variety, is *inferential statistics stood on its head. In probability theory, we make inferences about samples or individual events on the basis of knowledge about populations, but in inferential statistics, we use samples to generalize about populations. For example, if we know that a particular type of surgery is successful over 90% of the time, we might generalize to individual patients to say that the probability is over .90 that it will be successful for them.

Probability Value   The likelihood that a statistical result would have been obtained by chance (or *sampling error, or *random error) alone. Stated more precisely, it's the probability of the observed test-statistic value, or a more extreme value, *if the null hypothesis were true;* it's a conditional probability (i.e., the probability of the data given the condition of a true null). The probability value does not provide the probability that the null hypothesis is true, it does not provide the probability that the alternative hypothesis is true, and it does not provide the probability that the null hypothesis is false. It is just an estimate of how frequently the observed result (or a more extreme result) would occur *in the long run if the null hypothesis were true*. In *hypothesis or *significance testing, the probability value (*p* value) is compared by a researcher with an *alpha level to determine whether the result has *statistical significance. If the *p* value is less than (or equal to according to some) the alpha level, the result is judged to be statistically significant. For example, if the researcher decides to use an alpha of .05 and the calculated *p* is .022, the result would be declared statistically significant. Compare *posterior probability.

Probit Regression Analysis   A technique used in *regression analysis when the *dependent variable is a *dummy (or *dichotomous) 0, 1 variable. In the probit model, *independent variables influence an unobserved continuous variable, which in turn determines the probability that an observed dichotomous event occurs. Probit is short for "probability unit." See *logit. Compare *logistic regression.

   The questions you answer with probit regression are variants (in probability units) of the questions you answer with any regression analysis. The questions in probit regression language are these: (a) What is the change in the probability of the DV being 1 (e.g., yes, graduate) for a one-unit change in an IV? (b) What is the change in the probability of the DV being 1 (yes) for a one-unit change in an IV, while controlling for the effects of the other IVs? (c) What is the cumulative effect of all the IVs together on the probability of the DV equaling 1 (yes)?

Problem of Induction   Philosophical idea that the future might not always resemble the past. Suggests that evidence, and not final truths, is what can be provided by empirical research. In contrast, logic and mathematics are said to produce certain truth (as in "deductive truth"). Usually attributed to David Hume.

Procedure   Section in a journal article or other research report that explains how the research was executed. The goal is to include enough information that someone could replicate the study if needed. It includes information about materials, apparatus, and instruments, as well as the design used in the research study. It should include a step-by-step account of what the researcher did from the beginning to the end of the study, including what the researcher and the participants did during the study. This must be done briefly, however, because of space limitations in journals.

Process Research   Research examining *mediating and, to a lesser degree, *moderating variables, in an attempt to explain the mechanisms operating to produce change in the outcome variable.

Process Tracing In *case study research, analysis that seeks to discover and understand the causal mechanisms that led to an outcome. See *mediating variable.

Process Turtle Diagram A diagrammatic method of explicating a process in terms of with whom, with what resources, with what methods, and with what indicators. For examples, go to http://www.jhoti.com/turtle_diagram.asp

Procrustean Transformation or Rotation A technique used in *factor analysis to transform an empirical matrix so that it resembles a predetermined target matrix, such as a theoretically expected pattern. Often used in conjunction with *promax rotation.

Product The result of multiplying. For example, in the equation $9 \times 6 = 54$, 54 is the product.

Production Function An equation expressing the relationship between the output of a good and inputs needed to make it. This equation is frequently modeled using regression by economists. See *productivity, *econometrics.

Productivity Output per unit of input. The concept, originally developed in economics, has wide applicability in other fields.

Product-Moment Correlation See *Pearson's correlation coefficient (r).

Product Variable A variable obtained by multiplying the values of two other variables. Product variables are most often used to study *interaction effects. See *product vector.

Product Vector The result of multiplying two *vectors of scores on variables. It's a step in calculating the *covariance of two variables (but it should not be confused with vector multiplication in matrix algebra).

For example, in Table P.3, Vector 1 is multiplied by Vector 2 to get Vector 3, which is the product vector.

Table P.3 Product Vector

Case	Vector 1	Vector 2	Vector 3
	A	B	A × B
1	2	4	8
2	3	2	6
3	5	6	30
4	7	8	56

Profile Analysis   Data reduction technique for comparing groups of individuals on one dependent variable across multiple time points or for comparing groups of individuals on multiple dependent variables on the same or standardized scale at one time point. A graph is used so that the patterns can be depicted and viewed visually. When examining graphs, one looks to see if the lines are parallel (or not), if the lines have the same (or different) mean levels, and how flat the profiles are. Some computer software packages (e.g., SPSS, SAS, R) provide options for comparing group profiles to check for significant differences (e.g., using the multivariate approach to repeated measures analysis).

Program   A set of instructions, written in a *programming language, that tells a computer how to handle *data according to certain rules. Unless it is programmed, a computer cannot perform operations. Also called *software.

Program Evaluation   See *evaluation research.

Programming   Writing a set of instructions to solve a problem with a computer.

Programming Language   A *software program used to write other programs. Among *many* examples, some of the best known include FORTRAN, BASIC, Java, and C.

Program Theory   An explanation of how and why a social program should operate, including a *process* component (or "process theory") and an *impact* component (or "impact theory" showing early and later outcomes). An excellent way to depict a program theory is with a *logic model. Explicating program theory is important for designing and operating effective social programs; it also is important for interpreting results from an *impact assessment. For example, if data suggest that a program is not effective, this might be due to (a) implementation failure (i.e., the program services were not delivered as specified in the program theory) or (b) theory failure (i.e., the program was implemented correctly, but it was based on a poor or faulty theory).

Projective Tests   Psychological tests in which subjects are asked to describe what they see in pictures that can be interpreted in many ways. The idea is that subjects' interpretations will "project" their inner states. The Rorschach ("inkblot") test is a well-known example.

Promax   A method of *oblique rotation of the axes in a *factor analysis.

Propensity Score Matching   A form of subject matching most often used when random assignment is not possible. It is an advanced version of *matched pairs that uses multiple *covariates combined using *logistic regression to arrive at a propensity score, which is then used to match subjects. The goal of propensity score matching is to reduce bias in estimating the program effect in *quasi-experiments in which subjects cannot be randomly assigned

P

or in nonexperimental research such as a *case-control study. It is a powerful technique; its primary weakness is that it requires a relatively large number of subjects from which the matched pairs can be located. Compare *instrumental variable estimation.

Proportion   A number, ranging between 0 and 1.0, calculated by dividing the number of subjects having a certain characteristic by the total number of subjects. To get a percentage, you multiply the proportion by 100. See *relative frequency, *probability.

   For example, if the graduating class had a total of 948 students and 237 of those were business majors, the proportion of business majors would be .25 (237/948), and 25% (.25 × 100 = 25%) would be business majors.

Proportional Hazards Model   Another term for a "Cox model." See *Cox regression.

Proportional Reduction of Error (PRE)   A type of measure of *association that indicates how much you can reduce your error in the prediction of one variable by knowing the values of another variable. How much better can you estimate variable Y if you know variable X than if you do not? The answer is a PRE statistic. *Lambda is one example of a PRE statistic; the *Pearson r is not, but the r^2 is. Other examples are *gamma, $*R^2$, *omega squared, and *eta squared.

Proportional Stratified Random Sample   A *stratified random sample in which the proportion of subjects randomly selected from each category (stratum) is the same as in the *population. It's an *equal probability of selection method and, therefore, produces representative samples. Compare *quota sample.

Proportion of Variance Accounted for   See $*R^2$, *coefficient of determination, *coefficient of multiple determination.

Proportion of Variance Index   A synonym for *proportional reduction of error (PRE) measure.

Proposal   See *research proposal.

Proposition   A formal statement about the relationships among abstract concepts. Propositions usually occur early in an article or other research report. Subsequent parts of the report generally try to maintain or demonstrate the proposition. One type of formalized *theory is a set of related propositions.

   For example, "Cognitive sophistication fosters social tolerance" is a proposition.

Prospective Cohort Study   A *cohort study conceived and baseline data collected from before any of the people have developed the outcome(s) of interest. Compare *retrospective cohort study.

Prospective Power (also called A Priori Power)   Prospective power analysis is conducted *before* data are gathered in order to determine how large a sample needs to be to help avoid making a Type II error with the future research study. Many granting agencies now require that prospective power be reported. One popular and free program on the web for this purpose is G*Power (see the useful web resources section at the end of this book). You will have to tell the program what power level you desire (usually a minimum of .80 is recommended), the expected size of effect you expect to find, and the *alpha level you will use (.05 is usually recommended). From these three pieces of information, a power program will tell you the sample size needed to conduct the research. Compare *retrospective power.

Prospective Sampling   In clinical research, refers to selection of cases or participants based on whether they have been exposed to a risk factor, and after sampling the participants are followed forward to determine if and when the illness or condition of interest occurs. Compare *retrospective sampling.

Prospective Study   A *longitudinal study in which subjects are followed to see what will happen to them. Also called *panel study. The opposite would be a *retrospective study. The term is more commonly used in epidemiology than in the social sciences.

Protective Factors   See *risk and protective factors.

Protocol   (a) The plan for carrying out research, especially administering *experimental treatments and/or collecting data (e.g., *interview protocol). Sometimes a distinction is made between the *design, which is the overall plan, and the protocol, which is a document detailing the step-by-step procedures. Detailed protocols are especially important for reducing *random error and *bias when researchers hire others to collect their data and in multisite research in which treatments are administered by many different researchers. (b) The transcript notes of responses to think aloud questions are sometimes called "protocols."

Protocol Analysis   One of a number of techniques to analyze *think aloud, talk aloud, or interview data to determine descriptive/qualitative as well as quantitative characteristics of the verbal responses. An example of the former would be analyzing data in which people described their thinking while they engaged in problem solving. An example of the latter would be determining the exact stage of someone's moral development through application of a scoring rubric outlining responses characteristic of the stages.

Protocol Violation   A research protocol is a set of rules the researcher has for how a research study will be conducted. A protocol violation occurs when the researcher deviates from that protocol. For example, the researcher might include data collected before IRB approval, use a different data collection instrument, or fail to obtain informed consent from participants. Violations can vary from minimal (modifying the words on one item on a questionnaire) to severe (falsifying information, putting subjects at risk without their knowledge). When suspicions of protocol violation are present, an audit is conducted. Note that an original protocol can be modified, but the modification has to be approved by the *IRB.

Proxy Variable (or Measure) When one cannot obtain a direct measure of a variable, sometimes a closely related variable is used in its place (as its "proxy"). A proxy variable is an indirect measure of the variable a researcher wants to study; it is used when the object of inquiry is difficult to measure or observe directly. See *indicator, *operation. Also called "surrogate variable."

For example, in a classic study, Durkheim wanted to study the historical evolution of moral values in European societies. Since there was little directly available objective evidence about moral values, he studied the history of law. Laws, he believed, reflect moral values, and laws are easily accessible to the researcher. Another example: A measure of "free or subsidized lunch" might be used as a proxy for poverty in a research study of children in public schools.

Pseudo R^2 A "*true*" R^2 is routinely provided in regular *OLS regression; it indicates the proportion of the variance in the dependent variable that is predicted or explained by the independent variables. Unfortunately, this measure is not available in *logistic and *probit regression; these methods do not minimize error variance and instead rely on *MLE. Since there can be no variance from the mean with categorical variables, the R^2 estimate is spurious or "pseudo." As a result, several "*pseudo*" R^2 indexes have been developed to provide similar information (i.e., how well the model/equation fits the data). You can use the index in a similar way as you would use a traditional R^2. But because there are several ways to produce a pseudo R^2, and the different methods can produce quite different values, you must be careful to provide information about which specific pseudo R^2 you are using.

Pseudo-Random Numbers Numbers that approximate a set of true random numbers, usually as produced by a mathematical formula as generated by a computer. Random numbers have wide uses in statistics (e.g., in *simulations) and the demand for tables of random numbers used to be high. Today, however, multiple random number generators are available for free on the Internet (see web resources at the end of this book). Most of these are pseudo-random; that is, they are not produced by a truly *random process.

Pseudoscience Practices, beliefs, and procedures that claim to be scientific but are not scientific. Examples would include reinterpretation of negative findings as supporting a claim, continual creation of ad hoc hypotheses to explain away negative findings, absence of rigorous testing of claims, and overreliance on testimonials and anecdotal evidence while disregarding other evidence for the claim.

Psychometrician   Expert trained in measurement and *psychometric research. Usually PhD-level training is required.

Psychometric Research   Research on how psychological *variables are *operationalized for purposes of measurement, particularly measurement of individual differences among people. Focus is on psychometric properties (especially reliability and validity) of tests, personality inventories, and other measurement instruments.

Publication Bias   In *meta-analysis, the bias that arises from the fact that some types of study are more likely to get published than others and thus be more available for meta-analytic studies. The most frequently discussed source of such bias is the tendency for studies showing statistically significant results to be published more frequently than studies of equal importance that do not contain statistically significant findings. See *substantive significance, *file drawer problem.

Public Use Microdata Samples (PUMS)   Large samples of data from the U.S. Census Bureau's decennial censuses. They are available to any researcher and are designed for doing *secondary analyses with a personal (micro-) computer. Names, addresses, and other identifying data are deleted before the PUMS are made available to researchers.

PUMS   *Public use microdata samples.

Pure Research   Another term for *basic research; the opposite is usually *applied research. Some research studies are more pure (or applied) than others; therefore, it is helpful to view pure and applied as poles on a continuum rather than a binary choice.

Purposive Sampling   Sampling where the researcher (on purpose) specifies the characteristics of a population of interest (e.g., middle school students with ADHD) and then locates individuals with the needed characteristics.

   Technically, statistical inferences about a population cannot legitimately be made using a single purposive sample. On the other hand, identifying certain kinds of subjects of interest is an improvement over *convenience sampling.

PUS   Public use samples. See *public use microdata samples.

_p_ Value   Short for *probability value, that is, the probability that the value of a *test statistic, or a more extreme value, would occur by chance or *sampling error—if the null hypothesis were true. It answers this very specific question: "If the null hypothesis were true, what is the probability of my data (i.e., my result)?" It does *not* answer this question: "Given my data (i.e., my result), what is the probability that the null hypothesis is true?" In other words, the p value gives this $P(D|H_0)$, but it does not give this $P(H_0|D)$.

   For example, if a correlation between two variables in a sample of 100 cases were reported as $r = .43$, $p = .018$, this would mean the following: If there were no correlation in the population from which the sample was drawn (the null hypothesis), the probability of obtaining a correlation this size (.43) or larger in a sample this size (100) would be .018. Researchers sometimes round off a p value such as .018 to < .05, but the actual p value is more informative.

Note: In a probability distribution, such as a t distribution, the p value is the area in the tail(s) at and beyond the calculated value of the test statistic. In *hypothesis testing, researchers hope the calculated value of the test statistic will be large and the p value will be small, indicating *statistical significance.

Pygmalion Effect   Changes in subjects' behaviors brought about by researchers' expectations. See *self-fulfilling prophecy, *demand characteristics. Also called "Rosenthal effect."

The term originally comes from Greek mythology, and it was popularized in a play by George Bernard Shaw. It is perhaps best known to researchers in the form of a controversial study (by Rosenthal and Jacobson) in which teachers were told to expect some of their students' intelligence test scores to increase. They did increase, apparently because of teachers' expectations.

Q (a) Abbreviation for *quartile. Q1 is the first quartile, Q2 the second, and so on. (b) Symbol for the *studentized range statistic. (c) A measure of *goodness-of-fit for an *overidentified *path analysis model. It ranges from 0 to 1, with 1 indicating a perfect fit. (d) *Yule's *Q.* (e) *Cochran's Q test.

QCA *Qualitative comparative analysis.

QDA Miner Software Popular mixed methods data analysis software that includes a qualitative data analysis module (QDAMiner), a quantitative content analysis module (WORDSTAT), and a statistical analysis module (SIMSTAT). A free version of the qualitative module, called QDA Miner Lite, is available at http://provalisresearch.com/downloads/trial-versions.

Q Methodology A way of ordering or sorting the parts of objects of study. The most recognizable feature of Q methodology is that "subjects" sort cards (a Q sort) into a number of piles that represent points on a continuum. The sorters are most often not the subjects of the research; they are *respondents or even *informants. They sort statements into categories based on their personal understanding of the concepts being investigated.

For example, one might ask known conservatives and liberals to sort a group of cards on which are written the names of governmental policies. They would rank the policies on a scale ranging from most to least favorable. The researcher could use their rankings to test a theory of the components of liberalism and conservatism by seeing how the two groups of sorters differed.

Q-Q Plot Quantile-quantile plot. A method for comparing a sample distribution with a theoretical distribution, such as a *normal curve, by plotting them against one another. This is usually done with *percentiles as the quantiles. If the sample has been drawn from a normal distribution, the plotted values of the sample will approximate a straight line. Compare *normal probability plot, and see that entry for a graphic.

Q

Q Sort   See *Q methodology.

Q-Technique Factor Analysis   Type of factor analysis that focuses on relationships and clustering of cases instead of, as in regular *factor analysis, variables. This exploratory analysis identifies types or groups of people that are similar on the variables the researcher has the software use for clustering. Once the clusters of individuals are identified, they are further examined on descriptive variables to determine their demographic characteristics, in addition to their characteristics on the clustering variables. The technique is very similar to *cluster analysis. Compare *R-technique factor analysis.

Quadratic Form   See *quadratic relation.

Quadratic Relation   Said of a relation in a *regression analysis when one of the *independent variables has been raised to a power of 2 (X^2) and doing so produces a significant *regression coefficient. A quadratic relation indicates that there has been one departure from *linearity, that is, one turn or change of direction in the regression line. See *curvilinear relation, *polynomial regression analysis, *spline regression.

Qualitative   (a) When referring to *variables, qualitative is another term for *categorical or *nominal. (b) When speaking of kinds of research, qualitative refers to studies that rely on qualitative data. (c) When speaking of kinds of research, there is another stronger version, which is explained under the entry *qualitative research. See *participant observation, *ethnographic research, *focus group.

  The qualitative/quantitative distinction is often overdrawn. It is difficult to avoid *quantitative elements in the most qualitative subject matter; for example, "The painter entered his 'blue period' in the 1890s." And qualitative components are crucial to most good quantitative research, which begins with *theories, *concepts, and *constructs.

Qualitative Comparative Analysis   **(QCA)** A method of multiple case study analysis based on Boolean algebra, originally developed by Ragin. The emphasis is on demonstrating causal relations. Two versions exist: crisp-set QCA for use when the explanatory variables are dichotomous and fuzzy-set QCA for ranked explanatory variables. A relatively large number of cases can be handled with the method (roughly 20 to 50), and a free software package for conducting the analyses is available.

Qualitative Data   Data in the form of words, categories, and images. These data come from participant observations, field notes, in-depth interviews, and open-ended questions. The researcher is said to be the primary data collection instrument when collecting qualitative data.

Qualitative Data Analysis   The term is used to describe two broad categories of data analysis: (a) methods for analyzing verbal data, such as textual analysis or *grounded theory, and (b) methods for analyzing categorical data with statistical methods, such as *contingency tables and *odds ratios.

Qualitative Data Analysis Software   Computer programs designed specifically for the needs of qualitative research. Helps with tasks such as coding, linking multiple data sources, dividing, sorting, and relating data using *Boolean algebra operators, enumerating codes and categories, structuring visual models, drawing diagrams, creating memos and annotations, generating theory, and so forth. See *CAQDAS, *NUD*IST, *NVivo.

Qualitative Designs   Said of research designs based on qualitative data and/or that rely on the goals and purposes unique to a qualitative research study. A major part of most qualitative research and designs is to obtain *Verstehen and document the *emic perspective. The designs and methods of data collection vary depending on the qualitative method used. The most widely used qualitative research methods are *phenomenology, *ethnography, qualitative *case studies, and *grounded theory. Phenomenology and grounded theory rely heavily on in-depth interviews and open-ended questionnaires, ethnography relies heavily on field work and participant observation, and case studies rely on multiple kinds of data. Specific "designs" are sometimes delineated by the four major qualitative research methods. For example, case study designs include (according to one system) an intrinsic case study design (in which one is interested in only the specific case), an instrumental case study design (in which one hopes to understand something more general than the particular case), and a collective case study design (in which one studies multiple cases for comparative knowledge).

Qualitative Observation   Typically unstructured and exploratory observation. Also includes participatory observation whereby the researcher engages in the group practices in the natural environment to understand the group and phenomena "from the inside" and gain the *emic viewpoint.

Qualitative Research   In its "strong form," a research *paradigm that not only advocates the use of qualitative data (e.g., interviews, participant observation, open-ended questions) but also advocates a worldview supporting relatively strong forms of *relativism, *theory-ladenness of facts, *underdetermination of theory by evidence, *Duhem-Quine thesis, and the *problem of induction. Tends to take a *humanistic, *subjective approach to human science, rejecting the concept of *objectivity, and rejects all forms of *positivism and especially *scientism. Also is much more supportive of *idealism than *materialism. It is more popular in the humanities than hard sciences, and (in contrast to *mixed methods research and *multimethod research) qualitative researchers sometimes view the schism between the soft and hard sciences as unbridgeable.

Qualitative Variable   Another name for a *categorical variable or a *nominal variable, and in some instances a *rank order or *ordinal variable.

Quality Control Methods   Statistical procedures for checking the precision and accuracy of processes such as in manufacturing and research projects. Measurements are taken at regular intervals and are usually graphed to chart whether acceptable quality levels are being maintained.

Quantile   Any of several ways of dividing the total number of rank-ordered cases or observations into equally sized groups—into groups having the same quantity. *Quartiles, *quintiles, *deciles, and *percentiles are examples of quantiles. Quantiles indicate the proportion of scores located below (and above) a given value. For example, if you scored at the 80th percentile, your score would be above that of 80% of those who were tested.

Quantile-Quantile Plot   See *Q-Q plot.

Quantile Regression   A form of regression that gives more information about the effect or predictive power of independent variables on a dependent variable than standard *linear regression. A standard linear regression shows the conditional mean value of the dependent variable for each value of an independent variable or set of independent variables. The coefficients show, on average, the effect of the independent variables. In contrast, a quantile regression shows the relationship between the dependent and independent variables at five different levels of the dependent variable, specifically at five different quantiles (e.g., 5th, 10th, 50th, 90th, 95th). This allows one to see if the independent variables are more important at different levels of the dependent variable. That is, the regression coefficients will be different at different quantiles. We would not be surprised to see quantile regression used more frequently in the future.

Quantitative   Said of variables or research that can be handled numerically. Usually contrasted (too sharply) with *qualitative variables and research. Many research designs lend themselves well to collecting both quantitative and qualitative data, and many variables can be handled either qualitatively or quantitatively. For example, *naturalistic observations can give rise to either or both kinds of data. Interactions can be counted and timed with a stopwatch, or they can be interpreted more holistically. *Ordinal variables can sometimes form a bridge between quantitative and qualitative; see *qualitative comparative analysis.

Quantitative Analysis   Statistical analysis of quantitative data. Note that qualitative and categorical data can also be analyzed quantitatively (e.g., through counting).

Quantitative Data   Data in the form of numbers and variables. These data are collected using precise and structured measurement using data collection instruments and procedures that are high on reliability, validity, and cross-researcher agreement.

Quantitative Research   Term used as a contrast with *qualitative research. In its weak or soft form, quantitative research is research that is based on quantitative data. It refers to the research *paradigm that argues for social and behavioral scientific research that strives to accurately describe, predict, explain, and ultimately control (in a positive sense of solving problems) the natural and human world. Philosophically, quantitative research is generally supportive of a softer and updated version of *positivism known as *postpositivism*. In its strong or more aggressive form, quantitative research can take on characteristics of *scientism.

Quartile Deviation   Half of the range covered by the middle half of the scores in a *distribution; half of the distance between the first and third *quartiles. The advantage of the quartile deviation, in comparison to other measures of *dispersion, is that it is less influenced by *outliers (extreme values), certainly less so than is the ordinary *range. Also called "semi-interquartile range or "middle 50."

Quartiles   Divisions of the total rank-ordered cases or observations in a study into four groups of equal size. Technically, the three points that divide a series of ordered scores into four groups. Loosely, the groups themselves. The first quartile is located at the 25th percentile, the second at the 50th, and the third at the 75th. Compare *quantile, *quintile, *decile.

Quasi-experiment   A type of research design for conducting studies in field or real-life situations where the researcher may be able to manipulate some *independent variables but cannot randomly assign subjects to *control and *experimental groups. See *field experiment, *interrupted time-series design.

For example, you cannot cut off some individuals' unemployment benefits to see how well they could get along without them or to see whether an alternative job-training program would be more *effective. But you could try to find volunteers for your new job-training program. You could compare the results for the volunteer group (*experimental group) with those of people in the regular program (*control group). The study is quasi-experimental because you were unable to assign subjects randomly to *treatment and control groups.

Quasi-experimental Control Group   A control group that is not produced through the process of random assignment of participants to experimental and control groups. Often quasi-experimental control groups are *intact groups.

Quasi-experimental Design   A research design for a *quasi-experiment in contrast to, for example, a *randomized experiment. See *quasi-experiment.

Quasi-independent Variable   A variable treated statistically as independent but that cannot be manipulated by the researcher.

Quasi-random Sample   Another term for *systematic sample, perhaps because systematic sampling has only a small random component. However, systematic random sampling usually is an *equal probability of selection method and therefore produces representative samples.

Q

Questionnaire   A self-report data collection instrument, including a group of written items or questions to which subjects respond. A few researchers restrict the use of the term "questionnaire" to written responses, although this special case is probably better classified as a "paper-and-pencil questionnaire."

Quetelet Index   The *body mass index (BMI), named after its 19th-century creator.

Queueing Theory   The mathematical study of waiting lines or queues. Used most widely in economics and business, it can be applied to any waiting line from customers at checkout counters to aircraft on runways.

Quintiles   Divisions of the total rank-ordered cases or observations in a study into five groups of equal size. Technically, the four points that divide the observations into five groups. Loosely, the five groups themselves. Compare *quantile, *quartile, *decile.

QUOROM   Quality of reporting of meta-analyses. A checklist used to improve meta-analyses and their comparability by ensuring that they all report the same elements and in the same order. Used more in epidemiology than in the social sciences.

Quota Sample   A *stratified *non*random sample, that is, a sample selected by dividing a *population into categories and selecting a certain number (a quota) of respondents from each category. Individual cases within each category are not selected randomly; they are usually chosen on the basis of convenience. Compare *accidental sampling, *purposive sample, *random sampling, *stratified random sampling, *proportional stratified random sampling.

For example, interviewers might be given the following assignment: "Go out and interview 40 adults: 20 men, 20 women, with half of each 50-plus years old." Despite its superficial resemblance to *stratified random sampling, quota sampling is not a reliable method to use for making inferences about a population, but it is probably more useful than "Go out and interview the first 40 people you see."

Quotient   The number that results when one divides one number into another; the answer to a division problem.

r   Symbol for a *Pearson correlation coefficient, which is a *bivariate correlation (between two variables).

R   (a) Symbol for a *multiple correlation, that is, between more than two variables. (b) Abbreviation for *range.

R   A statistical software package available to download at no cost from the user group (Comprehensive R Archive Network, or R-CRAN) that built and maintains it. It is modeled after *S-PLUS. For several analytic techniques, R contains the most advanced programs available.

r^2 Symbol for a *coefficient of determination between two variables. It tells you how much of the *variability of the *dependent variable is explained by (or accounted for, associated with, or predicted by) the *independent variable. Sometimes written "r-squared."

For example, if the r^2 between students' SAT scores and their college grades were .30, that would mean that 30% of the variability in students' college grades could be predicted by variability in their SAT scores—and that 70% could not.

R^2 Symbol for a *coefficient of multiple determination between a *dependent variable and two or more *independent variables. It is a commonly used measure of the *goodness-of-fit of a *regression model. Sometimes written "R-squared."

For example, if the R^2 between subjects' personal (i.e., individual) income (the dependent variable) and subjects' education level, subjects' IQ, and their fathers' income was .40, that would mean that educational level, IQ, and father's income together explained (or predicted) 40% of the variance in personal income; conversely, it also would mean that the three independent variables did *not* explain 60% of the variance. The former is called the *coefficient of determination, and the latter is called the *coefficient of nondetermination.

r_{bis} Symbol for *biserial correlation coefficient.

r_{pb} Symbol for *point-biserial correlation coefficient.

r_s Symbol for *Spearman correlation coefficient (rho).

r_{tet} Symbol for *tetrachoric correlation coefficient.

R_c Symbol for *canonical correlation coefficient.

Radical   The *root of a number as shown by the radical sign √. A number (the "index") to the left of the sign shows the type of root. For example, $\sqrt[3]{}$ means the third (cube) root. If there is no number, the root is a square root.

Radix   In a life table, the starting number (100,000 in the example at the *life table entry). The number perishing at different ages is subtracted from the radix to obtain the number surviving.

R&D   *Research and development.

Random   Said of events that are unpredictable because their occurrence is unrelated to their characteristics; they are governed purely by chance. The opposite of random is determined.

The chief importance of randomness in research is that by using it to select or assign subjects, researchers increase the probability that their conclusions will be *valid. *Random assignment increases *internal validity, and random sampling increases *external validity. See *probability sample, *pseudo-random numbers.

Random Assignment   Putting subjects into *experimental and *control groups in such a way that each individual in each group is assigned entirely by chance. Otherwise put, each subject has an equal probability of being placed in each group. Using random assignment reduces the likelihood of *bias. It probabilistically "equates the groups" on all known and all unknown extraneous variables at the start of the experiment. Also called "random allocation." Several random number generators are available on the Internet (see the web resources section at the end of this book).

Random Coefficients Models   See *multilevel models and *HLM.

Random Digit Dialing   Approach to identifying a random sample of telephone numbers. Typically the first three digits are identified that are working, and then the last four numbers are determined randomly using a random number generator. This procedure can identify individuals regardless of whether their numbers are listed or unlisted.

Random-Effects Model   A design in which the *levels of the *factors are random in the sense that they are drawn at random from a population of levels rather than fixed by an investigator. Also called "variance components model" and "Model II ANOVA design." Random effects models are much less widely used than *fixed-effects models, in which researchers set the treatment levels or assume the levels to be fixed. Also sometimes used in analysis of longitudinal and nonexperimental data when the researcher wants to generalize to the population of values of an independent variable. Hand calculation of effects becomes more complex, but statistical packages usually allow one to specify whether an independent variable is fixed or random. In practice, many researchers and books make the assumption of fixed effects. Compare *mixed-effects model, *random variable.

The random-effects model is sometimes used when there are a large number of categories or levels of a factor. For example, say researchers in a survey organization wanted to see whether different kinds of telephone interviewers get different response rates. Because there is potentially a very large number of categories (differences in accent, quality of voice, etc.), perhaps as many as there are individual telephone interviewers, a sample is chosen randomly from the population of interviewers, which is also, in this case, a population of levels. On the other hand, if the survey organization were interested in only, say, the difference in response rate between male and female interviewers, it would use a *fixed-effects model.

Random Error   Another term for *random variation. Also called "unreliability" and *disturbance. See *reliability. "Error" without qualification usually means random error. Random errors are often assumed to have a *normal distribution. Random error cannot be eliminated, but it can be estimated. The opposite of random error is *systematic error, or *bias, which is usually more difficult to estimate.

Random Factor   (also called **Random Effects Factor**) A *factor in an *ANOVA in which the levels of the variable are points along a continuum and are viewed as representing the population of levels of the factor. If an independent variable had a range of 0 to 25, an example might be 0, 5, 10, 15, 20, 25 (where systematic "random" sampling was used to select the levels of the random factor). See *random-effects model.

Randomization   The use of a random process in assigning or selecting participants or other units in a research study. Often refers to *random assignment.

Randomization Tests   Another term for *permutation tests.

Randomized-Blocks Design   A *research design in which subjects are matched on a blocking *variable the researcher wishes to control. The subjects are put into groups (blocks) of the same size as the number of *treatments. The members of each block are assigned randomly to different treatment groups. Compare *Latin square, *repeated-measures ANOVA.

For example, say we are doing a study of the effectiveness of four methods of teaching statistics. We use 80 subjects and plan to divide them into

4 treatment groups of 20 students each. Using a randomized-blocks design, we give the subjects a test of their knowledge of statistics. The 4 who score highest on the test are the 1st block, the next highest 4 are the 2nd block, and so on to the 20th block. The 4 members of each block are randomly assigned, 1 to each of the 4 treatment groups. We use the blocks to equalize and reduce the variance within each treatment group by making sure that each group has subjects with a similar prior knowledge of statistics. The design enables comparisons between the treatment and control groups, holding constant the blocking factor (i.e., controlling for the blocking factor); it also usually provides a more *statistically powerful test of the treatment versus control conditions.

Randomized Clinical Trial (RCT)   Experimental methods applied to studies of the effectiveness of treatments, originally drug treatments in medical research. The first published results from an RCT appeared in a 1948 article, which reported the effects of streptomycin on tuberculosis. Considered the "*gold standard" in drug testing and sometimes in nonmedical fields, such as education. *Random assignment is used to form treatment and control groups, and *double-blind procedures are applied when possible. Randomized *clinical* and *controlled* trials are oftentimes used interchangeably, and both use the RCT acronym.

Randomized Controlled Clinical Trial   Synonym for *randomized clinical trial.

Randomized Controlled Trial (RCT)   Experimental methods applied to the study of the effectiveness of treatments. They can be conducted in a *laboratory or *field setting, such as a *field experiment of an educational intervention. Subjects are placed in *control and *treatment groups by *random assignment. The methods of the RCT are increasingly demanded in fields such as education and program *evaluation research.

Randomized Design   See *randomized experiment.

Randomized Experiment   An experiment in which subjects are randomly assigned to the treatment and control groups in order to equate the groups on all known and unknown variables. After equating the groups this way, the independent variable is manipulated (e.g., one group receives the treatment, and the other does not). Based on the logic of *Mill's method of difference. Usually considered the "*gold standard" for establishing causation (especially *descriptive causation). Also called *randomized clinical trial, *randomized control trial, *true experiment.

Randomized Field Trial   Another term for *randomized control trial, but one that does not take place in a laboratory or clinical setting.

Random Number Generator   A computer *program designed to produce a series of random numbers. These programs usually produce numbers in cycles.

This means that they generate numbers that are only "pseudo-random," but such numbers are often adequate for most purposes in social and behavioral research. See the web resources section at the end of this book for some random number generators.

Random Numbers   A sequence of numbers in which the occurrence of any number in the sequence is no guide to the numbers that come next. In the long run, all numbers will appear equally often. Tables of random numbers, found in most statistics texts, are frequently used to select random samples or assign subjects randomly. Random numbers generated by a computer are *pseudo-random, because they are produced according to a formula.

Random Process   A means by which random numbers or events are generated. Rolling fair dice is an example.

Random Response Set   A *response set that has no pattern, for example, not yea or nay saying, or attempting to appear desirable or attempting to support or go against the researcher's hypotheses, but simply responding in what is likely a meaningless pattern. This might happen when the participant is simply marking answers and is not interested or engaged in the study. Data for participants responding in this way should be discarded. The difficulty lies in determining whether a random response set is in fact present for a participant.

Random Response Technique   A method of asking survey questions on sensitive topics on which, the researcher believes, respondents might find it difficult to be forthcoming. The technique allows estimates about answers to sensitive questions while preserving the anonymity of those being surveyed. Respondents are randomly assigned to answer one of two questions; one is sensitive, and the other is not. The interviewer does not know which question has been assigned to the respondent and records only the answer, such as yes or no. The probability of being assigned the sensitive question, plus the probability of responses to the nonsensitive question, can be used to calculate the probability of responses to the sensitive question. Several studies have indicated that this method obtains better results than others (such as self-administered surveys) for collecting information about sensitive topics. Compare *survey experiment.

Random Sampling   Selecting a group of subjects (a *sample) for study from a larger group (*population) so that each individual (or other *unit of analysis) is chosen entirely by chance. When used without qualification, random sampling means *simple random sampling. Also sometimes called "equal probability sample," since every member of the population has an equal *probability of being included in the sample. A random sample is not the same thing as a

R

haphazard, whimsical, or *accidental sample. Using random sampling reduces the likelihood of *bias. Compare *probability sample, *cluster sample, *quota sample, *stratified random sample. See *random number generator for software useful for drawing random samples.

Random Selection   Another term for *random sampling. "Selection" is more often used in experimental research; "sampling" is the more common term in survey research, but the underlying principle is the same. See *random assignment, *probability sample.

Random Variable   A variable that varies in ways the researcher does not control; a variable whose values are determined by some chance process. You cannot predict the value of a random variable with certainty in advance because of this chance element. A random variable is one in which the observed values of the variable could have been different either because of the sampling process (*random error) or given the variation in the population. "Random" refers to the way the events, values, or subjects are chosen or occur, not to the variable itself. For example, men and women are not random, but gender could be a random variable in a research study; the gender of subjects included in the study could be left to chance and not controlled by the researcher. Also called *stochastic variable.

Random Variation   Differences in a variable that are due to chance rather than to one of the other variables being studied. Random variations tend to cancel one another out in the long run. A random variable can be discrete or continuous. Also called *random error.

For example, say you take two random samples of 100 workers from the same factory. You find that in the first sample, 52 are women and 48 are men. In the second sample, 49 are women and 51 are men. The differences between the sex compositions of the two samples would be due to random variation. See *sampling error.

Random Walk   (a) A series of steps in which the direction and length of each step is uninfluenced by the previous steps. (b) The random walk hypothesis states that because stock prices move randomly, in the long run an investor will do better choosing stocks at random (taking a random walk through the market) than by any other method.

Range   A measure of *variability, of the spread or the *dispersion of values in a series of values. To get the range of a set of scores, you subtract the lowest value or score from the highest.

For example, if the highest score on the political science final were 98 and the lowest 58, the range would be 40 (98 − 58 = 40).

Range Effects   *Floor and/or *ceiling effects.

Range Restriction   Occurs when, for some reason, the data have a very limited range on one or more variables. For example, education can be operationalized as ranging from 0 (no education) to 21 years (PhD), and this variable is correlated with individual annual income. However, if the range of education were restricted to 2 or 3 years (e.g., 3–6 years of education), it is likely that no relationship would be seen between education and income. Range restriction changes the observed relationship; it could reduce, eliminate, or even increase the size of a reported relationship. For another example, see Figure R.1.

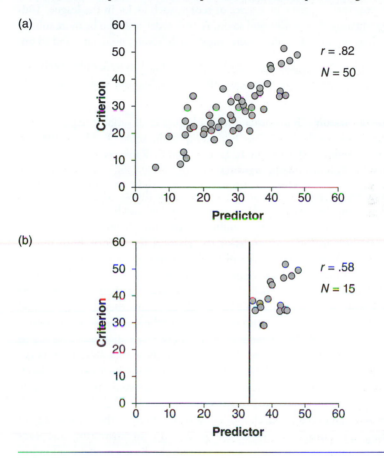

(a)

(b)

Figure R.1 Range Restriction Shown in Graph (b)

Rank Biserial Correlation Coefficient Correlation between dichotomous nominal data and ordinal data. For example, one might correlate participation in the experiment or not (dichotomous) with an ordinal variable such as rank of performance on a task (ordinal, first place, second place, third place, etc.).

Rank Correlation Correlation between variables that are in ranked units. Rather than varying in exact amount, the variable varies based on ranks. See *Spearman's rho and *Kendall's tau, which are the two most frequently used rank correlations.

Rank Data   Data measured on an *ordinal (or *rank order) scale.

Rank-Difference Correlation   Another term for *Spearman's rho. Compare *Kendall's tau.

Rank Order Scale   Another term for an *ordinal scale, that is, one that gives the relative position of a score in a series of scores, such as 1st in the league, 18th in the graduating class of 400, and so on. A rank order scale can be more subjective, such as severity of a pain: severe, moderately severe, moderate, and so on.

Ranks   Numbers assigned to a group of scores arranged in rank order, such as 1 for the highest score on a test, 2 for the second highest, and so on. Many *nonparametric tests are designed for use with ranks.

Rank Transformation   Transformation of a higher level variable (e.g., interval, ratio) to a rank (ordinal) variable. For example, the scores 1, 33, 55, 99, and 100 can be rank transformed to 1, 2, 3, 4, and 5. Rank transformations are often used in *nonparametric statistics.

Rasch Modeling   An early version of *item response theory (IRT) still much in use today. Named after its founder, Georg Rasch. Debates between proponents of Rasch and IRT models can be quite heated, though proponents of both agree that these methods are superior to *classical test theory. Both models involve methods for assessing the difficulty of test items and the ability or knowledge of the individuals responding to those items. The difficulty of items is judged by the number of individuals who get them right, and the knowledge of individuals is judged by how many items they got right. Good test items discriminate among the ability levels of the test takers. For example, a difficult item should be answered correctly mostly by individuals who scored well on the other items. Bad test items would be those that all test takers got right—or wrong—because these allow no distinctions in knowledge levels among the test takers. Another example of a bad item would be one that only high-ability test takers answered incorrectly.

   The basic data used in Rasch modeling is the *ratio of the *probability of answering questions correctly to the probability of answering questions incorrectly. Since the *log of this ratio is used, the Rasch model is a kind of *logit model.

Rating Scale   A *measurement technique for quantifying evaluations exemplified by the familiar "On a scale of 0 to 10 I'd give it a. . . ." Because the person doing the rating is the measurement "instrument," and because rating scales usually involve assigning numbers to nonnumerical phenomena, the process is often thought of as "subjective." But it can be quite *objective. Olympic judging is probably the best-known example of how a high level of consensus can be reached about the number to be assigned to something nonnumerical, such as a double backflip.

Ratio   A combination of two numbers that shows their relative size. The relation between the numbers is expressed as a fraction, as a decimal, or simply by separating them with a colon. The ratio of one number to the other is that number divided by the other. For example, the ratio of 12 to 6 (12:6) means 12/6, or 2:1. The statement "the ratio of X to Y" means "X divided by Y." A *slope is the ratio of the "rise over the run" (change in Y divided by change in X). Compare *proportion. See *odds ratio.

For example, say a bird watcher counted the visits to a backyard feeder by different types of birds; if one afternoon there were 50 visits by nuthatches and 20 by chickadees, the ratio of nuthatches to chickadees could be expressed as 50/20, or 50:20, or 5:2, or 2.5:1, or simply 2.5.

Rationalism   (a) An epistemological doctrine that maintains that reasoning is the main way we get knowledge. Its epistemological opposite is *empiricism (or a version of empiricism called *positivism). The assumption of rationalism lives on in much mathematical economic theory and is at the heart of *game theory. (b) The use of logical thought to produce theory. The most famous rationalist was René Descartes. *Postmodernism tends to reject both empiricism and rationalism. See *positivism.

Rational Number   An integer (a whole number) or a fraction composed of integers. Rational numbers can be expressed as *ratios; they are "ratio-nal." Compare *irrational number.

For example, 8,576 and −14 are rational numbers, as are 4/9 and 13/27. But 85.76, 4.9, and 1.3/2.7 are not.

Ratio Scale (or Level of Measurement)   A measurement or scale in which any two adjoining values are the same distance apart and in which there is a true zero point. The scale gets its name from the fact that one can make ratio statements about variables measured on a ratio scale. See *interval scale, *level of measurement.

For example, height measured in inches is measured on a ratio scale. This means that the size of the difference between being 60 and 61 inches tall is the same as between being 66 and 67 inches tall. And because there is a true zero point, 70 inches is twice as tall as 35 inches (ratio of 2 to 1). The same kind of ratio statements cannot be made about measures on an *interval or *ordinal scale. For example, the person who is second tallest in a group is probably not twice as tall as the person who is fourth tallest.

Ratio Variable   A variable that is measured using a *ratio scale, such as response time.

Raw   (Score or Data or Numbers)   Scores, data, or numbers that are in their original state ("raw") and have not been statistically manipulated. Note: The opposite of raw is not, in most cases, "cooked," since cooked implies dishonest manipulation of data. Usually, the expression "raw data" means data that need further work in order to be useful. Compare *derived statistics.

R

For example, if you got 23 out of 25 answers correct on a quiz, 23 would be your raw score. Other ways of reporting that score, such as 92% or 3rd in the class, would have to be calculated and thus would not be "raw."

RCT   *Randomized clinical trial, *randomized controlled trial, or, sometimes, *randomized controlled clinical trial.

RDD   Abbreviation for random digit dialing and *regression discontinuity design.

RDS   *Respondent-driven sampling.

Reactive Measure   Any measurement or observation technique that can influence the subjects being measured or observed, as when surveying respondents about an issue that influences their opinions about it. It is difficult to avoid such "reactivity." Reactivity is minimal when observing subjects in a *natural setting and in such a way that they are unaware that they are being observed. However, it is seldom possible to do such observing without becoming part of the setting and thus influencing the subjects indirectly. See *artifact, *Heisenberg principle.

Reactivity   An alteration in subjects' behavior or performance as a result of their awareness of participating in an experiment or being observed. It is similar to but broader than *Hawthorne effect.

Realism   (a) A philosophical doctrine holding that abstract *concepts really exist and are not, as *nominalism would have it, just names. Compare *holism, *methodological individualism, *latent variable. (b) A philosophical doctrine holding that the external world really exists, quite apart from our conceptions of it, and that the external world can be directly known by sensory experience. Often contrasted with *idealism. Compare *empiricism. Note that definitions (a) and (b) can be close to contradictory. In the West, philosophical arguments about realism go back to at least the ancient Greeks, and these debates continue today.

Real Limits (of a Number)   The points falling between half a measurement unit below and half a unit above the number.

For example, say you are measuring people's height to the nearest inch. The real limits of the height of someone whose height you record as 70 inches are 69.5 and 70.5; someone whose height falls between 69.5 and 70.5 will be recorded as being 70 inches tall.

Recall Bias   Intentional or unintentional distortions in *recall data typically due to imperfections in human memory. This is a threat to any research relying on self-report data, especially research asking retrospective questions.

Recall Data   Evidence provided by individuals based on their memories of past events. Virtually all data reported by individuals are recall data, but the term is usually reserved for data based on recollections of the relatively distant past. See *event history analysis.

Receiver-Operating Characteristic Curve (ROC Curve) A graphic plot showing the effectiveness of a classifier variable, such as a diagnostic test, for successfully identifying conditions or outcomes, such as survival/death/illness. It is a plot of the true positive rate against the *false positive rate and illustrates the tradeoff between the *sensitivity and *specificity of a test. The bigger the area under the curve, the better the test or classifying variable. The ROC curve is increasingly used in *data mining research to identify how well different classifying variables are working. An example is shown in Figure R.2.

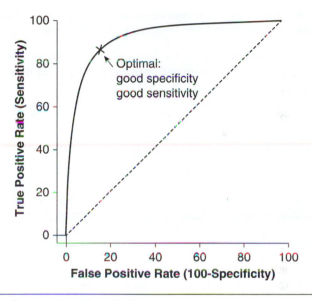

Figure R.2 Receiver-Operating Characteristic Curve

Reciprocal (of a Number) The reciprocal of a number is that number divided into 1 or (what amounts to the same thing) raised to the power of −1. For example, the reciprocal of 3 is 1/3 or 3^{-1}; the reciprocal of X is $1/X$ or X^{-1}.

Reciprocal Relation Said of a situation in which *variables can mutually influence one another, that is, can be both *cause and *effect. Reciprocal causation is common in systems theory. Compare *recursive, *interaction effect.

For example, say in an effort to lose weight, you've taken up running. Running and weight loss could be reciprocal: The more you run, the more you lose; the more you lose, the easier running is; so you run more, which causes you to lose more. . . .

R

Reciprocal Transformation   A *transformation of a data set by taking the *reciprocal of the members of the set. Can only be used with data that do not include zero.

Recode   See *coding, *transformation.

Record   A row in a computer matrix or *spreadsheet grid. See *case and, for an example, *data record. Cases are recorded in rows; variables are in columns or fields.

Record Linkage   Any procedure for merging data from one or more records, such as educational, medical, or census records. Of concern are ensuring that all individuals' records are used, that none are used more than once, and maintaining the privacy and confidentiality of the persons whose data are thus linked.

Rectangular Distribution   Said of a distribution of a variable when its values do not change; all outcomes are equally likely. When plotted on a graph, such a distribution forms a rectangle.

Rectilinear   (a) In a straight line; more often called *linear. (b) At right angles or perpendicular. See *orthogonal.

Recursive Model   A causal *model in which all the causal influences are assumed to work in one direction only; that is, they are *asymmetric (and the *error or disturbance terms are not correlated across equations). By contrast, nonrecursive models allow two-way causes. (See Figure R.3.) Contrast *reciprocal relation. Note: Readers are often confused by this term, because they take "recursive" to refer to recurring or repeating and therefore to mean a reciprocal relation.

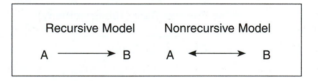

Figure R.3   Recursive Model

For example, if you were looking at the influence of age and sex on math achievement, your model would probably be recursive since while age and sex might influence students' math achievement, doing well or poorly in math certainly could not change their age or sex. On the other hand, your model of the relationship between achievement and time spent studying might not be recursive. It could be *reciprocal (or nonrecursive): Studying could boost math achievement, and increased achievement could make it more likely that a student would enjoy studying math.

Reduced Model In a *GLM the reduced model is a model with fewer independent variables in it. For example, you might want to know if a variable explains a significant amount of variance. In this case the "full model" would include all of the independent variables and the reduced model would exclude the independent variable in question. An F test statistic is readily available to test the reduced model.

Reductionism (a) A research procedure or theory that argues that the way to understand something is to reduce it to its smaller, more basic, individual parts—as organisms might be best understood by studying the chemicals of which they are made. Another example would be the view that the behavior of groups can be understood only by studying the behaviors of the individuals who make up the groups. The term "reductionism" is often pejorative; people who like such procedures more often call them *analysis or *methodological individualism. Compare *holism, *functionalism. (b) Reductionism can also be used to mean limiting explanations to a particular class of variables. For example, economic reductionism would be explaining everything by economic influences.

Redundant Predictor A variable in a *regression analysis that provides little or no additional ability to predict the value of the *dependent or *outcome variable. It is redundant because it is highly correlated with one or more other variables. Compare *confound, *intercorrelation, *multicollinearity.

Re-express To change, or *transform, values measured on one scale to another scale; for example, one might re-express speed in miles per hour as speed in kilometers per hour.

Reflexivity (a) Researchers' critical self-awareness of their biases and how these can influence their observations. (b) Difficulties of interpretation arising from the fact that researchers are almost always part of the context they are studying and thus cannot study it without influencing it. See *reactive measure.

Refusal Rate In survey research, the number of respondents who are contacted but refuse to participate in the survey; this number is divided by the initial sample size to get the rate. The nonresponse rate includes members of the sample who did not participate for any reason as well as those who refused. Refusers are usually only a relatively small portion of the nonresponse rate when a study is viewed as important and is endorsed by someone the subjects respect. See *nonresponse bias.

Region of Rejection An area in the tail(s) of a *sampling distribution for a *test statistic. It is determined by the *critical value(s) the researcher chooses for rejecting the *null hypothesis. Rejection regions are defined by values of the relevant probability distribution (e.g., z or t or F distributions). See Figure R.4 on page 372. Compare *one-tailed test, *two-tailed test.

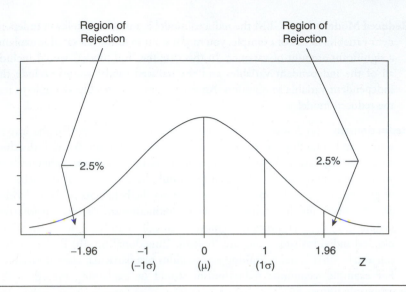

Figure R.4   Regions of Rejection

Regressand   Another term for the *dependent, *outcome, or *response variable in a *regression analysis.

Regression   Any of several statistical techniques concerned with predicting or explaining the values of one dependent *variable using information about the values of *independent or *predictor variables. Regression is used to answer such questions as "How much better can I predict the values of one variable, such as annual income (variously called the *dependent, *outcome, *criterion, *response, or Y variable), if I know the values of another variable, such as level of education (called the *independent, *predictor, *explanatory, or X variable)?" Regression can be used with *experimental and *non-experimental research data.

   The term "regression" originated in the work of the 19th-century researcher Francis Galton. In his studies of the heredity of characteristics such as height, he noted the phenomenon of *statistical regression, or regression toward the mean. Very tall people tend to have children somewhat shorter (closer to the mean) than themselves, and very short people tend to have children somewhat taller (closer to the mean) than they. Put more formally, extreme scores on a *predictor variable (parents' height) are likely to produce somewhat less extreme scores on a *criterion variable (children's height). Knowing how much regression toward the mean there is for a particular pair of variables gives you a prediction. If there is very little regression, you can predict quite well. If there is a great deal of regression, you can predict poorly, if at all. The r used to symbolize the *Pearson correlation coefficient originally stood for "regression." Indeed, a Pearson r is the same thing as a standardized regression coefficient between two variables.

Regression Analysis (a) Method of explaining or predicting the *variability of a *dependent variable using information about one or more *independent variables. Regression analysis can be used to answer three basic questions: (1) What is the predicted change in a dependent variable for each one-unit increase in an independent variable? (2) What is the predicted change in a dependent variable associated with a one-unit change in a particular independent variable—after controlling for other independent variables? (3) How much better can one explain or predict a dependent variable taking all the independent variables together?

(b) Technique for establishing a *regression equation. The equation indicates the nature and closeness of the relationship between two or more variables, specifically, the extent to which you can predict some by knowing others—the extent to which some are associated with others. The equation is often represented by a *regression line, which is the straight line that comes closest to approximating a distribution of points in a *scatter diagram. See *regression plane, *simple regression, *multiple regression.

Regression Artifact An artificial result due to *statistical regression or *regression toward the mean. Also called *regression effect.

Suppose a high school gave its students an English proficiency examination. The students with the very lowest scores were then assigned to a new tutorial program to help them prepare for the state-mandated graduation examination. If, after 3 months of tutoring, the students did better on a retake of the English proficiency examination, their improvement could be due to the effects of the program, but part of their improvement could also be due to regression artifacts. At least a few of the students probably got their original low scores through *random error (one wasn't feeling well the day of the test, another messed up the answer sheet, a third had her grade mistakenly recorded as a 68 when she earned an 86, and so on). Without a *control group, there would be no way to tell for sure how much of the improvement was due to regression artifacts and how much could be credited to the tutoring program.

Regression Coefficient A number indicating the average change in a *dependent variable associated with a one unit change in an *independent variable. A regression coefficient is part of a *regression equation. A *standardized regression coefficient (one expressed in *z scores) is symbolized by the Greek letter beta; an unstandardized regression coefficient is usually symbolized by a lowercase *b*. In *simple regression, the coefficient is sometimes called a simple regression coefficient; in *multiple regression, the coefficients are sometimes called *partial regression coefficients or multiple regression coefficients.

For example, if we were studying the relation between education (independent variable) and annual income (dependent variable) and we found that for every year of education beyond the 10th grade the expected annual income went up by $1,200, the (unstandardized) regression coefficient would be $1,200.

Regression Constants In a *regression equation, the *slope(s) and the *intercept. In the typical formulation, $\hat{Y} = a + bX$, a (the intercept) and b (the slope) are the constants; they are the same regardless of the values of the variables X and Y. These values are estimated based on the empirical data according to a rule (e.g., *OLS, *MLE), and they will vary from sample to sample. "The constant," without specification, usually refers to the intercept.

Note that this usage, while common, is loose by the standards of mathematics, where a "constant" would have neither a variance nor a standard error, as do both the slope and the intercept.

Regression Diagnostics Various statistical techniques used to check for violations of key regression *assumptions, that is, the assumptions of *linearity, *equality of variances, *normally distributed *errors, and, if possible, independence of errors/observations (e.g., *Durbin-Watson statistic in *time-series analysis). Also attempts to determine the *reliability of *regression equations, often with emphasis on assessing the impact of *outliers.

Regression Discontinuity Design (RDD) A research design that uses a break in a regression line to indicate the presence of a treatment effect. It is used particularly when subjects are placed in control and treatment groups according to a cutoff score (e.g., score on a diagnostic test) rather than by random assignment. It has been used most widely in the evaluation of educational programs. It is considered to be a relatively strong research design.

Regression Effect The tendency in a pretest-posttest design for the posttest scores to regress toward the mean. See *statistical regression. Also called *regression artifact; see that entry for an example.

Regression Equation An algebraic equation expressing the relationship between one *dependent variable and one (or more) independent variables. Usually written $Y = a + bX + e$. Y is the *dependent variable; X is the *independent variable; b is the *slope or *regression coefficient; a is the *intercept; and e is the *error term. If you leave off the e then it is written this way: $\hat{Y} = a + bX$, and it's now called a "prediction equation."

For example, in a study of the relationship between income and life expectancy, we might find that (1) people with no income have a life expectancy of 60 years, and (2) each additional \$10,000 in income, up to \$100,000, adds 2 years to the average life expectancy so that people with incomes of \$100,000 or more have a life expectancy of 80 years. This would yield the following regression equation: life expectancy = 60 years + 2 times the number of \$10,000 units of income. Put in equation form, $\hat{Y} = 60 + 2X$, where $\hat{Y}$ equals predicted life expectancy and X equals number of \$10,000 units. The intercept is 60.

Regression Estimate The estimated value of the *dependent (or *outcome) variable in a regression equation after the values of the *independent (or *predictor) variables have been taken into account. Also called *predicted Y.

Regression Line   A graphic representation of a *regression equation. It is the line drawn through the pattern of observed data points on a *scatter diagram that best summarizes the relationship between the *dependent and *independent variables. You can also view it as the line showing the *predicted *Y* value for each value of *X*. Yet another way of stating this is that the line shows the *expected value of *Y* for each value of *X*. It is most often computed by using the *ordinary least squares (OLS) criterion. When the regression line slopes down (from left to right), it indicates a *negative or inverse relationship; when it slopes up (as in Figure R.5), it indicates a *positive or direct relationship.

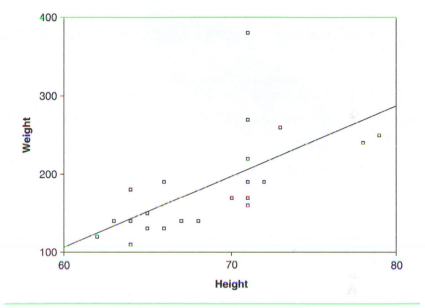

Figure R.5   Regression Line

Regression Mixture Modeling   See *latent class regression.

Regression Model   Another term for *regression equation, that is, an equation postulating the relationship between a continuous *dependent variable and an *independent variable or variables, plus an *error term. Regression modeling is a synonym for *regression analysis.

Sometimes the *Y* and *X* variables part of the model is called the "deterministic" part, and the rest is the "random error" part. That is, *Y* = Deterministic Component + Random Error (note: $\hat{Y}$ = Deterministic Component). One more way this idea is expressed is DATA = MODEL + ERROR.

Regression Plane   A graphic representation of the relation of two *independent variables and one *dependent variable. When a regression has two independent variables, they can no longer be represented graphically by a line. They can, however, be represented by a two-dimensional plane in three-dimensional space, as in Figure R.6. As the number of independent variables increases, the model goes into higher dimensions (e.g., 20 independent variables would take you into 21-dimensional space!).

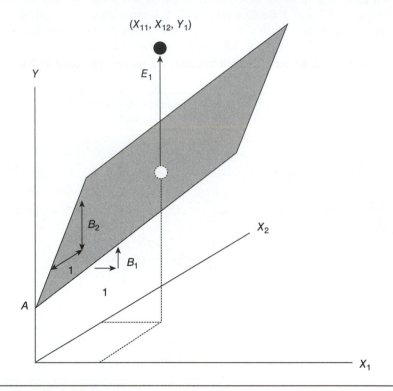

Figure R.6   Regression Plane

Source: From John Fox, *Applied Regression Analysis, Linear Models, and Related Methods* (Thousand Oaks, CA: Sage, 1997), p. 98.

Regression Sum of Squares (or Regression SS)   In *regression analysis, the sum of squares that is explained by the *regression equation. It is the regression version of the *between sum of squares in *analysis of variance. Abbreviated $SS_{regression}$ or $SS_{explained}$. Compare *residual SS.

Regression Toward the Mean   A kind of *bias due to the fact that measures of a *dependent variable are never wholly reliable, which results in later measures of a variable tending to be closer to the mean than earlier measures. This tendency is especially strong for the most extreme values of the variable. Another term for *statistical regression. See *regression artifact for an example.

Regression Weight   Another term for *beta weight or *regression coefficient.

Regress on   In *regression analysis, to explain or predict by. To regress Y on X is to explain or predict Y by X. One regresses the *dependent variable on the *independent variable(s).

For example, the statement "We will regress college grade point average (GPA) on SAT scores" means that we will try to explain (or predict) differences in students' GPAs by differences in their SATs.

Regressor   Another term for *independent variable or *predictor variable. See *regress on.

Reification   In *factor analysis and *principle components analysis, labeling the clusters of correlated variables discovered by the analysis (*latent variables) and treating them as though they were something concrete. As with reification more broadly, there is danger of overinterpretation when treating abstract theoretical entities as though they were substantive. Compare *realism.

Reinforcer Effect   The tendency of one variable to increase a causal influence between or among other variables. The opposite is a *suppressor effect. Compare *intervening variable, *interaction effect.

In Figure R.7, cognitive sophistication reinforces the causal link between education and tolerance.

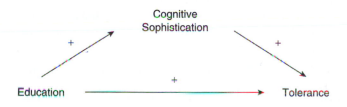

Figure R.7   Reinforcer Effect

Rejection Error   Another term for *alpha error or *Type I error. Compare *acceptance error.

Related Samples   (also called **Dependent Samples**) Data from the same participants (e.g., in a *repeated measures design, in a *pretest-posttest design) or participants that have something in common (e.g., see *matched pairs design). In these cases a *dependent t test or *repeated measures ANOVA would be used for statistical analysis.

Related Samples t Test   Synonym for a *dependent t test, for example, one used in a *repeated measures design or a *pretest-posttest design.

R

Relationship (or Relation)   A connection between two or more *variables, usually assessed by a measure of *association, such as a *Pearson r. The connection can indicate a causal link or a mere statistical association.

Relative Frequency   Another term for *proportion, that is, a number calculated by dividing the number of cases with a certain characteristic by the total number of cases. Relative frequency is often used as an estimate of *probability.

For example, if it rained on average 36.5 days per year, the relative frequency would be 0.1 (36.5/365). To get the percentage of days it rained, you would multiply the relative frequency by 100 (0.1 × 100 = 10%).

Relative Frequency Distribution   The proportion of the total number of cases observed at each score or value. For examples see *frequency distribution, *probability distribution.

Relative Risk Ratio   See *risk ratio.

Relative Standing, Measure of   A statistic that describes the comparative position (or rank) of one case or subject as compared to the others in the group. *Percentiles and *z scores are two widely used examples.

Relative Survival   Representation of survival in the absence of other causes of death. It is obtained by comparing percentage of people with a disease (e.g., cancer) that are alive (currently surviving) to the percentage of people who do not have the disease but are similar on all other characteristics. The relative survival rate is calculated by dividing the former by the latter. *Survival analysis can be used to study variables with a limited number of outcomes, or states, such as marriage or employment.

Relative Variation, Coefficient of (CRV)   See *coefficient of relative variation.

Relativism   A series of philosophical doctrines rejecting what it views as absolutism. (a) Relativism about knowledge is the philosophical doctrine that there are no universal truths and no objective knowledge. Knowledge claims are considered to be relative to something about the individual person, a social group, or a historical period such as personal beliefs, vested interests, or characteristics of a specific culture or historical period. (b) Relativism about morals (moral relativism) maintains that moral principles and beliefs are relative to individuals and/or cultures. According to this position, nothing is universally right or wrong; instead, what is right or wrong (or degrees in between) is determined by the particular culture or individual. One can distinguish soft relativism and strong relativism. Absolute relativism (the strongest form) is logically contradictory. Much *postmodernist thought emphasizes and celebrates various relativisms. See *cultural relativism.

Reliability   Freedom from measurement (or *random) error. In practice, this boils down to the *consistency* or stability of a measure or test or observation internally or from one use to the next. When repeated measurements of the same thing give highly similar results, the measurement instrument is said to be reliable. Compare *validity.

For example, if you got on your bathroom scale and it read 145 pounds, got off and on again, and it read 139, repeated the process, and it read 148, your scale would not be very reliable. If, however, in a series of weightings you got the same answer (say, 145), your scale would be reliable—even if it were not accurate (*valid) and you really weighed 120.

Reliability Coefficient   A statistic indicating the *reliability of a scale, test, or other measurement. Reliability coefficients range from 0, when the measure is completely unreliable (that is, when all observed variance is due to *random error), to 1.0, when it is perfectly reliable. Scales or tests with coefficients less than 0.7 are usually considered unreliable. Most reliability coefficients are *correlations between two administrations, versions, or halves of the same test. See *Cronbach's alpha.

Repeated Cross-sectional Design   Cross-sectional study conducted at two or more times, usually with different subjects. Also called serial cross-sectional design. See *trend study.

Repeated-Measures ANOVA   Analysis of variance in which subjects are measured more than once. For example, it is used to study a *within-subjects independent variable. It's also used for a *one-group pretest-posttest design to determine whether statistically significant change occurred from the *pretest to the *posttest. See *repeated-measures design. This research design goes by several different names, including within-subjects ANOVA and treatments-by-subjects ANOVA. See *randomized-blocks ANOVA.

Repeated-Measures Design   A research design in which subjects are measured two or more times on the *dependent variable (see Figure R.8, where O stands for observation). Rather than using different subjects for each *level of treatment, the subjects are given more than one treatment and are measured after each. This means that each subject is its own *control. See *correlated groups design. Also called *within-subjects design. Repeated-measures techniques are also used to study observational data, such as the effects (before and after) of a policy change.

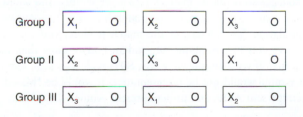

Figure R.8   Repeated-Measures Design

Source: Johnson, Burke. *Educational Research: Quantitative, Qualitative, and Mixed Approaches.* Thousand Oaks, CA: Sage, 2013.

Replacement   See *sampling with replacement.

Replication   Said of research that tries to reproduce the findings of other investigators so as to increase confidence in (or refute) those findings. Repeating
studies with different subjects or in different settings is especially important
for *experimental laboratory research, because it helps increase *external validity. Despite the undeniable importance of replication, it is not done as often
as it might be, largely because it is not considered high-status work. On the
other hand, almost all studies that build on past research are replication studies to some extent. Thus, replication is more a matter of degree than of kind.

For example, if one researcher found that people working in groups exerted
less effort than when they worked individually, other researchers would be
more likely to believe this finding if it could be replicated, particularly if it
could be replicated using different kinds of subjects: women rather than men,
adults rather than children, and so on.

Representational Validity   The degree to which a particular measurement
reflects, portrays, or indicates the thing being measured or assessed. It is present when an instrument measures, with a particular group of people in a
particular place, what it was supposed to measure.

Representative   (also called **Representative Sample**) Said of a *sample that is
similar to the *population from which it was drawn. When a sample is representative, it can be used to make *inferences about the population. The most
effective way to obtain a representative sample is to use *random methods to
draw it, in particular, to use an *equal probability of selection method
(EPSEM). Here are some sampling methods that produce representative
samples: *simple random sampling, *proportional stratified sampling, *cluster
sampling (when clusters are of equal size or when probability proportional to
size is used), and *systematic sampling (as long as the list is either stratified or
random). See also *probability sample.

For example, say you want to survey a sample of students on a college
campus in order to draw conclusions about student opinion. You would have
more confidence that your inferences were true of the student body as a whole
if the sample strongly resembles the population. Let's say you know that 45%
of all the college's students are male and 22% are seniors. You could then look
at your sample to see if there is a close match between your sample and these
known population *parameters. If the match is close, you can more confidently come to conclusions about the student body—more than confidently,
at any rate, than if your sample were, say, 80% male and 11% seniors. In that
case, your sample would not be representative; it would be *biased because it
would overrepresent males and underrepresent seniors.

Representativeness   The extent to which a study's sample results can be generalized to other situations or settings. Another term for *external validity. See
*representative.

Reproduced Correlation   Correlations implied by a *structural equation model (SEM). In SEM, model fit is determined by comparing the observed correlations to the implied or reproduced correlations. One hopes that the two sets of correlations will be similar. The null hypothesis is that they are the same, and one hopes *not* to reject this null hypothesis. It is tested using a *chi-square *test statistic.

Reproducibility   The tendency to obtain similar results when *replicating a research study. Compare *reliability.

Resampling   The process of repeatedly sampling from a sample in order to estimate what other samples from a population would look like were one able to take them. Rather than taking numerous samples from a population to determine the *standard error (something that is usually done only in theory), one draws one sample and repeatedly resamples from it. This group of (re)samplings is then used for *confidence intervals and other *inferential statistics. The two best-known techniques that use resampling are the *jackknife and *bootstrapping; bootstrapping is by far the more flexible and widely used of the two.

Research   Systematic investigation of a topic aimed at uncovering new information (discovering data) and/or interpreting relations among the topic's parts (theorizing). Major purposes include exploring, understanding, describing, predicting, explaining, and influencing or controlling. Research is done in hundreds of ways, ranging from lawyers searching among old court cases for legal precedents to physicists smashing atoms to study subatomic particles. While some research designs are clearly more effective than others for addressing particular sorts of problems, it is usually naïve (although perhaps not uncommon) to believe that there is one best way to conduct any research investigation.

Research and Development (R&D)   *Basic and *applied research aimed at inventing or designing new products. Thought of mostly in regard to manufacturing, perhaps especially to weapons manufacturing, R&D is increasingly common in service industries, such as banking and education, as well.

Research Design   The science (and art) of planning procedures for conducting studies so as to get the most valid findings. Called "design" for short. When designing a research study, one draws up a set of instructions for gathering evidence and for interpreting it. Compare *protocol.

One might view research designs including three major components: (1) the *research method* (e.g., *experiments, *quasi-experiments, *surveys, *A-B-A-B or single case, *phenomenology, *ethnography, *case study, *grounded theory), (2) the major *method(s) of data collection* (e.g., *interviews, *focus groups, *questionnaires, *tests, *observation including structured and *participant observations, *secondary or *existing data), and (3) the *sampling method* (e.g., *random,

R

*convenience, *purposive, *stratified, *cluster, *systematic, mixed). After carrying out the design, the data are analyzed, interpreted, and reported.

Researcher Bias   Similar to *experimenter bias but applicable to any kind of research, not just experimental research.

Research Ethics   The principles defining good and bad conduct that (should) govern the activities of researchers. See *ethics, *debriefing, *dehoaxing, *Milgram experiments, *IRB, *Nuremberg Code, *Helsinki Declaration.

Research Hypothesis   (a) A theoretically driven prediction about what will be found when data are collected and analyzed. The research hypothesis usually specifies a direction of relationship. For example, one might predict that education and income will be positively correlated, or one might predict that male nurses with 20 or more years of experience will earn more on average than female nurses of equal experience. (b) Sometimes used as another term for the *alternative hypothesis in statistical *hypothesis testing. In that context, it is the hypothesis that one hopes indirectly to substantiate by rejecting the *null hypothesis. The alternative hypothesis is the logical opposite of the null hypothesis.

Research Method   The overall research design and strategy used in a research study. Some examples of research methods are experimental research, quasi-experimental research, nonexperimental research, and single case research. Sometimes used as a synonym for research methodology.

Research Misconduct   Unethical or illegal conduct of research (e.g., fabrication of information, plagiarism, falsification of data, violation of the *IRB-approved research protocol).

Research Program   A plan for systematically addressing a related set of research questions. A *research design is a plan for one research project; a research program (sometimes called an "agenda") envisions a coordinated series of projects.

Research Proposal   The written document summarizing prior literature and describing the procedure to be used to answer the research questions, including the study instruments, IRB status, budget, and other supporting information.

Research Question   The problem to be investigated in a study stated in the form of a question. It is crucial for focusing the investigation at all stages, from the gathering through the analysis of evidence. A research question is usually more *exploratory than a *research hypothesis or a *null hypothesis.

For example, a research question might be: What is the relationship between A and B? A parallel research hypothesis could be: Increases in A reduce the incidence of B. The associated null hypothesis for significance testing might be: There is no relationship between A and B in the population.

Research Review   Another term for *literature review; often used in conjunction with a *meta-analysis.

Research Strategy   A general plan for conducting research. *Experimental, *longitudinal, and *mixed methods are examples of research strategies. Some distinguish a research strategy from a *research design, which in this usage would be a more specific and detailed plan (tactics) for conducting research.

Residual   The error or portion of the score on a *dependent variable not explained by *independent variables. The residual is the difference between the value observed and the value predicted (i.e., $Y - \hat{Y}$) by a *model such as a *regression equation or a *path model. Residuals are, in brief, errors in prediction. "Error" in this context usually means degree of "inaccuracy" rather than a mistake. It is sometimes assumed that unmeasured *residual variables could account for the unexplained parts of the dependent variable. See *error term, *deviation score. In ANOVA designs, residual means *error variance or *within-groups variance. In *contingency table analysis, residual refers to the difference between the observed and the expected frequencies. See *residual SS.

Residualize   To *control for or partial out.

Residualized on   Said of the variable that was *partialed out in a *semipartial correlation. Compare *regress on.
   For example, the semipartial correlation symbolized by $r_{1(2.3)}$ means the correlation between variables 1 and 2 after 3 was partialed out of 2—or after 2 has been residualized on 3.

Residual SS   In *regression analysis, the *sum of squares not explained by the *regression equation. Analogous to *within-groups SS in *analysis of variance. Also called "error SS."

Residual Term   Another expression for *error term, that is, the difference between an observed score or value and the score or value predicted by a model.

Residual Variable   In a *path analysis, an unmeasured variable; a residual variable may be assumed to cause the part of the *variance in each *endogenous variable that is not explained in the path model.

Resistant Statistics   Measures less likely to be influenced by a few unusual, extreme values (*outliers) in a *distribution. Compare the *median (a resistant statistic) and the mean in the two distributions in Table R.1. Increasing the

Table R.1   Resistant Statistics

	Median	*Mean*
X: 1, 2, 3, 4, 5, 6, 7	4	4
Y: 1, 2, 3, 4, 5, 6, 77	4	14

last number from 7 (the value in distribution X) to 77 (in distribution Y) does not affect the median at all, but it more than triples the mean. Compare *robust statistics. "Resistant" and "robust" are sometimes treated as synonyms.

Respondent   A person who answers questions in a survey or an interview or otherwise responds to a researcher's inquiry.

Respondent-Driven Sampling (RDS)   A statistically advanced version of *snowball sampling that is used to find members of hard-to-access populations through their social networks. As with any snowball sample, RDS starts with a set of respondents who serve as *seeds*. These seeds then recruit their acquaintances, friends, or relatives who qualify for inclusion in the study to form the first "wave." The first-wave respondents then recruit the second wave, who in turn recruit the third wave, and so on. What makes RDS more advanced than traditional snowball sampling is that it applies a (complicated) mathematical model that weights the sample to compensate for the fact that it was not obtained through simple random sampling. This enables researchers to make unbiased population estimates while using a method that has traditionally been regarded as merely a method of *convenience sampling.

Response Bias (or Effects)   Any biased outcomes due to interaction between interviewers and *respondents. For example, the ethnicity or sex of the interviewer might influence the way respondents answer questions.

Response Rate   The percentage or proportion of members of a sample who respond to a questionnaire. Low response rates are one of the more frequent sources of *bias in social science research.

Response Set (or Style)   (a) A tendency of subjects to give the same type of answer to all questions rather than answering questions based solely on their content. People who tend to say yes regardless of the question (yea-sayers) are a common example. (b) A tendency for observers to be influenced by an attitude toward the thing being observed. A prejudiced observer might, for example, rank some individuals lower than is merited by their actual behavior.

Response Variable   Another term for *dependent or *outcome variable; used most commonly in the context of *regression analysis. One might think that in this usage, the independent variable would be called the "stimulus" variable, but it is not. Rather, it is usually called the *explanatory variable.

Restriction of Range   See *range restriction.

Retrodiction   (a) In contrast to a traditional hypothesis (which focuses on predicting whether an event or relationship will be found in new data collected in the near future), a retrodiction is a "hypothesis" that "predicts" something that occurred in the past. A retrodiction must be tested with data, albeit data from or about the past. The retrodiction is based on factors that occurred even

R

earlier than the predicted event or outcome. Retrodiction relies on newer theories; it checks to see if they are supported by past data and determines how well they would have performed in the past. Used, for example, in historical sociology, archeology, and evolutionary biology/psychology.

Retrospective Cohort Study   A *cohort study conceived and started after some or all of the people have developed the outcome(s) of interest. Exposure and outcome data are collected retrospectively. Past data are identified and used in the study. Compare *prospective cohort study, *event history analysis.

Retrospective Power   Retrospective power (the probability, p, of rejecting a null hypothesis when it is false) analysis is controversial and is conducted after the data have been gathered. Many argue that conducting retrospective power is not needed because the statistical decision has been made, based on the p value. Also, rather than focus on retrospective power when statistical significance has not been obtained, it is better to examine the effect size estimate to determine what might be present in the population. Compare *prospective power.

Retrospective Sampling   In clinical research, refers to selection of cases based on their exposure to a risk factor (disease present or not), and participants are "followed backward" in time by obtaining the necessary independent/predictor variable data (risk factor present or not). Compare *prospective sampling.

Retrospective Study   Research that uses information from the past to draw conclusions. It is most widely used when the outcomes studied are long term, which makes *longitudinal or *prospective studies impractical. *Case-control studies are a common type of retrospective study, since in a case-control study, the events (at least the causal events) of interest in the research occur before the study begins. See *retrospective sampling.

   For example, if we were interested in the effects of early schooling on college graduation, we could conduct a prospective study by following students with different early school experiences to see whether and when they graduated from college years later. It would be easier and faster to conduct a retrospective study of graduates and nongraduates and compare their early schooling. See *recall data. Much research is in fact built on retrospective information, but the label is used mostly by those researchers whose data come from the distant rather than the more recent past.

Reversal Design   See *crossover design.

Reverse Coding   In multiple-item opinion and attitude scales, such as those using *Likert scales, positive opinions and attitudes are often studied using items in which agreement indicates a positive opinion or attitude. However, the coding may be and often is reversed for some items so that agreement indicates a negative opinion or attitude.

For example, say the response items were *strongly disagree, disagree, uncertain, agree,* and *strongly agree.* These are two typical statements to which a respondent would respond:

(A) The policy is an improvement over the old way of doing things.

(B) The policy will cause more harm than good.

The second of these, statement (B), is reverse coded since agreement indicates a negative belief about the policy. The two statements can be summed into a rudimentary scale if the numbers 1, 2, 3, 4, and 5 are the codes assigned to the responses to statement A, while 5, 4, 3, 2, and 1 are assigned to the responses to statement B. Note that you can have your statistical program do the reverse coding for you using this formula:

$$\text{New (converted) value} = (\text{Rating scale minimum value} + \text{Rating scale maximum values}) - \text{Old (unconverted)}$$

With a 5-point rating scale, you would subtract the old values from 6. The values 1, 2, 3, 4, and 5 will become 5 (6 − 1), 4 (6 − 2), 3 (6 − 3), 2 (6 − 4), and 1 (6 − 5).

Rho (P, ρ)   (a) A symbol for the *correlation coefficient for *population parameters; it corresponds to *Pearson's *r*, which is used for *sample statistics. (b) Abbreviation for *Spearman's (rank order) correlation coefficient.

Ridge Regression   An alternative to *OLS methods of estimating regression coefficients. It is intended to reduce the problems in regression analysis associated with severe *multicollinearity. See *lasso.

Right Censoring   Right censoring occurs in event history analysis (also known as *survival analysis and failure time analysis) when the individuals or subjects under study have not experienced the event by the time the study is concluded. For example, in a study of recidivism in which the event is being arrested after being released from prison, the data on the dependent variable are right censored for those individuals who have not experienced arrest by the time the study has ended. Note these people may or not be arrested after the study is completed, but this information is unknown. Compare *left censoring.

Rise   The change in vertical distance between two points on a *regression line; it is used to calculate the *slope. See *run and, for a graphic, *slope.

Risk   (a) The *odds or *probability of an unfavorable outcome, such as the value of your stock portfolio declining. Studies of risk usually involve statistical projections or modeling based on historical data. *Forecasts of the future are always uncertain, which is why acting on such predictions is risky. Calculations of risk are usually not simple probability estimates; they deal with probability and magnitude, such as your likelihood of losing money and, at each level of probability, how much you are likely to lose. Risk differs from pure uncertainty, where the probabilities of outcomes are completely unknown. See *hazard, *extrapolation. (b) The significance or *alpha level set by a researcher. This level is the researcher's statement of the acceptable level of risk of *Type I error.

Risk and Protective Factors   Factors that affect who gets what problem and how the problem is to be eliminated. *Risk factors* are biological, psychological, and environmental factors that put individuals at risk (e.g., low income, poor health care, lack of support systems, lack of coping strategies) for problems and disorders. *Protective factors* are factors that help prevent the problem or help people deal with it more effectively. Risk and protective factors have reverse effects; one hurts and the other helps an individual's or group's health and success in society.

Risk Difference   The level of risk for an outcome for one group (e.g., a treatment group) minus the risk for another group (e.g., a comparison group). Compare *risk ratio.

Risk Ratio (RR)   (also called **Relative Risk**) A ratio of two probabilities that is used with *categorical variables. The risk ratio is very common in medical research. It is used for similar problems as the *odds ratio, which is more common in social science research. Although calculated on the same data and convertible into one another, the two ratios are *not* identical and are sometimes confused. The differences are most easily described using an example.

Say we took two random samples of 100 students each at a particular university to measure the graduation rates of males and females. The hypothetical samples are described in Table R.2. The male odds equal .67, which we get by dividing Yes by No (40/60 = .67). The female odds = 75/25 = 3.0. The odds ratio is 3.0/.67 = 4.5, which means that the odds of females graduating are 4.5 times greater than the odds of males graduating.

Table R.2   Risk Ratio: Graduation Rates for Two Samples of Students

	Yes/Graduate	No/Not Graduate
Males	40	60
Females	75	25

By contrast, *risk ratios* are based on probabilities, not odds. And they focus on the unfavorable outcome—in this case, not graduating. Be careful to remember that, although they are built on the same information and can be easily converted into one another, odds and odds ratios are *not* the same as probabilities and probability ratios. The *probability* of a female not graduating is .25 (25/100). The probability of a male not graduating is .60. The *relative risk ratio* (risk of not graduating) is .60/.25 = 2.4. This means that the risk for males of not graduating is 2.4 times as great as the risk for females. The odds ratio, on the other hand, is 4.5; the odds of a male failing to graduate are 4.5 times as high. Which is the better way to report the relationship? The answer is found more in taste and tradition than in statistics. Odds ratios are used in *logistic regression and are more common in the social sciences. Probabilities and risk ratios are used in *probit regression and are more common in medical research. In both cases, the ratios range from zero to infinity, with 1.0 indicating equal risk or odds.

RMSEA *Root mean square error of approximation.

Robust (robust estimator) Said of a statistic that remains useful even when one (or more) of its *assumptions is violated—as long as the assumption is not violated too badly. Compare *resistant statistics.

For example, the *F ratio (or ANOVA) is generally robust to violations of the assumption of normality of the dependent variable within each group and the assumption that *treatment groups have equal *variances, especially when the sample sizes are equal.

Robust Regression Techniques used in *regression analysis to reduce the impact of *outliers on the estimates of regression coefficients. The usual method of calculating regression coefficients (*ordinary least squares [OLS]) is, like all measures based on *means, susceptible to distortion in the presence of extreme values.

Robust Standard Errors Methods of computing standard errors appropriate for robust regression coefficients. Robust regression is reliable in the presence of outliers; robust standard errors are reliable when the regression errors are correlated or are plagued by *heteroscedasticity.

Role-Playing In psychological investigations, researchers may assign roles for the research subjects to play, such as angry employer or defensive employee. Role-playing has many uses in therapy; in research, it functions much the same way as computer simulations. It enables the researcher to examine interactions in controlled and convenient contexts. *Game theory experiments often require the subjects to play roles. See *prisoner's dilemma.

Root A number that results in a given number when it is raised to a given *power. See *radical.

For example, 4 is the third root of 64, which means that $4^3 = 64$; also $\sqrt[3]{64} = 4$.

Root Mean Square (Error) Another term for *standard deviation, so called because the standard deviation is calculated by taking the square root of the mean of the squared errors.

Root Mean Square Error of Approximation Index (RMSEA)   A statistic used in *structural equation modeling to indicate model fit. It is an absolute-fit index, indicating how well the model reproduces the sample covariance matrix. It also is parsimony adjusted, meaning RMSEA decreases as the number of estimated parameters in the model decreases. Close model fit is indicated by RMSEA values less than or equal to .05. Reasonable fit is indicated by RMSEA values between .05 and .08. Values greater than .10 indicate poor model fit.

Rosenthal Effect   The influence of experimenters' expectations on outcomes of the experiment. The *Pygmalion effect is the best-known, but probably not the most important, example. See *self-fulfilling prophecy, *demand characteristics.

Rotated Factor   See *factor rotation.

Rounding   Expressing numbers in shorter, more convenient units, that is, with fewer numbers to the right of the decimal point than used when calculating the numbers.

For example, 13.834, 58.771, 61.213, and 97.098 could be rounded to 13.8, 58.8, 61.2, and 97.1, respectively.

Rounding Error   An error made by *rounding numbers before performing operations (adding, subtracting, etc.) on them.

Table R.3 shows the number of bowls of soup served in a restaurant and the percentage of each kind. "Percent (A)" shows the percentage of each flavor rounded to the nearest whole percent, but when totaled, this column adds up to 101% due to the rounding. To avoid that error, the restaurant owner would have to round to the nearest thousandth of a percent, as is done in "Percent (B)"—obviously, a silly level of precision in this case.

Table R.3   Rounding Error: Bowls of Soup Served, November 16–23

Kind of Soup	Number	Percent (A)	Percent (B)
Bean	46	14	13.855
Vegetable	72	22	21.687
Chicken Noodle	99	30	29.819
Tomato	115	35	34.639
Total	332	101	100.000

Row Marginals   The *frequency distribution of a variable shown across the rows of a *cross-tabulation. See *marginal frequency distribution for an example. Compare *marginal means, *marginal probability.

Row Percent   The number of cases in the row (in a *contingency table) divided by the number of cases in the row; the percents in each column row to 100%. Row percents are *conditional probabilities or rates and should be compared down the rows in each column. For an example of row percent, see Table C.10 with *contingency table. Also, see *cell percent, *column percent. Compare *row percent, *column percent.

RR   Abbreviation for *risk ratio.

***r*-Squared**   Another way of expressing r^2.

***R*-Squared**   Another way of expressing R^2.

RSS   Regression *sum of squares, that is, the *explained variance. See *sum of squared errors (SSE).

R-Technique Factor Analysis   An approach to *factor analysis that analyzes the correlations or items or variables, looking for *factors, that is, combinations of variables that "hang together." Compare *Q-technique factor analysis.

***r*-to-*Z* Transformation**   A way of transforming a *Pearson *r* correlation coefficient that enables the researcher to compute a *confidence interval and *confidence limits for it. The transformation is done using natural logs. By using an *r*-to-*Z* transformation, the researcher can also determine the *statistical significance of a Pearson *r* via a *z* test. For example, to test the null hypothesis that the population correlation is zero, the observed Z is divided by the square root of $1/(n-3)$, where n is the sample size. Using alpha = .05, the null would be rejected if this *z* test value (ignoring the sign if it's negative) is equal to or greater than 1.96. Note that this Z is not a *z* score or standard score. Also called *Fisher's *Z*.

Rule   In statistics and mathematics, as in other areas of conduct, a rule is a statement that tells us what to do.

For example, the *formula $A = B \times C$ tells us that to find A, multiply B by C. A rule is often a formula stated in words rather than in symbols.

Run   (a) Repeated values of a variable; for example, rolling dice and getting three 7s in a row would be a run. The *runs test is a *nonparametric test of the statistical significance of runs. (b) The change in horizontal distance between two points on a regression line. To get the *slope, divide the run into the *rise. See *slope for a graphic illustration.

Running Average   Another term for *moving average.

Running Median   A way of *smoothing a line composed of *medians. The techniques are analogous to those used for *moving averages, and the purpose is the same: to make a trend clearer by reducing the visibility of fluctuations.

Runs Test   Another term for the *Wald-Wolfowitz test.

Ryan's Method   One of several ways of adjusting *significance levels to compensate for testing *multiple comparisons. See *Scheffé test, *Tukey's HSD, *Dunn's multiple-comparison test.

S (a) Abbreviation for *subject. Usually Ss, for subjects. (b) Lower- or uppercase italicized *s*, *standard deviation of a sample.

S^2 Lowercase or uppercase italicized S^2, *variance of a sample.

Sample A group of *subjects or *cases selected from a larger group in the hope that studying this smaller group (the sample) will reveal important information about the larger group (the *population).

Sample Distribution A term sometimes used to refer to a *distribution of scores of a *variable in a *sample; an ordered array of the measurements or scores of a *sample of subjects. Not to be confused with a *sampl*ing* distribution or a *population distribution.

For example, if the U.S. surgeon general were to conduct a study of the birth weights of children, a sample of all the live births in a given time period could be taken; the weights could then be recorded and arranged in order, probably from heaviest to lightest, to facilitate study. This ordered arrangement would be the sample distribution and could be used, among other things, to calculate the relative frequencies of different weights.

Sample Mean The mean or average that is calculated on *sample data, in contrast to population data. Symbolized as M or $\overline{X}$ (pronounced "X bar"). Compare *population mean.

Sample Point In *set theory, any member of the *sample space. All possible sample points or outcomes would define the sample space. Also called *elementary event.

Sample Size The number of subjects or cases selected for inclusion in a sample. Compare *sampling fraction.

Sample Size Formulas Several formulas exist for determining an appropriate sample size for a study, particularly for determining statistical *power. Many of these require information that one will not have until after the sample has been identified and studied. However, reviews of the literature can often enable researchers to make good guesses about that information. The general rule for sample size is the bigger the better because the larger the sample, the smaller the *standard errors. However, in a search for practical limits to sample size, researchers have used several formulas that help them identify samples that will be adequately large for their purposes.

For example, one suggestion for multiple regression analysis is that this technique requires a minimum of 50 cases plus 8 cases for each independent variable. Other formulas are commonly used to calculate how big a sample needs to be to achieve a certain level of statistical *power. One software package, freely available on the Internet, for calculating sample size needed for a study is G*Power.

Sample Space   (a) In *probability theory, the group of *data points (*elementary events) that includes all possible outcomes of an experiment (*experiment [b]). See *underlying distribution for an example. (b) In sampling theory, all the possible *samples of a given size that can be drawn from a particular *population.

For example, when talking about the probability of drawing particular cards from a deck, the deck of cards is the sample space. It contains all possible outcomes of any drawing.

Sample Statistic   A numerical index based on sample data. Used to estimate a *population parameter.

Sample Survey   A survey in which a sample, not the whole *population, is studied. Compare *census.

Sample Weights   See *weighted sample.

Sampling   Selecting elements (subjects or other *units of analysis) from a *population in such a way that they are representative of the population. This is done to increase the likelihood of being able to generalize accurately about the population. Random sampling is often a more accurate and efficient way to learn about a large population than a *census of the whole population. See *attrition.

Sampling Bias   The problem that occurs in *nonprobability or *nonrandom sampling. The problem is that *systematic error enters into the process and the sample is not *representative of the population.

Sampling Distribution (of a Statistic)   A *theoretical* *frequency distribution of the scores for or values of a *statistic, such as a *mean. Any statistic that can be computed for a sample has a sampling distribution. A sampling distribution is the distribution of a statistic that *would be* produced in repeated *random sampling (with *replacement) from the same population. It is comprised of all possible values of a statistic and their probabilities of occurring for a sample of a particular size.

You can think of a sampling distribution as being constructed by drawing an infinite number of samples of a given size from a particular population and you record each of their distributions. Then the statistic, such as the mean, is computed for the scores of each of these hypothetical samples. *Then* this infinite number of statistics is arranged in a distribution to arrive at the sampling distribution. If we actually had this sampling distribution, we could determine how often our observed *sample statistic value would occur and whether our particular sample value was typical or rare.

In practice, we convert our sample statistic value to a *test statistic value that is known to follow (in repeated sampling) a particular probability distribution, such as a *t, F,* or χ^2 distribution. (In the distributions just mentioned, we also have to specify the *degrees of freedom [*df*] because the exact shape of those distributions varies according to their *df*.) Then, for the alpha level we are using, we obtain the *critical value based on the probability distribution (and reject the null hypothesis if the observed value of our statistic is greater than the critical value), or we use a statistical program to provide us with a *p* value (and reject the null hypothesis when this *p* value is smaller than the alpha level we have selected to use). Confidence intervals are constructed based on the estimated standard errors of the probability distribution we are using.

It is hard to overestimate the importance of sampling distributions of statistics. The entire process of *inferential statistics (by which we move from known information about samples to inferences about *populations) relies on sampling distributions.

Sampling Error   The inaccuracies in inferences about a *population that come about because researchers have taken a *sample rather than studied the entire *population. Sampling error is an estimate of how a sample statistic is expected to differ from a population parameter in a *random sample drawn from the population. Also called *sampling variability. See *random error.

For example, to find out how many students at a particular college cheated on their schoolwork in the past year, you survey 200 (a sample) of them. Suppose you find that 28% said they had cheated. If your sampling method were a good one, 28% would probably be close to what you would have obtained had you surveyed all the students at the college. But your figure is likely to be off, say, as much as 3% one way or the other (according to the 95% confidence interval given by your computer program). That would mean that your confidence interval is 25% to 31% (i.e., 28% ± 3%). The *sampling error* (i.e., *margin of error) is that plus-or-minus 3%. See *confidence interval, *margin of error.

Note that there are many other ways, besides sampling error, that your figure of 28% could be wrong. For instance, your questions could have been poorly worded, or some students could have lied about whether or not they cheated!

Sampling Fraction   The size of a *sample as a percentage of the *population from which it was drawn; the *ratio of sample size to population size.

For example, a sample of 1,000 of the residents drawn from a town with a total population of 50,000 would yield a sampling fraction of 2% (1,000/50,000 = .02 = 2%). A sample of the same size in a city of 1 million would result in a sampling fraction of one tenth of 1% (1,000/1,000,000 = .001 = .1%). Sample size is far more important than sampling fraction, so keep your focus on *sample size,* not sampling fraction; a sample of 1,000 can be just as reliable for making inferences about the city of 1 million as about the town of 50,000.

Sampling Frame   A list or other record of all the elements in the *population from which the *sampling units are drawn. It defines your *accessible population, which might be different from your *target population, depending on how good your sampling frame is.

For example, suppose you wanted to select a sample of all the students at a university. If you picked every 25th name listed in the student telephone directory, the directory would be your sampling frame, and it would define your accessible population.

Remember that a sampling frame might not include all members of the *target population of interest (in fact, it almost never does). In the present example, some students do not have telephones, and others enrolled after the directory was published; they are part of your target population, but they are not in the sampling frame. Other students have graduated since the directory appeared; they are in the sampling frame, but they are not part of the target population.

Sampling Interval   The population size divided by the desired sample size. Often symbolized by the lowercase letter k. A sampling interval is a key part of the *systematic sampling method.

Sampling Units (or Sampling Elements)   Items from a *population selected for inclusion in a *sample. Compare *unit of analysis.

For example, if the population were all the North American cities with more than 5,000 residents, and the sample were 200 such cities, they would be the sampling units.

Sampling Variability (or Variation)   (a) Differences in a *statistic when it is computed on two or more *samples drawn from the same *population. The value of this statistic will vary from sample to sample, but in the long run it will give you the correct value if it is an *unbiased estimator. (b) Differences between the value of a statistic computed for a particular sample and that same statistical index computed for the entire population. See *sampling error.

Sampling With (or Without) Replacement   When drawing a sample from a *population, one can replace or not replace subjects into the *sampling space after each draw. Many statistical procedures are based on sampling with replacement. Both provide unbiased estimates. However, sampling without replacement is slightly more statistically *efficient also, it is not desirable to include the same person in a sample more than once; therefore, researchers usually use sampling without replacement.

SARIMA   Seasonally adjusted *ARIMA.

SAS   Statistical Analysis System. A widely used *statistical package for data analysis in the social and behavioral sciences. Compare *SPSS, *R.

Saturated Model   (a) An estimation procedure that has zero *degrees of freedom. This is a problem; it can usually be solved by increasing the number of subjects and/or decreasing the number of parameters to be estimated based on your sample data. (b) In path analysis, the *just-identified model, that is, the model with all of the paths included. (c) In *factor analysis, a problem occurring when the number of factors to be estimated is equal to the number of observed variables. In the path analysis and factor analysis situations, one can judge the value of a simpler (unsaturated) model (with fewer paths or factors) by comparing it to the saturated model. (d) Refers to a model with all possible main effects and interactions and standard errors of zero.

Scalar   (a) Like or pertaining to a *scale. Said of questionnaire items that can be arranged in a definite logical order. See *Guttman scaling. (b) In *matrix algebra, a scalar is an ordinary number, not a matrix or a *vector. For example, when each component or element of a matrix is multiplied by a single number, this is called "scalar multiplication."

Scale   (a) A set of numbers or other symbols used to designate characteristics of a variable that is used in *measurement. For example, the numbers on a thermometer and the words "low, medium, and high" on an air conditioner are scales. See *level of measurement. (b) A group of related measures of a *variable. The items in a scale are arranged in some order of intensity or importance. A scale differs from an *index in that the items in an index need not be in a particular order and each item usually has the same weight or importance. For examples, see the *Bogardus, *Guttman, *Likert, and *Thurstone scales. Many writers do not distinguish between a scale and an index; it is fairly common to use the terms interchangeably to refer to any composite measure or *summated scale.

Scale Attenuation Effect   See *floor and *ceiling effects.

Scale Development   The process of developing an instrument to measure a construct. For the vast majority of constructs, multiple items are needed to measure the construct. Scale development includes identifying and testing items' *measurement properties, and includes determination of *validity and *reliability of the scale with the people in the *reference group. See definition (a) of *scale.

S

Scale Homogeneity   See *internal consistency.

Scale of Measurement   Another term for *level of measurement.

Scale Up   To take research findings and apply them more broadly. For example, findings from a learning laboratory might be used to guide statewide education reform, or discoveries in a chemistry lab could be scaled up to an industrial application.

Scaling   (a) Another term for *measuring. See *nominal, *ordinal, *interval, and *ratio scales. (b) The process of creating a *scale by putting a group of related items in a logical sequence.

Scan Statistic   A measure for detecting unusual (unlikely to have occurred by chance) clusters of events or data points in a data set. The null hypothesis is that the events or points are independent and identically distributed, or *i.i.d.

Scatter Diagram   See *scatter plot.

Scattergram   See *scatter plot.

Scatter Plot   Also called "scatter diagram" and "scattergram." The pattern of points that results from plotting two *variables on a graph (see Figure S.1). Each point or dot represents one *subject or *unit of analysis and is formed by the intersection of the values of the two variables. See *data point.

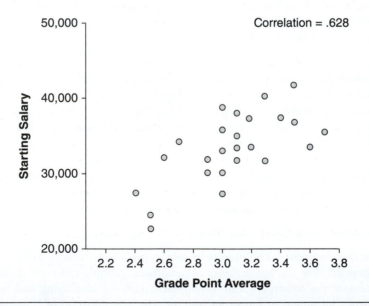

Figure S.1   Scatter Plot

Source: Johnson, Burke. *Educational Research: Quantitative, Qualitative, and Mixed Approaches.* Thousand Oaks, CA: Sage, 2013.

S

The pattern of the points indicates the strength and direction of the *correlation between the two variables. If you inserted a *regression line into the scatter plot, the more the points tend to cluster around a straight line, the stronger the relation (and the higher the correlation). If the line around which the points tend to cluster runs from lower left to upper right, the relation is *positive (or direct); if it runs from upper right to lower left, the relation is *negative (or inverse). If the dots are scattered randomly throughout the grid, there is no relationship between the two variables.

For examples of scatter plots, see *correlation coefficient, *heteroscedasticity, *intercept, and *regression line.

Scatter Plot Matrix   A display of scatter plots for all pairs of variables in a set of variables. If there are 10 variables, there will be a 10-by-10 matrix. Most often used in *regression diagnostics.

Scedasticity   The degree to which the values of a *dependent variable are scattered or dispersed across the values of an *independent variable. The question analysis of scedasticity tries to answer is: As the values of the independent variable change, does the degree of *dispersion in the dependent variable's values remain uniform? See *homoscedasticity and *heteroscedasticity; the latter entry includes a graphic illustration.

Scenario   An assumed or imagined sequence of events used to make decisions and contingency plans about future actions or events, often by contrasting two or more scenarios. Compare *decision table, *model.

Schedule   See *interview schedule.

Scheffé Test   A test of *statistical significance used for *post hoc comparisons of means in an *ANOVA. Among its main features are that it is a conservative test (it tends to err on the side of underestimating significance) and that it deals well with unequal *cell sizes. The Scheffé test involves calculating and using a new, more demanding *critical value for F. See *omnibus test.

Schema (plural: schemata)   Generally, a diagram, plan, or framework. In cognitive psychology, neuroscience, and related fields, a system for codifying concepts, experience, and data that organizes the way we perceive, learn, and remember. Compare *paradigm, *model.

Science   Most generally, the discovery, creation, accumulation, and refinement of knowledge. There are many controversies about what science is and about which disciplines, specialties within disciplines, and methods are "truly" scientific. According to most philosophers of science, there is no *perfect* criterion for demarcation of science from nonscience. One criterion might include cases that most agree should not be included, and another criterion might exclude cases that most agree should be included. See *epistemology, *paradigm.

Scientific Hypothesis   Another term for *research hypothesis.

Scientific Method   Technically there is no *single* scientific method for producing reliable and valid knowledge because scientists use a variety of methods. The term "scientific method" refers to the family of methods, including *hypothesis testing, and *inductive and *deductive approaches such as theory generation and theory testing.

Scientific Notation   Technique for reporting very small and very large numbers. The number is represented by taking the first digit and showing that it is multiplied by 10 raised to a positive or negative power. For example, 5.7×10^7 is equal to 57,000,000 (notice that we shifted the decimal 7 places to the right; this is also written as 5.7e+7). Likewise, 5.7×10^{-7} is equal to .00000057 (notice that we shifted the decimal 7 places to the left; this is also written as 5.7e−7).

Scientific Significance   Often contrasted with *statistical significance, scientific significance refers to the degree that a finding helps advance knowledge in a field. Scientific significance is decided by judgment, not statistical routines. See also *practical significance, *substantive significance, *clinical significance.

Scientism   (a) An extreme belief, according to which science is the *only* way to obtain knowledge. (b) A term used to belittle or dismiss theories and people who to tend to treat science as a religion or an ideology.

For example, people who believe that science is the highest human value, that it can solve all real problems, and that it is superior to any other form of knowledge or belief are likely to be accused of scientism. Compare *positivism.

Scope Conditions   The specifications or limitations on the applicability or *validity of a *theory and its *propositions. Scope conditions indicate the circumstances (e.g., times, places, kinds of subjects) under which a theory's propositions would hold true.

Score   A value of a variable. The term is used more broadly than when the value is a score in the ordinary sense of the term, such as a test score.

Score Test   See *Lagrange Multiplier Test.

Scree Plot   A plot of *eigenvalues in descending order. So called because of its resemblance to a geological scree, which is an accumulation of stones or other rubble at the base of a steep hill. Eigenvalues high up on the hill would be included as factors worthy of further analysis; those at the bottom would not. The division between the included and the excluded is the point where the eigenvalues level off.

The scree plot in Figure S.2 depicts the eigenvalues of 37 variables. Visually, the leveling-off point is at the fourth factor (actual eigenvalue for that factor = 1.8).

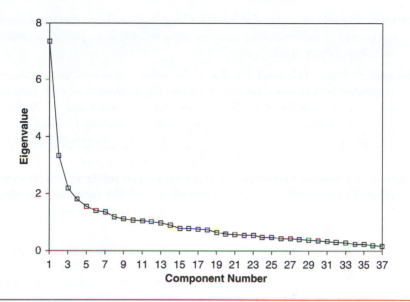

Figure S.2 Scree Plot

SD *Standard deviation (italicized). Also written *Sd* or *sd*.

SD *Semantic differential (not italicized).

SDT *Signal detection theory.

SE *Standard error, often standard error of the mean.

Seasonal Component Fluctuation of time-series data during the same month or months each year. It is one of the components that *time-series data are decomposed into. The components of the observed value are decomposed into *secular trend, *cyclical, *seasonal variations, and *irregular fluctuations.

Seasonally Adjusted Said of time-series data when regular, seasonal fluctuations are statistically removed. For example, if unemployment rates have regularly increased by 1% in the winter months, an increase in the winter months would have to exceed 1% before it would be interpreted as a true increase.

Secondary Analysis A type of research in which *data collected by others are analyzed. In some fields (e.g., sociology, economics), secondary analysis is a very common form of published research.

Examples of extensive and widely used data *archives available for secondary analysis include the U.S. Census *Public Use Microdata Samples (PUMS), the National Election Survey (NES) of the Inter-University Consortium for Political and Social Research, and the *General Social Survey (GSS) of the National Opinion Research Center (NORC). Secondary analysis in qualitative research can be thought of as having a long tradition (e.g., historians using documents in archives) or as emerging quite recently (e.g., publicly available oral history transcripts).

Secondary Data   Information collected by other researchers and available, sometimes in *databases, for use by others. Huge amounts of such data are available, for example, at the National Institutes of Health and the National Center for Education Statistics and in the Inter-University Consortium for Political and Social Research (ICPSR) collection. See *secondary analysis for other examples. Compare *primary data.

Secondary Prevention Research   Research focused on preventing the development of a problem/disorder among individuals with risk factors or early signs of the problem/disorder. Compare *primary prevention research, *tertiary prevention research.

Secondary Source   A source that provides nonoriginal ("secondhand") data or information. Compare *primary source, *original research report.

For example, if you wanted to study the city council, you could interview its members and attend its meetings, or you could read newspaper articles by a reporter who had interviewed the members and attended their meetings. In the latter case, you would be relying on a secondary source; you would not have obtained the information firsthand.

Second-Order Factor Analysis   Studying *correlations among factors so as to find factors that lie behind factors. See *factor analysis.

Second-Order Interaction   An interaction among three *independent variables. Also called a *three-way interaction, a triple interaction, or an A × B × C interaction. Compare to a *first-order interaction. See *interaction effect. Note: You can extend this terminology; a third-order interaction is the interaction among four independent variables, a fourth-order interaction is the interaction among five independent variables, and so forth.

Second-Order Meta-analysis   A meta-analyses of prior (first-order) meta-analyses. A meta-analysis of a set of independent, but methodologically comparable, first-order (i.e., standard) *meta-analyses that address the same relationship in different contexts. This helps one see how much variability there is in effect sizes across first-order meta-analyses and how conclusions should be qualified by context.

Second-Order Partial   Said of a *correlation or *regression coefficient when two variables are controlled. One can extend this logic to third-order, fourth-order, and, more generally, *higher order partials.

Secular Trend   A long-term trend or one of indefinite length, usually as opposed to a short-term trend or fluctuation. See *moving average, *time-series data.

Segmented Bar Chart   A bar chart in which each of the bars is made up of two or more parts ("segments"). This allows you to use a bar chart to compare both wholes and their parts.

The examples in Figure S.3 show the number of deaths per 100,000 attributable to heart disease for the entire population. The segmented bars and the clustered bars show the separate rates for men and women. While one or the other approach to graphing could be more effective for different purposes, here the choice is mostly a matter of taste or preference.

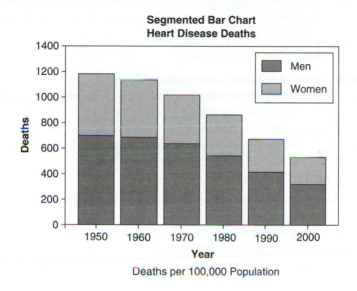

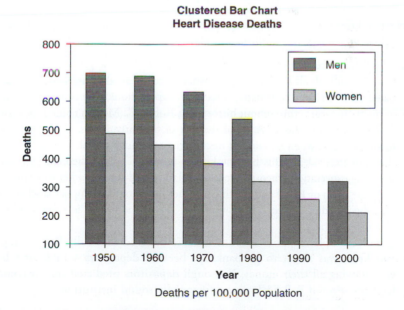

Figure S.3   Segmented Bar Chart (Compared to Clustered Bar Chart)

Selection Bias   (also called **Selection Threat (to Validity)** and **Self-Selection Bias**)
A problem that arises when the researcher cannot randomly assign subjects to
*control and *experimental groups.

For example, comparing the effects on academic achievement of attending
2-year colleges versus attending 4-year colleges would be difficult because
(among other reasons) students who chose to attend 2-year colleges might be
different in important ways (e.g., goals, income, motivation, aptitude) from
those who selected 4-year colleges.

Selection Effect   See *selection threat.

Selection Threat (to Validity)   Any "selection" procedure that causes comparison groups (e.g., treatment and control groups) to be different. This is a problem, because the researcher wants the groups to differ on only the manipulated
independent variable and not on any other extraneous variable. If the groups
differ on the independent variable and on an extraneous variable, then it will
not be clear which one produced any observed effect; that is, the variables will
be *confounded. See *selection bias.

Selective Dropout   In a research study with comparison groups, selective dropout occurs when the groups become increasingly different because of the
nature of dropping out of participants. It is a nonrandom loss of participants.
Even if one were to randomly assign participants to groups in an experiment
(to create "equivalent" groups), selective dropout would create a problem
because the groups would now be different on variables other than the independent variable, thus confounding the results. See *attrition.

Selective Observation   Observing only the cases or results that support one's
beliefs. It is a type of *confirmation bias.

Self-Fulfilling Prophecy   Something that happens because people expect it to
happen. Individuals don't just act on what is true in an absolute sense; they act
based on others' and, ultimately, their own expectations. The concept appears
in many literatures throughout history, but Robert K. Merton coined the term
"self-fulfilling prophecy." A social theorist of the early 1900s, W. I. Thomas,
made the point when he said, "If men define situations as real, they are real in
their consequences." This became known as the "Thomas theorem." In economics, "expectations theory" explains inflation and stock market movements
(e.g., the crash of 1929) and much consumer behavior. Karl Popper labeled the
idea the "Oedipus effect." In psychology, the phenomenon is known as the
*Pygmalion effect.

For example, suppose account holders believed that Billy-Bob Savings
and Loan was about to go bankrupt because depositors would soon be
withdrawing all their money. If enough depositors predicted this, it could
happen—even if B-B S&L were a financially sound institution.

Self-Report Inventory A type of instrument or questionnaire in which participants report, without the help of anyone else, their beliefs, attitudes, and behaviors. This would be in contrast to researcher *observation of participants for data collection.

Self-Selection Bias Another term for *selection bias.

SEM (a) *Standard error of the mean. (b) *Standard error of measurement. (c) *Structural equation modeling.

Semantic Differential Scale A question format in an interview or other survey instrument in which *respondents are asked to locate their attitudes on a scale ranging between opposite positions on a particular issue (described by bipolar adjectives), as in Table S.1. The interviewer or subject circles a number from 1 to 7 for each scale.

Table S.1 Semantic Differential Scale

			My Boss Is . . .					
Fair	1	2	3	4	5	6	7	Unfair
Passive	1	2	3	4	5	6	7	Active
Lazy	1	2	3	4	5	6	7	Hardworking
Efficient	1	2	3	4	5	6	7	Inefficient

Semi-interquartile Range The *interquartile range (IQR) divided by 2. In other terms, the difference between the 75th percentile and the 25th percentile divided by 2. Also called *quartile deviation.

For example, in the series 4, 6, 8, 10, the range is $10 - 4 = 6$; the IQR is $8 - 6 = 2$; the semi-IQR is $2/2 = 1$.

Semi-logarithmic Ruling Said of graph paper using *logarithmic ruling on only one *axis (usually the vertical or y-axis). See *logarithm. Such graph paper is often used for *time-series studies to compare trends for sets of data, especially when the sets of data are of different orders of magnitude, such as the populations of a city and of a nation. Since the advent of advanced computer graphics capabilities, such graph paper is used very rarely, but the scales are still quite important.

Semiology The study of signs and their meanings. A branch of linguistics and linguistic philosophy that some theorists believe has great promise as a model for how to study several aspects of human thought and action.

Semipartial Correlation A correlation that partials out (*controls for) a variable, but only from one of the other variables being correlated. Sometimes symbolized *sr*; in another notational system, the distinction is indicated by *r* with subscripts. For example, $r_{1(2.3)}$ refers to the correlation between variables 1 and 2 when variable 3 is removed from variable 2. For example, you might obtain the correlation between income (variable 1) and gender (variable 2), controlling for education (variable 3). The effect of education is *not* removed from personal income, but education *is* removed from gender, which produces a new "residualized gender variable" that is uncorrelated with education. The semipartial correlation is just the Pearson correlation between the unresidualized income variable and the residualized gender variable. Also called "part correlation." It is often computed in *multiple regression analysis and then squared. See *semipartial correlation squared. Compare *partial correlation.

Semipartial Correlation Squared   In *multiple regression analysis, the proportion of variance in the dependent variable that is explained by a particular independent variable beyond all other independent variables included in the analysis; it's the amount of variance in the dependent variable uniquely explained by a particular independent variable. It is a popular index of the relative importance of the independent variables or "variable ordering" in multiple regression and considered superior to using beta weights for the same purpose.

Semistructured Interview   A mixed form of interviewing in which some of the questions can be closed-ended and their ordering can be structured and other questions will be open-ended and/or unstructured in their order to be asked. Some of the questions will be determined beforehand, and some questions can arise during the interview process. Compare *unstructured interview, *structured interview.

Sensitivity   (a) The ability of a diagnostic test to identify the presence of a disease or condition. Sensitivity is the *conditional probability of the test giving a positive result if the subject does have the condition or disease; sometimes called "true positive." Originating in medical research, the term is now used more broadly. Compare *power of a test, *specificity. (b) Sensitivity is sometimes used by qualitative researchers to denote an ability of researchers to understand nuances in interviewees' accounts or to assume others' perspectives.

Sequencing Effects   Biasing effects that can occur when each participant must participate in more than one treatment condition, as in *repeated measures designs. There are three major kinds of sequencing effects: *order effects, *carryover effects, and *differential carryover effects. The problem of sequencing effects is usually resolved through the use of *counterbalancing.

Sequential Analysis   (a) A kind of investigation in which researchers decide as they go along (through periodic analyses of the data gathered up to that point) how much more and what kinds of data should be gathered next. Also called *interim analysis. Compare *negative case analysis, *post hoc comparison. (b) In experiments, a kind of statistical analysis that allows researchers to end the study when outcomes with the desired level of precision have been attained—when, for example, a treatment has been shown effective and it would make no sense (or would be unethical) to deny it to the control group. (c) Descriptions and analyses of the sequences in which behavior occurs; often conducted using data gathered from detailed observations of behavior in natural settings.

Sequential Sampling   Observations made until enough data have been gathered to make a decision. This contrasts with the more typical procedure of deciding on the number of observations (or sample size) before beginning the study. Compare *Pascal distribution, *theoretical saturation.

Serial Correlation   Another term for *autocorrelation, that is, correlation between earlier and later items in a *time series. It can be calculated by correlating a *time-series variable with a *lagged version of itself.

Serial Dependency   This occurs when behavior at later observations is dependent upon behavior at earlier observations. Compare *A-B-A-B design, *repeated measures design.

SES   *Socioeconomic status.

Set   A well-defined group of things. Events, objects, or numbers that are distinguishable from all other events, objects, or numbers on the basis of some specific characteristic or rule.

Examples of sets include all even numbers (those that are exactly divisible by 2), all murders (intentional illegal killings of persons, as opposed to all other forms of death), and all female physicians (contrasted with male physicians and/or females who are not physicians). Compare *sample space, *fuzzy set.

Set-Theoretic Model   An application of *set theory to the analysis of data.

Set Theory   A branch of logic and mathematics that deals with the characteristics of and relations among *sets.

Sex-Specific Rate   The ratio of the number of cases in some category (disease, births, deaths, personality type, etc.) to the total number of cases in the sex's population. It shows the percentage of males with the condition and the percentage of females with the condition. The male and female rates can be used to construct *risk ratios, which are similar to *odds ratios. Note: Sometimes the denominator is the total (combined) number of people (number of males plus the number of females). Often these rates are reported as "times a multiplier" such as times or per 1,000 people. See *segmented bar chart for a graphic.

Shapiro-Wilk Test   A statistical test of the *hypothesis that sample data have been drawn from a population with a *normal distribution. It can also be used to test for other population distributions. Usually abbreviated W. Compare *Lilliefors test, *normal probability plot.

Shotgun Approach   Said of research in which the investigator studies a large number of variables with no clear strategy or theoretical justification. The researcher points, so to speak, in a general direction and hopes to hit something. Also called "including everything but the kitchen sink" in your model. Compare *fishing expedition.

Shrinkage   The tendency for the strength of prediction in a *regression or *correlation study to decrease in subsequent studies with new data sets. The regression model derived from one set of data usually works less well with others. The degree of shrinkage is measured by change in R^2. Compare *regression toward the mean.

Sidak Technique   A correction technique used to adjust for inflated alpha when conducting *post hoc tests. It is not quite as conservative as the *Bonferroni technique.

Sigma (Σ, σ)   (a) The uppercase sigma usually means "sum of" and is thus an indication that the numbers following it are to be (or have been) added together. (b) Lowercase sigma is often used to symbolize the *standard deviation of a *population. See *standard score. (c) Lowercase sigma squared (σ^2) means population *variance.

Sigmoid Curve   A curve resembling the letter S.

Signal Detection Theory (SDT)   The theory that the detection of a signal, such as a sound, depends on sensory input and a decision process about whether one has heard something and/or what one has heard. It is interesting for methodology because of the parallels between the decision process of the subject in SDT and of the researcher in *hypothesis testing. When "signal" is interpreted broadly to include any outcome that can be present or not, such as a symptom of a disease, SDT can be used in many areas of research. SDT is not different in principle from *hypothesis testing, but most people find SDT easier to understand than the double and triple negatives used to describe hypothesis testing.

The matrix in Table S.2 shows the possible outcomes in a signal detection experiment. Compare this with the similar illustration of *hypothesis testing.

Table S.2   Signal Detection Theory

		Subject's Decision About Signal	
		Yes	*No*
Actual			
Presence	*Yes*	Hit	Miss
of Signal	*No*	False Alarm	Correct Rejection

Significance The degree to which a research finding is meaningful or important. Without qualification, the term usually means *statistical significance, but lack of specificity leads to confusion (or allows obfuscation). See *practical significance, *substantive significance, *significance testing. Researchers should usually specify the type of significance they mean to avoid confusion.

Significance Level The *probability of making a *Type I error that a researcher is willing to accept, that is, the probability at which it is decided the *null hypothesis will be rejected. Also called *alpha level. Compare *p value.

Significance Testing Another term for *hypothesis testing. Using statistical tests (such as the *chi-square test, *t test, *z test, or *F test) to determine how often the value of the test statistic observed in the *sample would have occurred if the *null (i.e., chance or "just *sampling error") hypothesis were true (i.e., if there is no relationship in the *population from which the sample was selected). This observed probability is called the *p value. If the observed value of the test statistic was unlikely to have been due to chance (i.e., if the p value is very small), the null hypothesis is rejected, and the finding is deemed statistically significant. See *hypothesis testing, *sampling distribution.

Sign Test The simplest and oldest of *nonparametric statistical tests. So called because plus and minus (+ and −) signs are used when this statistic is computed from sample data. The test relies on the binomial distribution. There are two main versions: (1) The one-sample version tests the null hypothesis that the population (from which your sample came) has the median value that you hypothesize. (2) The two-related-samples version tests the null hypothesis that the median difference between pairs of cases is zero (i.e., no difference) in the population.

Simple Correlation A *correlation between two variables only or a correlation that describes a *linear relationship. Also called "bivariate correlation." Contrasted with *multiple correlation and *nonlinear relation.

Simple Effect (also called **Simple Main Effect**) Effect of one independent variable on the dependent variable at a single level of another independent variable.

Simple Interaction Effect An interaction between two independent variables, in *ANOVA, at one level of a third independent variable.

Simple Multivariate (Form of the *General Linear Model) The generic name for any *GLM that has two or more *independent variables (or one categorical independent variable with three or more groups) and one continuous *dependent variable. The independent variables can be categorical or quantitative and can be *within-subjects or *between-subjects variables. A few examples are *multiple regression, *ANOVA (except for the two-group case), *ANCOVA, and *time-series analysis. If the dependent variable is not continuous, see *generalized linear model.

S

Simple Random Sampling   The most basic form of random sampling. It is analogous to randomly selecting names from a hat. Usually, selection is done without replacement so that the same person is not included in the sample more than once. Most statistical theory is based on sampling with replacement, but, in large samples, sampling without replacement works equally well. See *random sampling.

Simple Regression   A form of *regression analysis in which the values of a *dependent variable are attributed to (are a function of) a single *independent variable. Usually contrasted with *multiple regression analysis in which two or more independent variables are used to explain one dependent variable.

Simple-Simple Effect   In a three-way ANOVA (with three independent variables), this is a *simple effect within a two-way interaction at one level of a third independent variable.

Simple Structure   Desirable pattern in a rotated *factor loading matrix. The pattern is present when the following characteristics are present: (1) The loadings in each column (i.e., for a single factor) include only large loadings and small loadings, thus clearly showing the observed variables that do and do not load on the particular factor. (2) The loadings in each row (i.e., for a single variable) include just one large loading with the remaining loadings being small, thus indicating that the variable loads on only one factor (and does not double load or triple load). An example of simple structure is shown in Table S.3, the hypothetical results of an analysis of items based on a popular burnout scale.

Table S.3   Simple Structure

	Maslach Burnout Inventory (MBI)		
Item	Emotional Exhaustion	Depersonalization	Personal Accomplishment
Emotionally drained	**.98**	.00	.00
Used up	**.97**	.00	.00
Frustrated	**.90**	.02	.09
Callous toward people	.05	**.91**	.03
I don't really care	.01	**.92**	.00
Recipients blame me	.00	**.98**	.00
Accomplished	.02	.02	**.95**
I deal effectively	.01	.00	**.98**
I feel exhilarated	.00	.00	**.99**

Simpson's Paradox   A surprising or contradictory result that occurs when a relation between two variables is reversed by taking a third variable into account—or when the direction of the values for two groups taken individually is reversed when the groups are merged. *Lord's paradox is a variant. See *ecological fallacy.

Table S.4 illustrates Simpson's paradox. It gives the scores of two classes of 10 students in two different years. Students are in two groups, A and B, one of which scores substantially higher than the other. In the first year, the 5 students in Group A score a mean of 80, and the 5 in Group B get a mean of 60. In the second year, both groups raise their averages somewhat, to 81 and 62. And the gap between the groups narrows slightly, but the overall average goes *down* in year 2. That's the paradox: Both groups do better in year 2, but the overall mean goes down. The reason is that in the second year, there are 2 fewer students in the high-scoring group and 2 more in the low-scoring group.

Table S.4   Simpson's Paradox: Scores of Students

	Year 1		Year 2	
	Group A	*Group B*	*Group A*	*Group B*
	80	60	81	62
	78	65	79	67
	82	55	83	57
	75	58		64
	85	62		60
				63
				61
Group Mean	**80**	**60**	**81**	**62**
Overall Annual Means		**70**		**67.7**

SIMSTAT   See *QDA Miner.

Simulation   See *computer simulation, *Monte Carlo methods, *role-playing.

Simultaneous Equations   (a) Another term for "systems of equations" in decision analysis; used when one wants to find point(s) of intersection of several equations simultaneously to determine what is optimal and what decision should be made. (b) A type of *nonrecursive *regression analysis or *structural equation modeling (without latent factors). It is usually used with *cross-sectional or *time-series data when causation is believed to be bidirectional or *reciprocal. In this situation, *instrumental variables are used as an alternative to traditional *OLS estimation.

For example, if the number of crimes in a community goes up, the number of police may tend to be increased. But as the number of police goes up, the number of crimes may tend to go down. Or to take a second example, a drop in the level of rainfall can lead to the spread of the desert, which can lead to further declines in rainfall. In both cases simultaneous equations are sometimes used to attempt to untangle these bidirectional relationships.

Simultaneous Regression Analysis (SRA)   SRA is contrasted with the type of hierarchical regression in which the independent variables are entered into the analysis in more than one *block or set. In contrast to this hierarchical approach, in simultaneous regression the independent variables are entered into the analysis in a single block and then analyzed. When you use a single regression equation, that is what you are doing—you just don't put this long name on it.

For example, assume that you have one dependent variable and six independent variables. Perhaps these independent variables can be theoretically separated into two sets, with three being background variables and the other three being cognitive process variables. With hierarchical regression, you might decide to enter the first three independent variables in one set (the three background variables) and obtain the results (i.e., the regression equation with variables 1–3 included is obtained), then enter the remaining three independent variables (the cognitive-processing variables) into the regression (so that the equation now has all six independent variables in it). In this case, the researcher would be interested in the incremental variance (i.e., the amount of variance in the dependent variance that is explained by the second set of variables above and beyond the variance explained by just the first set).

In simultaneous regression, all six of the independent variables are entered in one step as a single set, producing just one regression equation. Both simultaneous and hierarchical regression can be used for explanatory and predictive purposes. In contrast, *stepwise techniques are used only for predictive and *variable selection purposes.

Single-Blind   A study design in which the subject or patient is kept ignorant of the treatment condition, but the researcher is not. See *double-blind, *triple blind.

Single-Case Design   An experimental design that uses a single participant to investigate the effect of an experimental treatment condition. Some examples are *A-B-A-B design, *A-B-A-C-A design, *multiple baseline design, and *changing criterion design.

Single-Classification ANOVA   Another term for *one-way ANOVA. Also called *single-factor ANOVA.

Single-Factor ANOVA   Another term for *one-way ANOVA. Also called *single-classification ANOVA.

Single-Factor Design   An *experimental design with a single independent variable manipulated by the researcher to determine its impact on the dependent variable. Also called a "one-way design."

Single-Factor Multilevel Design   An experimental design with one independent variable that has three or more levels (e.g., treatment condition 1, treatment condition 2, control group condition).

Single-Sample Runs Test   A *nonparametric test used to determine whether a series of numbers or events (e.g., heads and tails as in HTHTHHHHTHHT, or males and females as in MMFMFFFFFFMM) is randomly ordered. The null hypothesis is that the pattern of occurrence of numbers is determined by a random process. One might use this test to determine if a sample is actually random.

Single-Sample Test for the Median   *Nonparametric test used to determine whether the median is significantly different from some hypothesized median population value. The null hypothesis is that the median in population from which the sample median came is equal to the hypothesized value.

Single-Sample *t* Test   See *one-sample *t* test.

Single-Sample *z* Test   See *one-sample *z* test.

Single-Subject Designs (or Single-Case Designs)   The intensive study of single individuals receiving different treatments or in different settings. Two frequently used single-subject designs are the *A-B-A-B design and the *multiple-baseline design.

Six Sigma   A group of quality control measures that aims to ensure that there are at least 6 *standard deviations (sigmas) between the mean and the nearest specification limit. This translates into a tolerance for error of less than 4 per million. The term is generally used more loosely in the social and behavioral sciences, where very few phenomena can be measured to that degree of accuracy.

68–95–99.7 Percent Rule   An approximation rule for the normal distribution. It states that approximately 68% of the cases (or area under the curve) fall ± 1 standard deviation, 95% fall ± 2 standard deviations, and 99.7% fall ± 3 standard deviations.

Skewed   (a) Said of a set of numbers when their distribution is not a normal distribution or is nonsymmetrical. See *skewed distribution. (b) Sometimes used casually to mean unusual, odd, or nonrepresentative (e.g., "a skewed result").

Skewed Distribution   A distribution of scores or measures that, when plotted on a graph, produce a nonsymmetrical curve. In a unimodal skewed *frequency distribution, the *mode, *mean, and *median are different. When the skewness of a group of values is zero, their distribution is symmetrical.

   A positively (or upward or right) skewed distribution is one in which the infrequent scores are on the high or right side of the *x-axis, such as the scores on a difficult test. A left (or downward or negatively skewed) distribution is one in which the rare values are on the low or left side of the x-axis, such as the scores on an easy test. One way to sort out which is which is to remember that a skewer is a pointy thing; when the pointy end of the distribution is on the right, it is right skewed, and conversely for left skewed (see Figure S.4). Compare *normal distribution, *kurtosis.

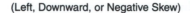

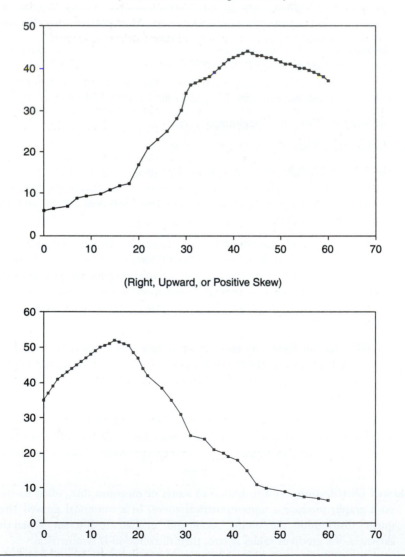

Figure S.4 Skewed Distribution

Skewness   The degree to which measures or scores are bunched on one side of a *central tendency and trail out (become pointy, like a skewer) on the other. The more skewness in a *distribution, the more *variability in the scores. See *skewed distribution for illustrations. Compare *kurtosis.

Computer programs often compute indexes of skewness. Positive values indicate a positive or right skew. Negative values indicate a negative or left skew. The value for a *normal distribution is zero.

Sleeper Effect   Originally used in mass communications theory to refer to a delayed reaction to propaganda or other message. More generally, any effect that becomes apparent only after the passage of time ("delayed causation").

Slope   Generally, the rate at which a line or curve rises or falls when covering a given horizontal distance. The most common reference is to the steepness or angle of a *regression line, usually symbolized by the letter *b* in a *regression equation. The slope of a line is calculated by taking any two points on the line and dividing the vertical distance (the "rise") between them by the horizontal distance (the "run") between them.

In a *positive or *direct relationship, the line slopes upward from left to right; in a *negative or *inverse relation, it goes down from left to right (called negative because the slope *b* is a negative number). Figure S.5 shows both.

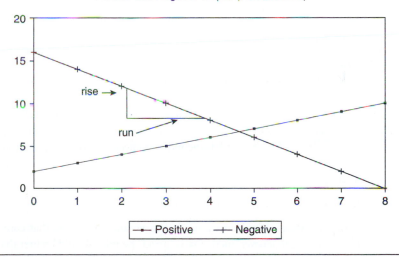

Figure S.5   Slope

Slope Analysis   Another term for *regression analysis, so called because regression analysis focuses on the angle or slope of a *regression line, the steepness of which indicates the strength of a relation.

Slutsky-Yule Effect   When *outliers occur in a *time series to which *moving average techniques have been applied, this can result in misleading fluctuations, especially when the outliers are random. Such changes in trend lines due to random outliers are called the Slutsky-Yule effect.

Small-*N* Problems   Difficulties in analysis that arise because a study contains too few cases for the appropriate use of the desired analytic method. For example, in a study with 20 cases and 6 independent variables, using regression analysis would be inappropriate; such a study would have inadequate *statistical power. (With 6 independent variables, about 100 cases are needed to obtain stable estimates.) See *sample size formulas.

Smoothing   Reducing irregularities (*fluctuations) in *time-series data, generally by using a *moving average. This is done to make long-term trends more apparent. See *ARIMA and, for an illustration, *moving average.

SMSA   *Standard metropolitan statistical area. Also called MSA for short.

Snowball Sampling   A technique for finding research subjects. One subject gives the researcher the name of another subject, who in turn provides the name of a third, and so on. This is an especially useful technique when the researcher wants to contact people with unusual experiences or characteristics who are likely to know one another (e.g., members of a small religious group). Also called *network sampling. Compare *respondent-driven sampling.

Sobel's Test   A statistical test used to check for mediation in a causal model. For example, theory might suggest that a simple bivariate relationship such as $X \to Y$ is incorrect and that the correctly specified model has an intervening variable I as in $X \to I \to Y$. One could run a regression of Y on X and run another regression of Y on X and I to see if the regression coefficient expressing the relationship between X and Y reduces when I is included. The degree to which the original XY relationship reduces with the intervening variable included is the *indirect* effect of X on Y. Sobel's test is used to determine whether the null hypothesis of no indirect effect can be rejected. If it is rejected, the indirect effect of X on Y is statistically significant. Sobel's test requires a large sample size, and, in general, *bootstrapping methods are preferred for testing mediation.

Social Constructionism   See *constructionism.

Social Desirability Bias   Bias in the results of interviews or surveys that comes from subjects trying to answer questions as "good" people "should" rather than in a way that reveals what they actually believe or feel. Because social desirability bias is very difficult to study, there is little evidence about its extent. Some researchers believe it is a big problem; others do not.

For example, if you asked people, "Are you a racist?" most would probably say, "No." Hardly anyone thinks it is acceptable (socially desirable) to admit to being a racist, including people who are racists, at least by some definitions.

Social Indicators *Statistics describing *variables that reflect social conditions, that is, that "indicate" something about the nature and quality of life in a society, often as it changes over time. The term is used by the U.S. Census Bureau as well as other researchers.

Examples of social indicators include per capita income, average life expectancy, median years of education, and infant mortality rate.

Social Science Citation Index **(SSCI)** An extensive source, compiled since 1966, of the citations of works in articles published in thousands of scholarly journals.

The SSCI has many uses. For example, if you found an excellent article on your topic published in 1990, you could use the SSCI to see where that article had been cited in the years since it was published. This would be one way to learn what work has been done on your topic since 1990.

Other commonly used indexes for determining the number of times and places where an article has been cited are Google Scholar, Web of Science, and Scopus; these can be found on the Internet. Google Scholar has become quite popular recently because it is easy to access, free, and often has direct links to the cited articles.

Social Sciences Any of several areas of study that focus on human interaction, institutions, and culture, including sociology, economics, anthropology, political science, history, social psychology, and some aspects of geography.

Socioeconomic Status (SES) Any of several composite measures of social rank, usually including income, education, and occupational prestige.

Sociogram Also called "sociograph." A graphic representation of the relations among individuals in a group—constructed on the basis of some *sociometric measure. See *network analysis.

For example, the answers to the question "Whom would you most like to work with?" for six people (see the example at *sociometric matrix) could be graphed as in Figure S.6.

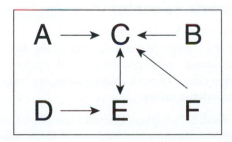

Figure S.6 Sociogram

Sociometric Matrix   A rectangular arrangement of *sociometric measures. Compare *sociogram.

For example, suppose that a manager asked the six members of one of her production departments two questions: Which member of your group would you most like to work closely with on a special project over the next year? Which one would you least like to work closely with? Answers could be useful in planning work assignments.

The results might look like those in Table S.5, where 1 = "most like to work with" and −1 = "least like to work with." The matrix can be read vertically (by columns) or horizontally (by rows). Reading horizontally, we see, for example, that A would most like to work with C and least like to work with B. Reading vertically, it becomes clear that A's choices are fairly typical. Most people choose C for "most like to," and most choose B for "least like to." We can also see that no one has strong feelings, one way or the other, about A or F and that opinions are evenly split about E.

Table S.5   Sociometric Matrix

	A	B	C	D	E	F
A	–	−1	1			
B		–	1		−1	
C			–	−1	1	
D		−1		–		1
E		−1	1		–	
F			1		−1	–

Sociometric Measure   Any of several ways to learn about the existence and the strength of relationships among individuals in a group.

For example, grade school students might be given a *questionnaire with items such as these: "Who is your best friend in the class? Who do you play with at recess?" Alternatively, similar *data could be gathered more slowly, but perhaps yielding results of greater *validity, by observing whom children play with at recess.

Sociometry   Any of a number of methods of gathering data on the attractions, repulsions, interactions, communications, and choices of individuals in groups. Most often called *network analysis today. See *sociogram, *sociometric measure, *sociometric matrix.

Software   Instructions, or *programs, that tell a computer how to perform tasks. Software is often contrasted with "hardware," which refers to the physical computer itself. Word-processing, spreadsheet, statistical analysis, and graphics programs are examples of software.

Solipsism   The philosophical doctrine that denies there is any reality outside one-self, or the belief that one can know nothing other than one's own reflections. *Relativism is sometimes accused of leading to solipsism by its opponents. In practice, no well-known writer has ever self-identified as being a solipsist.

Solomon Four-Group Design   An experimental research design that helps researchers *control for or measure *pretest sensitization. Subjects are randomly assigned to one of four groups. These receive different combinations of the pretest, treatment, and posttest, as shown in Table S.6.

Table S.6   Solomon Four-Group Design

	Pretest	*Treatment*	*Posttest*
Group 1	Yes	Yes	Yes
Group 2	Yes	No	Yes
Group 3	No	Yes	Yes
Group 4	No	No	Yes

Somers's *d*   An *asymmetric *measure of association for variables measured on an *ordinal scale. It is a *PRE measure.

Source Table   Synonym for *summary table. For an example, see *analysis of variance.

Span   The difference between the lowest and highest values in a distribution of values. More often called *range.

Sparse Table   A table with many empty *cells or with many frequencies of zero.

Spatial Autocorrelation   The relationship of a variable with itself, spatially. Used to determine the degree to which clustering is occurring spatially on variables of interest, such as income, politics, education, crime, or disease. The idea is seen in the popular statement "Everything is related to everything else, but closer things more so." For example, your political party or education or income level is more likely to be similar to those living near to than far from you. This kind of analysis is popular in geography, political science, and sociology.

Spearman-Brown Formula   Used to predict the approximate gain in the *reliability with which something could be measured by increasing the number of observations. Often used to adjust (upward) a *split-half reliability estimate.

Spearman Correlation Coefficient (rho)   A statistic that shows the degree of *monotonic relationship between two *variables that are arranged in rank order (measured on an *ordinal scale). Also called "rank-difference correlation." Abbreviated r_s. See *correlation coefficient, *Pearson correlation coefficient, *Kendall's tau.

For example, suppose you wanted to see if there was a relationship between knowledge of the political system and self-esteem among college students. You take a *sample of students and give them a test of political knowledge and a psychological assessment of their self-esteem. Then you rank each of the students on the two scales. Spearman's rho measures the association between the two sets of ranks. The *null hypothesis is that the two ranks are *independent.

Specification   Stating the propositions of a theory or model; saying (specifying) that a relation exists and indicating under what conditions it will be larger or smaller, such as describing how changes in the independent variable will result in changes in the dependent variable. In *path analysis, specification is drawing the path diagram. See *specification error.

Specification Error   A mistake made when deciding on (specifying) the *causal model in a *regression analysis, *path analysis, or *structural equation model. Common specification errors include leaving an important variable out of the causal model and, less crucially, including an irrelevant variable. The most important type of specification error is leaving out an independent variable that influences the prediction of the dependent variable. If, however, the omitted variable is not correlated with the other independent variables, it does not influence the estimate of their effect on the dependent variable. See *misspecification.

It can be very difficult to tell when such an error has been made because much of the purpose of regression analysis is to decide which variables are important and which are irrelevant. In other words, you have to know which variables are important, and include them in the model, in order to determine whether they are important and should be included in the model. See *paradox of inquiry.

Specification Problem   The problem of how to decide (how to specify) which variables to include and which to exclude in a *regression equation and, in a *path analysis, the direction of the causal arrows. See *specification error.

Specificity   The ability of a test to judge that subjects do not have a disease or condition, in other words, to avoid *false negatives. Specificity is the *conditional probability of a test giving a negative result when patients/subjects do not have a disease. Originating in medical research, the term is more broadly used today. Compare *sensitivity, which is the ability of a test to avoid *false positives.

Sphericity Assumption   A statistical assumption important for *repeated-measures ANOVAs; it supersedes the standard *homogeneity of variance assumption that is made with nonrepeated-measures ANOVAs. Sphericity refers to a condition called homogeneity of treatment-difference variances. If difference variables were constructed (where the difference was between the values of each pair of levels of the independent variable), the variances of these difference variables would have to be equal. Rather than examining sphericity, however, a sufficient but more conservative condition called *compound symmetry is usually examined. If compound symmetry is met, then sphericity is met. Note: When the *within-subjects independent variable has only two levels, sphericity is necessarily met.

*Mauchley's test for sphericity is the most common way to see whether the assumption has been met. When sphericity is violated, *F values will be positively biased, and the p values will be too small. Researchers adjust for this bias by raising the *critical value of F needed to attain statistical significance or by raising the p value using either the *Geisser-Greenhouse F test or the *Huynh-Feldt correction. A multivariate solution using MANOVA (which does not assume sphericity) is also available.

Spike   In *time-series data, a sharp increase followed by a quick decrease in a variable. See Figure S.7, in which the spike occurs at year 9.

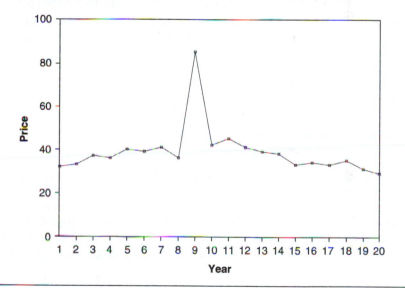

Figure S.7   Spike

Spline Regression   A technique used when the regression line, especially one representing change over time, contains bends or turns, in other words, when the regression line is not *linear. The points at which turns occur are called "spline knots." Different ranges of the independent variable are estimated, and each will have a different slope. Also called "piecewise polynomial regression." The main alternative, *polynomial regression, can be less effective because it might not fit the observed data pattern as well and is more vulnerable to *collinearity problems.

Split-Half Reliability   A way to check the *internal consistency (or *reliability) of an *index by seeing how well the scores on one half of the items *correlate with those on the other half. Compare *Cronbach's alpha, *KR-20.

For example, suppose you had 18 items on a questionnaire that you thought added up to a measure (or index) of racial prejudice. You could check the internal consistency of your index by seeing if respondents answered the odd-numbered questions the same way as the even-numbered questions. If there was not a strong correlation between the levels of prejudice as measured by the two halves, your index would not be very reliable, probably because it was measuring more than one thing.

Split-Plot ANOVA   See *mixed ANOVA, *mixed designs.

S-PLUS (or S+)   A programming language that includes statistical and graphics software. Compare *R.

Spread   Another term for *dispersion, or the *variability of a group of values or scores.

Spreadsheet   A *computer program that arranges *data and *formulas in a *matrix of *cells. Originally developed for accounting problems but now popular for organizing many kinds of data.

SPSS   Statistical Package for the Social Sciences. A widely used brand of computer *software that performs most standard statistical analyses of data. Compare *R, *SAS, *Minitab, *LISREL.

Spurious Precision   Said of results reported to more decimal places than is sensible given what is being described. See *rounding error for an example.

Spurious Relation (or Correlation or Association)   (a) A situation in which measures of two or more *variables are statistically related (they *covary) but are not in fact causally linked—often because the statistical relation is caused by a third variable. When the effects of the third variable are removed, they are said to have been *partialed out. See *confound, *lurking variable. (b) A spurious correlation, as defined in (a), is sometimes called an "illusory correlation." In that case, "spurious" is then reserved for the special case in which a correlation is not present in the original observations but is produced by the way the data are handled. Compare *artifact. Also called a "nonsense correlation."

For example, (a) if the students in a psychology class who had long hair got higher scores on the midterm than those who had short hair, there would be a correlation between hair length and test scores. However, not many people would believe that there was a causal link and that, for example, students who wished to improve their grades should let their hair grow. The real cause might be gender: Women (who had longer hair) did better on the test. Or that might be a spurious relationship too. The real cause might be class rank: Seniors did better on the test than sophomores and juniors, and in this class the women (who also had longer hair) were mostly seniors, whereas the men (with shorter hair) were mostly sophomores and juniors.

SQL   Standardized Query Language. A widely used database programming language. Such database languages are becoming increasingly important in quantitative analyses in social research with the growing use of *data mining of *big data.

Square-Root Transformation   Transformation of positive valued (nonnegative) data obtained by taking the square root of the dependent variable (most typically), independent variable, or both. This transformation of the dependent variable is sometimes done for count variables or for the goal of achieving linearity and reducing skewness.

SRC   Survey Research Center. Located at the University of Michigan, this organization is known for its many national longitudinal studies, such as the National Election Survey, the Survey of Consumers, and the Monitoring the Future Survey. See *archive, *secondary analysis.

SRMR   *Standardized root mean square residual.

Ss   Abbreviation for the *subjects in a study, as in "Ss were 147 sophomores taking introductory psychology." The abbreviation is not used much anymore.

SS   Sum of squares, that is, the sum of the squared deviations of scores from the *mean. For an illustration, see *sum of squares.

SSE   *Sum of squared errors. See also *error or *residual.

Stability, Coefficient of   See *coefficient of stability.

Staggered Implementation   A research design in which it is difficult to assign participants to control and experimental groups at the same time—often because everybody wants to be in the experimental group and receive the new software, training, equipment, screening program, or treatment. In staggered implementation researchers offer the treatment to *all* interested participants but randomly assign (often by a lottery) the date each group begins receiving the intervention: week 1, week 4, week 7, week 10, and so on. The groups that receive the treatment later serve as the control groups as well as, eventually, the experimental groups. This design has ethical as well as analytical benefits.

Standard   A criterion or outcome believed to be desirable. It is an agreed-on criterion, often established by an evaluator in conjunction with a stakeholder. Known published standards are provided by a standards body, such as the American National Standards Institute (ANSI). The goal in practice is to meet desired standard(s).

Standard Deviation (SD)   A *statistic that shows the *spread, *variability, or *dispersion of scores in a *distribution of scores. It is a measure of the approximate average amount the scores in a distribution deviate from the *mean. The more widely the scores are spread out, the larger the standard deviation. The standard deviation is the square root of the *variance. As a variable, it is symbolized: *SD, Sd, s,* or lowercase sigma (σ). Compare *Tchebechev's theorem. For an illustration, see *sum of squares.

The standard deviation is an important statistic both in its own right and because it is the basis of many other statistics such as *correlations and *standard errors, as well as for all other *standard scores such as the *stanine and the *z score.

When a distribution is normal or approximately normal, about two thirds (68%) of the scores in the distribution will fall between 1 SD below and 1 SD above the mean; about 95% will fall between 2 SD below and 2 SD above the mean; over 99% will be located plus or minus 3 SDs from the mean. For example, the height of women aged 18 to 24 in the United States is about 65 inches. The SD is 2.5 inches. Since the distribution is approximately normal, this means that 68% of the women are between 62.5 and 67.5 inches and 95% are between 60 and 70 inches.

In Table S.7, three distributions of scores, A, B, and C, are shown with their means and standard deviations. Like other measures of dispersion, the SD tells you how good the measure of *central tendency (in this case, the mean) is as an estimate of a value in the distribution. In distribution A, the mean is a perfect estimate and *SD* is zero. In distribution C, by contrast, *SD* is high and the mean of 35 is a poor estimate of any particular score in the distribution.

Table S.7   Standard Deviation

Distribution										Mean	SD
A	35	35	35	35	35	35	35	35	35	35	**35**	**0.0**
B	28	29	30	32	34	36	38	40	41	42	**35**	**5.2**
C	1	2	4	5	24	46	65	66	68	69	**35**	**30.6**

Standard Error   The standard error is the *standard deviation of the *sampling distribution of a statistic. It is a measure of *sampling error; it refers to error in our estimates due to random fluctuations in our samples. It is a measure of the predicted instability of a statistic from one random sample to another. It goes down as the number of cases (*N) goes up. The smaller the standard error, the better the *sample statistic is as an estimate of the *population parameter—at least under most conditions. See *standard error of the mean, *standard error of estimate.

Standard Error of a Proportion (SEP)   Analogous to the *standard error of the mean. The difference is that the SEP is the standard deviation of the sampling distribution of a proportion rather than the sampling distribution of the mean. See *sampling distribution of a statistic.

Standard Error of Estimate (SEE)   In regression, the SEE is the standard error of the *residuals. In simple regression, it is an estimate of the amount of variation around the population *regression line. The "error" is how much you are off when using the regression line to predict particular scores. More technically, the "standard error" is the *standard deviation of the errors from the population regression line (i.e., it tells you how much variation there would be around the population regression line over repeated sampling).

The lower the SEE, the higher the degree of linear relationship between the two variables in the regression. The SEE is used when placing *confidence intervals around the predicted mean value of Y for any particular value of X (i.e., if you put confidence interval around a point on the regression line). The larger the SEE, the less confidence one can put in the estimate (and the wider confidence intervals around these points on the line will be). As a variable, symbolized s_{yx} to distinguish it from s (i.e., the standard deviation of the scores—not the error scores).

Standard Error of Forecast (or Standard Error of Prediction) If a regression equation is used to predict the value on the dependent variable for a forecasted point using time-series data or for a future observation for a specific individual, this standard error is used to put the "confidence interval" around the predicted value. This prediction interval will be wider than one that is calculated using the *standard error of the estimate.

Standard Error of Measurement (SEM) This is a concept used in measurement or psychometric theory, and it is commonly used when reporting a standardized test result for an individual. You will recall that *confidence intervals are often placed around point estimates (such as the mean or a percentage) in inferential statistics to make sure readers do not overinterpret the point estimate (because we know point estimates vary from sample to sample). The analogous concept in testing is to put a "confidence interval" around an individual's score. SEM specifically refers to the value of the standard deviation that would be found for an *individual's* test score upon repeated testing (i.e., if that individual were to take the test an infinite number of times). The SEM must be estimated using group data.

Standard Error of the Difference Between Two Means Analogous to the *standard error of the mean. The difference is that this standard error is the standard deviation of the sampling distribution of the difference between two means. See *sampling distribution of a statistic.

Standard Error of the Mean A statistic indicating how greatly the *mean score of a single *sample is likely to differ from the mean score of a *population. It is the *standard deviation of a *sampling distribution of the mean. The standard error of the mean indicates how much the sample mean differs from the *expected value (which is the mean of the sampling distribution of the means). By so doing, it gives an answer to the question: How good an estimate of the population mean is the sample mean? It is calculated by dividing the standard deviation of the sample by the square root of the number of cases (*n). Compare *sampling error. See *sampling distribution of a statistic.

S

Standard Gamble   A *game theory concept referring to the risk a sick person is willing to take when the choice is between a treatment that can lead to improvement in the quality of life, but when there is also a possibility that the treatment will be fatal.

Standardization of Data   Turning scores or data points into *standard scores. See *z score, *stanine.

Standardized Mean Difference   Type of *effect size for comparing two means. Examples of this kind of effect size are *Cohen's *d,* Hedge's *g,* and Glass's delta. This popular type of effect size is used in *meta-analysis. It shows the difference between two groups in standard deviation units.

Standardized Measure or Scale   Any statistic that allows comparisons between things measured on different scales or using different *metrics. The best known is a percentage; others include *percentile ranks and *z scores.

Standardized Regression Coefficient   A statistic that provides a way to compare the relative importance of different variables in a *multiple regression analysis; comparison is possible because the *regression coefficients are expressed as z scores. Often symbolized as beta and called the *beta weight or *beta coefficient (not to be confused with the "beta" used to symbolize *Type II error). Also called standard partial regression coefficient (the term "partial" indicates that the effects of other variables have been held constant). The unstandardized coefficient *b* is an *asymmetric measure; beta is *symmetric.

Standardized Residual   Statistic for identifying outliers (and used in many plots for checking model assumptions). A *residual is Y minus Y-hat (i.e., $Y - \hat{Y}$), where Y is the observed value of the variable and $\hat{Y}$ is its *predicted value. It is standardized by dividing the observed residual by the standard deviation of the residuals. The result is a residual in z score units, with a mean of 0 and a standard deviation of 1. Values greater than 2.58 or less than −2.58 are often considered to be outliers.

Standardized Root Mean Square Residual Index (SRMR)   A statistic used in *structural equation modeling to indicate model fit. It is an absolute fit index, measuring the difference between the observed and predicted correlations. It is a mean absolute correlation residual. Reasonable fit is present when it is less than or equal to .08.

Standardized Score   A score coming from a set of scores that has been adjusted to have a particular mean and standard deviation. For example, *z scores have a mean of 0 and a standard deviation of 1, many IQ tests have a mean of 100 and a standard deviation of 15, and *T scores have a mean of 50 and a mean of 10.

Standardized Test   (a) A *norm-referenced test such as the SAT or the GRE. As in any norm-referenced test, an individual's grade is a measure of how well he or she did in comparison to a large group of prior test takers; that prior group was used to determine the norm (i.e., it is the group upon which the test has been "standardized").

(b) "Standardized" also refers to the conditions under which the test is taken (the same directions, materials, amount of time, and so on).

Standard Metropolitan Statistical Area (SMSA) A U.S. Census category designating an area made up of a central city of 50,000 or more residents and the surrounding region economically tied to it. The term was first used in the 1960 census, when 212 such areas were identified. Compare *census tract.

Standard Normal Deviate Another term for *standard score or *z score.

Standard Normal Distribution A *normal distribution with a *mean of 0 and a *standard deviation of 1.

Standard Partial Regression Coefficient Another term for *standardized regression coefficient in cases with two or more *independent variables; the coefficient is expressed as a *z score.

Standard Score Any of several derived measures of relative standing in a group; they are converted from *raw scores. Using standard scores allows one to compare scores from different *distributions. The most common standard score is the *z score or "sigma score." See also *T score, *stanine, *standard deviation. *Proportions and percentages are sometimes called "standard scores."

For example, suppose you are a student and you want to compare your scores on the final examinations in each of your five classes. This could be complicated, especially if each of the exams had a different number of questions and each of the classes enrolled a different number of students. You could convert your scores on each of your exams into standard scores. The higher your standard score for each class, the better you did in comparison to other students in that class. The examination with the highest of the five standard scores would be the one on which you did best.

Stanine Short for standard ninth or standard of nine. A *standard score scale widely used in school achievement tests. The scale has nine values or stanines: 1, 2, 3, 4, 5, 6, 7, 8, 9. Stanines 2 through 8 are one half of a *standard deviation wide. Stanine 5 straddles the mean (one quarter of a standard deviation above and below). Stanines 1 and 9 include scores that are, respectively, more than 1.75 standard deviations below and above the mean. Stanine distributions have a mean of 5 and a standard deviation of 2. Compare *z score, *normal curve equivalent.

STATA A statistics and graphics software package.

Stationarity A common assumption in *time-series analysis. It is the assumption that the variance, mean, and autocorrelation do not change over time in the series; when this is true the process is said to be stationary.

S

Statistic   A number, such as a *mean or a *correlation coefficient, that describes some characteristic of (the "status" of) a *variable or of a group of *data.

Strictly speaking, statistics are used to describe *samples and are usually abbreviated or symbolized by English (Roman) letters. *Parameters are equivalent measures for *populations and are abbreviated or symbolized by Greek letters. In common usage, "statistics" is used for both samples and parameters.

Statistical Conclusion Validity   The accuracy of conclusions about *covariation (or *correlation) made on the basis of statistical evidence. More specifically, inferences about whether it is reasonable to conclude that covariation exists—given a particular *alpha level and given the *variances obtained in the study. See *validity, *statistical significance.

Statistical Control   Using statistical techniques to isolate or "subtract" *variance in the *dependent variable attributable to variables that are not the subject of study. See *control for, *partial out, *ANCOVA.

Statistical Hypotheses   The two hypotheses used in statistical *hypothesis testing, specifically the *null hypothesis and the *alternative hypothesis. These statistical hypotheses are always expressed as *population parameters, not *sample statistics, because the hypotheses refer to properties of the *populations of interest.

Statistical Independence   A state in which there is no measured relation between two or more *variables. So called because the statistic describing one variable is independent of (has no association with) a statistic describing another variable or variables. See *orthogonal relationship.

Statistical Inference   Using *probability theory and information about a *sample to draw conclusions ("inferences") about a *population. Specifically, one asks the following question: How likely is it that this result (e.g., a mean difference, a correlation) in a sample of this size could have been obtained by chance—if there were no difference in the population from which the sample was drawn? If the probability is low (less than 5% is a common cutoff), then the results are declared statistically significant and are used to draw conclusions about the population. Sometimes called "statistical induction." See *sampling distribution, *external validity.

The same basic statistical concepts are used whether the research is on a representative sample of 1,500 adults surveyed about their attitudes toward political candidates or whether the research is about memory under three different experimental conditions tested on a group of 90 undergraduates. In the latter case, however, the investigators would put much more emphasis on internal than on external validity; that is, they would be more interested in establishing differences among the treatments than in directly generalizing the findings to a broader population.

Statistical Learning A set of prediction and classification techniques that involve first developing a model from *training data and then using what is learned on test data. Widely used in *data mining; also called "machine learning."

Statistical Package A type of *software that is a collection of *programs for doing statistical procedures with a computer. *SPSS and *SAS are among the more widely used statistical packages in the social and behavioral sciences. See also *R, *LISREL, *STATA, *S-PLUS, *MINITAB.

Statistical Power A gauge of the sensitivity of a *statistical test, that is, its ability to detect effects of a specific size, given the particular *variance and *sample size of a study. It is equal to 1 minus the probability of *Type II or beta error (e.g., if power is .80, then the probability of a Type II error is .20). One popular rule of thumb is to select enough subjects when planning your research study to help you achieve power of *at least* .80. See also *power of a test, *sensitivity.

For example, if power is .80, the probability of a Type II error is .20. In this case, you would reject the *null hypothesis 80% of the time that it is false and make a Type II error (fail to reject a false null) 20% of the time.

Statistical Regression A tendency for those who score high on any measure to get somewhat lower scores on a subsequent measure of the same thing—or, conversely, for someone who has scored very low on some measure to get a somewhat higher score the next time the same thing is measured. Also called *regression toward the mean because the second score is likely to move toward or be closer to the mean or average score. Compare *regression, *regression analysis, *regression artifact.

For example, someone who got a 150 on one version of an IQ test would be more likely to get a score of 149 or lower than a score of 151 or higher when taking a second version of the test.

Statistical Significance Said of a value or measure of a variable when it is ("significantly") larger or smaller than would be expected by chance alone. Compare *level of significance, *probability level, *practical significance, *substantive significance.

It is important to remember that statistical significance does not necessarily imply *substantive or *practical significance. A large sample size very often leads to results that are statistically significant, even when they might be otherwise quite inconsequential.

Calculations of statistical significance are most meaningful on samples that have been randomly selected or on groups that have been randomly assigned. They are of doubtful value without random selection or random assignment. That is because measures of statistical significance are designed to assess the probability of a result *in a random* sample.

Statistical Test Another term for *test statistic, that is, any of several tests of the statistical significance of findings. Statistical tests provide information about how likely it is that sample results are due to *random error.

Statistics   (a) Numerical summaries of data obtained by measurement and computation. (b) The branch of mathematics dealing with the collection and analysis of numerical data. "Statistics" originally meant quantitative information about the government or state—"state-istics." See *official statistics.

Statistics, Descriptive   See *descriptive statistics.

Statistics, Inferential   See *inferential statistics.

Stem-and-Leaf Display   A way of recording the values of a *variable, created by John Tukey, that presents *raw numbers in a visual, *histogram-like display. It is a *histogram in which the bars are built out of numbers.

   For example, if 40 students took a final examination in a course, their scores could be shown as in Table S.8. To represent the scores 56, 57, and 59, you put a 5 in the 10s column and a 6, a 7, and a 9 in the 1s column, and so on with the rest of the scores. The display makes it clear that most students scored in the 80s, not many in the 50s and 60s, and so on. The main advantage of a stem-and-leaf display is that it yields a clear picture of the frequency distribution, but unlike most graphic representations, it loses none of the numerical data. Turning the diagram on its side, it is easy to see, for example, that the distribution is *skewed to the left.

Table S.8   Stem-and-Leaf Display of Final Examination Scores

Stem (10s)	Leaves (1s) (Leaf Unit = 1)
5	679
6	02559
7	4466688
8	11233334444567799
9	22236778

Step Diagram (or Step Function)   A graph of a *cumulative frequency distribution. So called because when categorical variables are graphed, the result resembles (usually uneven) stair steps.

Stepdown Selection   Another term for *backward elimination.

Stepup Selection   Another term for *forward selection.

Stepwise Discriminant Analysis   *Discriminant analysis using a *stepwise procedure for *variable selection. Note: Stepwise procedures are not used for *variable ordering in *explanatory research.

Stepwise Regression   (a) A technique for calculating a *regression equation that instructs a computer to find the "best" equation by entering *independent variables in various combinations and orders. Stepwise regression combines the methods of *backward elimination and *forward selection. One by one, the variables are in turn subject first to the inclusion criteria of forward selection and then to the exclusion procedures of backward elimination. Variables are selected and eliminated until there are none left that meet the criteria for removal. Stepwise regression is often, but inconsistently, contrasted with *hierarchical regression analysis in which the researcher, not the computer program, determines the order of the variables in the regression equation. Although stepwise routines are widely available in statistical packages, nearly all statisticians recommend against using them, except perhaps for the most exploratory studies in which the researcher has absolutely no idea about how the variables might be related.

(b) A less common use of "stepwise" is to describe regression in which the researcher enters the variables in a logical, theoretical order. Note that this is almost the exact opposite of definition (a), and it should, to avoid ambiguity, be referred to as "hierarchical regression."

Stochastic *Random or *probabilistic. Thus, a stochastic variable is a *random variable. Said of a *model that is *probabilistic and contains *random elements—as opposed to a *deterministic model. Also used to refer to trial-and-error procedures—in contrast to *algorithmic procedures. Although the term has ancient Greek roots and originated in statistics in the 18th century (with Daniel Bernoulli), it wasn't until around 1900 that statisticians began, for unknown reasons, replacing the word "random" with the word "stochastic." The practice has spread enough that today these synonyms are about equally common in statistical discourse.

Stochastic Models Attempts to describe the structure of *systematic and *random error in a set of observations. Compare *ARIMA, *chaos theory.

Stochastic Process (a) A *random process. (b) When the *probabilities of the occurrence of an event change over time—particularly when the empirical probability approaches the theoretical probability—this is referred to as a stochastic process. See *Markov chain.

Stopping Rules Criteria, stated in advance, for ending an experiment early, as when one treatment is shown to be clearly superior to another or when a treatment causes harm to participants. Compare *sequential analysis.

Stratified Nonrandom Sample See *quota sample. Compare *stratified random sample.

Stratified Random Sample A *sampling frame is stratified, and then a random or *probability sample is drawn from each of the particular categories (or "strata") of the population being studied. You could stratify based on gender by sorting the sampling frame by gender (i.e., the females are followed by the males). The method works best when the individuals within the strata are highly similar to one another and different from individuals in other strata. Indeed, if the strata were not different from one another, there would be no point in stratifying. The strata have a function similar to that of blocks in *randomized-blocks designs. Stratified random sampling can be proportionate so that the sizes of the strata correspond to the sizes of the groups in the population—this is an *equal probability of selection method (EPSEM). It can also be disproportionate, as in the following example.

Suppose you wanted to compare the attitudes of Protestants, Catholics, Muslims, and Jews in a population in which those four groups were not present in equal numbers. If you drew a *simple random sample, you might not get enough cases from one of the groups to make meaningful comparisons. To avoid this problem, you could select random samples of equal size within each of the four religious groups (strata). In order to make this disproportionate stratified sample an *EPSEM, statistical *weighting would be applied.

Stratified Sampling   Usually short for *stratified random sampling.

Stratifying   Dividing a *population into groups or "strata" before doing research on it. See *stratified random sampling.

Stratum (plural: Strata)   A subgroup of a *population. Such groups are used, for example, in *stratified random sampling.

Strength of Association   The degree of relationship between two (or more) variables, as measured by statistics such as *R, *r, *eta, *phi, *regression coefficients (*standardized and *unstandardized), *structure coefficients, and *factor loadings. Often, strength of association indexes are converted to indexes showing the proportion of the *variability in a *dependent variable explained by or accounted for by the *independent variable(s). *Eta squared, *omega squared, and R^2 are common measures of strength of association converted to measures that account for the variance. Compare *coefficient of determination, measure of *association. Also called "strength of effect index."

Strength of Effect Index   Another term for a measure of *strength of association or variance-accounted-for indexes. See *effect size.

Structural Coefficients   Another term for unstandardized *path coefficients; they are *regression coefficients in *structural equation models and in path analysis.

Structural Equation   An *equation representing the strength and nature of the hypothesized relations among (the "structure" of) sets of *variables in a *theory or *model. Each *endogenous variable has a structural equation. See *structural equation modeling.

Structural Equation Modeling (SEM)   Models made up of more than one structural equation; thus models that describe causal relations among *latent variables and include coefficients for paths leading to *endogenous variables. SEM is a sophisticated statistical method for testing complex *causal models in which the dependent and independent variables (or endogenous and exogenous variables) are *latent. A latent variable is one that cannot be observed directly. It is a *construct, that is, a theoretical entity inferred from a pattern of relations (a *structure) among observable variables. SEM combines the techniques of *factor analysis, *path analysis, and *multiple regression analysis, thus allowing researchers to study the effects of *latent variables on each other. Analyses are frequently done with the *LISREL, *EQS, *Mplus, or *AMOS computer programs. Also called *analysis of covariance structures. See *confirmatory factor analysis. Compare *canonical correlation analysis.

*Model fit is determined using multiple fit indices, including *adjusted goodness-of-fit, *chi-square index for SEM, *comparative fit index, *goodness-of-fit index, *root mean square error of approximation, *standardized root mean square residual, *Tucker-Lewis index, and *weighted root mean square residual.

For example, take this apparently simple statement: The more intelligent a person is, the more likely he or she is to be successful. Both intelligence and success are constructs, latent variables that are constructed out of observations. To begin a study, one might sketch the relationship between intelligence and success in the kind of *path diagram shown in Figure S.8. (A full SEM path diagram would be much more complex and would include a detailed notation system.) Boxes stand for observed variables; those on the left are measurable aspects of intelligence; those on the right, measurable components of success. Circles represent the latent variables.

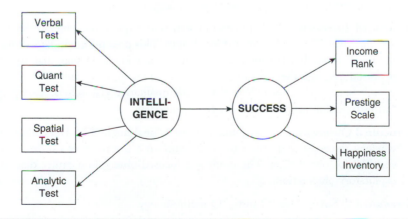

Figure S.8   Structural Equation Model

Note the direction of the arrows. Intelligence is hypothesized to cause success, so the arrow runs from intelligence to success. But the arrows run the other way from the latent variables (circles) to the observed variables (boxes). The verbal test scores, the spatial test scores, and so on do not cause intelligence. Rather, they are caused by it. Compare *principal components analysis, *factor analysis,

Structuralism An approach from anthropology, associated with C. Levi-Strauss, that investigates cultures by studying the structures of language. A main example is the structure of opposites in language-cum-culture, such as sacred-profane and raw-cooked. The structuralism of Levi-Strauss is one of the progenitors of *semiology and has been extended or opposed in recent times by *deconstructionism.

Structural Model The structural model, in *structural equation modeling, shows the relationships among the latent variables and is the substantive theory to be tested. Also called the "causal model." See *measurement model.

Structure Any underlying stable pattern among *variables in a system, such as a social, economic, political, or cognitive system.

Structure Coefficient A correlation between a variate or linear combination and a single variable. (a) In multiple regression, it's the correlation between a particular *independent variable and the *predicted Y (which is based on the entire set of independent variables). It is an alternative measure of the relative importance of the independent variable (see *variable ordering). (b) In *discriminant analysis, the structure coefficient (also called a discriminant loading) is the correlation between a predictor variable and the discriminant function scores. It is used to determine the nature of the dimensions on which the groups are differentiated. (c) In *factor analysis and *confirmatory factor analysis in *SEM, it's the correlation between a *latent variable (a *factor) and an observed variable; it also is called a *loading in this context.

Structured Interview An interview in which the questions, their ordering, and their wording are determined in advance. This presents a standard stimulus to all research participants, reducing certain kinds of bias that might be introduced into the data collection process. This approach is more popular among quantitative researchers than with qualitative researchers. Compare *semistructured interview, *unstructured interview.

Structured Observation A systematic observational method of data collection whereby the researcher enters the field with an a priori set of categories or variables for observation. The result is a focused observation rather than an exploratory observation.

Structured Q Sorts See *Q sorts, *Q methodology.

Studentized Deleted Residual (also called **Studentized Residual**) Statistic used in *outlier detection; it is the Studentized *residual (amount of unexplained variance) that would be found if the regression model were rerun without including the particular case or observation. It shows the influence of the case on the model. It approximately follows a t distribution, with $(n - 1) - p$ degrees of freedom, where n is the number of cases and p is the number of predictor variables plus 1.

Studentized Range Statistic   A t-like statistic used to determine the *critical value in the *Tukey HSD test. See *multiple comparisons.

Studentized Residual   A type of residual (unexplained variance) standardized using the *t distribution; specifically, it uses a *t distribution, with $(n - 1) - p$ degrees of freedom, where n is the number of cases and p is the number of predictor variables plus 1.

Student's t Distributions   A family of theoretical *probability distributions used in *hypothesis testing. As with *normal distributions, t distributions are unimodal, symmetrical, and bell shaped. Called Student's t because the author of the article that made the distribution well known (W. S. Gosset) used the pen name "Student."

The t distribution is especially important for interpreting data gathered on small samples when the population *variance is unknown; when it is known (which is rare), the z test is more appropriate. The larger the sample, the more closely the t approximates the normal distribution. For samples larger than 120, the z and t distributions are practically equivalent.

Subject   An individual who is studied in order to gather *data for a study. Often called a "research participant" or *participant. The individual is often a person, but it need not be; individual cities, occupations, small businesses, white mice, and so on can also be subjects. Compare *unit of analysis.

Subject Bias   See *demand characteristics.

Subjective   Having to do with inner, personal characteristics of an individual that characterize his or her experiences and decision-making process. Compare *objective. Often refers to data that can be obtained only from the subject of research, for example, in the answer to the question: "How would you rate your pain on a scale of $0 - 10$?" There is no objective "painometer" to rate the subjects' condition, only their subjective ratings.

Subjective Methods   Any approach to the analysis and evaluation of data based on the researcher's personal judgments, feelings, or intuitions about the topic being studied. Sometimes the term is used pejoratively and contrasted with scientific methods. Compare *qualitative.

Subjective Phenomenon   Something that can be learned only from a *subject; hence, something that is dependent on a subject's perceptions and self-reports and not on information that can be observed directly by someone other than the subject.

S

For example, the answer to the question "Do you *like* high-fiber breakfast cereals?" seeks subjective information. On the other hand, "Do you *eat* such cereals?" seeks *objective information; researchers might be able to check the answer to the second question if they doubt the accuracy of the subject's response. In medicine, to take an important example, pain research is based almost entirely on patients' subjective reports of the intensity of their pain; the same is true of measures of happiness in quality-of-life research. The branch of *qualitative research called *phenomenology focuses on subjects' reports of their experience of phenomena,

Subjective Probability   The strength of an individual's belief in the probability of an outcome. *Prior probabilities in *Bayesian inference are subjective probabilities. Also called "personal probabilities."

Subject Matching   See *matched pairs.

Subject Role   Problematic behaviors sometimes taken on by research participants, including, for example, *apprehensive-subject role, *faithful-subject role, *good-subject role, and *negative-subject role.

Subject Sophistication   (a) Ability of some research participants to figure out the detailed purposes of the study and to provide responses that would otherwise have been different. (b) Ability of participants to hide or lie about their true beliefs and deceive the researcher.

Subjects' Rights   See *research ethics, *IRB, *dehoaxing, *anonymity.

Subpopulation   A group in a population. A population often comprises multiple groups, such as those defined by gender, age, ethnicity, place of residence, occupation, and so on. Also called "subgroups" or "subpopulations."

Subscale   A part of a larger scale that measures a single, smaller, lower level factor. For example, the Organizational Commitment Scale includes three subscales, each measured by three items; the subscales measure commitment based on affiliation or pride in the organization, commitment based on satisfactory exchange with the organization, and commitment based on identification with the organization. Note that *Cronbach's alpha coefficients should always be computed for each of the subscales.

Subscript   A number or letter written below and to the right of a symbol to distinguish it from the same symbol with a different subscript.
For example, the number of cases in group 1 and group 2 might be written N_1 for group 1 and N_2 for group 2.

Subset   A *set contained within another set.
For example, if every *element in one set, accountants (A), is also an element of another set, human beings (H), then A is a subset of H.

Substantive Hypothesis Like any hypothesis, a substantive hypothesis is a conjecture about the relation between two or more variables. It is called "substantive" because it has not yet been *operationalized and in order to distinguish it from the kind of statistical hypothesis used in *hypothesis testing. See *null hypothesis.

For example, "Poor people have fewer 'life chances'" is a substantive hypothesis. To test it, we would need operational definitions of "poor" and "life chances." Perhaps we would use having an annual income less than half of the median for "poor" and average life expectancy for "life chances." We would then need to put the hypothesis into statistical form, perhaps as follows: The mean life expectancy for poor persons (MLP) is less than the mean life expectancy for non-poor persons (MLNP), or MLP < MLNP.

Substantive Significance Said of a research finding when it reveals something meaningful about the object of study. Often used in contrast with "mere" *statistical significance, which is present when a finding is unlikely to be due to chance alone. Of course, a result that is not statistically significant is often not substantively significant. Also called *practical significance.

For example, suppose we took large random samples of police officers in California and in New York. Comparing some of the data, we find that the mean weight of California officers is 173 pounds, while that of New York officers is 177 pounds. If the sample were large and representative, even this small difference would be unlikely to be due to chance, or *sampling error, alone; it would be statistically significant. But it would be hard to find someone who thought that the 4-pound difference in weight told us anything substantively significant about law enforcement officers in the two states.

Success In *probability experiments, an event that happens as predicted. The term "success" is usually applied arbitrarily to one of two ways a *Bernoulli trial can turn out. If success were drawing a black card, then "*failure" would be drawing a red card.

Sufficient Condition In *causal analysis, a *variable or event that, by itself, is always enough ("sufficient") to bring about a change in another variable or event. In practice, this is rarely achieved in social or behavioral empirical science because these disciplines routinely document probabilistic rather than deterministic relationships. The concepts of necessary and sufficient conditions are more commonly used in logical constructions of causation, which are popular in philosophy, political science, computer science, and decision science. Compare *necessary condition.

Many sufficient conditions are not exclusive. A patient might die of cancer, a heart attack, an infection, an aneurism, or any of several other ailments. These will not always lead to death because people sometimes survive these conditions (the conditions can be sufficient, but they are not necessary). Each of these sufficient conditions increases the probability of death but does not inevitably bring it about. Retrospectively, however, each of these ailments may be a sufficient *explanation* for a death. Thus, a condition that is sufficient to explain may not be sufficient to predict.

Loosely speaking, sufficient conditions are easy to find, but finding an *exclusive* sufficient condition, or even one that greatly narrows the range of possible sufficient conditions, is rare. If the sufficient causes of an outcome are very numerous, then they are not very instructive: A riot can be caused by a religious conflict, an election dispute, an encounter of opposing football fans, a food shortage, a rumor, and many other circumstances. But most religious conflicts, election disputes, and so on do not lead to riots. When the list of sufficient conditions is long and varies greatly from case to case, and any one of the conditions only occasionally brings about a particular outcome, sufficient conditions provide the researcher with very little clarification. This is the typical situation in the social and behavioral sciences.

Summary Table   Synonym for *source table. Table in *ANOVA including source, sum of squares, degrees of freedom, mean square, and F ratio. Users are advised to also include a column for effect size, preferably eta squared rather than partial eta squared. For an example of a summary table, see *analysis of variance. Compare to *analysis of deviance.

Summated Scale   A *scale or *index made up of several items measuring the same variable. The responses are given numbers in such a way that responses can be added up ("summated"). When this is done, it is typical, but not quite accurate, to treat the index as being measured on an *interval scale of measurement.

For example, say we have an attitude index about government responsibility made up of five questions in the following form: "The government in Washington should see to it that women and minorities do not experience job discrimination: strongly agree = 4; agree = 3; disagree = 2; strongly disagree = 1." Respondents' answers to the five questions can be added to arrive at a single number that measures the positive or negative strength of their attitudes. On a five-item index using the above numbers, the highest possible score would be 20—strongly agree (4) with all five statements: $4 \times 5 = 20$; the lowest would be 5—strongly disagree (1) with all five: $1 \times 5 = 5$.

Summative Evaluation   *Evaluation research conducted in the latter stages of a program to assess its impact or to determine how well it has met its goals. Summative evaluations are often undertaken to help policymakers decide whether to continue, expand, reduce, or terminate a program's funding. Compare *formative evaluation.

When assessing products, formative evaluation would be part of product development; one would find summative evaluations in *Consumer Reports* magazine.

Sum of Squared Errors (SSE) In a *regression analysis, the SSE is what you are trying to minimize when you use the *ordinary least squares criterion. The *errors in question are the vertical distances of the observed scores from the *regression line (or predicted scores). Also called the sum of squared *residuals. See *slope.

Sum of Squares (SS) The result of adding together the squares of *deviation scores. *Analysis of variance is in fact an analysis of the sums of squares, which are converted to variances by simply dividing them by their degrees of freedom. See *within samples, *between, *total, and *regression sum of squares. Not to be confused, when doing calculations, with the "square of sums," that is, all the scores first added together to get a sum, which is then squared.

For example, Table S.9 lists the scores on a test, calculates the *mean, subtracts the mean from each score, squares each of those results, and adds (sums) these numbers. Computing the sum of squares is a step on the way to calculating the *variance and the *standard deviation. The variance for a *population* is found by dividing the sum of squares by the number of scores. You use the number of scores minus 1 for the *sample* variance (238 divided by 6 = 39.67 in this example). The standard deviation is calculated by taking the square root of the variance (which equals 6.3 in this example).

Table S.9 Sum of Squares

Scores X	Minus Mean		Deviation Score $(X - \bar{X})$	Deviation Score Squared $(X - \bar{X})^2$
88	−80	=	8	64
86	−80	=	6	36
84	−80	=	4	16
80	−80	=	0	0
77	−80	=	−3	9
73	−80	=	−7	49
72	−80	=	−8	64
560			0	238
				(Sum of squares)

560/7 = 80
(Mean)

Superfluous Variable In *regression analysis, an *independent or *predictor variable that adds nothing to the total variance explained (*R^2) by the regression equation.

Superscript   A number or letter written above and to the right of a symbol; often used to denote its *power.

For example, the 3 in 8^3 is a superscript and means 8 times 8 times 8 (which equals 512).

Suppressor Effect   See *suppressor variable.

Suppressor Variable   A variable that conceals or reduces (suppresses) a relationship between other variables. Here's an example of "classical suppression": Suppose we were testing candidates for the job of forest ranger. We are sure that a good forest ranger must know a lot of botany; we also think that verbal ability has no effect on rangers' job performance. We give a written botany test to help us pick good rangers. But since the test is written, candidates with stronger verbal ability will tend to get higher scores, even if their knowledge of botany is no greater. In this example, verbal ability is the suppressor variable. It gets in the way of studying what we are interested in: knowledge of botany and rangers' job competencies.

To take another example, education tends to increase people's liberalism. But education tends to increase people's incomes, and increased income tends to reduce people's liberalism. In this case, income is the suppressor variable. See the illustration in Figure S.9 and compare it with the *reinforcer effect.

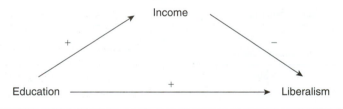

Figure S.9   Suppressor Variable

Sometimes specialized types of suppressor variables are discussed in the research literature. Here are the definitions that authors typically use for three major types of suppression: (a) Assume X_2 and Y are not correlated. If adding X_2 (to the original regression of Y on just X_1) increases the multiple correlation, then you have *classical suppression.* Alternatively stated, $R^2_{Y.12} > r^2_{Y.1}$ even though Y and X_2 are not correlated. (b) Assume X_1, X_2, and Y are all positively correlated. If X_2 has a negative *partial regression coefficient (showing the relationship between X_2 and Y controlling for X_1), then you have *net suppression.* (c) Assume that X_1 and X_2 are negatively correlated with each other. Also assume that X_1 and X_2 are both positively correlated with Y. If X_1 and X_2 each explain more of the variance in Y when included together (Y regressed on X_1 and X_2) than when each is included by itself (Y regressed on X_1 and Y regressed on X_2), then you have *cooperative suppression.*

Surrogate Variable or Endpoint   When an outcome of interest is difficult to study, researchers often use a surrogate. This is usually a presumed *mediating variable. For example, if the outcome of interest were whether a medication reduced death from heart disease, researchers might use lowering cholesterol level as a surrogate, because this is assumed to lead to the outcome of interest, lowering the number of deaths. Surrogate endpoints are usually faster and easier to measure, but they *assume* a causal link rather than test for one directly. The term is not widely used in social research, but the practice of using surrogate endpoints is fairly common there. Compare *proxy variable. See *social indicator.

Survey   A research *design in which a *sample of subjects is drawn from a *population and studied (e.g., via interviews or questionnaires) in order to make inferences about the population. A *census is a survey of an entire population; when contrasted with a census, a survey is then called a *sample survey. See *random sample.

Survey Experiment   A type of experiment conducted while administering a survey often to study the effect of different types of question or question wording. For example, respondents are randomly assigned to answer differently worded questions and their answers are compared. Survey experiments are one of the few research designs that commonly combine *random sampling and *random assignment.

Survival Analysis   The study of how long subjects persist ("survive") in a state, a *categorical* variable. By contrast, *time-series analyses examine change in a *continuous* variable over time. Survival analysis has been used in medical research to study the duration of illnesses, in demography to study life expectancy, and in organizational studies to analyze the survival of small businesses. Survival analysis is a variety of *event history analysis in which there are a limited number of states or conditions. Analytic techniques used in survival analysis are forms of *regression analysis. See *Cox regression, *discrete time event history analysis, *Kaplan-Meier analysis, and, for an example, *competing risks.

Survival Function   A function (or curve) describing the proportion of subjects remaining in a risk set for an event (e.g., marriage, divorce, death, airplane engine stops working, recidivism) that have not experienced a specific event by a specific time after they enter the risk set. The curve or function starts at 100% and shows the percentage, at successive times, of the population still surviving or in a particular state. Commonly used in *Kaplan-Meier analysis. Compare *hazard function.

Survival Rate   The proportion of people that don't experience the event (e.g., die of a disease) by a certain date. It's where the survival function (curve) levels off.

Survivorship Fallacy/Bias   The problem that occurs when one focuses only on survivors or winners, excluding those that are no longer visible. One might become naive or overoptimistic and not understand relationships among variables in science when only focusing on survivors (e.g., successful companies, successful students, survivors of war). There is nothing wrong with examining successful cases, but one also can learn from the other, more common cases.

Syllogism   A pattern of formal *deductive argument that contains a major premise, a minor premise, and a conclusion. If (but only if) the two premises are true, the conclusion necessarily (logically) follows.

For example:

Major Premise: All undergraduates like statistics.

Minor Premise: Mary is an undergraduate.

Conclusion: Mary likes statistics.

Symbolic Interactionism   An approach in sociology to the study of how people interact in groups of two or more people; the approach grew up in the context of *pragmatism in the 1930s. Most closely associated with the work of G. H. Mead and Herbert Blumer, it stresses close observation of how individuals in interaction use symbols to accomplish their purposes.

Symbolic Logic   A branch of logic that uses formal symbols, rather than ordinary language, to express its concepts. The purpose is to avoid the ambiguities of ordinary, informal, natural language. Compare *formal theory, *Boolean algebra.

Symmetric Measure   A *statistic that has the same value regardless of which *variable is thought of as *dependent and which is *independent. Compare *asymmetric measure. Examples include *Pearson's r and *Kendall's tau.

Symmetry   Property of being exactly similar or equivalent relative to an axis (e.g., in proportion, dimension, form, size, etc.). For example, the *normal curve is symmetrical around the mean because the two sides of the curve are mirror images of one another.

Synchronic   Said of research focusing on events that occurred at the same time. Usually contrasted with *diachronic. Compare *cross-sectional study.

Synechism   Term coined by Charles Sanders Peirce, referring to thinking in terms of continua rather than binaries (e.g., either/or, yes/no, true/false). Important because many behavioral and social science phenomena are best thought of as falling on continua rather than forming mutually exclusive categories.

Synergism   Term used to describe the increase in an effect when two treatments are administered jointly. Term for an *interaction effect used mostly in the context of drug testing.

Synthesis   Combining parts (e.g., *data, *concepts, *theories) to make a new whole. Sometimes contrasted with *analysis, which involves disassembling wholes to study their parts. In practice, analysis is often a step on the way to synthesis (and, over time, this synthesis will lead to a new stage of analysis).

For a statistics example, suppose we wished to calculate an average (*mean) income figure for citizens of all South American nations. Since nations report aggregate national income figures somewhat differently (some include transfer payments and others not), we might have to *disaggregate the figures. We could then analyze the parts that went into making up the total reported by each nation. Then we could perhaps figure out a way to synthesize them into a new, more general report about all the nations.

Synthetic Approach See *synthesis.

SYSTAT A statistical software package.

Systematic Error Measurement error that is consistent, not *random. See *bias. Compare *random error. Also called "invalidity." See *validity, *ARIMA.

For example, if you were to sample a population by dialing phone numbers at random, your sample would be biased; it would systematically overrepresent people who had more than one phone number and exclude people who did not have a phone.

Systematic Review Often another term for *meta-analysis. Systematic review can also refer to *literature reviews (whether using quantitative summaries or not) that stress clearly enunciated and replicable procedures for selecting studies to be reviewed and for drawing conclusions from them—as opposed to a more impressionistic approach.

Systematic Sample (also called **Systematic Random Sample**) A sample obtained by taking every "kth" subject or case from a list containing the total *population (or *sampling frame) of size N. The size of the sampling interval, k, is calculated by dividing the desired sample size, n, into the population size, N. The start point must be a *randomly* selected number between 1 and k. This type of sampling is an *equal probability of selection method, unless the sampling frame has a *periodicity problem. Systematic sampling works well when the sampling frame is in a random order. It works even better (i.e., more efficiently) if you can first stratify the sampling frame—for example, the sampling frame could be stratified by gender by listing the females and then the males, or it could be stratified by income by ordering the list from lowest to highest income level. Also called a "list sample."

For example, if you wanted to draw a systematic sample of 1,000 individuals from a telephone directory containing 100,000 names, you would divide 1,000 into 100,000 to get 100; hence, you would select every 100th name from the directory. You would start with a randomly selected number between 1 and 100—say, 47—and then select the 147th name, the 247th, the 347th, and so on.

S

It is always possible to do a simple random sample in cases where you can do a systematic sample (both require a complete list of the population). Some researchers consider simple random sampling to be more trustworthy, because its statistical properties are better known, but systematic sampling is often more convenient (if you are sampling by hand from a printed list or book), and it has the desirable property of *EPSEM in most cases.

Systematic Variance   Variance due to a cause that always influences values in one direction. It produces invalidity. Compare *bias, *cause, *systematic error.

Systems Theory   An approach or perspective in several disciplines that emphasizes studying the interrelations of the parts of a whole (the system) more than studying components in isolation from their position in an organized whole. Here's another way of putting it: A meta-theoretical approach for studying the operation and interrelations of many systems; studies subsystems and supra-systems. Tends to view phenomena as interrelated (open systems) rather than isolated (closed systems). The size of a system varies (e.g., subatomic system, solar system).

Tails (of a Distribution)   Values on the horizontal axis at the far right and far left ends of a graphic display of a distribution. If these values are extreme or "pulled" toward one end, the distribution is *skewed. The distribution represented by Figure T.1 is right skewed because it has a long, skinny tail pulled to the right (high X value) end of the distribution. The left (low X value) end of the distribution is more "fat tailed." See *two-tailed test of significance.

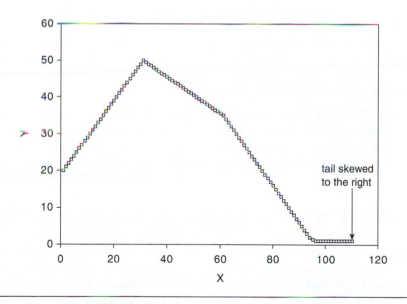

Figure T.1   Tails of a Distribution

Tamhane's T2 Post Hoc Test   Post hoc adjustment procedure in ANOVA that uses the Welch procedure and accounts for departures to homogeneity of variance. Similar procedures include *Dunnett's T3, *Games-Howell, and *Dunnett's C adjustments. Tamhane's T2 adjustment is slightly more conservative than the Games-Howell adjustment; therefore, the latter is usually preferred. See *homogeneity of variances, *violation of assumptions.

Target Population   The population about which a researcher wishes to draw conclusions; another term for a *population about which one "aims" to make inferences. Also called the "parent population."

Tau (T, τ)   (a) *Kendall's tau. (b) *Goodman and Kruskal's tau. (c) Symbol for the *population total, not the sample total. (d) A common symbol for "time" in a *time series.

Tautology   A statement or conclusion that involves *circular reasoning. This might involve, for example, taking the presence of an effect to argue for the presence of a cause, which is then claimed to bring about the effect. To avoid tautologies, one needs measures of causes and effects that are distinct, not redundant. See *training data.

Taxonomy   (a) A system of classification, originally of plants or animals; the term is sometimes used more broadly in the social and behavioral sciences to refer to classifications of personality types, political systems, and so on. (b) The systematic study of general principles of classification. Some draw a slight distinction between taxonomies and typologies, but both terms usually mean the same thing (i.e., hierarchical classification); different literatures or communities tend to prefer one term over the other.

Taylor-Russell Tables   Lists of calculations of predictions based on the *proportions of individuals who will be successful on a given *outcome, such as college graduation. The calculations involve using different cutoff scores on predictive tests, such as the SATs. These tables were important in the early history of *decision theory and are still used to illustrate some of its concepts.

Tchebechev's Theorem (or Inequality)   (See *Chebyshev's Theorem for alternative spellings.) A method for calculating the maximum *probability of a particular score in a *distribution of scores. It is used to set rough (and *conservative) outer limits for how many measurements will fall within 1, 2, and 3 *standard deviations from the mean, regardless of the shape of the distribution.

   For example, according to the theorem, at least 3/4 of the measurements in *any* distribution will fall in the range from −2 to +2 standard deviations from the mean.

t Distribution   See *student's t distribution.

T **Distribution**   The distribution used in *Hotelling's t^2 test. Also called "Hotelling's t^2 distribution." See *T test.

Temporal Precedence   Occurring earlier in time. Temporal precedence is one of the required conditions for making a claim of cause and effect. That is, changes in the independent variable must occur before changes in the dependent variable. (The other two required conditions are that a relationship between the variables must be present and there must be a lack of a plausible alternative explanation for the relationship.)

Temporal Validity   Type of *external validity, present to the degree that the results found in a study can be generalized across time. See *generalizability.

Term   Part of an *equation. For example, in a *regression equation, the *error term *e* is added to the other values in the equation.

Tertiary Prevention Research   Research focused on minimizing the consequences of a problem/disorder once it has occurred. Tertiary prevention research focuses on individuals who have the problem/disorder. Compare *primary prevention research, *secondary prevention research.

Tertiles   Divisions of rank-ordered scores into three groups of equal size. Compare *quartile, *percentile.

Test Battery   A collection of tests administered to a person or research participant to obtain a comprehensive assessment.

Testing Effect   Threat to *internal validity where the change in scores obtained on the second administration of the test is a result of having previously taken the test.

Test of Normality   Comparison of a set of observations to see whether they could have been produced by *random sampling from a *normal *population. A test of normality involves comparing the sample distribution with a normal distribution. Many graphical and statistical tests are available to check for normality (e.g., *normal probability plot, *histogram, *Kolmogorov-Smirnov test, *Shapiro-Wilk test).

Test-Retest Reliability   A *correlation between scores on two administrations of a test to the same subjects. A high correlation indicates high reliability. Squaring the coefficient and subtracting the result from 1 ($1 - r^2$) gives you an estimate of *random error. See *coefficient of stability.

Tests   The method of data collection in which a test, usually a standardized test, is administered to research participants. Compare *questionnaires, *interviews, *focus groups, *observation, *secondary or *existing data.

Test Statistics   (a) Test statistics are used to test a finding for *statistical significance—not to describe a *sample. They are based on sample data but are used to test hypotheses about population parameters. The *t test, *chi-square test, and *F ratio are examples of test statistics. The test statistic is the *calculated value* for the t, F, or chi-square, not the distribution. These statistics (t, F, and chi-square) have known probability distributions when the *null hypothesis is true, which means that they can be used to see if the calculated value based on the sample data conforms to the null hypothesis (or, more specifically, if the calculated value would be a rare event when the null is true). If the calculated value is more extreme than the *critical value (of the t, F, chi-square, or other distribution), then the null hypothesis is rejected; otherwise, you "fail to reject" the null hypothesis. See *hypothesis testing. (b) Statistics about tests and test items, such as statistical aspects of their *validity and *reliability. See *standardized test, *Rasch models, *item response theory.

Tetrachoric Correlation   A correlation between two *continuous variables that have been *dichotomized. Symbolized r_{tet}. It gives an estimate of what *Pearson's r would have been had the variables not been collapsed.

Before the availability of computers to do the grunt work, r_{tet} was frequently used for quick estimates of the Pearson r. It remains useful today mainly for data containing many gaps and errors, such as imperfect historical records. Compare the *phi coefficient, which is used for dichotomous, not dichotom*ized,* variables.

Texas Sharpshooter Fallacy   Fallacy of focusing on similarity but failing to notice differences. Can result in seeing patterns where there are none because the "pattern" is simply part of a larger chance process. See *cancer cluster. Named after the story of a shooter who randomly shot holes in the side of a barn and then drew a circle around the smallest cluster of holes and called it the bull's eye.

Text Mining or Text Analysis   A type of *data mining in which the data are texts that are studied using computer software. The goal is to make valid and reliable inferences about the content and structure of textual materials. Text-mining software makes vast amounts of verbal archival material available for detailed and rapid analysis. For example, if one wanted to study the differences in methodological approaches of psychologists, sociologists, and economists, one could undertake a text-mining analysis of prominent research journals in those fields.

Thematic Analysis   A common form of analysis in qualitative research whereby the researcher searches for and identifies patterns of meaning and themes (across sets of paragraphs, cases, participants, places, times) found in the data (typically transcribed textual data). Thematic analysis begins with coding of data (marking segments with categories or descriptors) and is followed by the search for thematic patterns that represent the data or parts of the data.

Theorem (a) A statement or formula in mathematics or logic deduced from other statements or formulas. A theorem is derived from premises; it is not an *assumption. (b) An idea accepted or proposed as a clear truth, often as part of a general theory. Compare *axiom, *postulate.

Theoretical Probability The number of ways that an event can occur divided by the number of possible outcomes. Alternatively stated, it's the expected probability of an outcome (or of a set of outcomes) based on a specific mathematical calculation or mathematically derived probability model.

For example, before you toss a fair coin 3 times, you can state that the probability of getting 3 heads in a row is $(.5)(.5)(.5) = .125$. Compare *empirical probability.

Theoretical Probability Distribution See *probability distribution (b).

Theoretical Sampling In grounded theory, a type of judgment or *purposive sampling in which the researcher seeks to refine theories, not to select a random representative sample.

Theoretical Saturation The point at which gathering more data is no longer informative. The term is usually associated with *grounded theory, but the concept is used quite broadly by researchers who collect qualitative data.

Theory A statement or group of statements about how some part of the world works, frequently explaining relations among phenomena. Theories explain "how" and "why" (and they can be big, small, or medium sized, and they can be about big objects all the way down to very small objects). While theory is usually distinguished from practice in ordinary language, Kurt Lewin's oft-quoted statement nicely captures the belief of most researchers: "There is nothing so practical as a good theory." Compare *hypothesis, *law, *realism.

Theory-Ladenness of Facts Philosophical position that observation and facts derived from observation are influenced by a researcher's beliefs, theories, and experiences.

Theory Trimming In *path analysis, deleting paths whose *coefficients are not *statistically significant.

Theta (θ) The symbol used for the ability score of an examinee in an *IRT analysis; also used for the trait score in an IRT measure of a psychological construct. Thetas usually range from -4.0 to $+4.0$ on the *logit scale. In *Rasch modeling, the comparable symbol is *beta*.

Thick Concepts Argument that sometimes facts and values are entangled and cannot be separated. Thick concepts conflate or mix the descriptive and the normative. Examples of relatively thick concepts might include research problem, achievement, evidence, justification, best explanation, good theory, War on Poverty, No Child Left Behind, and opportunity. Compare *Hume's law.

Thick Description   Used in *ethnography to refer to highly detailed, specific descriptions of cultural life that incorporate the *emic or inner perspectives of the individuals whose behavior is being observed. The term, coined by Gilbert Ryle, is most closely associated with the anthropology of Clifford Geertz, who specifically contrasted it with such "thin" descriptions as those implied by *behaviorism.

Think Aloud Technique   Data collection in which the researcher has participants verbalize their thoughts, perceptions, and reasoning while engaged in an activity.

Thin-Slice Analysis   A technique for interpreting observational data; very brief segments of behavior are observed and studied. The brevity can help decontextualize the behavior and sometimes make it easier to identify certain phenomena.

Third Variable   Another name for a *lurking variable or a *confounding variable.

Thought Experiment   Using one's imagination and reasoning skills to test a theory or hypothesis. Thought experiments have been widely used in the sciences (e.g., by Newton and Einstein) when actual experiments were impossible. They have been a key tool in building theories. Thought experiments may employ *counterfactual reasoning: "What would have happened if . . . ?" Despite their subjective and qualitative character, thought experiments have been widely used in the physical and social sciences.

Threats to Validity   Problems that can lead to false conclusions. The term was introduced by Donald T. Campbell and Julian Stanley to refer to the characteristics of various research methods and designs that can lead to spurious or misleading conclusions.

   Discussions of threats to validity often lead researchers to recommend using more than one method (see *mixed methods research, *triangulation). Because different kinds of research designs are open to different kinds of threats, you can reduce the *risk of error by using two or more methods. Researchers sometimes use a list of threats to validity as a checklist to review before putting the finishing touches on a design. See *mixed methods research, *multimethod research, *RCT.

Three-Parameter IRT Model   An item response model that includes the following three parameters: (1) item difficulty level parameter (the b parameter), (2) item discrimination parameter (the a parameter), and (3) guessing or pseudochance parameter (the c parameter). See *IRT.

Three-Period Crossover Design   A *crossover or *repeated measures clinical trial, typically including a placebo group and two treatment comparison groups. (Sometimes three treatments are compared without a placebo group.) This is a nice design because treatments can be compared (e.g., low dose vs. high dose, new drug vs. standard drug) with each other as well as to a no treatment placebo group. Comparison to the placebo group shows whether the treatments work. Comparison of the treatments shows which treatment works better. It also has the advantages of a crossover/repeated measures design, such as requiring fewer participants than an *independent samples design.

Three-Way ANOVA   *Analysis of variance with three *independent variables. Four interactions are possible in a three-way ANOVA (three two-way interactions and one three-way interaction), whereas in a two-way ANOVA only one is possible (a two-way interaction).

Three-Way Interaction   A three-way interaction is present when a two-way interaction (between two independent variables) changes at the different levels of a third independent variable. Note: This logic is easily extended; a four-way interaction is present when a three-way interaction (between three independent variables) changes at the different levels of a fourth independent variable; a five-way interaction is present when a four-way interaction (between four independent variables) changes at the different levels of a fifth independent variable; and so forth. See *interaction effect, *two-way interaction, *first-order interaction.

Three-Way Within-Subjects Design   A *factorial design that has three within-subject categorical independent variables and one quantitative independent variable.

Threshold Effect   An effect in a *dependent variable (DV) that does not occur until a certain level (threshold) has been reached in an *independent variable (IV). There are two general types. (1) Increases in the IV past the threshold continue to produce increases in the DV. For example, inflation may occur only when productivity drops below a certain rate, but then further productivity drops continue to increase inflation. (2) Additional amounts of the IV do not lead to increases in the DV, often because the DV exists in only one of two states (is *dichotomous). For example, a smoke alarm will not ring when there is very little smoke in the air, but once the threshold is met and it does ring, more smoke will not make it ring louder.

Thurstone Scaling   (a) A method of *scale construction in which judges assign weights or degrees of intensity to prospective scale items. The extent to which judges agree determines whether particular items are included in the scale. The method is seldom used today, largely because it is slow, expensive, and no more *reliable than *Likert scales. (b) A method of assessing the difficulty of items on a test pioneered by Thurstone; it employs paired comparisons between groups taking the test, and it is still widely used.

Tied Ranks   Ranked data in a variable to be used in description or in a nonparametric test that has some co-occurring ranks. When ties occur, those numbers are assigned the value that is the mean of their positions in ascending order of the ranks (i.e., if the ranks would not have been tied). For example, 1, 2, 3, 3, 8 would become 1, 2, 3.5, 3.5, 5; the numbers 1, 30, 30, 30, 45, 90, 100 would become 1, 3, 3, 3, 5, 6, 7; and the numbers 1, 1, 1, 2, 3, 4, 4, 5, 6 would become 2, 2, 2, 4, 5, 6.5, 6.5, 8, 9.

Time-Lag Design   Typically a *quasi-experimental design, and especially popular in developmental psychology research, a time-lag design examines individuals of the same age at different times (e.g., compare 18-year-olds in 1990, 2000, and 2010). It is good at examining generational or cohort differences, for example, identifying differences between age cohorts due to changes in the environment and culture over time. Compare *cross-sectional design, *longitudinal design, *cohort-sequential design.

Time-Lagged Correlation   The correlation of values on a variable at one point in time with values on the same variable at another point in time. Used, for example, in *cross-lagged panel designs.

Time Sampling   Conducting observations during specific time intervals (e.g., for the first minute of each 10-minute period). Compare *event sampling.

Time Series   A set of measures of a single *variable recorded periodically, over time, such as the annual rainfall in Miami from 1900 to the present. See *smoothing, *moving average. Time-series data for a variable are broken down or decomposed into four components: *secular trend, *cyclical, *seasonal variations, and *irregular fluctuations.

Time-Series Analysis   (a) Analysis of changes in variables over time. *Multiple regression is sometimes used for this purpose, but because of violation of the *independence assumption in *OLS regression, *ARIMA models are more often employed. (b) Any of several statistical procedures used to tell whether a change in *time-series data is due to some variable that occurred at the same time or was due to coincidence. See *interrupted time-series design.

Time-Series Data   Any data arranged in chronological order.

For example, the annual suicide rate in the United States from 1900 to the present would be time-series data, as would the Dow Jones daily averages for the last 18 months, as would the weekly spelling test scores of a class of sixth graders. Compare *survival analysis.

Time-Series Design   See *interrupted time-series design, *time-series analysis.

TLA   Three-letter acronym. Many fields, including research methods and statistics, make extensive use of TLAs.

TLI   See *Tucker-Lewis index.

Tobit Analysis A technique in *regression analysis used when the *dependent variable may be either zero or any positive number. For this kind of dependent variable, the *ordinary least squares criterion should not be applied. Also known as the "censored regression model."

For example, say the research question is "How much money will individuals spend on televisions this year?" The answer will fit into one of two categories: For most individuals, the answer will be zero; for the rest, it will range widely from a few hundred to several thousand dollars.

Tolerance (a) Support for the equal rights and liberties of others, usually others one finds threatening. (b) An allowable margin of error in measurement. (c) In *multiple regression analysis, the tolerance is the proportion of the variability in one *independent variable (IV) not explained by the other IVs included in the regression equation. The bigger the tolerance, the more useful the IV is to the analysis; the smaller the tolerance, the higher the *collinearity. According to one rule of thumb, a tolerance value of .10 or smaller indicates severe collinearity. Compare *variance inflation factor. (d) In some psychological studies, tolerance can mean ability to withstand some potentially harmful *treatment.

Total Determination, Coefficient of See *coefficient of total determination.

Total Effect In *path analysis and *SEM, researchers are sometimes interested in the total effect of a prior variable on a later variable in a *structural equation model. The total effect of the prior variable is the sum of its direct effect (if present) and its indirect effects (if present) on the latter variable. For example, one might be interested in the total effect of an *exogenous variable on an *endogenous variable occurring later in the model. See *path analysis for discussion of how to obtain direct and indirect effects; to calculate the total effect, just sum the values for the direct and indirect effects.

Total Sum of Squares The *sum of squares for a dependent variable. It is obtained by subtracting the mean from each score, squaring those scores, and then summing the squared scores. If you divide this by the *df*, you will obtain the total *mean square or, more generally speaking, you will have the *variance.

Training Data (or Sample) A data set or sample used to build a model; the model is then tested with different data. One way to implement this approach is to divide one's sample randomly into two. Use the first half as the training data to build a model, the second half to test the model. Building a model and testing it with the same data is a *tautology. See *cross-validation, *derivation sample.

Trait An enduring characteristic; it could be a physical characteristic such as sex or a psychological trait such as shyness. In contrast, a *state* is a less-enduring characteristic of someone. For example, trait anxiety is much more severe than state anxiety.

T

Trait-Treatment Interaction (TTI)   A *research design using *factorial ANOVA to determine whether there is an *interaction effect between *traits and *treatments, for example, whether a management effectiveness seminar has better results with women or men. Also called "attribute-treatment interaction."

Transformations of Data   Changing all the values of a variable by using some mathematical operation. One common example is changing proportions into percents by multiplying them by 100. Another widespread practice is to use a transformation to reduce the complexity of a table reporting large numbers, as when one reports income in thousands of dollars. In that case, the transformation is done by dividing each number by 1,000. Taking the *log (or the square root) of the values in a distribution is done to facilitate analysis, often by making distributions conform to statistical *assumptions. See *linear and *nonlinear transformations for more examples; also *logistic and *polynomial regression.

Transformed Standard Scores   *Transformations performed on *z scores, usually to eliminate decimals and negative numbers. For examples, see *Z score and *normal curve equivalent. Educational Testing Service transforms z scores by multiplying them by 100 and adding 500 to arrive at the familiar range from 200 to 800 used to report scores on the SAT and the GRE.

Translation and Back-Translation   Procedure used for translating a questionnaire or assessment instrument from one language into another language, in, for example, cross-cultural research. First the instrument is translated into the new language by a bilingual language expert; then the instrument is translated back to the original language by a different bilingual language expert. Last, the researcher checks for any differences between the original instrument and its translated-back version.

Transpose   A *matrix formed by interchanging the rows and columns (vectors) of another matrix. See *vector for an example.

Treatment   (a) In *experiments, a treatment is what researchers do to subjects in the *experimental group but not to those in the *control group. A treatment is thus an *independent variable. (b) Used broadly to mean almost any *predictor variable. For example, in a study of the effect on the traffic accident rate of changing the speed limit, the speed limit would be the "treatment." See *level, *condition.

Treatment Combination   See *cell mean for an explanatory example.

Treatment Group   Another term for *experimental group, especially in the context of a *clinical trial.

Treatments-by-Subjects ANOVA   *Repeated-measures ANOVA.

Treatment Variation Validity   Type of *external validity, present to the degree that the results found in a study can be generalized across variations in the treatment. See *generalizability.

Tree Diagram A way of depicting a series of possible events using "branches" to illustrate different outcomes. It is used in *probability calculations and *decision theory. See *decision tree.

For example, Figure T.2 shows the 6 possible outcomes, and their *probabilities, of a 2-out-of-3-set tennis match between A and B. A's record shows that she wins .70 (70%) of the sets she plays; B's set winning rate is 30%. The most likely outcome is that A will win in two sets (.49). The least likely is that B will win the match after having lost a set (.063).

Figure T.2 Tree Diagram

Trend (a) Movement in one direction of the values of a *variable over a period of time. See *secular trend and, for an example, *moving average. Compare *fluctuation. (b) The term "trend" is sometimes used to describe a research outcome that, if it were stronger, would be statistically significant—but it isn't.

Trend Analysis (a) A form of *regression analysis used to discover *nonlinear relations; frequently used when one has *time-series data. (b) A form of *analysis of variance with an *ordinal- or *interval-level independent variable. In other words, both regression and ANOVA are used for trend analysis.

Trend Line A line depicting a *trend. See *moving average, *ARIMA.

Trend Study An investigation of a variable over time in which the population studied does not remain the same. Also called a *repeated cross-sectional design.

For example, a study of college graduates' starting salaries in their first jobs from 1980 to the present would study a different group of graduates each year. Compare *cohort study, *panel study.

Trial Design   Synonym for *clinical trial.

Triangular Distribution   A *probability distribution of a *discrete variable that forms a triangle. The illustration at *underlying distribution is an example.

Triangulation   Using more than one method to study the same thing. The term is loosely borrowed from trigonometry, where it refers to a method for calculating the distance to a point by looking at it from two other points. See *mixed methods research, *multimethod research.

For example, if you were interested in people's attitudes toward environmental issues, you could look at patterns of voting behaviors on environmental candidates and issues; or you could interview leaders of the Sierra Club, the Nature Conservancy, and similar groups; or you could conduct a survey of a representative sample of the entire population. Or you could do all three and put the results together, in which case you could say that you had used a research strategy of triangulation.

Trimmed Data   The removal of a fixed percentage of extreme scores from each tail of a variable (e.g., the highest and lowest 5%). Statistics calculated on trimmed data are called "trimmed statistics." See *truncated distribution or sample, *Winsorizing.

Trimmed Mean   A *mean computed after removing the extreme observations. Thus, a trimmed mean is a measure of *central tendency that allows the researcher to deal separately with a *distribution's *outliers.

For example, an 80% trimmed mean would be the mean calculated using only the central 80% of the values in the distribution; the high and low 10% would be eliminated (trimmed). This is also called a 10% trimmed mean; a 5% trimmed mean would use the middle 90% of the distribution to calculate the mean. See *Winsorizing. Compare *interquartile range.

Triple-Blind Procedure   When all participants in an experiment are ignorant of which subjects received what treatment and which subjects were in the control group, this is called a triple-blind procedure. In a single-blind study, the subjects don't know. In a double-blind experiment, the experimenters also don't know (e.g., whether the red or the green pill has the active ingredient and which contains the *placebo). In a triple-blind procedure, the data analysts and any external committee monitoring the study are also ignorant of which subjects received the treatment and which did not. Of course, someone must know, or one could draw no useful conclusions from the study, but when the subjects, experimenters, and data analysts are in the dark, their prior knowledge cannot *bias the results of the study.

Trough   In a *time series, a point lower than the preceding and following points. Compare *spike.

True Experiment   An older name for a *randomized experiment, that is, an *experiment in which subjects are randomly assigned the treatment and control groups to equate these groups on all known and unknown variables prior to administration of the treatment. All experiments involve manipulation of the *independent variable (i.e., administration of some type of "treatment") by the researcher or by someone working with the researcher. "True" was contrasted with weaker experimental approaches such as *quasi-experiments and *natural experiments. Today it is helpful to think of experiments as varying from the strongest designs (*randomized) to weak designs (e.g., *one-group pretest-posttest design), with quasi-experimental designs (e.g., *nonequivalent comparison-group design) falling somewhere in between.

True Score   In *classical test theory, a score assumed to exist that constitutes the true amount of the attribute possessed by the respondent. It would be the average of the individual's scores obtained from completing an infinite number of *alternative forms of the test. The score we see is called the "observed score." The sum of the observed score and random measurement error is assumed to be equal to the true score.

Truncated Distribution or Sample   A distribution with data missing, nonexistent, or cut off at one end, such as an income distribution that omits anyone below or above a certain amount. Sometimes "truncated" and "censored" are used as synonyms. When a distinction is made, truncation usually refers to an incomplete sample, while censored refers to incomplete measurements of a variable. Compare *censored data or samples, *tobit analysis. In regression models data are truncated if when observations that have missing data on the dependent variable are excluded from the sample. Note that truncation reduces the sample size but censoring does not. Regression models with censored or truncated data must be estimated with Tobit models to ensure that the estimated regression coefficients are consistent and that the significance tests are correct.

Trustworthiness   The equivalent of *validity when referring to *qualitative research. The equivalency is conceptual. In practice, the means of assessing validity or trustworthiness vary between qualitative and quantitative approaches. Because of the special nature of qualitative data, standard quantitative techniques (*validity coefficients, for example) are inappropriate. On the other hand, many questions of the two research traditions are the same—for example, have researchers accurately recorded what they have been told by respondents or informants?

Truth Table   In logic and Boolean algebra, a list of all the logically possible combinations of categorical variables. This is usually combined with the number of empirical cases that fall into each category/combination. It is a key element in *qualitative comparative analysis.

T Score (uppercase T)   (a) The newer name for Z score (uppercase Z). See *Z score for fuller definition. Note: Not to be confused with z score (lowercase z). (b) Sometimes used to refer to the *normal curve equivalent. Note: Also not to be confused with the *t statistic or the *t test.

The T score (a) indicates deviation from a *mean. The mean is scored 50, and 1 *standard deviation is scored 10. Thus, a T score of 70 is 2 standard deviations above the mean; 40 is 1 standard deviation below.

TSS   Total *sum of squares.

t **Statistic**   The number that is tested in a *t test, that is, the number that is compared to the *critical region. Compare *F ratio, *test statistic.

t **Test**   A test of *statistical significance, often of the difference between two group *means, such as the average score on a manual dexterity test of those who have and have not been given caffeine. Also used as a *test statistic for *correlation and *regression coefficients. See *Student's t distribution. Compare z test.

A *two-tailed t test is used to test the significance of a "nondirectional" *alternative hypothesis, that is, an alternative hypothesis that says there is a difference between two averages without saying which of the two is bigger. A *one-tailed t test is called "directional" because it tests the alternative hypothesis that the mean of one of the two group averages is bigger. Generally speaking, the two-tailed test should be used so that science can discover *and* test hypotheses.

There are several formulas for t. The one to use depends on the nature of the data and the groups being studied, most often on whether the groups are *independent or *correlated.

T **test**   The uppercase T has been overused. It can mean (a) *Hotelling's t^2 test, (b) a rank order test of trends in a time series, and (c) a variant of the *Mann-Whitney U test. All these are quite distinct from the *T score and the *t test (lowercase t).

Tucker-Lewis Index (TLI)   A statistic used in *structural equation modeling to indicate model fit. It is an incremental fix index, which means it measures the increase in fit relative to a baseline model (usually an independence/null/not related model). Close model fit is indicated by TLI values greater than or equal to .95.

Tukey Line   A *regression line based on *medians (rather than *means, as is the *least squares criterion). It is more *resistant to *outliers than the ordinary least squares (OLS) regression line.

Tukey's Honestly Significant Difference (HSD) Test   After conducting an *analysis of variance of the differences in three or more group means, the researcher knows that at least two of the group means are significantly different.

To determine *which* means are significantly different, Tukey's HSD test can be used to locate the significant differences while maintaining the *familywise error rate at the desired *alpha level. It adjusts for the inflated alpha that would result if one simply conducted multiple *t* tests. See *post hoc comparison, *multiple comparisons test.

For example, suppose 150 overweight subjects were randomly assigned (30 each) to 5 different weight-loss programs to see if there were any significant differences among the programs. At the end of 10 weeks, the average weight loss for each group was computed, and an ANOVA *F ratio showed that there was an *omnibus effect (i.e., not all of the 5 population means were considered equal). However, to determine which pairs of means were significantly different, while holding the familywise alpha to, say, .05, Tukey's HSD could be used.

Two-Bend Transformation   A transformation for relations between two variables that, when plotted on a graph, produce a line with two bends. The most common transformations of this type are the *logistic and the *probit.

Two-by-Two Design   Said of a research design with two *independent variables, each with two values, and one dependent variable. See *N-by-M design.

Table T.1 is a two-by-two *factorial table (or "design layout") that shows the cell mean scores of the four groups produced by crossing sex and class. The independent variables are sex (men, women) and class (sophomore, senior), and the dependent variable is score on an achievement examination.

Table T.1   Two-by-Two Design: Mean Examination Scores

	Sophomores	*Seniors*
Men	40	62
Women	48	71

Two-by-Two Table   A two-dimensional matrix formed by crossing a row variable with two levels and a column variable with two levels. More generally, a matrix can have the dimensions of $r \times c$, where r stands for the number of rows and c stands for the number of columns. See *contingency table.

Two-Parameter IRT Model   IRT model that includes the item difficulty parameter and the item discrimination parameter. See *item response theory. Compare *one-parameter IRT model, *three-parameter IRT model.

Two-Sigma Rule   Rule of thumb that says 95% of the cases of a variable that is approximately normally distributed will fall within 2 standard deviations from the mean. In a fully normally distributed variable, 95.44% of the cases fall within 2 standard deviations, and 95% of the cases fall within plus or minus 1.96 standard deviations of the mean.

Two-Sided Test   See *two-tailed test of significance.

Two-Stage Least Squares Regression   In some path models, one variable affects another variable (variable A affects variable B), but the relationship also operates in the opposite direction (i.e., variable B affects variable A). Two-stage least squares regression is an advanced technique used, with *instrumental variables, to estimate the parameter going from A to B and the parameter going from B to A without violating the error term assumption that the error is not correlated with any of the independent variables.

Two-Tailed Alternative Hypothesis   An *alternative *statistical hypothesis stating that the outcome can fall in either tail of the distribution. This alternative hypothesis has a not-equal-to sign in it ($\neq$) (rather than a > or < sign as found in a one-tailed hypothesis). For example, in an *independent t test the *null hypothesis is that $\mu_1 = \mu_2$ and the two-tailed alternative is that these two population means are not equal ($\mu_1 \neq \mu_2$). This is a two-tailed alternative hypothesis because it does not state which mean must be greater in order to obtain statistical significance. A one tailed-test requires that the sample means fall in the expected direction if one is to obtain statistical significance. Most researchers use two-tailed alternative hypotheses because it allows hypothesis testing while still leaving open the discovery function of science that would be needed if the means were very different but in a different than predicted condition. See *two-tailed test of significance.

Two-Tailed p Value   The p value for a *two-tailed test. This is the standard p value provided in most statistical packages. It is the probability that the computed value of the test statistic (e.g., a t, z, or chi-square) would be equal to or greater than its observed value, in either (positive or negative) direction, under the assumption that the null hypothesis is true. See *p value. Compare *one-tailed p value.

Two-Tailed Test of Significance   A statistical test in which the *critical region (*region of rejection of the *null hypothesis) is divided into two areas in the tails of the *sampling distribution. A two-tailed test is slightly more conservative than a *one-tailed test. See *two tailed alternative hypothesis, *Type I error. Compare *one-tailed test of significance.

Two-Way Analysis of Covariance   Usually this means a *GLM that has one quantitative dependent variable and two categorical independent variables of theoretical interest and a quantitative independent variable as the *covariate. It's a *two-way ANOVA with a covariate added. The covariate might be a pretest measure or some variable the researcher wants to control for.

Two-Way ANOVA   *Analysis of variance with two categorical *independent variables. It is used to study the effects of two independent variables separately (their *main effects) and together (their *interaction effect). Compare *one-way ANOVA.

Two-Way Chi-Square Test   A *chi-square test for statistical significance on a *contingency table with two categorical variables. The null hypothesis is that the two variables are not related in the population; the alternative hypothesis is that the two variables are related.

Two-Way Interaction   A two-way interaction is present when the relationship between one independent variable and the dependent variable changes at the levels of another independent variable. For example, perhaps the relationship between education and income depends on ethnic group in a society with institutionalized discrimination. Specifically, perhaps there is a strong positive relationship between education and income for the dominant group, but there is little or no relationship for the discriminated-against group. Also called a double interaction, a *first-order interaction, or an $A \times B$ interaction. Compare *three-way interaction.

Two-Way Mixed Design   An experimental design and associated analysis of variance with one *within- and one *between-subjects categorical independent variable, and one quantitative dependent variable.

Type I Error   An error made by wrongly rejecting a true *null hypothesis. This might involve incorrectly concluding that two variables are related when they or not, or wrongly deciding that a sample statistic exceeds the value that would be expected by chance. Also called *alpha error or *false positive. Compare *Type II error. See *hypothesis testing.

Type II Error   An error made by wrongly accepting (or retaining or failing to reject) a false *null hypothesis. Also called *beta error or *false negative. Compare *Type I error See *hypothesis testing.

   In practice, Type I and Type II errors tend to be inversely related; however, you can decrease the probability of making a Type II error (while maintaining your same desired Type I error rate) by increasing the sample size in your research study!

Type III Error   There are several candidates for the definition of the third type of error. (a) Correctly concluding that there is a significant difference between experimental and control groups but being wrong about the direction of the difference. (b) Giving a correct answer to the wrong question; in Tukey's words, "A question not worth answering is not worth answering well." (c) Attributing a lack of results to the weakness of a treatment when, in fact, the problem was that the treatment was not administered properly. (d) Correctly rejecting the null hypothesis but for the wrong reasons.

Type I Sum of Squares   See *analysis of unweighted means.

Type III Sum of Squares   The type of sum of squares to be used when one does not have an equal number of participants in each condition or, more generally,

T

when the independent variables are correlated. This is the default on packages such as SAS and SPSS. When you have two or more independent variables, the significance test based on the Type III sum of squares compares the full model (the model with all of the independent variables included) with the reduced model that includes all of the independent variables except for the one of interest. This difference tells you if the variable adds anything to the model after accounting for or controlling for the other independent variables. It's the type of sum of squares that should be used in the vast majority of cases with general linear models such as ANOVA, ANCOVA, and multiple regression. Also called "enter method."

Typology   Literally, a study of types. A classification scheme involving a coordinated set of categories. It is often formed by cross-classifying two or more categorical variables; the cells in the cross-classification are named and become the categories in the typology. A typology is often used in the development of a theory. Compare *truth table.

U (a) Symbol for the *Mann-Whitney *U* test statistic. (b) Symbol for the *disturbance term in a *regression model. (c) In *path analysis, the symbol for unanalyzed effects or unmeasured variables. It is composed of both the effects of *variables not included in the *model and the disturbance or *random error. (d) In *factor analysis, the symbol for "unique factor," that is, the part not explained by the *common factors.

Unbalanced Designs Said of *factorial designs when the *cells contain unequal (or nonproportional) numbers of subjects. A common source of unbalanced designs is attrition or other missing data problems. Also called "nonorthogonal factorial designs."

Unbalanced Scale A *rating scale that has a negative and positive side of unequal size, as in (1) disagree, (2) neutral, (3) agree slightly, (4) agree, (5) strongly agree. Unbalanced rating scales are not recommended because they are nonparallel and can be used to "lie with statistics." If opinions are expected to mostly fall on one side of a scale, then simply increase the number of values/categories on a *balanced scale.

Unbiased Fair. Said of a research *design that is free from any characteristic that would misrepresent the evidence; also said of a method of analysis that does not distort the findings.

Unbiased Error Error that is *random in the sense that, in the long run, positive and negative unbiased errors cancel one another out and sum to zero.

Unbiased Estimator A *sample statistic that is free from *systematic error. Over repeated sampling (i.e., over the long run), the average value of an unbiased estimator will be equal to the true population parameter. Alternatively stated, the *expected value of an unbiased estimator is equal to the true population parameter. This is a very desirable property of for a statistical estimator. It will *not* tend to over- or underestimate the corresponding *population parameter. Unbiased estimators produce "unbiased estimates," that is, estimates that, statistically speaking, contain only random error.

461

U

Unbiased Sample   (a) A sample that is produced by an *equal probability of selection method. (b) A sample that contains only random error; that is, it is free of *systematic error. See *random sample.

Note: The use of an unbiased estimator cannot prevent the occurrence of a biased sample; that's because there are many factors that can cause you to end up with a biased sample. You might view the use of an unbiased estimator as a necessary but not sufficient condition for obtaining an unbiased sample. Compare *response rate, *nonresponse bias

Unbiased Sample Variance   A method of computing the sample variance so that it is an *unbiased estimate of the population *variance, usually by dividing the *sum of squares by $n - 1$ rather than n. Note that statistical packages and calculators usually use $n - 1$ by default even when it is not appropriate because the data are population, not sample, data (the package has no way of knowing).

Uncertainty   A state in which outcomes are unknown and in which there is no basis for calculating the *probabilities of outcomes. This contrasts with a situation characterized by *risk, in which the probabilities of at least some of the outcomes can be estimated. Sometimes the terms "risk" and "uncertainty" are used interchangeably.

Underdetermination   In philosophy of science, the position that it is possible for more than one theory to fit the evidence; also called "underdetermination of theory by evidence."

Underidentified Model   In *SEM, the model is underidentified when the number of variables is less than the number of parameters to be estimated; therefore, unique estimates are not available for all model parameters because there is too little information available. See *identification problem.

Underlying Distribution   (also called **Underlying Population Distribution**) The distribution of all possible outcomes of an *event.

For example, if the event is the result (sum) of a roll of two dice, there are 11 possible sums: 2, 3, 4 . . . 12, distributed as in Figure U.1 on page 463. The figure shows that there is one way to role a 2, two ways to roll a 3, six ways to role a 7, and so on. This is an example of a *triangular distribution.

Underspecified Model   A causal model in which important variables have been omitted. See *specification problem, *path diagram.

Unexplained Variance   A synonym for *mean square error. Scientists don't like *un*explained variance. Compare *explained variance, *variance explained.

Unimodal Distribution   A distribution with only one *mode. Compare *bimodal.

Union   In *set theory, a *set formed by including all of the *elements of two other sets. Symbolized $A \cup B$. Pronounced "A union B," or, alternatively, "A or B." Compare *intersection.

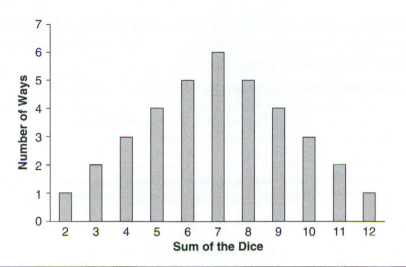

Figure U.1   Underlying Distribution of the Sum of a Roll of Two Dice

Unipolar Scale   Rating scale used to determine the degree or amount of a single quality or attribute. For example, see the 4-point effectiveness scale: (1) not at all effective, (2) slightly effective, (3) somewhat effective, (4) highly effective. Compare *bipolar rating scale.

Unit   A synonym for 1 in some statistical discussions. To say, for example, that the *standard deviation of a *normal distribution is "unit" means that it is 1. Compare *unity.

Units of Analysis   The persons or things being studied. Units of analysis in research in the social and behavioral sciences are often individual persons but can be groups, political parties, newspaper editorials, unions, hospitals, schools, monkeys, rats, reaction times, perceptions, and so on. A particular unit of analysis from which data are gathered is called a *case.

Unity   What statisticians sometimes like to call 1. For example, "This value approaches unity," means that it gets close to 1. Compare *unit.

Univariate Analysis   (a) Studying the distribution of *cases of one variable only; for example, studying the ages of welfare recipients but not relating that variable to their sex, ethnicity, and so on. Compare *bivariate analysis, *multivariate analysis. (b) Occasionally used in *regression analysis to mean a problem in which there is only one *dependent variable—a usage that conflicts with the more common meaning in definition (a).

Universal Constant   See *E (c).

Universal Set   All things to be considered in any one discussion. Usually symbolized: S. In *sampling theory, the universal set is the *population.

Universe   Another term for *population; the term is used more in logic than in statistics.

UNIX   A widely used *operating system.

Unobtrusive Methods   Procedures for collecting data, often about social life in natural settings, that are hidden or at least that do not interfere much with what is being studied. The chief benefit of these methods is that they reduce the influence of knowing that one is being studied on the results of the research. Measuring the popularity of museum exhibits by observing patterns of wear in the flooring is a classic example. Observing people in a public place, such as a coffee shop, while pretending to be an ordinary patron is another example, but one that may raise ethical questions about *informed consent.

Unsaturated Model   See *saturated model.

Unstandardized Regression Coefficient   A *regression coefficient, symbolized by b, based on data in their regular units (rather than standardized units). It is contrasted with a *standardized regression coefficient (also called a *beta coefficient).

Unstandardized Score   A score in the original *metric or units of measurement, one that has not been transformed into a *z score or other *standard score.

Unstructured Interview   An interview that operates like an informal conversation between the interviewer and the interviewee, allowing the interviewer to create questions and their ordering. This approach is popular in *qualitative research, especially during extended *field research. Compare *semistructured interview, *structured interview.

U-Shaped Distribution   A *frequency distribution in which the largest frequencies are at the extremes of the scores; this results in a graphic that resembles the letter U. The term "inverted U-shaped distribution" is sometimes used to describe frequency distributions in which the most frequent values are toward the middle and the least frequent at the high and low ends of the scores. Sometimes called a "goalpost distribution."

Figure U.2 on page 465 indicates the racial composition of high schools in Cook County, Illinois (Chicago and suburbs). The x-axis indicates the percentage of students attending the high schools who are black. The y-axis gives the number of high schools. Almost all of the high schools have less than 10% or more than 90% black students. Very few are in the middle range of 20% to 80%.

Utilitarianism   An ethical theory emphasizing outcomes or consequences of actions. It requires the identification and calculation of costs and benefits. If the benefits sufficiently outweigh the costs, the action should be performed. Some form of utilitarianism is frequently used in making policy decisions and is used by *institutional review boards in evaluating the ethical acceptability of proposals for research. Compare *deontology, *ethical skepticism.

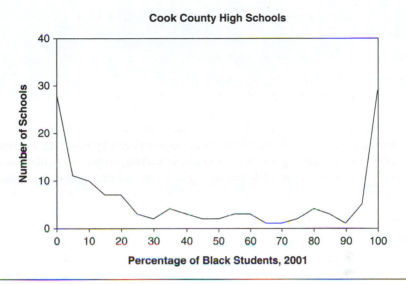

Figure U.2   U-Shaped Distribution

Utility   The usefulness or satisfaction derived from an outcome. Utility is sub-jective, but it is usually given a number. The satisfaction gotten from, say, a new pair of shoes may differ from one person to the next. Someone might say, "On a scale of 0 to 10, I'd give these shoes a 7," while you might have given them only a 4. In economics, utility is a determinant of the price a person will pay. In *decision theory, utility is combined (as a weighting factor) with the *probability or *expected value of an outcome to make a choice. Compare *minimax and *maximin strategy.

V See **Cramer's V.*

Validation Sample See **derivation sample for an explanation of both derivation and validation samples.

Validity The quality, accuracy, intersubjective agreement/approval, or truth value of or about some "object" of discussion (e.g., a measurement instrument, a research design, an inference, a claim, a conclusion). Validity is viewed and defined differently in different knowledge domains.

(a) In measurement or psychometrics, validity is traditionally viewed as the degree to which an instrument or test accurately measures what it is supposed to measure, or the extent to which the measure is free of *systematic error. Validity requires *reliability, but the reverse is not true. According to a more recent viewpoint, validity is the accuracy of inferences, interpretations, or actions that are made on the basis of test scores.

(b) In research *design, validity refers to the strength of the research design (invalid, quasi-valid, valid) for addressing a given research question or hypothesis.

(c) In the evaluation of published research, validity refers to the degree to which the researchers gathered data appropriate for answering their questions and how much one should believe their inferences and conclusions.

(d) In *qualitative research, validity has many additional definitions, but generally it refers to the *trustworthiness of the statements and findings provided by the research study.

For an example of (a), say we want to measure individuals' heights. If all we had was a bathroom scale, we could ask our individuals to step on the scale and record the results. Even if the measurements were highly reliable, that is, consistent from one weighing to the next, they might not be very valid depending on the accuracy of the scale.

Social scientists have not found it easy to define validity. To try to explain it, they have created numerous subcategories, including *content, *consequential, *construct, *convergent, *criterion-related, *discriminant, *ecological, *external, *face validity, *internal, *population, *predictive, and *statistical conclusion validity. There are many additional "validities"!

Validity Coefficient   A *Pearson correlation between two sets of scores, such as scores on an old and a new version of a test, or between a *predictor and a *criterion variable.

Validity Generalization Study   A type of *meta-analysis in which a validity coefficient computed in multiple studies is treated as a dependent variable and one searches for independent variables that predict variations in the validity coefficients. Validity generalization is present to the degree that the validity coefficients cannot be predicted by other variables and operate well in multiple contexts. See *metaregression analysis.

Value Added   Increase in worth or value. The difference between input value and output value. In manufacturing, this would mean the costs minus the selling price. In education, it might mean the difference between students' achievement at the beginning and the end of a year of schooling.

Value-Added Models   In educational measurement, a statistical model (often a *hierarchical regression model based on *longitudinal data) used to determine the unique contribution (or "value added") to student achievement of schools, classrooms, and teachers. Value-added models attempt to *control for all other variables that might also affect achievement. The models are used to determine the relative effectiveness of different schools, classrooms, and individual teachers. The logic of *value added also is used in other research domains such as business and government products and programs.

Value-Free   Goal of science when researchers attempt to keep their personal values out of the collection and interpretation of evidence. As Max Weber pointed out long ago, value-free means that researchers place the values of science above their other values, not that they have no values. Contrast *value-laden, *theory-ladenness of facts.

Value Judgment   A belief or statement that something is good (or bad), beautiful (or not beautiful), and so on. All value judgments are opinions, but not all opinions are value judgments. Value judgments are usually contrasted with statements of fact, but in practice the distinction is often unclear. See *objective.

Value-Laden   Said of any research or theory that contains (is weighed down by) the values of the researcher or theorist. Often contrasted with *objective and *value-free.

Variability   The *spread or *dispersion of scores in a group of scores; the tendency of each score to be unlike the others. More formally, the extent to which scores in a *distribution deviate from a *central tendency of the distribution, such as the *mean. The *standard deviation and the *variance are two of the most commonly used measures of variability. For an example, see *standard deviation.

Variable (a) A condition or characteristic that can take on different categories, levels, or values. (b) Loosely, anything studied by a researcher. (c) Any finding that can change, that can vary, or that can be expressed as more than one value or in various values or categories. The opposite of a variable is a constant. (d) In algebra, a variable is an unknown.

Here are some of the major types of variables: *categorical, *continuous, *dependent, *independent, *moderator, *mediating, *intervening, *endogenous, *exogenous, *random, *extraneous, and *confounding.

Examples of variables include anything that can be measured or assigned a number, such as unemployment rate, religious affiliation, experimental *treatment, grade point average, and so on. Much of social science is aimed at discovering and demonstrating how differences in some variables are related to or explain differences in others.

Variable Analysis Data analysis in which relationships between and among variables are examined. This is the standard approach used in *quantitative research. Compare *qualitative research, *case study analysis.

Variable-Centered Analysis Data analysis focused on relationships among variables (rather than individuals), such as *factor analysis, *path analysis, and *general linear models (e.g., *ANOVA, *regression). The variable-centered approach typically considers the effect of each variable holding all others constant. Contrast *person-centered analysis, *case-oriented research, *case study analysis.

Variable Ordering In *explanatory research, one often wants to determine which variables in the set of independent variables are the most and least important. Variable ordering is the ranking of the independent variables from least to most important. This activity also is known as determining the "relative importance" of the independent variables. In *regression analysis, the *semipartial correlation squared statistic is calculated for each independent variable, and these are then ranked to make a judgment of relative importance. *Beta coefficients also are sometimes used for this purpose. See *dominance analysis. Compare *variable selection.

Variable-Oriented Research A term introduced by Ragin to describe research that focuses on aspects (variables) of cases, usually numerous cases, rather than on cases as a whole. The distinction between *case-oriented research and variable-oriented research is closely parallel to what is often meant by quantitative (variable) and qualitative (case) research.

Variable Parameter Model A model in which the *population *parameters being estimated are assumed to be variable, not constant. For example, this occurs in *Bayesian but not *frequentist (i.e., classical) statistics.

Variable Selection In *predictive research, data are sometimes available on many predictor variables. Variable selection is the search for a subset from the total set of variables that performs well on some criterion such as *R^2. For example, perhaps a large corporation has fully 75 *predictor variables available for predicting interest rates; it might save time, money, and energy if a particular set of 20 variables explains nearly as much variance as the full set. Variable selection relies on algorithmic procedures such as *stepwise, *forward selection, *backward elimination, and *all subsets regression. Compare *variable ordering.

Variance A measure of the spread of scores in a *distribution of scores, that is, a measure of *dispersion. The larger the variance, the farther the individual cases are, on average, from the *mean. The smaller the variance, the closer the individual scores are to the mean.

Specifically, the variance is the mean of the sum of the squared deviations from the mean score divided by number of scores. That is, it's the average distance from the mean in squared units. (See *sum of squares for an example.) Taking the square root of the variance gives you the *standard deviation (i.e., it converts the variance into regular, nonsquared units). A variance cannot be less than zero, nor can the standard deviation.

Variance Components Analysis Another term for *random effects model or *Model II ANOVA.

Variance-Covariance Matrix A square matrix in which the entries on the diagonal are *variances and the others are *covariances of the variables measured. The top triangle (above the diagonal) of the matrix is a mirror image of the bottom triangle. Widely used in *factor analysis and *structural equation modeling. Compare *correlation matrix (a correlation is a "standardized covariance").

Variance Explained In *regression analysis, the variance in the *dependent variable that is associated with or accounted for by the independent variables. *R^2 is a common measure of the variance explained.

Variance Inflation Factor (VIF) A measure of *collinearity in multiple *regression analysis. This statistic is 1 divided by the *tolerance. Therefore, low tolerances result in high VIFs, and vice versa. The lowest possible VIF is 1.0 when there is no collinearity. If the tolerance were 0.2, the VIF would be 5.0 (1.0/0.2 = 5.0). The smaller the VIF, the less collinearity is present; hence, smaller is better. According to one rule of thumb, VIF should be less than or equal to 10.

Variance of Estimate A measure of the *variability of the points around a *regression line or surface. The square root of the variance of estimate is the *standard error of the estimate, that is, the standard deviation of the *residuals. The variance of estimate is also called the *mean square residual (MSR) or *mean square error (MSE).

Variate (a) A *canonical correlation is the correlation between two or more combinations of variables; in factor analysis, a *factor is a variate. In *SEM, a *latent variable is a variate. In multiple regression, *predicted Y is a variate (composed of the linear combination of the observed values of the variables multiplied by their coefficients plus the y-intercept). (b) A type of *variable. (c) Another term for *random variable. See *multivariate analysis, *univariate analysis, *covariate.

Variation (a) The extent of the "variety" in a *variable, such as the spread of values in a *distribution of the values for a particular variable. (b) Used to refer loosely to any measure of *dispersion. (c) In the *variance and *standard deviation, variation is the total of the squared deviations from the mean score (that is, the *sum of squares). Since adding up all the squared deviations from the mean can produce a huge sum, the number is divided by the number of cases (minus 1 for a sample) to get the variance. To get the standard deviation, one takes the square root of the variance.

Variation, Coefficient of (CV) See *coefficient of variation.

Variation Ratio A measure of *dispersion typically used with *categorical variables. It is the *relative frequency of the nonmodal scores or values.

For example, if the relative frequency of the modal score were .40 (as it is in the example at *frequency distribution), then the variation ratio would be .60.

Varimax A widely used method of *orthogonal rotation of the axes in a *factor analysis. As its name suggests, it maximizes the variances of the factors.

Vector (a) In *matrix algebra, a column (or a row) of a *matrix, or a matrix with either one column or one row. Any particular value in a vector (e.g., 7 in the example in Table V.1) is called an "element" of the vector. Loosely speaking, the number of elements in the vector is its "dimension"; there are five elements in vector b. (b) Geometrically, a vector is a set of ordered values with a length and direction. (c) In a standard data set used for statistical analysis, the data for a case are contained in a row vector, and the data for a variable are contained in a column vector.

Table V.1 Vector

Column vector

$$b = \begin{bmatrix} 3 \\ 7 \\ 9 \\ 4 \\ 8 \end{bmatrix} \quad \text{Row vector } b^T = [3\ 7\ 9\ 4\ 8]$$

Note: b^T is the *transpose of b.

Venn Diagram   A type of graph using circles to represent variables and their relationships. The rectangle represents the *universal set (*population), and the circles inside the rectangle are sets (variables). Shown in Figure V.1, the *intersection (stated "*A* and *B*") is the area of overlap (marked by the letter *b*). The *union (stated "*A* or *B*") is all of the area covered by either circle (*a*, *b*, and *c*; or *A* and *B* minus the overlapping part *b*).

For example, in Figure V.1, the rectangle *U* represents the "universe" of all the adults in a particular city. The circle *A* stands for all of the registered Republicans, and the circle *B* stands for the city's adult African Americans. The intersection of *A* and *B* (i.e., *b*) indicates those African Americans who are registered members of the Republican Party. The union of registered Republicans and African Americans is *a* + *b* + *c*.

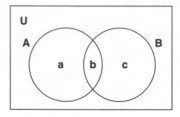

Figure V.1   Venn Diagram

Verisimilitude   (a) The state of being close to or similar to the truth; competing scientific theories are sometimes thought of as having different degrees of verisimilitude. (b) Used in qualitative methods to refer to a narrative that appears to be true and/or a text that adheres to the norms of a writing genre.

Verstehen   A German word meaning "understanding." It was used by Max Weber and Wilhelm Dilthey to refer to a method of interpreting social interaction that involves putting oneself in the place of another. Broadly today, any method using empathetic means of gaining insight into the experiences, meanings, motives, and behavior of others, such as *role-playing. See **Geisteswissenschaften*.

Vicious Circle   (a) A definition or an argument that assumes what it is trying to prove. Compare *tautology. (b) A negative feedback system that gets worse and worse.

VIF   *Variance inflation factor.

Vignette   A brief story or hypothetical set of events depicting a situation. Survey researchers, for example, might present a vignette and ask respondents to describe their reactions to the events and/or indicate what they would do in such a situation.

Violation of Assumptions   Statistical tests make a variety of assumptions about the population from which the data were selected. For example, in *ANOVA standard post hoc tests such as *Sidak and *Tukey's HSD assume homogeneity of variance or *homoscedasticity, but in the presence of unequal variances the *Games-Howell post hoc test should be used because it adjusts for lack of homoscedasticity.

Visual Analog Scale   A line with only the left and right poles marked, where participants are asked to mark on the line where their personal rating falls.

Vital Statistics   Statistics about births, deaths, marriages, and divorces. So called because they have to do with life (*la vita*). Also used more loosely to include information about health and diseases.

Vogt's Correlation Paradox   A paradoxical result that occurs when the correlation between two variables is positive despite the fact that the trends in values for the two variables are in opposite directions: The trend in one variable is upward, while the trend for the other variable is downward. The paradox occurs with change scores rather than absolute values and can occur because the Pearson r is in part based on ranks in the data and not only on absolute values.

For example, in many U.S. states between 1980 and 2000, gross state product (GSP) moved upward on the whole, while the trend for state appropriations for higher education (AHE) was downward. But the positive correlation was strong between these two trends moving in opposite directions. The paradox occurred because in any one year the two variables tended to move in the same direction, but in those years when AHE went up it increased more slowly than GSP, and in those years when AHE went down it decreased more quickly than GSP. Compare *Simpson's paradox.

Volatility   Another term for *standard deviation, especially when used to describe stock market prices.

Volunteer Bias   Any of several problems that arise in drawing valid conclusions from research because participation in the research is voluntary. Since people cannot ethically or legally be compelled to be research subjects, volunteer bias is always a potential source of inaccuracies in generalizing from research samples to broader populations. See *research ethics, *sampling error, *unobtrusive methods.

For example, if you are studying authoritarianism in college students and if volunteers for studies tend to be less authoritarian than those who refuse to participate, your sample will not be representative.

Vulnerable Populations   Potential groups of participants in research whose freedom of choice or capacity for protecting themselves in the course of research is limited. Examples include children, poor people, prisoners, and other institutionalized persons. Research on such populations is usually given close scrutiny by *institutional review boards.

W Symbol for (a) the *Wilcoxon test of statistical significance, (b) *Kendall's coefficient of concordance, and (c) the *Shapiro-Wilk test.

Wait-List Control Group Sometimes participants wanting to participate in an experimental research study are told that they must go on a wait list while also responding to the research protocols. They are, in effect, a control group. Typically this group will later be given the intervention when it is considered unethical to withhold treatment from any of the research participants. Compare *staggered implementation.

Wald Statistic (also called **Wald's Test**) A *test statistic used for assessing the *statistical significance of individual *coefficients in a *logistic regression. It answers the question: Does the particular variable contribute significantly to the model? It follows a chi-square distribution.

Wald-Wolfowitz Test A *nonparametric test of the *null hypothesis that two *samples have been drawn from *populations with identical distributions. Sometimes called the "runs test."

Ward's Method A *hierarchical, *agglomerative approach to *cluster analysis that uses the logic of an analysis of variance (maximizing between group sum of squares and minimizing within group sum of squares) rather than using a distance measure of association. It tends to produce clusters of approximately equal size (which may or may not be appropriate), and outliers can have a greater than desired influence on the resulting clusters.

Washout Period In a clinical trial, it's the time before the study when participants receive no active medication (allowing any previous medications or treatments to be eliminated from their system) and baseline data are collected. More generally, in a *repeated measures design, it is the period between treatment conditions. The goal is to reduce *carryover effects.

W

Wave   In a *panel or longitudinal study, when the same subjects are interviewed more than once, each session is called a wave.

Wavelet   A formula used to represent *time-series data. Several varieties of wavelet exist.

Web-of-Beliefs   Holistic idea that all ideas are part of a larger set. The term was coined by W. V. O. Quine. In hypothesis testing, it leads to the claim (called the *Duhem-Quine thesis) that a single hypothesis cannot be tested in isolation from all other factors, hypotheses, or assumptions.

Web of Causation   A term for a theory of multiple and linked causes, such as the causes of a disease in epidemiological research. See *causal diagram, *path diagram.

Weighted Average (or Mean)   A procedure for combining the means of two or more groups of different sizes; it takes the sizes of the groups into account when computing the overall or grand mean. If groups are of equal size, you just take the average of the group means. However, if the groups are not the same size, which is generally the case in research, you need to weight the group means based on the number of people in them; then the larger groups will get more weight than the smaller groups.

For example, say 239 students in Economics 201 took the midterm and you know the average grade of each of three groups: economics majors, economics minors, and others (as summarized in Table W.1). You want to know the grand mean of all 239 students. You can't just add up the three groups' means and divide by 3 (which would give you an average of 83.2). There are more "majors" than "minors," and there are more "minors" than "others" in the class. To get the average of all students, you would weight each group's mean by the number of people. Specifically, for each group, you multiply the mean (column B) by the number of people in the group (column A), add up this result for all three groups, and then divide by the total number of students: $(21,228.4/239) = 88.8$. Notice that this new mean, 88.8, is quite a bit bigger than the original unweighted mean, 83.2. That's because in the unweighted mean of 83.2, the "others" (who had lower test grades) had too much influence and the "majors" (who had higher test grades) had too little influence on the grand mean.

Table W.1   Computing a Weighted Average

Group	A Number	B Mean Grade	C = (A × B)
Majors	168	93.2	15,657.6
Minors	51	78.8	4,018.8
Others	20	77.6	1,552.0
Total	239		21,228.4

Weighted Data   (a) Any information given different weights in calculations, as when the final examination counts twice as much as (is weighted double) the midterm. (b) Data whose values have been adjusted to reflect differences in the number of *population units that each *case represents. See disproportionate *stratified sampling, *weighted sample.

   For example, suppose we want to generalize about the attitudes of all 90-year-olds. We have a *sample of 100 men and 100 women, all of whom are 90 years old. We will need to give the women's attitudes more weight, because in the general population, there are many more 90-year-old women than 90-year-old men and the goal is to generalize to the attitudes of all 90-year-olds.

Weighted Least Squares   A version of *ordinary least squares regression in which the variables are multiplied by a particular number or "weight." This is sometimes done to correct for *heteroscedasticity. Compare *generalized least squares. See *loess.

Weighted Moving Average   See *moving average, *smoothing.

Weighted Root Mean Square Residual Index (WRMR)   A statistic used in *structural equation modeling to indicate model fit. Reasonable fit is indicated by WRMR values less than or equal to 1.00.

Weighted Sample   In survey research, a sample in which *weighting has been applied to different categories (e.g., ethnicity) to make the overall sample representative of the population. For example, if a group were known to comprise 10% of the population but only 8% of the survey sample were from that group, then the researcher could weight that group's responses more heavily when computing statistics for the sample as a whole. The actual numbers used to adjust the figures are called "sample weights." See *weighted data.

Weighting   (a) Multiplying a variable by some amount to make it comparable to other variables. See *weighted average. (b) The number by which the variable is multiplied. *Predicted Y is a weighted mean provided by a regression equation.

Welch Test   A test of statistical significance used to test the difference between *means when the data violate the assumption of *homogeneity of variance required of other tests, such as the *F and *t tests.

White Noise   Completely *random variation, that is, variation containing no *systematic variance. The term is used often to describe randomness in *time-series data. See *noise.

Widespread Biserial Correlation   A measure of *association, which, like the ordinary *biserial correlation, is used when one *variable is *continuous and the other has been dichotomized by the researcher. In the widespread version, the researcher is interested in extremes in the dichotomized variable, but not in the middle range of scores.

W

Wiki   A collection of web pages that allows any authorized user to contribute to the collection, including by revising the content. Wikis are used by virtual communities of researchers to post ideas that are in development. The term comes from the Hawaiian word for "fast." The online encyclopedia Wikipedia is probably the best-known example.

Wilcoxon-Mann-Whitney Test   Test used to see if the medians of two independent samples of ranked data come from the same population (*null hypothesis) or not (alternative hypothesis). This is a nonparametric version of an *independent *t* test. It is a combination of the *Wilcoxon rank-sum test and the *Mann-Whitney *U* test.

Wilcoxon Matched-Pairs Signed-Ranks   Test used to see if the median of the differences between the dependent/related pairs of scores is 0 or significantly different from 0. This is a *nonparametric version of the *dependent *t* test.

Wilcoxon-Pratt Test   A modification of the *Wilcoxon test used to deal with tied ranks.

Wilcoxon Rank-Sum Test   A nonparametric version of *independent *t* test. Similar to *Wilcoxon-Mann-Whitney test and *Mann-Whitney *U* test.

Wilcoxon Signed-Ranks Test   Nonparametric test to determine if a single sample median comes from a population with a value hypothesized by the researcher. It's a nonparametric version of the parametric *one-sample *t* test.

Wilks's Lambda   A widely used *test statistic for equality of group means (*centroids) in a *MANOVA and in other multivariate tests. The test yields an *F* ratio, which is then interpreted in the same way as any other *F* ratio. Samuel Wilks, of this lambda, and Martin Wilk, of the *Shapiro-Wilk's test, are often confused.

Winsorizing   *Trimming data of a percentage of their highest and lowest values and replacing the trimmed observations with the highest and lowest values remaining in the *trimmed data. This reduces outliers and skewness, but it also restricts the range and it throws out data. Statistics such as means, variances, and standard deviations can be Winsorized; that is, they are calculated on a Winsorized sample.

Within-Group ANOVA   Another term for *repeated-measures ANOVA.

Within-Group Difference (or Variance or SS)   In an *ANOVA, the part of the total *variance attributable to differences among the subjects in a (*control or *experimental) group. The within-group variance is compared to the between-group variance. If the between-group variance is large relative to the within-group variance, this indicates that the groups (e.g., treatment and control groups) were significantly different (i.e., more different than from what would be expected to occur by chance). See *F* ratio.

W

Within-Group Sum of Squares   The *error sum of squares in *ANOVA. It indicates the amount of variation of the scores within the groups from their group means (in squared units).

Within-Samples Sum of Squares   Another term for *error sum of squares.

Within-Subjects ANOVA   Another term for *repeated-measures ANOVA.

Within-Subjects Design   A research procedure that compares the same subjects in more than one condition or at more than one time. It has a *within-subjects independent variable. Also called *repeated-measures design.

Within-Subjects Variable (or Factor)   An *independent variable or factor for which each subject is measured more than once—at different *levels or *conditions. Compare *between-subjects variable. See *counterbalancing for an example.

WLS   *Weighted least squares.

WordStat   See *QDAMiner.

WRMR   See *weighted root mean square residual.

X The letter commonly used to symbolize an *independent, *predictor, or *explanatory variable. When one discusses more than one such variable, they are usually called X_1, X_2, X_3, and so on.

χ^2 *Chi-square.

***x*-Axis** The horizontal axis on a graph. Also called *abscissa.

***X*-Bar** An X with a line over the top of it ($\bar{X}$); this is an often-used symbol for the *mean of a *sample. The mean score for a *population is usually symbolized by the Greek letter *mu (μ).

***X* Variable** The *independent or *predictor variable (or cause). So called because when graphed, it is plotted on the *x-axis (also called the "abscissa" or "horizontal axis").

Y   Letter commonly used to symbolize the *dependent, *outcome, or *criterion variable.

$\hat{Y}$ or $\hat{y}$ Called "Y-hat." The uppercase refers to the *predicted value of Y in the population, and the lowercase refers to the predicted value in the sample.

Y'   Called "Y-prime." An older symbol for the predicted value of Y, that is, the predicted value of the *dependent variable in a *regression equation. Also Y-hat ($\hat{Y}$) and sometimes Y^*.

Yates's Correction (for Continuity)   An adjustment in the computation of the chi-square test statistic to improve its accuracy for 2×2 tables, especially those with small cell values. "Continuity" refers to the fact that the correction is made because one is using a continuous distribution (chi-squared) to estimate a discrete distribution.

　　Yates's continuity correction is less widely used than it once was, largely because many statisticians think that it overcorrects for the possibility of *Type I error and thus increases the chances of *Type II error. Compare *Fisher's exact test.

y-Axis   The vertical axis on a graph. Also called the *ordinate. The *dependent variable is usually plotted on the y-axis. See *x-axis.

Yield Curve   A line on a graph that results when the interest rate for bonds or other securities is plotted against the length of time they have to be held before they pay off. These curves generally slope upward because the longer investors must hold investments, the higher the rates they want.

y-Intercept   The point where a *regression line intersects the *y-axis. Sometimes referred to simply as the *intercept. In a *regression equation, it is symbolized by the letter a, α, or β_0. The intercept is the value of the dependent (Y) variable when all the independent (X) variables are zero. The use of the term "y-intercept" is specific to regression. "Constant" is the more generic term used in other multivariate methods. See the graphic at *intercept.

Yoked-Control Technique A matching technique to control for the possible influence of the temporal sequencing of an event. Each control participant is "yoked" to an experimental participant so that whenever the experimental participant experiences a specific event the control participant also experiences the event. The key is that it is an action or inaction on the part of the experimental participant that determines when the event occurs. To control for and rule out the temporal sequencing of the occurrence of the event from the dependent variable, the control and experimental participants have to experience the event in the same temporal sequence.

Yule's Q A measure of *association for two *dichotomous variables. It is a simplified version of *gamma for 2 × 2 tables. It is a *PRE measure.

Y Variable The *dependent or *outcome variable (or effect). So called because when graphed, it is plotted on the *y-axis (also called the *ordinate or vertical axis).

z   See *z score.

Z   See *Fisher's Z.

z-Axis   The vertical axis in a representation of a three-dimensional space.

Zero-Order Analysis   Analysis of original data. If you use that analysis to do another analysis, the second analysis would be a first-order analysis. If you used the first-order analysis to do another, that would be second-order, and so on.

Zero-Order Correlation   A correlation between two *variables in which no additional variables have been *controlled for (or held constant or partialled out). A *first-order correlation is one in which one variable has been controlled for, a second-order correlation controls for two, and so on. Zero-order associations are the opposite of those measured by *multivariate analysis.

Zero-Sum Game   Any game (or, more broadly, social situation) in which one player (or social actor) can gain only at the expense of another and in which one player gains exactly as much as another loses. More informally, it refers to any "win-lose" situation, as contrasted with a "win-win" situation.

   For example, if you and I were to play poker for money, it would be a zero-sum game; the only way you could win money would be for me to lose it, and vice versa. The term "zero-sum" comes from the fact that if you add my losses to your winnings, the result, or sum, is zero. Certain forms of social interaction (such as poker) are clearly zero-sum games, others (such as donating blood) may benefit both the giver and the receiver, and for others (such as affirmative action), the extent to which they are zero-sum situations is open to debate.

z Score (lowercase z)   The most commonly used *standard score. It is a measure of relative location in a *distribution; it gives, in *standard deviation units, the distance from the mean for a particular score. If you convert a set of numbers to z scores, the set of new numbers will always have a mean of 0 and a standard deviation of 1. A z score of 1.25 is 1¼ standard deviations above the mean; a z score of −2.0 is 2 standard deviations below the mean. Therefore, z scores are especially useful for comparing performance on several measures, each with a different mean and standard deviation (i.e., you would convert all of the measures to z scores, and then you could make comparisons). Compare *effect size.

For example, say you took two midterm exams. On the first, you got 90 right; on the second, 60. If you knew the *means and *standard deviations, you could compute z scores for each of your exams to see which one you did better on. The procedure is to take your score, subtract from it the mean of all the scores, and divide the result by the standard deviation (in symbols, $z = X − M/SD$), where X is your score, M is the mean, and SD is the standard deviation. Table Z.1 shows how to compute your z scores and compare them. In this example, you did better (ranked higher in the class) on your second midterm. Your score of 60 was 2 standard deviations above the mean; your 90 was only 1 standard deviation above.

Table Z.1   Computing Your z Score

First Midterm	Second Midterm
$X = 90$	$X = 60$
$M = 80$	$M = 42$
$SD = 10$	$SD = 9$
$(90 − 80)/10 =$	$(60 − 42)/9 =$
$10/10 = 1$	$18/9 = 2$

Z Score (uppercase Z)   An older name for a T score. It is a *standard score in which the mean of the distribution is 50 and the *standard deviation is 10. The Z score is obtained by transforming the z score (multiplying z by 10 and adding 50), which is why the Z score is called a *transformed standard score. The only advantage of this transformation is that it eliminates decimals and negative numbers. See *T score.

z Test   A test of *statistical significance that is used when the population standard deviation is known, when sample size is very large, or when the sampling distribution of the test statistic is believed to follow the normal distribution (with a mean of 0 and a standard deviation of 1). It is less frequently used than the t test, because the researcher rarely knows the population standard deviation, and the t test is more accurate with small samples. There is little difference between the two when samples are large (greater than 60 or so).

z Transformation   Another term for *r-to-z transformation.

z Value   A *z score (lowercase z) used as a *test statistic when the *sample distribution is assumed to equal or approximate a *normal distribution.

Suggestions for Further Reading

Readers wishing to consult statistics and methodology texts to supplement this dictionary have *many* works from which to choose. Listed below are works that are very clearly written and/or are widely cited accounts and/or are representative of some of the many disciplines that use the methods defined in this dictionary.

The suggestions are in four categories. The more elementary books in Group I are basic enough that most readers can read them without help. Group II contains more advanced volumes that, while usually starting with the basics, move quickly to more difficult topics and examine them in greater depth. Group III lists other dictionaries and reference works that contain methodological and statistical terms. Group IV lists useful websites for methodological and statistical reference.

Special mention should be made of the SAGE series Quantitative Applications in the Social Sciences. Works in this series introduce readers to advanced topics in short booklets. By focusing on concepts rather than proofs and derivations, the booklets can cover advanced topics without requiring more than basic statistical knowledge of readers.

I. Elementary Methodology and Statistics

Babbie, E. (2012). *The practice of social research* (13th ed.). Belmont, CA: Wadsworth.

Black, T. R. (1994). *Evaluating social science research: An introduction.* Thousand Oaks, CA: Sage.

Christensen, L. B., Johnson, R. B., & Turner, L. A. (2014). *Research methods, design, and analysis* (12th ed.). Boston, MA: Pearson.

Creswell, J. W. (2013). *Research design: Qualitative, quantitative, and mixed methods approaches* (4th ed.). Thousand Oaks, CA: Sage.

Freedman, D., Pisani, R., & Purves, R. (2007). *Statistics* (4th ed.). New York, NY: W. W. Norton.

Gall, M. D., Gall, J. P., & Borg, W. R. (2006). *Educational research: An introduction* (8th ed.). New York, NY: Pearson.

Huck, S. K. (2011). *Reading statistics and research* (6th ed.). Boston, MA: Pearson, Allyn & Bacon.

Jaeger, R. M. (1990). *Statistics: A spectator sport* (2nd ed.). Thousand Oaks, CA: Sage.

Johnson, R. B., & Christensen, L. B. (2014). *Educational research: Quantitative, qualitative, and mixed approaches* (5th ed.). Thousand Oaks, CA: Sage.

King, B. M., Rosopa, P. J., & Minium, E. W. (2010). *Statistical reasoning in the behavioral sciences* (6th ed.). Hoboken, NJ: Wiley.

Moore, D. S. (2012). *Statistics: Concepts and controversies* (8th ed.). New York, NY: W. H. Freeman.

Neuman, W. L. (2009). *Social research methods: Qualitative and quantitative approaches* (7th ed.). Boston, MA: Pearson.

Norusis, M. J. (2009). *SPSS 17.0 guide to data analysis.* Upper Saddle River, NJ: Prentice Hall.

Ramsey, F. L., & Schafer, D. W. (2012). *The statistical sleuth: A course in methods of data analysis* (3rd ed.). Pacific Grove, CA: Brooks Cole.

Sirkin, R. M. (2006). *Statistics for the social sciences* (3rd ed.). Thousand Oaks, CA: Sage.

Urdan, T. C. (2010). *Statistics in plain English* (3rd ed.). New York, NA: Routledge.

Utts, J. M., & Heckard, R. F. (2014). *Mind on statistics* (5th ed.). Belmont, CA: Thomson.

Vogt, W. P. (2007). *Quantitative research methods for professionals.* Boston, MA: Pearson, Allyn & Bacon.

Vogt, W. P., Gardner, D. C., & Haeffele, L. M. (2012). *When to use what research design.* New York: Guilford Press.

II. More Advanced Works on Methodology and Statistics

Agresti, A., & Finlay, B. (2009). *Statistical methods for the social sciences* (4th ed.). Upper Saddle River, NJ: Pearson.

Chernick, M. R., & Friis, R. H. (2003). *Introductory biostatistics for the health sciences: Modern applications including bootstrap.* Hoboken, NJ: Wiley.

Cohen, B. H. (2013). *Explaining psychological statistics* (4th ed.). Hoboken, NJ: Wiley.

Cohen, J., Cohen, P., West, S. G., & Aiken, L. S. (2003). *Applied multiple regression/correlation analysis for the behavioral sciences* (3rd ed.). Mahwah, NJ: Lawrence Erlbaum.

Fisher, R. A. (1970). *Statistical methods for research workers* (14th ed.). New York, NY: Holt, Rinehart & Winston.

Fisher, R. A. (1971). *The design of experiments* (9th ed.). New York: Macmillian.

Fox, J. (2015). *Applied regression analysis and generalized linear models.* Thousand Oaks, CA: Sage.

Glass, G. V., & Hopkins, K. D. (1995). *Statistical methods in education and psychology* (3rd ed.). Boston, MA: Allyn & Bacon.

Greene, W. H. (2011). *Econometric analysis* (7th ed.). Upper Saddle River, NJ: Prentice Hall.

Hair, J. F., Black, W. C., Babin, B., Anderson, R. E., & Tatham, R. L. (2009). *Multivariate data analysis* (7th ed.). Upper Saddle River, NJ: Prentice Hall.

Hays, W. L. (1994). *Statistics* (5th ed.). Fort Worth, TX: Holt, Rinehart & Winston.

Hesse-Biber, S. N., & Johnson, R. B. (Eds.). (2015). *Oxford handbook of multimethod and mixed methods research inquiry.* New York, NY: Oxford University Press.

Keppel, G., & Zedeck, S. (1989). *Data analysis for research designs.* New York, NY: Freeman.

Kleinbaum, D. G., Kupper, L. L., Nizam, A., & Muller, K. E. (2013). *Applied regression analysis and multivariable methods* (5th ed.). Boston, MA: Cengage Learning.

Kline, R. B. (2010). *The principles and practice of structural equation modeling* (3rd ed.). New York, NY: Guilford Press.

Knoke, D., Bohrnstedt, G. W., & Mee, A. P. (2002). *Statistics for social data analysis* (4th ed.). Belmont, CA: Wadsworth.

Kutner, M., Nachtsheim, C., & Neter, J. (2004). *Applied linear statistical models* (5th ed.). Boston, MA: McGraw–Hill/Irwin.

Lance, C. E., & Vandenberg, R. J. (2009). *Statistical and methodological myths and urban legends: Doctrine, verity and fable in the organizational and social studies.* New York, NY: Routledge.

Maxwell, S. E., & Delaney, H. D. (2004). *Designing experiments and analyzing data: A model comparison approach.* Mahwah, NJ: Lawrence Erlbaum.

Mendenhall, W., & Sincich, T. (2011). *A second course in statistics: Regression analysis* (7th ed.). Upper Saddle River, NJ: Pearson.

Mohr, L. B. (1990). *Understanding significance testing.* Thousand Oaks, CA: Sage.

Myers, J. L., Well, A. D., & Lorch, R. F. (2010). *Research design and statistical analysis* (3rd ed.). New York, NY: Routledge.

Newton, R. R., & Rudestam, K. E. (2012). *Your statistical consultant: Answers to your data analysis questions* (2nd ed.). Thousand Oaks, CA: Sage.

Norusis, M. J. (2009). *SPSS 17.0 advanced statistical procedures companion.* Upper Saddle River, NJ: Prentice Hall.

Pedhazur, E. J. (1997). *Multiple regression in behavioral research: Explanation and prediction* (3rd ed.). Fort Worth, TX: Wadsworth Publishing.

Pedhazur, E. J., & Schmelkin, L. P. (1991). *Measurement, design, and analysis: An integrated approach.* Hillsdale, NJ: Lawrence Erlbaum.

Shadish, W. R., Cook, T. D., & Campbell, D. T. (2002). *Experimental and quasi–experimental designs for generalized causal inference.* Boston, MA: Houghton Mifflin.

Sharma, S. (1996). *Applied multivariate techniques.* New York, NY: Wiley.

Sheskin, D. J. (2011). *Handbook of parametric and nonparametric statistical procedures.* Boca Raton, FL: Chapman & Hall.

Tabachnick, B. G., & Fidell, L. S. (2012). *Using multivariate statistics* (6th ed.). Boston, MA: Pearson.

Tukey, J. W. (1977). *Exploratory data analysis.* Reading, MA: Addison–Wesley.

Vogt, W. P., Vogt, E. R., Gardner, D. C., & Haeffele, L. M. (2014). *Selecting the right analyses for your data: Quantitative, qualitative and mixed methods.* New York, NY: Guilford Press.

Wooldridge, J. (2012). *Introductory econometrics: A modern approach* (5th ed.). Mason, OH: South-Western Cengage Learning.

III. Dictionaries and Reference Works

American Psychological Association. (2014). *APA dictionary of statistics and research methods.* Washington, DC: American Psychological Association.

Andrews, F. M., Klem, L., Davidson, T. N., O'Malley, P., & Rodgers, W. (1981). *A guide for selecting statistical techniques for analyzing social science data* (2nd ed.). Ann Arbor, MI: Institute for Social Research.

Bannock, G., Baxter, R. E., & Davis, E. (2011). *The Penguin dictionary of economics* (8th ed.). London, UK: Penguin.

Black, J. (2012). *Dictionary of economics* (4th ed.). Oxford, UK: Oxford University Press.

Blackburn, S. (2008). *Oxford dictionary of philosophy* (2nd ed.). Oxford, UK: Oxford University Press.

Borowski, E. J., & Borwein, J. M. (1991). *The HarperCollins dictionary of mathematics.* New York, NY: HarperCollins.

Calhoun, C. (2002). *Dictionary of the social sciences.* Oxford, UK: Oxford University Press.

Cramer, D., & Howitt, D. (2004). *The SAGE dictionary of statistics.* London, UK: Sage.

Dodge, Y. (2006). *The Oxford dictionary of statistical terms.* Oxford, UK: Oxford University Press.

Everitt, B. S. (2002). *The Cambridge dictionary of statistics* (2nd ed.). Cambridge, UK: Cambridge University Press.

Everitt, B. S. (2006). *Medical statistics from A to Z* (2nd ed.). Cambridge, UK: Cambridge University Press.

Lewis-Beck, M. S., Bryman, A., & Liao, T. F. (2004). *The SAGE encyclopedia of social science research methods* (Vols. 1–3). Thousand Oaks, CA: Sage.

Miller, R. L., & Brewer, J. D. (2003). *The A–Z of social research: A dictionary of key social science research concepts.* London, UK: Sage.

Porkess, R. (2006). *Web-linked dictionary: Statistics.* Glasgow, Scotland: HarperCollins.

Porta, M. (2014). *Dictionary of epidemiology* (6th ed.). New York, NY: Oxford University Press.

Salkind, N. J. (2007). *Encyclopedia of measurement and statistics* (Vols. 1–3). Thousand Oaks, CA: Sage.

Schwandt, T. A. (2015). *SAGE dictionary of qualitative inquiry* (4th ed.). Thousand Oaks, CA: Sage.

Scriven, M. (1991). *Evaluation, thesaurus* (4th ed.). Thousand Oaks, CA: Sage.

Sullivan, L. E., Johnson, R. B., Mercado, C. C., & Terry, K. J. (2009). *The SAGE glossary of the social and behavioral sciences.* Thousand Oaks, CA: Sage.

Upton, G., & Cook, I. (2014). *A dictionary of statistics* (3rd ed.). Oxford, UK: Oxford University Press.

Weisstein, E. W. (2009). *CRC concise encyclopedia of mathematics* (3rd ed.). London, UK: CRC Press.

IV. Some Useful Websites on Statistics and Methodology

Selecting the Appropriate Statistical Test

http://www.ats.ucla.edu/stat/stata/whatstat/default.htm

Statistical Calculations

For links to multiple webpages that perform statistical calculations:

http://statpages.org/javastat.html

http://www.danielsoper.com/statcalc/

Indirect effects: http://www.danielsoper.com/statcalc3/calc.aspx?id=32

Free Statistical Software

For access to the premier collection of free software programs for statistical computing and graphics: http://www.r-project.org

More free software: http://statpages.org/javasta2.html

Statistical Packages

Tutorial for SAS and STATA: http://www.unc.edu/~nielsen/soci708/odocs/stata_sas_guide.pdf

Tutorial for SPSS: http://www.spss-tutorials.com/data-analysis/

Tutorial for SAS: http://www.umass.edu/statdata/software/handouts/sas_online/index.html

Tutorial for STATA: http://data.princeton.edu/stata/

Applets Demonstrating Statistical Concepts

http://wise.cgu.edu

http://onlinestatbook.com/stat_sim/

http://www.stat.tamu.edu/~west/applets/

http://it.stlawu.edu/~rlock/maa51/java.html

http://www.methodsman.com

http://vogtsresearchmethods.blogspot.com/

Intervening Variables and Mediation

An excellent and continually updated website on mediation, maintained by David Kenny: http://davidakenny.net/cm/mediate.htm

Preacher and Leonardelli provide a program to calculate the *Sobel test for mediation and macros for bootstrapping tests for the same purpose: http://www.danielsoper.com/statcalc3/calc.aspx?id=31

Sample Size Determination, Power Analysis, and Effect Size Calculation

G*Power: http://www.gpower.hhu.de/en.html

Another power program: http://www.stat.uiowa.edu/~rlenth/Power/

Power for ANOVA: http://www.math.yorku.ca/SCS/Online/power/

Effect size: http://people.cehd.tamu.edu/~bthompson/effect.html

Randomization (Assignment and Selection)

Random number generators easy to use for random selection and random assignment:

http://randomizer.org

http://random.org

http://psychscience.org/random.aspx